Teaching

LANGUAGE, COMPOSITION, AND LITERATURE

Teaching

LANGUAGE, COMPOSITION, AND LITERATURE

Mary Elizabeth Fowler

Professor of English
Central Connecticut State College

McGraw-Hill Book Company

New York, St. Louis, San Francisco, Toronto, London, Sydney

TEACHING LANGUAGE, COMPOSITION, AND LITERATURE

Library of Congress Catalog Card Number 64–66201

21715

345678910–CO–10987

To Elizabeth

Preface

The idea for this book was born more than six years ago out of a desire to help young teachers work out a philosophy of teaching English which combined important psychological and sociological insights with the study of language and literature. The untimely death of Elizabeth Rose during the first year of the writing meant reshaping the original plans for a collaborative effort, but her deep concern for the young student and his language as well as her part in the initial planning and point of view are reflected in its design and content.

During the past six years the teaching of English has been radically improved. During these years, ideas and materials which seemed revolutionary have become commonplace in many schools. Despite the strides which have been made in curriculum revision and the upgrading of standards for work in English, much remains to be done. Curriculum revision is still in many schools a patchwork affair, a replacement of some parts rather than a rethinking of the whole sequence of secondary English.

In the national concern for education of the gifted, the real and necessary needs of slow, terminal, and culturally disadvantaged students have, until recently, been largely overlooked. The designing of a curriculum for one year, three years, or six years frequently proceeds without much recognition of the ways in which students learn, or of the very real needs and interests of young people which might make learning more fruitful and relevant. Research, new methods and materials in English, and the recommendations of leaders in the field have been frequently ignored or imperfectly understood. "Raising standards" is too frequently interpreted as the need to teach college-level classes in the high school by emphasis on complicated literary criticism before the student has read widely enough to acquire his own standards of literary judgment.

This book attempts to explore new materials, and to bring together the suggestions of master teachers for ways of encouraging students to read to the best of their ability, to speak and write the language with clarity and power, and to develop discriminating tastes in literature and the popular arts. It considers that the aim of the English program is to produce literate, well-read young people, and to lead to the development of mature, thoughtful adults. It sees the English the student learns in the classroom as an integral part of a process of using language which continues long after the student has left school requirements behind. Finally, it conceives of the student's use of language as a necessary means to his intellectual growth, and the development of a set of values by which to live.

The book is intended to provide practical suggestions for beginning teachers of English, experienced teachers engaged in curriculum revision, and those engaged in the development of sequential programs.

The first section of the book, called "Preview," attempts to set the framework for the book by discussing the issues, problems, and trends in the teaching of English, the context of the society in which the teacher works, the implications of adolescent needs and interests for the program in English, and the nature of language as the central study in the program.

The second section, "Process," includes a discussion of the problems of teaching in two parts: the first deals with the skills of comprehension and expression, and the second with the development of appreciation of literature, of the ability to read intelligently and critically, and of an understanding of its humanistic values. Each chapter discusses problems and aims of teaching, the process of teaching (including recommended assignments and activities for students), and ways to evaluate growth.

The section called "Program" attempts to give suggestions for planning and curriculum building, for a program of individualized reading, and for the professional growth of the kind of teacher needed for today's demanding English curriculum. Suggested sequential and "spiral" programs in language, composition, and literature are included in various chapters of the book.

The ideas about teaching English in this book represent a synthesis of those accumulated over the years from the talk, writings, and practice of numerous excellent classroom teachers, and from the readings in various areas which have shaped a philosophy of what good teaching of English should be. Many ideas have come from the student teachers who have translated theory into practice in their own teaching. Conscious debts have been acknowledged; unconscious borrowings may be forgiven, I trust, because of the difficulty of tracing just how or where such ideas became part of the whole pattern.

Among the debts too numerous to be acknowledged, some deserve particular mention. The ideas about teaching English in this book have been particularly influenced by my earliest teacher of English, my father, Herbert Eugene Fowler, and by the books, teaching, and friendship of Lou La Brant and Louise Rosenblatt. My deepest appreciation goes to Mary Houston Davis of Finch College and Marjorie B. Smiley of Hunter College for constructive and perceptive criticism of the whole manuscript through numerous revisions. Hastings L. Dietrich, formerly of The Macmillan Company, and Estelle Pollack, a former student, have provided intelligent and painstaking comments on the whole book. Others who have provided helpful criticism for individual chapters include Hal Dorsey, Margaret Early, Brobury P. Ellis, John and Frances Hunter, Joan Kerelejza, Elizabeth Martin, Jean Parsons, and Priscilla Tyler.

I am grateful to the teachers of methods who tried early drafts of several chapters in their classes, and whose students provided helpful suggestions: Mildred Abbott (Western Reserve University), Virginia Alwin (Arizona State College at Flagstaff), Richard Corbin (Hunter College High School), Margaret Early (Syracuse University), M. Agnella Gunn and Gertrude Callahan (Boston University), and Priscilla Tyler (then of the Harvard Graduate School of Education). To others for kindnesses too numerous to mention, I owe thanks: H. D. Welte and W. B. Fulghum, my colleagues, my friends, and the members of my family. Finally, particular thanks are due to my typist, the efficient and imaginative Rosemarie Sammataro, who helped to bring order out of chaos in the manuscript.

Mary Elizabeth Fowler

Contents

Today's teacher, in schools without blackboards, or before an automated electronic "teaching console," or facing a television camera, still points to the far horizon, still makes the same promises, still is gratified as the child grows into the man.

The finest instrument the teacher possesses is his own mind with its capacity to project an image of man that is appropriate to his age. This image of what the child might become expresses the basic human values and ideals, the things most worth doing, the goals worth striving for.

FRANK G. JENNINGS [1]

The subject and the challenge

English in a changing world

To understand the subject we teach, we must view it against the background of a world in rapid change. The contrast between the world of sixty years ago, described in Thornton Wilder's *Our Town*, and our world of today serves to show some of the differences. In that play, Emily claims to have been almost run down by a horse in the main street of town; today, jet planes cross continents and oceans in a few hours, and the first American astronaut to make an orbital flight saw three dawns in less than four hours. The people of *Our Town* were born, lived, and died in Grover's Corners. Americans today—students, teachers, businessmen, diplomats—work, study, and spend vacations almost all over the world; village herdsmen and African tribal chiefs tour America, and students from villages of all the continents attend American high schools and colleges. Modern transportation and communication have telescoped time and space and brought peoples in all corners of the world closer together.

---

[1] "Teaching of Man," *Saturday Review*, vol. 52, Feb. 14, 1959, p. 30.

Our era is one of astonishingly rapid social and technological change. Within twenty years we have seen the creation of new states, the independence of countries from colonial rule with the social and political upheavals attendant on such changes, and the rapid conversion of Stone Age cultures to modern technology. The age of automation makes it possible for thousands of men to be thrown out of work by a few highly developed machines. Electronic brains have been invented which can translate languages, predict election results, and do fifteen years of mathematical computation in two minutes.

The communication revolution

Modern technology has dramatically changed the world of business and transportation, but even more important is the way in which it has revolutionized our communications. Typed messages can now be sent and answered immediately by the recipient. Satellites now circling the earth are reporting information which will revolutionize space travel, communications, and our concepts of geography and astronomy, and will make possible man's flight to the moon.

We live in an increasingly oral world. By far the largest proportion of our verbal communication is through speaking and listening. From the pre-breakfast radio or television news to the late, late show in the family living room, a continuous stream of language assaults our ears. A great deal of information which came to former generations through newspapers, books, and periodicals comes to us today through radio and television. Where much of our information used to be received after a delay of hours or days, communication today is instantaneous. We can dial a number and hear a voice almost anywhere in the United States, and place calls to be answered within minutes to almost any part of the globe. United Nations deliberations are translated simultaneously into five languages. Television tapes of history-making events are flown from distant countries to be broadcast within hours, and Telstar, our first communications satellite, has inaugurated global television.

The phenomenon of instantaneous communication is perhaps the most significant part of the communication revolution. So far-reaching are its effects that it is rapidly changing our ways of living, our modes of government, and our prospects of international cooperation or conflict. With the technology for instantaneous world communication have come increased responsibilities. As Norman Cousins has pointed out, Telstar may become "nothing more than a device for showing 'Gunsmoke' simultaneously in six countries," but it has the potential for "creating a world-wide audience for genius." [2]

As the arena of modern warfare shifts from the battlefield to the conference tables of the United Nations, the burden of world safety rests on the verbal skills of statesmen, diplomats, national leaders, and delegates to inter-

[2] "Short Strokes," *Saturday Review*, vol. 55, July 28, 1962, p. 29.

national conferences. Tomorrow's diplomats and statesmen, the students who will use our miraculous new inventions, are in our English classes today. Will their study of language assist them in using language more accurately, wisely, or responsibly?

We have hardly begun to assess the impact of the electric age on our culture, our mores, our speech, and the education of our children. Further, the age of electricity and automation will bring about world-wide changes in our relations with all mankind: "Men are . . . involved in the total social process as never before; since with electricity we extend our central nervous system globally, instantly interrelating every human experience." [3]

Of far-reaching implications for the teacher of English and his students is the fact that English has become a world language, spoken by one in ten of the world's people, and operating as one of the five working languages of the United Nations. In some countries it is the only medium of communication between groups speaking different languages or dialects. The language we speak is taught and spoken all over the globe. It has been suggested as the international language for Telstar. Our culture, too, has become a world culture. The writings of American authors have been translated into dozens of languages; our movies are shown all over the world; American plays are produced in many countries. Eugene O'Neill is a favorite dramatist in Stockholm; *Porgy and Bess* received acclaim in Moscow; Hemingway, Faulkner, and Steinbeck are favorite American writers abroad, and European youth are said to be more familiar with their writings than are our own adolescents. We need to ask whether our students are aware of the importance of their own language and culture abroad.

Changing times—changing subject

Viewed against the background of such breathtaking social, technological, and verbal change, the subject we teach has until recently changed little since the days of *Our Town*. The Emilys and Georges of today still read—in many schools—*The Lady of the Lake, Evangeline, Silas Marner, Julius Caesar,* and the *Idylls of the King*. American literature is a relative newcomer to the literature program, and until World War II, American boys and girls knew almost nothing of any literature besides English and American. Despite the evidence that the teaching of formal grammar does not help students write better, a large portion of time in English classes is still spent in drill on formal grammar, just as surveys reported it was in 1917 and 1938.[4] New studies in language have greatly changed our concept of the way language works, but the findings of these studies have had until recently little impact on courses of study.

---

[3] Marshall McLuhan, *Understanding Media: The Extensions of Man,* McGraw-Hill Book Company, New York, 1964, p. 358.
[4] See page 131 for a discussion of this research.

Despite recent dramatic improvements in English programs throughout the country, the heart of the English curriculum in the space age is still, in too many schools, the reading of a few nineteenth-century classics and the study of a grammar we inherit from the eighteenth century.

English for American youth

In a period of rapid cultural change, reassessment of the process of education is inevitable. English teachers today are reformulating aims for their subject within the context of an age of automation. The topics and problems addressed in this book are those for which we search for answers: a redefinition of the English curriculum for today's youth, and the aims of English instruction today. The basic issues of goals, content, and methods demand thoughtful examination.

Criticisms of public education and the unfavorable comparisons of American schools to those of Europe have often overlooked the important factor of the different roles school systems play in a society. In the United States the goal of education for all American youth, aimed at developing each individual to his full potential, is quite different from that of the education of a leisure class, or a social and economic elite. Teachers in American schools must meet and teach all kinds of young people of widely differing abilities and widely varying backgrounds. Our schools retain and teach students who would drop out early from schools in other societies. The recent focus of national attention on the education of culturally disadvantaged youth in an attempt to discover potential excellence at all social and economic levels is having its impact on schools and education.[5]

The kinds of teaching described in this book aim primarily at providing materials and methods in English which will assist all students to achieve their maximum growth and development in the skills and arts of using, understanding, and appreciating the language and its literature. Programs for superior students, those which challenge the indifferent and stimulate the slow learner to work up to capacity are urgently needed. In a democracy the abilities of all youth deserve equal opportunity for development.

A description of the physical, emotional, and intellectual differences of youth is given in Chapter 2. The chapters on teaching in the various areas of English suggest ways in which teachers can provide for these three large ability groups common in our classrooms: the bright, the average, and the slow learners. A report on the most pressing problems facing America's educational system points to the need for a different kind of education for youth to

[5] A President's conference on educating culturally disadvantaged youth under the direction of Dr. James B. Conant explored such problems, as did his book *Slums and Suburbs,* McGraw-Hill Book Company, New York, 1961. See also Educational Policies Commission, *Education and the Disadvantaged American,* National Education Association, Washington, D.C., 1962.

prepare for tomorrow's automated civilization. It calls for an understanding of the nature of change and the ability to adjust to it. It holds that the trend toward highly specialized technical training has "created an extraordinary demand for gifted generalists—managers, teachers, interpreters, critics." [6]

The pursuit of excellence is democracy's business. Today's educators are in quest of new definitions of excellence, and new ways of identifying those who may achieve it. The discussion of this problem in Chapter 2 (page 44) raises important questions for teachers.

The product of the program

A look at the students who emerge from twelve or fourteen years of the study of English in our schools and colleges suggests that some of the criticism of English teaching today is justified. College teachers complain that students who enter can neither read efficiently nor comprehendingly, speak effectively, spell or punctuate correctly, write clear, coherent expository prose, or command a fair level of standard English. Many businesses and industries find their employees so lacking in verbal skill that they provide post-public school instruction for them. Surveys of the reading habits of our school and college graduates show appalling figures: not one in ten college graduates reads one book a month; few know how to use their leisure time in reading, viewing movies or television discriminatingly, or how to keep up to date on newspaper and magazine reading. Many homes contain no reading matter of any kind except the daily newspaper. About one-sixth of the child's waking hours from age three until nearly the end of high school are devoted to television,[7] and the fare the networks claim the public demands has been called television's "wasteland."

Although there is evidence that the reading of teen-agers is more extensive and of higher quality than ever, there is little question in the minds of English teachers that we could be doing a more effective job of training modern youth to handle their language with more skill, sensitivity, and understanding.

Where does the difficulty lie? Is it in our programs, our selection of subject matter, the kinds of teachers we have, or the ways in which they were trained and in which they now teach? This chapter and this book examine these questions.

It seems evident that change is in order. What is needed in today's complex and rapidly changing world is not a return to English programs of the

[6] Rockefeller Brothers Fund, *The Pursuit of Excellence: Education and the Future of America,* Doubleday & Company, Garden City, N.Y., 1958. See also The President's Commission on National Goals, *Goals for Americans,* Prentice-Hall, Inc., Englewood Cliffs, N.J., 1960.
[7] Wilbur Schramm, *The Impact of Educational Television,* The University of Illinois Press, Urbana, Ill., 1960, p. 216.

turn of the century, but a reexamination of what English includes, and a thoughtful study of the best available recommendations as to programs productive of maximum skill in reading, writing, speaking, insight into literature, and understanding and command of the complex processes of human communication.

What is English?

English is a central humanistic study in the schools during the child's educational career from elementary school through college. It is taken by all children, of all ages, abilities, backgrounds, and goals. The study of their own language and literature is, for American children, the doorway to all other subjects in the curriculum. Yet one of the exasperating things about this central subject is the difficulty of agreement about its definitions.

The past fifty years have seen a swing from a narrow conception of English, focusing on spelling, reading a few pieces of literature, and studying grammar, to courses which include practically everything and cross the boundaries of many other subjects in the curriculum.

During 1958, a Committee on Basic Issues in the Teaching of English met in a series of conferences to attempt some "definitions and clarifications" about the teaching of English. That committee compiled a list of thirty-five basic questions which need to be answered by research and experiment in order to design a constructive program in English and to train enough adequately prepared teachers to administer it.

Among these are questions about the goals, content, and teaching problems in the field: a definition of English; the possibility of developing sequential programs; a definition of content and method in teaching of literature and language; a discussion of how writing should be taught; whether national standards for writing can be set up; the effect of the work load on student achievement; and the contributions of modern technology to the teaching of English.[8]

The committee charged with defining the most serious problems in the field listed the question, "What is English?" as its first issue. Although no final definition of the subject can be universally agreed on, most teachers of English would probably accept the statement of the Commission on English of the College Entrance Examination Board (CEEB) that the three central subjects of the English curriculum are language, literature, and composition.

A backward look

One of the earliest attempts to redefine English and to suggest changing aims and content was that of a joint committee of the National Education

---

[8] George Winchester Stone, Jr. (ed.), *Issues, Problems, and Approaches in the Teaching of English,* Holt, Rinehart and Winston, Inc., New York, 1961, pp. 7–19.

Association (NEA) and the National Council of Teachers of English (NCTE) in 1917.[9] The report stressed the importance of relating items of knowledge to the students' daily experience, and identified cultural, vocational, social, and ethical values as desired outcomes of English. Various committees since 1917 have attempted to redefine the basic aims of English instruction and the content of the curriculum. Some have had far-reaching effects: the NCTE's *Experience Curriculum in English* (1935) emphasized the importance of language experiences as the center of the curriculum; its *Conducting Experiences in English* (1939), and *A Correlated Curriculum* (1940), described various kinds of correlated and integrated high school programs in English.

The Eight-year Study of the Progressive Education Association carried on experimental programs in thirty cooperating schools during the 1930s, following its students into college to show that the graduates of the most experimental schools were "strikingly more successful" in college than students in matched control groups.[10]

In the period after World War II, concern for improvement of communication skills increased as the need for sharper critical appraisal and understanding of language was dramatically highlighted by wartime experience with propaganda. Many colleges experimented with programs in communications skills. At the secondary level, curriculum programs were designed. One of the most influential of the postwar definitions was the report of the Harvard Committee, *General Education in a Free Society*.[11] The report urged the use of great works of literature in courses in secondary schools as well as in colleges, intensive close reading of some well-written paragraphs, training in reading at different speeds and for differing purposes, a constant practice in writing on exercises close to student interests, and the study of grammar only in relation to structural weaknesses in speech and writing.

The Commission on the English Curriculum of the National Council of Teachers of English, founded in 1945,[12] drew together teachers from different levels of instruction from kindergarten through college to produce a series of volumes on the English curriculum.[13] The first of the five volumes represent-

---

[9] James F. Hosic, *The Reorganization of English in Secondary Schools,* Government Printing Office, Washington, D.C., 1917.

[10] Wilford M. Aiken, *The Story of the Eight-year Study,* Harper & Row, Publishers, Incorporated, New York, 1942, p. 110.

[11] Paul Buck (ed.), *General Education in a Free Society,* Harvard University Press, Cambridge, Mass., 1945.

[12] The Commission appointed in 1945 was disbanded in 1962 at the NCTE Convention at Miami Beach, and a new one was appointed. The new Commission on the English Curriculum will work on additional publications which present sequential programs and incorporate some of the new trends in the teaching of English.

[13] NCTE Curriculum Series: Commission on the English Curriculum, vol. I, *The English Language Arts,* 1952; vol. II, *Language Arts for Today's Children,* 1954; vol. III, *The English Language Arts in the Secondary School,* 1956; and Alfred H. Grommon (ed.), vol. V, *The Education of Teachers of English for American Schools and Colleges,* 1963; all volumes published by Appleton-Century-Crofts, Inc., New York.

ing common areas of agreement between teachers at different levels attempted to suggest ways of ensuring steady and developmental progress in related language skills throughout the years of schooling. The Commission's volume I, *The English Language Arts*, outlines a sequential program in the language arts from kindergarten years through college. Volume III, *The English Language Arts in the Secondary Schools*, suggests practices, units, curriculum plans, and developmental programs which have been tried in different parts of the country and gives the research that is the basis for recommended practices.

These books, representing as they do areas of agreement among teachers with widely varied backgrounds, interests, and philosophies, have provided direction for curriculum makers. The emphasis in volume III on unit teaching, the inductive method, and on varied programs in literature, speaking, listening, and writing designed for students of all capacities, has had far-reaching effects on teachers and courses of study.

Present trends strongly favor a more careful definition and delimitation of the responsibilities of the English teacher and the content of the courses we call English. They call for giving a more prominent place to composition and for raising standards so that more is demanded of students.

The task of defining and clarifying the nature and content in English for a constantly changing society is a continual process. One group succeeds another as rapid cultural changes suggest changes in the content and methods of the subject. Each generation will probably continue the process of asking and answering for itself the question, "What is English?"

A forward look

Even though many school programs remain outdated and static, changes in the English programs throughout the country during the last decade have been many and dramatic. Recent recommendations about the teaching of English have already resulted in significant improvement in many schools. The two reports on American high schools by James B. Conant,[14] with their emphasis on composition, have already had strong impact on many high school programs, as parents and administrators recognize the need for better training in composition for all students.

American awareness of contrasts between our system of education and European systems, particularly since the launching of the Soviet satellite Sputnik in 1957, has been heightened; we have seen evidence of superior results in teaching languages, science and mathematics. The Conference on the Academically Talented presided over by Conant in 1958 has led to the introduction in our schools of programs for the gifted, honors courses, and Ad-

---

[14] *The American High School Today: A First Report to Interested Citizens*, McGraw-Hill Book Company, New York, 1959, and *Education in the Junior High School Years*, Educational Testing Service, Princeton, N.J., 1960.

vanced Placement Programs providing college-level instruction for gifted high school seniors and allowing them exemption in some freshman college subjects. The upgrading of work for superior students has resulted in the raising of standards for all grade levels. Colleges report that high school students are better prepared. Increasingly high standards for college admission and the excellence of courses for superior students have begun to exert pressure on the colleges to give more demanding courses.[15]

We are in the midst of a searching examination of the English program and a serious search for answers to the questions being raised about the present content and methods of English teaching. The new designs for learning are imaginative and challenging. To see them in context we must take a backward look at what English programs used to be.

Designs for learning

If students cannot read, write, or spell as well as they should after twelve or more years of experience in English classes, the fault may be in the ways in which we have traditionally organized materials in the subject. One teacher, describing how it was twenty years ago, says, "On Mondays we had literature or book reports, on Tuesday, spelling, on Wednesday, vocabulary drill, on Thursday, composition, and on Friday, tests." A very common pattern of organization is still that which allots certain blocks of time to one aspect of the subject: five weeks to a novel, six to a Shakespearean play, five or six to a review of grammar, four or five to a "unit" on poetry. There are usually no cogent reasons for allocating time in these ways. If one asks the teacher, the reply is apt to be either that the course of study demands it or that this particular five weeks has been allotted to his class to use the thirty-five copies of *Ivanhoe* (which must be returned on Monday at the end of the five weeks). Some argue that students must have a change of subject every few weeks, lest they get bored.

This kind of organization does not take into account patterns of language growth and development, the interrelationships between the language arts, the interests or needs of students, or the individual differences within the class.[16] Often the motivating factor is the coverage of the textbook in literature or grammar or the demands of an outdated course of study.

Core and communications programs

The fragmented programs described above led many thoughtful teachers to plan ways of studying English that would show students how the various

[15] See Fred M. Hechinger, "The New Student," *New York Times*, April 22, 1962, p. E9; and *The Principals Look at the Schools*, NEA, Washington, D.C., 1962.
[16] The following chapter will explore these differences more deeply.

ways of using language were related, and further, the relationship of English to other subjects in the curriculum. Out of their efforts came two kinds of programs: those in communication skills and the core program. The former focused on language as communication, and attempted to train students in the skills of reading, writing, speaking, and listening.

Although the influence of the communication-skills programs was never strongly felt in the secondary schools, from the thirties to the fifties many schools adopted core programs of different types. The commonest kind of course was that in which a block of two periods was set aside in the school day during which one teacher might teach both history or social studies and English, or two teachers might teach the course cooperatively. The advantages were an uninterrupted block of time in which the teacher might work with a class on units or projects, the possibilities of showing relationships between English and other subjects, and the provision for meaningful use of reading, writing and, speaking skills in the study of history, geography, or social studies. Although many core programs tended to be diffuse in content and often limited work in English to the teaching of skills, many of the best of these included thought-provoking and challenging units of a kind not often experienced in the more traditional, fragmented programs. Here everything depended on the skill and breadth of background of the teacher, his ability to work in flexible patterns, his careful planning of materials to serve individual differences, and his ability to develop in students habits of self-discipline and intellectual curiosity.

The integrated program

Many teachers had the skill and courage to attempt a more freely planned kind of integrated program, and some of these were exciting in the hands of imaginative, skillful teachers. In these, individual reading programs proceeded according to student interest, guided by the teacher, but without being limited by topics, units, or assignments. A continuous flow of writing throughout the year proceeded without definite teacher-dictated assignments largely through student interests in self-expression or topics related to class discussion or subjects of study. Much student-teacher planning allowed students to recognize their own needs for study, often to set their own assignments and goals, and frequently to work at their own pace. The description of such a program appears in the book *Were We Guinea Pigs?* written by the class members.[17] The success of this program in producing pupils whose learning has continued is indicated in the follow-up study of the class twenty years later.[18]

---

[17] Class of 1938, Ohio State University High School, *Were We Guinea Pigs?*, Holt, Rinehart and Winston, Inc., New York, 1938.
[18] Margaret Willis, *The Guinea Pigs after Twenty Years*, Ohio State University Press, Columbus, Ohio, 1962.

Today's integrated programs attempt to provide learning activities or units of study in which students observe and practice the skills of language. The preparation for a panel discussion may involve reading books, writing an outline or a report, speaking as a member of the panel, listening critically and thoughtfully to the arguments of others, and evaluating the use of language in each of these acts. The student learns to think of the many uses of language —spoken and written—as part of the process of communication.

Unit teaching

The use of thematic and other kinds of units in the English program has increased as teachers have found in such organization a method of integrating the work in the areas of English, showing interrelationships, and providing a flexible arrangement of content to allow students to work according to their individual ability. In the view of many teachers, unit teaching "places the skills of communication where they belong—in purposeful activity in a social setting." [19] The use of thematically organized sequences is a common form of organization recommended for Advanced Placement Programs. Following this trend, many literature anthologies began organizing their selections in thematic units, and paperback publishers, too, have made units available. Illustrations of thematic units are given in Chapters 13 and 15.

The recommendations of the NCTE's Commission on the English Curriculum for integrated rather than fragmented programs, for a developmental sequence of learning experiences in English, and for a method which emphasizes inquiry and inductive teaching have been widely accepted by leaders in the profession.[20] Research shows that two of the major trends in curriculum building are the ordering of materials into growth sequences with provision for individual differences (the sequential program), and the integrated program, which emphasizes the interrelationship of the language arts to one another and teaches them together rather than in isolation, often in problem-solving and interest-centered units.[21]

An English program which raises questions, stimulates students to observe and generalize about their own experiences, and attempts to build concepts rather than to teach rules and definitions is characteristic of the methods of modern English teachers.

The sequential program

One of the most significant developments in the teaching of English since World War II has been the movement to design programs in English which

---

[19] Commission on the English Curriculum, *The English Language Arts in the Secondary Schools,* p. 112.
[20] Cf. *ibid.,* p. 376, and Walter Loban et al., *Teaching Language and Literature: Grades 7–12,* Harcourt, Brace & World, Inc., New York, 1961, p. 81.
[21] Chester W. Harris (ed.), *Encyclopedia of Educational Research,* 3d ed., The Macmillan Company, New York, 1960, p. 459.

would provide for sequential growth in language arts and skills from the early elementary years through college. Many forces combined to give impetus to this movement, now gathering momentum, which has been implemented by the work of regional, state, and local English organizations cooperating to bring closer together instructors at all levels to work together in designing new programs.

The NCTE Commission on the English Curriculum has been a major force working to help teachers develop sequential programs in English from the kindergarten through the college years. The volumes published by the Commission include a general statement of the aims, procedures, and designs for English programs, and examples of curricula already in operation.[22]

The curricula being produced in the CEEB summer workshops, in centers set up under the Office of Education's Project English, and those in preparation by regional, state, and local English organizations can be expected to provide new directions in teaching to ensure a steady progress in the development of English curricula. The "Articulated English Program" drawn up by the Conference on Basic Issues in the Teaching of English is another attempt to provide recommendations and directions for those who would redesign the curriculum.[23]

The "spiral curriculum"

Concept learning and inquiry, as well as delight in discovery, play a central role in the thinking of the distinguished scientists and educators who worked together on a conference on new educational methods held in Woods Hole, Massachusetts, in 1959. The concept of the spiral curriculum developed by this group emphasizes teaching the underlying structure of a subject, its basic principles, and its relation to other subjects. The basic premise of the conference report is that there is no subject which cannot be taught in some form at all age levels, given teachers with skill to translate its principles and concepts into understandable language.[24] The conference made no attempt to suggest a spiral curriculum in English, but teachers are exploring the implications for their subject and experimenting with ways of applying these concepts to the study of language and literature.[25]

Advanced placement programs

Since they were first established, Advanced Placement Programs have been pacesetters for the rest of the curriculum. Where students have been

---

[22] See the discussion and the list of publications on p. 7.
[23] "An Articulated English Program: A Hypothesis to Test," in Stone, *op. cit.*, pp. 234–246.
[24] Jerome S. Bruner, *The Process of Education*, Harvard University Press, Cambridge, Mass., 1960.
[25] See pp. 65–68 for a sample pattern of concepts in language.

carefully selected, and teachers with special qualifications and reduced loads given the responsibility for teaching them, they have offered gifted students college-level work in the close reading and analysis of style and language and careful training in composition. The "Acorn" syllabus, discussing the requirements of the program, and the frequent conferences calling together those directing and teaching the programs have provided an important kind of in-service training for capable teachers. Inaugurated in 1955, the program was launched as a project of the College Entrance Examination Board to "encourage schools and colleges to work together and stimulate students and teachers to higher achievement." [26]

Humanities programs

The development of humanities courses in many schools in recent years has grown out of efforts to break down the rigid barriers of subject and time in the school day and to help students understand the relationships among the arts. Such programs may bring together literature, theater arts, ballet, art, music, architecture, philosophy, and history for students in the course. Teachers from several departments frequently cooperate to plan the program, and often guest lecturers, films, and field trips to visit concerts, museums, or theaters are included. Such programs attempt to develop in students "a sensitive appreciation of the great heritage of human experience known as the humanities, the record of what men over the centuries have felt, thought, and done in their increasing quest for the good life." [27] Boldly designed programs in Pennsylvania, Oregon, Michigan, Wisconsin, New Jersey, and Connecticut have demonstrated what kinds of programs are possible.

American studies

The correlation of the eleventh-year courses in American history and American literature into an American studies course has provided a pattern of integration for some schools. In some, it has become a kind of American humanities course, teaching concepts of American culture and ideas unique to our tradition, and including music, the visual arts, the dance, journalism in all its forms, religion, and education. [28] Others have focused on American ideas and traditions explored through readings in history and literature.

---

[26] *A Guide to the Advanced Placement Program,* CEEB, Princeton, N.J., 1961. See also *Advanced Placement Program: Course Descriptions,* College Board Advanced Placement Examinations, Box 592, Princeton, N.J., 1960. Essay questions from the examinations may also be obtained from the same source.

[27] Brochure of the John Hay Fellows Program, Rockefeller Plaza, New York 20, N.Y.

[28] Craighill S. Burks and R. Lawrence Dowell, "We Have Left No Art Unturned," *NEA Journal,* vol. 53, May, 1964, pp. 22–24.

New directions

The problem of education in our age is complicated by the demands of a rapidly growing society. The population explosion hit the schools with dramatic force when the war babies began to go to school. Many of them reached the junior high schools in 1953–1954. Ideas about class size and methods of teaching have had to undergo rapid revision recently as teachers and administrators have attempted to meet these changes.

In addition to the problem of population expansion, the demands of education have changed. Where schools in 1940 expected 10 per cent of their students to enter college, some schools now prepare 90 per cent or more of their students for higher education, and more and more college students go on to graduate school. In the near future, more than 50 per cent of public high school graduates will pursue some kind of higher education.[29] Postwar demands for better teaching for gifted children have resulted in honors courses and Advanced Placement Programs. In addition to making new provisions for identifying and training the academically talented, schools have faced the problems of providing for culturally deprived children of slum and high-delinquency areas, and for more and more non-English-speaking children: war refugees, displaced persons, and other immigrants. Dr. James Conant has described the problem of slum children who drop out of school as "social dynamite," and estimates that over half the boys between sixteen and twenty-one in some slum neighborhoods are out of school and out of work. This building up of a mass of unemployed and frustrated youth in crowded slums is a "social phenomenon that may be compared to the piling up of inflammable material in an empty building in a city block."[30] The problems resulting from rapid linguistic, social, and cultural changes have posed serious questions for the schools, and particularly for English teachers charged with the primary responsibility of helping all children become literate.

The shape of things to come

Radical changes in the English curriculum and in methods of teaching English are underway. New schools will be larger and serve more students, as more and more boys and girls enter classrooms from kindergarten to college. Schools are now being built, organized, and staffed for large-group instruction, team teaching, and closed-circuit television. In the future we may see increased use of language laboratories for remedial help in reading and speech, flexible classrooms which can be altered by movable walls to accommodate fifteen

[29] *Progress in Education,* U.S.A., Department of Health, Education and Welfare, Washington, D.C., DE 10005-61 B, p. 19.
[30] Conant, *Slums and Suburbs,* p. 18.

or five hundred students, teaching machines which may take over much of the work teachers are now doing, and classes taught by television. The comprehensive high school recommended in the Conant reports may gradually replace the small-town high school. Some communities are experimenting with the ungraded high school, in which each student may proceed in each course according to his own rate.[31]

A wide variety of elective courses in English and opportunities for independent study are being offered in high schools as well as in the colleges. Under such programs, as one college dean points out, "Students learn first that they must, and then that they can, read serious books without a teachers' gloss." [32]

School days have been lengthened in many communities, and some have planned a longer school year. Summer schools offering remedial work, classes for students with special interests, and accelerated or advanced work for superior students are common.[33] Some universities have offered gifted high school seniors the opportunity to enroll in summer-school Advanced Placement classes.

Well-planned new schools will include a different kind of English classroom. It is recommended that such classrooms have facilities for classroom libraries, flexible seating arrangements, films and slides, overhead projectors and TV, recording equipment, and files that teachers might use for displaying books, periodicals, and students' work; for large-group instruction or small-group conferences; for illustrating structure and organization; for evaluating oral work; and for filing students' compositions.[34]

Teaching English as a second language to thousands of today's youth will undoubtedly assume a larger place in the curriculum of the future. New textbooks, materials, language laboratories, and methods of teaching will make it possible for non-English-speaking children to gain mastery of their adopted tongue and become literate users of the English language.[35]

Textbooks of tomorrow may be different, too. Paperback texts in units of instruction prepared for schools by several publishers have provided a new flexibility for English curricula.[36] New books designed for children from culturally different backgrounds[37] may open the doors of reading for many more

[31] Abraham Lass and Jerome S. Bruner, "The Nongraded High School: Two Views," *Saturday Review,* vol. 47, Jan. 18, 1964, pp. 70–72.

[32] John S. Diekhoff, "Teacher Go Home," *Saturday Review,* vol. 44, July 15, 1961, pp. 52–54.

[33] *Extending the School Year,* Association for Supervision and Curriculum Development, Washington, D.C., 1961.

[34] Grommon, *op. cit.,* p. 373.

[35] See C. C. Fries, *Teaching and Learning of English as a Foreign Language,* The University of Michigan Press, Ann Arbor, Mich., 1963.

[36] See the bibliographies of chapters on literary forms, and Chap. 15.

[37] For instance, the *Gateway English* anthologies, developed at the Project English Center at Hunter College, New York City.

American youth. Books are being designed and written in response to the need voiced by Dr. Otto Klineberg and other critics of contemporary textbooks for books displaying our diversity and cultural pluralism.[38] Books which reflect the excitement and fascination of the study of language, and texts which offer young people much of the heritage of the world's great literature, are beginning to be written for tomorrow's students.[39]

Large-group instruction

Experiments in variations of class size have been carried on in numerous schools, often with the aid of foundation grants. Beginning with the assumption that there is no optimum class size for all subjects and levels, teachers have tried to identify topics and subjects which might be taught in large classes, by lecture, or by television; those which would most profitably be taught in small groups of twelve or fifteen; and those which could be explored in independent study by mature students.

Large-group instruction in English is often given in practical matters such as outlining, dictionary work, punctuation, note taking, and the like. This use of one teacher for 100 to 300 students makes possible small-group meetings for informal discussion of literature and student writing.

Team teaching

Theoretically, large- and small-group instruction allows master teachers to give demonstration lessons, permits interns during their first and second years of teaching to work with them, and allows much of the practical detail work of the classroom to be carried on by teacher aides.

Teacher aides

Along with the rapid increase in class size, demands for increased quality of instruction and more attention to reading and composition have compounded problems. The recommendations of the Conant high school report that composition make up half the curriculum in English and the recommendation there and by the Commission on English of the College Entrance Examination Board that students write a theme each week imply a workweek for the English teacher of nearly sixty hours.[40]

---

[38] Otto Klineberg, "Life Is Fun in a Smiling, Fair-skinned World," *Saturday Review,* vol. 46, Feb. 16, 1963, pp. 75–77, 87.
[39] See bibliography in Chaps. 3, 7, 8, 10, 11, 12, and 13.
[40] Commission on English of the College Entrance Examination Board, *Preparation in English for College-bound Students,* CEEB, Princeton, N.J., 1960, p. 2. See also the California study reported in William J. Dusel, "Determining an Efficient Teaching Load in English," *Illinois English Bulletin,* vol. 43, October, 1955, pp. 1–19.

Teaching by television

Teaching by closed-circuit television is still too expensive a mode of instruction for the majority of public schools, but many have tried it. In the mid-sixties an estimated 15 million students in elementary schools through college received part of their instruction daily by television. It is estimated that by 1971 television will be used during about a third of the students' class time. The telephone, too, has been pressed into educational service, and teachers have experimented with lectures via telephone broadcast over school public-address systems. Most experiments have indicated that skills in punctuation, mechanics, spelling, and the like can be taught as successfully by television as by regular class procedures.[41] Although the results in composition, poetry, and such subjects are more difficult to measure, educational television programs in the techniques of poetry, contemporary literature, and others have been offered by universities with dramatic success, and Boston's pilot course on the humanities, shown to high schools throughout the Boston area, gained enthusiastic response from teachers of both college-preparatory and terminal classes who saw the films *Our Town, Oedipus Rex,* and *Hamlet.*[42] As experiments become more widespread and carefully set up and controlled, new answers may be forthcoming to the question of the effectiveness of televised teaching in such a subject as English.

Teaching machines and programmed instruction

Schools are investigating teaching machines which provide the student with a means of instructing himself, checking his answer to find whether he has made an error. Proponents of teaching machines maintain that the saving of teacher time and the help given students who may learn with only the aid of the machine will be important factors in providing instruction in a period of overcrowded classrooms. At the present time such machines are expensive and relatively rare in the classroom. Except for machines which are designed to improve the speed of reading and reading skills, the majority of topics in the English classroom lend themselves better to programmed instruction by books.[43]

---

[41] *Compendium of Televised Education,* vol. 11, Sept. 1, 1964, Michigan State University Press, East Lansing, Mich., foreword. See also *Teaching by Television,* Ford Foundation and Fund for the Advancement of Education, New York, 1959.

[42] Miriam Goldstein, "Humanities through Television," *English Journal,* vol. 49, April, 1960, pp. 250–255.

[43] The principles of the teaching machine or of programmed learning emphasize the need for dividing the thing to be learned into very small sequential steps and the necessity for immediate reinforcement of learning through correct responses. (See B. F. Skinner, "The Science of Learning and the Art of Teaching," in Arthur A. Lumsdaine and Robert Glaser (eds.), *Teaching Machines and Programmed Learning: A Source Book,* NEA, Department of Audio-Visual Instruction, Washington, D.C., 1960, pp. 99–113.)

Programmed texts have proved valuable as a method of breaking down subject matter into simple and logical learning steps, providing instruction in which students may proceed as quickly or as slowly as they are capable, and providing homework, laboratory exercises, and other materials which can supplement the exchange of ideas between student and teacher and leave the teacher free to invest his best energies in creative teaching.[44] To the texts in grammar, vocabulary, spelling, and linguistics have been added imaginatively designed texts in such subjects as poetry, prosody, and composition.[45]

Some advantages of such texts are that they permit individualized instruction, allowing each student to proceed at his own pace; they ensure that every student in the class answers every question; and they enable the teacher to detect trouble spots.

New programs demand new teachers

The ideal of competence in the areas of English outlined above will be reached in varying degrees by the youth of widely differing backgrounds and abilities who attend our schools. Increasing understanding of the different backgrounds, abilities, and needs of adolescents, the problems of slow learners, and the need for challenging the gifted have in recent years resulted in a new awareness of the teacher's task.

The need for change is dramatically outlined in the 1961 NCTE report on the status of the profession. This suggests that public support, funds, and research are urgently needed to achieve important goals, among them improving the education of English teachers, recruiting and preparing more teachers, encouraging research about English teaching, and designing sequential English programs.[46]

The follow-up report published in 1964 showed that serious deficiencies still exist. Only 50.7 per cent of teachers of English in secondary schools were English majors in college, and since the first report, 30.4 per cent had taken no course work in English, and 25.7 none in education. Nearly half the teachers interviewed reported feeling they were not well prepared in literature, language, composition, or the teaching of reading.[47]

[44] Edward Fry, *Teaching Machines and Programmed Instruction,* McGraw-Hill Book Company, New York, 1963, p. 41.
[45] Among the new texts are the programmed courses in grammar and usage, *English 2600* and *English 3200,* by Joseph C. Blumenthal, Harcourt, Brace & World, Inc., New York, 1962; *Poetry: A Closer Look,* by James M. Reid et al., Harcourt, Brace & World, Inc., New York, 1963; and *The Programmed Approach to Writing,* by Edward J. Gordon et al., Ginn and Company, Boston, 1964.
[46] Committee on National Interest, *The National Interest and the Teaching of English: A Report on the Status of the Profession,* NCTE, Champaign, Ill., 1961, chap. 2.
[47] Committee on National Interest, *The National Interest and the Continuing Education of Teachers of English,* NCTE, Champaign, Ill., 1964.

Government support has led to the improvement in the teaching of the sciences, mathematics, and foreign languages, but congressional bills proposed to aid the teaching of English and school libraries have lagged far behind. The extension of the National Defense Education Act in 1964 to include support for college and school programs in English makes possible similar improvements in the teaching of the humanities.

Project English

So urgent is the problem of designing new curricula and preparing teachers that funds have been made available by the Congress through the Office of Education's Cooperative Research Branch to establish curriculum centers for working on methods, materials, and research. As research, experimentation, and demonstration continues, improved curricula for sequential patterns of teaching reading, composition, language skills, and the development of new materials may be expected to come from these centers.

The CEEB

Further efforts to give support and direction to curriculum revision in the schools have been made by the Commission on English of the College Entrance Examination Board. The first summer institutes designed to develop sample curricula leading to integrated and articulated English programs for all four high school years were begun in 1962 under the Commission's direction. In the summer institute workshops directed by the CEEB, teachers develop materials for use in their own schools. In addition to the summer workshops, the Commission's program includes a series of kinescopes designed for teacher-training classes and English department meetings; a collection of *End-of-Year Examinations in English*[48] written by the Commission and tested in pilot schools, sample syllabi in literature, language, and composition prepared through summer institutes and the follow-up program, and continuing guidance for teachers of English who wish to grow in the profession.

Other efforts

Other groups are participating, too, in the efforts to improve the education of teachers of English and to provide opportunities for study, research, and curriculum planning. The NCTE regularly sponsors summer workshops in cooperation with colleges and universities, as well as a series of three-day workshops preceding the national convention at Thanksgiving. The NEA's Project on English Composition has set up nine centers to offer summer workshops and develop in-service training programs. Since 1951, the John Hay

---

[48] See example on pp. 235–236.

Fellowships offered to outstanding high school teachers have provided opportunities for study to hundreds of American teachers. Yale University's annual English conference conducted since 1955 has produced a collection of reports of speakers and committees on the problems in English.[49] Local, state, regional, and university conferences and workshops have provided continuing education for teachers in almost every region of the country.[50] Kinescopes demonstrating methods of English teaching have been developed by the CEEB and by the University High Schools of the University of Illinois and Minnesota.

Tomorrow's teachers

Some facts are inescapable, and schools and teachers must find some ways of dealing with them. Millions more children will be attending our schools and colleges in the next few years. Some ways of meeting the crises of inadequate staffs and larger classes will have to be found. Of the ways that have been suggested, some seem to automate our most humane subjects, and others, such as the use of master teachers, suggest that teaching may become more of an art and a profession than it has been.

In a sketch of the "brave new world" of our automated future, Dr. Robert Pooley counsels us to use machines wisely, but to remain what "machines can never be: intelligent, educated, warmly human beings . . . igniting others with the same undying fire." [51]

The kind of English teacher envisioned by the present book is one with adequate background in language and literature, knowledge of the science and art of teaching these subjects, a knowledge of adolescents, their interests, and ways of learning, and a dedication to humanistic values. Chapter 17 suggests the kind of education the teacher of English needs and the programs underway for in-service training of teachers.

The recommendations in the Conant report on the education of American teachers and those in volume V of the NCTE curriculum series deserve serious attention by those who are responsible for educating tomorrow's teachers of English. Chapter 17 examines current suggestions for the education and certification of teachers of English.[52]

Tomorrow's teachers will need to explore all the ways and resources through which they can work toward the new goals set by the exacting and rewarding profession of teaching English. The years ahead will bring dramatic

---

[49] Edward J. Gordon and Edward S. Noyes (eds.), *Essays on the Teaching of English,* Appleton-Century-Crofts, Inc., New York, 1960.

[50] See Grommon, *op. cit.,* part 3.

[51] Robert C. Pooley, "Automatons or English Teachers?," *English Journal,* vol. 50, March, 1961, p. 173.

[52] James B. Conant, *The Education of American Teachers,* McGraw-Hill Book Company, New York, 1963, and Grommon, *op. cit.*

"I'm in love with my teaching machine."
Drawing by J. G. Farris;
© 1964 *Saturday Review*.

changes to schools and to the profession. The teachers of tomorrow, better prepared and better educated than those of today, will bring a new sense of dedication to meet the challenge.

Selected bibliography

Jerome S. Bruner, *The Process of Education,* Harvard University Press, Cambridge, Mass., 1960. The report of the Woods Hole Conference of scientists, scholars, and educators who met to discuss the improvement of science teaching in the public schools.

Commission on the English Curriculum of the NCTE, *The English Language Arts,* Appleton-Century-Crofts, Inc., New York, 1952.

——, *The English Language Arts in the Secondary School,* Appleton-Century-Crofts, Inc., New York, 1956.

Committee on National Interest, *National Interest and the Continuing Education of Teachers of English,* NCTE, Champaign, Ill., 1964.

——, *National Interest and the Teaching of English: A Report on the Status of the Profession,* NCTE, Champaign, Ill., 1964.

James B. Conant, *The American High School Today: A First Report to Interested Citizens,* McGraw-Hill Book Company, New York, 1959.

——, *Education in the Junior High School Years,* Educational Testing Service, Princeton, N.J., 1960.

————, *The Education of American Teachers*, McGraw-Hill Book Company, New York, 1963.

————, *Slums and Suburbs*, McGraw-Hill Book Company, New York, 1961. A study of the large metropolitan high school and the problems of culturally disadvantaged youth.

Albert R. Kitzhaber et al., *Education for College*, The Ronald Press Company, New York, 1961.

Marshall McLuhan, *Understanding Media: Extensions of Man*, McGraw-Hill Book Company, New York, 1964. A thoughtful discussion of the impact of the electronic age on our culture.

The President's Commission on National Goals, *Goals for Americans*, Prentice-Hall, Inc., Englewood Cliffs, N.J., 1960.

Rockefeller Brothers Fund, *The Pursuit of Excellence: Education and the Future of America*, Special Studies Project Report V, New York, 1958.

George Winchester Stone, Jr. (ed.), *Issues, Problems and Approaches in the Teaching of English*, Holt, Rinehart and Winston, Inc., New York, 1961.

Lloyd J. Trump and Dorsey Baynham, *Guide to Better Schools: Focus on Change*, Rand McNally & Company, Chicago, 1961.

Alfred North Whitehead, *The Aims of Education*, The Macmillan Company, New York, 1929.

What do you care for Caesar, who yourself
Are in three parts divided, and must find,
Past daydream and rebellion and bravado,
The final shape and substance of your mind?

CONSTANCE CARRIER [1]

CHAPTER *2*

The learner and his world

Youth in the world of today

The adolescents between the ages of thirteen and eighteen in our schools are often, like Peter, in conflict between the imperious demands of their personal and social needs and the intellectual development through which, if they are successful, they will find the "final shape and substance" of their minds. It has long been recognized that schools and teachers must provide conditions favorable to the personal and social as well as intellectual growth of boys and girls. Recent research in adolescent psychology has indicated ways of utilizing knowledge about adolescent growth to provide the most favorable environment for learning, and to select the materials for teaching which engage young people most completely and absorbedly in the tasks of learning.

The children now in our junior and senior high schools were born shortly after World War II. They have never known a world in which a war, cold or hot, was not going on; they have grown up in an era of postwar prosperity. The adolescents in our classes must be viewed against the background of rapidly shifting economic, social, and political patterns: a world of more cars, more TV sets, newer and larger schools, and larger classes than any other generation has known. They are the children of the atomic age, brought into the world in the dark shadow of Hiroshima and inevitably influenced by

---

[1] From "To Peter at Fourteen," in Rolfe Humphries (ed.), *New Poems by American Poets*, copyright by Ballantine Books, Inc., 1953; reprinted by permission of Constance Carrier.

all that atomic power and the race for space imply. Theirs is the age of the beatnik, the angry young man, the existentialist. But it is also the world of an ever more powerful United Nations, of the Peace Corps, and of the atom test-ban treaty. Today's youth is interested in space ships and jet airplanes, hot-rod cars and drag races, but also in idealistic youth movements, in working with underprivileged children, and in classes and summer-school work for the gifted.

Achieving maturity in our contemporary culture involves stresses unknown to other cultures, where adolescence seems to be a less stormy period of life than it is in ours. Some of the contrasts between these cultures and our own provide instructive insights for teachers.[2]

The nature of the world in which he grows up presents problems and obstacles to an easy growth into maturity for the young person today. The complex automated world described in Chapter 1 has meant a decrease in vocational opportunities for many. A future of making parts on an assembly line or of routine office jobs without responsibility involves a loss of identity which does not challenge the best energies or the creativity of many young people. "The closed college door" represents another kind of limitation, as increased numbers of young people vie in the highly competitive scramble for admission to crowded colleges.

For large numbers of our youth, school life is something to be endured until they reach their sixteenth birthday. In city slums nearly half the children drop out of school in grades nine, ten, eleven, and twelve.[3] The lengthened period of compulsory schooling and diminishing employment for the young has resulted in such large numbers of jobless youths under twenty-one that the President proposed in 1961 that Congress take action. The Economic Opportunity Act of 1964 provided for a Job Corps to train such youth for employment. The search for individuality in a mass culture, and for satisfying, significant, and responsible work and family life are major tasks for today's youth. In addition to the diminution of vocational opportunity and responsibility, growing up today involves problems not characteristic of simpler societies or of an earlier era. Many are common to a mass culture: the mobility and consequent rootlessness of many families, increasing disorientation of family life, the prolonged period of youth's economic dependence on the family, the change from a largely rural to a largely urban population, racial tensions—all these aspects of today's culture combine to complicate the task of growing from childhood into maturity.

The teacher of English today recognizes the interplay of physical, emotional, intellectual, and social factors in learning and the roles of each in adolescent growth. He is aware, too, of the problems of the emotionally dis-

[2] As Margaret Mead has pointed out in *Coming of Age in Samoa: A Psychological Study of Primitive Youth for Western Civilization*, William Morrow and Company, Inc., New York, 1928. (Paper: Mentor Books, 1949.)

[3] James B. Conant, *Slums and Suburbs*, McGraw-Hill Book Company, New York, 1961, p. 2.

turbed children who are found more and more frequently in the average class-room of today's crowded schools. The gifted, the retarded, the children of the slums, those of various racial, ethnic, and national backgrounds, the aggressive child, and the juvenile delinquent all spend time in our classrooms and demand recognition and understanding.

The teacher of adolescents who has had in his college training a course in child development or adolescent psychology has a useful context in which to view the students he meets in the classroom. As he faces boys and girls of twelve or fourteen or sixteen, the abstractions of the psychology text become translated into reality. Often he goes back to the books he has read and looks at them in a new light, that of the life situation in which he leads those under his direction to learn about the English language and its litera-ture. All he can remember about what he has learned and all he can add to that knowledge will be important. The teacher with an understanding of youth and its development has in his grasp the means of leading individual boys and girls to find enchantment in books, to master the written and spoken language, and to enjoy using their minds to question, to think, and to learn.

While he does not confuse his role as teacher of English with that of the physician, psychiatrist, or the sociologist, he realizes that his role as an under-standing adult who offers both support and firmness plays an essential part in the young person's growth. His encouragement of the shy and withdrawn child may be the key which unlocks the ability to express thoughts in writing or speaking; his acceptance of the hostile and rebellious disturbed youth may be the first step toward socialization and subsequent intellectual achieve-ment.

We are realizing today that many potentially gifted youth remain un-identified in school or achieve little because of social and emotional handicaps. The child from the slums often does not look at academic achievement as a goal worthy of his effort or is incapable of believing he can attain success in school or in a career; children from broken families and disturbed homes carry too much anxiety to be able to do well in school. Many gifted young people have emotional problems which stand in the way of learning.

The program in English, enlisting the students' own drives toward maturity, recognizing current interests, and creating new ones, can lead youth to intellectual excellence even as it serves their emotional need to grow from dependence into maturity. The teacher's awareness of adolescent growth, needs, and interests can provide an invaluable guide for selecting materials, methods, and content in the English curriculum. The following pages sug-gest ways in which this understanding of the developmental tasks of youth[4]

---

[4] The discussion of these developmental tasks is drawn from many of the excellent studies of adolescent growth and development, but particularly from the treatment of the necessary steps to maturity in Robert J. Havighurst, *Developmental Tasks and Education,* Longmans, Green & Co., Inc., New York, 1953.

and of cultural, social, and intellectual differences may be made to serve individual growth.

Physical development

The teen-ager may worry considerably if the physical changes of adolescence occur in him more or less rapidly than in his peers; teachers, too, may fail to understand the significance of these differences in students, especially during the junior high school years. Problems of inattentiveness, daydreaming, childishness, irresponsibility, and attention-getting aggressiveness are often by-products of these concerns. The small, underdeveloped boy often becomes unbearably troublesome in the classroom in order to compensate for his uncertainty about his masculinity. Girls whose figures mature more rapidly than those of their peers often grow round-shouldered or refuse to do the kind of classwork which requires that they stand before the class. Others, proud of their emerging femininity, emulate movie idols by wearing tight sweaters and narrow skirts.

Teachers of early adolescents often see the most startling evidence of the differences in physical development and growth. Pictures of a seventh-grade class often show boys varying from each other as much as fifteen inches in height, and ranging from plump, childish bodies and faces to tall, gangling, definitely masculine ones. Some girls at this age are still little girls, with the straight-up-and-down figures of the ten-year-old; others have the rounded curves of young women and show skill in wearing lipstick and varied hairdos. Our English programs very often ignore these startling maturational differences and present both children and the precociously mature with the same fare: the same theme topics, the same grammar drills, the same books to read.

During the period of rapid physical development and consequent awkwardness and self-consciousness, youth should find speaking as comfortable an experience as possible. The comfort offered by the group in panel discussion or choral speaking, or that of sitting behind a desk rather than standing before the class, helps awkward youth gain ease in speaking.

Reading, too, should serve adolescent growth. Teachers are aware of the fact that physically immature girls are probably not yet ready for books containing a frank treatment of adult relationships and that physically underdeveloped boys may find satisfaction in reading about the exploits of very masculine adventurers, muscular sports heroes, and those who have demonstrated physical courage and prowess.

Some of the brief, ungraded papers used for writing practice may well give expression to some of the very real adolescent worries about height, weight, complexion, posture, sexual development, and what the boys call "body built." [5] Particularly during the junior high years, some attention given

---

[5] The teen-agers interviewed in a survey by social scientists at Purdue University listed anxieties about growth among their most pressing problems. Psychologists, too, point out the

to reassuring youth about the normality of its concerns about growth takes little time in the year's program but may have important effects in lessening worry and freeing the young person to develop more intellectual interests.

Emotional development

The physical changes of adolescence have their psychological parallels. Wide variations in emotional development exist. The fifteen-year-old kept dependent by his parents may think and feel as a child, while the boy or girl of the same age who has had to assume serious responsibilities early may be a nearly mature adult.

The staggering cost to human happiness of mental illness today both to the individual and to society is ample evidence that schools and society are rightfully concerned about including in the curriculum materials and activities which promote mental health. Teachers spend much of their time in today's schools struggling to teach children with emotional problems that block learning, produce reading disabilities, result in aggression or withdrawal, and produce disruptive disciplinary problems. Emotional problems in adolescence are enormously costly to the individuals who wrestle with them, to the welfare of other adolescents with whom disturbed children associate, and to the society of which they will be members and raise families who will suffer the damaging consequences of their conflicts.

Such children can effectively prevent the progress of those who want to learn. Many of these young people carry heavy burdens of anxiety: they worry over parents who are ill, physically or mentally; divorces or separations, whether they have occurred or are impending; financial insecurity, parental alcoholism, or the desertion of the family by a parent. Their relations with parents, brothers, or sisters are often strained to the breaking point. Neither the teacher nor the schools can change the home situation, but there are ways in which teachers can help such students.[6]

What the teacher can do

For many a troubled youth the first step to social adjustment and school achievement has been the establishment of a relationship with an understanding teacher to whom he could look for acceptance, support, direction, and encouragement. For such young people, talking and writing about pressing

seriousness of these concerns for adolescents. See H. H. Remmers and D. H. Radler, *The American Teenager,* The Bobbs-Merrill Company, Inc., Indianapolis, 1957, chap. 3, and Lawrence R. Frank and Mary Frank, *Your Adolescent at Home and at School,* The Viking Press, Inc., New York, 1956, chap. 2.

[6] In many schools there are no provisions for such children, and teachers must find ways of handling them in the regular classroom. Some helpful suggestions are given in Fritz Redl and David Wineman, *The Aggressive Child* (including *Children Who Hate* and *Controls from Within*), The Free Press of Glencoe, New York, 1957.

problems, sometimes with classmates and sometimes in private conferences with a teacher, along with reading about those who have had similar problems has provided the first step to rehabilitation as it did with the delinquent in jail who turned to books, talks with other prisoners, and writing for self-understanding.[7]

Understanding from classroom teachers has resulted in gains in academic achievement, prevention of failures and dropouts, and more positive attitudes toward work, school, and society. Since the English teacher deals more directly than most teachers with the thoughts and feelings of youth, he can play an important role in salvaging many adolescents who would otherwise be lost or fail to reach their potential for living and learning.

The teacher of English can offer help with some of the common conflicts of adolescence often merely by "listening with the third ear," by providing an accepting audience—of one person or of the class—for talking and writing, and by recommending the right books at the right time to the right person. The major energies and interests of adolescents are turned toward the following developmental tasks through which the individual must work in his progress toward maturity.

Achieving independence. The tensions resulting from the adolescent's battle to become independent of his parents and family produce so much anxiety that these problems rank high on every list of adolescent difficulties. The amount of freedom or discipline, the having and managing of allowances, privileges, and responsibilities, and the attempts to decide on career goals are often the basis for argument or outright conflict. Closely related to these are his relationships with brothers and sisters, his rivalry with them for parental affection, scholastic achievement, material possessions, and social success—all more important goals during adolescence than during childhood. Units on family life and problems of growing up, frequently included in the early junior high school curriculum, provide valuable opportunities for talking, writing, and reading about such matters. Class reading of such books as Rawlings' *The Yearling*, Steinbeck's *The Red Pony*, Steffens' *Boy on Horseback*, as well as other books which show adolescents struggling with their problems, inevitably results in discussion of the problems of the readers themselves. The

---

[7] Two examples are instructive here. On a televised documentary program, "Youths Anonymous," filmed at the Boys' Republic in Detroit, the viewer saw troubled youths in a voluntary group-therapy meeting, and heard the slow, hesitant verbalizing of their hostility. The value of this kind of talk is expressed in the words of one boy: "What you say helps me; what I say may help you to look at things differently." The role of the adult leader was that of the accepting adult: a listener, sometimes a questioner, but never a judge.

A sociological study conducted at Harvard University showed that juvenile delinquency may be reduced simply by talking. A group of boys talked about themselves in tape-recorded interviews; it was observed that typically they passed through five stages during the series of interviews: apathy, anger, despair, insight, and transformation. The delinquency rate after a year was half of what might have been expected for such a group. (News item in the *New York Times*, August 5, 1962, p. 1.)

young adult must win his independence not only from the parents but also from the need for control by other adults. His training during the high school years should help him move from dependence on authority for control and discipline to self-sufficiency, or the ability to set his own tasks and goals; he must learn to discipline himself, to accept responsibility, and to direct his own actions wisely. He must move, in Riesman's phrase, from "other-directed-ness" to autonomy; from the need to conform in order to be popular or loved to the ability to stand alone, if need be, and to obey his inner controls.[8] The giant step the adolescent takes toward maturity by becoming capable of regulating his own life and actions, making his own decisions, and living independently as an adult is a result of a series of smaller steps taken during the years from twelve to eighteen.

Adjusting to sex roles.   Psychologists see adolescence as a transition from childhood to the time when the youth adjusts not only to a changing and maturing body, but also to a concept of himself as an adult who accepts his sex role with satisfaction. Many men and women never fully adjust to their masculinity or femininity and spend their lives warring against the role into which their biological makeup has cast them. The overprotected boy, inclined to effeminacy, may find satisfaction in biographies and novels about fully masculine men who have achieved in the field of the arts, literature, or intellectual activity rather than in athletic prowess, battle, or dangerous adventure; the tomboy, reluctant to abandon blue jeans for more feminine attire, needs assurance that her feminine role is a worthy one in the eyes of her peers, and evidence of the satisfactions of womanhood and motherhood. Books have provided this for many girls. Sigrid Undset's *Kristin Lavransdatter,* Willa Cather's *My Antonia,* Jessamyn West's *The Friendly Persuasion,* and others offer portraits of fully maternal women, finding satisfaction and joy in family life. The sudden metamorphosis of the heroine of Carson McCullers' *The Member of the Wedding* from the tomboy Frankie to the lipsticked "F. Jasmine Adams" is the perfect example of the working out of this youthful dilemma.

For older boys and girls during the senior high school years, reading and writing may explore patterns of family life and of marriage. Mann's *Budden-brooks,* Tolstoi's *Anna Karenina,* and Galsworthy's *The Forsyte Saga* have helped many young adults clarify their own sense of values about marriage and the family.

Searching for identity.   The basic task of adolescence is self-identification.[9] Our culture does not encourage the building of a clear self-image, yet psychologists today maintain that it is the concept of self which determines the way the adolescent views himself in his relation to society. His sex role,

[8] David Riesman et al., *The Lonely Crowd,* Anchor Books, Doubleday & Company, Inc., Garden City, N.Y., 1956.
[9] Edgar Z. Friedenberg, *The Vanishing Adolescent,* Dell Publishing Co., Inc., New York, 1962, p. 17.

his status as an independent, self-directed, or dependent person, his belief in his ability to learn and to achieve, his role as a delinquent, a "tough guy," or a contributing member of society are all manifestations of his deepest feelings about himself.[10]

The eternal problems of the search for identity are the universal questions of man, reflected in literature for centuries: Who am I? What is it to be a man? Of what am I capable? What am I here for? Every adolescent asks these age-old human questions, and it is the responsibility of the English teacher above all others to assist in the search by first directing youth to the literature in which such problems are explored, and by then guiding his talking and writing in such a way that he clarifies the answers for himself.[11]

A characteristic expression of these adolescent feelings is this uncorrected paper by a tenth-grade girl:

Who Am I?

I am an average teenage girl and I feel this is quite an experience. I cry at movies and get dramatic and dig Elvis and anything with a calypso beat. I read books by Hemingway and Buck. I also enjoy the ballet, and love to talk for hours on the phone.

Being a teenage girl I associate with other teenagers. We go to parties, dances, and church. We have erratic eating habits, potato chips, ice-cream, choclate, and cucumbers all at one sitting.

We dress to suit all the latest fads which I must admit, are rather ridiculous at times. The girls like nothing better than to get all dressed in a new party dress, or wear bermuda shorts wherever they go. The boys wear white buck snapjacks and novel cufflinks, or their comfortable pair of old dungarees.

We like to laugh, enjoy ourselves, and have a good time.

There is one part of the teenager that not everyone knows. That is the serious part. In a few years I'll have to go out into the world. Will I be a success? What's happening in the world? Everyone seems to be opposing everybody else. Why can't we live in peace and harmony? Why am I here and what is my purpose in life? I am glad and proud to be an American and to be free, but why can't all the people everywhere be free? These are just a few of the questions that run through a teenager's mind. At times we are confused and mixed-up about things that we don't comprehend. All this makes a teen-ager a teenager and a young person on the brink of adulthood.

Yes, I feel that being a teenager is quite an experience.

In his struggle to clarify his concept of self, the young person often begins by conforming to the image his parents have of him; later the role he assumes with friends is all important. Still later, he chooses young adults with whom to identify and fictional or real-life heroes and models to emulate. Gradually,

---

[10] Ruth Strang, *The Adolescent Views Himself: A Psychology of Adolescence,* McGraw-Hill Book Company, New York, 1957, develops this point of view.

[11] A discussion of literature as a means of obtaining insight into self is given in Chaps. 9 and 15.

however, he must crystallize in his own thinking the role he wishes to play, the kind of person he wants to be; he must formulate his own ideals, standards, and philosophy of life. As psychologists have pointed out, the dark view of the world held by many adolescents is subject to change.[12] Writing, reading, and group discussion of goals and standards have helped many young people take a more positive view of the future.

Clarifying vocational goals. The young idealistic adolescent, emerging from childish fantasies about the glamorous romantic adult roles he wishes to assume, must gradually form a realistic idea of his abilities and limitations and learn to accept them without loss of self-respect. Not many would-be doctors or lawyers have the ability to take the rigorous training these professions demand. Not all girls are fitted to be nurses or airline hostesses. Psychologists point out the romantic quality of many early vocational choices (ballet dancing, missionary work, medicine) and suggest that while these choices may not be practical in themselves they may be useful in providing a basis for a shift to related but more realistic goals.[13] Confused, immature thinking about vocational aims often finds expression in writing, as in this brief, uncorrected paper by a fourteen-year-old girl:

My Plans for the Future

As for my plans in the future, I would like to be an airline hostess. My first reason is that I like airplanes. I always like to go up in an airplane and when I look down I can see many things. My second reason is that I like many people who are traveling. I would like to help these people who are traveling. I think it would be wonderful because I like people. Also a hostess will have a chance to travel to many strange places. I know that to be a hostess I will have to have college work. But I will need nursing experience to. I'm not quite sure how much nursing I will need or what college I will go to. I think it is one year. I would like to be many things but I like this in perticular. After this I would like to be a nurse if I can not be a hostess.

Such papers need examination and discussion to clarify the student's thinking and to lead to the reasoned search for a satisfying career which will challenge the individual's best abilities. The exploration of the world of work and the choice of worthwhile vocational aims involve the realistic assessment of capabilities and aptitudes. The course in English need not and should not become a course in psychology, but recognition of the role of the emotions in language and literature and awareness of the individual's need to perform his developmental tasks can help adolescents to greater acceptance and understanding of themselves and of others and can thereby ensure them of more satisfying lives as human beings. Reading, writing, and talking have always served such ends.

[12] Strang, *op. cit.*, chap. 3.
[13] Frank and Frank, *op. cit.*, p. 72.

Social development

A number of factors in addition to biological inheritance and emotional makeup affect the intellectual growth of youth. Each stage of development is related to the life of the boy or girl as a member of the group. The need to belong, one of the most powerful of adolescent drives, affects attitudes toward school, toward learning, and toward authority. It is helpful to the teacher to recognize that during adolescence the social group becomes the most important influence in shaping the standards, values, ideals, and often the vocational, educational, and social goals of boys and girls. The group to which the adolescent owes his allegiance—the boys and girls with whom he studies, dates, and socializes—plays an important role in his development.

Belonging to such a group is the first step toward independence of the child, who heretofore has been most strongly influenced by his home environment and parental approval. In attempting to free himself from parental control, the young boy or girl takes group behavior as a model. Conflict between the values of the group and its pressures and individual standards often becomes acute during adolescence. Although the siren song of the peer group is irresistible, especially for the youngster unsure of himself, individual consciences are frequently strong, and the young adolescent is usually eager to do right. The Franks observe:

> . . . very often young people get caught up in a pattern (not in their own group) that puts heavy accent on popularity: who dates and who doesn't, who is sought after, who is most reckless, and so on. The incredible fact is that each one of these adolescents may have high standards and ideals for himself, but seeing his world as it is represented by his peers, he must, as he thinks, conform.[14]

Because the admiration and approval of the group is so essential to the young person, many disciplinary behavior problems arise from the fact that adolescents prefer the authority of the group to that of teachers or administrators. Many somewhat antisocial children band together to make life miserable for their teachers. Schools and administrators who recognize the pressures of the peer group make use of its leaders to influence other young adolescents and work for ways in which group activities and group decisions may be constructively pursued.[15]

Attitudes toward leadership, toward the prestige of athletes or scholars, toward certain vocational goals, toward gangs and their achievements are all far more powerfully conditioned by the group than by any other single factor. To be useful, attempts to change attitudes must include ways in which the

[14] *Ibid.*, p. 303.
[15] Sociometric techniques have provided some useful ways of doing this. See discussion in Chap. 4.

approval of more socially desirable goals and achievements may come from the groups young people associate with.[16]

Riesman points out that language, too, is a powerful peer-group tool:

> For the insiders language becomes a chief key to the taste and mood currents that are prevalent in this group at any moment. For the outsiders, including adult observers, language becomes a mysterious opacity, constantly carrying peer-group messages which are full of precise meanings that remain untranslatable.
>
> . . . Language . . . is used in the peer-groups today much as popular tunes seem to be used: as a set of counters by which one establishes that one is "in" and by which one participates in the peer-group's arduously self-socializing "work." [17]

The language of the group is so special, such a hallmark of the students' current stage of adolescence, that the teacher may find in it a rich mine of material for language study. The currency and transitoriness of teen-age slang, the vividness of teen-age metaphor, and the use of language to signal membership in various groups can be studied from the resources of the students' own language in or out of school. Exercises in Chapters 3, 6, and 7 contain suggestions for such study.

Teachers in large metropolitan schools often are called upon to deal with near-delinquent youth or children from culturally deprived backgrounds. The teacher's understanding and successful handling of these adolescents is often the deciding factor in their staying in school, and at times may be the deciding factor in their transition to acceptable adult society rather than to delinquency. As one perceptive teacher observes of the children in a "blackboard jungle" school in Manhattan:

> . . . these kids with the black leather jackets and shaggy haircuts and booing, jeering voices . . . are really the most pitiful group of scared lost mixed-up kids that ever were turned, unwanted, out into a big dirty city. When taken away from the protective gang, they are not only amazingly defensive and frightened, but also almost afraid to admit or believe that their names are Joe or John. . . . They seem to crave affection, admiration, understanding, and when sure that these are being genuinely offered, thrive on them and drop the loud cruel protection of the gang.[18]

One teacher with long experience in working with adolescents from foreign backgrounds makes a plea to teachers to respect the cultural integrity of such children, who often use language "as a weapon and a wall" to preserve the dignity of self.[19]

---

[16] James S. Coleman, *The Adolescent Society: The Social Life of the Teen-ager and Its Impact on Education,* The Free Press of Glencoe, New York, 1961, p. 320.

[17] Riesman et al., *op. cit.,* pp. 105–106.

[18] Suzanne Nemser, "Two Graduates Cultivate Gardens in 'Blackboard Jungles,'" *MAT Newsletter,* Yale University, October, 1956, pp. 6–7.

[19] Charles J. Calitri, "Language and the Dignity of Youth," *Saturday Review,* vol. 46, July 20, 1963, pp. 46–61.

In general, it is not difficult to understand the steps that youth takes on the way from peer group to gang. The need for belonging, coupled with rejection by many of the closed social groups in schools, when combined with parental indifference, neglect, or abuse, makes the gang powerfully attractive to many youths from all strata of society. As the boys in the musical *West Side Story* say, "A guy's an orphan without a gang." The gang offers the solidarity of the group; it thrives on and is united by conflict; it offers outlets for the tensions and aggressions of adolescence; it intensifies and extrapolates normal adolescent rebellion against parents and teachers to include almost all authority figures in society.

In some measure, these tensions operate in the growing up of all youth. The difference between the normal youth and the delinquent lies most often in the availability of some kind of help with these problems, and the presence of a strong, supporting adult who can reinforce the young person's striving for socially acceptable values. One of the tragic themes in reports about delinquents is the frequency with which the attempt to break away from the gang fails for lack of such support. When the break is successful, it is most often because some adult helped the youth bridge the gap between asocial living and socially approved goals.

The program in English can provide reading and topics for discussion which help youth work toward constructive rather than asocial group and individual behavior. Student discussions about goals and values can be of positive value in the English class. Ruth Strang says:

> When young people discuss topics relating to themselves, they speak from the vantage point of their own first-hand experiences. . . . Panels of gifted children have given keen insight into school procedures that bore or frustrate them; they present a sound blueprint of the kind of education they want and need. Juvenile delinquents tell us about blighting conditions in their lives and give us glimpses of their need for attention, respect, and responsibility. Panels of high school students who have reading difficulties make a plea for understanding and for more effective instruction and meaningful reading material.[20]

Intellectual development

The widening intellectual interests of young people during adolescence make these years exciting adventures for both student and teacher. Thoughtful college teachers point out that it is during the secondary-school years that the young person's values, tastes, and intellectual interests are formed. The development of the student's language is of primary concern to the teacher of English, and determines to a large extent the materials he studies at the various stages of his development. Knowledge about the ways in which students learn affects curricular content and design, and determines choices of materials appropriate to youth of differing intellectual capacities and interests. Related to

[20] Strang, *op. cit.*, pp. 17–18.

the process of learning, too, are the cultural attitudes toward intellectual achievement which often determine the success of the individual in learning and the choice of his intellectual goals.

The adolescent and his language. Language is the learner's most important tool and the key to his intellectual development. His ability to think effectively depends in great part on his skill with language. For many years the verbal aptitude test of the College Entrance Examination Board has proved the most reliable index of academic success. The teacher of English will have a significant role in furthering the language development of boys and girls. Some understanding of the linguistic road the learner has traveled is helpful to the teacher who plans the content of the course.

Much that has been learned in recent years about the language of children is useful in illuminating the language behavior and attitudes toward language of adolescents. Early studies in children's use of language have revised drastically our notions about children's vocabularies. Studies estimate that the first-grade child knows 24,000 basic and derivative words, and the twelfth-grade child, 80,000.[21] The steps from the birth cry to the child's first recognizable word have been charted by observers who have shown how the babbling of the infant reproduces all the speech sounds which are articulated in any language. As the child learns through the stimulus of the adult speech around him, he selects the speech sounds of his family language. By the time he reaches adolescence, he loses the plastic ability of the infant to articulate the phonemes common to languages different from his own.

Psychologists have shown what a miraculous feat the child's early learning of language is: by the time he is six he is in command of most of the basic sentence structures and can generate sentences of his own based on their patterns. The role of babbling is of the utmost importance to his language development; without these years of practice and pleasure in the sound and articulation of words, he does not learn to speak. Without any formal study of sentence structure or vocabulary, the child, in six years, learns more about the language than we succeed in teaching him during twelve or fourteen years of study in English. His language grows and develops through his constant use and practice of it, through his high degree of motivation to use language for his personal and social needs, and through his eagerness for response from those with whom he wishes to communicate. Jesperson, the Danish grammarian, quoting a Slavic proverb, says, "If you wish to talk well, you must murder the language first." Through continuous practice and responsiveness from those who encourage his talking, the young child learns almost by himself to eliminate errors through his curiosity about correct forms. Usually no one teaches him that "Birds flied away," is incorrect; he soon observes others saying *flew*. Never again in school or in life is he in such a favorable environment for language learning.

---

[21] George Miller, *Language and Communication*, McGraw-Hill Book Company, New York, 1951, p. 150.

The child's sentence structure shows steady maturation, too. His first words are complexes of meaning: *da* for "doll" may mean "I want my doll," and perhaps even have additional refinements, "Not that old rag doll but the new doll I got for my birthday yesterday." His early sentences may be rudimentary ones of two or three words; compound sentences begin at about age two, and the first complex sentence after he is three. There is a steady growth in the maturity and complexity of his sentences.[22]

It is clear that many of these facts about language development in the child have significance for the teacher of adolescents. Of first importance, perhaps, is the role of motivation and satisfaction in early language learning: the child gets recognition, praise, and satisfying response from his early efforts to learn language, or he does not learn well. Studies have shown that children brought up in institutions are retarded in language growth, as are children from lower socioeconomic levels. Dorothea McCarthy has suggested that parental indifference or neglect in homes where mothers work and the lack of stimulation in such environments are the most important factors contributing to the language retardation of such children.[23] The emotional and personal character of the child's early language is also of foremost importance. Since his earliest affectional memories are associated with his learning of language, emotional overtones and connotations cling to many of the words he knows. When the speech of the home becomes a subject for correction or contempt, as it frequently is in schools, his resistance to change may be increased.

The adolescent and his learning. The discussion of language and thinking in Chapter 3 outlines the major concepts of recent learning theory. As has been indicated in the discussion of language, the young person's command of language grows as he matures; the steps in this intellectual maturing have been summarized for parents and teachers by psychologists.[24] Teachers familiar with these patterns of intellectual growth provide the maximum stimulation for curious minds during the adolescent years, without demanding achievement too advanced for particular age levels.

The process of learning. Students learn and retain, so we are told, that which enhances their concept of self—the young person wants to learn that which will make him more worthy in his own eyes, in the eyes of his friends, and in society's view.[25] He responds to learning and standards of conduct which he perceives as making him more mature. To be recognized as an adult is his strongest desire.

---

[22] See the instructive study of the language development of adolescents in Lou La Brant, "A Study of Certain Development of Language of Children in Grades Four to Twelve Inclusive," *Genetic Psychology Monographs,* vol. 14, November, 1933, pp. 387–494.

[23] Speech at the Workshop on Language and Linguistics in School Programs, NCTE Convention, Nov. 22, 1961, Philadelphia.

[24] Harold W. Bernard, *Adolescent Development in American Culture,* Harcourt, Brace & World, Inc., New York, 1957, chap. 9.

[25] Strang, *op. cit.,* chap. 3.

The adolescent years are those in which the young person, rightly challenged, will attempt prodigious feats of reading and learning to test his powers. He may attempt to read books beyond the limits of his comprehension: Tolstoi's *War and Peace,* Proust's *Remembrance of Things Past,* or Kant's *Critique of Pure Reason.* He may read voraciously in subjects that interest him and change these interests every few months. He may reject the tasks which seem meaningless and irrelevant only to seek out those which are important to him at the moment, though they are, perhaps, more difficult. Gilbert Highet tells of Jesuit schools in which boys challenged each other to "feats of brainwork which would astonish us nowadays," for example, memorizing long passages and debating important problems. He observes that "really interesting challenges are required to elicit the hidden strengths of really complex minds." [26] For some students, pressure to attain high standards is often effective. Albert Schweitzer claimed that a new teacher changed his life at fourteen by demanding the best from the dreamy boy threatened with losing his scholarship. The teacher's words, "You have no right to have me give you beautiful music when you spoil everything you play," were the challenge needed to produce the desire for perfection.

The process of ordering knowledge into some kind of meaningful structure is essential for enduring learning. The importance of structure and the disastrous effect of lack of organization in the learning process is emphasized by Bruner: "The poor teacher permits so much irrelevant action to occur in such self-obscuring sequences that only a genius could give a coherent account of what he had been up to. . . ." [27] Piecemeal and fragmented programs fail to provide the learner with a meaningful framework for what he learns. Students may experience pattern and order in perceiving the relationship between the nature of language and its spoken and written uses, and may also experience order and design in the forms of literature and writing studied during each year. Enduring learning takes place when the young student sees his own growth through sequences of learning experiences leading to clearly defined goals.

As we have seen in Chapter 1, the emphasis today on concept learning, on immediate reinforcement of learning by the rewarding of correct responses, and on problem solving, inquiry, and discovery rather than the mastery of fact, is shaping the methods and materials we use for teaching. Because many concepts develop slowly in children's thinking, psychologists advocate the enrichment of programs of learning by concrete experience and by numerous examples and illustrations of the concepts to be learned.[28]

[26] *The Art of Teaching,* Vintage Books, Random House, Inc., New York, 1954, p. 149.
[27] Jerome S. Bruner, *On Knowing: Essays for the Left Hand,* The Belknap Press of Harvard University Press, Cambridge, Mass., 1962, p. 101.
[28] Helpful studies of learning are John Dewey's *How We Think,* D. C. Heath and Company, Boston, 1910; David Russell's *Children's Thinking,* Ginn and Company, Boston, 1956; and Jerome S. Bruner et al., *A Study of Thinking,* John Wiley & Sons, Inc., New York, 1956.

Cultural attitudes toward learning.   Family and cultural attitudes toward learning are influential in determining the strength of the motivation to learn and the intellectual goals toward which the individual is willing to work. In a situation where "all pressures of the culture unite to impress on the child the value of learning," where learning is the pathway to the most valued male roles, and where it is accorded deep respect in the family and in society, children were found to be highly motivated to intellectual achievement despite a school environment of physical hardship, punishment, and backbreaking, often monotonous work.[29] In families in which parents have little education and resent children who surpass them, in which study and intellectual achievement are devalued and status is accorded to physical rather than intellectual achievement, children with high IQs are frequently found to be underachievers. Children whose motivation is poor, who fear failure, and who lack self-esteem often "set their levels of aspiration relatively low." [30]

The culture as a whole affects the intellectual aspirations and achievements of youth. Sociologists and writers have shown how the relatively classless society of childhood shifts quickly into rather rigidly stratified social classes during the years of secondary school. Hollinshead pointed out the powerful effect of social class on the adolescents he studied. He noted that lower-class children who found themselves pushed out of things in school while honors and special privileges accrued to upper-class students, were more likely than others to drop out of school early.[31] Davis believed that intelligence tests discriminated between children from the highest and lowest socioeconomic levels, and indicated that schools have not learned much about the kinds of rewards and motivations which are successful with lower-class children.[32] According to Coleman, in the high school society in most schools, rewards for scholastic achievement have consistently lower status than those for athletic prowess.[33]

Youth in the classroom

Today we recognize that young people of the widely varying backgrounds, interests, capabilities, and goals described in the preceding pages have different motivations for learning and therefore require the use of different teaching materials and different approaches. Teachers frequently think of their

[29] Dorothy Lee, "Developing the Drive to Learn and the Questioning Mind," in *Freeing the Capacity to Learn,* Association for Supervision and Curriculum Development, 1960, pp. 10–21.

[30] Strang, *op. cit.,* p. 111.

[31] August B. Hollinshead, *Elmtown's Youth,* John Wiley & Sons, Inc., New York, 1949, p. 202.

[32] Allison Davis, *Social Class Influences on Learning,* Harvard University Press, Cambridge, Mass., 1955, p. 41.

[33] Coleman, *op. cit.,* p. 302.

teaching tasks in terms of three large and frequently overlapping groups: the above-average and superior students (most, but not all, college-bound); the large average group, including many whose education will end with the twelfth grade or their sixteenth birthday; and the slow learners, separated in most schools and frequently given remedial work.

Any attempt at a three-group classification of the large, heterogeneous, widely varied aptitudes and interests such as those of our high school students is bound to present difficulties. Classes often contain students with IQ ranges of fifty or sixty points and differences of five or six grades in reading ability.

There is much overlapping in the groups. Many of those whose parents insist on their placement in college-preparatory classes are not intellectually capable of college work. Many of the terminal students are of superior ability but are limited in aspiration or barred by financial status from going to college. Many of the slow learners are merely indifferent; rightly challenged, they might accomplish much.

Superior students

Recently, Advanced Placement Programs and honors classes for the gifted have provided enriched curricula for intellectually able students. Some schools have attempted to increase the prestige accorded by adolescent society to intellectual achievement by giving school recognition through awards, letters, honors, and privileges. Scholarship grants and achievement awards for the sciences, mathematics, and English are increasing, and seem to be gaining increasing respect in the high school group.

Programs for the intellectually able might be much more stimulating than they frequently are. Some teachers believe that because of this a great many such students take far too little responsibility for their own learning and perform required tasks without pursuing any individual inquiry of their own. Jacques Barzun has commented on the deadly character of many of the routine tasks we set for students, and the general lack of passion for intellectual inquiry which makes work and study "habit-forming and indeed obsessional." [34]

The problem of providing the best education for the gifted is very serious. Measures of achievement now available cannot distinguish effectively between the so-called "school-bright" children—those who do well by academic standards—and those whose creativity cannot be adequately measured by any educational instrument yet devised. Albert Einstein, Winston Churchill, Thomas Edison, and Thomas Mann are among those who were not successful in school. The potential talents of the creative student may be overlooked in schools, where he is frequently punished for nonconformity, lack of neatness, and daydreaming. Terman's studies of gifted children found that teachers'

---

[34] Jacques Barzun, *The House of Intellect,* Harper Torchbooks, Harper & Row, Publishers, Incorporated, New York, 1961, p. 125.

estimates of genius were often inaccurate; they graded low for carelessness, lack of neatness, and behavior problems.[35]

Teachers have observed that many children maintain high academic ratings through conforming to teacher expectations, through agreeing rather than questioning, and through their ability to perform many rote learning tasks. Many students in this group are governed by the desire for grades rather than by the thirst for learning. One study indicates that highly creative youth are less interested in conforming to the teacher's demands, are far more imaginative, more given to humor, and more wide-ranging in their interests. Those who were high in creativity were not especially high in IQ, and those high in IQ were not especially high in creativity.[36]

Another difficulty with the academically able group is that because of the pressure for achievement, we sometimes risk doing serious damage by ignoring the personal-social aspects of development. One young man, graduated from high school with honors in English, science, and mathematics, had, ten years after graduation, not succeeded in making any adjustment to college, to a job, to the opposite sex, and had suffered a mental breakdown. He says of his experience:

> In school, I held in contempt the use of the hands and of the body. When I was most ill, I was planning the organization of the world, not understanding that I was dealing with myths and fancies. Part of my therapy had to do with withdrawing from the world of unreality, which I was trying to organize by living largely in physics where I worked with facts that are measurable in a world that is controllable.[37]

The intellectual and the emotional needs of the individual are both interdependent and strong: "the teacher must be a quickener of that impulse-life through which thought can grow, indeed a shaper and molder of impulse into the rationality which comes from a healthy craving for contact with reality." [38]

English programs for today's youth must provide an intellectual challenge to the gifted, encourage individual responsibility for learning and habits of inquiry, and stimulate creativity. We need more English teachers who can recognize and provide for the creative and highly individualistic student, as well as for the more conventionally successful; teachers who are willing to measure their teaching success not by requiring advanced college work from

---

[35] Lewis M. Terman and Melita Oden, *The Gifted Child Grows Up,* Stanford University Press, Stanford, Calif., 1947, p. 26.

[36] J. W. Getzels and P. W. Jackson, "The Study of Giftedness," in *The Gifted Student,* Cooperative Research Monograph no. 2, U.S. Department of Health, Education and Welfare, Washington, D.C., 1960, pp. 1–18.

[37] James E. Spitznas, "General, Special, and Vocational Education: An Exploration of Distinctive Differences," *What Shall the High Schools Teach?* Yearbook of the Association for Supervision and Curriculum Development, Washington, D.C., 1956, p. 207.

[38] Gardner Murphy, *Freeing Intelligence through Teaching: A Dialectic of the Rational and the Personal,* Harper & Row, Publishers, Incorporated, New York, 1961, p. 22.

high school students but by stimulating them to acquire a broad background of critical reading, writing, and thinking which will enrich their college experience.

The middle group

Even more diversified in membership than the groups of the superior and the ungifted students is the broad middle group, which includes a large variety of young people with widely differing capabilities, backgrounds, and interests. Many of these students need a far richer curriculum than the rather thin content of the general or terminal courses usually provided for them. Under the guidance of teachers who understand their aspirations, interests, and motivations these students can read widely in good literature, write well,[39] and learn to handle their oral language with skill.

Some of the chief differences between the members of this group and the superior group are those of goals: Those in the general or terminal group, in which the average student is often found, usually have more immediate, practical goals than the superior group. They do not look forward to the delayed satisfactions of college or a career, but to the immediate ones of a job and early marriage. They are less interested in and less capable of abstract thinking but can often be challenged to explore those philosophical questions which concern them deeply. They need more individual guidance from teachers, more encouragement, more understanding, and more experiences of successful learning than their more able classmates.

The problems which challenge them may not be of the most abstract kind, such as speculation about the nature of good and evil (although many can engage in these, too, with interest), but those which they can talk about in more concrete terms: what makes a good life for them; what values and standards are worth having or working for; what kinds of personal relationships in marriage and family life are important; how one can find work which will yield satisfaction over a lifetime. There are still many in our secretarial, general, and vocational programs whose work in English is neither vitally significant in relation to their life goals nor stimulating intellectually. Teachers call many of these students the "terminal students who go to college." Many of them do not decide until late in their high school careers to further their education, and find themselves entering college with backgrounds of scanty reading and almost no writing. Even those who do not go on to higher education are capable of much greater effort and more challenging and interesting work, which will prepare them to enter business or vocations and adult life as educated people.

Many teachers who are sympathetic to these youngsters and like to teach

---

[39] Carl Wonnberger has shown how students failing English in his classes were able to write prize-winning poems and prose ("They All Can Learn to Write," *English Journal*, vol. 45, November, 1956, pp. 455–461).

them are seriously troubled by the poverty of their experiences in English in many present courses of study. Good teachers who care about teaching young people, rather than securing the prestige of teaching the college-bound, have shown what can be done to stimulate such students to achievement which surpasses expectation. Good general or secretarial classes have frequently proved more exciting to teach than the college groups: often these young people are less inhibited, more emotionally responsive to prose and poetry, more eager to learn, and more capable of growth because they are less self-satisfied than their intellectual superiors. Such students, too, are particularly responsive to the teacher who obviously enjoys working with them.

Teachers often encourage snobbish attitudes toward non-college-bound students. They may address one class by saying, "You're my bright college class; I expect more of you," and the slow group by saying in their hearing (perhaps to visitors), "These students are my dull group. There isn't anyone in this room with an IQ higher than 90. I just try to keep them quiet." These are not isolated or exaggerated instances; such remarks are heard frequently in many of our high schools.

A report of the NCTE Committee on English in Terminal Secondary Education makes some of the following observations about terminal students: they are poor readers, reading chiefly digests, sports, or home and fashion magazines; they have "little understanding of the world scene and their relations to it"; they are almost wholly unaware of the human values literature has for them; and they feel that they should have been taught more in English, chiefly more speech, vocabulary, punctuation, and letter writing, both business and social.[40]

The "ungifted"

What of the commonly designated "slow groups" in our schools? Again, it is common to find impoverished English programs for these young people, with little content which can stimulate curiosity or the drive to learn. Often youngsters in these classes have long histories of rejection and of lack of understanding, encouragement, or even acceptance by teachers. They tend to be both social and intellectual underdogs; they comprise the classes that are distributed to the losers in the competition among teachers for college and upper-level general courses. Many teachers consider their time wasted in teaching them. Slow groups are often considered a symbol of failure or punishment for the teachers assigned to them. Few actively seek such groups or have much understanding of them or their needs. Often it seems as though only the most gifted and humane teachers look on such classes as a challenge and receive satisfaction from teaching them. Yet there are many fine, creative teachers who feel their greatest rewards come from changing the apathy and

---

[40] "Terminal and Preparatory: A Report of the NCTE Committee on English in Terminal Secondary Education," *English Journal*, vol. 43, December, 1954, pp. 488–515.

rebellion in such youngsters to satisfaction in achievement. One such teacher, speaking of the black-leather-jacket crowd described earlier, says:

> In my English class I have found to my great joy that many of these kids are very sensitive to rhythm, colors, beauty, and have the emotional maturity (due to many hard knocks) to tackle poetry that might confuse a group with a higher IQ. I have also found that if handled gently and if talked to on an adult level, these kids will, even in a class of thirty-five, get down to work and genuinely seem interested in creative writing, poetry, social problems.[41]

Studies in class influences on learning by Davis and others have shown that the majority of our slow learners, at least in metropolitan schools, are of low socioeconomic status, and that many of them come from slum neighborhoods. Hollinshead, Davis, and others have shown how schools are oriented to middle-class values and standards, with the majority of both teachers and students drawn from that class.[42] Lower-class children find tests, textbooks, courses of study, and reading materials geared to a middle-class culture. From the beginning, their reading experiences deal with worlds completely unknown to them, for the white-picket-fenced-in world of Dick and Jane is as foreign a world as is that presented in most of their subsequent reading. Research is at present attempting to find some answers to the problems of presenting materials which are more meaningful to such young people.[43] In the meantime, some successful teachers have suggested learning experiences which can engage the interest and challenge the learning ability of these students.[44]

The challenge to the teacher

The teacher who respects each young person as an individual, helping him to feel his worth, may contribute more than he knows to society. Ralph Bunche, formerly Under Secretary for Special Political Affairs of the United Nations, tells of his sixth-grade teacher in Albuquerque, New Mexico, who treated all of her sixty-five students as equals and gave each a feeling of individual importance. He says, "She influenced me decisively at a formative stage of my life. For the first time, I found someone who treated me just like everybody else." [45]

---

[41] Nemser, *loc. cit.*
[42] See studies by Davis, *op. cit.* and Hollinshead, *op. cit.*
[43] See Educational Policies Commission, *Education and the Disadvantaged American*, NEA, Washington, D.C., 1962, and Conant, *op. cit.*
[44] Morris Finder, "Teaching English to Slum-dwelling Pupils," *English Journal*, vol. 44, April, 1955, p. 200.
[45] "Belle Sweet: Ralph Bunche's Favorite Teacher," *Saturday Review*, vol. 45, Apr. 21, 1962, p. 60.

Awareness of the kind of world today's adolescent lives in, and sensitivity to the pressures, influences, and events which are shaping his life, are perhaps more important for the teacher of English than for almost anyone else in the child's school life. For it is this teacher who deals with matters most deeply personal to the student: the language by which he lives, the literature which moves his heart and shapes his mind, his values, and his goals. This realization must force us as teachers of English to feel a sense of great responsibility in handling the students and materials we work with, for we have it in our power to shape the thoughts, the attitudes, the feelings, the ideals, and the values of youth during the most formative years.

Teachers in today's world may find pleasure in teaching the gifted because they almost seem to teach themselves. Today, when the majority of youth seem to be college-bound, such classes are in many schools a mark of prestige for the teacher; a large number of our best teachers have not taught average or ungifted children for years. Many teachers, striving for status themselves, resent and reject slum children, those who are culturally apart, or those who are indifferent to the hallmarks of academic success. Too often, in schools where teacher and administrative attention focuses on the college-bound, such children encounter little but discrimination, rejection, hostility, and neglect. Nothing in the curriculum is geared to their interests or capacities, and little effort is made to provide the kinds of school experiences which could help them learn. As Conant's *Slums and Suburbs* points out, society and its teachers cannot afford such neglect of potential excellence. Provided with the right materials and stimulation, these children are capable of much. The achievement of Higher Horizons programs and the success of the experimental prefreshman program at Dillard University in New Orleans in enriching the backgrounds of Negro youth entering college have shown new directions to the teacher.[46]

Teaching these students is a challenging and satisfying enterprise, demanding those who can, in Bruner's words, "practice the canny art of intellectual temptation." The truly gifted intellectually can thrive on many different kinds of programs and with many different kinds of teachers. The unmotivated, the "academically untalented," the average, and the "generals" need understanding and supporting teachers to achieve their full potential for learning. It is primarily sociological and psychological understanding in the teacher who knows his subject that has led to the success of such programs as the Higher Horizons[47] in increasing the level of aspiration and raising the educational goals and motivation for learning of culturally disadvantaged youth.

The English teacher who knows and understands adolescents and the various aspects of their development and who is aware of their needs, goals,

---

[46] See Frank G. Jennings, "For Such a Tide Is Moving . . . ," *Saturday Review,* vol. 47, May 16, 1964, pp. 74–88.

[47] Described in "The Search for Hidden Talent," in Arthur D. Morse, *Schools for Tomorrow —Today!* Doubleday & Company, Inc., Garden City, N.Y., 1960.

and interests, can utilize this knowledge to select and shape the materials of the courses he teaches. He meets the requirements of developing adolescents of differing abilities and aspirations by providing an easy atmosphere in which youth may speak and find an attentive audience; stimulation, encouragement, and guidance for its writing; and a forum for the challenge of ideas generated by its reading. His choices of activities, units, and topics for speaking, writing, or reading are chosen carefully, not only with an eye to their literary or intellectual worth, but also to the moment of growth they may serve.[48] The teacher challenges, guides, provokes the intellectually lazy to thought, and offers tactful understanding of adolescent shyness and uncertainty. He does not attempt to mold the student but to assist him in developing his own individuality. Such teachers may have the satisfaction of contributing significantly to new generations of youth—not apathetic or defeatist—but idealistic, creative, and intellectually productive.

Selected bibliography

Elizabeth Berry, *Guiding Students in the English Class,* Appleton-Century-Crofts, Inc., New York, 1957. Useful suggestions showing the relationship of guidance and the study of English.

Educational Policies Commission, *Education and the Disadvantaged American,* NEA, Washington, D.C., 1962.

Marynia Farnham, *The Adolescent,* Harper & Row, Publishers, Incorporated, New York, 1951. A psychiatrist discusses adolescent problems and behavior. A helpful and informative book for teachers.

Lawrence R. Frank and Mary H. Frank, *Your Adolescent at Home and in School,* The Viking Press, Inc., New York, 1956. (Paperback.) A down-to-earth discussion of adolescent development and behavior by two psychiatrist parents.

Edgar Friedenberg, *The Vanishing Adolescent,* Beacon Press, Boston, 1959. (Paper: Dell Publishing Co., Inc., New York, 1962.) An important study of adolescents in today's culture and their relation to teachers and schools.

Arnold Gesell, *Youth: The Years Ten to Sixteen,* Harper & Row, Publishers, Incorporated, New York, 1956. The study of the psychological and physiological development of adolescents.

Robert J. Havighurst, *Developmental Tasks and Education,* Longmans, Green & Co., Inc., New York, 1953. Havighurst defines ten important developmental tasks each adolescent must perform on the road to maturity.

Arno Jewett, (ed.), *English for the Academically Talented Student in the Secondary School: A Report of the Committee on English Programs for*

---

[48] The chapters on speaking, reading, and writing and the study of literature (4–6 and 9) provide illustrations of such activities.

High School Students of Superior Ability, NCTE and NEA, Washington, D.C., 1960.

————, *Teaching Rapid and Slow Learners,* U.S. Office of Education, Bulletin no. 5, Government Printing Office, Washington, D.C., 1954.

H. H. Remmers and D. H. Radler, *The American Teenager,* The Bobbs-Merrill Company, Inc., Indianapolis, 1957. A summary of the findings of the Purdue opinion polls which surveyed the opinions of adolescents about their problems, attitudes, prejudices, and beliefs.

Ruth Strang, *The Adolescent Views Himself: A Psychology of Adolescence,* McGraw-Hill Book Company, New York, 1957. The author studies written comments of teen-agers that illuminate the way in which they perceive themselves and their problems. An enlightening book for teachers.

CHAPTER 3

Language is, without a doubt, the most momentous and at
the same time the most mysterious product of the human
mind.

SUSANNE LANGER [1]

The nature of language

Our language is that intricate, delicately interwoven system of symbols, gestures, and sounds by which the mind of man reaches out to the minds and
hearts of other men to communicate feelings, thoughts, desires, and dreams.
The magical capacity of the human brain to invent such symbols and to
translate them into thoughts, ideas, and emotions makes possible the true
brotherhood of man, linking men around the world and the minds of men dead
with those of men living. Language is man's greatest invention, guns, bombs,
and automatic brains notwithstanding. It has made possible all human progress
and human destruction; it makes possible war and peace, faith and doubt, the
development of institutions, governments, education, trade, science, art, and
a hundred other aspects of a culture. With the oral language of the storyteller,
or a written language to preserve thought, a culture may endure for a thousand
years; without these, it may be obliterated in a brief time.

From the first precivilization beginnings of human speech to the present
when man's voice is transmitted all over the world in an instant, the history
of language is the history of communication. The ways in which we use language today will largely determine the future of our civilization, and shape
its destiny, either survival or destruction. What children learn in schools today

---

[1] *Philosophy in a New Key,* Mentor Books, New American Library of World Literature, Inc.,
New York, 1948, p. 83. (Paperback.)

about language and the way it affects human thought and behavior will help to determine this future.

Language and the English program

The whole program in English is a language program. The frequent separation of the curriculum into literature, composition, grammar, and speech implies a division of the language process which does not exist in life. Whether the language we use is heard, spoken, read, written, or studied, the intricate, flexible, and plastic material with which we work is the same: a system of symbols made up of sounds, signal systems, and large and small units of written and spoken words. The modern English program is designed to help the student understand the structure and meaning of the language he speaks, to bring to awareness the unconscious processes he has been using since infancy, and to assist him in using language maturely, responsibly, and effectively.

The value and effectiveness of the English program may rest on how much the English teacher understands and applies learnings about language as a process, a product, and an art. To understand the nature of language as a symbolic system and its development in the young learner is to be familiar with the process. To understand the spoken and written language, its history, its structural patterns, and the myriad ways that words acquire meanings is to know something of the product, language, as it is used in man's communication. To understand the subtleties of the relationship between the word, its meanings, and what verbal symbols can tell us about man's thoughts, feelings, and dreams is to know something of language as an art. But the uses of language as process, product, or art are intricately interwoven in human communication, and any division for discussion or teaching is simply a matter of convenience. The interrelationships between language and literature, and among the various language skills, understandings, and appreciations, should be clearly observable in a modern English program. For this reason, the integrated program seems to many teachers to provide the most natural setting for the kind of development of competence with language that is our aim.

A second fact with important implications for the teacher of English is the highly verbal nature of the culture in which we live. Man, the handler of things in early times—the plow, the plantings, the animals, seeds, shelters, and clothing of his world—has become largely a symbol handler in our society, cut off to a large extent from nature and the world of objects. In today's world, much of man's life is carried on by means of words, whereas in earlier times, direct experience was his central teacher. A few hundred years ago, men learned to farm, to build, or to handle tools and machines through watching and sharing the actions of their elders. They learned trades and crafts as apprentices on the job, rather than in technical schools. Women learned to cook, to knit, and to sew in their mothers' kitchens or living rooms, rather than out of cookbooks or handbooks of sewing and knitting instructions.

Today, what we understand of the world we live in, its nations, its peoples, its government and politics, its wars, comes to us through the medium of words, filtered through the thinking, speaking, and writing of many other persons. The nature of the culture in which today's youth live demands a language program much more inclusive and comprehensive in nature than the traditional program of sentence analysis and the study of punctuation.

Knowledge about how children learn has further changed the emphasis and method in modern language programs. Present-day learning theories point to the importance of the development of concepts as a primary factor in children's thinking—the "structural steel" of thought, as one author calls them.[2] As the discussion of learning in Chapter 2 points out, concepts develop slowly after much real and vicarious experience. The shift in emphasis from rule and prescription to inquiry and discovery in learning is nowhere more important than in the language program. As students learn to observe the way people use language, they grow more aware of educated usage, of the many purposes for which people use words, and of the complex nature of the process of communication.

Finally, as has been emphasized in the first chapter, the most significant need today in the field of English is that of a sequential program, one which begins early to develop concepts about language in the young learner, provides practice in skills, and covers work that increases in difficulty and complexity throughout the years of schooling. This chapter suggests practices and activities in all areas of English which may help to develop the kind of command over language which we hope for in our students.

To understand the language he speaks, the student must understand it as a symbolic process. Both students and teacher need to understand the personal nature of language in the individual and the role of language as a social and cultural force. The student must learn how to speak so that others can understand him, to listen without being swayed by his emotions, to write with awareness of the reactions that his written words may produce in his audience. All these can help him to read literature critically and appreciatively. This chapter attempts to present some important concepts about language, showing how the teacher's understanding of language processes shapes and informs his teaching of each of the areas of English, and provides a context for the study of language, composition, and literature.

The teacher of English is first of all a teacher of language. He must understand language and the way it operates in human beings if he is to teach effectively the skills of reading, writing, and speaking, and to lead students to the enjoyment of literature. Language is the lens through which we study the nature and structure of the written and spoken word, the ways in

[2] David H. Russell, *Children's Thinking*, Ginn and Company, Boston, 1956, p. 122.

which men communicate, and the way in which the artist uses patterns of words to create literature. Further directions in the study of language are provided in Chapters 4 to 14.

Language and critical thinking

Two major kinds of thought processes are generally recognized in human beings: analytical or critical thinking, and creative or imaginative thinking. Although schools have been urged to pay more attention to the latter type of thinking, it is primarily with developing and sharpening the critical faculties and with training in logical modes of thought that modern education is concerned.

The central obligation of the teacher of English today is the teaching of critical thinking. Whether the teacher is dealing with the skills of comprehension in the areas of English, the appreciation of language in works of literature, or the processes of writing and speaking, his major concern is with the thoughtful, critical evaluation of words and meanings.

To train students in habits of critical thinking, the teacher draws on techniques and materials from a number of areas and disciplines. Some teachers have successfully taught the ancient art of logical analysis in simplified form to high school students. The techniques of propaganda analysis are frequently included in social studies classes, and English teachers have used such devices as the "bandwagon technique," "name calling," and others to teach students how to approach critically the uses of language they meet in advertising, political speeches, and other prose designed to persuade through emotion. Most commonly included in texts for the study of language in the high schools are some of the principles of general semantics, which have become a basic part of language study in many classrooms. The teacher of English draws on all of the above materials to help students. Three major areas of language study throughout the secondary school years are language as a symbolic process, the major uses of language, and the relationship of language and thinking.

Language as a symbolic process

Man, the symbol-making animal, is unique in his ability to use verbal signs representationally; they "stand for" things in the world of experience as signs in the animal world do not. The animal may respond to sensory messages like the smell of food, or smoke, or a whistle; an intelligent dog or cat may learn to respond to the word *dinner* by looking for his food, or to the word *out* by going to the door and crying to be let out. But no animal except man can talk *about* going out or *about* last night's or next week's dinner, or tell his grandchildren *about* the kind of dinners mother used to cook. Words can make us think of things which are not present to our senses. This ability to symbolize experience through making words stand for things and ideas is basic to human thought, essential to man as a means of communication, cooperation, and control. Symbolization is the function which distinguishes man from animal.

A system of agreements. Human language is possible because of agreements among men to have certain sounds or symbols represent things they need to talk about. Some of the first words may have been name words, as men looked about them and agreed on certain sound symbols to stand for *man, woman, child, fire,* or *dog.*

We frequently forget that the matter of agreement is basic in determining the meanings of the words we use. Words stand for things because we agree to call these things by a particular sound: a kind of four-footed animal is called *dog,* the thing we sit in is called a *chair.* Agreements in different languages produce words like *chien* or *hund, chaise* or *stuhl,* for the same objects. People who cannot agree about meanings are in trouble with language. Students of words have pointed out how difficult it is to come to agreement about the meaning of the word *democracy* when it is used to signify very different concepts by Russians, by Germans, by the ancient Greeks, and by Americans. Young people can readily understand the importance of agreement in assigning meanings to words when they analyze their teen-age talk, in which certain words have meanings only for those initiates who understand them, or as they look back at the special words they use in their own families, which only the family members can recognize.

Words and things. The process by which man agrees to let certain symbols of sound or print represent things often leads to confusion in the way we teach language to the very young. "This is a dog," or "this is dog," mother may say, pointing to the picture of the dog or the word *dog* in his ABC book. The child, assuming that there is a real and necessary connection between the symbol (the picture or the word) and the thing, often learns to respond to the word symbol as though it *were* the thing, withdrawing his hand from the word *dog* in his book if he has been nipped by a dog which frightened him or crying at the word *shot* if he remembers the painful shot the doctor gave him. Parents often encourage this kind of thinking by teaching him to withdraw his hand from an object he is forbidden to touch by telling him it is "hot." Words are learned by the infant in close association with experiences of love, hate, fear, anger, or security. The verbal symbols carry this emotional freight throughout his life. His cry of "Mama" causes Mama to appear magically, and is analogous to the magical beliefs primitive peoples hold about words. For them, as for children, the word does not "stand for" the thing in any symbolic sense; it *is* the thing itself.

The term "word magic" is often used to describe the feeling that words are magical symbols which might control us or events. The primitive tribesman who refuses to utter the name of the tiger or the crocodile for fear that the animal will hear him, or who calls him polite names such as "grandfather" or "my lord," is attaching magical significance to his use of words. Sophisticated modern man is troubled by many of the same verbal taboos. Like the infant or preliterate man, we feel that the word symbol itself contains magical powers: there are words for everyday human acts and functions which we cannot print in books or say over the airwaves. Every so often a man shoots another man for calling his dog a "mutt" or for calling his sister or his wife by a name usually applied to an animal. The word used in each case is merely a symbol; it does not change the genealogy of the dog nor the character of the woman. Yet, many modern men still react to it as though it did.

This fact that language is a system of symbols and that the symbol merely stands for the thing it symbolizes is a basic concept about language to be developed in the English program. Some of the most serious causes of tensions and controversy in modern life are affected by our failure to distinguish clearly between symbol and thing. Words representing death, disease, and sex among other things are often subject to strong verbal taboos, preventing us from dealing realistically with the facts they represent. We know of people who cannot bring themselves to make wills, to mention death, cancer, or mental illness, or to talk about bodily functions even with their doctors.

A study of euphemisms and circumlocutions commonly used in our everyday speech is an illuminating area for research and understanding of language.[3] Recognizing the power of word magic over our lives and clarifying understanding about the nature of language may break the power of verbal taboos over thinking and lead young people to healthier uses of language.

Words and feelings. The child's meanings for the words he uses are the product of the experiences he has associated with that word. Since no two people have identical experiences, the language of each individual is unique; the meanings for the words he uses lie deep in his own nervous system. Thus his "meaning" for the word *dog* may include affectionate feelings for a gentle playmate or fear of a neighbor's dog which bit him. Young people learning about language need to recognize that words mean different things to different people and that the meanings for the words we know come from our own experiences and carry with them many emotional colorings. To illustrate this fact about language, the teacher may ask a class to write down the pictures which come into their minds for each word from a list he dictates, including such words as *dog, vacation spot, car, child, school, dinner, kitchen, teacher, book,* or *dress.* The wide variety of responses will provide material for discussion about the personal nature of the meanings of the words we use.

The experiences which give meaning to the words in our vocabulary add emotional coloring, associative meanings which are not part of the denotative or lexical meaning of the words. The word *sea* has different meanings to the prairie child, the city child, and the coastal child who has, perhaps, lost a father or brother in a storm. The words *school* and *book* have different emotional values for the scholar and the truant. Even seemingly neutral words like *desk* or *pencil* may carry an emotional charge for those who have strong

[3] Students will find H. L. Mencken's discussion of euphemisms (indirect expressions substituted for direct ones) both entertaining and rewarding (*The American Language,* 4th ed., Alfred A. Knopf, Inc., New York, 1936).

"Well, here we go again. Another discussion about the meaning of 'as is.' " Drawing by J. Mirachi; © 1963 The New Yorker Magazine, Inc.

associations with these objects. To help students understand this aspect of language, called *connotation*, the teacher may dictate a list of words such as *book, desk, pencil, kitchen, house, home, teacher*, and *school* and ask students to comment on those which arouse favorable feelings, those which arouse negative feelings, and those which do not seem to call forth any response in them. As students discuss their reactions to these words, the role that feelings and experience play in determining the meanings of words becomes clear.

Symbols and meanings. Although the process of assigning meanings to verbal symbols has gone on since men started to talk, we still have a very limited number of words to stand for an unlimited number of things: the actions, events, ideas, relationships, and processes of a world in constant change. Men have been naming things, describing and qualifying them since the world began. Yet our stock of words is inadequate to represent the complexity of the physical world we perceive through our senses and the myriad feelings, dreams, and ideas of which man is capable. Every user of language is continually frustrated by the inadequacy of words to convey his thoughts. The simple attempt to describe the way we react to everyday happenings baffles every man as it baffles the poet. How does one describe the feeling evoked by a kiss or a sunset, the sensation of sunbathing or of skiing against a cold wind, one's idea of God or conception of beauty? Trying to put into words what happens when one ties a shoe, bites into an apple, or cuts a finger quickly shows us how inadequate is our stock of words to represent what we experience through our complicated patterns of nerve and brain. The teacher may ask students to try to describe one of these acts to illustrate this fact about language.

Each word often serves to communicate myriad meanings. The symbol for man designates Stone Age man, Renaissance man, the nineteenth-century Victorian, and the man of the space age. Our word-symbol "city" stands for Alexandria, the Athens of 500 B.C., the Jerusalem of Biblical times, or Tel Aviv, born yesterday. We speak of wars and with a single three-letter word refer to the Punic Wars, to World War I, to a cold war of ideas, or to a war on disease.[4]

The word *love* means something quite different when we use it to refer to love of God, of country, of Yale, of woman, of child, of a favorite food. It has different meanings in the mouth of child, patriot, Hollywood producer, lover, or saint. The words do not change much; their meanings are constantly changing and extending, as are the things the words stand for. Yet we handle the words unthinkingly, as though the things they represented were static. Much of the student's understanding of literature and his skill in writing and speaking will depend on his ability to understand this concept about language. He should have numerous chances to use words like *city, man, house, table,* and *book* in as many senses and contexts as he can imagine. Through comparison within the class and discussion of student examples, he will come to understand that the words he knows stand for things which are constantly changing.

Language and metaphor.   "Language is fossil poetry," declared Emerson. Because we commonly think of metaphor as a device used in poetry to be studied as such in school and then forgotten, the average user of English is little aware of the metaphorical quality of his everyday speech. Metaphor is at the root of extensions of meanings in our language. One simple illustration is the use of words for the parts of the body in everyday speech: *hand, heart, head, foot, arm, toes.* Even young children learn to use these word metaphors as they speak of the hands of the clock or the foot of a sock. From our feet comes the extension of meanings of the word *foot* to include *foot of the mountain, foot of the class, foot it to town, footwork,* and so on. Such words

---

[4] Alfred Korzybski (*Science and Sanity,* International Non-Aristotelian Library Publishing Company, Lakeville, Conn., 1933) used the map-territory analogy and suggested a system of dating and indexing abstractions to remind the user of their differences: cow[1] is not cow[2]; Britain[1066] is not Britain[1960]; automobile[1915] is not automobile[1970]. The concepts about language and behavior discussed in this chapter are derived chiefly from his book, and from those who have popularized his theories: Hayakawa, Chase, Lee, and others (see bibliography).

may range in meaning from the literal and concrete (the valvular human heart) to the most abstract: *the heart of the matter, giving one's heart away, putting one's heart into the effort, a heartless girl.* Such words stand not only for physical objects (the human heart) but for very abstract phrases that have no physical referent (*heart of the matter*). Metaphor is the device by which we use words which signify objects in the physical world to imply a comparison and to express the unknown in terms of the known.

It has been called the device by which we express the inexpressible: our notions of God ("the Lord is my shepherd"), of space ("starry vaults of the heavens"), the passage of time ("time's winged chariot"), and so on. The language of literature and poetry employs this means to deal with man's subtlest and most complicated thoughts and with his notions of abstract beauty, love, or faith. By this means he communicates intense feelings about something or someone by means of comparison with a familiar object: Browning apostrophized his wife as "My Star"; Tennyson viewed God as a pilot and his death as "Crossing the Bar." This primary understanding about the way in which language works is often neglected in schools.

Students need much practice in learning to recognize metaphor in everyday speech. Such understanding is essential to the comprehension of literature and the spoken word. Frequent exercises in gathering metaphor from advertising, from the sports column of the newspaper, from slang, and from school jargon will make this concept meaningful. The power of the compact metaphor to convey almost instantly a strongly emotionally tinged idea, to compress much meaning into one or a few words is another way in which metaphor operates in our language, as with the phrases *iron curtain, cold war, brainwashing.*

Students may be asked to make lists of words like this which have become metaphorical nouns, verbs, or adjectives: "he *dogs* my footsteps," "he made a *pig* of himself," "he is a *clown*" (or a *lemon,* a *doll,* a *heel,* a *peach*), "he *drummed* it into my head," "it *threw* me off the *track,*" "she *blossomed* out," "he gave me the *green* light." Even our commonest words may be used in a metaphorical sense, and the student must learn to understand this early in his reading experience: "I saw the *point* of the joke," "*give* him enough *rope,*" "his *head* was in the *clouds,*" "we were *given* equal rights."

The study of metaphor can enrich every facet of the study of language, composition, and literature in the English program. Young people expand their vocabularies as familiar words acquire metaphorical meanings. They may see how the writer employs metaphorical language to add color and vigor to his language and learn from him how to employ such language in their own writing. They may study the connotative effect of the writer's use of *shouted, shrieked,* or *thundered* (instead of *said*) to convey character. Along with this kind of study should go the critical analysis of metaphor to determine whether the writer is attempting to sway the reader's opinion with loaded words ("the czar of the labor unions," "Nazi tactics"). The student must learn to discriminate between the legitimate use of metaphorical and connotative language in poetry and in adding color to language, and its questionable use to arouse feeling where the appeal should be to reason.

Meanings and contexts. A primary source of meaning of the words we use in discourse is that of context. The function of context to determine meaning is a basic principle of the English language. We cannot tell what part of speech any single word in our language is until we see it used in a sentence or phrase, where it may become noun, verb, or perhaps adjective or preposition. Our dictionaries list sometimes hundreds of meanings for a simple preposition or adverb, meanings determinable only by context. The many meanings of words like *run, man,* or *fall* make a formidable task for the young learner of language until he begins to learn to guess from context. *Hand* may mean first to him the part of his body with which he touches or picks up things; later he learns about the hands of a clock; still later he is asked, "Hand me this." Anyone watching a small child struggle with words will understand how complex is the concept that the same word may be used to point out something, to express an idea, to describe an action, or to indicate a relationship.

Sometimes very small children can tell by context of gesture, tone, or facial expression whether the "I'm going to spank you" of a parent is threat, promise, joke, or affectionate banter. Contexts may thus be physical (situation, gesture, expression) or verbal (the meaning of a word as it is used in sentence patterns or longer passages of the spoken or written word). Sometimes one must read a whole book in order to determine the meaning of a key word to a writer as "nature" in Wordsworth or "the oversoul" in Emerson. Critical readers learn early to look for contexts in evaluating the meanings of excerpts from book reviews, movies, advertisements, and political speeches. The study of context as it relates to meaning is an important part of our lifelong study of the language we speak. The critical user of language must constantly be on guard against those who, quoting out of context, distort meanings of words and passages for their own particular purposes.[5]

Two major uses of language

Students of language generally agree that there are two broad functions of language: its referential function, in which it purports to inform or state facts; and its emotive function, through which it moves or sways the emotions. The language of fact, sometimes called referential language, is designed to describe, to state facts, or to record data as accurately as words will allow; emotive language may express feelings or attempt to sway them—its purposes may range from the representation of a mood in a lyric poem, to a propaganda piece designed to stir people to anger and hatred. These two quite different functions of language need to be clearly understood by the critical user of

[5] See Chap. 5 for further illustrations of words and contexts.

words. The two are not mutually exclusive; often the functions overlap. Sometimes a bare statement of fact may be used to evoke emotion, as does Warren's
laconic answer "Dead," to Mary's question about Silas, in Frost's "The Death
of the Hired Man." The line, " 'Dead' was all he answered," tells us of the
factual response of Warren to Mary's question about Silas and evokes compassion for Silas.

Denotations and connotations. Learning the distinctions between the
denotations and connotations of words is an essential step in clarifying differences between the emotive and referential uses of language. Words commonly
carry both kinds of meaning and critical thinking about language and literature depends on the reader's ability to distinguish between these meanings.

The denotative or dictionary meanings for the word *house* or *baby* are
very different from the connotative meanings of these words or the associations
they arouse in the reader or hearer. *Rabbit* and *ermine* both denote kinds of
fur; yet the latter connotes wealth and luxury while the other does not. Both
peso and *doubloon* denote kinds of coin, but the first suggests Mexican peons
while the other almost inevitably conjures up images of pirates.

Denotative meanings are referential; connotative meanings are deeply
personal and usually emotive. They cluster around the words we know, adding emotional overtones to our meanings. In the work of the literary artist,
they add depth and power to poetry and prose. In the mouth of the rabble-
rouser or the propagandist, they may be used to manipulate emotions, rouse
hatreds and passions, and obscure reason. For some persons, words so used
lose their denotative meanings almost entirely, as when the dominant association a person may have for the word *red* is a rabid hatred of Communists.

Facts and judgments. A second aspect of this twofold function of language is the distinction between the statement of fact and that of judgment. The
statement of fact is an assertion which can be checked by objective means.
The common dictionary definition of "fact" as something which "is true"
does not allow for change in a world where the facts of today are the fictions
of tomorrow. Our facts are "true" until research proves them false and substitutes new facts. Judgments or statements of opinion are intended to express
our evaluations or feelings about people, events, or things. They often sound
as though they were fact, but the critical reader or listener learns to distinguish
statements such as "the book is five inches long" from such judgmental statements as "the book is good" or "the book is interesting." An argument about
the first statement may be settled by using a tape measure or a ruler; a dispute
about the latter two may be resolved only through agreement about an
opinion.

Scientific statements require continuous checking of experience by objective means. If the report of a scientific experiment is accurate, it may be
duplicated by someone following the directions in any country and in any
language. Franklin's experiments with electricity were checked and duplicated
in London and on the continent, as were Marie Curie's with the isolation of

radium. Exact descriptions of procedures in science are verifiable. Persons hostile to scientific ideas and processes, as persons have been toward vaccination, sterile techniques in surgery, and the idea that the earth is not flat, have been slowly forced to yield before the pressure of scientific evidence. Where arguments grow warm as to whether one country has a better form of government than another, neither agreement nor any verifiable conclusions may be reached. Most of the areas of violent controversy in the world today arise in the area of such judgments as these.

The making of sound judgments, based on adequate factual evidence, is one of the attributes of the trained critical mind. Students need continuous practice in speaking, writing, and thinking if they are to learn to use both kinds of language well and to be aware of the strength or weakness of the evidence on which their value judgments rest. Critical thinking is taught in classrooms where such judgments are continually examined and challenged and where writers and speakers are pressed to present supporting evidence for these judgments. The facts supporting such statements as "X high school is better than Y high school," "Mr. X is an unfair marker," "*The Yearling* is a better book than *Johnny Tremaine*," must be assessed, and the speakers (or writers) held responsible for presenting adequate evidence.

Command of the language of fact, commonly called report language, is of basic importance in business, medicine, international relations, science, and government. It is the language which most closely fits the objective world, the world of objects and things, as opposed to the inner world of the human mind and the imagination. Unsupported judgments often pass for fact rather than opinion, and they mislead both speakers and hearers. The psychiatrist's judgments about insanity, the doctor's judgments about disease, and the lawyer's about criminal intent are only as sound as the basis of fact on which they rest. Sound judgmental thinking, based on careful study of facts, is one of the greatest intellectual achievements of the human mind. The professions of medicine, law, and diplomacy have as their primary goal the training of individual minds to make sound judgments. Here is a major area of English study for students learning to use the language critically.

Students need to practice distinguishing between facts and judgments in their own reading, writing, and speaking. One of the chief difficulties reported by scientists, professional people, and businessmen is the inability of high school and college graduates to write clear, accurate reports, in factual language, of an event, an experiment, or a process. Evaluations become mixed with the language of the report; the writer stops describing the event or the process and begins to tell how he feels about it. Practice in report writing and in giving factual oral reports should be provided in the English program throughout grades seven through twelve. Students should have opportunities to analyze newspaper writing, both reporting and editorials, and the language of persuasion in advertising and political speeches, to assess the balance of fact and judgment, and the evidence offered for the judgments made.

The relationship between language and thinking

Students whose work in English has developed their awareness of the processes of their thinking through which they sort, classify, and order their experiences have gained a measure of control over the capacity for clear and critical thinking. The processes of classifying, abstracting, and generalizing are primary functions in thinking and using language, developed through the study of their functioning in speaking and writing, and the study of literature. The capacity of the brain to classify, to generalize, and to think abstractly is its most human characteristic, a true measure of intelligence. These are thinking processes which good teachers attempt to teach when they ask students to outline a paper, to organize a piece of writing or a speech, to select important information in taking notes, to see relationships between different subjects, themes, and ideas. Other important characteristics of clear and critical thinking are the drawing of valid inferences, the recognition of directive statements, and the avoidance of two-valued thinking.

Classification.   Man's power to categorize or classify is a central human process, a way of mastering and ordering his environment through language. Classifying objects, people, and events is a way of sorting out an unassimilable series of things into a manageable assortment of classes. Through classifying, man reduces multiplicity and complexity to something like a pattern of order and system.

We often forget that our simplest words—those which stand for common objects—are class names: *chair* or *table* may refer to individual objects, but the words are used also to classify a group of things of various shapes, sizes, materials, and colors which look very different to the eye. The difficulty the infant has in learning such classes as *dog* and *cat* remind us of differences: at first all four-footed animals may be *dog;* soon cows and horses are excluded, and the term is narrowed down to include dogs and cats. A further refining of the concept of "dogginess" leads to recognition that the word refers to things as varied in appearance as great Danes, dachshunds, and Chihuahuas. The mastering of all our usual classifications involves such complicated processes, but as adults we frequently forget the many differences that classifications cover and tend to think in terms of similarities only.

Young people should become aware of the process of classification as an essential language tool for making our environment manageable. Classifications are often vital to life itself, as we realize from the way we classify things as poisonous-not poisonous, dangerous-not dangerous, malignant-benign, insane-sane. Often, however, we fail to realize that we specify classifications for a particular purpose and that a single entity may be classified in several different ways. Still more important is the realization that classifications help determine how we feel about the person and thing classified.

The problem of classifications and the way they affect our feelings toward things and particularly people is a matter for discussion with frequent classroom examples, many of which can be drawn from literature. Students may discuss how their expectations about people change as soon as they have classified them as "Jewish," "Catholic," "Republican," "Italian," "Irish," "odd ball," or class "brain." They may profit from discussion of the errors in classification they have made.

The student may profitably learn to observe that classifying an object or a person often determines how we think of what has been classified. If he decides that Miss X is a hard teacher or that physics is a hard subject, he may find himself acting as if his classifications were facts. Students should have some experience with the effects of classifying on our thinking about the members of racial and national groups. When we cannot tell how we feel about a person until we know his nationality, race, or religion, we operate in terms of a verbal symbol rather than the reality of the worth of the person. It is this kind of thinking which leads to stereotyping and invalid generalizations.

Generalizations.   Habits of generalizing and making judgments on insufficient evidence are common in student thinking, writing, and speaking, well into the college years. Broad generalizations seldom challenged in the classroom appear in almost every paper: "teachers are grouchy," "women drivers are reckless," "*David Copperfield* is the greatest of Dickens' novels" (the student has read no others), "*War and Peace* is the greatest war novel of all time" (the student has skimmed this and read a review of *All Quiet on the Western Front*). Teachers, too, frequently encourage the judgment and generalization which passes for thought by assigning such topics as "A Typical Teen-ager." Much talking and writing goes on about high-level abstractions which are never defined: "school spirit," "Americanism," "democracy," "realism," "style," and "literary classics."

Invalid generalizations often lead to stereotyped thinking: "teen-agers are wild," "blondes are dumb," "Italians are musical." Students need to learn that "teen-agers" and "blondes" are broad abstractions covering many individuals with differing characteristics. The word "Texan" may refer to any one of several million people living in Texas, some of whom brag about their state and wear ten-gallon hats, and some who do not. Stereotyped thinking sets up road blocks to critical thinking.

The abstracting process.   In the process of developing his concept of *dog*, the young child learns to abstract certain qualities which assist him in recognizing the classification: legs, hair, barking, and so on. This process of abstraction is an essential part of learning and using language for the purposes of classifying and thinking about the world in which we live. The word symbols "teen-ager," "Texan," "Southerner," or "Irishman" are abstractions of a much larger order, standing for thousands, perhaps millions of individuals who make up the group classified by that term. Such abstractions are in themselves broad generalizations obscuring the important differences between the individuals in the category and leading to thinking in terms of the symbol rather than the individuals for which the symbol stands.

The awareness of the process of abstracting is essential, then, to clear thinking. Hayakawa's now-famous abstraction ladder[6] moving from the cow as an organism (a collection of atoms and electrons), to the cow we perceive with our senses, to the word *cow*, to *livestock*, to *farm assets*, to *asset*, to *wealth* is a useful device for showing students how one can move from the thing itself to the word for the thing and through increasingly abstract terms in which more and more characteristics of the object are left out—in other words, symbols which have moved further and further away from reality.

Even young students have worked out their own abstraction ladders with familiar objects, beginning with something like their own two-year-old brown male bull terrier named Butch through successively abstract terms: bull terrier (including females), terrier (including other kinds of terriers), dog (including collies, dachshunds, and others), animal (including horses and cows), pet (including birds and turtles), mammal (including whales and man), to living creature (including everything in Noah's ark). As students construct similar ladders with such words as *car* and *school* and *house*, they begin to develop an awareness of the level of abstraction they are using. They see how at times it is useful to move toward more abstract words in order to talk about ideas (*democracy, justice, truth*), and how necessary it is to move toward the more specific word in writing and speaking when accurate communication is at stake.

Inferences.   The drawing of conclusions or inferences from the objective data our senses perceive is a continuous part of the process of thinking. The young child learns to infer parental pleasure, anger, or amusement from smiles, frowns, sharp words, or laughter. Much of our personal and social life is based on inference: from actions, words, gestures, looks, tones of voice, we infer friendliness or hostility, laziness or energy, brilliance or stupidity. When we make inferences, we project the known facts to a guess about the unknown; we may infer that the house is on fire from smelling smoke and that an accident has occurred from hearing the ambulance siren. Our inferences may not be correct: the smoke may come from burning leaves; the ambulance may be making a test run for civil defense.

Since much of the data on human behavior are relatively inaccessible, hidden under layers of social form and custom, our inferences often go seriously astray and endanger interpersonal relations. Wrong inferences and "snap" judgments result from drawing too hasty or illogical conclusions from consideration of incomplete facts. Police officers have frequently arrested epileptics for supposed drunkenness; emotionally disturbed children have been judged as retarded; the realistic representation of an invasion from Mars on a radio program once caused mass hysteria.[7] In making factual statements we attempt to report objectively: John broke three windows in the school. Our resulting judgment may be "John is naturally destructive," and we may infer,

[6] S. I. Hayakawa, *Language in Thought and Action,* rev. ed., Harcourt, Brace & World, Inc., New York, 1964, p. 169.
[7] Orson Welles caused panic all over the nation with his October, 1938, radio broadcast of a dramatization of H. G. Wells' *The War of the Worlds.*

rightly or wrongly, that John dislikes schools and teachers. The fact (John broke three windows) does not warrant either the judgment or the inference. More evidence is needed. Good inferential thinking watches for clues, collects and weighs evidence, and arrives logically at a valid reasoned conclusion which does not go beyond the evidence available. Practice in inferential thinking is an essential step in critical thinking and in intelligent reading.

Directive statements.   The normative or directive statement often proves a block to clear thinking. The tendency to interpret directive statements as factual has led to serious misunderstandings about language. Students and teachers need to recognize that an important function of human language is to bring about desired goals or actions and that such language cannot be interpreted literally. The mother who claims that "All little boys love to go to school" is not making a statement of fact but one which is calculated to bring the reluctant scholar safely within the doors of the first-grade room. There are those who forsake democracy because it has not lived up to its belief that "All men are created equal." They fail to recognize in that statement a directive or goal toward which to work rather than a literal statement of fact. So with many of the statements with which a society ensures that its citizens will work for desired goals: "All men are brothers," "A Boy Scout is clean, courteous, and obedient," "America is the land of freedom and opportunity."

"Either-or" thinking.   The human habit of thinking of problems, events, people, and things in terms of two solutions, two values, or two categories lies deep in human experience. We tend to classify things in terms of two values: right-wrong, good-bad, yes-no, pro-con. Our very language is set up in terms of these polarities; most of our evaluative words have their opposites: beautiful-ugly, bright-dull, strong-weak, rich-poor, black-white. Our language pulls us in the direction of seeing things in terms of black or white and discourages us from looking at the many shades of gray which form the continuum from black to white which fits more clearly the facts of the natural world.

The approach to problem solving for young people has proved fruitful when they have been trained to consider varying possibilities for solution rather than to search for the "right" one. School children are often encouraged in school to believe that their answers to questions must be either "right" or "wrong"; they tend to seek in literature or in popular drama assurances that characters are either villains or heroes, "good guys" or "bad guys." Such oversimplification of problems and judgments leads to a limited kind of thinking, and blocks exploration of many possible answers, judgments, and values; it leads to rigidity rather than to the flexibility needed to face the highly complicated problems in today's world.

The more the school can do to encourage consideration of many sides to a question, many solutions to a problem, many possible explanations of human behavior in life or in books, the greater are the possibilities for clearer thinking and sounder judgments. Schools do not divide students into "bright" and "dull" as two mutually exclusive and immutable groups, but assess intelligence on a many-valued scale and take into account such factors as willingness to work, achievement in different subjects (often quite different from intelligence), and others. Colleges do not choose applicants on the basis of grades and test scores alone, but consider recommendations from principals and teachers, study habits, personality factors, and extracurricular interests. A student's themes are not simply good or bad, but a complex of achievements (or errors) which can be looked at individually and considered in his composite grade. In every area of language study and use, either in school or life situations, teachers can help students move away from the primitive kind of either-or thinking to a more flexible and realistic kind of thinking which takes into consideration the many shifting complexities of today's world.

It is the primary responsibility of the teacher of English to be aware of and to pass on to his students a deep respect for language, its wonder and power, and a sense of responsibility in using it wisely, thoughtfully, and honestly. If we do not do this, whatever we teach about the agreement of nouns and verbs, about types of literature, and about topic sentences will have little meaning. If they cannot read today's newspaper and sift from its maze of fact, judgment, and inference enough about what is going on in the world to be informed citizens, it will not seriously profit our students to have read *Macbeth* and *Silas Marner*. If they cannot sift the grains of fact from the chaff of words designed to move, persuade, coerce, or manipulate their thinking, to distinguish distortions and untruths in the beguiling words designed to please, it will not matter whether they have gained skill in recognizing figures of speech or in scanning a sonnet.

The necessity for rethinking the language program is imperative. In this world of words in which our very survival depends on the critical and thoughtful use of language, we spend far more time in our schools teaching children where to put commas than helping them think critically and responsibly about the potential weapon they handle daily. Education for today's world demands a greatly enriched language program, broad in scope, and designed to help young people understand the ways in which human beings use language for different purposes, to move, control, and persuade as well as to inform. It should teach them how language can be used to communicate ideas more clearly and responsibly and enable them to understand and evaluate its use whether in the world about them or in the literature they read. It should be a program designed to lead to maturity: "When I was a child, I spake as a child, I understood as a child, I thought as a child: but when I became a man, I put away childish things" (I Corinthians 13:11).

Concepts about language for an eleventh-year program

The following concepts about language were developed by one teacher as the basis for a year's work in English in the eleventh grade. The student papers that follow were based on these concepts.

Language is a means of revealing an individual's values.

Tone and approach in language vary with the person to whom one is communicating.

Spoken and written language differ in certain ways.

Even between two individuals in the same family language varies.

Language changes to accommodate a change in society.

Professions, trades, and occupations have individual languages.

Dialects are prevalent.

Cultural referents enrich language.

Maturational, cultural, and artistic development in the use of language result in good composition.

Mass media of language impose certain forms.

The sound of language affects the meaning.

The observance of the rules of language helps good writing.

A combination of grammatical, lexical, and metaphoric meaning results in colorful language.

Effective language is composed of skills gained from wide reading, thoughtful listening, and experimental writing.[8]

Sample student papers

The following papers, written on the concepts, are samples of the kinds of exercises which help students develop an awareness of language, its many functions and varieties. (Further discussion of these concepts will be found in Chapters 7 and 8.)

Commercial for *Gringle* Brand Shlepkins in Double Talk

"Ladies, have you ever pundled the adveniences of owning a *Gringle* shlepkin? *Gringle* shlepkins are the most fantassible ever to be put on the starken. They're sloogy— they're flimboyant—they're tinglish—they're even plinchy! *Gringle* shlepkins come in a multity of glashish dranions—rabbish red, yaggle yellow, grunky green, and blishy blue. They are presible in many punchions also, ranging from twinky-six to fundy-four. Rush down to your blundest troogle and parshish one—right *Kling!*"

Genesis 23:1–6 and as It Might Be Written in Today's Language

And the life of Sarah was a hundred and seven and twenty years; those were the years of the life of Sarah. And Sarah died in Kiriath-arba—the same is Hebron—in the land of Canaan; and Abraham came to mourn for Sarah, and to weep for her. And Abraham rose up from before his dead, and spoke unto the children of Heth, saying: "I am a stranger and a sojourner with you; give me a possession of a burying-place with you, that I may bury my dead out of my sight." And the children of Heth answered Abraham, saying unto him: "Hear us, my lord, thou art a mighty prince among us; in the choice of our sepulchres bury thy dead; none of us shall withhold from thee his sepulchre, but that thou mayest bury thy dead."

At the age of one hundred twenty-seven years, Sarah died in Kiriath-arba, other-

[8] Concepts and student papers from the class of Elizabeth G. Norwood, Bancroft School, Worcester, Mass.

wise known as Hebron, which is located in Canaan. Abraham went there to mourn for Sarah. He explained to the inhabitants that he was a stranger, but he needed a place to bury his wife. The people, who admired Abraham greatly, told him of their admiration and said that he could bury her anywhere that he wanted.

(The student concluded that she liked the Biblical version better.)

Old Age*

Fie,
Gangrenous harlot,
With noxious breath foully
Reeking from tainted lips
And mangy, black-baked gums,

Fie,
Macabre strumpet,
With fossil frame nearly
Piercing dry, ashen skin
And leprous, degenerating limbs,

Fie,
Accursed slattern,
With glassy eyes grimly
Peering through mangled lids
And gaunt, pock-marked cheeks,

Was yours the face that launched a
thousand ships
and burnt the topless towers of Ilium?

Homer keeps Helena immortal, and
Only mortal things grow old.
Abominable toad,
Fie.

Basic concepts about language: a sequential program

The program described here outlines major concepts and information about language to be developed throughout the years of secondary school through assignments in speaking and writing, and by activities, readings, and discussions. Materials suggested in other chapters in this book may be added to these assignments. Many of the suggested activities are designed for continued practice during the six years, and may be adapted to different grade levels by the choice of simpler or more complex materials. The study of American regional dialects is suggested for grade eleven, and the history of the English language and its changes for grade twelve, where the student frequently encounters Beowulf, Chaucer, and the various translations of the Bible. The arrangement of concepts and assignments is in sequential order of difficulty. Further discussion of such assignments will be found in Chapters 7 and 8.

---

* Exercise in figurative language.

Concepts about language	Assignments and activities
Language is a symbolic process. *Learnings:* There are many nonverbal or non-linguistic "languages." Verbal symbols (words) stand for things and ideas. Language is a system of agreements about meanings. One word may stand for many things or meanings. Meanings grow through metaphorical extension.	A study of nonlinguistic systems of "language" and the way sounds, colors, visual symbols, and gestures symbolize meaning: animal language, insect, fish, and other communication systems, codes, signal systems, visual symbols (road signs, advertising symbols, clothes, uniforms, pins). Study of the symbols of mathematics and science. Words such as *tree, house, animal,* or *man* may stand for many different kinds of entities. Study of different kinds of things words may stand for: *animal, bird, flower, tree.* Common words may acquire metaphorical meanings, such as body terms like *head, foot, toe, hand, heart.*
All languages change; change is normal. *Learnings:* Languages grow through the addition of loan words and other vocabulary changes. Languages change through the influence of social, political, and economic events.	A study of word origins and shifts in meaning of loan words and borrowings from American Indians, and French, Spanish, Dutch, and German immigrants. A study of functional shift, or the way words shift their form classes: words used as different parts of speech (*ball, fire, run, set, strike*). A study of changing usage: the study of changing status of words and expressions; observation of usage in everyday speech, in mass media, fiction, and drama. A study of the shift of levels of usage according to situation: formal and informal standard, colloquial, slang, and substandard. A study of the processes by which new words are added to the language: coinages, compounds, analogy, erroneous utterances, portmanteau words, and others. Study of changes and words added from new inventions and social movements: machines, aviation, atomic, and electronic inventions, wars, changes in government. Study of loan words in English from Latin, Anglo-Saxon, Danish, and Norman French. Study of changes in the form and structure of the language characteristic of English from Anglo-Saxon times to the present. Study of changing usage, of amelioration and pejoration, of shifts of status from slang to standard.

Concepts about language	*Assignments and activities*

Words acquire meanings from varied sources.

Learnings:

Meanings develop through experience; individuals may have different meanings for the same words.

The meanings of words are determined by their context; contexts may include gestures, tones of voice, silence.

Structure and word order determine meanings.

Papers on "What ——— means to me" (school, camp, homesickness, fear, Christmas); "An experience that changed the meaning of the word ——— for me"; "A word that caused misunderstanding"; "My picture of a (cowboy, Texan, Southerner, Irishman)."

Exercises in slanted writing, associating words with other favorable or unfavorable words.

Study of shifts of meaning of commonly used words and expressions: *freedom, democracy, socialism, liberal.*

Study of ways in which gestures, intonation, and facial expressions determine the meaning of words or sentences.

Student-written political speeches providing both favorable and unfavorable contexts for the same name.

Students work with lists of words from the four form classes, arranging them into sentences with different meanings suggested by different orders (*man bites dog; dog bites man*).

Language shapes thinking.

Learnings:

Words affect the way we feel about things.

Words are used at different levels of abstraction.

Generalizations lead to uncritical thinking.

Words are used to group and classify; classifications shape thinking.

Study of emotional associations for words: denotations and connotations, name calling, euphemisms, loaded words.

Study of word magic and verbal taboos.

Constructing abstraction ladders (see page 61).

Study of abstract and concrete words; general and specific words.

Examination of sweeping generalizations about women drivers, blondes, teen-agers.

Study of stereotypes which influence thinking and feeling about people, ethnic groups, races.

Spoken language is different from written language; spoken language is of primary importance.

Learnings:

Written language cannot fully convey the speaker's intonation and gestures.

Study of the sound symbols (phonemes) represented by many written symbols (graphemes): e.g., *s* has 33 different spellings).

Study of the relationship of punctuation symbols to the tones, pauses, and inflections of spoken language.

Listening to the sounds of poems, plays, and fiction read aloud.

Practice in reading passages in several different ways to convey different meanings: anger, sorrow, pleading, irritation.

Concepts about language	*Assignments and activities*
Language has order, structure, and pattern.	A study of grammar and syntax, of the relation of word order to meaning, of varieties of sentence patterns and their possible modifications.
Language is used for different purposes. *Learnings:* Factual language attempts to record, explain, or convey information. Judgments indicate the way the speaker evaluates things, people, and situations. Inferences state conclusions inferred from situations or words. Emotive language attempts to affect the feelings of listener or reader. Directive language is used to influence others to act. Language is used both literally and figuratively.	Writing statements of fact or judgment and distinguishing between them. Analyzing news media and TV for both kinds of language. A study of poetry, drama, fiction, or persuasive writing for emotive language. Discussion of pledges, vows, oaths, and other statements designed to influence behavior. Study of cartoons, ads, and mass-media sources to analyze inferences intended or desired. Study of literal and figurative language in literature, mass media, and everyday speech. Analysis of literal and figurative use of the same words: *cool, blast, hot, star, doll, ball.*
Language changes according to the sex, education, home and social environment, occupation, geographical region, and social and economic status of the speaker.	Words, expressions, and language characteristic of the sexes: description of a dance, a ball game, a school, as a boy and a girl would describe it. Writing paragraphs or bits of dialogue illustrative of the usage of different educational levels. Usage studies focusing on shoptalk, usage characteristic of different social and occupational groups. The special languages of the family, the neighborhood gang, the teen-age crowd, the club group. Study of readings and recordings illustrating dialect and regional speech. Study of different forms of address, greetings, familiar and polite society idioms, and folk usage. Study of variations of language of the same individual in different situations: family, school, informal groups, business meetings, formal gatherings.

Selected bibliography

The teacher will find the following books useful and illuminating, providing some important insights into the nature of language, meaning, and human behavior. Some of the exercises in these books are useful for high school classes at all grade levels.

Monroe C. Beardsley, *Thinking Straight: Principles of Reasoning for Readers and Writers,* 2d ed., Prentice-Hall, Inc., Englewood Cliffs, N.J., 1956. Exercises in logic and critical thinking.

Max Black (ed.), *The Importance of Language,* Prentice-Hall, Inc., Englewood Cliffs, N.J., 1962. (Paper: Spectrum Books.)

John B. Carroll, *The Study of Language: A Survey of Linguistics and Related Disciplines,* Harvard University Press, Cambridge, Mass., 1959. Discusses important psychological studies of language.

Stuart Chase, *The Tyranny of Words,* Harcourt, Brace & World, Inc., New York, 1938. (Paper: Harvest Books.)

————, *The Power of Words,* Harcourt, Brace & World, Inc., New York, 1954. An economist looks at the language and deals in these two popularly written books with its uses and abuses in politics, government, economics, and sociology.

Walker Gibson (ed.), *The Limits of Language,* Hill and Wang, Inc., New York, 1962. (Paper: American Century). Most interesting and important for a philosophy of language or the relation of language to the way we think and how we see the world.

Edward T. Hall, *The Silent Language,* Premier Books, Fawcett Publications, Inc., Greenwich, Conn., New York, 1961. (Paperback.) A most interesting study of the language of gesture, posture, facial expression (kinesics) and its significance in human behavior and communication.

S. I. Hayakawa, *Language in Thought and Action,* Harcourt, Brace & World, Inc., New York, 2d ed., 1964. (Paperback.) A popular presentation of Korzybski's theories for the layman. Excellent teaching exercises.

————, *The Use and Misuse of Language,* Premier Books, Fawcett Publications, Inc., Greenwich, Conn., 1962. (Paperback.) A collection of essays on semantics originally appearing in the magazine *ETC.: A Review of General Semantics.*

Wendell Johnson, *People in Quandaries,* Harper & Row, Publishers, Incorporated, New York, 1946.

Susanne Langer, *Philosophy in a New Key,* Mentor Books, New American Library of World Literature, Inc., New York, 1959. (Paperback.)

Irving J. Lee, *Language Habits and Human Affairs,* Harper & Row, Publishers, Incorporated, New York, 1941. Excellent examples of semantic confusion as it affects human behavior.

————, *The Language of Wisdom and Folly,* Harper & Row, Publishers, Incorporated, New York, 1949.

Catherine Minteer, *Words and What They Do to You: Beginning Lessons in General Semantics for Junior and Senior High School,* Harper & Row, Publishers, Incorporated, New York, 1953.

C. K. Ogden and I. A. Richards, *The Meaning of Meaning: A Study of the Influence of Language upon Thought and of the Science of Symbolism,* 8th ed., Harcourt, Brace & World, Inc., New York, 1962. Difficult but important. A pioneer study of meaning.

Anatol Rapaport, *Science and the Goals of Man,* Harper & Row, Publishers, Incorporated, New York, 1950. Challenging materials for young scientists and mathematicians.

Cleveland A. Thomas, *Language Power for Youth,* Appleton-Century-Crofts, Inc., New York, 1955. Thought-provoking exercises in language and meaning; semantic concepts for high school students.

PART 1

Language:

SKILLS AND UNDERSTANDING

CHAPTER 4

"Really, now you ask me," said Alice, very much confused, "I don't think———"
"Then you shouldn't talk," said the Hatter.

LEWIS CARROLL [1]

"Remember that you are a human being with a soul and
the divine gift of articulate speech . . ."

GEORGE BERNARD SHAW [2]

Speaking and listening: a two-way process

The oral tradition

Western civilization has moved from the oral tradition of classical and medie-
val times when most teaching and learning was oral, through the typographical
culture of the Renaissance, in which books and libraries were created, back to
an oral culture in which by far the greatest amount of our teaching and the
dissemination of information and learning is again oral, by way of the spoken
word and the listening ear.

In today's world oral communication is increasingly important. Today

---

[1] *Alice's Adventures in Wonderland*, chap. 7.
[2] *Pygmalion* in *Selected Plays*, vol. I, Dodd, Mead & Company, Inc., New York, 1948. By
permission of The Public Trustee and the Society of Authors.

"Lord knows we've tried, mother. We just can't seem to communicate." Drawing by William P. Hoest; © 1964 *Saturday Review*.

each child in our public schools has heard, during a good part of his life, the general American dialect spoken by most national news broadcasters and commentators and by many entertainers. Today's child has listened during much of his early life, but he has also learned not to listen; he can tune out sounds which drive his elders to distraction.

Ironically, in an age in which oral language has become more quickly and widely disseminated than ever before, communication has become increasingly difficult. A central theme in modern literature is the inability of men to communicate their deepest thoughts and feelings to one another. T. S. Eliot's hollow men "grope together and avoid speech"; Prufrock dreams of talking with his lady but fears she will answer "that is not it at all, that is not what I meant, at all." Critics have seen Samuel Beckett's *Waiting for Godot* as an illustration of the disintegration of language, an "indication that language has lost its function as a means for communication. . . ."[3] The novelists Carson McCullers in *The Heart Is a Lonely Hunter,* James Joyce in *A Portrait of the Artist as a Young Man,* Franz Kafka in *The Castle,* and many others explore the same theme. The failure of communication in a depersonalized and mechanized age gives meaning to the primary objective of human language: the attempt to send a message to another human mind, and to have that mind

[3] Martin Esslin, *The Theatre of the Absurd,* Anchor Books, Doubleday & Company, Inc., Garden City, N.Y., 1961, p. 45. (Paperback.)

respond with understanding. Only when there is interaction between the sender and the receiver of the message is the act of speech meaningful and complete. If the receiver does not listen or understand, a two-way conversation may turn out like some of the dialogues in *Alice in Wonderland* between Alice and the Mad Hatter, in which people talk past, rather than with, each other: "The Hatter's remark seemed to have no meaning in it, and yet it was certainly English." The use of language to communicate meaningful ideas which can be understood by the hearer is a primary need in today's world.

Because speaking and listening occupy primary places in the giving and getting of information and the conduct of life in the modern world, both deserve attention in the English program. The ability of the individual to express ideas in such a way that others will listen and understand is a basic need of his social and personal life. His ability to establish close and satisfying personal relationships, and to find a place in the business and social world depends primarily on speech. He needs enough facility with his native tongue to enable him to use it freely and adequately for his personal relations. If he is too inhibited to speak with any but his best friends, if he cannot talk about personal matters, if he is not free to agree or disagree with others without becoming angry and emotional, he will not have acquired the necessary speech skills.

Since speech is an important social and economic index, every child in a democracy should acquire, through his schooling, a command of language which will allow him to choose freely the groups he wishes to belong to, and the careers he desires. Chapter 7 explores this problem in greater detail. Furthermore, in a world in which important decisions are frequently arrived at on the basis of information given orally, accurate and critical listening becomes a necessity.

Speech and listening in the English program

The first contact between ourselves and the world is established through speaking and listening. As the infant listens to the sounds in his early environment, he begins to associate feelings of comfort and security with the voices of those who care for him. His early childhood years are devoted to his major problem: that of deriving meanings from the streams of sounds reaching his ears, and learning to reproduce those sounds in order to make his wants, needs, feelings, and wishes known to others. Without normal development of ear, tongue, and vocal cords, he does not attain normal speech, and has lifelong difficulty in becoming a member of the human society. The poignant story of Helen Keller, the small savage civilized through learning language,[4] shows the essential roles speaking and hearing play as the cornerstones of that process.

[4] William Gibson, *The Miracle Worker,* Atheneum Publishers, New York, 1960.

The human infant reproduces the speech he hears about him in his earliest years: it may be American English, British English, Chinese, Spanish, or Hindustani. His native vocal equipment permits him to produce a wide variety of sounds, pitches, stresses, inflections, pauses, and tones, many of which he will never use. Able to imitate any speech sound known to men, he sorts out by ear those which his culture has determined as part of its language, but by the time he is fourteen or fifteen his ear and tongue have lost the ready ability to imitate many sounds. Not only does the child reproduce the language of the culture into which he is born, but his imitations include the accents and speech peculiarities of those from whom he learns his language. His early speech will reflect his loves, loyalties, and admirations—parents, the children he plays with, the adults who were important to him in early life.

English teachers today accept the view that a fair command of standard English[5] and the ability to use it with ease and self-confidence in speaking is the right of every child in our public schools. However, a child's language is an important part of his personality. The attempts of the school to change it may be interpreted as criticism or contempt for him as a person, or for his family, whose speech patterns he reflects. Most educators agree that it is the responsibility of the schools, and primarily of the English teacher, to bring each child as near to the goal of a general standard speech as possible. Problems lie in the frequent disagreements about how these goals shall be attained and in the relative importance of the speech problems we meet in our schools today.

Designing a program to develop speech in all children means providing for many different needs: activities to develop the speech of above-average and superior children from among whom the leaders of tomorrow may come and provision for the steady improvement in diction, pronunciation, usage, and ease in speaking of those with nonstandard usage. In addition, most of our schools must provide for the large groups of those young people whose speech problems are of a special kind, requiring concentrated or specialized attention: children of foreign-born or first-generation parents whose first language is not English; children whose speech difficulties stem from psychological problems ranging from the shyness of those with slight lisps to the deep-seated problems of those with severe speech retardation, blocking, or stuttering; physically handicapped children whose defective speech may be the result of birth injuries, brain damage, or disease; and those whose speech development has been impaired by hearing difficulties.

Goals for the program

Acceptable speech, free from attention-getting irregularities, solecisms, mannerisms, and locutions which would bar the user from certain vocational

---

[5] Standard English is commonly defined as the language of educated speakers, those prominent in business, public, and cultural affairs of the community. See Chap. 7, p. 165 for an expanded definition, and for further illustrations about teaching usage.

goals or social groups, is the goal for instruction in speaking and listening. The English program must provide the opportunity for each individual to come as close to this ideal as possible.

In addition to this over-all aim for the program, goals for speech work and training in listening will include the following:

Ease and fluency.   Boys and girls should have ample opportunity to practice speaking until they develop a natural, comfortable ease of speaking to small groups and larger audiences. They need to develop the confidence which grows through practice.

Clarity.   Discussion in the English classroom should give students needed practice in the logical organization of ideas needed in clear thinking.

Responsibility.   Good speech training emphasizes the speaker's responsibility for accurate, thoughtful speech, rather than that designed primarily to persuade, to dazzle with rhetoric, or to control others.

Critical listening.   The need to develop skills of accurate and critical listening is a primary aim for the program. Students need to learn to evaluate the words and intentions of the speaker, and to ask, "Who said it? Why is he saying it? What does he stand to gain by it?" and "What is his authority for saying it?"

Principles underlying the program

Good speech and good listening habits are not automatic, but must be taught. Speaking and listening activities in the integrated program become a natural part of the uses of language in the English course. Instead of special units, or a series of three-minute talks tucked in when convenient, speaking becomes a normal part of the everyday work in English as students meet in groups, plan panels, or round-table discussions, give oral reports, make tape recordings to improve their use of language, and read literature aloud. Listening, too, becomes a part of the program, with time spent in analyzing listening skills, practicing for improvement in accurate and critical listening, and learning to listen for appreciation of language and literature.

Program into practice

The teacher may start by making his own diagnosis of the speech and listening abilities of his class. Students should share in this estimate and add their own ideas about their needs. Since boys and girls speak most easily and competently about what interests them, an important part of the teacher's task will be finding a range of stimulating topics about which they can exchange ideas. Effective speaking and listening demand that the teacher be primarily responsible for making the class into an audience for its members and for assisting students in talking freely with others in the class and participating in group discussions. His skill in getting students to work effectively in groups is essential to successful learning. Finally, the program should provide for a wide range of individual differences in speaking and listening abilities and for diagnosis and referral of speech-handicapped children.

Diagnosing needs. During the early part of the school year, informal discussion with students about their tastes and interests serves many useful functions. The alert teacher may make mental notes of the lines of communication in his class. Do boys talk to girls? Are some students silent while others constantly demand to be heard, even though they may have little to say? Are some students ignored? Do students listen to one another, or is there competitive effort to get attention without listening to the points others are making? Is there a real exchange of ideas, or is the talking in the familiar traditional pattern of recitation—question and answer? [6] Are there young people whose speech shows the influence of non-English-speaking backgrounds? Do students use inaccurate, accented, unidiomatic speech with many nonstandard locutions? Obviously each class will require different approaches and procedures, as well as different plans for speech and discussion activities.

The students' own appraisal of their individual and group speech needs provides an opportunity for formulating goals and bringing to consciousness many of the needs for good speech in today's world. As students make lists of speech habits they wish to change, skills they wish to master, or patterns of speaking in people they desire to emulate, they begin to realize the practice that is necessary if they are to achieve their speech goals.

The use of the tape recorder to record speech patterns of individuals and group sessions provides the teacher with an excellent means of gathering data on the speech needs of students. Such recordings show the kinds of usage habitual with class members, speech difficulties needing correction, habits of discussion to be changed, and individual speech patterns which need improvement. Such recordings, too, provide the individual student with one of his most powerful motivations for speech change. As he hears himself speak for the first time on tape, he becomes aware, usually, of the difference between the sound of his own voice as others hear it and the sound he hears within his own ear. His usual reaction—"Do I sound like *that?*"—provides a powerful stimulus for improvement. Similarly, groups that use recordings of class discussions for study soon recognize the kinds of speaking skills with which they need help. Here, too, is powerful motivation for learning.

In addition to notes on these observations, the teacher's informal written records of the students' social skills in speaking and listening can be extremely valuable. Notes on poor usage, on inability to articulate certain sounds, or the overhesitant speech of the shy person—all these may go into the planning record. Although the teacher's own observations are a good guide, standardized diagnostic tests can be useful, too. A test of listening may be used to

---

[6] See the illustrative flow charts on pp. 92–93.

help students find out how good their listening skills are and to provide useful motivation for improvement.[7]

For the class to gain the most from work in speaking and listening, students should share in determining needs and objectives. Boys and girls need to become aware of the limitations of their own language habits and usage and envision their goals clearly enough to work toward them. Most young people realize the value of good speech in their future careers. It is the teacher's job to help them become aware of their needs and the limitations of their language patterns, and to strengthen their desire to put the necessary effort into improvement.

Stimulating interest.   The child practices and improves his language because he wants to talk as others do and because his impulse to communicate with others is so strong. The incentive to talk in the youngsters in our classrooms is nearly as strong as it was in childhood. Where topics of interest and importance to adolescents are discussed in the classroom, there is little problem in stimulating interest. This does not mean that the only possible topics are techniques of dating and getting a driver's license. Students have become enthusiastically involved in discussing social issues, current problems in education, and public affairs, and in exchanging ideas about values. Good discussion of these topics demands critical and logical thinking. The thoughtful teacher suggests such topics, or seizes the moment when they arise out of classwork in writing or literature. Every unit of study provides opportunities for panels, reports, and discussions. The following chapters contain suggestions for such topics and kinds of discussion. A classroom which is a stimulating environment for exchanging ideas, opinions, and beliefs provides the kind of setting needed for good development of speaking and listening.

Young people may become aware of their own need to develop acceptable speech patterns by formulating criteria for good speech and by analyzing models of good speech and usage they hear around them. They may learn something of the demand for good speech as a requirement for most jobs and professions. Through analysis of their speech as they hear tape recordings of their voices or through discussions and oral reading or dramatizations of plays in which they have participated, they grow critical of their own voices. Speech experts tell us that the individual never hears his voice as it sounds to others. Listening to a record or tape, he hears for the first time what his voice sounds like to others, and gains powerful motivation for speech improvement.

Establishing the audience.   Respect for and attention to the opinion of others should be requisites of class discussion. The teacher can help students understand the importance of a feeling of comfort and friendliness in the class. Since most young people struggle to some degree with stage fright, it may be important for teacher and class to talk over these feelings and their causes and suggest remedies. Many classes have learned to encourage the reluctant,

[7] See those listed on p. 91.

shy speaker and to provide the kind of audience which encourages good speech. The teacher may have to step in when discussion grows heated to remind them of the necessity for allowing dissenters to be heard. The tendency of young people in excited discussion to grow personal or aggressive needs firm handling if democratic and fruitful discussion is to take place.

Working with groups. The skills involved in working in groups provide the basis for effective discussion in all areas of English. The ability to resolve problems through discussion, to arrive at group decisions, to talk with those who hold different views or come from different backgrounds is an essential skill of democratic living. Further, working with groups within the English class makes it possible for the teacher to use different kinds of instruction for differing purposes, and often for differing needs of individual students. It makes possible a kind of diversity and flexibility within the classroom, and permits the use of materials of differing levels of difficulty and complexity.

In a few English classes, working in groups is so natural that students are used to moving into a group-work session and changing back without noise, lack of control, or waste of time. In others, students have had so little practice that teachers are hesitant about trying the experiment. A little preventive strategy and some carefully worked out procedures can make the transition from the formal class setting to working effectively in groups a smooth one.

The teacher must know the class and assess its ability to assume responsibility and to govern itself. Most young students consider working in groups a privilege worth working for. The teacher can utilize the students' wish for this kind of discussion to emphasize standards of conduct and responsibility. Although some classes take longer than others to become ready for the kind of self-discipline the process requires, teachers can train most students to accept the disciplines of group work. Group processes provide important training in discussion techniques and the skills of working with others.

The short buzz session of ten minutes or so provides a good introduction and testing ground for group work. When students engage in heated class discussion of an issue or a topic and there is not time for all to contribute, the teacher may say, "Since you all have something to say about this and we have only ten minutes left in the period, we will divide the class into four (or five) groups, in order to give everybody a chance to have his say." A quick arbitrary division by the teacher with a reminder about lack of time is often sufficient to carry students through the first trial. A follow-up session the next day may elicit suggestions as to how group discussion can be carried on more effectively.

Group work can be prepared for by a discussion with the class about the opportunities it presents for exchanging ideas about books or student writing. Students can help with the planning of ways in which they might assist in assuming the responsibilities necessary to make such a process work. A class secretary may list on the board the things the class suggests as conducive to good group work: moving chairs and forming groups quietly, keeping conversation low, getting to work quickly without wasting time, helping to draw out the nontalkers, listening to others when they are trying to speak.

If the class decides it is mature enough to undertake a group-work session, the teacher may challenge them to live up to their outline of good procedures and give them a trial. If students are unable to use their freedom wisely, the teacher may bring them back into regular class formation, asking why they were unable to carry out their plans. Junior high school students should be given several chances to learn these rather difficult skills. Each bit of progress in self-discipline and improvement in discussion should be called to their attention and praised. Some classes, especially of older, more emotionally mature students, can learn in a few trials to conduct orderly, businesslike meetings.

At its best, group discussion can teach students how to conduct committee work rapidly and efficiently without losing time, how to measure progress, how to sense the amount of agreement there is in a group, how to cut off the loquacious without seeming arbitrary, how to vote on an issue rather than on feelings and personalities, and how to talk to the point, argue, discuss, and challenge without incurring hurt feelings. Gradual improvement in these skills may progress during the six years of secondary school until students are ready to move into adult life to work effectively in many adult groups. Continual practice, discussion of successes and failures, and skillful leadership by the teacher will assist students to learn these much needed skills of democratic living.

Teachers using these techniques suggest that students can learn best to collaborate with a number of other people if the group structure is changed from time to time. Different types of grouping serve different needs in the classroom and may be adapted to many kinds of work. Among these are interest groups (students interested in exploring a particular problem or topic); special-skill groups (students who like to write, to do art work, to interview, etc.); ability groups (students grouped according to ability and the difficulty of the topic); or sociometric groups (students choosing those with whom they would like to work as first, second, or third choices).[8]

In the chapters that follow, suggestions are included for kinds of topics which lend themselves well to group discussion methods, whether writing, drama, poetry, thematic units, or other topics are the center of classwork.

Overcoming speech difficulties. The English teacher who encounters a student with a speech problem may confer with the speech therapist in the school or town, or, if there is none, may ask the consultant in the State Department of Education for assistance or for resources available in the state for therapy. Many colleges and universities now have speech clinics; speech

[8] Discussion of those techniques may be found in Jean D. Grambs, *Group Processes in Intergroup Education,* National Conference of Christians and Jews, New York, 1951, pp. 64–66. See Helen H. Jennings, *Sociometry in Group Relations,* American Council on Education, Washington, D.C., 1948, for techniques of constructing sociograms for sociometric choices.

therapists for elementary schools and consultants for elementary and secondary schools are becoming more common. School principals and guidance personnel often know the resources in the state. For the teacher without background or training in diagnosing speech problems, the first step is to find help from a professional.

Speech therapists recommend some general principles which the teacher can follow in meeting speech problems in English classes. These are, in general, the basic principles which operate to improve the speech in all adolescents: building of confidence, developing a feeling of freedom and ease in speaking with and to others, lessening tension in speech situations, building a receptive attitude in the class so that aberrations, distortions, or mistakes are accepted and never become an occasion for giggles or ridicule.

Some of the commonest problems and steps which may be taken to alleviate them are the following:[9]

Articulation problems. These are among the most common problems in our classrooms. Distortions of single sounds—*r, w, l, s, z,* and others—sometimes persist into the high school years unless the child has had therapy as early as the third grade. The lisp—the distortion of *s* and *z*—is handled better, therapists think, if the label is not attached to it. If clinical help is not available, the child may be told that he distorts these sounds in such a way as to attract attention. The main problem here is for the teacher to recognize the distortion and make a tactful referral to the consultant. This kind of problem is not usually difficult to correct; there is not much danger in doing the wrong thing, unless the overzealous teacher calls too much attention to the matter and embarrasses the child. Although practice in articulation and in oral and choral reading are helpful, the teacher needs a course in speech correction or direction from the consultant before any more specialized attention is given.

Stuttering. This is perhaps the most baffling problem the teacher has to deal with. Since the stutterer often wants to recite, to read aloud, and to contribute to the class, teachers (and often students) frequently wait in discomfort while he attempts to get the words out. Such children should be treated like others in the classroom and every effort should be made to help build their confidence and to release their tensions and nervousness. This problem, of course, requires the attention of a therapist, and professional help should be obtained, if available. In the regular classroom, participation in choral speaking (where group support lessens tension), creative dramatics, role playing, reading a part in a play, sociodrama—any activity in which the stutterer can lose his identity in an assumed role—often gives him the chance to speak entirely without stuttering. Puppetry, in which the individual is

[9] The suggestions given here for diagnosing and working with speech problems were largely made by Dr. Hal Dorsey, Director of Speech and Hearing Clinic, Central Connecticut State College, New Britain, Conn.

hidden from view, has been used as therapy for many children with speech difficulties. Choral speaking, particularly, often develops the feeling of fluency so important to stutterers.

"Cluttering." A less commonly understood, but frequently found, speech irregularity among adolescents is one commonly confused with stuttering: the too-rapid speech of the child whose words tumble out, literally becoming "cluttered" in delivery. This often occurs in the teen-ager, probably as a part of the awkwardness common to adolescence. The speech activities discussed above are helpful for this kind of speaker: often reading a part in a play or assuming the character of a slow, deliberate speaker in one of the other role-playing activities gives needed practice. So too does choral speaking, particularly of the slow, measured music of the psalms, and serious, stately, or elegiac verse. It is important that the teacher recognize the difference between stuttering and cluttering, obtain therapeutic treatment for the one, and provide relaxing and tension-releasing activities for the other.

Hearing difficulties. The hard-of-hearing child often goes undetected in school or family, sometimes for as long as four or five years. Where yearly or biennial hearing tests are common, as they are in many communities, these difficulties may be diagnosed early and treated. Often teachers (and parents) blame a child for inattention or disobedience when his real problem is hearing loss. Often such loss results in a too loud or too soft voice, which may be one of the clues to diagnosis. Testing and referral to a hearing specialist is essential for the young person with this difficulty.

Other problems. Inability to hear the students who are speaking is a real problem in some classrooms. The wee small voices often result from a classroom atmosphere in which students are reciting, rather than talking or discussing. Often they are speaking to the teacher alone, without consciousness that others are listening. When students speak informally in group discussion, or face others in the class to communicate ideas in which they are interested, there is little trouble with inaudible voices. Reminding the student to face others to whom he is speaking is often helpful in assisting the really shy student to consider his listeners.

Other speech-related problems can be remedied through the regular program in speech. Severe chronic hoarseness or hypernasality of tone may be helped by exercises in individual oral reading and in choral reading to improve both voice and articulation. The too soft or too loud voice, often troublesome in the classroom, can be improved by specific attention to pitch, loudness, and tone. Sometimes the teacher who can take time to be a willing listener as the stage-fright victim talks out his problem can be of help—chiefly by listening.

The important thing for teachers to remember and to teach their students is the concept that voice quality and speech are learned behavior, and, therefore, susceptible of improvement. Difficulties such as stuttering, lisping, nasality, and others are acquired, not inherited. The classroom in which speaking, rather than reciting, is a natural, important part of classroom work provides the best therapy and the optimum setting for good speech.

Speaking and listening activities

In planning the year's activities, the English teacher works to see that students are given opportunities to engage in spontaneous speech activities and to take part frequently in informal discussion; to engage in more formally planned speech activities, such as making announcements, giving reports, or taking part in planned discussions; to take part in interpretive activities, such as oral reading or choral speaking of literature; and to take part in activities for practicing and improving their listening skills.

Spontaneous speech activities

Some of the activities during each year include the kinds of informal talks and discussion in which the student expresses his own thoughts and ideas. Usually, these activities are in the majority in most classrooms where students engage freely in discussions about literature, writing, and other topics. The teacher aware of the needs of adolescents to gain practice in speaking frequently and informally can arrange for some kind of speaking to go on during almost every class meeting. The occasions for public speaking at the secondary level are relatively few. The most frequent opportunities for giving talks and speaking before a group are those in which students give oral reports, make announcements, and the like. Unit activities lend themselves naturally to discussion in committees, small groups, whole-class discussions, and forums in which speeches are unrehearsed.

Conducting class business and making announcements. There are many occasions in which young people may practice the needed skills of speaking briefly and clearly before the group through learning to conduct the business of a classroom. Being chosen to make announcements or read daily bulletins provides real incentive for clear and audible speech. In many classrooms, the class operates as a club, with different persons being chosen each day to call the class to order, agree on class business, and sometimes to summarize what has gone on the day before.

Informal speaking and discussion. Many opportunities for informal class discussions will arise during the course of the year's work in English. Young people learn through practice the importance of examining all aspects of a problem, listening to the ideas of others, seeking for areas of agreement, and keeping the discussion to the point. As students gain skill and maturity, more difficult discussion techniques may be learned: drawing out the timid, tactfully diverting those who wish to monopolize discussion, summarizing points of agreement or steps of progress in thinking, and sensing when the discussion has reached the point of diminishing returns or consensus. The teacher who can provide topics and problems for discussion at differing levels of difficulty will be preparing youth for successful practice in one of the most important kinds of communication.[10]

Classes may be divided into small groups from time to time for any of the following activities:

Committee work. Planning bulletin boards, class parties, group reports, field trips, and class projects. The teacher will see that the membership of the group lends itself to providing good experience for beginners learning to talk and work together.

Small-group discussions. The simplest kind of discussion arrangement is the informal small group organized quickly from time to time for a specific purpose: discussing and criticizing student papers, talking about books or the meaning of a poem, dramatizing a scene from a play, organizing a discussion for tape recorder, or talking over ideas as a preliminary step to writing a paper.

Planned speech activities

Panels, forums, and round-table discussions. These types of discussion represent an advance in formality of structure and operation. Since real give and take in talking together is a sophisticated skill, these discussions should emphasize exchange of thought and idea rather than individual talks by students. Even so, some planning of individual talks must take place.

Discussion of speech standards, suitable levels of usage, the responsibility of the speaker to support assertions, offer evidence, and to check facts and give sources are important language problems which come up during analysis of such presentations. The discussion of discussion, circular as it seems, provides valuable opportunities to assess the quality of thinking, to exercise critical judgment about the speakers' points of view, and to raise questions about points not clearly made or about illogical or uncritical thinking.

Planned speeches. At a slightly more formal level are the planned and perhaps rehearsed panel discussions for which students write out a presentation of a point of view from reading or research, or the oral talks in which planning and perhaps rehearsing takes place: giving oral reports from written notes, making a speech before the class, the student council, an outside audience, or a club meeting. When the student's interest is deeply engaged and he is called on to talk to the class about something he knows well and is interested in, he has the best chance of speaking with creditable ease and effectiveness.

Interpretive activities

Some activities require the speaker to interpret the thoughts and ideas of another person. Choral speaking of poetry, oral reading of literature, drama-

---

[10] Suggestions for such topics are given in Chaps. 6 to 14.

tization of plays, role playing, sociodrama, and creative dramatics require the speakers to assume another role and to interpret the moods, feelings, and ideas of another person.

Choral speaking.   The choral speaking of poetry and rhythmic prose provides valuable experience in speaking and hearing literature. In addition, students in a group often find it possible to read well and speak better than they do individually. Group support lends comfort to the shy and the inhibited and provides camouflage for the vocal uncertainties of young adolescents. The demands of literature and poetry for words spoken rhythmically, articulated cleanly, and spoken clearly set a standard of good speaking difficult to attain in everyday situations. Slovenly speech and poor diction show immediately; the effort to get the nonsense or patter poems right encourages clean articulation, and the satisfying sound of lines well spoken is the reward for effort.

Achieving good choral speaking with a class is an art which many teachers learn through experimenting on the wonderfully adaptable and frequently cooperative human beings in their classrooms. Creative leadership is essential; too often teachers attempt to conduct group reading merely by giving students an opening cue and letting voices rise and fall where they will. The ragged, cluttered effect of such spoken verse is discouraging. Some rehearse too diligently on fine points of diction and sound until the pleasure in reading has evaporated for the speakers, and the poetry has become deadened by routine. The teacher who wishes to lead choral speaking successfully should listen to some of the recordings of verse choir skillfully done, read some of the books by master teachers of the art,[11] and practice with the class until both he and they feel easy and unembarrassed about trying various readings and vocal effects. Chapter 11 gives some suggestions about choral speaking and the appreciation of poetry.

Some teachers who have been successful with choral speaking offer these suggestions to beginners who would learn its techniques:

1. Act as leader, not dictator: ask the group how certain words and lines should be said, and how different readings would affect the meaning.

2. Emphasize meaning, always. Students cannot read intelligently what they do not understand. Questions like "What do you think this line means?" "How should it be read?" "Does the break in thought come at the end of the line, or in the middle of the next? Why?" or "What image do you think the poet is suggesting by this phrase?" are essential. Too often students and teacher plunge into a poem which young people plainly fail to understand. Reading then becomes mere rote work—sound and fury signifying nothing.

3. Encourage the students to put their own poem together by offering

---

[11] See also the suggestions for work in speech and listening, including the arrangement of Poe's "The Bells" for speech choir, in Commission on the English Curriculum, *The English Language Arts in the Secondary School*, Appleton-Century-Crofts, Inc., New York, 1956, chaps. 7 and 8, and the bibliography at the end of the chapter.

different interpretations and readings of various lines. Understanding of the poem will grow as they learn to read verse more skillfully together.

4. Choose poems carefully. Choice is all important. Many leaders of choral speaking have their groups perform with great beauty much magnificent prose and verse: parts of the Psalms, Ecclesiastes, and other sections of the Bible; Donne's "No Man Is an Island," the poems of Cummings, Eliot, Sandburg, Lindsay, Millay, MacLeish, and other modern writers whose verse lends itself well to this kind of reading. Poems should be chosen for sound as well as for meaning. The beauty of young voices reading powerful and memorable verse in unison is moving to the speakers themselves and to the audience. Groups that are willing to practice to bring their reading to a high level of accomplishment should have the satisfaction of a larger audience than the class. Recordings may be preserved on tape and played for other classes; students may do "live" readings for other classes in the school; and a good group should be able to appear in school assembly at least once a year. Many slow learners do well in this kind of performance and find satisfaction in the achievement. Interest in poetry throughout the school has often been kindled by such a program.

Oral reading and dramatics.   Teachers find many occasions for oral reading in situations which give purpose to the speaker and ensure an attentive audience. The study of literature calls for illustration from selections being read: bits of dialogue which illuminate or reveal character, good descriptive passages, memorable moments, thought-provoking or inspiring lines, passages communicating mood, setting and tone. Reading aloud when these passages are under discussion brings literature to life for many students who have difficulty with the printed symbol.

Laughter in the English classroom is much too rare a commodity. The sharing of humor increases appreciation and teaches the student something of the fun to be derived from silent reading.

One of the most enjoyable forms of oral reading for young people and adults is that of play reading or dramatics. It is difficult to understand why the study of a play is often limited to the printed word. Teachers who believe that plays are meant to be heard make the reading of the play, with parts assigned to class members, an important part of the study. Some students can read well at their seats; others do better in groups seated in front of the class, while the extroverts enjoy dramatizing.

One of the chief difficulties teachers encounter in play reading and dramatics with adolescents is the frequent inhibition of those who are reluctant to throw themselves into a part. Often play reading becomes wooden and painful. If the teacher can help to make the atmosphere of the class informal and receptive, even the inhibited sometimes relax, particularly under the infectious influence of some of the extroverts. Sometimes if the teacher takes a role it helps draw the class into the spirit of the thing. Students should not be asked to read parts without being given a chance to prepare or to know what they are reading. Assigning scenes to a group to prepare for dramatization or reading before the class a day or so in advance, and often under a student director, is advisable. Reading for ideas and meaning can make oral, choral, and play reading a way to enjoyment and understanding of literature, rather than a deadening, word-for-word, literal rendition of the text without the informing spirit which brings it to life.

Role playing, sociodrama, and creative dramatics. Role playing and sociodrama are important tools not only for the social scientists and psychologists who originated these techniques, but also for English teachers, who may adapt them to help students understand the role of language in interpersonal relations and gain insight into the motivation and feelings of characters in literature. In role playing, informal situations are set up in which students play the roles of characters or participants. The role playing of situations involving conflicts between adolescents and their parents allows young people to explore various tactful ways of explaining a point of view or making a request, and also to experience, as they play the parent roles, how it feels to be in the position of parent. Teachers often make up more formal role-playing situations which are really miniature plays or sociodramas to enable students to work through a problem in human relations by exploring different solutions, and always by discussing the importance of language in such situations. As students talk over what might have been said and how a situation might have been handled differently, they may replay the situation with the insights they have gained to experience the difference that changes in the use of words or in attitudes make.[12]

Both students and teachers can invent role-playing situations which provide practice in language use and illustrate the effects of language on human actions and feelings. The role playing of social situations such as introductions, telephone manners, being interviewed for a job, asking a girl for a date, or meeting her parents provide natural settings for practice of speech in which all may take part in a brief time. Although the student's words are unrehearsed in such activities, he speaks not in his own person, but in that of another whose ideas and attitudes he interprets.

The teacher may give each student a separate slip of paper indicating the role he is to play and put a group of players together to act out the scene, using the words, actions, and character which the real-life persons may be expected to use. The discussion of the feelings of the players should occur after they have played their respective roles. The players may simulate a life situation in which several people are thrust together and must rise to the occasion by talking to each other. Students may take any of the following roles to gain useful practice in improving conversation habits:

[12] The teacher may find some useful illustrations of the uses of role playing and sociodrama with an eighth-grade class in Hilda Taba and Deborah Elkins, *With Focus on Human Relations: A Story of an Eighth Grade,* American Council on Education, Washington, D.C., 1950; and in Hilda Taba et al., *Curriculum in Intergroup Relations: Case Studies in Instruction for Secondary Schools,* American Council on Education, Washington, D.C., 1949.

1. A loquacious featherbrained girl who gushes and doesn't allow anyone to get past the introductory clause of a sentence before she tries to get the conversation turned back toward herself: "That reminds me of the time when I . . ."

2. The shy, inarticulate boy who hesitates and doesn't know what to say at a dance.

3. The teen-ager forced to entertain his parents' older visitors while the parents are dressing to go out.

The following role-playing situations, involving several players, may be played several times, with different players, while the class observes the differences that language makes in the human relations involved:

1. Father wants his son to go to college because he did; he wants him to follow in his footsteps to become a doctor, lawyer, teacher. Son does not make good enough grades to get into college. (Or son wants to be a veterinarian, gardener, contractor, or salesman.) Players: father, son, mother, teacher or principal.

2. A bright student with family problems at home wants to drop out because he doesn't like school. Players: student, student's friend, teacher, principal, parent, guidance officer.

3. A problem student, acting up in class, disturbing others, trying to keep the spotlight on himself, feels unjustly punished by the teacher. Players: students, teacher, principal.

4. A discussion between two or three teen-agers and their parents (and/ or grandparents) on the question of whether today's children have too much freedom. Players: grandmother, mother (who understands), teen-age daughter or son.

5. Boy (or girl) attempts to convince father or mother that he (she) is mature and responsible enough to get a driver's license.

6. Students play one of the problems in Margaret Culkin Banning's *Letters to Susan*[13] (problem of allowances, going steady, early marriage, etc.).

7. Students may choose to play roles in scenes from short stories, plays, or popular books: Clarence Day's *Life with Father*, Frank Gilbreth and Ernestine Carey's *Cheaper by the Dozen*, Mr. Collins' proposal from Jane Austen's *Pride and Prejudice*.

Role playing in the English class provides the teacher with a useful teaching technique for the following purposes:

1. To provide junior high school students with speech situations in which they can overcome awkwardness, gain confidence, and begin to gain some insight into human behavior.

[13] Harper & Row, Publishers, Incorporated, New York, 1936.

2. To provide an opportunity at any grade level for students who are having difficulty understanding why people behave as they do, either in literature or in life.

3. To assist students to understand the complexities of human reactions and the role language plays in complicating or clarifying human relationships.

4. To enable students to gain sensitivity to the way other people feel, through living through their roles or figuratively "stepping inside their skins" for a brief time. Role playing is the best means for human beings to understand "how it feels" to be someone else: a parent, teacher, another classmate.

The teacher may choose to have students play problem situations, make up sociodramas involving students who are having difficulty communicating, or gain understanding of short stories or novels by having students play roles of characters and act out the dilemma in the story or go beyond it to show how it might have been handled differently.

Listening activities

Training the student's listening ear to distinguish fine points in speech and dramatic interpretation may be achieved by some of the following exercises:

Asking students to listen in the classroom with eyes closed to sounds heard in the halls or outdoors and to list and describe these sounds. As students compare lists, they discover that some are more acutely aware of such noises than others and more accurate about identifying them.

Students may listen to compare two readings of a short story, a poem, or a speech from a Shakespearean play to discern differences in reading words or lines, observing phrasing, intonation, emphasis, and other means readers use to convey meaning.

The students' performance as speakers and listeners may be used to improve participation in panels and discussions. Students may discuss speaking and listening habits and learn to watch for improvement. As they observe their own performance in discussion and those of others in discussion, there should be opportunity for class discussion of such habits. Through self-analysis, students may learn to become aware of habits to avoid: interrupting speakers, failing to listen, talking others down, talking around the question rather than to the point, making appeals to emotion rather than to reason.

Junior high school students may learn to practice listening skills by exercises during which class members are introduced to each other, and students are asked to remember names and brief facts about each individual given in the introductions.

The give and take of good conversation—a lost art, according to some critics of modern culture—may be practiced in the classroom as students engage in informal discussion or exchange of opinions on a variety of topics.

Evaluating speaking and listening

Growth in power over oral language is demonstrated in performance of students individually and in groups. Those whose speaking habits have improved during the year in command of greater ease and fluency, in ability to speak before a group without hesitancy or embarrassment, or to speak effectively, with a comfortable and appropriate level of usage have made significant gains. Often progress will come in several of these areas. Improvements in articulation, diction, usage, tone of voice, and tempo of speech are also important evidences of growth.

The teacher who makes up a diagnostic chart of speech characteristics of students early in the year has something with which to evaluate progress as the year goes on. Students' recordings of their own voices at the beginning and the end of the year provide a most useful check of growth and progress. Teachers suggest the following techniques of evaluating speech activities:

1. Observing professional speakers, actors, commentators, and the like and from such observation developing standards for critical examination of what is said and how it is said.

2. Making speech recordings for purposes of record and evaluation.

3. Evolving cooperatively sets of standards for various speech activities and applying them to activities in progress.

4. Setting goals for future performance in the light of the results of the evaluation.[14]

The teacher may want to use one of the following useful standardized tests for measuring listening skills:

. . . *Brown-Carlsen Listening Comprehension Test*, grades 9–13, fifty minutes, Harcourt, Brace & World, Inc., New York, 1953.

. . . *Brown-Carlsen STEP Listening Comprehension Tests*, level 2 (grades 10–12), level 3 (grades 7–9), Cooperative Test Division, Educational Testing Service, Princeton, N.J., 1957.

The teacher may find it useful to evaluate progress in classroom discussion by using the flow charts that appear in the accompanying figures. In charting the give and take of discussion in the class, the teacher can observe how much participation by students takes place, and how much of the discussion is dominated by the teacher. (See Figures 4-1 to 4-3.)

Figure 4-1 shows a double-circle arrangement of a classroom containing thirty pupils. The letter T indicates the teacher's seat; C indicates the location of the class chairman; R shows where an invited resource person is sitting. The double-headed arrows show an interchange between two persons. It is ap-

---

[14] Summarized from Commission on the English Curriculum, *op. cit.*, p. 208.

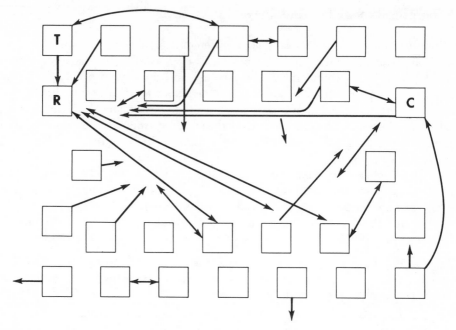

Figure 4-1 **Flow chart showing participation in discussion in a seventh-grade class-room.**

parent that, in this classroom situation, the teacher really allowed the chairman to assume the role of leader, that the pupils were free to approach the resource person directly, and that only two pupils made irrelevant remarks. The group dynamics of the situation were apparently good: a wide distribution of response, a democratic atmosphere, and close adherence to the topic of discussion.

Figure 4-2 depicts a situation in which a group of pupils is seated around a table under the direction of a teacher who dominates in a question-and-answer type of discussion. There is little opportunity for the pupils to challenge or reinforce one another's statements, to interpret, to think independently, or to learn democratic procedures.

Quite different is the flow chart shown in Figure 4-3. Here there is free interchange between pupil and pupil as well as pupil and teacher. In this situation, the teacher is still needed to guide the discussion, as is shown by the arrows that lead to and from him in a number of instances.[15]

Students may evaluate their growth subjectively in written comments for the teacher. Do they feel more comfortable and less nervous speaking in front of the class? Have they engaged in some new speech activities during the year

[15] Charts and comments from Marian Zollinger and Mildred A. Dawson, "Evaluation of Oral Communication," *English Journal*, vol. 57, November, 1958, pp. 503–504.

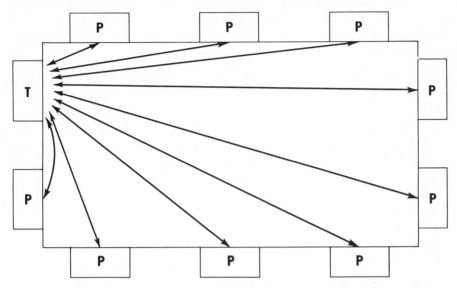

Figure 4-2   **Flow chart showing a completely teacher-dominated discussion.**

(acting in a play, reading a role, giving a report to the class, taking part in a panel discussion)? What gains do they see in their own use of speaking-listening skills during the year? What do they need more practice in? What was the most helpful speech activity they engaged in?

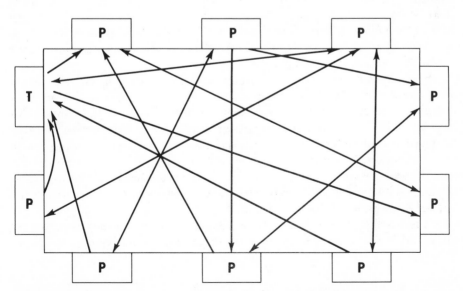

Figure 4-3   **Flow chart showing a democratic group discussion where pupils freely exchange ideas and where the teacher gives considerable guidance.**

A check list formulated by students is helpful as a means of evaluating themselves on their work in speech and discussion. One such list, evolved by a class for use by individuals, contained these questions (to be answered *none, some, much*):

1. What part did I play in this group discussion? (Was I an active participant? Was I an active listener to the contributions of others? Was I willing to respect the point of view held by others? Was I willing to weigh the varying points of view before arriving at a final conclusion?)

2. Was I well prepared for participating in the discussion? (Did I have adequate facts to support my statements? Did I use reliable sources of information for the facts I needed? Did I base my opinion on sound reasoning? Did I find questions unanswered in my mind because of insufficient data? Did I select and organize my facts to make a clear presentation? Did I make effective use of demonstration, illustration on the board, analogy, or other devices to clarify my ideas for others?)

3. How carefully did I speak? (Did I use approved language? Did I pronounce words correctly? Was my enunciation clear? Could everyone hear me? Did I hold attention with my eyes and voice as well as my ideas?) [16]

Students may construct a similar rating chart for listening in discussion. A sample check list might include these questions: Do I help to improve listening conditions by minimizing distractions? Do I look directly at the speaker? Do I show him I am interested? Do I ask questions which help the speaker to clarify his meaning? Does my attention wander? Am I so intent on my own contribution to the discussion that I do not concentrate on others' contributions? If the discussion tends to ramble, do I help tactfully to turn it back to the point? When it is necessary to disagree with a speaker, do I do so courteously? Do I take notes to aid my attention and comprehension? Am I ready to summarize the main points? [17]

Since students are likely not to take seriously subjects in which they are not given a grade, discussion and evaluation throughout the year should make it evident that their progress in speaking and listening is as important as that in other skills. Their own self-evaluations, conferences with the teacher, and their observations of individual and class improvement may be made a matter of importance through keeping records in their folders of work for the year. Grades for individual speeches are of minor importance. The real value of such techniques is to keep before the student's awareness his steady improvement in these two important skills.

The English classroom should be a place where the student can find his voice and learn to use it to express the ideas he is formulating as he thinks,

---

[16] *Ibid.*, p. 501.
[17] Olive S. Niles and Margaret J. Early, "Adjusting to Individual Differences in English," *Journal of Education,* Boston University, vol. 138, December, 1955, p. 53.

reads, writes, and listens to others. It should be a forum for ideas rather than a showcase for performance; it must be a place where young people can be assured of a receptive, attentive audience as they gain practice in shaping thoughts into spoken words.

Student activities and assignments

The following exercises, activities, and assignments are planned to assist students in developing good speech habits and gaining practice in speaking and listening. Other exercises are given within the chapter.

Developing clear speech

. . . Students may develop the "lost art of conversation" as they engage in panels modeled on popular television shows: radio, sports, and news broadcasts, interviews with celebrities, or youth forums. Models (some currently available, and some on records or tape) may be "Meet the Press," "Author Meets Critic," "Open End," "Small World," "Invitation to Learning," and "New England Town Meeting." Audiovisual departments have tapes of many of these.

. . . Students may write their own broadcast of news or commentary and produce it for the class. The job of selecting, editing, and highlighting the news, or distinguishing between editorializing and reporting involves important language skills.

. . . Shy and withdrawn students find it easier to speak with something in their hands. When students feel the need of such practice, oral talks in which the speaker demonstrates how something works provides the best bridge to solo speaking. Students may demonstrate how something works (an outboard motor, an abacus, a new camera), or show an object of interest (a doll from a foreign country, a rare book, a Civil War sword, a stamp collection).

. . . Small-group discussion topics may include reading general books (on a simple topic), reading the books of a single author, discussing different reactions to the same book, talking about a community, regional, national, or international problem.

. . . Students often record discussions, talks, readings, or dramatizations on tape, and then exchange tapes with other classes, schools in the community or in other regions, or schools abroad. Organizations which will arrange for the exchanges are International Tape Exchange, 834 Ruddiman Ave., North Muskegon, Mich., and World Tape Pals, Inc., Dallas 15, Tex.

. . . Students may act as directors for choral speaking. The results may not be professional, but students will learn much. A class of thirty may divide into three groups with student directors, and each group of ten students may read its choices for the other twenty.

. . . Provide a chance for students to enrich their appreciation of humor through choral reading of nonsense verse. Such selections as Lewis Carroll's

"Jabberwocky," many poems from Milne's *When We Were Very Young*, Lear's "The Jumblies," and others provide engaging nonsense for laughter and enjoyment. Numerous anthologies contain suitable poems; *The Oxford Book of Light Verse* is valuable in this regard.

. . . Teachers may provide opportunities for students to read stories to young children. In schools with elementary grades under one roof or nearby, visits can be easily arranged. Many high schools plan to have groups do such reading at Christmas. Older students may present oral-reading programs of poetry, prose, and plays to other grades in the school. Talking to a younger audience is easier than talking to peers, especially for the less able students.

Developing skills of diction

. . . Allow students to listen to a recording of *My Fair Lady* or read together Shaw's *Pygmalion* as background for a discussion about the relationship between speech and social status.

. . . Verse choir, oral readings, and creative dramatics may provide helpful activities for the improvement of enunciation and substandard articulation or pronunciation.

. . . Encourage students to enjoy some of the tongue twisters children use in games for practice in diction. Nursery rhymes and speech texts offer many choices besides the ubiquitous "Peter Piper." Listening to and practicing some of the patter songs from the Gilbert and Sullivan operettas highlights the importance of masterly articulation.[18]

Listening activities

. . . The importance of listening with a purpose may be dramatized if teachers divide the class into two groups to listen to a recording of a play, speech, or short story. Half the class may be given questions directing students to listen for certain points; the other half may be asked to listen for pleasure. A brief quiz on content at the end of the session usually points out dramatically the difference in understanding and remembering what has been heard.

. . . Accurate listening may be practiced as students write a series of directions for actions that can be performed in the classroom and work in pairs, with one person reading the steps of directions while the other follows the instructions.[19]

. . . Give students ample practice in recording assignments accurately, getting the main facts from a lecture or selection read to them. They should have a chance to evaluate their success, compare their notes with the original, and discuss whether they have heard the main ideas or have confused principal ideas and details. Tapes of controversial discussions and political

---

[18] See the selection of patter songs in Marjorie Gullan, *The Speech Choir*, Harper & Row, Publishers, Incorporated, New York, 1937.

[19] Niles and Early, *op. cit.* Other excellent listening exercises are included in this article.

speeches provide excellent opportunities to listen to get facts straight and to observe and discuss distortions and misunderstandings.

. . . Teachers develop critical listening by encouraging examination of the ideas in student reports, newspapers, radio and television broadcasts, and assembly lectures. Questions of "What was said?" "By whom?" "Why?" and "How does he know?" should become basic.

. . . Encourage students to listen critically and analytically to radio and television speakers on programs of news, opinion, and controversy. They should look for propaganda devices, faulty logic, loaded words, appeals to emotion rather than reason, half truths, omissions, and quoting out of context. Comparing the first impression of the spoken words of a political speech with the transcript of the full speech in the newspaper provides a valuable check on content.

. . . Teach listening for main ideas by having students make a list of language signals pointing to chief ideas. Students have noted such signals as "first," "there are several ways," "the two main ideas are," "in the first place," "the one thing," "next we find," and others.[20]

. . . Students may practice listening for organizational patterns of speeches heard on radio, television, recordings, or in assembly or lectures. This practice helps in learning to distinguish between main idea and supporting details, to determine whether ideas are supported by reasons, facts, examples, or illustrations, and to decide whether the conclusion is clearly made. Students may also be asked to make notes of the main arguments in an announced television speech on national policy or foreign affairs.

Selected bibliography

Harlen Martin Adams and Thomas Clark Pollock, *Speak Up!* The Macmillan Company, New York, 1956. Speaking and listening activities in the classroom: a text for high school students.

Willard J. Friedrich and Ruth A. Wilcox, *Teaching Speech in High Schools,* The Macmillan Company, New York, 1953. A good discussion of the speech activities commonly taught in high schools.

Jean D. Grambs, *Group Processes in Intergroup Education,* National Conference of Christians and Jews, New York, 1951. The writer provides assistance to teachers who wish to use group work to improve group relations in the classroom.

Helen Hall Jennings, "Sociodrama as an Educative Process," *Fostering Mental Health in Our Schools,* 1950 Yearbook of the Association for Supervision and Curriculum Development, NEA, Washington, D.C., 1950.

Irving J. Lee, *How to Talk with People,* Harper & Row, Publishers, Incorporated, New York, 1952.

[20] Stanley B. Kegler, "Techniques in Teaching Listening for Main Ideas," *English Journal,* vol. 45, January, 1956, pp. 30–32.

Walter Loban et al., *Teaching Language and Literature: Grades 7–12,* Harcourt, Brace & World, Inc., New York, 1961, chaps. 4 and 9.

Ralph G. Nichols and Leonard A. Stevens, *Are You Listening?* McGraw-Hill Book Company, New York, 1957. Helpful discussion of problems involved in teaching listening.

Olive S. Niles and Margaret J. Early, "Listening," *Journal of Education,* Boston University, vol. 138, December, 1955, pp. 41–55. Excellent suggestions for classroom exercises in listening.

George Shaftel and Fannie R. Shaftel, *Role Playing the Problem Story,* Commission on Educational Organizations, National Conference of Christians and Jews, New York, 1952. Offers helpful suggestions about the uses of role playing in teaching.

Speech in the English Classroom, NCTE, Champaign, Ill., 1961. A portfolio of twelve articles reprinted from the *English Journal.*

CHAPTER 5

If we think of it, all that a University, or final highest School can do for us, is still but what the first School began doing,—teach us to read.

THOMAS CARLYLE [1]

Reading: symbol into thought

Despite the evidence that young people in our high schools are reading more and better books than ever before and that children who have never owned books are starting their own paperback libraries, teachers and administrators usually feel that some attention to reading skills is essential to most high school youth. Most of our students, even the able ones, can be taught to read better. For many, what is needed is help in increasing the speed of reading so that as adults they will be able to keep abreast of a flood of printed materials. Many very bright young people need specific instruction so that they may improve reading skills already working well for them if they are to succeed in college. They may endeavor to improve their reading rate or to learn more subtle skills of comprehension and literary analysis. Many, chiefly interested in science or mathematics, need to experience pleasure in reading as a means of enriching their adult lives.

The broad average group, including terminal, vocational, and business students and many who will drop out of high school before graduation, needs specific help and instruction in reading, too. For many of these, what is needed is a program in literature and guided reading which stimulates their desire to read and helps them build independent reading habits. For most of these, instruction in the English classroom should help establish such habits and provide practice in developing vocabulary and comprehension skills. The

[1] "The Hero as a Man of Letters," *On Heroes and Hero-Worship*, Estes and Lauriat, Publishers, Boston, 1886, p. 385.

majority of these students need training in reading in all their subjects. Poor reading habits and lack of interest are handicaps to their academic success in science, history, and mathematics, as well as in English.

The group which needs specialized help at the secondary level includes those students who are seriously retarded in reading. These usually require more individualized remedial work than the teacher is trained to give or has time for in English class. Opportunity for individual reading and participation in discussions of books stimulates the desire to read, but for many of these students a special class must provide the individual attention most English teachers have not time to give.

Backgrounds: reading and cultural attitudes

The attitudes of adults have great influence on the reading of young people. Although figures on increased book buying are encouraging, there is a darker side to the picture. American adults—even college graduates—read little. In the homes of such graduates there are often few books. Adult indifference toward reading is reflected in the feeling of adolescents that reading is not an important part of life.

These widespread cultural attitudes affect most of the children in our schools. There is another, less understood way in which cultural attitudes strongly affect just those young people who have the most difficulty with reading. The high school dropout rate is highly correlated with slow-learning pupils whose outstanding characteristic is an extremely low reading level.[2] The seriousness of the problem with these children is closely related to family and class attitudes toward school, toward learning, and toward reading. Teachers in slum schools report that "when children leave the school they never see anyone read anything—not even newspapers," and observe that "If we could change the family attitude toward reading, we could accomplish much."[3]

Reading specialists have speculated about the effect of the materials generally used in teaching beginning reading on lower-class children, the group from which many of the slow readers come.

Other factors may be important in the adolescent's attitudes toward reading. One study exploring the role of the adolescent's concept of self in reading improvement found that those who interpreted demands for improvement as a personal threat rejected the demands in order to keep intact their concept of themselves. When remedial reading methods were nonthreatening, the adolescent was able to respond to them and to accept himself as a student

---

[2] James B. Conant, *Slums and Suburbs,* McGraw-Hill Book Company, New York, 1961, p. 50, and Ruth Penty, *Reading Ability and High School Dropouts,* Bureau of Publications, Teachers College, Columbia University, New York, 1956.
[3] Conant, *ibid.,* p. 25.

and a reader.[4] The effect of the attitude of the group, too, has been little explored, but some experiments suggest that this has a highly significant influence on reading, particularly during the adolescent years.[5]

Plainly, much research is still needed to point the way to better reading
methods and to find ways to stimulate interest in and change attitudes toward
reading. It is imperative that such changes come soon, for, as many educators
have pointed out, the cost to society of potentially educable youth who cannot learn or who drop out of school is staggering.[6]

Reading: an all-school problem

More and more schools are becoming aware of the fact that the task of improving the reading of students in secondary schools is not the province alone
of the English teacher, but a problem in which the whole school is involved.
In some school systems the faculty has cooperated in planning for reading
improvement in all classes. Recognition of the need for such programs and cooperation in putting them into practice are difficult to secure, however. In a
survey of 147 schools in 1956, 86 reported "no program for reading instruction," and "no schools claimed to have achieved a total developmental program." [7]

Two other factors may affect the status of the reading program in the
school. In some schools reading instruction is provided in a separate program
outside the English department, taught by reading specialists who are not
department members and who may not be English teachers. Often there is
little relation between the instruction in reading classes and that in English,
and little communication between teachers in each area. Often, too, reading is
given as a separate course from English, and in some schools "Reading," "Literature," and "English" are separate courses. Until teachers of English become more skilled in giving instruction in important aspects of reading in
their own courses, the trend toward separation of the two areas may become
more prevalent. The English teacher who disclaims responsibility for improving the reading of students may assist the process of specialization which
moves reading into a separate part of the program.

Although renewed emphasis is being placed today on the teaching of
literature, most teachers of English recognize that this program has three important, often interrelated strands:

[4] Robert M. Roth, "The Role of Self-concept in Achievement," *Journal of Experimental
Education*, vol. 27, June, 1959, pp. 265–281.
[5] See the classroom illustrations in Chap. 15.
[6] See Chap. 1, p. 4.
[7] Margaret J. Early, "About Successful Reading Programs," *English Journal*, vol. 46, October,
1957, pp. 395–405.

1. A reading-skills program designed to increase speed and improve comprehension, to teach students how to adapt their reading approaches to a variety of materials, and to improve the reading of students of all abilities.

2. Training in close reading of prose and poetry for appreciation and esthetic enjoyment.

3. A program of individual reading, encouraging the student to read widely and enabling him to develop into an independent and discriminating lifetime reader.

Although there is much overlapping among these three strands, each deserves the teacher's attention. The discussion of the program in literature in this book looks at each in different chapters. The present chapter deals with the reading-skills program. Chapters 9 through 13 discuss the teaching of close reading of the different types of literature, and Chapter 14 points out the relation of the mass media and of visual and oral literature to the development of taste and appreciation. Chapter 15 outlines an individual reading program designed to encourage the development of lifetime reading habits.

Teachers of reading generally consider three kinds of attacks on the problems of reading. The terms frequently confused should be clearly differentiated in the teacher's mind:

Corrective reading.   This term includes remedial activities carried on by regular class instruction.[8]

Remedial reading.   By this term is meant remedial activities which take place outside the framework of class instruction, in reading laboratories, or in individual tutoring or small-group instruction when the rest of the class is not present.[9] Most teachers reserve the term for the work done with the "students whose development of reading skills is below the normal (those students being retarded readers) of performance for his age or grade." [10]

Developmental reading.   This is the term applied to the whole program of reading improvement for all readers, regardless of grade level or intelligence, who have failed to master some of the skills necessary to good reading. This kind of reading is generally looked on as an all-school program, including the bright, the average, and the slow learners. In many schools a good part of the best energies of the teacher, the best equipment, and the most individualized instruction is given to just those students whose serious retardation in reading makes it unlikely that they will achieve much gain. Some of these readers limited by lack of intelligence will never read much better than they do. The English teacher must decide what kind of help can be given most productively to the students in his classes and provide help as it is needed—even for the gifted who need to read better. Every reader can learn to read better, except

[8] Albert J. Harris, *How to Increase Reading Ability: A Guide to Developmental and Remedial Methods,* 4th ed., Longmans, Green & Co., Inc., New York, 1961, p. 21.
[9] *Ibid.*
[10] *Ibid.,* p. 17.

those so limited in intelligence that they already read as well as they ever will. The responsibility of the teacher of English is largely with developmental and corrective, rather than with remedial, reading.

Variations in ability

A major responsibility for teachers is that of providing for the wide range of reading abilities and interests which usually exist in most classes. Even homogeneously grouped classes often contain a range of four or five years in reading ability. In a tenth-grade college-preparatory class, some students may be reading at the college level, others may be considered average readers, and still others may not be able to read books of more than eighth-grade difficulty. In average or slow classes, the range may be even wider—often as much as six years. Such differences present many problems in the selection of materials for English classes.

Poor readers are not necessarily slow learners; many have average, above-average, and even superior intelligence. Bright students often read much too slowly and painfully to tackle difficult reading in literature and the sciences. Others, gifted in mathematics and the sciences, might almost be considered nonreaders. They look at reading as a waste of time. Correction of poor reading habits and practice in rapid reading assists many of these to make signal gains.

Among the average and above-average students are many whose basic reading skills in phonics and word-attack methods are so inadequate that they lag several grades behind their classmates in reading ability. Emotional and psychological problems retard many otherwise able learners. Teachers recognize that the slow learner cannot progress beyond the limits of his intelligence. He may never get beyond the basic skills in reading. Students with average intelligence or above may make important gains during a program of corrective reading and can at least be brought up to grade level.

Standardized tests give only a rough indication of the reading level of the student. Separate scores for rate, vocabulary, and comprehension are desirable. At the high school level, the use of grade scores is particularly misleading, and wide variations are possible. A student with an IQ of 150 may test at an eighth-grade reading level. The results of several IQ tests are usually better than one. Those which involve little or no reading, like the Wechsler-Bellevue Intelligence Scale, the nonverbal section of the California Mental Maturity Test, or portions of the Science Research Associates Mental Abilities Test have been recommended by teachers of reading. The latter two may be administered by the classroom teacher.

Many reading teachers point out that grade scores for reading are often misleading; they measure the student only against those in his own class and give only a rough indication of his reading ability. Percentile scores are more useful as a general index of the student's ability to read. Grade-level scores are useful to show how a class stands and how the individual performs in relation to his class. Separate scores for speed, comprehension, and vocabulary are available on most tests.

Vocabulary has often been found to be the best single index of verbal skill. Some useful tests are the following:

. . . *Cooperative English Tests: Reading Comprehension:* Part I: Vocabulary; Part II: Reading (yields scores on both speed and comprehension). Cooperative Test Division, Educational Testing Service, Princeton, N.J., 1960.

. . . *Doren Diagnostic Reading Test,* Educational Test Bureau, Philadelphia, 1956.

. . . *Roswell-Chall Diagnostic Test of Word Analysis Skills,* Essay Press, Box 258, Cooper Station, New York, N.Y., 1956–1958.

. . . *School and College Ability Tests (SCAT),* Educational Testing Service, Princeton, N.J., 1952. Levels 1–5 cover grades 4–14.

. . . *STEP Reading Comprehension Tests* (Sequential Tests of Educational Progress). Four levels: 1, grades 13–14; 2, grades 10–12; 3, grades 7–9; 4, grades 4–6. Educational Testing Service, Princeton, N.J., 1956–1959.

Both the estimates of reading grade level of the students and the recommendations of book lists that estimate the suitability of a book for a certain grade level need to be considered tentative. Such estimates are usually made through the use of one of the popular reading formulas indicating the vocabulary level. Books like Harper Lee's *To Kill a Mockingbird,* or Twain's *The Adventures of Huckleberry Finn,* placed on some lists at the seventh-grade and sixth-grade levels, respectively, obviously involve more serious problems of comprehension than recognition of vocabulary.

Program into practice

The teacher attempting to plan for the improvement of reading of the students in the English class must take the following steps: (1) diagnosing reading abilities of the students in the class; (2) clarifying the aims of the program needed to improve attitudes and skills; (3) providing resources to challenge readers of varying abilities; (4) finding time to include practice of reading skills in an already crowded program; (5) providing for differences in reading ability in the students; and (6) stimulating interest and encouraging the desire to improve in the members of the class.

Diagnosing reading abilities

Most schools give schoolwide standardized tests to measure reading ability, and the results of these are easily accessible to the teacher. Such tests usually include scores for speed, rate, comprehension, and vocabulary.

Many teachers feel that listening tests[11] provide excellent tools for reading diagnosis. They supplement this information with informal diagnostic procedures of their own to determine types of reading difficulty and to make more precise diagnoses in particular areas such as vocabulary, speed, and the guessing of words in context. Informal diagnostic measures include the teacher's observation of students' oral reading as opportunity is given early in the year for students to read to the class. If an informal natural reading situation is set up and students are unaware that they are being observed, the teacher may make some helpful notes about their capabilities. Many teachers feel that they can learn much about the student's reading level through such observation.

More accurate results for purposes of placement may be obtained through the use of a good oral reading test which the teacher may give to students individually.[12] Several observations should be made with those students who feel increased anxiety about reading to the class, and with those who are uneasy about reading for the teacher.

The teacher may make observations about the students' level of vocabulary by allowing the class to read silently a paragraph or two from a text they are using and asking them to make a list of the words they do not understand. Brief vocabulary quizzes on a reading assignment of a short story or essay may also be informative.

Teachers of reading use some of the following diagnostic techniques to determine the reading abilities of students in their classes:

1. Observing the students' reactions in the classroom to oral reading, to reading situations, and to comments revealing reading attitudes.

2. Observing the phrasing, intonation, word-by-word reading, and understanding of sentence structure shown by students in the class.

3. Asking each student to appraise his own reading in written or oral autobiographies which deal with such questions as how his reading started, what are his leisure interests, what has his reading experience been, what are his reading likes and dislikes, and so on.

4. Asking students to write (or describe to the teacher) a self-appraisal of their reading practices: do they skip words, do their eyes regress or skip lines, do the thoughts go ahead of the eye span, do the thoughts wander as the student reads?

[11] For instance, *Brown-Carlsen Listening Comprehension Test*, Harcourt, Brace & World, Inc., New York, 1953.

[12] William S. Gray, *Standardized Oral Reading Paragraphs*, grades 1–8, Public School Publishing Company, Bloomington, Ill., 1915; *Gilmore Oral Reading Test*, grades 1–8, Harcourt, Brace & World, Inc., New York, 1951–1952. See also George D. Spache, "Clinical Diagnosis in the Classroom," in M. Jerry Weiss, *Reading in the Secondary Schools*, The Odyssey Press, Inc., New York, 1961, pp. 54–59, and Ruth Strang, *Diagnostic Teaching of Reading*, McGraw-Hill Book Company, New York, 1964.

5. Interviewing individual students or students and parents and trying to estimate the students' reaction to reading and the parental demands made on him.[13]

The writing of the retarded reader sometimes provides clues for diagnosis of causes of reading disability. It often reveals a good deal about his difficulty in recognizing the shapes of words and the forms of letters. The following theme by a seventeen-year-old boy (with some translations of words by his teacher) indicates something about these difficulties:

> The most inbineraly [embarrassing] I think I over had is at a dances. I had just began to no horo [know how] to dance. It happen that they was a gril I had since [seen] damce and I wish I have one to. I ask her ploin to have ad dansee and she refure they were other gril around her to that I new so I was very indenersly it happen that it was do no the gril at all I had alway dance with gril that I nero well this happen last year at a school damce. One thing I can say that I hope it dont happen again becauld it makes you fel like a baby the first time sautt [that] it happen to a lot of people but it cant be help by the gril some time becauld she have damce.

Here are letter reversals (gril), letter substitutions (damce), and general difficulty in translating sounds into symbols. The boy was tested at the Harvard Reading Clinic, where the examiner's report revealed that the boy had transferred his handedness from left to right for most activities (except shooting, shoveling, and batting balls). Vision was more acute in the left than in the right eye, and there was marked loss of vision in both eyes, even with glasses. The report pointed to numerous difficulties involved in his reading problem: transference of handedness, visual defects, loss of schooling from illness, and psychological conditions growing out of these conditions.

Clarifying aims

The kinds of reading attitudes and skills the program needs to work for are suggested by a synthesis of the characteristics of mature readers by Gray and Rogers:

1. A genuine enthusiasm for reading.
2. Tendency to read (a) a wide variety of materials, (b) serious materials on many problems, and (c) intensively in a particular field.
3. Ability to understand words, meanings, and ideas, and to sense mood and feeling intended.
4. Capacity for and making use of all that one knows or can find out in interpreting or construing the meaning of the ideas read.
5. Ability to think critically and analytically about what is read.
6. Tendency to fuse new ideas acquired through previous reading and to translate these into improved behavior.

[13] Summarized from Strang, *ibid.*

7. Capacity to adjust one's reading pace to the needs of the occasion and to the demands of adequate interpretation.[14]

Attitudes determine to a large extent how students approach reading. Classes include those who will read with zest and maturity, the indifferent who never read voluntarily, and the nonreaders with a long history of reading failure behind them. The attitude toward self often determines the will to improve: ". . . the slow-learning adolescent who has not learned to read not only feels inadequate as a reader but also as a person. . . . Many youngsters come to a reading clinic or special reading class with a fixed idea of themselves as persons who cannot learn to read. Until they obtain a more hopeful concept of themselves they will make little progress." [15] Emotional and psychological problems are also of primary importance among the causes of reading disabilities.[16]

The feelings of anger, resentment, hopelessness, and frustration which characterize poor or nonreaders are familiar to every teacher who has tried to work with them. Most of these students have felt themselves slipping further and further behind their classmates as school subjects get harder and demand more reading, and the gap between their abilities and those of their classmates becomes more noticeable. Many or most of them face days devoted to unceasing, unrewarding labor for no discernible purpose. They are regarded and they regard themselves as hopeless.

Yet, in many schools these boys and girls are learning to read, and some have achieved notable gains in reading. Young people themselves need to realize that such achievement is possible for most of them, and English teachers need to know about the materials and means by which they can be helped.

Need, interest, the drive to know—these are the things that give impetus to more and better reading and make lifetime readers out of today's teen-agers —the eager and gifted, in love with life and learning; the solid average group, willing to search for meaning in life; and even the hostile, the resentful, the leather-jacket crowd who present a tough face to the world. Boys who would not learn to read have been taught by patient and understanding teachers who unearthed their interests and devised materials to stimulate them.

The primers of such students have been cookbooks, racing sheets, *Hot Rod Magazine*, driver-training manuals, *Sports Illustrated* or *Popular Mechanics*, stories about boxing, baseball, horse racing, cars, or airplanes. The teacher needs to know such materials.

[14] Summarized from the characteristics of mature readers formulated by such reading experts as Stella Center, Mortimer Adler, Ruth Strang, and others in William S. Gray and Bernice Rogers (eds.), *Maturity in Reading: Its Nature and Appraisal,* The University of Chicago Press, Chicago, 1956, pp. 54–55.
[15] Ruth Strang, *The Adolescent Views Himself,* McGraw-Hill Book Company, New York, 1957, p. 69.
[16] See Beulah Kanter Ephron, *Emotional Difficulties in Reading: A Psychological Approach to Study Problems,* Julian Press, Inc., New York, 1953.

Providing resources

A primary problem in providing instruction for reading improvement is that of inadequate resources, not only for remedial readers but for all young people in the school. School libraries are often heavily weighted with textbooks, outdated reference books, and encyclopedias, with a meager collection of fiction and nonfiction. In many libraries, much of this is dated, and little is chosen by a trained person familiar with the reading interests of adolescents. Anyone looking at the supplies of books provided for leisure reading in many high school libraries will find little to challenge the interest of young people. Even with the advent of inexpensive paperback books, few classrooms have an array of attractive, stimulating titles. Still more meager fare is offered in many a room set aside for classes in improvement of reading or remedial reading. Young people are put to work on reading drills, or at machines in rooms bare of any reading materials.

If the concern of the school is to provide a sound developmental reading program for all students, good and poor readers alike, an adequate school library, well stocked with books for leisure reading and staffed by a trained librarian interested in adolescents and familiar with their reading habits, is a primary requirement. Desirable provisions for instruction of below-grade readers include a room with reading materials at various grade levels, paperback books, magazines, newspapers, and other testing and teaching materials. The classroom teacher of English should have had training in teaching reading skills as well as literature and know the kinds of books adolescents like.[17] The ample resources of recordings in fiction, nonfiction, and drama can be tapped for these students.

Reading machines to increase the rapidity of eye fixations do not create readers. Schools spend hundreds of dollars on do-it-yourself kits and reading machines to improve reading, but often offer a pittance to the English teacher and the librarian with which to buy books for bare shelves. Magazines and newspapers still carry something of the stigma of the hardly respectable, perhaps because they are associated with reading for pleasure. Many young people in secondary schools grow up in an almost bookless world, except for the ponderous literature anthology in which they must read according to assignment. Practice in reading is the only sure road to improvement. An environment in which students can find the books which interest them and time and a place to read are essential ingredients of a good reading program.

Finding time

Teachers ask, "How do I find time to include the teaching of reading in an already crowded program? What can be left out?" Many answers are

[17] See also the discussion of an individual reading program and suggested book lists in Chap. 15.

possible. Good teachers are already teaching reading. As they teach vocabulary, they develop concepts about the meanings of words in literature, the sea terms in *Moby Dick,* literary words like *irony* or *realism,* or words which need explanation or visual aids: *heath, moor, battlements, prairie.* As they teach literature, they call attention to the differences involved in reading a play, a poem, or a short story.

Teaching reading skills can be closely related to the teaching of literature at every point. The chapters on literature (9 to 14) in this book include skills leading both to comprehension and appreciation. The individual reading program described in Chapter 15 provides a framework for growth in developmental reading throughout the six years of secondary school.

Providing for differences

Most conscientious teachers realize that they could be doing a better job of teaching reading. Often the bright nonreader is ignored or bored in the English classroom. Many students might quickly be brought to read better through directed practice and focus on needed skills by a teacher trained to diagnose and deal with reading difficulties. Attacks on reading skills may find their place in each of the traditional areas of English. The teacher familiar with a wide range of reading materials for both good and slow readers, aware of some of the problems which produce reading disabilities, and dedicated to the proposition that all readers can improve, will find time for the needed activity at the right moment even in a crowded program.

Reading instruction for each group may include some of the following:

For bright students who are good readers. Practice in skimming and sampling books, in reading rapidly for main ideas, in developing locational skills (finding topics in library reference materials); learning to guide independent reading through intelligent selections; a concentrated effort to improve speed and develop the comprehension needed for college work.

For bright students who are nonreaders. A large part of the reading program should be devoted to developing interest and independent reading habits, according to the program described in Chapter 15.

For average readers reading below grade level. Teachers should provide much opportunity for vocabulary study and for reading practice to develop speed and comprehension in newspapers, magazines, and a wide range of literature within their capacity. There should be concentration on such skills as reading for main ideas, noting organization of paragraphs, observing transitions, learning the basic sentence patterns, and developing and maintaining interest through discussion of books with peers.

For slow readers who are also slow learners. There is a need for much teaching of word attack skills, basic sight and recognition vocabulary, and phonic drill. These students often must start with beginning reading instruction on the primary level. They require practice with vocabulary cards, with simple dictated stories, with easy reading books high in interest for teen-agers, and with materials of consuming interest which will drive them to read. They need practice to increase eye span and to break habits of finger pointing and vocalizing.[18]

Many teachers teach the use of the typewriter to improve ability to recognize letters and words, and to enable students to read stories composed on the typewriter.[19]

For all above-average students. Teachers need to teach the SQ3R study formula to develop good study habits. The emphasis is on the formula: study and survey the material, question the material, read, recite, and review. This formula provides a usable pattern to guide students in studying to retain what they have read.[20]

Stimulating interest

The problem of stimulating the desire to read in adolescents varies according to differences in ability. For the intellectually superior, what is needed is a teacher who knows enough books to recommend a succession of challenging novels and biographies which deal with interests already strongly established.[21]

The range of interests in the middle group is narrower, and fewer students are open to intellectual challenge. More individual guidance is usually needed, and more stimulation and support from classmates who are also reading.

Because slow readers have met little but frustration in their efforts to read, individual guidance and instruction and conference work will be necessary. Direct appeals to their interests, encouragement and experiences of success, evidence of progress, however slight, and much more training in basic reading skills will be needed with this group.

Few schools are provided with sufficient reading materials for such youth. Some teachers adapt them or write their own. One teacher in a school for socially maladjusted boys in Manhattan remembers teaching Floyd Patterson

---

[18] Some teachers ask students to demonstrate the irregularity of eye movements and eye fixations per line by having two members of the class demonstrate, with one holding a mirror to observe the eye movements of the other as he reads silently. Walter Loban et al., *Teaching Language and Literature: Grades 7–12*, Harcourt, Brace & World, Inc., New York, 1961, p. 245.

[19] Helen Rand Miller in *The Clearing House* (vol. 34, October, 1959, p. 94) tells of a fourteen-year-old boy who could neither read nor write primer words, but whose consuming desire for a driver's license drove him to ask for help. His fascination with the typewriter and his learning to type provided the first step in reading and led to the reading of his own typed stories.

[20] Francis P. Robinson, *Effective Reading*, Harper & Row, Publishers, Incorporated, New York, 1962, chap. 2.

[21] See Chaps. 13 and 15 for examples.

to read by hand-printing stories about boxing, and compiling spelling lists of words drawn from the vocabulary of boxing.[22]

Other teachers have typed students' dictated stories about sports, adventure, or animals to provide reading materials for such readers. Some classes have produced their own books in mimeographed form, books the members can read. Since nonverbal boys are usually fascinated by machines, teaching them to type has often brought results in helping them to read what they have written.

In such ways have understanding teachers attempted to deal with one of the most serious problems faced by those trying to teach older boys and girls to read. Fifteen-year-olds with mature bodies and interests and the reading level of third graders find little to challenge their desire to read. Only recently have there been attempts to provide for these readers materials with simple vocabularies within the range of adolescent interests.[23]

The major steps in reading

The ability to read rapidly with full understanding of meaning and a critical attitude toward what is read is a complex process involving many related skills. The tasks of reading with which the present chapter is concerned are those which involve basic skills of comprehension: understanding and developing vocabulary, adjusting the speed of reading to subject matter of differing types and purposes, and mastering the many ways in which the reader understands the meaning of what he reads. These include recognizing organizational patterns, distinguishing between facts and judgments, following the author's reasoning, and discerning his purpose.

Improving comprehension

Comprehension involves the development of a wide vocabulary which enables the reader to understand the meanings of single words and the ability to understand words in the syntactical relationships of the sentence or paragraph. Each of these basic tasks is composed of a number of smaller skills which can be improved through training and practice. To these might be added a third category: reading between the lines to determine the author's purpose and examine his reasoning. These skills are discussed chiefly in the chapters devoted to teaching the different types of literature and also in Chapter 14. The development of vocabulary and the skills of understanding meanings of the printed words are the primary concerns in improving reading.

[22] *New York Times,* June 25, 1960, p. 23.
[23] See Ruth Strang et al., *Gateways to Readable Books,* 3d ed., The H. W. Wilson Company, New York, 1958, and similar works in the bibliography at the end of the chapter.

Improving vocabulary. A continuing need from the beginning of the teaching of reading throughout the college years is the development of the student's vocabulary. Individual vocabularies owe their richness not to the number of different words, but to the number of meanings for each word as well. It is as important to a good reader to know eight or ten common meanings of the words *run, take,* or *off* as to know an equal number of different words.

Other key vocabulary tools used by teachers of reading to build word concepts and word meanings are a familiar part of the curriculum: the study of word origins, roots, prefixes and suffixes, words used figuratively, and borrowings and derivations from other languages. Teachers use all these areas of study from time to time to keep interest in words alive. Continual reference to such areas of language study in the context of ordinary class activity is more meaningful than the concentrated attack of a unit on prefixes and suffixes which lasts for several weeks. The discussion in class of a few words each day, with several meaningful contexts provided by the teacher, helps the student associate the new word with something in his experience and provides a surer means to vocabulary growth. Too much school vocabulary work is circular and abstract: words are defined by other words existing only in books or in the students' minds and are seldom attached to their physical referents.[24]

Because so many words are learned from books alone, schools should help slow learners extend their range of experience. It is common practice in many schools to reserve the field trips for the honors and Advanced Placement classes. The trips to the city, to museums, to plays, to art galleries and libraries are provided for the more gifted children whose experiences, generally, are already rather wide. For the underprivileged pupils whose meager vocabularies and interests are limited by the poverty of their environments, enrichment of experience is a key means of developing vocabulary and of enlarging interests and horizons.

To keep students aware of words and curious about them, teachers should make constant reference to words in the news, words encountered in the reading or study of the class, or on television. Representatives of the College Entrance Examination Board have repeatedly stressed the fact that such classwork, combined with wide reading, is better preparation for the verbal factor test of those examinations than rigorous vocabulary study from word lists. Vocabulary improvement is most successful when it proceeds from the work the class is doing and when the student associates the new words with the contexts which make them memorable.

Developing dictionary skills. Developing the habit of dictionary use may be taught at every grade level. Many students do not use the dictionary because they are baffled by it. Poor students, frustrated by marks which are

---

[24] Chapters 3 and 8 suggest other ways of developing power over words and meanings.

meaningless to them, give up rather easily, preferring to blunder their way through pronunciation and meaning.

A dictionary for every student is useful standard equipment in many schools, and in others there are sets which can be shared by classes. Often maximum use is not made of these resources. Often, too, students are kept on beginners' dictionaries long after they are ready to move to more adult ones and miss the challenge of knowing a really good dictionary. Every school with a substantial book budget should have one or two copies of *Webster's Third New International Dictionary* in the library, along with the one-volume *Shorter Oxford English Dictionary.*

Teachers should make sure that students know how to use these books and make some assignments during each school year to encourage students to develop the dictionary habit. The teacher whets curiosity by asking, "I wonder when this word came into our language?" "Do you know where to find the original meaning of this word?" or "From what language does this word come?"

Practicing dictionary skills may provide many of the common but necessary techniques for efficient use of the dictionary. As English teachers, we often take for granted the fact that our students know their alphabets. A brief competitive timed game in which students are given a list of words or the names of the students in the class to alphabetize may reveal that some are unknowing and some extremely slow about performing this simple skill. Students who master such a task quickly may be sent on to more complicated study; those who are slow or muddled must drill themselves or work in teams until they master a ready use of the alphabet.

Using context clues.   Ability to guess words from context is another skill needed in comprehension, a skill most poor readers and many good ones have not mastered. Poor readers take a rigid rather than a flexible approach to guessing. They are unwilling to take a chance. Yet, the good reader has been for years a guesser of contexts; instead of stopping in defeat over an unfamiliar word, he plunges on and makes the most of context clues. Some time needs to be spent in helping readers of all levels of ability to develop a more adventurous attitude toward guessing words. The teacher will need to help some strike a balance between the completely freewheeling, wild, and illogical guessing characteristic of many poor readers and the fear of guessing at all. Students need to know that both careful and systematic vocabulary building, and practice in making reasoned guesses at words which can be understood from fairly clear contexts, are basic to good vocabulary development.

Teachers of reading list a number of types of clues used in guessing words from contexts.[25] Among these are the following:

[25] Constance McCullough, "Learning to Use Context Clues," *Elementary English Review,* vol. 20, April, 1943, pp. 140–143, and others cited in Commission on the English Curriculum, *The English Language Arts in the Secondary School,* Appleton-Century-Crofts, Inc., New York, 1956, p. 170.

1. The synonym clue: The word is explained by a synonym used in the same sentence: "The story of the courageous men who climbed Annapurna will go down among the annals of *intrepid* adventurers."

2. The experience clue: "Fish begins to *deteriorate* quickly if it is not kept on ice."

3. The comparison-and-contrast clue, in which the antonym is given in the same sentence: "Although the Indians appeared friendly, *hostile* tribes were known to live in the area."

4. The word-summary clue, in which the details preceding or following the word explain the meaning: "The floors were washed, the furniture oiled and polished, and the curtains freshly laundered; the whole house was in *immaculate* condition for the holidays."

5. The association clue, in which meaning is clarified through the associations the word suggests to the reader: "The *roseate* hues of the sunset faded into darkness."

The teacher who can supply or elicit from the class six or seven memorable contexts for the words being studied may provide useful help for the student. Common words which college students have reported they did not know— *procrastinate, timorous, irascible, evoke, impeccable*—may be fixed in the memory by such associations. The students may mention characters in fiction or on television who could be described as *timorous* or *irascible;* they may discuss different things about which they *procrastinate:* homework, getting up in the morning, writing thank-you letters, going to teachers for help.

The study of vocabulary involves this kind of association with many contexts and practice in using words correctly as different parts of speech. Command of language demands that the student be sensitive to whether a word commonly used is a transitive or intransitive verb, an adjective, adverb, or a noun. More study of this kind helps such students as the one who vaguely connected the word *fickle* with the meaning "to change" and wrote the sentence, "Dr. Jekyll fickled into Mr. Hyde."

Understanding thought relationships. As important as the recognition and understanding of individual words is in the reading process, the major problem of the reader is that of understanding words in larger thought units— phrases, sentences, and paragraphs. Part of the task of following the writer's meaning is understanding of such transitional words as *then, however, moreover, nevertheless,* and others. Slow and sometimes average readers frequently need practice in thinking through and understanding coordinating and subordinating words, even those as common as *so . . . as, not only . . . but also, since, if, because,* and *although.* Such common words express important relational concepts which students often fail to grasp. Even the sense of negation in *but* or the qualifying tone of *however* escapes poor readers. Students should do much close reading and discussion of words in such sentences to develop control over their meanings. Understanding qualifying words like *some, many, always,* and *almost* is essential. Good critical reading focuses on the presence or absence of such words in statements of opinion, facts, and generalizations. Teachers will find lessons in general semantics helpful here in teaching young readers to evaluate dogmatic statements and broad generalizations prefaced by such words as *always, every,* or *all.*[26]

Recognizing organizational patterns. Helpful to the student's progress in speaking and writing as well as in reading is an understanding of the common organizational patterns of expository prose. Understanding these patterns is of particular help to the reader in assisting him to comprehend quickly the trend of thought in exposition and in helping him follow the organization of the writer's ideas. Students need to learn to distinguish between the main idea, or thesis sentence, and supporting details. They must observe whether the paragraph being read is organized with main ideas stated first and details following, or whether the main idea is given in a summary topic sentence. The good reader can skim quickly by following main ideas as he grasps the thought pattern of the author's paragraphs. He also recognizes the various means of support for generalizations and thesis sentences: details, reasons, examples, or illustrations. The teacher may illustrate paragraph patterns by listing on the chalkboard a series of examples leading to a conclusion (inductive paragraph), and a contrasting pattern for the deductive paragraph: conclusion, followed by examples.[27] All students need practice in developing this sense of paragraph organization, but average and slow readers need frequent occasions for looking at materials they are reading to observe how paragraphs are put together.

Senior high school students who are good readers may study such expository devices of prose as comparison and contrast, time and space devices, ideas leading to climax, and others. Patterns and examples of these may be found in most freshman English college texts.

Mastering interpretive skills. The skills of critical and interpretive reading are most commonly taught in the context of the study of literature. It is in these areas that students gain practice in such literary skills as reading for clues to time and place of the story, novel, or play and understanding tone, atmosphere, point of view, characterization, and plot structure. Reading to detect irony, satire, wit, or pathos is also part of this study.[28]

Teachers may help students prepare for the close study of literature in the senior high school by helping them with some of the simpler literary skills during the junior high school years. Among these is understanding the

---

[26] See suggestions in Chap. 3.
[27] See J. N. Hook, *The Teaching of High School English,* 2d ed., The Ronald Press Company, New York, 1959, p. 280.
[28] See Chaps. 9 to 13.

figurative language of everyday speech. Students may approach the complex language of poetry and literary prose through the study of slang, advertising language, and everyday speech, learning to recognize that common phrases are not meant literally. Such expressions as the *melting pot,* getting a new government *launched,* cutting official *red tape, steamroller* tactics, *high-pressure* salesmen, and others are seldom recognized as figurative by poor readers.[29]

Varying reading approaches. Teaching students how to read for specific purposes is an important and usually neglected part of the teaching of comprehension. Students should have numerous chances in each grade to practice efficient reading by defining a specific purpose: reading to pick out main ideas, to note specific details, to follow directions, to predict outcomes, to find specific answers, to find proof for an argument, to observe the organization of ideas and supporting evidence, to make critical comparisons between two accounts of the same event in different newspapers, to take notes, to analyze the meaning of a short story, a poem, or a passage of prose. Most of the good texts on reading suggest methods of helping students attain these comprehension skills.

Studying textbooks. One of the chief reasons for failure of freshmen having difficulty with college work is lack of familiarity with the makeup of textbooks and with library reference tools. Although teachers often spend time in close reading of literature, they frequently forget that students seldom learn by themselves to use a textbook wisely, or remember to familiarize themselves with the instructional aids such books provide. One tenth-grade girl having difficulty with biology revealed that she did not know that the summary section of her text was important and had overlooked it.

Students frequently refer to their literature books or their grammar texts as "that green book" or "the one with the picture of a sailboat on the cover." Teachers need to take the time to explore the text with students, teaching them how to examine the organization of the material by looking at the table of contents. They should learn how to discover the resources for vocabulary study by examining the glossary; how to use the index, the list of illustrations, the title and author index, the biographical notes, and the questions at the ends of chapters. Discovering order in the makeup of textbooks in English (and in all subjects) should be a part of instruction in every class.

Using the library. Just as students seldom know how to use a textbook wisely, so many of them know little or nothing about the use of the library. Even though the research paper is commonly assigned in many high schools, students often lack skills in using the standard library tools useful in English: the card catalogue, *The Readers' Guide to Periodical Literature, The Education Index, The Book Review Digest,* the standard reference tools such as the *Encyclopaedia Britannica,* the *Encyclopedia Americana, Collier's Encyclo-*

---

[29] A more detailed discussion of figurative language is given in Chaps. 3 and 11.

pedia, almanacs, *Who's Who* volumes, biographical dictionaries, and other resources.[30]

Some English teachers design class periods to be used as a library treasure hunt. The teacher prepares dozens of cards, each directing the student to find a particular source or bit of information in the library. Each student takes a card from the teacher, accomplishes his task, exchanges that card for another, and continues until, at the end of the period, the person who has located the highest number of sources has the best score. (Teams may play, too.) Sample questions are "Locate three biographies of Albert Schweitzer," "Find a sequel to *Little Women*," "Find a book of criticism on television," "Find an article about India in each of two encyclopedias," "Locate one article on censorship in *The Readers' Guide to Periodical Literature*." As students become more skillful in using the library resources, the assignments may grow more difficult.

Increasing speed

Skimming and rapid reading are important skills for today's readers. Research shows that when students read faster, comprehension increases. The deliberate word-by-word reading habits of poor readers are a primary reason for their failure to grasp the meaning of sentences or paragraphs. They often cannot see the forest for the trees. Most poor readers, and many good ones, read all material at the same speed—usually a snail's pace—the cartoon page, an editorial in the *New York Times*, the news story about the latest sensational murder, a poem by T. S. Eliot, or a passage from Plato.

Even good and skillful readers often need to retrain their reading habits. The rapid reader who spends a good deal of time on research often finds his reading markedly slowed down and needs to practice to gain speed for less concentrated reading. The student accustomed to conscientious plodding as the single approach to all print needs training to learn to skim for rapid review of materials already read, for light fiction requiring little thought, or for time-saving sifting of the newspaper for important facts. Much the student encounters in schools needs to be read at different rates: he must read poetry or a concentrated prose passage much more carefully than he reads a series of pamphlets or magazine articles to gather material for a report.

Teaching skimming. Skimming is one of the most useful techniques a teacher can train students to master. Rapid skimming is necessary to keep abreast of the times and to find the news worth remembering in the spate of words designed to fill the daily newspaper. In skimming, the reader runs his eye over the page rapidly to find information, or to locate passages which he

[30] Jean Key Gates, *A Guide to the Use of Books and Libraries*, McGraw-Hill Book Company, New York, 1962, is an invaluable guide for students and teachers. Jessie Boyd et al., *Books, Libraries and You*, Charles Scribner's Sons, New York, 1941, is a simpler reference book, designed for high school readers.

wants to read carefully. The reader whose eye moves rapidly down the telephone book page to locate a name is skimming, rather than reading.

The teacher may give students many chances to practice the skills of skimming during the regular English class. Some of the following exercises are helpful.

Skimming newspapers to locate articles on a particular subject and to digest the main points.

Skimming new books of light fiction to sample a writer's handling of plot and character.

Skimming pages in a textbook to locate the treatment of a subject or a point not listed in the index.

Skimming an encyclopedia article to find relevant biographical facts about a writer or historical personage.

Skimming articles in a number of magazines to gather points on a topic for a report or a research paper.

Teaching rapid reading.   Students need to learn the skills of rapid reading for much light fiction, or easy informational materials. They can learn to increase speed in many ways. For instance, it almost always increases when students improve their powers of concentration and learn to shut out distractions. Some class periods given to practice in rapid reading may show them how to improve on their own. They may take an informal speed test to see how many pages of a book they can read in thirty minutes of class time. During the next trial they may consciously try to push their speed faster by putting a bookmark five pages ahead of the number of pages they read in the first attempt and try to work toward it. Consciously striving to read faster, with the resultant improvement in concentration, usually makes improvement possible.[31]

The spectacular gains in speed claimed for those who have taken speed-reading courses make difficult any realistic estimate of averages based on rate alone. The normal reading rate for high school students and adults has been estimated at 250 words per minute. Those who read slower than this in easy material—light fiction or easy nonfiction—may be considered slow readers. Reading experts say that the superior reader should be able to read light fiction or easy nonfiction at a rate of 400 words per minute, and rates of 1,400 words per minute have been reported, though they are extremely rare.[32] Although recent speed-reading programs indicate that most people can make dramatic gains in learning to read faster, critics of such programs point out that rapid reading is not as necessary to the literate reader as the ability to read important

[31] Students may estimate their own reading rate by timing themselves on the reading of a page and estimating how many pages or words per hour they normally read. See Paul Witty, *How to Become a Better Reader*, Science Research Associates, Inc., Chicago, 1953, chap. 7.

[32] Harris, *op. cit.*, pp. 508–509.

Drawing by Robert Day; © 1963 *Saturday Review.*

books slowly and with comprehension. The ability to adapt rate to content is of major importance to the good reader.

In the recently developed programs of "reading dynamics," speeds of 20,000 words have been claimed. One well-known teacher of reading, interviewed about the possibilities of speed reading, pointed out that people who claim to read by sweeping the eye down the middle of the page are probably skimming instead of reading, since research studies show that the most the eye can assimilate in rapid reading is about 1,450 words per minute.[33]

Teachers of reading believe for the most part that although almost all readers can be taught to read faster and more efficiently, the way to improved reading lies not in quick and dramatic increases in reading speed, but in patient teaching of skills of word analysis, vocabulary, and comprehension—all

[33] Helen M. Robinson, quoted in Ellen Lamar Thomas, "What about High Speed Reading for Our Schools?" *Bulletin of the National Association of Secondary-school Principals,* vol. 46, March, 1962, pp. 112–116.

prerequisites for speed.[34] Caustic skeptics have suggested that at the high speeds claimed by speed readers, it should be possible to read *The Decline and Fall of the Roman Empire* over a cup of instant coffee. Those who read *Crime and Punishment* or *Doctor Zhivago* in an hour remind most teachers of literature of the cartoon of the breathless tourist dashing into the Louvre and asking, "Which way to the Mona Lisa? I'm double parked."

Reading machines to develop speed are in frequent use in many schools. The Controlled Reader[35] forces the reader to increase his speed by requiring him to read at a speed slightly more rapid than his usual rate. A bar moves down the page, revealing one line at a time, and as it does the reader must increase his pace to keep up with it. (The technique is similar to that used in the movies, when an introductory prose passage too long for a single frame exposure is shown on the screen.) Reading accelerators and tachistoscopes (used during the war to train the Air Force plane-spotting teams by flashing quick images on the screen) are other such devices. Often good readers use these machines to speed up their reading. Their motivation is high, reading is satisfying to them, and the desire to read faster is strong. Slow readers sometimes approach these devices in the same spirit, but many strongly resist the machine approach.

Using many approaches. Fortunately, research is beginning to bear out what teachers of literature have long suspected: a book-centered course may be more effective than a machine-centered course in increasing speed.[36]

Although many methods to improve the speed of reading exist, the real danger is that schools and teachers may seek one simple panacea: the machine, the prepared unit, reading laboratory, or reading films. Many of these are expensive, and they are purchased in many schools instead of books for the library or school classrooms. Many young people respond to the novelty of films, machines, or self-help exercises, but when the materials are misused, as they often are, they lose their effectiveness. The retarded reader, directed to sit alone in a laboratory booth, or to work alone in a room with a reading laboratory, may quickly become bored. The teacher's individual attention in conferences and through supervision of reading activities provides needed help for such readers.

Reading speed improves when students do any of the following:

1. Learn the possibilities of varying approaches to different kinds of reading; most untrained students use one speed for all printed matter.

2. See the possibility of improvement, learn how to practice, and observe their own growth.

[34] *Ibid.*, p. 114.
[35] Educational Laboratories, Huntington, N.Y.
[36] Constance M. McCullough, "What Does Research Reveal about Practices in Teaching Reading?" in *What We Know about High School Reading*, NCTE, Champaign, Ill., 1957–1958, p. 26.

3. Learn the significance of such interfering factors as daydreaming, wandering attention, background noise of radio or television, and lack of interest.

4. Discipline themselves to practice continually to increase speed.

5. Learn that forcing the eye down the center of the page, as well as exercises designed to increase eye span, will help develop speed.

6. Learn to watch for such habits as vocalizing while reading or reading with the finger moving across the page.

Reading laboratories[37] have proved useful in many classrooms. The reading laboratory is a collection of graded reading materials in boxes which allows the student to work through the exercises at his own rate, to check his accuracy, and to recognize his gains in reading. In too many schools, however, they become the whole reading program, or a substitute for classroom libraries; teachers report that they sometimes become stultifying for poor readers to use year after year.

Successful teachers of reading do not believe in one cure-all for reading troubles, but in a variety of approaches to assist and stimulate the reluctant reader. Many of the new instructional materials being developed by publishers are helpful adjuncts to the classroom library. Used wisely, they may help readers develop needed skills of comprehension and improve their rate of reading. The teacher of reading remembers that not all students respond alike to the same materials, and that the search for the method which will help is especially important with young people whose reading difficulties are often complicated by emotional problems. Many of the aids to instruction—films, texts, both standard and programmed, skill builders, and reading materials for poor readers—should be part of the classroom equipment or available in schools. Additional suggestions for these are given in the bibliography of this chapter.

Classroom materials for teaching may well include the following:

Literature units prepared by publishers (*Scholastic Literature Units, Bantam Learning Units,* paperback collections of short stories, novels, poetry, and plays).

Current magazines of interest to slow readers: *The Reader's Digest, Scholastic Magazine, Hot Rod Magazine, Seventeen, Scientific American, The Saturday Evening Post, Read Magazine.*

Collections of short stories and brief biographies adapted for poor readers.

SRA Reading Laboratory or *Tactics in Reading.*

Selected novels of high interest and low vocabulary.

Evaluation of the reading program

Standardized reading tests probably give teachers the most accurate picture of the reading gains a child has made during a year's work in English. Some of

[37] Don H. Parker et al., *SRA Reading Laboratory,* Science Research Associates, Inc., Chicago, 1957.

the tests give separate scores in speed, comprehension, and vocabulary. Such tests carried on yearly in schools give a useful check on the effectiveness of the total reading program. Where scores do not advance much for most children, it is evident that more work in reading needs to be done in the English classroom and probably means that schoolwide attention to reading should be encouraged. Such tests identify those boys and girls who make no progress or fall further behind their classmates and who probably need some expert remedial instruction in reading.

Informal methods of testing reading comprehension, speed, and vocabulary improvement are used in the English class to determine the achievements in reading during the year. Teacher-made quizzes on reading are used by most teachers as a check on understanding the literature read in class. The student's individual reading record shows the number of books he has read during the year and enables the teacher to observe whether he has grown in ability to read more difficult books. The teacher's observation of students' class contributions, participation in discussion, and ability to talk with more perception about more complex books provides another important measure of reading gains.

Weiss points out that a reading program "permeates the entire curriculum and can be evaluated only in the total framework." He suggests these questions for evaluation:

> How well does he [the student] perform in each of his classes? What new skills has he attained? How effectively does he use these skills? What new insights and values has he gained through his reading? What new attitudes has he formed? How has his behavior changed as a result of his learning? Does the student find adequate practical reward and pleasure in reading so that he will continue to read throughout his lifetime? [38]

Probably one of the least used and most valuable indices of student growth in reading is change in attitude and behavior. Teachers attempt to find out something about whether the year's work in reading and the study of literature has resulted in more positive attitudes toward reading, toward the possibility and desirability of growth in reading, toward the literature read in class, and the books read for pleasure. Teachers who encourage students to write out honest answers to these questions often get some revealing responses.[39] Such evaluations provide the best possible means for planning a future program of reading with the student.

Student attitudes toward reading, the development of an interest in reading that appears to carry over from year to year, increased library circulation, the improvement of vocabulary, reading rate, and comprehension skills, and growth in independence, judgment, and discrimination in reading are some of the most useful measures of the success of a year's reading program.

[38] M. Jerry Weiss, *op. cit.,* p. 439.
[39] See the sampling of student responses in *ibid.,* pp. 441–442.

The student who has a chance to profit from a carefully planned developmental reading program in which he grows in ability to read throughout his secondary years is likely to become an adult who reads with more efficiency, comprehension, and pleasure, either in business or in college work. He will be better able to achieve the maximum growth of which his intellect is capable, and have at his command a skill which will add an important dimension to his life.

Student activities and assignments

The activities suggested here are designed to present ways in which students may develop reading skills and practice speed in reading. Since the skills the student needs are many, this limited sampling must be supplemented by the teacher's study of the materials, books, and resources suggested in the bibliography which contain further suggestions for ways to improve reading.

Improving vocabulary

Many different approaches to extending vocabulary through reading and study may be used:

. . . In composition, students may be urged to think of synonyms for overworked nouns, verbs, and adjectives; the study of grammar yields information about changes in word meanings and the derivations of interesting words; the course in literature yields idiomatic expressions and words common to various regions. Discussion may arouse curiosity about these words and lead to acquisition of some which will become part of the students' working vocabulary.

. . . The study of roots, prefixes, and suffixes provides clues to unknown words for the reader. Students often enjoy the competition of making lists of derived words from a common root. For instance: (1) *graph: telegraph, graphic, seismograph;* (2) *duco: educate, induct, conductor;* (3) *terra: terrestrial, territory, subterranean;* (4) *porte: transport, portable, import.* Particularly appealing to slow learners is the idea that each root, suffix, or prefix learned may unlock meanings to several other words. Some of the most useful prefixes are *ab-, ad-, com-, dis-, en-, ex-, in-, pre-, sub-,* and *un-* and suffixes such as *-tion, -ment, -ize, -ise, -able.*[40]

. . . Gifted students may extend vocabulary through the study of Biblical and mythological allusions, through learning about the history of the language, and through making a particular study of word changes, of derivations from different languages, and of words contributed to English by various national groups and conquering tribes.

. . . Other sources of vocabulary growth include the study of new words (*astronaut, blast off, countdown*); words which have changed connotations

---

[40] See Chap. 8, pp. 203 and 205, for a discussion of prefixes and suffixes in spelling.

(*lady, villain, knave, propaganda*); words with the same referent but different connotations (*teacher, pedagogue, educationist, schoolmarm*); and others.[41]

Developing comprehension

. . . The teacher may clip and mount cartoons illustrating situations from which the reader is to draw any inference about the people involved or the situation pictured. These may be shown on the overhead projector, and the implied inference discussed. *New Yorker* cartoons often offer considerable opportunities for subtle inferential thinking.

. . . The teacher may read to the class, or project on the overhead projector, a poem such as Robinson's "Richard Cory" or Browning's "My Last Duchess," and discuss the inferences to be drawn from Cory's suicide, the Duke's treatment of the Duchess, or the behavior of the Duchess.

. . . Divide the class into groups of four or five, give each group a set of five or six words each, and let each group see how many different sentences they can construct. Such words as *set, beat, ball, strike, run, still, down, fast,* and *point* serve to illustrate the process of functional shift, or the use of one word as different parts of speech.

. . . Study the newspaper with the class to distinguish between the use of fact and judgment in news stories and editorials. Note the balance of supporting fact for the judgments offered.

. . . Ask students to make lists of vivid adjectives from advertising in popular magazines; concrete verbs from sports writing; concrete versus abstract nouns.

. . . Ask students to write sentences using common words with both literal and figurative meanings and to explain the figurative use. Example: Literal: "I went fishing yesterday." Figurative: "She was just fishing for a compliment." Illustrations of papers on such a topic may be found in *End-of-Year Examinations in English,* College Entrance Examination Board, Princeton, New Jersey.

. . . Encourage slow readers to listen to recordings of short stories, plays, and selections from novels: Basil Rathbone reading Poe's short stories, Hal Holbrook reading from Mark Twain, Don Spark reading H. G. Wells' *The Time Machine,* and others, will encourage students to go on to read the books. The NCTE's *Studies in the Mass Media,* vol. 4, October, 1963, lists many such recordings.

. . . Give better students the opportunity to interpret irony and satire by reading aloud some of the following kinds of materials: columns from the newspaper in which a feature writer assumes an ironic tone toward his subject; Siegfried Sassoon's "Does It Matter?," Wilfred Owen's "Base Details," Swift's "A Modest Proposal," W. H. Auden's "The Unknown Citizen."

---

[41] *Word Study* of the G. & C. Merriam Company, *Words at Work* of Scott, Foresman and Company, and *Inside the ACD* of Harper & Row, Publishers, Incorporated, give frequent examples of such areas of word study. They are supplied to teachers on request.

Varying speed of reading

. . . Provide students with practice in skimming rapidly for facts, news items, or particular details in newspapers or in literature being studied in class.

. . . Develop skimming skills by arranging class sessions for browsing, sampling, and skimming books and articles in order to find some that students want to read carefully.

. . . Encourage students to use varying speeds as they change from news to sports to editorials in reading the newspaper.

. . . Try a class experiment in concentration with poor readers. Assign them a short story to read, allow them to read for fifteen minutes, and then ask each member to note how many pages he read. Then ask them to read further, trying this time to concentrate during the entire time of reading, to tune out distractions, irrelevant thoughts or ideas, and to resist all disturbance. Let them count the pages read during the last fifteen minutes. For most of them, there will be a dramatic improvement.

Developing vocabulary and dictionary skills

. . . The recency-frequency law states that we remember best those words which we use most frequently and recently. Encourage students to record words they do not know on cards, along with illustrative sentences, and practice using them frequently for mastery.[42]

. . . Give each student a mimeographed copy of the suggestions for word study in this chapter or the language projects in Chapter 3 or Chapter 8. Number each suggestion, tell students to keep the list in their notebooks, and use it as a resource for brief paragraph assignments to be handed in at least once a week. The student may choose an assignment, identify it by the number, and try his hand at many different kinds of word and language study.[43]

. . . Divide the class into two to four competing groups (teams) equipped with dictionaries. Give each group ten minutes to explore and note some interesting facts about derivations or meanings. Each group may contribute an interesting word, a derivation, or fact about a word.

. . . Ask students to collect the names of products which are derived from Greek myths and to explain the suitability of the names.

. . . Read to the class some excerpts from Frank Sullivan's "cliché expert" articles in *A Pearl from Every Oyster* (Little, Brown and Company, Boston, 1938). Suggest an assignment in which they describe something, a sunset, a

[42] James I. Brown and Rachel Salisbury, *Building a Better Vocabulary*, The Ronald Press Company, New York, 1959, p. 39.
[43] The teacher may also find fruitful suggestions to add to the list from *Word Study; Words at Work; Inside the ACD;* Luis Muinzer, "Historical Linguistics in the Classroom," *Illinois English Bulletin*, vol. 47–48, November, 1960, pp. 24–58; and Verna A. Hoyman, "An Evaluation of Methods of Teaching Vocabulary in the Secondary School," *Illinois English Bulletin*, vol. 49, November, 1961, pp. 1–28.

spring morning, a walk in the fall) in clichés, and then rewrite it in fresh imagery.

Mastering derivational suffixes

. . . Ask students to observe in newspapers and advertising, coinage, a functional shift, the making of new words by adding suffixes, and other manipulations of language: *comfort-conditioned air, conversation-quiet, jet-smooth Chevy; It was go all the way* (astronaut language); *He cadillacs to work; He jets here tomorrow; He emceed the show; He jeeped all over India.*

. . . Have students work in groups to list as many nouns as possible which are formed with the noun suffixes *-eer, -ess, -ist, -or, -er,* or verb suffixes *-ize, -ise, -fy, -en, -ate.*

. . . Encourage students to learn the meaning of common prefixes or suffixes:

Negative or reverse: *anti-, de-, dis-, in-, mis-, non-, ob-, un-.*

Act of, state of, or quality of: *-y, -ity, -ness, -ice, -ation, -ion, -tion, -ment, -ant, -ism.*

Full of: *-ful, -ous, -ulent.*

Having: *-ate, -ive, -ed.*

Resembling: *-ish, -ic, -ical, -ly, -like.*

. . . Suggest that they invent some nonsense words with these derivational suffixes, and classify them as parts of speech according to the endings. The student paper advertising "Gringle Shlepkins" on page 64 illustrates the possibility that some students may go on to put the words in context.

The teacher may divide the class into four groups as teams and set a time limit for their learning prefixes and suffixes and their meanings, or common Greek and Latin roots. At the end of the allotted time the groups may play against each other after the manner of a spelling bee.[44] Among the roots to be learned and illustrated with words derived from the roots are the following:

Latin	*Greek*
dicere: say, speak	*demos:* people
caput, capit: head	*aster:* star
audire: hear	*chron:* time
cantare: sing	*glot:* tongue
pendere: hang	*anthropos:* man, human being
credere: believe	*derma:* skin
mors, mortia: death	*optikos:* vision
loquor: speak, tell	*neo:* new
ducere: lead	*polis, polit:* city, citizen
aqua: water	*phil:* friendly

. . . A similar quiz arrangement may be used in encouraging students to learn many of the interesting word derivations. They may like to draw illus-

[44] Resources for study will be found in Donald W. Lee, *Harbrace Vocabulary Guide,* Harcourt, Brace & World, Inc., New York, 1956.

trations modeled after those of James Thurber in Margaret Ernst's and James Thurber's *In a Word*.[45] Some of the derivations of the following words have interesting word histories: *alimony, alphabet, assassin, astonish, bedlam, auspicious, biscuit, book, capricious, cynic, dexterity, ecstasy, lady, lunatic, muscle, radical, salary, supercilious*. (All of these may be found in *In a Word*.)

. . . Divide the class into groups and ask them to list all the words they can think of that are derived from a group of five Greek or Latin roots. The group presenting the longest original list of words is the winner.

Selected bibliography

Glenn Myers Blair, *Diagnostic and Remedial Teaching*, rev. ed., The Macmillan Company, New York, 1956. "Outstanding," according to one reviewer.

William S. Gray and Bernice Rogers (eds.), *Maturity in Reading: Its Nature and Appraisal*, The University of Chicago Press, Chicago, 1956.

Agnella M. Gunn (ed.), *What We Know about High School Reading*, NCTE, Champaign, Ill., 1958. (Pamphlet.)

Albert J. Harris, *How to Increase Reading Ability: A Guide to Developmental and Remedial Methods*, 4th ed., Longmans, Green & Co., Inc., New York, 1961. Particularly helpful for the secondary English teacher.

George Spache, *Good Books for Poor Readers*, Reading Laboratory and Clinic, University of Florida, Gainesville, Fla., 1955. An invaluable list of reading materials classified according to interest and reading levels.

Ruth Strang et al., *Gateways to Readable Books*, 3d ed., The H. W. Wilson Company, New York, 1958. Lists graded reading materials for poor readers.

————, *The Improvement of Reading*, 3d ed., McGraw-Hill Book Company, New York, 1961. New edition of *Problems in the Improvement of Reading*, long a standard text on methods of teaching reading.

M. Jerry Weiss, *Reading in the Secondary Schools*, The Odyssey Press, Inc., New York, 1961. A useful compendium of articles about reading.

Materials for teaching reading skills

Olive S. Niles et al., *Tactics in Reading, I and II*, Scott, Foresman and Company, Chicago, 1961. Exercises in word attack, dictionary study, comprehension. (Keyed to *Vanguard* and *Perspectives* anthologies.)

Don H. Parker et al., *Reading for Understanding*, Science Research Associates, Inc., Chicago, 1958. Emphasis on understanding the ideas and meaning words convey. A reading comprehension program indexed from the third through twelfth-grade levels.

---

[45] Alfred A. Knopf, Inc., New York, 1951. See Chap. 8, p. 208, below.

————, *Reading Laboratory, Secondary Edition,* Science Research Associates, Inc., Chicago, 1957.

Reader's Digest Reading Skill Builders, Grades 2 through 8, Reader's Digest Educational Department, Pleasantville, N.Y.

CHAPTER *6*

I haven't written for a few days because I wanted first of all to think about my diary. It's an odd idea for someone like me because it seems to me that neither I—nor for that matter, anyone else—will be interested in the unbosomings of a thirteen-year-old schoolgirl. Still, what does that matter? I want to write, but more than that, I want to bring out all kinds of things that lie buried deep in my heart.

ANNE FRANK [1]

Writing: thought into symbol

The bringing out of all kinds of things that lie buried deep in the heart, with the attendant satisfactions and releases that such writing brings to the human mind and spirit, is the wellspring out of which all good writing comes.

For the teacher of English, helping young people to write implies much more than acting as a guardian of the language, protecting it from such assaults as dangling modifiers and sentence fragments. No one else in the school, perhaps, deals so closely with the thoughts, heartaches, and joys of youth during the brief years when the child turns into the young adult.

Writing may serve the child's emerging individuality as can no other kind of study. In no other medium can he examine so carefully his developing ideas and values, recognize so clearly his kinship with the joys and pains of the human condition, or gain so much insight into his own mind and heart and those of his fellows.

Writing during the adolescent years can be for both student and teacher a richly rewarding experience. At its best, it becomes a means of individual growth and a challenging intellectual exercise for the exploration of ideas.

---

[1] *The Diary of a Young Girl,* by Anne Frank. Copyright 1952, by Otto H. Frank. Reprinted by permission of Doubleday & Company, Inc., Garden City, N.Y. and Vallentine, Mitchell & Co., Ltd., Publishers, London.

Writing in our culture

Although speaking and listening occupy a large proportion of the time human beings spend in communication, writing is, as we have seen, a complex process, far more demanding for most people than speaking. Whereas practice in speaking and listening begins early in the child's life, writing is the last of the language skills to receive attention in school, and even the thirteen- and fourteen-year-olds entering high school often find writing a paper of one hundred words a difficult task.

Even though we have seen the tremendous emphasis on the spoken word in our culture, it is obvious that we live in an age in which the written word is of primary importance in the conduct of education, business, and cultural affairs. We are accustomed to regard the ability to write clear, coherent prose as a hallmark of the literate, educated man. Today we are finding that the command of the written word is in increasing demand in the business world, both as a key to a job and to success in it. A recent survey of educators, businessmen, administrators, and members of the professions placed improvement in written composition first in their recommendations about English teaching today. According to them, the ability to write clearly, concisely, and accurately is the qualification most needed for success in business, education, or the professions.[2]

The nature of the process: basic questions

Writing is an attempt to record human speech; in teaching it we are teaching a new language. The written language is a kind of notation of the sounds, pauses, inflections, stresses, tones, gestures, and facial expressions which transmit meaning in speech.

The child who grows up speaking English has heard and practiced the infinite complexities of a human language since his cradle days and mastered them with seemingly effortless ease. Writing requires close coordination between brain and hand—attention to spelling, punctuation, neatness, margins, sentence structure, and choice of words—and is therefore more complicated for the young learner.

There are three central problems that face teachers of English planning programs in writing. First: how do students learn to write? In the face of controversy about methods of teaching writing, the kinds of writing students should do, and the amount of time to be allotted to composition, we need to know what answers research has found to these questions. Second, busy teachers want to know how to find time for writing in an already crowded program. A third and final question every teacher must face is that of deciding what kinds of writing students should do.

[2] Joseph Mersand, *Attitudes toward English Teaching*, Chilton Company—Book Division, Philadelphia, 1961.

How do they learn to write?

Many unanswered questions face the teacher of English who tries to discover how students learn to write.[3] On one matter research is clear. Students do not learn to write better by drilling in grammar exercises or learning prescriptive rules about formal grammar. Summaries of research on the relation of the knowledge of formal grammar and the ability to write have been accumulating for more than twenty-five years. They have been reported in the *Encyclopedia of Educational Research* in the editions published in 1941 and 1960. Comprehensive reports of research on grammar and composition reveal the same findings. Ingrid Strom summarizes the studies in this way:

> Research reveals that a knowledge of classificatory grammar has little measurable effect on the ability to express ideas accurately or precisely in writing or speaking. Grammatical errors are individual matters and are best attacked through individual instruction. Children and adolescents improve their sentences by having many opportunities, with the guidance of the teacher, for structuring their own thoughts into their own sentences.[4]

More recently, the committee studying research on the teaching of composition evaluated 485 studies with this conclusion:

> In view of the widespread agreement of research studies based upon many types of students and teachers, the conclusion can be stated in strong and unqualified terms: the teaching of formal grammar has a negligible, or, because it usually displaces some instruction and practice in actual composition, even a harmful effect on the improvement of writing.[5]

Despite this overwhelming and incontrovertible evidence, large amounts of class time are still being spent on the study of grammar to the neglect of practice in writing and reading. In 1938 Dora V. Smith reported that surveys of English class activities showed that more classroom time was spent on drill in grammatical forms and workbook exercises than on any other single phase of instruction.[6] In many English classrooms, perhaps the majority, this picture has not changed for the better.

---

[3] The Committee on the State of Knowledge about Composition of the NCTE was assigned the task of examining research on this problem; its findings indicate that relatively few carefully controlled or definitive studies of methods of teaching and evaluating composition have been made. The summary of its findings can be found in Richard Braddock et al., *Research in Written Composition,* NCTE, Champaign, Ill., 1963.

[4] Ingrid M. Strom, "Research in Grammar and Usage and Its Implications for Teaching Writing," *Bulletin of the School of Education,* Indiana University, vol. 36, September, 1960, p. 14.

[5] Braddock et al., *op. cit.,* p. 37.

[6] Dora V. Smith, "English Grammar Again," *English Journal,* vol. 27, October, 1938, pp. 643–649.

The current assumption behind recommendations about the amount of time to be spent on composition in the English course is that "the way to learn to write is to write." Dr. James B. Conant's report recommends that the time devoted to English composition during the four years "should occupy about half the total time devoted to the study of English" and that each student "should be required to write an average of one theme a week." [7] The Commission on English of the College Entrance Examination Board recommends that writing should take one-third of the school week in class and outside. [8] There is fairly general support in the profession for this emphasis on writing in the English curriculum. One study found that writers whose papers received critical comments and who revised their papers during a class period after reading and discussion of papers made significant gains over the group that received only praise and encouragement and a third group which wrote one essay during the term. [9] Even though most teachers feel that frequent writing and the correction of papers are the mainstays of the program, one careful study carried out by a Project English found "no evidence to warrant affirmative replies" to the question whether more writing produces better writing, or whether more careful correction yields better results in student writing than less correction. [10]

As yet, little seems to be known about the relationship between writing and reading. Most teachers feel that students who read widely in good literature tend to write better than those whose reading is limited. Although research is not decisive, the experience of the majority of teachers at the secondary and college level indicates that students learn to write by reading widely and by frequent guided practice in writing, accompanied by suggestions for revision and through discussion and revision of papers.

How do we find time?

If students learn to write by writing and if papers should be carefully evaluated, the increased load for the English teacher becomes staggering. The National Council of Teachers of English, many other state and regional organizations, and the College Entrance Examination Board have all reinforced the

[7] James B. Conant, *The American High School Today*, McGraw-Hill Book Company, New York, 1959, p. 50.

[8] Floyd Rinker, "Priorities in the English Curriculum," *English Journal*, vol. 51, May, 1962, p. 312.

[9] E. W. Buxton, "An Experiment to Test Effects of Writing Frequency and Guided Practice upon Students' Skill in Written Expression," unpublished doctoral dissertation, Stanford University, 1958.

[10] Dwight L. Burton and Lois V. Arnold (The Florida State University), *Effects of Frequency of Writing and Intensity of Teacher Evaluation upon High School Students' Performance in Written Composition*, Cooperative Research Project no. 1523, supported by the Cooperative Research Program of the Office of Education, U.S. Department of Health, Education and Welfare, Government Printing Office, Washington, D.C., 1963.

demand for a class load of four classes with not more than twenty-five students each for the teacher of English. A study carried out by California teachers in an effort to estimate the number of hours per week it would take a conscientious teacher to mark papers in such a way as to teach writing and thinking estimated a total of 50.8 hours.[11] The matter of class size and teacher load is probably the foremost problem faced by teachers of English today. Unless English teachers have a reasonable teaching load, they cannot find it possible to produce students who have an adequate command of the skills and arts of language. There is evidence that the resolutions of groups recommending reduced loads for teachers of English are slowly making headway, but ways of meeting the problem need to be found now.

Even with conditions as they are in many schools—teachers carrying five classes of English with 150 to 175 students—much may be done. Recommendations for adding to the teachers' theme load must be balanced by a close look at the curriculum to see what can be subtracted. It is probable that much we try to teach in English classes is expendable and that much, too, is clearly a waste of time. Little use of the findings of research about materials and methods for teaching is reflected in the average course of study. Teachers wishing to find and make time for writing, revision, discussion of writing, conferring with students, and the marking of papers must weigh the importance of what they teach and ruthlessly eliminate the nonessential, the inaccurate, and the unprofitable. In the first category, sometimes overlapping the second, is much that we teach about grammar and punctuation;[12] much of our teaching about form deals with peripheral matters, and neglects the heart of the matter, the teaching of logical thinking and clear expression.

Until the day when the public is willing to support a reasonable teaching load, there are many possibilities for reducing the present load to a workable size. Possible solutions which have been tried in some schools are mentioned on pages 147 to 148. The need for clearly defined, sequential programs in composition is great. Some new programs are described on pages 390 to 393 and 403 to 405.

Goals for the writer

Organization, accuracy, clarity, and economy are probably the virtues most in demand in writing today. In addition to these, most thoughtful teachers wish to encourage students to write honestly and responsibly, using language with care, integrity, and sensitivity. Some writing experiences in every year of the secondary school may aim at developing these qualities in young writers. Some

[11] William J. Dusel, "Determining an Efficient Teaching Load in English," *Illinois English Bulletin*, vol. 43, October, 1955, p. 15. See also "Class Size and Teacher Load in High School English," *English Record*, Monograph no. 8 of the New York State English Council, 1964.

[12] See Chap. 8.

of them are emphasized in every assignment; others develop through slowly growing awareness of the responsibilities of the writer to his audience. Thoughtful teachers can plan writing assignments that stimulate the imagination and intellects of their students. Careful revision and class discussion keep the goals clearly defined.[13]

Basic principles for the writing program

A sound writing program may be based on a few important principles:

Writing is a two-way process.   Writers are continually sending "letters to the world," but few are like Emily Dickinson—content to keep writing without any response. The young writer needs an audience—not only the teacher, but the wider audience of the young people he knows.

Writing is based on experience.   The debate over the values of "creative" versus expository writing is waged wherever English teachers meet and talk. Experienced teachers usually agree that a major source of writing should be the young writer's own experience. Papers about trips to Mars, explorations under the ocean, and similar topics suggested in some "creative writing" assignments send the students off into fantasy before they have learned to deal with reality. Even when the student writes about literature, his paper should reflect his own experience with reading rather than the abstractions about literary style and theme he borrows from someone else.

Writing improves through practice.   Only the act of writing—continual writing—can develop fluency, skill, and control over language and idea, and help banish the paralyzing fear that confronts many young people when they write.

Meaning comes before form.   The young writer must care about what he has to say before he can be led to an interest in the form of his writing. Over-attention to form has done more harm than good to many students in our classes. The struggle to express meaning and thought is the primary goal for the writer during the secondary years.

Program into practice

A program of composition designed to produce students with the skills demanded by colleges or the adult world must be planned to provide students with challenging theme assignments and opportunities for free writing. In the integrated program, composition is an integral part of the year's work, rather than a sporadic affair with themes assigned irregularly and related to little else the student is doing. One day a week is little enough to devote to such

---

[13] See pp. 142–146 and 153–156 for suggestions about teaching toward these goals.

work, and more time is desirable if students are to have time for writing in class, for reading and discussing papers, and for conferences with the teacher. In many programs weekly writing is part of the student's regular work in English; topics are drawn from his work in literature, or the study of language, and his theme folder contains a cumulative record of his year's work in composition and his spelling and vocabulary assignments.

The process of writing: six sequential steps

The process of writing may be seen as a series of six sequential steps in which teacher and students work together toward the production of a finished composition. Much of this takes place as a kind of dialogue between students and teacher. The steps are: (1) general discussion brings up possible topics for writing; (2) the student must write his rough draft and polish it to the best of his ability; (3) then the teacher reads and comments on the papers. (4) Discussion of papers takes place in class, in small groups, or in conferences; (5) the teacher uses the set of papers to determine matters for teaching; and (6) the students revise the papers, profiting by the suggestions made in class discussion or in conference.

Some changes in the order of this sequence are often desirable. Ideally, the student should have a chance to profit from all the possible suggestions teacher and classmates can make before he hands in a final draft of his paper for a grade. In the world of publishing the writer may submit his work for criticism and act on suggestions by friends, critics, and editors before the final product is evaluated. Yet in the classroom, we almost always confront the student with criticism *after* his work has been evaluated and seldom give him credit for careful revision. If possible, the class should read and discuss papers *before* they are handed in for the teacher's criticism and grade.

Step one: Generating ideas.   Much of the writing at the beginning of any school year may be brief and informal, suggested by the teacher in the effort to help instructor and class know each other better. The teacher will want to know many things about the young persons who will be with him during the year: their goals, something of their interests and recreations, their personalities and feelings, their intellectual interests. The dullness of stereotyped papers on "My Hobby," "My Chosen Career," and "My Autobiography" result not so much from the topics as from our notions that each bit of writing on these subjects must be a finished paper. Writing of this informal kind provides an excellent collection of diagnostic materials for a planned program to improve skills. The teacher may frankly enlist the aid of the class in the project by asking each student to write briefly each day or so on something about himself that he thinks is imporant in helping the teacher to get to know him.

The teacher genuinely interested in young people will think of many things he would like to know, and the young, sensing interest, will generally respond. The "brainstorming" techniques of Madison Avenue have something to offer the teacher of composition. He may, by stimulating excited talk about problems and topics of interest and concern to young people, start the flow of ideas through the freer medium of speech and, when many voices are clamoring to be heard, ask students to write their points of view so that all may have a chance to express their opinions.

Topics may grow out of the need to talk, think, or exchange ideas about something of importance to the writers. Younger students are absorbed in immediate and often personal problems: working out with adults the amount of freedom or responsibility they may have; improving their relations with parents, brothers, sisters, teachers; deciding what to do about cheating, about dating, about choosing friends, about setting standards of behavior for themselves. Writing which allows them to think through and exchange ideas with others about the significant problems of growing up is worth working on and worth taking trouble with. Senior high school students are interested in thinking through their roles as future adults, as individuals trying to find a satisfying career, to work toward marriage and a family, to find values to live by, and to explore and discuss ideas which excite them. Teachers who understand adolescents can think of dozens of topics on which young people will want to write if they have a chance to talk over their ideas with others.

Step two: Composing and prevision. Anyone who has ever written knows the desperate feeling of panic many writers experience at the sight of a blank page on which one must shape one's inner thoughts. The task of the writer is a lonely one—there is only the writer and the blank page of paper in front of him. John Mason Brown has aptly called it "pleasant agony." The good teacher of writing will provide the learner with a favorable setting for getting started with his writing. First, there is the possibility of providing time for discussion before the cold task of putting pen to paper takes place. Secondly, class time for writing can provide the learner with time for the rough draft, which gives him something to work with when he finishes his paper at home.

The teacher may help the unskillful young writer by suggesting that he postpone thinking about mechanics and spelling until he gets his ideas worked out on paper. One man, now on the editorial staff of a well-known weekly magazine, remembers himself as an awkward thirteen-year-old, struggling with ideas, and recalls gratefully the teacher who said, "Never mind the commas, the ink smudges, or the misspellings. We can fix those up later. Just write about something that means a good deal to you."

Many teachers see the writing period as a valuable time for helping the young writer organize, clarify, amplify illustrations, support arguments, and notice sentences which need punctuation changes. This process, often called "prevision," prevents errors and prods students to think carefully during the composing process. Students can be given help in choosing a subject, in narrowing the subject, in organizing thoughts according to some pattern of order. Many teachers provide check lists for students to initial and clip to their papers on which they answer questions about organization, topic sentences, punctuation, and grammatical matters. The clean, "polished" copy of the rough draft, whether written in or outside of class, should be as free from error as prevision can make it.

Step three: Marking papers.   The task that looms largest for the teacher of English is the reading of the flood of papers that come to his desk. Reading and commenting on the written ideas of young writers are twin responsibilities not to be lightly undertaken. The teacher who wants his students to attain skill in writing and to find continuing satisfaction in writing must treat these papers with consideration. The student who wants to write can accept much rather caustic and harsh criticism; the game is worth the candle to him. But most of our students are not writers; writing is not important to them. Certainly our teaching of composition does not often turn out writers; rather it turns out many students so fearful, so inhibited about writing, so conditioned to think of writing as a painful experience, that many of them never willingly set pen or pencil to paper again.

When the set of themes is handed in, the teacher's task is to read and make comments on them and to hand them back as quickly as possible. Young people do not have long memories; papers returned after the lapse of more than a week are almost forgotten. Then the student looks merely for the grade and disregards the teacher's carefully written comments.

Careful planning can aid the process of grading and marking. The teacher may plan a schedule for papers so that each class has papers due on a different day. (There is a psychological advantage for the teacher in facing one pile of themes; five sets at once compounds the difficulty of getting started.) Then, too, most teachers have overworked consciences about correcting every error. This habit prolongs the time it takes to grade papers and, more seriously, confronts the learner with an almost impossible task of revision. When everything is wrong (as it seems to be with some students), where is the inept student to start?

Some system of minimum standards may be set up by which the teacher judges the paper in terms of the writer's skill with form and the conventions, as well as in handling ideas. He should be helped to gain command of the most common conventions and problems before he is asked to proceed to revision of matters of greater complexity.

Comment on the student's thought may be in the form of marginal responses to ideas. Even some brief notations such as "Yes," or "I agree" is very satisfying to the writer. Even "No" may be valued; it lets him know he is being listened to. Students who are used to having teachers respond to thought very quickly learn to value such comment more highly than a good grade. The process of commenting, raising questions, stimulating students to further thought, making suggestions that will help the student see how to revise—all this takes time, teaching skill, and understanding of the individuals who are writing. Above all, even the brief word of praise for a phrase or an idea makes the labor of writing rewarding for the student.

Teachers can direct the attention of students to places where papers need revising by some such comments as these: "Can you add a few more details?"

"How can you make your readers see this (person, scene, event)?" "Have you given enough evidence here to prove your point?" "Haven't you overlooked an important point?" "Your point is not clear to me." "This paragraph needs further development; three examples are not enough to prove your case." "Can you rearrange the order so that each step in your argument becomes clear?"

Sample comment. The teacher's terminal comment should give the writer help in improving the style and content of his paper and suggestions for revision. It ought to send him on toward the next paper. Some sample teacher comments on the following paper by a slow seventh grader suggest what may be helpful to the young writer:

If I Had a Million Dollars

I'd buy all the schools in the world, and then I'd fire all the teachers, and then I'd put them in an underground jail, so no one could look at them. Then I'd buy a Jet bomber and bomb the jail. Then I would give Mr. _____ a real torture, I'd build a school after I got through bombing all the others, and I'd make him go to school all over again, let him know how it feels. Then I'd buy a whole lot of land, and make a country of my own. And then I'd make a police force, but of all the things I'd buy a carnival. Then a big sail boat and I'd hire a crew, and every day I'd go sailing. But most of all I'd want a dog. A nice rusty colored dog. By then I would have spent my million.

Sample terminal comment: "I'll bet you feel much better now that you have taken care of schools, teachers, and principals. At the end of your paper you seem to think of some nice things to do with your money. I'd like to know more about that country of your own. Perhaps you may want to write another paper sometime describing it."

Purpose of teacher's comment: A slow seventh grader who has stored up this kind of bitterness about schools and teachers is not ready to think about sentence structure and punctuation. The teacher who accepts this outburst without alarm, but with suggestions for more constructive thinking, may, with patience, get more and better writing.

Grading student papers demands a clear formulation of criteria for the class. Much ink has been spilled in argument over what kind of grading system is best. Most teachers reject the numerical grade; unless one counts comma faults, it is difficult to reduce anything so complex as human thought and emotion to numbers or percentages. The simple letter grade with a plus or minus tells the student little about his paper unless it is accompanied by some kind of evaluative comment. Perhaps a little better is the fractional grade in which a student may get an A— above the line for thought, idea, content; and a B or a C below the line if form, mechanics, and sentence structure are not equal to idea. Thus, an A— over C+ means that the thought expressed on the paper is superior, but there are mechanical or grammatical errors which keep the paper from being considered above average.

Some teachers reject this kind of grade, feeling that form and idea are inseparable. Form and content *are* inseparable in a work of art that is to be judged, but in the themes of adolescents, both seldom develop at the same rate. Almost all teachers have seen themes in which a student struggled with a significant and challenging idea, too complex for the form at his command. To penalize him for this disparity may be to send him back to the simple and banal thought which can be written easily and to which his form is adequate or to simple, primer sentences rather than complex ones. Frequently, too, the writing of those youngsters whose spelling is horrendous and whose sentence structure is hardly better shows flashes of individuality, concreteness, and rhythmic phrasing that lifts a composition out of the ordinary. These are the important matters in writing. We can be fairly sure the command of mechanics will improve when the writer realizes he has something of importance to say.

Useful teacher comment is largely a matter of raising the right questions, and then following through to see that the learner has answered them through revision. Suggestions which direct attention to his thought and help make his meaning clearer are usually accepted with good grace.

Marking and commenting on themes should be a teaching-learning process. Our tendency to use the word *correction* for our handling of papers suggests the concept most conscientious teachers have about their duty: weeding out errors, correcting and revising imperfect sentences. If the larger part of our attention, however, is turned to commenting instead of correcting—to questioning, arguing, suggesting, guiding—we then turn the responsibility for improved writing back where it belongs—to the writer. In turn, we may require that such effort on our part result in attempted improvement on his and that each paper or at least many of those kept in his folder be revised.

The bibliography of this chapter lists several excellent pamphlets on the problems of theme evaluation which have been done by teachers in English organizations. The teacher of English will find these worthy of study and thought. The sample papers, with grades and teacher comments, provide useful models for evaluation. The writers of these pamphlets agree, for the most part, that the terminal comment the teacher puts on the student's paper may be the most valuable part of the teacher's marking. An example of a paper marked for revision and of the teacher's terminal comment is given on page 144.

In general, teachers who have worked on theme evaluation agree on some such standards as the following for grading papers for college preparatory students:

A papers.   The paper worthy of an A grade should be one lifted above the ordinary by most of the following: the expression of thought of some maturity, forceful language, maturity of sentence structure, mechanical competence, concrete, lively illustration or detail. It should be readable, clear, and logical. For the grade and ability level of the students, such papers should be well organized, with smooth transitions, precision of words, and a good beginning and ending.

B papers. Such papers are above the ordinary in many of the above characteristics, but may lack a few of these strengths. The writer should say something of importance in a paper worth a B, but he may say it less clearly or forcefully, or with less command over the style and mechanics of composition, than the writer whose paper is worth an A.

C papers. The C paper is usually average in every way. The ideas it expresses may be trite or undistinguished; the language unfelicitous, awkward, or insensitive; the mechanics careless.

D papers. These papers are those which are clearly lacking in clarity, forceful expression, ideas, and form. The thought may be not only banal, but illogical; there may be serious or repeated errors in spelling, mechanics, punctuation, or sentence structure. Organization may be weak or largely lacking.

F papers. These papers fail not only in expressing any coherent thought worth attention (for the grade and ability level of the student), but in mastery of a minimal competence in form, mechanics, and logic. Such papers may be filled with careless errors, but generally they are written by students who haven't grappled honestly with an idea worth putting on paper and whose writing is incoherent, unidiomatic, and nearly illiterate.

Although no system of grading papers is absolute, this description represents a reasonable norm against which teachers can measure the writing of their college-bound students.

Any system of standards for papers such as that above must be considered in relation to the maturity and intellectual capacity of the group. The thought which seems banal to the teacher fresh from college may be freshly minted by the ninth grader just experimenting with words; command of sentence structure and punctuation must be measured against the student's chronological age. The surest way to the kind of evaluation which will help a student grow is the teacher's knowledge of good writing and his awareness of the level of performance in style and structure which can reasonably be expected of pupils of each age group. The teacher's ability to distinguish felicitous phrase or genuine thought, is of major importance. In criticizing teachers' criteria for grading, one teacher says: "Without turning a hair they will swallow cacophonous wording, disorganized paragraphs, and strings of eight or ten consecutive prepositional phrases, but they will strangle on a supposed misuse of *shall* or *will*. Still others, it must be suspected, simply do not know good writing when they see it." [14]

Step four: Discussing. Early in the year, many papers may be read by the teacher for general comment and discussion, with the writer remaining anonymous if he wishes. It is often better to offer the young writer the cloak of anonymity and keep the focus of attention on the paper before we take the next step of asking that he have the courage and self-confidence to read his

[14] Albert Kitzhaber, *Themes, Theories, and Therapy: The Teaching of Writing in College,* McGraw-Hill Book Company, New York, 1963, p. 129.

paper himself to the group and lead group discussion of his ideas. This act requires more courage than one imagines. It takes time for the teacher to help learners develop techniques of constructive criticism and offer tactful suggestions which will be helpful to the writer: "Could you tell us more about this?" or "I'd like to know more of the reasons why you think that," or even, "I don't agree with what you said here, because . . ." Pressing the writer to become more concrete, more specific, to back up generalizations with facts, to make clear his point of view, statement, or explanation is one of the most valuable services the group can perform.[15]

Another service to the developing writer that the teacher must often perform is that of protecting him from harmful criticism that would damage his self-confidence. The young are innocently or deliberately cruel, and often free discussion can be used as an opportunity to settle grudges, attack the scapegoat, or make fun of the unpopular member of the class. This can be disastrous to the writer and is harmful to the spirit of the class in general. The establishment of respect and acceptance for every student's honest ideas must be a cardinal principle of the English program, and the skillful teacher will provide experiences in which this kind of attitude may develop. The audience should feel that it has an important part to play in assisting the writer in clarifying his thinking; it should never feel that its role is simply to point out flaws.

Step five: Teaching.   Each set of papers written, polished, and discussed becomes a matter for teaching before the papers are revised as well. Many good teachers believe that the study of grammar, sentence structure, and style comes after writing, not before. The impulse to improve form comes after the desire to have something to say and the struggle to try to say it. The most meaningful teaching about grammatical matters, sentence structure, punctuation, spelling, and the conventions is based on the kinds of difficulties exhibited in student papers.

Ideally the teacher will wait until writing is relatively free and students are accustomed to writing frankly to either the teacher or the class as audience, before much concentrated work on mechanics and grammar proceeds. Then the process of choosing sentences for revision, putting them on the board, or duplicating them on sheets for each student will provide the class with materials for language study for an almost indefinite period. The revision of sentences will inevitably bring up innumerable problems of grammar and rhetoric: the desirability of sentence variety, word order, difficulties with modification, tenses of verbs, wordiness, and agreement of subject and verb.

As the student looks at the sentences and paragraphs he or his classmates have written, the study of how to rephrase them becomes more meaningful. Grammatical topics need not be taught in textbook order; the process can be inductive and questioning. Because one does not revise writing according to any rigid system—deleting words in one paper and changing organization in

[15] An account of such class procedures is given in Belle McKenzie and Helen F. Olson, *Experiences in Writing*, The Macmillan Company, New York, 1962.

the next—students should learn that many matters of form and structure need to be considered together in good revision. Careful writers take many steps to improvement: attacking redundancy, checking agreement, changing sentence order for emphasis, providing transitions.

This kind of revision is an infinitely harder and more demanding intellectual process than learning about language in a textbook, where types of errors are so neatly grouped together that we may be sure of finding a misplaced modifier in every one of twenty-five sentences in the appropriate section. The problems raised by this kind of revision and the discussion and revision of paragraphs in class can provide, as Arthur Mizener points out, "the easiest way to interest students in the game of composition, to make him take pleasure in the craft of composition." Mizener's belief that the five- or six-sentence paragraph can present students with all the problems of a long essay,[16] has been put into practice with rewarding results by many teachers of English.

The use of the overhead or opaque projector for projecting student themes for group discussion and analysis is an invaluable aid to the teacher of composition. Through this means, each member of the class may see the theme under discussion and observe such matters as spelling, handwriting, punctuation, organization of topic sentences and details, sentence structure and diction, analysis of the student's reasoning and logical development of his theme.

Problems in rhetoric. The study of rhetoric during the high school years cannot profitably be devoted to the formal college-level composition drill on the familiar patterns of process, description, narration, and argument, and developed by illustration and example, comparison and contrast, or other methods. Few practicing writers start writing in the ways such books suggest. What the student chiefly needs to learn about clear and thoughtful writing can be dealt with in a few useful principles which he learns to practice over and over, in more and more complicated patterns, as his skill in shaping sentences and paragraphs begins to keep pace with his maturing thought. Some rhetorical problems for continuous work in each grade, with topics of increasing difficulty, are the following:

Stating an idea clearly and concisely. The young writer needs practice in saying what he thinks. One of the problems of the unskilled writer is the circumlocution of ideas. The sound of the writer's voice making a firm, crisp statement of belief or conviction is the thing the student must learn to listen for in written prose. It is the sound, as one student observed, of "a fist banging on a table."

Supporting the idea. Once the writer has stated his idea or proposition clearly, it is up to him to offer support for it. He needs to show the logical

---

[16] See examples in "The Craft of Composition," in Edward J. Gordon and Edward S. Noyes (eds.), *Essays on the Teaching of English*, Appleton-Century-Crofts, Inc., New York, 1960, p. 178. (Copyright © 1960, The National Council of Teachers of English.) See also the description of this process of revision in Edwin Sauer, *English in the Secondary School*, Holt, Rinehart and Winston, Inc., New York, 1961, chap. 6.

basis for his opinion. Frequently student writing is a string of ill-considered judgments and wild generalizations strung together with some connectives. A major matter for teaching with almost every set of papers is the recognition of the clear pattern of expository prose—the statement of opinions, points of view, propositions to be validated, or arguments to be supported with reasons, examples, or details. Group discussion and analysis can be profitably brought to bear on the matter of logical, reasoned support for ideas. In class discussion of such a paper as "Foreign Cars" (see page 144), students soon point out that the main proposition is indefensible, and that none of the supporting arguments offers proof of the proposition, but merely generalizations without evidence ("foreign" cars are less expensive to run, and so on).

The teacher may draw on the standard composition texts to help students become aware of different methods of support. Models of prose in which support is given by illustration and example, by particulars and details, by presenting reasons or offering logical proof—all these may be studied, practiced, discussed, and rewritten in class.

Discriminating between facts and judgments.   Essential training in rhetoric and in logical analysis depends to a great extent on the writer's ability to distinguish between the statement of fact and the statement of opinion or judgment. The student must learn how much evidence is required to support a particular statement. "Team X has a better record than team Y" can be quickly settled by turning to baseball facts and figures; "Poem X is better than poem Y" demands a much subtler array of facts for support.

Using concrete detail.   A major matter for practice is the handling of concrete detail in the development of paragraphs of description or narration. The student writer who can muster three details per paragraph usually feels he has exhausted the topic. Study of prose models illustrating a writer's command of detail can be used profitably for discussion or as models for analysis. The topics for writing on pages 153 and 157 suggest assignments in developing skills in using details.

Teaching economy, sensitivity, and clarity.   It is painful for the writer to learn to cross out words which have been set on paper only at the cost of agonizing thought. Editing is a ruthless but necessary job for the person who strives for well-ordered concise prose. Students should strive for economy by holding to rather rigid minimal word limits in assignments, by revising their papers to eliminate all unnecessary words, and by condensing long passages.

Writers today need to be sensitive to the kind of impact their words will make on the reader. In face-to-face speech, we often know instantaneously, because of the expression on the listener's face, whether we have been misunderstood, whether we have hurt others' feelings, whether clarification or soothing words are in order. The permanence of the written word makes sensitivity to the audience a primary obligation of the writer and a matter for teaching and discussion.

Foreign Cars

Which ones?   *Which ones?*

Foreign cars offer advantages, many of which are not found in American made

a Rolls-Royce?

models. Foreign cars are small and compact. The size enables the drivers to handle them

Which? All?   *agr?*

with ease. The American cars, on the other hand, are much bigger. The addition of

unnecessary parts, such as "wings," (add to the bulk of the car, making it difficult to

ever try to park a Rolls-Royce?

handle. The driver of the (forign) car has no trouble getting into parking areas, while

Rambler? Comet?

the driver of the American car often must struggle for a time before realizing that his

are all American cars "monstrosities"?   *all?*

monstrosity just will not fit into the space. Foreign cars, unlike American cars, are very

a Mercedes-Benz? an M.G.?   *Ford?*

economical. A foreign car gets more mileage on a gallon of gas than does an American

Friends of mine send to England and Japan for parts!

car. Oil, tires, and repairs cost less with the foreign cars. The price of a new foreign

Are you sure of this?

car, compared to the price of a new American car, is much lower. *Have you ever compared the price of a Rolls or an M.G. with that of a Ford? My guess is that you've fallen in love with a VW and hope to get one as a graduation present. If you plan to use these arguments with your father, you'd better check some facts. You probably have a specific car in mind, but your reader may be thinking of a different one. Can you check this paper to be more specific about what you mean?*

In an age of continual attack against jargon and "gobbledygook" in the writing of adults, it is certain that clarity in writing should be emphasized from the early junior high school years on. Even young students can be taught to avoid awkward passive constructions, to value writing that is concrete over that which is wordy and abstract, to revise their papers in such a way that readers can understand what they are trying to say.

Mastering the "speaking voice." Walker Gibson points to the necessity for the writer to engage in role playing, to ask himself, "Who am I in this situation, what is the situation, and who is the audience?" The writer, he believes, must overcome the lack of gesture, tone, and facial expression; his task is to "surround his words with other words on the page that his reader may infer the quality of the desired speaking voice." [17] He suggests that students and teachers may profitably ask questions about the speaking voice in the papers they discuss. What kind of voice is it? How does the listener know? How is the speaker's personality conveyed?

Improving organization. The struggle to order thought is perhaps the most demanding task the writer knows. The good writer must learn to reduce complexity to simplicity, to see logical relationships between the steps of his thinking, to grasp the sequence of thoughts which leads to emphasis. Like most of the other tasks mentioned here, the ordering of thought in discourse, both oral and written, is a continuous matter for teaching through all the grades and with each level of ability. The materials will differ; the basic principles remain the same.

Outlining can be a help in the process, but as most teachers know, those the students make are generally appalling muddles. The working through of outlines on the chalkboard with discussion about grouping of ideas according to topics and subtopics, the searching to see whether each point is related to the idea under which it comes, and the seeking of logically reasoned steps in thinking can be worked out until an acceptable outline is evolved. The formal matters of parallel structure and three-level development need not concern the group until a reasonable grasp of a simple four- or five-point topical outline with some supporting points is achieved. Familiar topics may lend themselves to this kind of thought-provoking analysis: arguments for higher insurance for teen-age drivers, for lowering the voting age to eighteen, for or against a longer school day or year—topics which are matters of lively discussion and on which all have opinions and some ready facts to be fruitfully used. A parallel project is the working with duplicated copies of some student outlines.

Certainly a matter for teaching is the concept that the plan is a means to an end; that the writer who can sketch out a kind of design for his paper may save much valuable time. The skillful writer carries his scheme in his

[17] Walker Gibson, "The Speaking Voice: A Kinescope," produced by the Commission on English of the CEEB, *English Leaflet,* vol. 42, Winter, 1963, pp. 14–23.

head; the novice must get his on paper where he can move the parts about and objectify the relationship of part to whole.

It is doubtful that most student writers ever see the outline as an integral part of the writing process, something that may be shaped and changed and reworked as his paper grows. For most, it is a chore to be dashed off, handed in if the teacher insists, and forgotten. For many, it is written *post hoc*, as a concession to teacher whim. It is the teacher's job to show students the relevance of the outline to the paper and to help him develop his skill in using it as a tool to achieve order.

Teaching about grammar and usage.   Matters of mechanics, the conventions of punctuation and capitalization, spelling, problems of sentence structure, and the like may be made matters for teaching as they arise in the papers. There is no need to spend class time on structures that young people do not use or on problems of complicated syntax when the writers have difficulty in recognizing a finite verb. The teacher may mark with a specific color or symbol some sentences that contain grammatical problems as he reads the papers and these—either duplicated for the class, written on the chalkboard, or shown by opaque or overhead projector—can provide the material for class discussion. Common errors such as the comma splice may be illustrated by several sentences from papers, the principle clarified through discussion, and mastery ensured by an assignment in which students write a number of sentences of their own in that pattern. Before much class time is spent on punctuation of common structures, the teacher will want to check in an up-to-date handbook on changing usage.[18]

Step six: Revising papers.   The young writer must know that a good paper is usually written in rough draft and may be corrected several times before a satisfactory copy may be obtained. He may learn that it is possible to proofread for punctuation errors, to watch for misspellings he knows he is likely to make, and to guard against generalizing without support or failing to provide illustrations or concrete detail. He should learn that the paper should be free from errors he knows how to deal with before he turns it over to the teacher.

The teacher's time and energy spent on marking papers has only one legitimate goal: assisting the young writer with the process of revision. Grades are really side issues, however reluctant the writer, teacher, parent, and principal are to regard them as such. Careful revision alone can produce real growth in the writer. It is true that many papers are not worth revising; many may be written quickly and discarded. But during each school year, some papers, increasing in length and complexity, need to be written, rewritten, and thought through again if the student is to know what it means to the writer to strive for a finished piece of prose. Students often learn little about real revision beyond correction and recopying. Teachers report that many of

---

[18] See the suggestions in Chap. 8 about teaching grammar and punctuation.

them think of the process as one of correcting punctuation and spelling errors and altering a sentence fragment or two. The real work of revision—cutting words, phrases, and paragraphs; rearranging word and sentence order; amplifying underdeveloped paragraphs; eliminating redundancies, abstract language, and clichés—all this the young writer must be taught.

Handling student writing

We have seen earlier in this chapter estimates of the proportion of the English teacher's time spent on evaluating papers. The task that looms largest for every teacher is what Thomas Wolfe in his teaching days called "the huge damnation of that pile of unmarked themes." If the teacher is to have time to read widely and to give attention to other important aspects of the curriculum, he must work out some timesaving devices to use in managing student writing. Ingenious teachers have worked out a number of ways to ensure that students write frequently and that their writing finds an audience and as often as possible frequent criticism and comment.

Here are some of the ways teachers have developed to bring the job of handling student writing down to manageable proportions:

Reducing the paper load.   Writing done in class may be used for practice and discarded or kept, uncorrected, in the student's folder. Many sets of papers may be corrected for one or two problems; some may be read for ideas and not for form; the teacher may announce that students will not know which set is to be marked carefully and thoroughly.[19]

Much informal writing may be demanded almost daily; and most of this need not be graded or marked. We need not feel obligated to give every paper a grade because "students want them." Students (and often parents) frequently demand that every scrap of paper the student writes be corrected. Such practice makes a travesty of education and makes collective bargaining for grades more important than learning. Students whose chief interest in life is haggling for grades (and many of our brighter students are in this group) need to be brought up sharply by a teacher who will help them examine their attitudes and values and the real goals of learning.

Many schools have used lay readers—trained college-educated housewives who assist the teacher in the task of reading papers, allowing him to increase the amount of writing students will do.[20] In one program the lay readers corrected twelve to sixteen papers each year, and the regular teacher four to six. Usually the teacher reads the papers handled by the reader but

[19] See Eric Johnson's "Avoiding Martyrdom in Teaching Writing: Some Shortcuts," *English Journal,* vol. 51, September, 1962, pp. 68–76, for ingenious shortcuts in grading papers and holding conferences.

[20] See Paul M. Ford, "Lay Readers in the High School Composition Program: Some Statistics," *English Journal,* vol. 50, November, 1961, pp. 522–528, and Virginia M. Burke, "A Candid Opinion on Lay Readers," *English Journal,* vol. 50, April, 1961, pp. 258–264.

does not mark them, and uses some of the time saved from detailed correcting for conferences with students. Many teachers feel that turning this amount of student writing over to an outsider to read prevents the teacher from doing one of the most important jobs—working with student writing. Although little research on the effectiveness of lay reading programs has been carried out, many teachers feel that a well-directed program can aid the teacher of writing.

Student correction. Many teachers have found it profitable to divide classes into small groups for frequent reading and commenting on papers. Such practice has advantages: it means that one more paper can be assigned and find response without adding to the teacher's burden; it provides a student audience and assures that each paper is heard by at least four or five people.[21]

Planning conference time

Conference time may be managed, even in the usual crowded day, and under the far from ideal conditions of teacher load that exist at present. The last fifteen minutes of the period during which papers are returned may be used for help as the teacher moves about the room responding to students who wish to raise questions about their papers. This is a good time for the other students to start revising or correcting. Again, time may be gained by allowing a class period every week or two to in-class writing. This kind of use of class time may be much more productive than the time spent on spelling and vocabulary lists and on workbook drills. While the class is busy writing, the teacher may move around the room, offering help or talk with students at the desk. Frequently small-group conferences are meaningful. The teacher may select three or four students who have similar problems—poor organization, generalizing, thin writing, and the like. Students learn from each other, usually without embarrassment.

Handling plagiarism

The problem of plagiarism, which commands attention at all levels, is much wider than the English class; its causes are to be sought in general cultural attitudes. The student is aware of "payola," of gifts and graft in business and politics, and of evasion of income taxes. In our day, when it seems fair to get something for nothing, and the only crime is getting caught, honesty becomes difficult.

Responsible teachers of writing believe in training students in habits of honesty and in challenging what they feel to be abuses of integrity. Many teachers sidestep the problem of investigating when they suspect dishonesty through their fear of parental wrath or administrative pressures to avoid trouble. Conscientious teachers make no charges without strong evidence, but

[21] See the suggestions in Emily Betts Gregory, "Managing Student Writing," *English Journal,* vol. 44, January, 1955, pp. 18–25, and those in McKenzie and Olson, *op. cit.*

they can often extract the truth from the reluctant culprit by skillful questioning: there was a baseball game so mother wrote the theme; the encyclopedia article on his topic said the thing much better than he could; this week's magazine or Sunday sermon had ideas which could be neatly appropriated. Teachers of English have an obligation to emphasize honesty in writing and to help young people develop the attitudes which will make cheating or plagiarism unpopular. Insistence on recognition of source materials, questioning when plagiarism is suspected, and valuing honest expressions of opinion can encourage students to value their own integrity.

Publicizing writing

Reaching a wider audience than the few who usually read his papers provides an important means of satisfaction for the young writer. Good themes may be posted on the bulletin board, although this practice often rewards writers who are already skillful and may put more distance between them and the less skillful. Another way of preserving and publicizing writing (and a powerful incentive to revision) is to collect folders of themes according to types: short stories, poetry, or autobiographical papers class members have written. One teacher suggests that the class may form a class publishing company (with editors, rewrite men, proofreaders, and illustrators) to write and publish a book—an anthology, a "how-to-do-it" manual, a biography, an encyclopedia, or a novel.[22]

Numerous publications for student writing encourage the student with a gift for creative writing. Some possible outlets for such writing are:

. . . *The Student Writer*, 2651 North Federal Highway, Fort Lauderdale, Fla.

. . . The *Atlantic Prize Essays, Prize Stories, and Prize Poems* (published annually), 8 Arlington Street, Boston 16, Mass.

. . . *The Literary Cavalcade* (Scholastic Magazines Writing Awards Issue), 33 West 42d Street, New York 36, N.Y.

Other ways of reaching an audience are class magazines or newspapers (easy to run off from time to time in duplicated form), letters to pen pals in other regions or abroad, letters to newspapers or magazines (surprisingly many find their way into print, especially in local papers), or letters to authors, actors, or officials.[23] It is good for students to learn that such letters in our society are an important channel of public opinion.

---

[22] William J. Dusel, "Planning the Program in Writing," *English Journal*, vol. 45, September, 1956, p. 325.

[23] Teachers know that authors may be reached through their publishers, but they may be reminded of the protests of John Steinbeck, Thornton Wilder, and others, warning them of the cruelty of motivating student writing at the expense of the weary author. Such letters should contain the tactful reminder that no reply is expected. Miraculously, some busy people do respond to children: President Eisenhower, Albert Einstein, and even former Premier Khrushchev have been known to answer letters of unusual appeal.

Letters can be levers to effect action. They have kept alive plays about to close on Broadway, brought television programs to communities which did not have them, changed the times of important programs, or ensured repeat performances; they have brought about legislation and appropriations for teachers' salaries, better schools, educational funds, and the preservation of historical sites and shrines.

Letter writing is a key activity in democratic action. It is the citizen's privilege in a democracy to let his voice be heard, but too many thoughtful citizens are inarticulate or passive. Since congressmen and legislators often answer letters, the real force of this kind of communication should be sensed by tomorrow's citizens.

Evaluating growth in writing

Efforts to find reliable objective means of evaluating the ability to write have been discouraging. The interlinear composition test developed by the Educational Testing Service as part of the College Entrance Board Examinations is reported to have high reader reliabilities of .95 to .96, and is regarded by the service as a useful predictor of success in college composition classes.[24] High reader reliability has been found in some of the research in composition which attempted to measure students' skill in writing through their performance on an essay test.[25] Reader reliability on tests of student writing has been notoriously suspect, however. In one study, English teachers and others who marked 300 compositions by giving them one of nine grades rated 94 per cent of the papers with either seven, eight, or nine of the possible grades; and no paper received less than five different grades.[26]

The classroom teacher is likely to find the following standardized tests useful in assessing student ability and achievement in writing:

. . . *School and College Ability Tests* (SCAT). Five levels: level 1, grade 12 and freshman and sophomore years of college; level 2: grades 10–12; level 3: grades 8–10; level 4: grades 6–8; and level 5: grades 4–6. Educational Testing Service, Princeton, N.J.

. . . *STEP* (*Sequential Tests of Educational Progress*). Four levels: freshman and sophomore years of college, grades 10–12, 7–9, and 4–6. Essay Writing and Writing tests. Educational Testing Service, Princeton, N.J.

. . . *English Expression Tests,* Cooperative Test Division, Educational Testing Service, Princeton, N.J.

---

[24] Braddock et al., *op. cit.,* p. 40.
[25] *Ibid.,* p. 4.
[26] Paul B. Diederich et al., *Factors in Judgments of Writing Ability,* Research Bulletin RB-61-15, Educational Testing Service, Princeton, N.J., 1961.

The difficulty of the trained testing staff of the CEEB in validating its grading of student themes suggests the greater difficulties facing English teachers who attempt to measure growth of students in writing during a year's work. Such evaluation is necessarily subjective, just as is the attempt to judge other intangibles, such as appreciation of poetry and taste in good literature. Although some standardized tests provide useful estimates of competence, the only significant test is that of performance—the writing the student has done over a period of time. The validity of the grading will depend on the teacher's ability to recognize good writing and to estimate its worth.

Pupil-teacher evaluation

The conference between student and teacher concerning the theme folder which represents the writing of a few months or the school year provides one of the most useful kinds of evaluation of writing. Such a folder is usually ample testimony to the fact that individual composition grades mean little. The review of many themes gives a much better overview of the student's work. Both students and teachers usually find that estimating a fair letter grade on the theme folder is a relatively easy task; more often than not, the student will arrive at the same grade as the teacher and understand clearly why he is receiving a grade of C or B or even D. If some evaluating device is used on each theme—a check list, Ideaform paper,[27] or a rating scale—basic difficulties in writing will be easily recognized.

Self-evaluation

The teacher who requires students to write an evaluation of their theme folders at certain intervals—each marking period, perhaps—forces them to analyze their composition problems and provides them with a clarifying device to guide work toward improvement. Conferences often allow teachers to make more meaningful comments to the student than is possible with written corrections, and to help the student plan his next steps in improving his writing.

The teacher's evaluation

The teacher is eventually responsible for the evaluation of student progress in writing in the English class. The student's theme folder is primary evidence, but much more than an average of individual grades on papers must be taken into consideration. The student folder, if carefully kept, should tell much about the student's attitude toward writing, and the conscientiousness with which he tries to improve.

[27] The Ideaform paper, available through the NCTE, provides a cover sheet the student may use for each theme, with an evaluation scale allowing for ratings for both form and content of the paper.

Real growth in writing can only be judged as the teacher observes the increasing maturity of the student's ideas, his growing skill in varying and perfecting his sentence structure, his increasing command of the conventions, his improved ability to organize his thoughts, and his increased sensitivity to word, phrase, tone, and meaning. Judgment depends finally on the competence of the teacher as writer and critic. Although theme grading can never be an objective process, the evaluation studies worked out by various teacher groups[28] provide a reputable consensus of opinion and an invaluable help for the teacher who wishes to check his judgments against those of his colleagues. Teachers in any school system will do well to study these to discuss and compare theme evaluation in department meetings and teachers' groups, and to observe, in such a publication as *End-of-year Examinations in English,* the really distinguished writing of which some students are capable.

There is probably no part of the English teacher's work more demanding or more satisfying than the teaching of writing. The discussion in this chapter has indicated ways to lighten the teacher's load of composition correction, and pointed to some of the kinds of writing which both students and teachers find rewarding. The teacher who can assist a young person to find satisfaction in writing his feelings, thoughts, and ideas has enabled him to enter more deeply into self-discovery. No part of his education is of greater value.

Student activities and assignments

The following assignments are designed chiefly to stimulate the student to think, to use his imagination, and to write about matters of importance to him. Although the student will often write about language and literature, the topics for such papers are suggested in the appropriate chapters devoted to those areas of study. The writer's critical, problem-solving, and imaginative abilities are those to be developed by the papers suggested here.

Exploring the writer's resources

Teacher and class may develop together a list of ideas and topics students would like to hear about from other members of the class. The list may be copied from the chalkboard into student notebooks, where each writer may add to his list as the year progresses.

. . . As the members of the class come to know each other, the teacher may encourage writing about personal matters: family relationships, experiences of rejection, images of self, problems, values, standards, ideals, or goals. The teacher may help students feel free to write about such matters, without assigning these topics. He should remember that the young dislike feeling that the teacher is prying or asking personal questions.

. . . Teachers may encourage students to keep journals into which they

---

[28] See bibliography for a list of these.

record their observations of people, scenes, or incidents; their thoughts, worries, fears, high or low moments; their comments on life and people.

. . . Teachers often need to help students get started in writing. For those who complain that they "don't know anything" about a topic, a few minutes of talk with the teacher, or the class, often shows how much they do know.

. . . To emphasize the value of writing from experience, teachers may read from Twain's *The Adventures of Tom Sawyer*, Gilbreth and Carey's *Cheaper by the Dozen*, Day's *Life with Father*, or other books which draw on the everyday happenings common to adolescents.

Developing observation and perception

Sharpened observation is one of the writer's most important resources. Conrad's words might be used for every class in composition: "My task is . . . to make you hear, to make you feel—it is, before all to make you see." [29] Practice in observing the physical world and communicating the experience to others is basic to imaginative and expository writing. For accuracy of observation and skill in using detail, students may try the following writing assignments:

. . . Writing verbal snapshots of small scenes: the locker room before a game, the cafeteria at 11:30 A.M., Nancy's bedroom before the prom, backstage before the play.

. . . Writing descriptive paragraphs that include fifteen details in one hundred and fifty words. They may compare their efforts with those the teacher may read from authors who have mastered the use of concise and concrete detail.

. . . Writing descriptions of people or places in terms of interest and previous experience. (Watching any crowd in the park, some people notice pretty girls, some, children at play, some, boys playing baseball, some, the clothes people wear. The painter notices color and shape of features, the dancer notices ways of walking and moving.)

Teaching expository skills

Assignments to develop clarity, economy, and accuracy:

. . . Write a do-it-yourself paper, giving clear directions for something you know how to do well: baiting a fishing rod, sailing a boat, starting an outboard motor, dressing a baby, making a cake, knitting a sweater, making a pizza, combing hair into a French twist.

. . . Bring something small and simple to operate to class, choose a partner to work with you, and write directions telling him how it works. As he attempts to follow your directions, let the class observe how specific, accurate, or misleading your directions are. Suggestions: loading a camera,

---

[29] Joseph Conrad, Preface to *The Nigger of the 'Narcissus,'* Doubleday & Company, Inc., Garden City, N.Y., 1937, and J. M. Dent and Sons, Ltd., Publishers, London. By permission of trustees of the Joseph Conrad Estate.

operating a light meter, playing on a recorder, using a needle threader.

. . . Explain to someone who has never seen them the following artifacts of American culture: bubble gum, a ball-point pen, a lipstick, ice cubes.

. . . Practice brevity. Write a fifty-word description used to sell a popular book or product. Then exchange descriptions with a classmate and cut the descriptions to twenty-five words for an ad.

. . . Write a fifty-word night letter on a common problem: a college boy needs money for a tuxedo; a girl wires parents for permission to go to Florida with a group of girls; a student who has failed a course wires that he must attend summer school. Exchange telegrams with a classmate and cut the telegram to fifteen words so that it may go as a day message. Compare the edited version with the original to see whether the heart of the message has been kept.

. . . Practice accurate report writing: go in pairs or groups to one familiar place: the gym during a basketball game, the local ice-cream hangout, a pizza palace, the "Y" on "Y-Teen night." Spend fifteen minutes taking notes about things seen, heard, smelt, or felt. Write a theme organized around one dominant impression; use sensory details to communicate the idea.

Assignments in letter writing

Letter-writing assignments should emphasize real letters which will be sent to a reader and which will, perhaps, get a response. Some letters which will actually be sent are these:

. . . Students may adopt a ship for letter writing. One teacher reports that her class joined the Adopt a Ship Plan, writing letters to the sailors on board, and receiving letters in return.[30]

Other letter-writing assignments give students valuable practice in developing sensitivity to the audience they are writing for.[31] Real and important problems in language may be attempted and the author's success evaluated in class discussion in assignments such as the following:

. . . Write to a parent (who is out of town) asking for an increase in allowance; attending a college weekend with a boyfriend; buying a dress for the senior prom; getting a driver's license.

. . . Write to a teacher asking to be excused for a misdeed, for rudeness, or for failure to accept an important responsibility.

[30] The Adopt a Ship Plan, sponsored by Peter Moreno, Propeller Club, 17 Battery Place, New York 4, N.Y. Described by Hazel M. Mortimer, "English Motivation by Adopting a Ship," *English Journal*, vol. 50, November, 1961, pp. 560–561.

[31] See Erwin Steinberg, "Teaching Expository Writing," *The Clearing House*, vol. 35, November, 1960, pp. 163–168, for the point of view that the chief complaint of employers about the writing of engineering students is their lack of sensitivity to the audience. The above topics present problems in communication which may help students develop such sensitivity through increased awareness of words and feelings.

. . . Write a letter to a friend refusing an invitation you do not want to accept, or explaining to grandparents why you prefer to visit friends during the summer, rather than to visit them.

. . . Write a letter of apology to the parents of your girl for keeping her out past the deadline they set; for breaking something of value in their house.

Pen-pal letters

. . . Teachers may encourage students to write pen-pal letters. A class may adopt a school in another country, or another part of the United States— a region which students may have read about. Let groups give reports on the regions they have chosen, exchange book lists, records of readings, and interviews with groups in other schools.

. . . Similar letters may be written to students in other countries,[32] and the letter exchanges may become useful stimulants to reading books with foreign settings. Letters to students abroad should be carefully written; writers must think of the responsibility they are undertaking when they try to describe life in America to people in another country.

Problems in argument

The teacher may give students valuable practice in handling logical and valid argument through setting such problem-solving assignments as the following:

. . . A friend who is not doing well in school has decided to drop out at the end of his junior year. Write him your opinion about his decision.

. . . Write a letter of opinion on the decision of a friend or relative in which you argue with his decision to join the army before finishing school, to get married before finishing college, to take a job rather than to go to college.

Write an argument for or against:

. . . A needed change (in television, in our home, in our school, in education).

. . . Something you believe your parents are wrong about.

. . . A minority point of view: something you believe in that your friends don't believe in.

. . . A prejudice, cheating, the grading or testing system, going to college, joining a sorority.

---

[32] Organizations sponsoring pen-pal correspondence will make names and addresses available. The Junior Red Cross translates letters from abroad, but most exchanges are carried on in English. Some useful addresses are the following: International Friendship League, 40 Mt. Vernon St., Boston 8, Mass., Student Letter Exchange, Waseca, Minn., Dyer's Pen-Pal Service, R.F.D. 3, Seguin, Tex.; Letters Abroad, Inc., 45 East 65th St., New York 21, N.Y.; Crusade for World Peace, Box 6993, Washington 20, D.C. (members of the People-to-People Program); International Junior Red Cross, 131 Livingston St., Brooklyn, N.Y.

Encouraging critical thinking

Students may be assigned critical and analytical papers, forcing them to think through difficult issues and problems. Papers should present arguments and give valid support for judgments. Papers or letters to various groups or organizations which support the banning of books like *1984, The Adventures of Huckleberry Finn, The Merchant of Venice,* and others may present arguments for or against the point of view taken by the banning group.

Topics may be assigned to stimulate discussion of critical standards in the study of literature. The imaginative teacher may think of topics such as these:

. . . The Voice of America is told that it will have just one hour more to broadcast before the program is banned in Russia and the satellite countries. How should it spend that hour? Supposing it were up to you to choose readings to reflect the American spirit, what pieces of American literature would you choose?

. . . What play, movie, novel, or author would you send on a cultural-exchange program in Russia? Africa? India? Japan? Why?

Stimulating imaginative writing

The principles of Yale's Daily Themes course may be helpful to teachers who want students to write imaginatively: (1) individualize by specific detail, (2) verify by range of appeal (smell, sound, touch); (3) establish a point of view; (4) use the indirect method (show, don't tell); (5) characterize by speech and gesture; (6) use words for connotation; and (7) unify by a single impression. Senior high school students will be capable of using some of these principles; others, such as "individualize by specific detail," are useful at all levels.[33]

. . . Ask students to describe their earliest memory and check with their families for accuracy. Memories of happy moments, of exciting events, of places and persons are favorite topics.

. . . Stimulate less able students to write imaginatively by showing them few pictures of family or teen-age situations from *The Saturday Evening Post* covers, each of which presents an idea easily converted into a story. The differences in what students "see" in the same picture are worth discussion. (*The New Yorker* covers will challenge more able students.)

. . . Use poetry as a means of reaching personal experience and teaching that poetic metaphors have personal applications. The title of the poem may suggest the title of the subject of the paper: "The Soul Selects . . ."; "My Own 'Desert Places'"; "My 'Road Not Taken'"; "'Proud Words' in My Life."

. . . Increase sensitivity to human relationships in literature through writing. A discussion of short stories such as Irwin Shaw's "Strawberry Ice Cream Soda" or Morley Callaghan's "The Snob" may be followed by papers examining a relationship in the writer's life which could be improved.

[33] Richard B. Sewall, "The Content of Student Writing," in Gordon and Noyes (eds.), *op. cit.* (Copyright © 1960, The National Council of Teachers of English.)

. . . Give students this assignment: "Describe the face of a person you know, odors in the kitchen on Christmas, something large (ocean, sky), something small (anthill, flower, snowflake), something you have felt (the feel of sand, of a snowball, of wet grass, of going barefoot on a dusty road). Looking back into memory, compare something you remember then with your perception of it now: my backyard at six, and the way it looks to me now; a favorite trip taken at ten, and taken again now; a well-known person as he appeared to me as a child, and as he appears now. School— then and now; church—then and now."

. . . Read the scene of Emily's twelfth birthday from *Our Town*,[34] and ask students, "Do any of us really see one another? Take a real look at a member of your family to see whether you can observe him or her as Emily would, on such an occasion, and write about it."

A sequential program in composition

The program suggested here is designed to develop essential skills in writing, thinking, and reasoning through practice in the kinds of writing commonly emphasized in composition programs. The arrangement of assignments is, in general, from simple to complex, from easy to difficult, from brief papers to longer ones, and from papers focusing chiefly on the exploring of the writer's own world of experience and thought to increasingly challenging topics demanding logical thinking about readings in language and literature.

The program is arranged by levels rather than by specific grades. Some students may never be capable of progressing beyond the third or fourth level of difficulty; others may be ready for practice in the kinds of writing and topics suggested in levels five or six before they leave junior high school. Teachers will therefore want to select materials or assignments from any level according to the needs and abilities of a class or the kind of practice the class seems to need.

Although the program is arranged "horizontally" to provide for growth during a period of several years the student spends in the secondary school, the "vertical" arrangement suggests the kinds of writing during any one year with which the student might reasonably be expected to have practice. The series of writing tasks, then, should provide opportunity for the development on the Brunerian premise that "the foundations of any subject may be taught to anybody at any age in some form," [35] and is therefore both "spiral" in its arrangement in progressively difficult assignments and sequential in the development of important writing skills.

[34] See p. 290.
[35] Jerome S. Bruner, *The Process of Education*, Harvard University Press, Cambridge, Mass., 1960, p. 11.

General principles for the program

During each year, students should have experience in writing both brief and long papers, learning to edit wordy pieces by careful revision, and to develop brief, thin papers with richer detail and more supporting evidence. Each year's work should include:

. . . Some free and spontaneous informal writing, both in and out of class. The subject matter may be the feelings, reactions, opinions, memories, thoughts, fantasies, or insights of the writer. The practice of keeping journals, diaries, or "thought books" should be encouraged.

. . . Some imaginative writing, free as to form and length, possibly unscheduled, and perhaps ungraded, often personal and private. Such writing can provide release and offer a chance for creative expression and imaginative invention.

. . . Much expository writing in various forms to provide for development of the essential skills of using language accurately and honestly, and exercising critical faculties of logical reasoning and analytic thinking.

. . . The research paper (usually a misnomer for a paper patched together out of materials lifted directly from encyclopedias and reference books) is discussed here as the library report. The skills of gathering and documenting materials should be taught throughout the six years, but most students will not be capable of real research until the college years.

Each year's work should include a balance of single sentences and paragraphs (especially at the beginning of each year), longer papers of two and three paragraphs, and 500-, 600-, and 1,000-word themes at levels four through six. Emphasis should be on the relation of length to the demands of the subject and the method of development, rather than on an arbitrary number of words.

Kinds of writing	Level one	Level two	Level three	Level four	Level five	Level six
Simple Exposition Skills: using clear, concise, specific language; following logical order; writing directions or accounts of processes; writing clear definitions	Giving directions for a simple act or process: tying a shoe, starting an outboard motor . . .	Writing definitions of everyday words (door, chair, pencil) and comparing with the dictionary definition. Writing personal definitions of abstract words: *happiness, friendship, beauty* ("What _____ means to me")	Same, with more complicated topics: directions for going from a known location to an unknown; processes such as developing a film, changing a tire	Explaining the organization and work of a club or group: Boy Scouts, PAL, Boys' Clubs, etc.	Describing and explaining the function of a well-known activity to someone who has not had experience with it: a pep rally, a square dance, a religious festival or ceremony	Clarifying the meaning of complex abstractions (*democracy, liberalism, prejudice, integrity*) by giving many specific illustrations and exploring the diverse meanings of these terms
Narration Skills: handling of different kinds of order; selection of detail to develop one central theme	Accounts of family of school incidents, of family trips or celebrations; narratives of personal experience or incident			Describing an incident from a particular point of view; selecting details about a complex event to convey a single theme		
Reporting Skills: using the language of fact with clarity and precision	Factual reporting of simple incidents, school trips, accounts of firsthand observations, family or school incidents. Writing reports of class meetings, keeping notes on class discussion and assignments			Reporting discussions of controversial issues in student council or committee meetings, town meetings, community groups. Factual reporting of speeches and events. Note-taking on lectures, assignments, and readings		
Description Skills: use of concrete words, selection of detail to support a single impression; accurate use of language	Brief papers describing familiar scenes, places, or persons	Descriptions emphasizing sensory impressions with concrete detail	Descriptions of place or scene to evoke mood; character sketch to emphasize a dominant trait	Longer papers of more complex descriptions: a holiday celebration, a person, a group of people in action	Description of something minutely observed: an animal, bird, flower, anthill. Technical descriptions, as of laboratory equipment, mechanisms, etc. Description of the dramatic, the violent, the unusual: an accident, a storm, a street fight, a group in a moment of crisis	

159

Kinds of writing	Level one	Level two	Level three	Level four	Level five	Level six
Library Reports Skills: learning the techniques of summarizing, paraphrasing, and interpreting reference materials for reports; learning the differences between honest borrowing and plagiarizing; gaining skill in documenting sources and mastering conventional form in footnoting and bibliography	Brief reports on the history and derivation of one word	Report on the history of a custom, a superstition, place names, or similar language investigations	Investigation of topics suggested by assignments in the study of language and literature; report on a mythological, Biblical, historical, or other reference in literature	Report on an aspect of the history of the language or of a point in changing usage	Using reference materials to gather and organize a report on an investigation related to work in language: the invention of the printing press, the development of the alphabet, manuscript writing, code systems, Biblical analysis, problems in translation from a foreign language	Biographical report on a person who made significant contribution to a development of language: Braille, Caxton, Gallaudet, Helen Keller; teachers, writers, inventors. Biographical paper on the works of a single writer or group of writers: the Brontë sisters, Frost, Dickens, Emily Dickinson
Writing about Books Skills: dealing with literature from the critical and analytical point of view rather than the retelling of plot; writing honest reactions to literature; searching for author's purpose and theme; examining dominant tone, mood, symbolism	Personal reactions to characters and situations in books; agreement or disagreement with the choices or decisions characters make	Observing the steps through which a character changes or develops	Comments on the relationships between characters; observing the writer's description of place and character	Observing the conflict between forces in the piece of literature; analyzing the author's purpose; discussing the relation of the endings to the development of character and action	Discerning the writer's theme and how it is illustrated in the book; observing and analyzing stylistic characteristics	Analyzing the writer's central symbols in the book; developing thematic statements made by the author; commenting on books which illustrate a universal human plight or illuminate a major literary theme. Analysis of a literary theme developed in several readings, both fiction and nonfiction (for instance, the theme of racial injustice)
Argument and Opinion Skills: practice in supporting opinion and argument by adequate evidence, in logical thinking and writing. The audience for the early years may be the writer's classmates; later, receptive adults; lastly, he may address an unknown audience: contemporaries outside his own school, unknown adults	Papers on such topics as "I believe my parents (teachers, etc.) are wrong about . . ."; pro or con arguments on problems of allowances, dating, chores, homework, school responsibilities or rules; letters to editors of school paper on school or teen-age problems	Arguments pro or con school requirements, policies, punishments, rules	Pros or cons of cheating, school and civic issues. Matters of school policy, changes needed, etc.	Pros and cons of personal standards and values	Argument and opinion about national or international issues: political, social, ethical, or moral issues; questions of human rights, educational goals, questions of values and beliefs. Papers should offer specific illustrations and deal with specific situations	

Kinds of writing	Level one	Level two	Level three	Level four	Level five	Level six
Critical Writing and Analysis Skills: exercise in critical thinking and writing about problems increasing in complexity; analysis of literary and mass-media sources to develop awareness of logical fallacies, semantic traps, propaganda techniques, and of stylistic features of literature	Practice in critical analysis of advertising appeals, TV stereotypes in family and western programs	Analysis of commonly used abstractions: success, *integrity, school spirit*	Analysis of the reality of characters in literature, credibility of motivation and dialogue, consistency of endings of fiction or drama	Analysis of newspaper editorials and mass-media materials for balance of fact and judgment; examination of such materials for validity of evidence. Analysis of a prejudice, a deeply held belief, an important value	Interpretation of a passage from literature, an aphorism, a parable, a folk saying, a well-known quotation, or a general truth. Interpretation of a poem or a short story. Critical review of a TV program, a play made from a book, or the film version of a classic	Critical analyses of some difficult poems, short stories, plays, and novels, with emphasis on theme, symbolism, structure, and style
Exercises in Style Skills: developing sensitivity to a variety of styles in literature through "trying them on" in practice. Although the student's major problem in writing is to develop a style and voice of his own, occasional attempts to write paragraphs or brief bits modeled after well-known stylists may help him develop an ear for style, and perhaps increase his own command of language. The writing of paragraphs modeled on the sentence patterns of a prose passage from literature may develop sensitivity to word order, syntactical patterns, and choice of words	Writing brief paragraphs in Madison Avenue English, sportswriter's or TV commercial language, or Mad magazine satire	Writing dialogue in the style of movie or TV romances, westerns, or mysteries; teen-age fiction or popular magazine romance; trying New Yorkerese or Timestyle	Writing a well-known piece (a fairy tale, fable, or parable) in several styles	Attempting pieces of character description, dialogue, or action, modeled on the prose of Hemingway, Salinger, Lardner, Conrad	Attempting writing closely modeled on paragraphs from 18th, 19th, or 20th century prose masters: Johnson, Lamb, Stevenson, E. B. White, Mencken, and others (the teacher can find a wealth of examples for models)	

Selected bibliography

Don P. Brown et al., *Writing: Unit-lessons in Composition,* a graded sequence of three books (I, II, III), with three separate editions of each book (A, B, C), Ginn and Company, Boston, 1964.

Edward J. Gordon and Edward S. Noyes (eds.), *Essays on the Teaching of English,* Appleton-Century-Crofts, Inc., New York, 1960. (Part II, "The Teaching of Writing.")

J. N. Hook, *Teaching High School English,* 2d ed., The Ronald Press Company, New York, 1959, chaps. 9 and 10.

Lou La Brant, *We Teach English,* Harcourt, Brace & World, Inc., New York, 1951, chaps. 10 and 11.

Hart Day Leavitt and David A. Sohn, *Stop, Look, and Write,* photographs to stimulate high school writing, Bantam Books Inc., New York, 1964. (Paperback.)

Walter Loban et al., *Teaching Language and Literature: Grades 7–12,* Harcourt, Brace & World, Inc., New York, 1961, chap. 10.

Belle McKenzie and Helen F. Olson, *Experiences in Writing,* The Macmillan Company, New York, 1962. Helpful instructions about how to organize a class in writing in high school.

Edwin Sauer, *English in the Secondary School,* Holt, Rinehart and Winston, Inc., New York, 1960, chap. 6.

Wallace Stegner et al., *Modern Composition: Books 1 through 6,* Holt, Rinehart and Winston, Inc., 1964.

Pamphlets

The following pamphlets on evaluating student writing are available through the National Council of Teachers of English, Champaign, Ill.

"Evaluating Ninth Grade Themes," *Illinois English Bulletin,* vol. 40, March, 1953.

"Evaluating Twelfth Grade Themes," *Illinois English Bulletin,* vol. 40, April, 1953.

Lois Grose et al., *Suggestions for Evaluating Junior High School Writing,* Association of English Teachers of Western Pennsylvania, n.d.

Helen Hillard et al., *Suggestions for Evaluating Senior High School Writing,* Association of English Teachers of Western Pennsylvania, n.d.

"Principles and Standards in Composition," *Kentucky English Bulletin,* vol. 6, Fall, 1956–1957.

A Scale for Evaluation of High School Student Essays, California Association of Teachers of English, 1960.

Standards for Written English in Grade 12, Indiana English Leaflet, vol. 4, June, 1962.

Ednah S. Thomas, *Evaluating Student Themes,* The University of Wisconsin Press, Madison, Wis., 1960.

CHAPTER 7

The definitive grammar of English is yet to be written, but the results so far achieved are spectacular. It is now as unrealistic to teach "traditional" grammar of English as it is to teach "traditional" (i.e., pre-Darwinian) biology or "traditional" (i.e., four-element) chemistry. Yet nearly all certified teachers of English on all levels are doing so. Here is a cultural lag of major proportions.

W. NELSON FRANCIS [1]

Mastery of language: the study of usage

Overview: the revolution in usage and grammar

The study of language today stands at a new frontier. It has wide horizons; it draws on a range of materials of a vitality and richness and flexibility undreamed of in an earlier era. It emphasizes creation rather than dissection. Instead of handing the student a narrow list of prohibitions to memorize, the teacher sends him to language in use—his own and that of others—for the purposes of exploring, discovering, observing, and finally creating an infinite variety of patterns of language possible for the users of English.

In many English classrooms today, the student looks at his language not as a series of sentences in his grammar book to be diagrammed, a list of pitfalls of usage to avoid, or words to fill in the blanks of workbooks, but as a vital form of human activity. He becomes aware of the stream of language that flows around him continually and observes its uses in the television commercial, the sports writer's column, a speech by the President of the United States, the sentences from his own themes, or a poem by E. E. Cummings. Through working with language-in-use, his ears become opened to the many

---

[1] "Revolution in Grammar," *Quarterly Journal of Speech,* vol. 40, October, 1954, pp. 229–312.

ways of saying things; his eyes are alert for the new word, the vivid phrase, the arresting image; his tongue acquires the fluency that comes from acquaintance with a broad range of usage; his brain discerns differences between truth and nonsense.

The frontiers of language are being expanded today by new developments in modern linguistic science. Instead of one grammar—literary, frozen, and formal—we have today numerous "new" grammars of English, representing different points of view about language, different analyses of English and the way it works. Each of these new grammars has contributed something of value to the material the English teacher uses. It matters little that disagreements lead to excited controversy wherever students of language meet. Here are men and women deeply absorbed in the study of a live and changing language and able to generate the excitement of discovery in the process.

The subject called grammar in the schools generally includes both the study of grammar and the study of usage. The grammar of a language is the description of the way the language operates; in the study of grammar we attempt to bring to the conscious level an understanding of the system the individual uses unconsciously to produce the sentences of his language. The study of usage is concerned with the choices the individual makes in selecting from a variety of words and constructions those appropriate to his use.

We saw in Chapter 3 a discussion of the English curriculum as a language curriculum. Language may rightly be considered as the broad base of the triangle, the key to the rest of the program in composition and literature. It should be clear, however, that the study of language is not synonymous with the study of grammar and usage. Familiarity with the distinctions made by linguists about the different branches of language study may clarify the discussion.

In Chapter 3 we viewed language as a social and cultural phenomenon shaping human behavior, thought, and feeling. Chapters 4, 5, and 6 showed how the student gains control of its spoken and written forms: listening and speaking, his primary language experiences; reading, his mastery of the symbolism of print; and finally, most difficult of all, the conversion of thought into the written symbol. When the student has progressed through the elementary grades in our schools and has acquired some facility in writing, he is ready to look at his language from a different point of view, to study its varieties of expression and its structure. The chapter examines the first part of the student's mastery of language—the problem of usage, both written and spoken. Chapter 9 deals with the problems involved in his mastery of the structure and mechanics of the language. Since the teaching of usage and grammar is interrelated at most important points, some basic concepts may be examined first.

For the purposes of this discussion, the following definitions will be helpful:

Language includes speech and its recorded forms. There are human societies without an alphabet or without a written language, but there is no society without a spoken language. The written language is an attempt to record in a series of written symbols the stream of sound shaped by millions of human lips into the language of a culture.

Grammar is the study of the way the language works. The study of grammar in schools is designed to make the child aware of how the system of grammar operates in him as a speaker of English and to teach him something of the workings of the signals, structures, and patterns of words which make up his language. For instance, the child who observes that a basic pattern in English sentence structure names first the doer of the action, next, the action, and then the goal, is studying the grammar of English whether in or out of school.

Usage refers to the choices speakers make in the forms and meanings of words and the appropriateness of these choices to the situations in which they are used. The speaker's choice between *I fetched the paper* or *I brought the paper*, between the standard word *children* or the colloquial *kids* in a particular context is a matter of usage rather than of grammar.

Standard English is the dialect of educated speakers, those prominent in business, and in public and cultural affairs of the community. Standard English is ". . . the English that with respect to spelling, grammar, pronunciation, and vocabulary is substantially uniform though not devoid of regional differences, that is well-established by usage in the formal and informal speech and writing of the educated, and that is widely recognized as acceptable wherever English is spoken and understood." [2] Standard English in this sense of the term is the "consensus language of literary and literate users of English the world over in the twentieth century." [3]

Colloquial usage. English teachers need to be clear, too, about the status or usage labels used to describe varieties of usage. Linguists have complained that even college teachers of English are uncertain about what the dictionary status labels mean, as can be seen from the following:

> Even teachers of English frequently misunderstand the application of the label *colloquial* in our best dictionaries. Some confuse it with *localism* and think of the words and constructions marked "colloquial" as characteristic of a particular locality. Others feel that some stigma attaches to the label "colloquial" and would strive to avoid as incorrect (or as of a low level) all words so marked.
>
> The word *colloquial*, however, as a label in a modern, scientifically edited dictionary has no such meaning. It is used to mark those words and constructions whose range of use is primarily that of the polite conversation of cultivated people, of their familiar letters and informal speech, as distinct from those words and construction which are

[2] By permission. From Webster's *Third New International Dictionary*, copyright 1961 by G. & C. Merriam Company, Publishers of the Merriam-Webster Dictionaries.
[3] Priscilla Tyler, "An English Teacher Looks at *Webster's Seventh New Collegiate Dictionary*," by permission from *Word Study*, vol. 38, April, 1963, p. 4, copyright 1963 by G. & C. Merriam Company, Publishers of the Merriam-Webster Dictionaries.

common also in formal writing. The usage of our better magazines and public addresses generally has, during the past generation, moved away from the formal and literary toward the colloquial.[4]

The role of context in governing the status of a word as colloquial or slang is recognized in many recent dictionaries. Webster's *Third New International Dictionary* maintains that there is "no satisfactory objective test" for slang. It abandoned the label *colloquial* because it felt that "it is impossible to tell whether a word out of context is colloquial." For modern lexicographers and linguists, usage is relative, choice is a matter of taste and appropriateness, and correctness depends upon context.

Substandard usage. According to Webster's *Third*, the *substandard usage* label designates "Status conforming to a pattern of linguistic usage that exists throughout the American language community, but differs in choice of word or form from that of the prestige group in that community: *drownded; hisself.*[5] Substandard usage calls attention to the speaker's lack of education, and for this reason it is the chief concern of the program in improvement of usage.

As teachers of English, we need to be clear about our role as teachers of language. We are not guardians of the language, protecting it from change, defending the ramparts against the split infinitive and the misuse of *whom.* Nor can we legislate the forms our students will choose by forbidding them to use certain locutions. The English teacher can be a creative and stimulating teacher of a great language if he can successfully open the ears of his students to the many varieties of linguistic usage which constantly flow about us. If he can impart to them his own fascination with the history and changes in words and syntax of the language, if he can challenge his students to experiment with many usages and many styles and master them for his use, he will have accomplished much. He should teach awareness, sensitivity, taste, and discrimination, rather than rules, a few fixed and invariable forms, and a narrow range of choices. The user of English should not be cabined, cribbed, and confined in a strait jacket of "proper" forms, but enjoy the flexibility of expression and the vivid word and phrase that make American English vigorous and alive.

Sound teaching of usage involves more than filtering out the impurities which educated parents dislike in their children's speech: "between you and I," *like* as a conjunction, or mispronunciations. Such surface changes are merely patchwork on the fabric of language, likely to wear through and show the speaker's level of education, as does Eliza's slipping back into her Cockney dialect in a moment of excitement at Mrs. Higgins' tea party. Students must understand that the development of good language patterns depends on sensitivity to educated speech and the making of informed choices among the many varieties of English.

[4] Charles Fries, "Usage Levels and Dialect Distribution," *The American College Dictionary* (copyright 1947, © copyright 1964) by permission of Random House, Inc.
[5] *Ibid.,* p. 19a.

Language change: a basic point of view

We cannot begin to ask the questions that most teachers want answered—what grammar shall I teach, and how shall I teach it?—without looking briefly at the history of language to gain perspective. The one basic concept which underlies all teaching of language today is that of linguistic change. Although a vocal group holds that the English teacher's job is primarily to "maintain standards" and to "resist change," the informed teacher knows that all languages change during the course of their histories and that such change is normal and inevitable.[6]

Languages are continually being shaped by custom and tradition and by the political, economic, and social histories of the peoples who speak them. No legislation, no fiat of government or academy has served to fix the language and stay the process of change. Dr. Samuel Johnson confessed that he had hoped to stabilize and regulate the language when he started his great dictionary but soon found that no dictionary could "embalm his language and secure it from corruption and decay," and that to attempt to do so was to try "to enchain syllables and to lash the wind. . . ."

Aims of instruction in grammar and usage

Modern teachers agree generally on three central aims for the teaching of grammar and usage: helping students understand the nature and structure of their language; establishing desirable habits of usage; and developing the command of language in speaking and writing.

Understanding the structure of English

The focus of instruction in grammar should, so teachers believe, help the student understand the basic patterns and structure of the language he speaks. As he begins to observe that most sentences he writes or speaks can be reduced to common structural patterns[7] or to "kernel" sentences and transformations of these sentences,[8] he observes the underlying structures of English discourse

---

[6] The statement of basic concepts about grammar and usage agreed on by linguists has been widely accepted: (1) language changes constantly, (2) change is normal, (3) the spoken language *is* the language, (4) correctness rests upon usage, and (5) all usage is relative. (Commission on the English Curriculum, *The English Language Arts* (copyright 1952, National Council of Teachers of English), Appleton-Century-Crofts, Inc., New York, pp. 274–277.

[7] The concept of patterns of sentence structure is utilized in the books for high school students by Paul Roberts, and by Neil Postman et al. (see bibliography).

[8] The theory of transformational grammar is advanced by Noam Chomsky, *Syntactic Structures*, Janua Linguarum No. 4, Mouton and Company, 'S-Gravenhage, the Netherlands, 1962.

and is presumably better able to utilize these structures to generate sentences of his own.

Establishing desirable habits of usage

Since command of informal standard English is absolutely necessary for economic advancement and social prestige, schools in a democratic society must attempt to give each student as firm a grasp of the standard spoken and written language as he is capable of attaining. It is evident that in our culture the young person whose speech is substandard will have doors closed to him in many kinds of employment and many social groups. Although we cannot enforce standard usage, we can muster all the means at our command for making young people aware of the cultural importance of standard English and the limitations they will face without it. They may also be brought to understand the need for flexible rather than arbitrary standards and learn to choose discriminatingly those which are most appropriate.

Improving command of language

The student gains command over his language through observing his own usage, evaluating it, and practicing to change substandard locutions in speaking and writing. His study of grammar focuses first on the patterns of his own sentences. As he reads literature, listens to its oral forms, and gains practice in generating sentences on good models, his own language and structure change, and he is able to use a wider range of expressive forms.

The program in usage

For most of the young people in our schools, the improvement of usage is the paramount practical problem. It is chiefly usage, rather than grammar, that marks the speaker as educated or uneducated, that calls attention to his social, economic, and cultural backgrounds, and it is therefore usage that is the primary, continuing concern of the schools for all students of all abilities. When parents demand that the schools teach their children "good grammar" it is usage that they really mean.

Grammar as a theoretical study is a subject that each child should know something about; it is a significant part of his liberal education. However, the close analytical study of the grammar of a language as complex as English is abstract and difficult; many of the children in our schools are too limited in intelligence or linguistic background to profit from great amounts of time spent on this area. For them, time is more profitably spent practicing speaking and writing and thereby gaining familiarity with, and command over, the consensus language—standard English.

Schools, then, have two jobs to do in teaching usage. For all students, acquaintance with standard English is of primary importance. Observation and practice lead to the habitual use of socially and culturally approved forms and acquaintance with the language of educated speakers.

Secondly, schools must provide acquaintance with the many varieties of English in common use in differing groups and speech communities of American life. In the United States, where various regions have been settled by immigrants from different parts of the world, and life and customs vary widely, many different speech patterns flourish. Most Americans are familiar with some of these: the dialects of Boston, New York City, or the deep South. On the other hand, most Americans are unaware of the dialect differences of vocabulary and pronunciation which characterize the speech of many other areas: the terse, laconic speech of the Maine man, the idiom of much Midwestern speech, or that of regions of the Southwest.

In *Travels with Charley*, John Steinbeck, a writer with an ear for American regional speech, laments its passing as a cultural loss of major proportions. In an earlier book, he has one of his characters comment on regional differences:

> "I knowed you wasn't Oklahomy folks. You talk queer, kinda—that ain't no blame, you understand."
>
> "Ever'body says words different," said Ivy. "Arkansas folks says 'em different, and Oklahomy folks says 'em different. And we seen a lady from Massachusetts, an' she said 'em differentest of all. Couldn't hardly make out what she was saying." [9]

Class dialects exist, too, even in what we like to think of as a classless society. Although in the United States the social gulf between an Eliza Doolittle and a Mrs. Higgins is not as wide or as pronounced as it is in England, substandard and illiterate dialects do reveal important differences in education, social and cultural background, and occupational status.

W. Nelson Francis, Chairman of the NCTE's Commission on the English Language, distinguishes differing dialects in this way: *regional* dialects spoken in speech communities in differing parts of the country; *social* or *class* dialects (spoken by different social groups within the same region); *prestige* dialects (those admired and emulated by the speakers of other dialects); the *standard dialect of a language* or the standard language (that used by the educated and ruling classes); and a *literary* dialect (that used primarily by writers and scholars).[10]

Recognition and study of such dialects is part of the content of new cur-

---

[9] From *The Grapes of Wrath*, by John Steinbeck, copyright © 1939, by John Steinbeck. Reprinted by permission of The Viking Press, Inc. (Compass Books edition, p. 184.)
[10] Based on W. Nelson Francis, *The Structure of American English*, copyright © 1958, The Ronald Press Company, New York, pp. 48–50.

ricula in which the student learns something of the varieties of English.[11] His skill in adapting his usage to the occasion is a measure of his literacy and his mastery of the language.

Program into practice

Children come to the schools with many different kinds of linguistic backgrounds. Few come from homes where generations of educated users of English have shaped the speech patterns of the present generation. Many do not have homes in which good books and graceful and cultivated conversation prevail, and it is these that ensure an easy command of the standard language. Children from such "good" backgrounds normally speak a more acceptable English at the age of five than the majority of others will do after five, ten, or even fifteen years of schooling. They will need little of the detailed attention to usage and grammar usually included in most curricula. Their chief need will be increased experience in reading and practice in speaking and writing.

Children with less favored cultural backgrounds—the majority in our schools—need a much different kind of instruction. Parents who have little education or are not native speakers of English set substandard speech patterns for their children. The street and the playground leave their impress on speech habits, too, and make more difficult the task of the schools and the English teacher. The child's home environment and the language of friends or the gang exert such a powerful force on his language that unless we train him in patterns of observation and practice which will operate outside the classroom, we can hardly expect the few minutes a day spent in the English class to change habits of long standing.

Furthermore, teachers today are beginning to understand the deep psychological importance of language to the child. The adolescent's language is colored by deep emotional associations—those of home, family, and close friends. When the English teacher rejects or condemns such language, he often appears to reject an important part of the child's life. Part of the resistance to change in such children is probably a reaction to the labeling of such usage as "bad" or "wrong."

Society's rejection of substandard usage may have more damaging consequences than we suspect. For the child with a foreign-language background, such an attitude forces an untenable choice. He may choose to accept the language of the school, turning his back on the language of home and friends. Or he may retain his close emotional bonds and reject not only the language the school tries to force on him, but also the tasks of reading or writing the school sets for him.

As one teacher of such children has pointed out, the price we ask is often too great: "An individual's linguistic usage is among other things the outward

[11] See Jean Malmstrom and Annabel Ashley, *Dialects—U.S.A.*, NCTE, Champaign, Ill., 1963.

sign of his most deepseated group loyalties . . . the blunt fact is that only if his loyalties shift will his grammar change." [12]

An important part of the teacher's task is developing the understanding that "correct" usage is not the measure of worth of the individual, even though many fine people are penalized by society for substandard usage. Literature provides bountiful examples of the admirable person whose worth cannot be measured by the single criterion of standard usage. Penny Baxter of *The Yearling,* Mama of *Mama's Bank Account,* Huck Finn, and numerous others weigh more heavily in the scale of human values than Macbeth or Richard III, who spoke the King's English well. Good usage is important because it confers prestige on its user, but it does not change his character. If the young people in our English classes can understand this, they will have developed sound attitudes for good language learning.

Usage: depth or surface?   The broad range of habitual choices of words and phrases make up the deep stream of the speaker's normal level of usage, whether standard English, a regional variation of standard, or the substandard usage characteristic of those with little schooling. In addition to this range of depth usage, there are also rapid surface changes as the normal speaker adapts quickly to his audience or his situation.[13] As he moves in different social or occupational groups, formal or informal social situations, he adapts vocabulary and style to the occasion, often without conscious effort.

The study of usage in the classroom attempts to offer the student enough practice in using language to make his command of the consensus language a natural part of his behavior. At the same time, it should familiarize him with enough of the range of varieties of usage to allow him to exert conscious control over language. This is a task of considerable dimensions.

Diagnosing usage levels.   Classes may contain some students who easily use a good level of the informal standard language in speaking and writing— those who may profitably use their time improving command of sentence patterns and developing fluency and power in writing. A second large group in most classes includes those whose language may be relatively free from substandard elements, but is limited by impoverished vocabulary and awkward and confusing sentence structure. The third group is that of the speakers of substandard English. Their linguistic performance is marked by impoverished vocabulary, limited command of sentence structure, heavy reliance on slang and colloquial usage, and habitual use of substandard forms (those often called nonstandard or illiterate in levels of usage scales).[14] Examples may be found among the forms of the past tenses of verbs: *clumb, drownded, had went,*

---

[12] Allan F. Hubbell, "Multiple Negation," © *Inside the ACD,* Random House, Inc., New York, vol. 10, October, 1957, p. 3.
[13] The concept of "depth" and "surface" usage comes from conversations about usage with Dr. Priscilla Tyler, now of the University of Illinois, Department of English.
[14] See Charles Fries, *American English Grammar,* Appleton-Century-Crofts, Inc., New York, 1940, for the distinguishing characteristics of this group.

"Who or whom do I see about the adult English course?" Drawing by Alan Dunn; © 1963 The New Yorker Magazine, Inc.

brung, I seen it, he come; double negatives: *can't hardly, ain't got no;* and such pronominal forms as *hisself* and *yourn.* For such students, enriching their range of expression, sentence patterns, and vocabulary is the goal of "good" English, rather than painstaking—and often unnatural and erroneous—mastery of "good" usage. The teacher may himself distinguish carefully between literary and informal usages and teach them to some students, but for the student who is still saying "I done it," or "he give me the book," they waste time needed for other kinds of practice. The elimination of emphasis on such matters as use of *shall* and *will,* or *who* and *whom* would greatly simplify the tasks of both the English teacher and the student who must master standard English.[15]

[15] The teacher who is not conversant with current studies in usage should read Margaret Bryant's *Current English Usage,* Funk & Wagnalls Company, New York, 1962; Bergen Evans and Cornelia Evans, *A Dictionary of Contemporary American Usage,* Random House, Inc., New York, 1957; and Margaret Nicholson, *A Dictionary of American-English Usage* (based on Fowler's *Modern English Usage*), Oxford University Press, Fair Lawn, N.J., 1957. (Paper: New American Library, 1958.) Teachers should also read sections 1 ("Dic-

Gaining support for good usage. With some students, the teacher may find that making them aware of the limitations of their substandard dialect may be the first step toward change. The teacher may read a short story in which such usage is common: Hemingway's "My Old Man," Thurber's "You Could Look It Up," Lardner's "Haircut," or "Some Like Them Cold," or Twain's "The Celebrated Jumping Frog of Calaveras County." If students are asked to tell what kind of person is speaking, they will often realize that the speaker's usage marks him as a man with little education and that speech is one of the most direct clues to educational and social background. Observation of the differences in usage of characters on television's "The Beverly Hillbillies" or "Gomer Pyle, USMC" may illustrate the same thing. Substandard speakers may be asked to study their vocational choices to find out whether good usage and clear speech is an essential qualification. The skillful teacher can lead students to see that, rightly or wrongly, society does judge the individual by his usage and that poor usage may lead to false estimates of real worth. Substandard usage, according to employers, gives a misleading estimate of ability and frequently discriminates against the applicant for a job.[16] Today, with emphasis on providing educational opportunity for disadvantaged youth, the problem of improved usage assumes major importance. It is the responsibility of the school to make available the opportunity to learn standard English, but only the student himself can guarantee that any learning will occur.

Choosing items for study. The notion that all English usage is divided into two categories—correct and incorrect—is still prevalent in many schools despite the increasing emphasis on flexible standards of usage during the past thirty or forty years. The problem of teaching usage to all the students in our classes could be greatly simplified by some realistic evaluation of the usage items which will call most unfavorable attention to the user's speech or writing and those commonly used among educated speakers and writers which need little attention in the classroom. The most serious effect of the confusion over the status of usage items is the waste of time that could be well spent on reading and writing.

The pronouncements about acceptable or "correct" usage in many textbooks and composition handbooks encourage confusion. Recent studies have shown that such texts do not agree about what is acceptable usage,[17] and that "the majority of the teachers still reject most usage that published information

---

tionaries, Words, and Meanings") and 4 ("Usage") in Leonard Dean and Kenneth G. Wilson (eds.), *Essays on Language and Usage*, Oxford University Press, Fair Lawn, N.J., 1963, and part 4, "Linguistics and Usage," in Harold B. Allen (ed.), *Readings in Applied English Linguistics*, Appleton-Century-Crofts, Inc., New York, 1958.

[16] See discussion of the problem of usage as a factor in vocational discrimination against youth in Ruth I. Golden, *Improving Patterns of Language Usage*, Wayne State University Press, Detroit, 1960, chap. 2.

[17] See Jean Malmstrom, "Linguistic Atlas Findings versus Textbook Pronouncements on Current American Usage," *English Journal*, vol. 48, April, 1959, pp. 191–198.

tends to support as acceptable." [18] Many reject items which were voted "acceptable" by the jury of scholars and writers in one of the earliest usage studies more than thirty years ago.[19]

Improving usage.   The program in usage should include numerous activities designed to develop sensitivity to language. All students, whatever their command of English, may profit from observation, comparison, and discussion of usage and pronunciation. The teacher who promotes this kind of inquiry is assisting students to acquire important skills: the development of awareness about language, sensitivity to the many ways in which it is used, and an alert ear to the habits and customs of speakers of English. The student who is curious about language, and who has learned to listen and observe, has developed the tools which will serve him the rest of his life. The teacher may start this kind of inquiry at any grade level.

Students may record their own observations of characteristic usage on *ain't, it's me,* and other controversial items and indicate the speaker's background, occupation, and educational level. At either the junior or senior high school level, there is almost unlimited scope for student inquiry and research into dozens of areas of language which can help develop awareness of language in general and usage in particular: historical studies, various kinds of word study, semantics, and dialect and regional speech. Some of the many possible topics for inquiry are listed in the exercises at the end of this chapter and in Chapter 3.

Changing the student's depth usage.   Two approaches to the problem of improving usage seem to produce the best results, according to teaching studies. One is that of placing both the right and wrong forms before the student to assist him in making a conscious choice. The other recommends much oral practice as the path to improvement.[20] Not until the usage sounds familiar is the student likely to change. He must hear standard English until it "sounds right" and practice it until it feels comfortable to the tongue. His problem is, like that of Shaw's Eliza in *Pygmalion,* that of learning a new dialect.

Classroom activities include frequent practice in speaking with opportunity for classmates and teacher to make tactful suggestions about improvement of usage. Listening to tapes of his own performance in discussion, practicing with a fellow student who speaks well, or working with a classmate on such matters

---

[18] Thurston Womack, "Teachers' Attitudes toward Current Usage," *English Journal,* vol. 48, April, 1959, p. 188.

[19] Sterling A. Leonard, *Current English Usage,* Monograph No. 1, NCTE, Champaign, Ill., 1932.

[20] See Percival M. Symonds, "Practice versus Grammar in the Learning of Correct English Usage," *Journal of Educational Psychology,* vol. 22, February, 1931, pp. 81–96, and Prudence Cutright, "A Comparison of Methods of Securing Correct Language Usage," *Elementary School Journal,* vol. 39, May, 1934, pp. 681–690.

as distinguishing between *lie* and *lay*, *sit* and *set*, *learn* and *teach*, can be helpful. Also valuable are class sessions in which all those who need practice with a particular form receive help from the teacher in finding a commonsense approach to the problem, as with the agreement of subject and predicate when a phrase intervenes: "one of the boys was (were) lost."

Work in English may emphasize group practice in which students say aloud together sentences with correct forms of commonly misused verbs. Whatever practice the teacher can invent that focuses attention on hearing standard forms and practicing them in a classroom situation where students and teacher work together for improvement will assist the substandard speaker to master and feel at ease with a new dialect which may open for him the door to opportunity. The teacher who can help students change their depth usage must help them get new patterns, words, and phrases in their mouths and on their tongues, as well as in their ears.

Surface usage: the varieties of English. Earlier descriptions of "levels of usage" have been supplanted today by the concept of varieties of English that range from the most formal or literary dialect of the language through informal standard, colloquial, slang, and regional to illiterate. Instead of the value judgment implied in the idea of "levels," modern linguists prefer to think of varieties on a continuum that extends from nonstandard (chiefly spoken, the characteristic speech of uneducated persons) to formal standard (used in restricted groups in formal speech and writing). Table 7-1 shows the range of such usage.

Linguists point out that just as the speaker chooses evening dress for some occasions and dungarees for another, each "right" in one situation and "wrong" in another, so he also varies his speech and written language according to the formality or informality of the occasion, the audience he tries to reach, and the purpose of his discourse. This idea, generally accepted by scholars and teachers today, recognizes the importance of context and appropriateness in dictating choices in usage.

The teacher who recognizes this modern point of view toward usage helps students see that it is natural, reasonable, and customary to say "Hi" to one's friends and "good morning" to the principal and unnatural to reverse the two kinds of greeting. By assisting a student to observe the differences in the way he chooses usage for family, friends, older persons, strangers, or possible employers, the teacher emphasizes the necessity for developing control and a range of idiom from colloquial to formal standard and for accepting the responsibility of making appropriate choices in usage. For many students, the comparison with changes in dress is instructive. Classes may discuss varieties of usage appropriate to situations in which blue jeans are standard dress and those requiring dinner jacket or a formal evening gown. They will see that to insist on one right and invariable form for every speaker, usable in all circumstances, is as misguided as requiring a single way of dress in all social situations.

Table 7-1. **Summary of the Principal Varieties of English**

Nonstandard English (Limited use)	Informal English (Limited use)	General English (Unlimited use)
Chiefly spoken Language not much touched by school instruction; often conspicuously local; not appropriate for public affairs or for use by educated people	*More often spoken than written* Speaking and writing of educated people in informal situations; often includes shop-talk or slang and some localisms	*Both spoken and written* Speaking and writing of educated people in their private or public affairs
Typical uses Conversations of many people at home, with friends, on the job Representations of this speech in stories, plays, movies, comic strips, on radio and television	*Typical uses* Casual conversation Letters between intimates; diaries, personal writing; writing close to popular speech, as in fiction and some newspaper columns	*Typical uses* Conversation; talks to general audiences Most business letters and advertising News and feature stories, newspaper columns Magazine articles and books on subjects of general interest Most fiction and other literature for general circulation

SOURCE: Porter G. Perrin, *Writer's Guide and Index to English,* 3d ed., Scott, Foresman and Company, Chicago, 1959, pp. 18–19. Copyright © 1959 by Scott, Foresman and Company.

The teacher's language

The most effective teacher of English may well be he who is master of a range of varieties of usage and able to change easily from clear, informal standard into a vigorous colloquial speech and even now and then (for special effect) into the slang or argot of the young. Such teachers break the stereotype of the precise, correct speech of the English teacher without lessening respect

Formal English (Limited use)	Comments	
More often written than spoken	1. Informal, General, and Formal English together make up Standard English.	"gobbledygook") may be regarded as the extreme of Standard English.
Speaking and writing for somewhat restricted groups in formal situations	2. The varieties are to be thought of as shading into each other—not as sharply defined and mutually exclusive. A passage might be regarded as Informal, for instance, if it had several conspicuous traits characteristic of that variety even though the greater part of the passage was in General English.	5. The varieties are characterized by some differences in word forms, in pronunciation, in vocabulary, in grammatical constructions, and by the avoidance of certain locutions (as Standard English avoids double negatives). The chief differences, and the easiest to discuss, are in vocabulary.
Typical uses Addresses and lectures to special audiences		
Some editorials and business writing		
Literature of somewhat limited circulation: essays and criticisms, much poetry, some fiction		
Academic writing: reference works, dissertations, term papers, some textbooks	3. Usage is said to be *divided* when choices exist between two usages in General English, both of which are in good standing (for example, the spellings *catalog* or *catalogue*, or a comma or no comma before the *and* of the last item in a series).	6. Labeling a usage as belonging to any one of the varieties is meant to indicate that it is characteristically used as the description of that variety suggests, that its connotation comes from this use, and that it is not characteristic of another variety. Such labeling is not intended to prevent a word's use under other conditions but does suggest that it may be conspicuous in another variety and that its connotation should be intended.
Scientific and technical reports		
Books and articles dealing with special subjects for professional groups and experts		
	4. *Slovenly* (impoverished speech, often including obscenity and profanity) may be regarded as the extreme of Nonstandard, and *Stilted* (pretentious and unnecessarily heavy speech or writing—	

for the range and nuances of English that should be the pattern for youth. When one asks students whose speech they admire, they invariably cite teachers such as these. English teachers and administrators who believe in the desirability of one narrow range of "correct" speech for English teachers forget the richness of American colloquial speech and the poetry of much folk usage. The teacher who is himself able to move from formal to informal or colloquial speech as the occasion warrants sets a desirable model for the young people who hear him.

Student activities and assignments[21]

The student activities suggested here are designed to help students develop sensitivity to usage, awareness of the varieties and purposes of language, and discrimination about their own choices of words.

Build respect for good usage

. . . Let students write or talk about their favorite radio or television news announcer and compare his usage with that of other announcers.

. . . Let students analyze the usage of characters in current television serials, and discuss the ways in which it reflects occupation, social and economic status, education.

. . . Encourage students to form a habit of listening to the usage of announcers on the major networks, to top-flight news analysts, and actors in television and radio, and to the speeches, programs, or recordings of those who are known for their command of the language: Adlai Stevenson, the late President Kennedy, the late Edward R. Murrow, Walter Cronkite.

. . . Especially useful is practice in telling anecdotes in which conversation is quoted in order to improve on the substandard "he says" and "she says to me."

Developing an awareness of varieties of usage

. . . Ask students to write an account of a high school social, sports, or school activity in three different levels of usage. Specify the audience in each case: small sister, college friend, elderly relative.

. . . Let students write in class in answer to the following questions: When is your English most relaxed? Most formal? When do you choose words and connotations most carefully? When do you make a special attempt to speak "down" or "up" to someone (that is, using simple, formal, or literary language).

. . . Students may list usages they would include under each of these levels of usage: Blue-jeans English; shirt-sleeve English; high-heels English.

. . . The class may compile their own list of "barbarisms" or expressions, words, and usage they particularly object to, and discuss why. These may include such expressions as "man," " 'bye now," "like man," "like a cigarette should," or others.

. . . Assign these topics for papers: Dialect differences in the speech of someone I know (family, friend, teacher); the semantics of our family; "home" English versus "school" English; the kind of English I would like to use; I have modeled my speech on . . . ; language which has kept me out of something; language which has helped me to get into something; dialect differences between two parts of the country in which I have lived.

[21] The discussion of evaluation of mastery of language usage, grammar, and mechanics is included at the end of Chap. 8.

. . . Paired practice is helpful to many students who have trouble with substandard usages. Students whose own usage is well established may be encouraged to work with those students who have trouble with a particular problem: verb tense, agreement of subject and predicate, pronoun with antecedent, and others. Work sheets, workbooks, or grammar handbooks may provide exercises for review, and the tutor may ask the student to respond orally with the approved (standard) form. When the tutor can certify that his student has mastered the form being taught, he may refer him to the teacher, who will test him for mastery of these usage problems.

. . . Approach the teaching of usage through common sense and meaning. In the sentence "(She, Her) and Mrs. Perkins bake the best cookies in town," tell students to choose the form they would use with one subject alone: "She bakes," not "her bakes." It is usually more effective to teach such problems through meaning and common sense than through the roundabout way of case, number, and definition.

. . . Many teachers keep files with folders of work sheets on usage practice. Students learning to type may copy some of these exercises or drill questions on dittoes and file them in folders where they are accessible for oral practice for those who need them.

. . . Senior high school students may make a study of slang from one of the points of view suggested in one of the books on the subject (Eric Partridge, *Slang Today and Yesterday*, The Macmillan Company, New York, 1934; Lester V. Berrey and Melvin Van den Bark, *American Thesaurus of Slang: A Complete Reference Book of Colloquial Speech*, 2d ed., Thomas Y. Crowell Company, 1953, or the chapter on slang in H. L. Mencken's Supplement II, *The American Language*, Alfred A. Knopf, Inc., New York, 1948).

Some of the suggested areas for study are the slang of different groups: cockney, public house, workmen, radiomen, commerce, publicity, journalism, theater, sports and games, circus life, sailors, soldiers, Yiddish, cant, and others. (See the suggested categories in Partridge.) Another may be a study of the purposes of slang (employed for such reasons as "high spirits, . . . belonging to a trade, . . . social set, class; . . . to be novel, different" [22]).

. . . Students may study dialect differences in American regional speech through one of the new linguistic geographies available.[23] One junior high school class studying dialect differences in pronunciation wrote its own short anecdotes using a list of test words for pronunciation, chose the best of their own stories, recorded them on tape, and exchanged the tapes with students in a school in Texas which had undertaken the same project.[24]

[22] Eric Partridge, *Slang Today and Yesterday*, The Macmillan Company, N. Y., 1934, p. 6.
[23] Reference materials include Hans Kurath, *Handbook of the Linguistic Geography of New England*, American Council of Learned Societies, Washington, D.C., 1954; and *A Word Geography of the Eastern United States*, chap. 3, Studies in American English I, The University of Michigan Press, Ann Arbor, Mich., 1949, by the same author.
[24] Students at Long Lots Junior High School, Westport, Conn. See also Evelyn Gott, "Teaching Regional Dialects in Junior High School," *English Journal*, vol. 53, May, 1964, pp. 342–363.

. . . Students studying American literature may choose to study regional speech as recorded by an American author: Sinclair Lewis, Jesse Stuart, Harper Lee, William Faulkner, Willa Cather, Eudora Welty, Ring Lardner, Mark Twain, Sarah Orne Jewett, Hamlin Garland, John Steinbeck, and others.

. . . The relationship between language and status may be explored by senior high school students. Some may wish to read Nancy Mitford's *Noblesse Oblige*,[25] with its discussion of "U" and "non-U" speech, and the accompanying articles on the subject. The students might make up their own glossary of language as an index to class (for instance the pronunciation of *vase, aunt,* or other test words.)

. . . Junior high school students may make up their own glossaries or dictionaries of words in special areas: teen-age slang, sports slang, the slang of dating, school life, college life, army, navy, marine or air-force slang. Their examples may illustrate uses of language (from slang to colloquial) to indicate status or group membership.

. . . Other exercises to develop the student's ear for language, and his awareness of its varieties, can be found in some of the newer language texts, and in some of the high school and college English textbooks suggested in the bibliography.

Emphasize oral practice

. . . Students may make up oral stories for practice in avoiding double negatives. Example: "X went on a camping trip with his brother and his father. When they got to the camp site, they found that they *didn't have any* . . ." (Students may add examples using the full pattern *they didn't have any* _____.)

. . . During role playing of conversations of characters in short stories and other situations, students may pay particular attention to usage. The listeners may observe inappropriate language and discuss whether the level of usage is out of place in the situation in which it is spoken or for the character portrayed.

. . . Focus attention for one week on one particular problem, such as the usage of the six commonest irregular verbs: *do, come, run, see, go, give.* Let students practice the right forms by saying or reading sentences aloud or by making up impromptu stories in which they are used.

. . . Ask students to read themes aloud in small groups, paying particular attention to usage problems: agreement of subject and predicate, accurate use of verb forms and objects of prepositions.

. . . Let students listen to tape recordings of a class discussion, taking notes on usage which could be improved, and discussing them in class.

. . . Students may make up sentences using the various tenses of commonly misused irregular verbs, such as the thirteen similar verbs having past

[25] *Noblesse Oblige: An Enquiry into the Identifiable Characteristics of the English Aristocracy,* Harper & Row, Publishers, Incorporated, New York, 1956.

participles ending in *n* or *en: break, drive, eat, fall, fly, give, grow, know, see, speak, take, throw, write.* Grouping the irregular verbs so that students practice those with similar forms at one time and having them notice the differences between the standard and substandard forms helps through association of those with similar forms.

Selected bibliography

Harold B. Allen (ed.), *Readings in Applied English Linguistics,* Appleton-Century-Crofts, Inc., New York, 1958, part 4. (Paperback.)

Margaret M. Bryant, *Current American Usage,* Funk & Wagnalls Company, New York, 1962.

David A. Conlin and George R. Herman, *Modern Grammar and Composition,* American Book Company, New York, 1965 (grades 9–12).

Richard Corbin et al., *A Guide to Modern English Series,* Scott, Foresman and Company, Chicago, 1960–1963 (grades 9–12).

Leonard Dean and Kenneth G. Wilson (eds.), *Essays on Language and Usage,* Oxford University Press, Fair Lawn, N.J., 1963, part 4. (Paperback.)

Bergen Evans and Cornelia Evans, *A Dictionary of Contemporary American Usage,* Random House, Inc., New York, 1957.

Ruth I. Golden, *Improving Patterns of Language Usage,* Wayne State University Press, Detroit, 1960.

Lou La Brant et al., *Your Language Series,* McGraw-Hill Book Company, New York, 1956–1962 (grades 7–12).

Charlton M. Laird and Robert M. Gorrell (eds.), *English as Language: Backgrounds, Development, Usage,* Harcourt, Brace & World, Inc., New York, 1961.

Jean Malmstrom and Annabel Ashley, *Dialects—U.S.A.,* NCTE, Champaign, Ill., 1963.

Margaret Nicholson, *A Dictionary of American-English Usage,* Oxford University Press, Fair Lawn, N.J., 1957. (Paper: New American Library of World Literature, Inc., New York, 1958.)

Thomas C. Pollock et al., *Macmillan English Series,* 2d rev. ed., The Macmillan Company, New York, 1964 (grades 9–12).

Robert C. Pooley, *Teaching English Usage,* Appleton-Century-Crofts, Inc., New York, 1946.

Neil Postman et al., *Discovering Your Language,* Holt, Rinehart and Winston, Inc., New York, 1963 (junior high school level).

James Sledd and Wilma Ebbitt, *Dictionaries and THAT Dictionary,* Scott Foresman and Company, Chicago, 1962. Collects many of the most important articles representing the controversy over usage on the appearance of Webster's *Third New International Dictionary.*

Louis Zahner et al., *The English Language* Series, Harcourt, Brace & World, Inc., New York, 1962 (grades 9–12).

CHAPTER 8   So long as the language lives the nation lives too.

CZECH PROVERB

Mastery of language: the study of grammar, punctuation, and spelling

The second major phase of the student's mastery of language is his study of the structure of English. Chapter 7 has shown how he gains familiarity with the varieties of English, and gains command of standard English through observation and practice. The present chapter is concerned with the analysis of language provided by the new grammars of English, and with the insights they supply teacher and student for the study of the language.

Since there is little doubt that the language program in schools will continue to explore and use the new research in grammar, there is little profit in repeating here methods of teaching traditional grammar, already admirably handled in earlier texts. Beginning teachers, those planning to start programs in linguistic grammar, and those who wish to keep abreast of new developments in their field will want to explore some of the ways in which teachers have experimented in classrooms with the new concepts and materials.[1]

Although few textbooks in linguistics for high school students are available at present, recent texts and revisions of older handbooks on grammar and usage are including linguistic approaches, and new books are on the way. Courses, workshops, and summer language institutes for teachers of English

[1] See Chap. 16 for a discussion of national recommendations that all teachers of English acquire such preparation.

are becoming available in many communities for teachers who want to learn the new techniques. Others have pioneered by using a text with the students in a learn-as-you-go process. Although more background is desirable, many of the teachers now using the new methods have learned them in this way. Those who start their students on the road to discovering language find themselves caught up in the fascination of its study and continue to explore the wealth of materials now available which can reveal to us the workings of the language we speak and write.

The English teacher needs to be familiar with the following terms:

Grammar is the study of the way a language works. It includes two main branches: morphology and syntax; linguists would add a third, phonology.

Morphology is the study of the changes in form of words and the meanings of these changes: for instance, the addition of *s* to form the plural of most English nouns or the *-ed* suffix indicating past tense of verbs. The minimal meaningful units in the language are called *morphemes.*

Syntax is the study of the order of words in meaningful discourse, and of the relationships between word order and meaning. It includes the study of varieties of sentence structure, including the modification and subordination of words and phrases.

Phonology is the study of the sounds of a language, of the stresses, pauses, rising and falling intonations, and the melody of speech. The significant units of speech sound are called *phonemes.*

Traditional grammar. The grammar taught in schools is still, in most of the country, traditional (often called formal) grammar; that is, an analysis of the language according to classifications and definitions based on Latin grammar and formulated in the eighteenth century or earlier by writers of handbooks attempting to offer a linguistic leg up the social ladder to members of a rising middle class. Modern grammarians have pointed out that some of the rules and definitions sprang from the minds of the writers rather than from a systematic observation of the language.

Traditional grammar is largely *prescriptive:* it presents rules and offers advice as to how things should be said, or words should be used. The new grammars are *descriptive:* they formulate generalizations about language as it is used, and describe the way it works.

The program in grammar

Traditional grammar has been taught in the schools in two ways. Such "formal" grammar offers the students rules and definitions to learn, and sentences to analyze according to these rules. More recently, schools have taught "functional grammar," in which the emphasis for the student is not on learning the rules, but on practicing approved forms in his speaking and writing. Traditional grammar presents classifications and definitions based on meaning; the new grammars present analyses based on the structure of English sentences.

The "new" grammars

The major forces shaping language study today are the systems of grammar formulated by the structural linguists and, more recently, by the generative or transformational grammarians. Structural grammar attempts to analyze the living spoken language to determine the basic structures of English sentences, the stress and intonation patterns which signal meaning, and the words which act as markers or signals to indicate parts of speech (*the* before a noun, *was* or *have* before a verb). Generative grammar seems to have even more in common with traditional grammar than that of the structuralists; it suggests that English consists of two kinds of sentences: basic or simple ("kernel") sentences and transformations of these sentences. From the kernel sentences, the infinite variety of complicated sentences which we use in English can be generated.

Generative grammarians argue that if preschool children of even limited intelligence can unconsciously learn to generate thousands of new sentences based on the early sentence structures they have learned, there must be an underlying process which can be explained. The basic sentences and transformations are suggested as the result of such a process which goes on in the native speaker of a language. The transformation of a basic sentence pattern—subject, verb, object—into the passive voice results from such a process: *the dog bit the man* into *the man was bitten by the dog.* Whatever the type of analysis proposed, the new grammars attempt to offer a clearer and more precise description of the operation of the language.

Those today who look for new materials and methods in the teaching of grammar are understandably reluctant to scrap the old ways before they know what the new grammar offers. However, teachers who have adapted new methods and materials to the programs of grammar now being taught in schools believe that much of the old may be retained and blended with the new. Some use the most workable parts of the three systems: the traditional approach, structural linguistics, and generative grammar.

Certainly, as many teachers have shown, we can draw from the new methods much that can be helpful without seriously contradicting what students have learned previously about grammar, or confusing students who may move on to study more traditional grammar. The shift to a linguistic point of view about grammar can be accomplished without learning an entirely new vocabulary; some books use many traditional terms. Students who have learned traditional grammar find the linguistic approach a new way of looking at the grammar with which they are already familiar. Some understand for the first time the way the language works. For many, the study of grammar, formerly codified, formal, and little related to the use of words in live language, becomes a lively, fascinating study, sensitizing them to the language they speak and arousing a curiosity about it which will endure as a lifetime habit. New language curricula being prepared for use in many secondary schools today make use of all three of these grammars. The three have much in common, and there is overlapping at many points.

Program into practice

The content of the program in grammar was determined for many years by the assumption that students needed to learn the rules of traditional grammar in order to learn to write and in order to pass college entrance examinations. An analysis of college placement tests in English made as long ago as 1936 showed that 96 per cent of the items dealt with usage exclusively, that 75 per cent of the tests did not contain any technical grammar, and that colleges were concerned with the student's ability to use language correctly and effectively rather than with his mastery of grammatical terminology or his ability to classify forms.[2]

The assumption that a knowledge of formal grammar helped students to write better has also been dismissed as a valid reason for its emphasis in the English program. (See the discussion in Chapter 6, page 131.) Furthermore, according to studies of what colleges expect of students, the following grammatical skills are important: the ability to write full sentences rather than fragments; the ability to construct sentences with more than one clause and to exhibit control over coordinate and subordinate clauses; acquaintance with current usage in punctuation; an elementary knowledge of grammar (either traditional or structural); acquaintance with educated usage; awareness of varying American speech communities rather than insistence on textbook standards of usage.[3]

Furthermore, research has shown that students who study the problems of sentence structure from the standpoint of clear, effective expression of thought performed better on tests of grammar and sentence structure than did those students who were taught to approach such problems through grammatical definition.[4] One study using three different methods of teaching

[2] Dora V. Smith and Constance McCullough, "An Analysis of the Content of Placement Tests in Freshman English Used by One Hundred and Thirty Colleges and Universities," *English Journal*, vol. 25, January, 1936, pp. 17–25. Twenty years later, a repetition of the same test showed similar results and disposed of the notion that mastery of formal grammar is necessary for college entrance: ". . . it may be stated confidently that colleges no longer are interested in whether an entering student knows technical grammatical terminology, punctuation rules, evanescent pronunciations, or the like, but rather colleges are concerned with proof that a student can actually *use* language to good effect." (Donald M. Litsey, "Trends in College Placement Tests in Freshman English," *English Journal*, vol. 45, May, 1956, p. 250).
[3] Summarized from "High School Preparation for College English in Ohio," *English Association of Ohio Bulletin*, vol. 4, June, 1963. (Unpaged reprint.)
[4] Ellen Frogner, "Grammar Approach versus Thought Approach in Teaching Sentence Structure," *English Journal*, vol. 28, September, 1939, pp. 518–526.

sentence structure found that the method which related instruction to the actual errors students made in their compositions got results in one-third of the time spent on the other two methods—all using the thought approach.[5]

Time may be saved for writing by eliminating the long weeks often spent in the classroom in teaching students to diagram sentences. Current summaries of research on the teaching of diagramming have shown that "sentence structure is taught as effectively by the composition method as it is by the diagramming of sentences," and that diagramming is a sterile skill.[6]

All students can, to some degree, understand the nature and structure of the language they speak. Traditional grammar, with its many generalizations, definitions, and abstractions, posed almost insuperable difficulties for the child of low or average intelligence. Both structural and transformational grammar demand that the student experiment with the parts of language to see how they work, and thus are not beyond the capacity of most students in our schools. The major areas of grammar which the student needs to explore are (1) the word classes (parts of speech); (2) the basic sentence patterns and syntactical structures; (3) the operations of coordination, subordination, and modification; (4) the intonation patterns, pauses, and stresses which operate as a signal system in English; and (5) the "mechanics" of transcribing speech into writing: punctuation and spelling.[7] Dictionary study, an essential tool for the study of the language, has been treated in Chapter 5, but some additional suggestions are given in the exercises of this chapter.

The words of English: locating parts of speech

As most teachers know, it is quite possible for a child who has been through "grammar review of parts of speech" every year for six years to be unable to tell a noun from a verb when he arrives in the twelfth grade. Part of the difficulty is in the process of definition. "The noun is the name of a person, place, or thing," does not really help a student locate a noun in discourse. Is *beauty* a thing? Is *love?* Is *justice?* The addition of *quality* to the definition does not help the young learner to any great extent. To many young people, the *thing* talked about in *The boy was running away* would be *running away,* and not *boy.*

[5] Silvy Kraus, "A Comparison of Three Methods of Teaching Sentence Structure," *English Journal,* vol. 46, May, 1957, pp. 275–281.

[6] See studies summarized in Ingrid M. Strom, "Research in Grammar and Usage and Its Implications for Teaching Writing," *Bulletin of the School of Education,* Indiana University, vol. 36, September, 1960, p. 9.

[7] The treatment of grammar in this chapter is derived from and patterned closely after the presentation in the two texts for high schools by Paul Roberts: *Patterns of English* (1956) and *English Sentences* (1962), Harcourt, Brace & World, Inc., New York. It makes no attempt to offer an original presentation, but is intended to present to teachers some of the highlights of structural and transformational grammar now being used experimentally in many schools. The teacher will want to read extensively and intensively in the books recommended at the end of the chapter to gain a working understanding of the new grammar.

Nouns.   The student of the new grammar locates nouns, verbs, adjectives, and other parts of speech, not by definitions, but by using an analogical test. He finds that nouns are words like *orange, truth, pencil,* or *book;* they are words which occur after *the* or *an* and fit into a test blank such as *He wanted the* ———; *She likes* ———. Students may quickly fill in such frames with a list of words which function as nouns in these frames:

He wanted the (*book, glove, ball, food, orange, truth*).

She likes (*gravy, boys, lessons, beauty*). Words like *dancing, walking,* and *shouting* are also possible choices for the latter.

If the word can be changed to indicate plurality or possession, it is a noun: *balls, boys', girls, ladies'.*

Verbs.   The student learns that verbs are words that work like *talk, go, move,* or *think* in these test frames: *They* ———; *They* ——— *often;* or *The people* ——— *it* (*love, answer, notice, like, want, serve*). Some words can be used in either frame: *They* (*love, walk, grow,* or *answer*); *The people* (*love, walk, grow,* or *answer*) *it.* These frames provide a simple test for locating transitive and intransitive verbs. A second test is inflection. If the word changes from past to present or adds *s* when used with *it, he,* or *she* it is a verb.[8]

Other kinds of verbs which work or pattern in such frames as *The cake* ——— *good; The girl* ——— *pretty;* or *The book* ——— *interesting* are linking verbs. Common ones are the forms of *to be—am, is, was, were, are—*and others which may be followed by adjectives or nouns in the complement: *appear, become, feel, grow, look, remain, smell, sound, seem, taste.* When such verbs occur before adjectives, they are linking verbs; when they pattern with adverbs, they are nonlinking (intransitive). Such verbs are often followed by noun complements: *The boy is my brother; he is my teacher; John is my friend.*

Adjectives.   An adjective is a word that behaves like *lovely, sad, thoughtful,* in such positions as these: *They were very* ———; *He appeared* ———; *They saw a very* ——— *child.* The final test for adjectives is whether they pattern with the intensifier *very.* We do not say *a very soon girl,* but we say *a very beautiful girl.*

Adverbs.   An adverb is a word that behaves like *down, often,* or *happily: She danced* ———; *He ran* ———. (Words like *gaily, hopefully, swiftly, gracefully, in, up,* or *over* may thus be adverbs.)

Some linguists call these word groups the four *form classes.* They are open classes of words—we keep coining new nouns, verbs, adjectives, and adverbs, and words which began as one part of speech may function in any one of the other form classes.

Structure or function words

Functioning differently from the expandable form classes are the groups of words the linguist calls *structure* or *function words*—those which act as

---

[8] The exceptions are *to be* and the modals (see list on p. 188).

signals or markers of nouns and verbs. Among these classes are the determiners, serving as markers of nouns and pronouns, and the auxiliaries, serving as markers of verbs. Intensifiers (markers of adjectives and adverbs), prepositions, conjunctions, and subordinating words also belong to the structure-word class. Students learn that structure words belong to closed classes. We do not invent new prepositions or conjunctions.

Determiners.   The structure words called *determiners* serve as markers of nouns. The student may easily recognize in his daily language that words like *the* or *an* signal the advent of a noun. The list of determiners includes *the, a, an, every, each, this, that, these, those, my, our, your, their, his, her, its, no, both, some, many, much, few, several, any, all, most, more, either, neither, one, two, three, four.*

To become familiar with this concept, students may practice using determiners from the list in sentences like these: ——— *girls rode* ——— *bicycles;* ——— *dogs ate* ——— *sausages rapidly; mother did* ——— *marketing in* ——— *store,* and so on. Next, they may try filling in sentences where determiners have been used and nouns left out such as: *The* ——— *showed his* ——— *a* ———.

Pronouns.   Pronouns are sometimes treated as a subclass of nouns, and sometimes as structure words. Teachers develop the concept of the pronoun by calling attention to the behavior of proper nouns, which ordinarily do not pattern with determiners: *Mount Everest* (not *the Mount Everest*), *New York City* (not *the New York City*), and *Bill* or *Mary* (not *the Bill* or *the Mary*). Pronouns include a group of words which pattern without determiners almost exactly as proper nouns do. The student can experiment by interchanging pronouns with proper nouns in numerous sentences to see how they work in noun positions in the sentence: *that girl is beautiful* (common noun); *Alice is beautiful* (proper noun); *she is beautiful* (pronoun). The teacher will have to point out, too, that some words can occur as both determiner and pronoun: *these, those, this, that, all, any, his, her,* and others.[9]

Auxiliaries.   A second large group of function words, the *auxiliaries,* act as verb markers and signal the coming of a verb in the sentence. Auxiliaries like *do, be, have,* and *can* act as verbs also and only two—*be* and *have*—pattern with the past forms of the verb. The auxiliaries called *modals* constitute a special group of verbs which do not take the inflections *-ing* or *-s: shall, will, can, may, should, would, could, might, must, dare, need,* and *ought. Dare* and *need* also function as auxiliaries.

The purpose of modals is to indicate moods, emotions, and attitudes toward happenings. This group of words provides part of the wide range of expression in English verbs: I *must* go to work; I *ought* to go to work; I *might*

---

[9] Roberts, *Patterns of English,* pp. 37–38. Roberts calls attention to the fact that though most books treat pronoun pairs like *my-mine* together, they pattern quite differently. *My* works like *the; mine* patterns like *I* or *me* or *Jack.*

go to work; I *may* go to work; I *could* go to work; I *can* go to work; I *will* go to work; I *should* go to work.

Intensifiers.   *Intensifiers* such as *very, rather, quite,* and *somewhat* pattern with adjectives and adverbs. Thus in the frame *He was very* ———; or *He walked very* ———; we can fill in *interesting, wonderful, handsome,* or *honest* for the first frame, and *slowly, rapidly, mincingly,* or *vigorously,* for the second.

Prepositions.   Another group of words signaling the coming of a noun in the sentence is the *prepositions.* They commonly introduce prepositional phrases and function as noun or verb modifiers. Nine prepositions are used in 92 per cent of all phrases with prepositions; in order of frequency of use they are *of, in, to, for, at, on, from, with,* and *by.*[10]

Conjunctions.   The system of conjunctions (linking words) serves to connect or join words and word groups. Coordinating conjunctions linking equal grammatical units include *and, but, yet, nor, or, for, so* and pairs such as *either . . . or, both . . . and.*

Subordinators.   The system of linking words which commonly joins subject-predicate word groups includes those commonly called relative pronouns (*who, which, what, that, whoever, whichever, whatever*), and basic subordinating conjunctions (*after, although, as, as if, because, before, how, if, since, that, unless, until, when, whenever, where, wherever, whether, while*). This basic group of function words links an independent subject-predicate word group to a dependent (subordinate) subject-predicate word group.

Lexical and structural meanings

The structure words discussed above are "empty words." They have little meaning in themselves, but act as useful signals to clarify the structure of the sentence and to indicate the form classes.

Teachers use two devices to illustrate the function of structure words in the language and to show the differences between lexical (or dictionary) and structural meanings. As students learn that many words can belong to two or more form classes, they recognize the semantic difficulties presented by ambiguous headline or "telegram" word groups.[11] *Cook ducks fast* may refer to the process of cooking or ducking. The meaning is clarified by the addition of words that mark either nouns or verbs: *the cook ducks very fast; the cook will duck fast, cook those ducks fast.* In each case, structure or function words indicate the form class of words and mark the structural pattern of the sentence. (Let students try such often-used examples as *ship sails today, army plans move, slum houses poor, bank gains fast, time flies, plan moves slowly,* and others.

---

[10] Verna Newsome, *Structural Linguistics in the Classroom,* The University of Wisconsin Press, Madison, Wis., 1961, p. 31.

[11] See discussion of headline words in Roberts, *Patterns of English,* chap. 2.

A second kind of teaching device might be called the "Jabberwocky" test. Lewis Carroll's poem has been frequently used as an instructive example of the way structural signals operate in a sentence to indicate the form classes without reference to meaning.[12] Even students who have never heard of structural linguistics can locate the nouns and verbs and tell which words are adjectives and adverbs; they will note that *toves* must be things or nouns, that *gyre* and *gimble* must be verbs (because of the auxiliary *did*), that *mimsy* and *slithy* are adjectives, and *borogroves* is a noun.

Their primary language learning stands them in unconscious stead as they recognize *the* as a noun marker, *did* as a verb marker, *mimsy were the borogroves* as an inversion of the common linking-verb pattern: *the borogroves were mimsy.* They recognize these not by lexical meanings (we don't know what *borogroves* are) but by the structural signals. *Outgrabe* is something *mome raths* do, therefore a verb. *Mimsy* and *slithy* seem to be adjectives by virtue of position and the *y* suffix (similar to *pretty, happy,* and *jaunty*).

Both teachers and students can invent sentences in which the form classes are filled with nonsense words and students may be asked to construct several different sentences on each pattern. Some examples follow.

The peebles are corkling arkily on the pollygish may yield such varied meanings as the following:

The girls are walking happily on the boardwalk, or
The cats are yowling unmelodiously on the fence, or
The mothers are gathering angrily on the schoolgrounds, or
The children are wandering aimlessly on the beach.

The structural patterns of these sentences are the same; the lexical meanings are quite different. As we have seen, the form words without the structural signals communicate meanings (as they do in headlines), even though at times those meanings may be ambiguous, as in *army demands change.* A sentence with no form words at all communicates nothing; it simply provides a frame into which the lexical meanings may be poured:

The ———— are ————ing on the ————.

Basic sentence patterns

Although linguists differ as to the number of patterns which can be called "basic," the notion that certain structures or patterns do recur with great frequency and that innumerable sentences can be modeled on these patterns is common to both structural and generative grammars.

Working with patterns can be an important part of language study throughout the junior and senior high school years. Once students understand the form classes and the basic function words, they can go on to construct a rich variety of syntactical structures on these models.

---

[12] See Donald A. Lloyd and Harry Warfel, *American English in Its Cultural Setting,* Alfred A. Knopf, Inc., New York, 1956, p. 98.

Pattern 1. The first, irreducible basic sentence pattern is that of subject-predicate or noun-verb: *boys run, dogs bark, the child cried, birds fly.* The student may be reminded that these are the basic kinds of sentences to the child learning the language, whose first sentences are likely to be *baby go, daddy come,* or *doggie bite.* The noun plus verb combination may include a determiner (D) before the noun and an adverb: *the boy runs fast* or *the dog barked fiercely.* The words which do not always occur in the pattern are put in parentheses: (D)LV(ADV). The basic formula for Pattern 1 is NV.

Pattern 2. Pattern 2 may be expressed symbolically as $N_1V_tN_2$. The subject-predicate-object (or noun-transitive verb-noun) pattern, perhaps one of the most widely used in English, is another basic structure. N_1 and N_2 mean that the first noun in the pattern is different from the second.

N_1	V_t	N_2
John	*hit*	*Jack.*
Jane	*studies*	*Latin.*
Susie	*dates*	*boys.*
The cat	*caught*	*mice.*

Through filling in these patterns with new sets of nouns and verbs, students learn inductively the functional differences between intransitive and transitive verbs. Some verbs can be used in both patterns: *birds fly* (Pattern 1) or *men fly planes* (Pattern 2); some only in Pattern 1 (*hens sit*) or in Pattern 2 (*she fries potatoes*). By observing which verbs work in one pattern only and which work in both, students can grasp the concept of the intransitive verb.

Patterns 3 and 4. The third and fourth most frequently used patterns in English involve linking verbs. Teachers have found that the concept of the linking verb, often very difficult for students to grasp, can be observed in practice with these two patterns: noun-linking verb-adjective, and noun-linking verb-noun.

Pattern 3:

N	LV	A_j
Games	*are*	*interesting.*
Roses	*smell*	*sweet.*
Jane	*is*	*studious.*

Pattern 4:

N_1	LV	N_2
Jane	*is my*	*sister (friend, supervisor, aunt).*
Miss X	*is my*	*teacher (sister, tutor, counselor, friend).*
The building	*was a*	*church (college, factory, tenement).*
My dog	*is a*	*collie (mongrel, show dog, rover).*

Pattern 5. A fifth pattern uses a transitive verb and two objects, the first called indirect and the second direct (or inner complement and outer complement):

(D)N₁	Vₜ	N₂	(D)N₃
He	*gave*	*Jane*	*the letter.*
Mother	*bought*	*David*	*a car.*
The roses	*gave*	*me*	*hay fever.*

Several other patterns are suggested in the discussions of basic patterns in various books, but most of these are less frequent in use and involve small classes of verbs such as the linking verbs *seem, become, remain.* The students who are ready for some of the less frequent patterns may look for them in the texts suggested in the bibliography. For most students, mastery of these five patterns and practice in expanding and subordinating them will provide ample opportunity to develop skill in using the language in everyday speech and writing.

Expanding sentence patterns

Once the student has grasped the essential elements of the first five basic sentence patterns, he is ready for continued practice in expanding patterns through the addition of words and groups of words which add to, but do not change, the basic structure of the pattern. He learns that the two chief methods in English of expanding and adding complexity to simple statements are compounding and modification. Subordination provides another way of modification by adding ideas of lesser importance than the main pattern.

Compounding. The writer or speaker many compound elements of the sentence in several ways.

Compounding subjects:

birds fly . . . birds and bees fly . . . birds, bees, and mosquitoes fly

Compounding predicates:

birds fly . . . birds fly and sing . . . birds fly, sing, and build nests

Compounding objects:

John studies mathematics . . . John studies mathematics and science . . . John studies mathematics, science, and history.

John studies history, science, and mathematics; reads poetry and drama; and enjoys football and basketball.

Jane takes care of the baby, sweeps the floor, and gets dinner.

Compounding whole sentences:

John studies history, science and mathematics, but Jim enjoys football and basketball.

Our class won the pennant for softball, but the seniors defeated the juniors in the basketball tournament.

Predicates can be expanded by adding modals—*shall, will, can, may, must, should, would, could, might*—as in these examples:

Pattern 1: *babies cry; babies must cry.*
Pattern 2: *the boy shot a bear; the boy might shoot a bear.*
Pattern 3: *the girls are pretty; the girls could be pretty.*

Modals may be added in any of the patterns. Forms of the verb *be* may be added to expand a pattern: a form of the verb *be* precedes the verb, and the verb takes the present participle form:

Judy dates boys.   *Judy is dating boys.*
They go tomorrow.   *They are going tomorrow.*

Although the possible patterns of verb expansion are too numerous and complex for elaboration, the teacher can encourage students to experiment with modals, forms of *be* (plus *-ing*), or *have* plus *-en* which may produce verb clusters (the verb plus its auxiliaries) like:

The girls	*may have been walking*	*too long.*
	could have been walking	*too long.*
	will have been walking	*too long.*

Modification.   The second basic method of expansion is modification. Students may begin expanding patterns through the simple process of adding word modifiers—adjectives, adverbs, determiners (*a, the*), and intensifiers (*very, rather*), and proceed to add prepositional phrases, participial and infinitive phrases, appositives, and dependent clauses.

The noun with its modifiers is called a *noun cluster.* When students have become familiar with the modifiers which may precede a noun, they may work with noun clusters to see how such a unit may be used as various parts of the sentence: subject, object, or complement. Practice in using clusters in different sentence positions helps develop a sense of the flexibility of sentence structures in variable positions which is an essential characteristic of English. For instance, they may experiment with patterns like these:

The three pretty girls were walking home.

He happened to see *three pretty girls.*

He noticed that *three pretty girls* were absent.

Prepositional phrases, or the structures often called *P groups,* are among the most common word groups used for modification and expansion of sentences. Students may experiment with these in sentences to see how they function as adverbs and adjectives and observe the relations of these groups to the words they modify.

Subordination.   Among the structures frequently modifying noun headwords[13] are the relative clauses, beginning with *who, which,* or *that.* Students

---

[13] *Headword:* the term used by linguists to denote "that which is modified." Roberts uses the term S *group* to denote subordinate clauses.

may learn to expand sentences by adding clause modifiers after the noun headword:

The boy   who was in my class   *broke his leg.*
　　　　　　⎵⎵⎵⎵⎵⎵⎵⎵⎵⎵⎵⎵⎵⎵⎵⎵
　　　　　　　　　S group

The test   which was given in the school auditorium   *was difficult.*
　　　　　⎵⎵⎵⎵⎵⎵⎵⎵⎵⎵⎵⎵⎵⎵⎵⎵⎵⎵⎵⎵⎵⎵⎵⎵⎵⎵
　　　　　　　　　　　　　S group

The school   that wins the local basketball championship   *gets to*
play games out of state.
　　　　　　　　　　　　S group

Clauses may also modify the verb headword:

When we reached the school   *the bell had already rung.*
⎵⎵⎵⎵⎵⎵⎵⎵⎵⎵⎵⎵⎵⎵⎵⎵⎵⎵⎵⎵
　　　　　S group

We were greatly puzzled   for he had never behaved like this before.
　　　　　　　　　　⎵⎵⎵⎵⎵⎵⎵⎵⎵⎵⎵⎵⎵⎵⎵⎵⎵⎵⎵⎵⎵⎵⎵
　　　　　　　　　　　　　S group

Composing sentences

Emphasis in teaching grammar has turned from analysis (taking a sentence apart to see how it works) to synthesis (building a sentence by putting its component parts together). The student learns to handle structures by composing his own sentences on various patterns and gains practice and familiarity with his language by experimenting with these patterns. The ingenious teacher may provide students with a year's language study by giving them basic patterns and asking them to alter, expand, and vary these structures, discussing their revisions for style, meaning, emphasis, and conciseness. Other suggestions for studying parts of speech and sentence structure will be given at the end of the chapter.

Much of the work in grammar may profitably be practice with patterns of coordination, modification, and subordination. As students gain familiarity with basic sentence patterns, they may see that each is expandable in many ways, but that there is always order in the methods of expansion. Familiarity with this order is the link between the study of grammar and the improvement of composition. Although little research has been done on the relation of structural linguistics or generative grammar to the improvement of writing, many teachers believe that students gain flexibility and control over their own structures by such study.

Transformations of basic patterns

Although transformational grammar has, as yet, not been widely introduced into schoolroom use, many linguists think it holds much promise for clarifying students' concepts about how the language operates. The key concept of transformational (generative) grammar—that the language consists of kernel or basic sentences and transformed sentences built on these basic patterns—throws light on some of the troublesome places in grammar for young people. For instance, it is fairly easy to show how the passive construction derives from a kernel sentence according to this description:

Kernel (basic) sentence: *The dog bit the man.*
Passive transformation: *The man was bitten by the dog.*

The transformational rule: make the second noun (*man*) the subject; add a form of the *be* verb, plus *-en* (sign of the past participle), plus *by*, plus the original subject (*dog*). The transformational rule may be abbreviated to:

$$\text{Object} + \text{be} + V_t + \text{-en} + \text{by} + \text{subject}$$

The simple transformations which students may practice, illustrated in sentences, are these:[14]

Transformation	Basic, kernel, or source sentence	Transformed sentence
Passive	He broke the vase.	The vase was broken by him.
Yes/no	The girl has lost her book.	Has the girl lost her book?
		Hasn't the girl lost her book?
WH question	He will show something.	What will he show?
DO	He liked the party.	Did he like the party?
	He likes olives.	He does like olives.
Imperative	You will close the door.	Close the door.
Negative	He can walk the dog.	He can't walk the dog.
Expletive IT	The girl is lost.	It is a girl who is lost.
Expletive THERE	Three bears were here.	There were three bears here.

Students may also find the following pattern helpful in filling in the subject-predicate, and subject-predicate-object patterns (Patterns 1 and 2):

Someone or *something*   *did something*   *to*   *somebody* or *something*   (sometime, someplace, in some manner, for some reason).[15]

[14] Adapted from unpublished materials presented by John Mellon at the Linguistics Workshop, NCTE Convention, Miami Beach, Fla., 1962.
[15] *Ibid.*

The sound of English

Intonation. The emphasis in the new grammars on spoken English has led us to realize the importance of stress, pitch, and pause in signaling meanings in English. Punctuation attempts to substitute written symbols for the pauses, stresses, and pitch of the spoken language. When students understand something of the patterns of intonation in spoken English and the relationship of this sound-signal system of punctuation, they can often gain a firmer grasp of the system.[16]

The teacher can help the student understand the importance of intonation, pitch, and stress in the spoken language by asking them to read the same printed symbols in varying ways: *We fail, you'll pay for this, he went with her, I'm coming,* and so on. They can see how many different meanings can be implied by the voice with the same symbols. Lady Macbeth's "We fail?"

may be WE fail? or we FAIL?

The accent in *What are you doing?* may fall on any one of the words, giving a different meaning to the sentence by a shift in stress: *Whát are you doing? What áre you doing? What are yóu doing? What are you dóing?*

Although the complexities of intonation in English speech are too many for the secondary student to master completely, there are some important ways in which the study of sound patterns can help him in writing. The patterns of intonation serve as an invaluable guide in clarifying the ambiguities of meaning; they often offer clues to punctuation, and they serve to help the student sense the structure of English sentences. The three parts of the intonation system of English are stress, pitch, and juncture.

Stress. Teachers and many students are already familiar with the patterns of stressed and unstressed syllables traditionally marked in the pronunciation of English words. Stress indicates the degree of loudness or softness of the syllables we utter. Our scansion of English poetry usually works in a pattern of accented and unaccented syllables. Some dictionaries (and some systems of scansion) also recognize tertiary stress, or secondary accent. Linguists, however, identify four stresses in English, usually marked primary (/), secondary ($\wedge$), tertiary (\ ), and weakest, or zero, stress ($\cup$).

These patterns play an important role in the sentence melodies of English

---

[16] The main features of the intonation system of English described here are derived from the two books already cited by Paul Roberts, who in turn acknowledges indebtedness to George Trager and Henry Lee Smith, Jr., *An Outline of English Structure,* Battenburg Press, Norman, Okla., 1951.

speech, and provide invaluable clues to meaning. They often mark the differences when the same word is used both as noun and verb:

/ \ \ / / \ \ /
contrast, contrast; address, address

Stress also indicates the difference between adjectives and nouns used as modifiers:

/ \ \ / / \ \ /
White House, white house; bluebird, blue bird

Pitch. The variation in tones of voice from low to high in the sentence melody of English speech is called *pitch*. Four levels of pitch in English are generally distinguished; for convenience they are numbered from 4 (the highest) to 1 (the lowest). When we mark sentences in a pitch pattern, we can indicate the tones from high to low by these numbers:

4 2   2   3   2   3   1
Nancy, come here this minute.

3   2   2   3 1
What are you doing? or

2   4   2   3 1
What are you doing?

Pitch is also indicated by lines drawn above and below the letters to indicate variations from low to high. Linguists use a line well above the letters for pitch /4/; a line just above for pitch /3/; a line just under the letters for pitch /2/; and a line well below them for pitch /1/.[17] We may have the same phrase or sentences said in several different ways. The meaning of each sentence differs with the pitch used to express the emotion of the speaker:

Where|are|you going?   (exasperation)

Where are|you|going?   (annoyance)

Where are you|going?   (surprise)

Where|are you|going?   (insistence)

Juncture. The pauses in the stream of speech sounds make up the system of *juncture* in English intonation. Linguists recognize four kinds of juncture: open, or plus, juncture—the breath pause which cuts up the speech flow into words—and three terminal junctures which indicate different kinds of sentences: falling ↘ (double-cross juncture #), rising ↗ (double-bar juncture //), and sustained, or level → (single-bar juncture /).

Falling juncture signals the dropping of the voice at the end of the sen-

---

[17] Roberts, *Patterns of English*, p. 229.

tence in statements, requests, and those questions introduced by a question word and not answerable by *yes* or *no*:

    He was going home. ↘ *Open the door.* ↘ *Who is going?* ↘

Rising juncture marks the sound of the rising inflection after the yes/no question sentence: *Did he come?* ↗ *Do you like it?* ↗ Within the sentence, it marks the slight rising inflection accompanying nouns in a series: He likes chocolate, ↗ doughnuts, ↗ and pickles. ↘ It is this juncture in speech which usually corresponds to the comma in writing.

Level or sustained juncture (single bar), as its name implies, is the slight break or pause of breath without rising or falling pitch. The long sentence that includes a restrictive clause is illustrative of level juncture: *The man who waited on us yesterday has gone home.* → It usually indicates no punctuation.

We have seen how intonation patterns operate as a clue to meaning, both in the stresses marking words and the rise and fall of the voice that turns a
                     3   2 1 2   1   2   2 1 2 3
statement into a question: *You're going with her.* ↘ *You're going with her?* ↗

Recognition of intonation patterns can also help the student in punctuation. He will see that the rising juncture calls usually for commas, that falling junctures usually demand a semicolon or a period, and that level junctures indicate that no punctuation is necessary. The student who can master the high-low intonation patterns of the declarative sentence has grasped a basic concept about sentence structure and punctuation.[18]

Finally, since intonation indicates important syntactic relationships in English, the student who masters the essentials of the system understands more clearly the structures he reads and writes. Intonation provides some of the most helpful clues to the recognition of sentence fragments, restrictive and nonrestrictive clauses, appositives, and the like. As the student trains his ear to observe the way his voice works in the intonation of the sentence patterns he utters, he understands how to read by structural patterns rather than single words, and how to write and punctuate by the syntactical groupings of words in sentences.

The mechanics of writing: punctuation and spelling

The system of punctuation and spelling of English which we must teach our students is a matter quite different from that of helping them acquire approved usage or construct better sentences. Much of our time in English is spent on the mechanical conventions of transcribing speech into writing. Modern punctuation is less than 250 years old; our system of spelling, less than 600 years old. Both are imperfect notations of speech, and both are

---

[18] The teacher who wishes to pursue the study of intonation in more detail may find helpful suggestions for teaching in Roberts, *English Sentences,* Whitehall's *Essentials of English,* and Lloyd and Warfel's *American English in Its Cultural Setting* (see bibliography).

frozen by printers' forms. They consume a great deal of time which might more profitably be given to other aspects of reading and writing. Nevertheless, an adequate command of the conventions of English punctuation and spelling is an important criterion of educational and cultural background. At least minimal competence in the mechanics of English is demanded by industry, the professions, or almost any position requiring more than mechanical skills.

Much of the drudgery young people connect with the study of punctuation and spelling might be minimized if the task were simplified for them. It is possible to identify the basic kinds of punctuation which serve in most English sentences. Experienced teachers believe that mastering 100 commonly misspelled words may eliminate a large per cent of the spelling errors made by students. When the task is analyzed, the subject may be reduced to learnable proportions for most young people.

Mastering punctuation

It is essential to decide which basic marks of punctuation students should learn first. Handbooks contain all the possible varieties of punctuation, and many of the rules are outdated today. For example, the comma after introductory words and clauses and often before *and* or *but* in compound sentences is frequently omitted in modern usage.

The student learns to punctuate for two reasons: to convey written thoughts with accuracy, and to appear literate and educated to the audience for which he writes. Spelling and punctuation may be false indices of education and literacy; many people think they are. Yet the fact remains that employers, and even friends, continue to judge the individual by such measures. The student who wants to pass the test had better learn the system. If he follows good advice and streamlines the process, he will be able to become competent, but he has to perceive the order in the system and to have some hope that he will be able to master it.

A few simple rules will help the learner. Some of these are:

1. *Don't* overpunctuate. When in doubt about a mark of punctuation, leave it out. Of the twenty-three rules for the comma in some composition handbooks, only five or six are commonly used in good contemporary writing and publishing.[19] Learn those first.

2. *Do* observe current usage in punctuation. Watch your textbook, the daily newspaper, the magazines you subscribe to, the modern novels you read. You can learn much by observation, even though many handbook rules may

---

[19] One college handbook lists four:

> You need only four rules to use the comma expertly, and the last two employ the same principle. Use a comma: (I) before *and, but, for, or, nor, yet, still* when joining independent clauses; (II) between all terms in a series, *including the last two;* (III) to set off parenthetical openers and afterthoughts; (IV) before and after parenthetical insertions (use a *pair* of commas). [Sheridan Baker, *The Practical Stylist,* Thomas Y. Crowell Company, New York, 1962, pp. 48–49.]

disagree with what you read. Since printers have simplified much modern punctuation, there is little merit in learning outdated forms. Other things are more important.

3. *Do* learn the basic syntactic structures and sentence patterns of English. Unless you can recognize English sentences, clauses, phrases, verb and noun clusters, adjectives, and adverbs, you will not make much headway with the rules of punctuation. If you do know the basic structures, your job of gaining command of the techniques of marking them should be relatively simple.

4. *Do* recognize the fact that writing is recorded speech. Since the intonation, stress, and pause patterns of the human voice in speech are the original source of our system of punctuation, it makes sense to realize that awareness of intonation can help in punctuation. Learn the basic intonation patterns of English and use them to assist you in punctuating.

5. As with spelling, realize that a large percentage of errors can be dealt with by using a basic group of concepts and guiding rules. Master this group before you go on to the finer points.

Punctuating by structures. Most students enter junior high school with some basic concepts of punctuation. They recognize and use the minimal system: beginning sentences with capital letters, ending with a period or a question mark, commas to set off words in a series. Many know far more than this, of course, and others are still in relatively shaky command of capitals, periods, and commas. The student needs first to learn the various marks which signal the basic sentence patterns of his writing.

As he begins to expand basic sentence patterns by compounding, he may, in some related lessons, learn how to punctuate such structures. If, as is suggested here, the emphasis is on having him write his own sentences, learning the punctuation system for these takes on significance as it becomes related closely to structure and meaning. He sees that compounding subjects, predicates, adjectives, or adverbs requires the separating comma to clarify meaning:

She was pretty, pert, and popular. (Pretty *and* pert? Or pretty pert?)

Teen-agers like doughnuts, soda, ice cream, and pickles. (Not ice cream *with* pickles).

Mary, Jo, Keith, and Tom are in my class at school. (Four people or two? Mary, Jo, and Keith, or Mary Jo Keith?)

Punctuating interrupted patterns. As students work at expanding simple patterns—NV, NVN—they will see that modifiers, verb or noun clusters, phrases, or clauses may interrupt the basic pattern. They learn that such words or word groups are commonly set off by commas to indicate an interruption of the basic structure:

Interrupting word: *He showed, nevertheless, a fine cooperative attitude.*

Appositive phrase: *His sister, a brilliant student in the senior class, has won a scholarship.* (Added information interrupting the NVN pattern.)

Subordinate clause: *We started out and, because we had no place in particular to go, drove to the beach.* (Clause interrupting compound sentence.)

Punctuation also sets off introductory words, clauses,. and phrases to indicate the beginning of the main structure:

Instead, he walked slowly over to the bleachers.

Instead of going right home, we went down town to get some ice cream.

Students should be reminded that a single comma never separates the basic structural elements of the sentence: subject and predicate, predicate and object, or linking verb and complement.

One of the chief systems of punctuation, then, is that which marks off the structural elements of the sentence: subordinate from main structures, words and modifiers in unexpected places, modifiers of word groups placed between, before, or after basic NV, NVN, or linking-verb structures. Students should learn the basic patterns and observe the ways of setting off interrupting clauses and phrases.

Punctuating by intonation patterns. The teacher who can train his students to hear intonation signals in speaking may provide them with useful clues to punctuation. Such training is not an infallible guide, but it is often useful. It may often work better in helping the student punctuate restrictive and nonrestrictive clauses than any group of rules he may learn. The most useful clues are these:

1. The falling juncture signaling the end of a declarative sentence and calling for a semicolon or period:

We are going to dinner.

2. The level juncture signaling the restrictive clause or phrase versus the rising inflection and the three stresses which signal the nonrestrictive clause:

My sister, who lives in Texas, owns a Thunderbird.
(Three stresses, slight rising juncture marked by commas.)

My sister who lives in Texas owns a Thunderbird.
(Level juncture; no distinctive pauses; no punctuation.)

3. The comma after long introductory clauses or phrases, sometimes called sentence modifiers:

Because he never thought of anyone but himself, most people did not like him.

Since we are driving down to the shore on Tuesday, we will bring the beach chairs with us.

Intonation and sentence structure. Perhaps the most difficult problem in punctuation for the student is that of the semicolon between two independent clauses without a conjunction. Here again, recognition of structure and attention to intonation may help. Fading or falling juncture indicates the terminus of a thought unit. Often the sentence fragment results from inattention to the oral sentence melody. The student frequently cuts into two structures one that should be punctuated by a comma. When the sentence is read aloud, falling juncture indicates the structure and the required punctuation.

She was a popular senior. A girl who had been elected to almost every important office in the school.

Often, too, the comma fault, or comma splice, joins two independent structures which demand the semicolon:

We didn't want anyone to come with us, we were quite eager to go alone.

Mastering spelling

George Bernard Shaw's benevolent gift to found a Society for Simplified Spelling, and the efforts of other spelling reformers have made little impact on our culture. Old habits of spelling, inherited with the history of the English language, seem deeply rooted in our culture. To retrain the users of English to employ the best system of simplified spelling would be almost as difficult a job as to change our way of walking or our alphabet. It would mean rewriting and reprinting all our books, rebuilding typewriters and printing presses, and changing habits developed by dozens of years of schooling. The student who resists learning to spell accurately may be asked to imagine how the worlds of business, communications, and education would be affected if we were to try to change our system. Then he may be confronted with a piece of writing by an illiterate speller to observe the effect on the reader of the maverick who doesn't play by the rules. The problem speller warrants our sympathy: if he is not visual-minded, he has much learning to do. But since adequate spelling is demanded of those who would be considered literate in our society, he has no choice but to learn to spell adequately.

English spelling is immeasurably more difficult than that of languages whose spelling is phonetic. English contains forty-four sounds that can be represented by 250 spellings. Linguists have pointed out that today's spelling does not spell today's language, but the Middle English (London dialect) of the late fifteenth century when printers attempted to work out ways of representing sounds in print. Words imported from other languages brought with them their spellings based on the sounds of the parent language: thus we have *recognize* from Latin (with its *-ize* form) and *surprise* from French (with its *-ise* form). The illogicality in English spellings has infuriated generations of impatient learners, but definite patterns do exist. Some spellings contain the buried history of the language—for instance the silent *gh* in *night,* or *k* and *gh* in *knight,* sounded in Chaucer's day.

Linguistic approaches to spelling. Recent linguistic research into pronunciation and spelling has pointed out many patterns in English spelling which can be profitably learned by the poor speller. Probably all students should be taught some of these patterns. They should understand the relation of sound to writing and the fact that problems in English spelling arise from the fact that many speech sounds (phonemes) have as many as twelve or fourteen graphemes (written symbols). Many teachers recommend developing rules inductively by having students supply examples of the numerous ways we use to spell words with the long vowel /ey/ ($\bar{a}$): a (*gravy*); ai (*raise*); ay (*payment*); ea (*steak*); ei (*veil*); ey (*whey*). Students may also write variants of /ow/, /iy/, and /ey/.[20]

Reasons for poor spelling.   What are the reasons for poor spelling? Carelessness seems to be a major factor in the case of the poor speller who often habitually misspells simple words. To improve, he must be urged to feel some responsibility for spelling well.

The first job of the problem speller is recognition of the fact that he *can* learn to spell. The teacher can show him that what seems a formidable job, without beginning or end, is actually one which can be attacked in common-sense ways. He must learn that knowing a few rules will help him master dozens of words, that learning a small group of words will help him eliminate as much as 75 per cent of his errors. He must realize that mastery of a relatively small group of prefixes and suffixes will give him control of hundreds of other spellings. The teacher can help him cut the task to size and show him that recognizing some of the general patterns of English spelling will assist him to spell most of the words he will ever need to write. Above all, he must be urged to tackle the problem systematically and with self-confidence. Many teachers have shown that poor spellers can be taught to spell adequately when they settle down seriously and in earnest to the task of learning.

Streamlining the problem.   Numerous studies of the allotment of curricular time indicate that in relation to the results achieved, a disproportionate amount of time is given to spelling. Research studies indicate that heavy time allotments produce no better results than smaller amounts of time.[21] We can no longer afford such a sacrifice of time needed for reading and writing. Students spend much time in school studying and being tested on dozens of words they never misspell. A common sense time-saving approach to the problem would suggest locating the words which the student habitually misspells and concentrating on these. Since numerous studies exist which have shown what

[20] The following discussions of applications of linguistic theory to spelling are valuable: Margaret Kemper Bonney, "New Roads to Rome: A Linguistic Approach to Spelling in Secondary Schools," *English Leaflet,* vol. 42, Winter, 1962; Ralph M. Williams, *Phonetic Spelling for College Students,* Oxford University Press, Fair Lawn, N.J., 1960; and Robert A. Hall, Jr., *Sound and Spelling in English,* Chilton Company—Book Division, Philadelphia, 1961. The teacher should also be familiar with the section on spelling in *Webster's Third New International Dictionary,* G. & C. Merriam Company, Springfield, Mass., 1961.

[21] Ernest Horn, "Spelling," in Chester W. Harris (ed.), *Encyclopedia of Educational Research,* 3d ed., The Macmillan Company, New York, 1960, p. 1346.

spelling demons exist for students at different grade levels,[22] we should start with these commonly misspelled words. A pretest will indicate which words individual students need to work on; they should keep a list of these in their spelling notebooks and be encouraged to master these errors. Spelling research suggests these procedures:

1. Students should be encouraged to concentrate on words or parts of words which the pretest or errors in written work show are trouble spots.

2. Careful pronunciation of words is an important factor in good spelling.

3. Distributed learning is more productive than mass learning: students should focus on fewer words at one time and have opportunity for practicing these at intervals for recall.

4. Words should be *overlearned*—that is, learned beyond the point of one successful recall.

5. Teachers should not overvalue spelling. Emphasis on spelling as a matter of first importance has given poor spellers strong inhibitions about writing. Since many good students are poor spellers, primary emphasis should be on good writing.

6. The presentation of words in context is less effective than presenting them in list form, except as the context is necessary for identification.

7. Pretests corrected and studied provide the most effective learning.

8. Primary emphasis should be on visual imagery, but for many students audile and kinesthetic methods increase the effectiveness of learning.

9. The only rules that should be taught are those applying to a large number of words and having few exceptions. The most useful of these is the one for adding suffixes by changing *y* to *i*, dropping the final silent *e*, and doubling the final consonant. Three other rules are that the letter *q* is always followed by *u*, that English words do not end in *v*, and that proper nouns and most adjectives formed from proper nouns begin with a capital letter.

10. Recommended procedures for teaching rules: teach rules inductively and develop them in connection with the words to which they apply; teach one rule at a time; emphasize both positive and negative aspects. When a rule has been taught, it should be systematically reviewed and applied. Emphasis should be on use of the rule rather than on memorization of a verbal statement.[23]

Teachers may also tape sentences using 100 spelling demons, and allow students to take this taped test at intervals, until they can spell all the words. Spellers who have made a good score at the beginning of the year may be required to take it later in the year to check their retention.

---

[22] See Thomas Clark Pollock, *Teachers Service Bulletin in English,* High School Edition, vol. 8, no. 1, The Macmillan Company. (Unpaged reprint.)
[23] Summarized from Horn, *op. cit.,* pp. 1345–1346.

Helping poor spellers.   Teachers can help the poor speller to attack his problems constructively by assisting him to see the patterns and regularities in many seemingly chaotic spellings. The student may also learn something about the language, which will help him with some problems. Among the suggestions made by experienced teachers of spelling are these:

1. Encourage students to work out simple mnemonic (memory) devices which will help them associate ideas with correct spelling. Commonly used devices which have worked for some students are the following: notice *pa* in *separate; ma* in *grammar;* scientists *labor* in the *laboratory; pie*ce of *pie;* one writes letters on station*e*ry (notice the *e's*); the princi*pal* is the student's *pal.* Students may make up their own mnemonics; often the sillier they are, the more memorable they become.

2. Teach students how prefixes and suffixes operate with the root to form correct spellings. The teacher may write a list of words on the board and ask them to add prefixes and suffixes to show the spellings: dis/agree/ment, dis/satisfy, mis/spell, dis/appoint/ment, drunken/ness. The prefix plus root accounts for the double *s* in *misspell* and double consonants in numerous other words.

3. Teach students to pronounce carefully, even exaggerating or deliberately mispronouncing certain troublesome words. Have poor spellers sound out silent letters in *gnaw, knight, phlegm, diaphragm, pneumonia.* Meticulous pronunciation of words with syllables commonly slurred by most students may help: *February, sophomore, government.*

4. Teach students to make a methodical attack on spelling. The process combines pronouncing the word, looking at the word, closing the eyes to visualize it, writing it, and checking the result.[24]

5. Teaching students the derivations of some words may assist them in remembering the spellings. They may learn that we get *Wednesday* from the name of the Norse god Woden; that a play*wright* is like a ship*wright* in that he constructs plays as the latter constructs ships (from Middle English *wright, wrighte,* Old English *wyrhta,* a worker, maker); that *Mediterranean* comes from the Latin *medius,* middle, and *terra,* land. Sacrilegious is derived from Latin *sacer,* sacred and *legere,* to gather up, take away.

6. Common misspellings are likely to be analogical: thus we get *speach* on the analogy of *speak, fourty* on the analogy of *four, pronounciation, curiousity,* and others. Teachers may call attention to the probable reasons for these spellings to help students master them.

7. One way to simplify the task of spelling for poor students and save time for more important work is to teach students to look for the accepted variants in spelling of many English words. Lists of demons commonly taught and retaught every year are full of words listed with alternate spellings in several

---

[24] Julia McCorkle, *Learning to Spell,* D. C. Heath and Company, Boston, 1953, pp. 32–34.

reputable collegiate dictionaries. Accepted variants are the *e* in such words as develop(e); judg(e)ment, and many words ending with the suffix *-able:* blamable, likable, movable, etc. Both teachers and students should be familiar with these accepted variants.[25]

Evaluation

The student's real command over language, his knowledge of the structure of English, and his skill with punctuation and spelling are best demonstrated in his writing. The objective tests of writing ability mentioned at the end of Chapter 6 provide some of the best measures of the student's command of grammar in use. Numerous informal tests may enable the teacher to judge recognition of structure, knowledge of the parts of sentences and their relationships, and of punctuation. Some of the exercises given in this chapter and in Chapter 6 can be used to estimate these abilities.

The student's command over language may be observed by his degree of mastery of some of the following skills, demonstrated in practice exercises or tests:

Writing sentences in the basic patterns (see pages 190 to 192).

Writing parallel models of various sentence patterns.

Adding elements to basic patterns, such as Pattern 1 plus an S group, or NV plus P group, etc.

Composing sentences in parallel structure or in patterns of gerunds, infinitives, or other word groups.

Elaborating sentence patterns by adding modifiers.

Distinguishing between figurative and literal meanings of words.

Recognizing varieties of usage and the appropriateness of each in writing, in listening to speeches or recordings, in speaking, or in reading literature.

The teacher will want to look for the following skills in attempting to evaluate what students have achieved in their language study during the year:

Increased variety, complexity, and maturity of sentence structure.

Increased command over punctuation according to structural patterns.

Increased awareness of appropriate usage.

Increased vocabulary and sensitivity to words and connotations.

Increased fluency in speaking and writing and command over a range of language varieties.

A sample question on language in the CEEB's suggested *End-of-Year Examinations in English* asks students at the ninth-grade level to write two sentences for each word illustrating the literal and nonliteral uses of five of the following: *astronomical, antidote, ballast, Cassandra, colossus, doldrums, foggy, Rubicon, oasis.* A second part of the question asks them to explain the

---

[25] The teacher should know the study by Donald W. Emery, *Variant Spellings in Modern American Dictionaries,* NCTE, Champaign, Ill., 1958.

source or derivation of four new words made up from other words in the language and to give an example of another word formed in the same way, choosing from *astronaut, do-it-yourself kit, fallout, Mercury station wagon, NATO countries, Salk vaccine.*[26] From this question teachers can see the range of information about the language which capable ninth graders may be expected to demonstrate.

The teacher who desires to use standardized tests of grammar and usage should check carefully with a reliable evaluation to determine whether the test calls for mastery of formal terminology, or includes as wrong usages items established by recent studies as acceptable.[27] Among the tests which may be used to measure competence in these areas are the following:

. . . *English Expression; Cooperative English Tests,* grades 9–12, 13–14, Co-operative Test Division, Educational Testing Service, Princeton, N.J., 1960.

. . . *Science Research Achievement Test,* Science Research Achievement Series: Language Arts, grades 6–9, Science Research Associates, Inc., Chicago, 1954–1957.

Tests at the beginning, middle, and end of the year may provide valuable indication of student progress in spelling. The Administrative Management Society (AMS) spelling tests, commonly given in high schools, allow the teacher to measure the achievement of students against national norms.[28]

Increased curiosity about words, their etymologies, connotations, and nuances of meaning, and understanding of the structure of the language can result from the student's investigation of his own language. Students can be stimulated to excited inquiry about language by observing its changes, its history, its current coinages, and its social, psychological, and personal uses. As this chapter has tried to point out, the study of grammar and usage must be more than the memorization of a few prescribed forms. It must educate the student to observe a living language, constantly in flux, and train him to observe, listen, practice, and record its varieties until his own use of words is flexible and discriminating. Such study puts responsibility on the speaker and the writer to make informed choices. As one linguist says:

No man should let another choose his language for him; for speech and reason make us human. The choice is never easy, partly because no linguistic form is good in itself, absolutely, and for all purposes, partly because the determinants of choice are various—the character of the speaker (or writer), the nature of his audience, the relation between them, the situation, the subject, the speaker's intent, and so on.[29]

---

[26] *End-of-Year Examinations in English for College-bound Students, Grades 9–12,* CEEB, Princeton, N.J., 1963, p. 47.
[27] See Oscar K. Buros (ed.), *Fifth Mental Measurements Yearbook,* Gryphon Press, Highland Park, N.J., 1959.
[28] Administrative Management Society, Willow Grove, Pa.
[29] James Sledd, postscript to *Dictionaries and THAT Dictionary,* by James Sledd and Wilma Ebbitt. Copyright © 1962 by Scott, Foresman and Company, Chicago, p. 274.

LUNATIC

ASTONISH

"Lunatic. Latin *iuna,* moon. There was a belief that *lunacy* was caused by sleeping with the moon full on your face and that the condition followed the moon's phases. The *lunatic* was moonstruck. *Loony,* the slang abbreviation, has got itself associated with the Scotch word *loon,* which meant lout, from the Anglo-Saxon *lutan,* to bend low, the posture of an inferior order. With all that we now know about the influence of the moon on human cycles, perhaps those antique medicine-men weren't so far off."

"Astonish. Latin *extonare,* to strike by thunder. This word has become a great deal milder in the course of its history. An astonished person is more surprised than stunned. *Thunder* itself comes from the name of the Norse god Thor, the Thunderer. In the sixteenth century, a blow on the head *astonished* a man. Perhaps it still does today, though we'd say it knocked him cold. *Stun* was a Middle English word which meant to make a din."

Illustrations by James Thurber for *In a Word,* by Margaret S. Ernst and James Thurber, Alfred A. Knopf, Inc., New York, 1939. Copyright, 1939, by Margaret S. Ernst ©, 1960, by Joan E. Goldstein.

"Senate. Latin *senex,* old; *senatus,* council of old men. A slander on those legislative boys in Washington equal to calling the members of the Supreme Court the "nine old men." In Rome the senate was the council of the elders. *Congress* comes from the Latin *congressus,* a coming or walking together."

SENATE

The student who is given the chance in the English classroom to explore the many aspects and varieties of language will find in this study an illuminating area of intellectual inquiry and gain command over the tool which allows him to function most completely as a human being.

Student activities and assignments

The student's study of language should give him the opportunities for practice in using the structures and conventions of the language, and engaging in group or individual language projects which enable him to study the language analytically. The new language textbooks now being produced will offer many additional suggestions to the teacher (see page 181).

Projects for language study

Individual students, groups of students within a class, or whole classes may be started on the path to inquiry and discovery about language through assignments and projects leading to interesting research about language, its history, development, and change. The list of suggestions offered here is indefinitely expandable as teachers and students learn more about language and discover new topics to study. Here are some projects individual students or small groups might undertake:

. . . Students in a twelfth-grade English literature survey course may work on comparing linguistic differences in several versions of the same writer: Chaucer (in Middle and Modern English); *Beowulf* in Old English and modern English; comparisons of various translations of the Bible; Malory's *Le Morte d'Arthur* in the original and in a modern version, and so on. Old English poetry, Shakespeare, *Gawain and the Green Knight,* and other classics which mark various stages of the language may also be used to show linguistic and stylistic changes.

. . . The flavor of English dialects may be sampled in such writers as D. H. Lawrence (*Sons and Lovers*), Eric Knight (*The Flying Yorkshireman and Other Stories*), Emily Brontë (*Wuthering Heights*), Hardy (Dorset novels), Shaw (*Pygmalion*), and others.

. . . Encourage students to develop a continuing awareness of the language by working at long-term projects which may go into a language notebook, an oral report, or a written paper. Word collections of this kind have been gathered by a class for a dictionary as a class project. Thoroughgoing research by a senior high school student might be written up and submitted to *Word Study,* published by the G. & C. Merriam Company, Springfield, Massachusetts, or *Inside the ACD,* Harper and Row, Publishers, Incorporated, New York. Some of the areas of word study may be the following:

1. Borrowings or loan words: the words English has borrowed from other languages—names of foods, clothes, inventions, customs, activities: *pizza, fricassee, chemise, skiing, garage, table d'hote,* etc. The class may construct a "tree" of such borrowings.

2. Words derived from new technologies: television (*telecast, televise, televiewing*), aviation (*dive bombing, takeoff, tailspin*), nuclear

energy (*fallout*), space satellites (*launching pad, blastoff, orbit*—both as noun and verb—*countdown, astronaut*).

3. Names of products: *nylon, Dacron, Kodak, Fiberglas.*

4. Phonetic economy: *lab, prof, bio, math, soc, psych.*

5. Place names in the language: *bayonet, cantaloupe, calico, tuxedo, gypsy, damask, satin, frankfurter.*

6. Words from proper names: *bloomers, boycott, marcel, silhouette, maverick, derrick, sadist, nicotine.*

7. New words added to the language: *beatnik, sit-in, drip-dry, airlift, integrationist, globalize.*

8. Coinages from initials: *NATO, deejay* (disk jockey); *emcee* (master of ceremonies); *veep, CARE.*

Language problems

. . . Ask students to write dictionary-style definitions of five common words or to meet in groups to write definitions—five words for each group—that include the different senses of each word and its use as different parts of speech. *Door, kitchen, ball, dog, point, dig, house, fish, word, run* may be used as examples. Groups may then compare their definitions with those given in several dictionaries.

. . . Ask students to discover facts about grammatical functions of language by setting them some of the following problems:

   1. Make a list of several ways to form noun plurals.

   2. Make a list of all the ways you can think of to express differences in time of an action in English ("I saw John yesterday," "I will see him tomorrow," and so on).

. . . Give students groups of sentences from a first-grade book and ask them to rewrite them varying sentence structure and using more grown-up words. Select the best sentences in terms of order, emphasis, rhythm, and clarity.

Understanding language history and change

. . . College-bound students may be capable of an assignment in which they study some of the principles of historical development of changes of meaning. Some of these are (1) *extension,* in which the meaning of the word has widened; (2) *restriction,* in which it has narrowed; (3) *pejoration* (degeneration); (4) *amelioration* (elevation); (5) *folk etymology;* (6) *euphemism* by phonetic distortion: *darn, heck,* and others.[30]

. . . Students should understand the principle of the etymological fallacy, or the notion that words must continue to mean what they originally meant. Illustrative words to be studied are *dilapidated, holiday, bonfire, arrive,*

---

[30] See David DeCamp, "The OED in the Classroom," *College Composition and Communication,* vol. 12, December, 1961, pp. 227–229, for useful exercises.

candidate, lady, knight, angel, knave, lust, villain. They may collect other examples in their language notebooks.

. . . Let students compile their own lists of words which have changed in meaning. Let them collect slang terms used differently today from the way they were ten years ago (*cool, blast, ice, with it, have a ball*); slang metaphor (*cat, alligator, egghead, goof, fink*).

. . . A study of the special vocabulary of a particular field: science, television, medicine, space research, nuclear physics, jazz, "beat" language, army, navy, etc.

. . . Let students study advertising to see how new products are named by coinages adding traditional suffixes and prefixes. They may then try to invent names for imaginary new products, using some of these prefixes, suffixes, or roots. Such words as *Kleenex, Trimex, Sominex,* and *Bab-o,* utilize *-ex* and *-o* endings.

Enjoying language

Much of the verbal play of the teen-ager contributes to his sensitivity to and awareness of language. Word games are growing in sophistication and some present opportunities for invention and observation.

. . . Students may adopt the word game, "Conjugation of Irregular Verbs," said to have been invented by Sir Bertrand Russell on the British Broadcasting Company's Third Programme:

A junior English class wrote these:

I am uninformed; you are unaware; he is ignorant; I am well-rounded; you are obese; he is fat.[31]

. . . Junior high school students will enjoy language games similar to the recently popular one called "Tom Swifties," with its emphasis on the punning relationship of verbs and adverbs to the situation in the sentence. The humorous exaggeration of the style of the Tom Swift books is imitated in these samples from a junior high school: *"I'm going to die," he said gravely; "Do I have to hunt Moby Dick," he wailed; "Please pass the sugar," he said sweetly; "Get me the latest file," he rasped.*[32]

Composing sentences

. . . Give students exercises of this kind:

Complete the following verbals by adding a sentence pattern. Be sure the verb in the pattern specifies the doer of the action:

After washing the dog, ———; Having written my theme, ———; Being only six years old, ———.

. . . Encourage students to compress sentences by the use of a single word modifier:

[31] Verna A. Hoyman, "An Evaluation of Methods of Teaching Vocabulary in the Secondary School," *Illinois English Bulletin,* vol. 49, November, 1961, p. 12.
[32] From *Pegasus,* vol. 1, June, 1963, King Philip Junior High School, West Hartford, Conn., pp. 34–35.

She looks as though her skin had been tanned by the sun. (She looks suntanned.)

She talked in a voice that sounded like that of a small child. (Her childish voice . . .)

. . . Let students practice mastery of parallel structure by constructing sentences on the following patterns:

He was late for school *because* (add three *because* clauses). Example: *He was late for school because he was very tired, because he had been working late for weeks, and because his alarm clock did not go off.*

Junior high school students who have not been taught some of these grammatical forms may need a little more assistance with directions:

He liked to ———, ———, and ——— (add three *to* verbs); or *He liked* ———*ing,* ———*ing,* and ———*ing* (add three *-ing* words).

The policeman saw him steal the money (add a clause beginning with *moreover, however, nevertheless, because, after, since,* or *when*).

. . . Students may learn something of the principles of emphasis by placing the clause before or after the main clause:

After ———*, Tom was afraid. Tom was afraid after* ———. (Try other sentences with *when, since, because, nevertheless, yet.*)

. . . Students may be taught to write adverbial clauses by providing them with a main clause and having them add clauses telling *when, why, where,* or *how.*

. . . Students may practice adding relative clauses as modifiers:

The boy (who ———*) won the game.*
The team (which ———*) lost.*
My bicycle (that ———*) is broken.*

Restrictive and nonrestrictive patterns may be developed from these sentences as students observe whether the clause is essential to the meaning of the sentence or gives added information.

Teaching sentence structure and modification

Use the flannel board to demonstrate word order, mobility of modifiers, and ways of expanding patterns. Sometimes teachers use red or green cards for words forming the basic pattern parts, yellow for modifiers, and move the cards to show the many possible arrangements of words.

Deriving grammar lessons from student themes

Use one group of papers early in the year to illustrate punctuation conventions needing review: apostrophes, capitals, punctuation of restrictive and nonrestrictive modifiers, comma faults, and sentence fragments.

Selected bibliography

Every teacher of English needs to know the basic books in the field he teaches. This list includes the books generally considered of signal importance in the development of modern theories of grammar and linguistics.[33] Articles on linguistics in recent issues of the *English Journal* and *College English* should also be consulted. The high school language texts listed in the bibiography of chapter 7 offer rich suggestions for teaching the new grammar.

Grammar and linguistics

Harold B. Allen (ed.), *Readings in Applied English Linguistics*, Appleton-Century-Crofts, Inc., New York, 1958. (Paperback.) (8)

Leonard Bloomfield, *Language,* Holt, Rinehart and Winston, Inc., New York, 1933. Some linguists call this "far and away the best book on the subject written in the twentieth century," serving as a basis for most of the work on linguistics since its publication.

Winthrop Nelson Francis, *The Structure of American English,* The Ronald Press Company, New York, 1958. Linguistics for teachers of English. (7)

Charles C. Fries, *American English Grammar,* Appleton-Century-Crofts, Inc., New York, 1940 (English Monograph No. 10, National Council of Teachers of English). Every teacher of English should know this pioneer study of American English.

————, *The Structure of English,* Harcourt, Brace & World, Inc., New York, 1952. Fries' second analysis of modern American English, based on recordings of conversations, is a basic source book for many of the studies of structural linguistics. (6)

H. A. Gleason, Jr., *An Introduction to Descriptive Linguistics,* rev. ed., Holt, Rinehart and Winston, Inc., New York, 1961. (9)

————, *Linguistics and English Grammar,* Holt, Rinehart and Winston, Inc., New York, 1965.

Hans P. Guth, *English Today and Tomorrow: A Guide for Teachers of English,* Prentice-Hall, Inc., Englewood Cliffs, N.J., 1964, chap. 1.

Robert A. Hall, Jr., *Linguistics and Your Language,* Doubleday & Company, Inc., New York, 1960. 2d rev. ed of *Leave Your Language Alone.* Many English teachers will not agree with Hall, but they and their students will find him interesting and enlightening on the subject of language. (4)

Otto Jespersen, *Growth and Structure of the English Language,* 9th ed., Doubleday & Company, Inc., Garden City, N.Y., 1956. One of the most influential books in this century for its concise, appreciative treatment of the history and development of English.

Donald A. Lloyd and Harry Warfel, *American English in Its Cultural Setting,* Alfred A. Knopf, Inc., New York, 1956. Excellent chapters on the conventions of writing and spelling.

Walter Loban et al., *Teaching Language and Literature: Grades 7–12,* Harcourt, Brace & World, Inc., 1961, chap. 11.

Robert C. Pooley, *Teaching English Grammar,* Appleton-Century-Crofts, Inc., New York, 1957.

[33] The books numbered 1 through 9 are suggested minimal readings for the beginning teacher of linguistics, in the order recommended by some teachers of the subject.

Paul Roberts, *English Sentences,* Harcourt, Brace & World, Inc., New York, 1962. Transformational grammar for high school students. (2)

————, *English Syntax,* Harcourt, Brace & World, Inc., New York, 1964. A programmed transformational grammar text for high school students.

————, *Patterns of English,* Teacher's ed., Harcourt, Brace & World, Inc. New York, 1956. Structural grammar for high school students. (1)

————, *Understanding English,* Harcourt, Brace & World, Inc., New York, 1958. A modern approach to grammar. (3)

Edward Sapir, *Language: An Introduction to the Study of Speech,* Harcourt, Brace & World, Inc., New York, 1921. (Paper: Harvest Books, 1955). One of the first and most important books on modern linguistics by a brilliant scholar. (5)

James A. Sledd, *A Short Introduction to English Grammar,* Scott, Foresman and Company, Chicago, 1959.

Ingrid M. Strom, "Research in Grammar and Usage and Its Implications for Teaching Writing," *Bulletin of the School of Education,* Indiana University, vol. 36, September, 1960.

Harold Whitehall, *Structural Essentials of English,* Harcourt, Brace & World, Inc., New York, 1951.

History of the language

Albert C. Baugh, *History of the English Language,* Appleton-Century-Crofts, Inc., New York, 1935. A standard text in the history of language.

Margaret Bryant, *Modern English and Its Heritage,* rev. ed., The Macmillan Company, New York, 1962. Full of details about the historical development of the language and the development of English vocabulary.

Margaret Schlauch, *The Gift of Language,* The Viking Press, Inc., New York, 1942. (Reprinted as *The Gift of Tongues,* Dover Publications, Inc., New York, 1956.) A lively, popular history of the language, with excellent chapters on the relation of language to society.

PART *2*

Literature:

APPRECIATION, INSIGHTS, AND VALUES

CHAPTER *9*

I believe that man will not merely endure: he will prevail. He is immortal, not because he alone among creatures has an inexhaustible voice, but because he has a soul, a spirit capable of compassion and sacrifice and endurance. . . . The poet's, the writer's duty is to write about these things. It is his privilege to help man endure by lifting his heart, by reminding him of the courage and honor and hope and pride and compassion and pity and sacrifice which have been the glory of his past. The poet's voice need not merely be the record of man, it can be one of the props, the pillars to help him endure and prevail.

WILLIAM FAULKNER [1]

The nature of literature

Literature is the record of the attempt of writers to express and communicate their ideas about man's hopes, dreams, ideals, feelings, thoughts, and experience, and his relationship to society. Literature deals with the life of man in moments of crisis and anguish, with his most intimate relationships, with his innermost thoughts and his deepest loves and hates, with his "courage, honor, hope, pride, compassion, pity, and sacrifice."

This chapter is devoted to the nature of literature, its importance for the reader, and basic concepts about the literature program in the secondary school. Purpose, organization, selection of literature, and approaches for developing understanding and appreciation are considered. The chapters that follow deal with various aspects of teaching the important literary types and include suggested student activities and units for teaching. In studying these chapters on the teaching of literature in Part 2, the reader will want to return

[1] Nobel Prize Speech, reprinted from *The Faulkner Reader,* copyright 1954 by William Faulkner (Random House, Inc.).

from time to time to the discussion of the development of language skills in Part 1, particularly the chapter on reading (Chapter 5).

Why study literature?

To make literature live for young people, it is necessary that we be clear ourselves about why we teach it and what it has to offer them. One important aim is often lost sight of in the numerous reasons we advance for the reading of books: the "exposure" to certain classics or the mastery of literary terminology. Most teachers, whatever their commitment to any particular approach may be, would agree on the following goal for the teaching and study of literature in the high schools: we want the young to become readers, to find delight and value in literature, and to remain readers throughout their lives. If we keep this clearly in mind, much else about selection of material and approach and method will fall into place. We will understand that only through challenging and pleasurable experience with reading and the feeling that reading is of vital importance in their lives will the young continue to find time for books after they leave our classrooms. The fact that existing programs have often failed to produce lifetime readers indicates that our methods and approaches need revising.

But we realize immediately that we want more for the young than pleasure or a lifetime habit of reading books. We hope for continued growth in taste and discrimination. We ask not only that they read, but that they read thoughtfully and critically. Traditional programs emphasizing the painstaking dissection of a few "classics" have done very little to ensure that habits of critical reading will continue after the school years. Studies show that we have produced readers who read chiefly to satisfy their appetites for sex and violence, to identify themselves with glamorous and improbable fictional characters, or to escape from the pressing problems and issues that concern mankind.[2]

Literature as experience

Our principal aim, then, in teaching literature, may be to produce critical, mature, and thoughtful readers, but we cannot expect that the young will

---

[2] See the studies which have attempted to explain why people read: William S. Gray and Bernice Rogers, *Maturity in Reading: Its Nature and Appraisal,* The University of Chicago Press, Chicago, 1956, pp. 27–28; and Douglas Waples et al., *What Reading Does to People,* The University of Chicago Press, Chicago, 1940, p. 13. Research on the nature of critical reading is summarized in E. Elona Sochor et al., *Critical Reading: An Introduction,* (1959), and the nature of the reader's involvement, of misinterpretations which affect judgment, and of psychological reactions of readers are analyzed in James R. Squire, *The Responses of Adolescents While Reading Four Short Stories* (1964), Research Report no. 2, both from the NCTE, Champaign, Ill.

accept this goal for their own in the beginning. We must offer them something much more immediate and vital. Only when we offer them in literature
something as intense and meaningful as life itself can we be sure that we will
make readers out of the young people in our classrooms.

Literature as vicarious experience provides young people with important
insights by means of which they can see and understand much about themselves and society. Through reading widely in books which deal honestly with
life—all of life—and through guidance and discussion with wise and mature
teachers, they can grow to understand not only themselves and their relationships to the society in which they live but also the craft of the artist.

One of the most important reasons we can offer the adolescent for reading
is that through books he can live many lives. Through discussion he can come
to see the limitations of one man's experience: a few family relationships, a
few jobs, a small sampling of all that life has to offer. The reader, however,
can experience vicariously all the events and the lives he would like to live.
He can, through identification with the brave or the great, climb mountains,
perform heroic deeds, fall in love with beautiful women. By acknowledging and
serving the tremendous appetite for life in youth, we can help them experience
through reading all that one life can never hold and extend their knowledge
of themselves, other men, and other lives.

Literature as individual insight.   It is through literaure that we see into
the heart and mind of man. The masks each man wears in real life, the various
roles he plays as he presents himself to the world, allow us to see little of the
real self of our fellow men, or even to know ourselves with any degree of
completeness. The mist the heart wears disguises the deepest feelings we have,
and our greatest human failures are those in which we cannot share our feelings with those closest to us. It is the privilege and the mission of the artist
to lift the veil that hides the human heart and give us our closest looks at
man's innermost thoughts, feelings, and dreams. The mind of the artist illumines
the complexities of human character: we know the hidden thoughts, feelings,
and desires of few people in the real world as we know those of Eugene Gant
of *Look Homeward, Angel*, Stephen Dedalus of *A Portrait of the Artist as a
Young Man*, Anna Karenina, or Emma Bovary. By showing us the interior of
one human heart, the artist illuminates for us the experience of every man.
Through fiction, poetry, and the drama, we come to know the loneliness, the
beauty, the courage and pain of the human condition.

Literature as social insight.   Literature offers us also knowledge of man
as a social being, caught up in a complex of social issues and problems. We
see him continually against the backdrop of the society he has evolved, watch
his reactions to war and peace, to authority and economic privation. Literature
can interpret imaginatively the basic human situations: man's suffering of
injustice, his struggle for power, his conflict with his fellows, his rebellion
against the laws of God and man. The facts we learn from geography, sociology, history, and science become invested with human significance as we

live through drought and famine, the devastation of an atomic bomb, life in a Civil War prison, or racial conflict in South Africa. Such pictures of life can illuminate moments of history or serious social problems; they have their own human truth, different and more moving than the historian's document or the sociologist's report.[3]

There are few young people in our society who have not been touched in some way by the social problems explored in literature. As they search to define their own social values and to understand the problems of their age, they gain understanding and clarify their thinking through reading and discussing the books which present these problems in a human context. Today, when America's treatment of minorities is a major cause of distrust of democracy among the new nations and a threat to international peace, it is important that they gain insight into the human dilemmas resulting from complex social and economic issues.

Many young people in our schools have experienced hurt or rejection because of prejudice against their color, religion, or nationality. Through reading and discussing literature they share the feelings experienced by those who have been rejected: the heroine of Willa Cather's *My Antonia*, Florence Means' *Alicia*, the Mexican teen-agers in Beatrice Griffith's *American Me*. Boys and girls to whom Bergen-Belsen and Auschwitz are only names may experience through Anne Frank's story the suffering of exclusion and fear-darkened years of hiding, the tortured waiting for the sound of the storm trooper's boots on the stair. The passionate search for a homeland and the emotional significance of the founding of the state of Israel to Jews all over the world is humanized for readers in Leon Uris' *Exodus*. James Baldwin's *Notes of a Native Son* explores what it feels like to be a Negro in a white America.

Literature and international understanding.   The need teachers feel today to introduce young Americans to literature of foreign peoples and their cultures raises other questions about teaching. Good readers may be moved to deeper understanding and empathy by such pictures of other lives and peoples as Pearl Buck's *The Good Earth*, Kamala Markandaya's *Nectar in a Sieve*, or Knut Hamsun's *Growth of the Soil*. Without the guidance of a teacher who can help them see the common human problems beneath cultural differences, many students may read such books without understanding them. Immature readers have been known to reject Alan Paton's fine novel, *Cry, the Beloved Country*, because they didn't want to "read about people who lived like that." Such understanding comes to students through the widening of experience with books reflecting different cultural patterns, through discussion and understanding of such differences, and the guidance of a teacher who can help

---

[3] The treatment of the teacher's role in such situations is based primarily on the discussion of Louise Rosenblatt's *Literature as Exploration*, Appleton-Century-Crofts, Inc., New York, 1938. This book provides a valuable introduction for beginning teachers to the teaching of literature which deals with personal, social, and cultural problems.

them see the common human needs, joys, and sorrows which unite the human family.

The problems of racial tensions and the implications of *apartheid* are humanized through the sufferings of one man in *Cry, the Beloved Country.* We experience the torture of political imprisonment in Arthur Koestler's *Darkness at Noon,* the extermination of the Warsaw ghetto in Hersey's *The Wall,* the impact of war on civilians in his *Hiroshima* or *A Bell for Adano,* and in Steinbeck's *The Moon Is Down;* we understand Russia better for having read Tolstoi's *War and Peace* and Sholokhov's *And Quiet Flows the Don.* Through the availability of inexpensive paperback editions the great literature of the entire world is now within easy reach of our students. American boys and girls must know something of the world in which they will live, and whose future they will shape. And that future will probably depend, at least in part, on the understanding and imagination they display about the peoples and cultures whose future in that world they share.

Literature as esthetic experience.   The reader's involvement in the literary experience as pleasure, insight, and idea comes usually before interest in form, or in the art through which the writer expresses his ideas. The sense of form grows slowly in most readers, coming from wide and varied reading and much discussion and comparison of such matters as characterization, plot, structure, setting, tone, style, and mood. Awareness of form and content do not develop simultaneously in immature readers. Only gradually, and through skillful teaching, does the young reader acquire a sense of how a writer handles structure and plot, of how he orders the parts of a work into a harmonious whole.

During their study of literature, students should gain some insight into the creative process. Such a study as John Livingston Lowes' *The Road to Xanadu*[4] gives us glimpses of the breadth and depth of Coleridge's reading in books of travel and exploration that were assimilated in the "deep well of unconscious cerebration" and emerged synthesized into "The Ancient Mariner." A study of Keats' craftsmanship gives us the account of his search for the precise word in the revisions of "The Eve of St. Agnes." Both John Holmes and John Ciardi have written accounts of Robert Frost's search for pattern and rhyme in the composition of "Stopping by Woods on a Snowy Evening."[5] The seriousness and dedication with which the artist searches for the perfect form

---

[4] Vintage Books, Random House, Inc., New York, 1959.

[5] See M. R. Ridley, *Keats's Craftsmanship,* University of Nebraska Press, Lincoln, Nebr., 1963; John Holmes' analysis of Frost in Charles W. Cooper, *A Preface to Poetry,* Harcourt, Brace & World, Inc., New York, 1946, pp. 603–607; and John Ciardi, *How Does a Poem Mean?,* Houghton Mifflin and Company, Boston, 1959. Melville Cane, *Making a Poem: An Inquiry into the Creative Process,* Harcourt, Brace & World, Inc., New York, 1953; Stephen Spender, *The Making of a Poem,* W. W. Norton & Company, Inc., New York, 1962; and Malcolm Cowley (ed.), *Writers at Work,* The Viking Press, Inc., New York, 1958, all throw light on the artist's craftsmanship.

can be instructive for the adolescent who struggles with the writing of brief paragraphs.

Emphasis on insight and idea, rather than on the formal aspects of play, novel, or poem, should be, for most students, the central experience with literature during the high school years. For average and slow readers, the problems of comprehension of meaning and the beginnings of critical reading are the basic tasks. Only on a sure mastery of these can the subtler appreciations of the work of art be built.

The sense of form grows as the teacher leads students to see how the writer arranges the events in the plot of a novel or play or orders the lines of a poem. Sometimes the teacher can help them experience this order by showing them a different possible organization: they may be given a quatrain with its lines rearranged, a passage with words left out or changed. They may be asked what difference it would make if a particular scene came after or before another in a play or a novel, or they may discuss a different kind of ending. For instance, at the beginning of Edith Wharton's *Ethan Frome*, we meet Ethan, but we do not see Mattie or Zeena. What would it do to the novel if the door were to open at the beginning (as it does at the end), and Ethan were to introduce us to "Miss Mattie Silver"? Through such discussion of the appropriateness of the order of events, the contrasts of characters, the rightness of mood, tone, and atmosphere, teachers can develop in students a sense of the importance of form in all good writing as an inseparable part of the meaning of the piece of literature.[6]

Literature and values. In the study of literature, the adolescent encounters the values men live by. His reading about men and women who have made moral and ethical choices and his evaluation of these and their results provide him with a measure for thinking about his own choices and their consequences. The natural idealism of youth responds to the images in books of those who have lived lives of purpose, who have demonstrated personal, physical, or moral courage, or dedicated their lives to serving others. The adolescent, searching for heroes among worthy adults after whom he may model his own life and conduct, finds these in books in fuller dimension, often, than in life. Reading, thinking, and talking about literature are primary ways through which the maturing adolescent accomplishes one of the most important tasks of his development, the discovering and organizing of his own values and the formulating of his own philosophy of life.

The program in literature

The kind of readers we want to produce after six years of experience of literature—mature, independent readers of discriminating tastes, critical judgment, and sound appreciation—are those who have found increasing satisfaction in

[6] Further discussion of form is given in Chaps. 10 through 13.

reading and developed the ability to react honestly and think critically about what they have read. Such readers develop not through forced reading of required lists of classics or an accumulation of facts about history and biography, but through a planned progression of experiences in selecting, sampling, judging, reading, and discussing literature. They require the sure guidance of teachers who can help them take three important steps leading to good reading: comprehension of the written word, critical and analytical reading, and the development of esthetic appreciation.

The growth of literary comprehension

The foundation of literary appreciation is built on the skills of comprehension. Some of these have been discussed in Chapter 5, but others are basic to the understanding of the literary work of art in whatever form it appears. Understanding a novel, short story, or play involves accurate reading and understanding of clues pertaining to setting and to time. Reading often involves analysis of character, which is revealed through speech and action, through what other characters say, or in other indirect ways. Readers need to develop skill, too, in recognizing that fiction may be narrated from different

"When I read it at home, I didn't know it had all that stuff in it. Irony and metaphor and all that." Drawing by Saxon; © 1963 The New Yorker Magazine, Inc.

points of view. Understanding who is telling the story is essential to meaning.

Other skills of comprehension are involved, too, in creative reading of literary works. The reader must be sensitive to the denotations and connotations of words, for through these he discerns atmosphere, tone, mood, irony, and satire. He must be able to read figurative language with understanding and grasp the central metaphors in prose, poetry, or drama. An understanding of symbolism is a more complex matter and may develop slowly in the young reader, who tends to be literal-minded.

Irony and satire, always difficult for literal-minded students, may be experienced in a range of materials from the obvious to the subtle and complex. Much ironic comment on everyday life is available in contemporary journalism, and students may be asked to read and interpret such passages. The teacher may present for class discussion such a poem as Sassoon's "Does It Matter?" in which the ironic comment is fairly obvious as the poet dramatizes the maimed soldier thinking of the "splendid work for the blind," and the kindness of those who will assist the crippled.

Allied to this and to the study of figurative language is the ability to discriminate between levels of meaning: to understand when the words must be read at the literal level and when a figurative or symbolic level is implied. Sometimes both levels operate at the same time, adding complexity to the work of literature and to the reader's task. The development of these skills of comprehension will be treated in the succeeding chapters dealing with literary types.

The development of critical reading

Students do not become critical readers merely by reading a list of classics or by being told which are the great books. The ability to develop independent judgments about literature, to become sensitive to style, and to tell the differences between the good, the poor, and the mediocre grows slowly and sometimes haltingly, and it must be based on wide experience in reading, judging, and discussing these books with other readers. During the adolescent years, many of our students become omnivorous readers, devouring indiscriminately everything from the mediocre and ephemeral to some of the world's greatest classics. For the student who continues to read widely, some kind of judgment usually emerges slowly as the good literature makes the bad seem dull and cheap by contrast.

But not all readers achieve this state of discrimination by themselves. Some continue to read anything in print simply for escape long into the adult years. They have the ability to forget *War and Peace* and remember the plot of the mystery thriller they read years ago. They read omnivorously, and almost without any sense of critical evaluation. They remain immature readers all their lives. Such readers have seldom been given a chance to examine their own responses to literature and learn to make judgments about books instead of accepting the judgments of teachers or literary critics.

Critical readers can learn, too, that although personal identification makes literature compelling for us, we often tend to identify with characters whom we might not admire in real life: Macbeth, Hedda Gabler, Becky Sharp, Scarlett O'Hara, Eustacia Vye. The power of fictional characters may cast such a spell on us that we uncritically condone their failings and often fail to see them as the author intended us to. Students must learn to understand without condemning, although in literature, as in life, this is difficult to do. One may understand Anna Karenina without either condemning or condoning her leaving her husband and child.

As readers mature, it will be necessary for them to gain insight into more and more complicated characters about whom their judgments cannot be simple: Emma Bovary, Lord Jim, Anna Karenina, Ahab, or Beret of *Giants in the Earth*.

When we identify too strongly with a character or read our own wishes and emotions into the novel or play, we distort and frequently fail to understand what the author wrote. Students have been known to read regret or shame for adultery into the behavior of an unfaithful wife; they are certain that Rhett Butler will return to Scarlett O'Hara or that Eustacia and Wildeve could have been happy together. They may even project into the story or novel their own religious beliefs, as when they decide that the dying man in Hemingway's "Snows of Kilimanjaro" is experiencing a religious conversion. Reading with critical faculties intact is a mature achievement.

The development of appreciative reading

The reader who has felt the impact of good literature may well be a confirmed book addict for life. It is probable that unless his reading does have this kind of impact, probably during the secondary years, reading may never become an important part of his life. More important than any other experience in his English classes, perhaps, is that sense of living in literature which he must feel if he is to remain a reader. At times it is the sense of brilliant illumination of character—fascinating, deadly, or tragic. Sometimes it may be the sense of a life so vivid in books that real-life experiences lack luster beside it. Often our most admired friends are dull beside Becky Sharp, Cathy Earnshaw, Lord Jim, Raskolnikov, and Captain Ahab.

Literature captures us because of the flash of imaginative insight it affords. The reader's response is often a complete engagement of heart, mind, and imagination; often, too, it is a visceral response: we may weep or laugh, feel sick or recoil in revulsion. This identification of the reader with the experiences and emotions of fictional characters is a first important step to appreciative enjoyment.

The long tradition of literature that starts from Achilles dragging the body of Hector around the walls of Troy in the *Iliad* and comes right down to Michener's *The Bridges at Toko-ri* has engaged the feeling of readers who respond to physical action. The immature reader demands from novels action, and often physical violence: cowboy-and-Indian skirmishes or wars, old or new. Even more significant for mature readers is the impact of an idea, a glimpse into the depths of a human heart, or a revelation of character. The moment when Huck Finn decides not to betray Jim, when the police come for Tess as she sleeps on the altar at Stonehenge, when Heathcliff flings himself on Cathy's grave—all these are what make literature live.

The fully appreciative reader responds to the author's imaginative insight into character as well as to thrilling action. As students gain in the ability to read with depth and perception, they relish the story in which little happens on the physical level because so much is happening in the character's mind. The reader who has passed through experiences of reading, judging, and comparing books with his friends, under the guidance of skillful teachers, may be ready during his senior high school years to read and enjoy complex and subtle novels and short stories with enjoyment and insight.

The mind of the reader trained to notice the way in which an artist achieves his effects responds fully to the writer's craft. He notices skillful handling of dialogue, the symbolic use of setting, the music of words, and the rhythm of great descriptive prose. The mature reader delights in the pattern and order of the work of literature and responds to the unity of design and idea. In a real sense, then, he responds to the power of literature to challenge the mind to think, the heart to feel, and the senses to respond to the writer's art.

Organizing the program in literature

The way we teach literature at the secondary level reflects what we think is most important about it and how we believe students develop comprehension and appreciation of what they read. The numerous possible patterns of organization—a chronological survey, types of literature, selected classics or a program organized around themes and units—may profitably be examined in some detail. Each has values and limitations and many programs use a combination of these patterns during the year.

The historical or chronological approach

The frequent use of this approach to literature results in part from the complaints of college instructors that their students completely and appallingly lack any historical sense in the study of literature. For many high school students, Chaucer walks hand in hand with Milton and Dryden, and Jonathan Edwards with Whitman and Stephen Crane.

Admittedly, at some point in his education, the student needs to learn literary history. The chief limitation of such courses at the secondary level lies in the immaturity of the student and the magnitude of the task. Modern learning theories suggest that students learn and remember best as facts fall into meaningful contexts. Appreciation and understanding of literature involve more than a mastery of names of authors and their works and the ability to sort them out into the appropriate centuries; all too frequently, such courses demand little more of students. The study of literature may result in a mere name-dropping acquaintance with authors, dates, and titles, frequently without the reading of more than a brief fragment of an author's work in an anthology. Furthermore, the learning task confronting immature students is formidable. Having read little, they are asked to learn *about* authors instead of reading them. The breakneck pace of such courses and the lists of facts to be learned frequently leave the student with little more than a dizzy impression of scattered details. Without wide reading of many whole books or any historical framework or context in which to fit new facts, students, even at the college level, achieve little growth in awareness of chronology. Such courses have been in increasing disrepute at the college level; at the high school level they do little to develop appreciation and comprehension of literature.[7]

Organization by types

The generic approach to the study of literature often suggests that what is most important about literature is its form. Although students may develop skills in recognizing the various genres through such study, they do not usually emerge with the feeling that literature is chiefly concerned with communicating the experience of man. Study by types provides a neat packaging of literature into units: six weeks may be spent on the novel, on poetry, or on the short story. This approach often ignores or overlooks an important concept in literature—the same literary theme may be expressed in poetry, the drama, fiction, or the essay. One of the purposes of the student's study of literature is to enable him to observe the relationships of great literary themes which are expressed in various types of literature.

Students need close study of plays, fiction, the essay, and poetry under teacher guidance for appreciation and understanding of literary forms, and this close reading is usually part of every year's work in the study of literature. Most teachers feel today that a combination of approaches to literature serve the young student's literary development better than a year's focus on genre alone.

[7] See the discussion of the American literature survey in Thomas J. Wertenbaker, Jr., "A Surfeit of Surveys: Thoughts on Chronology and Theme in American Literature," *English Journal*, vol. 52, January, 1963, p. 9: "A survey tends . . . to inculcate in him [the student] the worst possible reading habits while it slights its subject and cheats him, unsuspecting, of his literary heritage." See also, Commission on the English Curriculum, *The English Language Arts*, Appleton-Century-Crofts, Inc., New York, 1952, p. 133: "The survey should await the maturity of college years."

Selected classics

The view that there is a core of great pieces of literature which all readers should know dominated the planning of programs of literature throughout the early years of this century, and is still prevalent in many schools. The influence of the early college board examinations kept a small list of selected classics in the curriculum of many schools long after the College Entrance Examination Board had abandoned tests which required students to give evidence of mastery of certain works. The chief strength of this plan of organization is its attempted provision for cultural continuity in an all-too-often fragmented culture.

The chief limitations of such a program, in the eyes of many teachers today, are found in the difficulties faced in presenting students of widely varying abilities, backgrounds, stages of development, and interests with the same books at the same time. Such programs do not provide for the large majority of students who are indifferent, reluctant, or poor readers. For able students, some effort to provide knowledge about great literary works is common today, as many programs include mythology, the Bible, Greek plays, the *Odyssey* and the *Iliad,* the plays of Shakespeare, and great world novels. An NCTE survey found that colleges do not require that students be familiar with any particular list of books, although they expect general acquaintance with literature of real merit; about 15 per cent of the colleges polled emphasized the essay.[8]

The integrated program: unit teaching

The general outlines of the integrated program are described in Chapter 1. Many teachers of literature believe that the flexible plan of an individualized reading program, such as that described in Chapter 15, and some teaching through thematically organized units, offers the maximum opportunity for students to achieve their best growth in reading skills and in the development of appreciation of literature.

The approach to literature through thematic units has clear advantages in flexibility and comprehensiveness. It allows the teacher to bring in biographical and historical facts where relevant; it focuses now on one single piece of literature, now on a group of poems, plays, or short stories, and now on a combination of these expressing a common theme. It allows for a maximum of flexibility in planning, grouping, and handling of individual differences. Surveys have shown that the traditional literature program which used to present all students with a standard list of selected classics has changed in many schools and that, as paperback books become more easily available, the use of thematic units is becoming more widespread at both junior and senior high school levels.[9]

---

[8] *High School–College Articulation of English: Reports by the NCTE Committee on High School–College Articulation,* NCTE, Champaign, Ill., 1961–1963, pp. 1–7.

[9] Arno Jewett, *English Language Arts in American High Schools,* U.S. Department of Health, Education and Welfare, Washington, D.C., Bulletin no. 13, 1959, p. 76.

Although overemphasis on the didactic, biographical, historical, and technical approaches has been criticized, each of these is appropriate in some classroom situations in connection with some literary works. Few teachers would think of beginning the study of *A Tale of Two Cities* without acquainting the student with the historical context. Biographical information has significance in a study of the themes of the Jesuit poet Gerard Manley Hopkins; one can hardly detach Fitzgerald's *The Great Gatsby* from the social setting of the 1920s; Paton's *Cry, the Beloved Country* and Steinbeck's *The Grapes of Wrath* grow out of a particular economic and social setting in a particular country at a particular time. Only the teacher's understanding of literature and of students can finally answer the question of which method or approach will serve best with a particular class in teaching a piece of literature.

What literature shall they read?

One of the most dramatic changes in the teaching of English in the last few years has been the increasing range of selections offered to young readers. We have seen a growing number of contemporary novels added to the books which used to be standard classics. *Ivanhoe, Silas Marner,* and *A Tale of Two Cities* are still widely taught, but they have been joined in many, if not most schools, by Hawthorne's *The Scarlet Letter,* Willa Cather's *My Antonia,* Crane's *The Red Badge of Courage,* Steinbeck's *The Pearl,* Hemingway's *The Old Man and the Sea,* and Rolvaag's *Giants in the Earth,* among others. The range of selection, made possible by the low cost of paperback books and the availability of inexpensive hard-cover volumes, has made it possible for many teachers to meet the wide range of differences in their classes with varied choices.[10]

Censorship and the teacher

The listing of such books brings us to one of the most perplexing problems the modern teacher must deal with in selecting literature for adolescents. With an unlimited supply of modern realistic novels available at the corner drug store, the narrow range of life offered in some of the standard nineteenth-century classics seems remote from the interests of today's adolescents. Many teachers, believing that students should read challenging modern books, have found themselves in trouble with school boards, administrators, and parents.

---

[10] One study of books mentioned by superior students in Advanced Placement examinations illustrates the variety. Among books mentioned more than once were such difficult works as *War and Peace,* Stendhal's *The Red and the Black,* and Virginia Woolf's *Mrs. Dalloway.* The mention of such books as Jones' *From Here to Eternity,* Wright's *Native Son,* Huxley's *Point Counterpoint,* Hemingway's *The Sun Also Rises* and Faulkner's *Light in August* suggests an increasing liberalism in reading lists. Albert B. Friedman, "The Literary Experience of High School Seniors and College Freshmen," *English Journal,* vol. 54, December, 1955, pp. 521–524.

Books such as Uris' *Exodus*, LaFarge's *Laughing Boy*, and Lewis' *Main Street* have been removed from the shelves of high school libraries; authors declared unsuitable for school use include Chaucer, Plato, Mann, Faulkner, Thoreau, Twain, Whitman, Huxley, Wolfe, and others. Homer's *Odyssey* has been attacked as "unchristian." Groups of parents have objected to Hawthorne's *The Scarlet Letter*, Pearl Buck's *The Good Earth*, and Walter Edmonds' *Drums along the Mohawk* because they are said to contain "pornography" and "obscene language." [11]

Other books perennially under attack or banned in many communities are *The Catcher in the Rye, The Grapes of Wrath, 1984,* and *Brave New World.* The restrictions on reading lists and books available for use in classes and school libraries have become so disturbing that the American Library Association has issued a Freedom-to-Read resolution, and the Committee on Censorship of the National Council of Teachers of English has published a statement, "The Student's Right to Read," which indicates steps teachers, librarians, and students may take in choosing books or in meeting criticism of choices. Both statements have been endorsed by publishers and educational groups. The 1960 NCTE Convention renewed the stand taken in 1953 when it resolved to "reaffirm its trust in the right of teachers to select books most appropriate to their teaching without interference from either administrators or outside groups intent on any form of censorship." The Meeting on Book Selection and Censorship of the 1963 NCTE meeting urged that teachers of English consider the contribution which each work may make to the education of the reader, its esthetic value, its appropriateness to the curriculum, and its readability, both in structure and content, for a particular group of students.[12]

Since any program in literature designed to encourage wide reading and to assist students to select independently and read more maturely may encounter such problems, teachers are rightfully concerned about the stand they should take in using a book in the classroom, ordering it for the school library, or recommending it in a reading list.

Although both parents and teachers probably underestimate the knowledge and experience of life of teen-agers, few teachers would recommend either Lawrence's *Lady Chatterley's Lover* or Miller's *Tropic of Cancer* for classroom discussion. Yet many feel that *1984* and *The Catcher in the Rye* strongly support moral values and consider *The Adventures of Huckleberry Finn,* banned in some schools, an eloquent plea for brotherhood.

Here the NCTE's support of the teacher's right to judge is of great importance. Teachers in turn must assume the responsibilities involved in free-

---

[11] Reported in *Council-Grams,* NCTE, Champaign, Ill., issues of December 31, 1960, and February, 1964 ("Summary of Proceedings of Meeting on Book Selection and Censorship"). See also Lee A. Burress, Jr., *How Censorship Affects the School,* Wisconsin Council of Teachers of English, Special Bulletin no. 8, October, 1963, and continuing reports in the *Newsletter on Intellectual Freedom,* American Library Association, Chicago.
[12] *Ibid.*

dom to teach by being sure not only of the literary quality and the worth of the books they choose to recommend or to teach, but of their ability to discuss such books with a class in such a way as to lead to increased maturity. Important, too, is their careful consideration of the impact such books will make on immature readers. Probably some balance is the wisest course. It is not the teacher's role to campaign militantly for freedom to teach any book despite community mores; yet many teachers feel it is an abdication of responsibility to yield to pressure from a minority and withdraw a book which can make a significant contribution to the student's maturity.

It should be our aim in teaching literature to raise a generation of readers who will be able to read a book and understand the author's purpose and the book's meaning. It is plain that many adults who object to *1984, The Catcher in the Rye, The Adventures of Huckleberry Finn,* or *Brave New World* have not understood them; some have not even read them. Some of the teachers who are contributing most to the development of mature habits of reading and the development of judgment of young people are teaching such books so that young people understand them. As one such teacher says, "Our students are reading books in which they are finding answers, good, bad, or spurious. We bring these books out from under the table, out of the area of the forbidden, and talk about them." The consensus, then, of many teachers of English is that we ought to avoid novels which overemphasize or distort sex or violence or those whose characters are too neurotic for young readers to understand as are some of Faulkner's and Sherwood Anderson's.

The teacher is not a crusader. The mature teacher will tread softly, choosing books which can help young readers grow in experience and judgment, but refusing to insist that all students read a book—even a good one—to which a number of parents object. There are always other books to choose.

Some experienced teachers who have successfully taught controversial books in their communities make the following suggestions:

1. Have the principal read the book.

2. Don't require the book of all students.

3. See that no child reads a book to which his parents object.

4. Allow such children to be excused when the book is discussed.

5. Invite parents to join in an evening discussion of books their children are reading.

6. Use tact and taste in discussing delicate problems.

7. On occasion, invite male teachers to discuss a boys' book with the boys or a woman teacher for a discussion with the girls. (Principals and guidance counselors have helped in this way.)

8. Be honest. If they want to read the current salacious best seller, say "No, not for required reading. It gives an ugly and distorted picture of the relations between men and women; erotic scenes seem to be included every few pages to keep the reader interested. If you want to read it on your own,

come in and talk it over." The teacher may then suggest good modern fiction in which relations between men and women are treated honestly.

Other problems of selection

Another important question of selection deals with the desirable balance of American, British, and world literature in the curriculum. The dominance of British literature in the curriculum has long ago given way to a representative selection of the standard American authors during each of the high school years, taught today perhaps even more frequently than selections by British authors. In most schools, the eleventh-year American literature surveys seems to be the rule, although many use thematic units rather than the chronological survey as an organizing principle.

The trend to include more world literature in the curriculum is a promising one. Although some teachers argue that much is lost in literature in translation, few would suggest that American students remain unfamiliar with some of the great books of our Western heritage: Homer, Stendhal, Tolstoi, Dostoevsky, Mann, or Ibsen. Foreign educators visiting this country have criticized this insularity of American students, and accused them of ignorance of great European writers.

Although the tendency seems to be to include world literature chiefly in the twelfth year, it seems desirable to include some world literature at each level of the secondary years. Frequently, thematic units include outstanding pieces of world literature among the selections offered; units on international understanding, world literature, or a group of books about foreign countries are often used at each grade level. Sample units of this kind are suggested in Chapter 15.

Should the emphasis in the secondary school be on contemporary literature or the classics? Here again, opinions are mixed. Criticism of the tendency to include too much avant-garde contemporary literature before students are widely read in more traditional writings is common today. Conversely, some critics of American education have deplored the fact that European youth seems to know much more about American contemporary writers than our own adolescents do. Faulkner, Hemingway, Steinbeck, and Caldwell are widely known and read abroad but seldom included in American courses of study. At present it is probable that Faulkner's *Intruder in the Dust,* Hemingway's *The Old Man and the Sea,* and Steinbeck's *The Pearl* are the only commonly taught novels of these three writers.

There are at least two possible solutions to the problems of selection touched on here. The first is to suggest a balance of contemporary and nineteenth-century literature for the reading which all students will do together. Emphasis should probably be on contemporary literature for the average and slow groups. An individualized reading program and the inclusion of thematic units during each year of the secondary school makes it possible for students to select a balance of readings for themselves and to determine the areas in which their reading needs enrichment. If there is discussion in class of the values of a broad background in American, British, and world literature and the desirability of understanding both contemporary and older literatures, many students will take the responsibility for planning their own programs of independent reading.

Are there any books all students should read? There is no easy answer to this question. College professors say that there is no single piece of literature in our heritage which all students—even at the graduate level—can be assumed to know: not Shakespeare, not the Bible, myths, or Greek plays. Many, therefore, have urged that schools teach a basic list of books to fill this need. Good students can no doubt be encouraged, even required, to read the great books which are part of the educated man's heritage. Forcing poor readers to do so has led to the substitution of watered-down classics for simple but well-written books which they might read and enjoy.

Considering the wide individual cultural and educational differences among students, it seems impossible to agree on any books all American students should read during a particular year. College board examinations have not based tests on such standard pieces for many years. Lists of "great books" and masterpieces of fiction are plentiful.[13] The teacher who guides college-bound students, or others who desire to read classics, should introduce the students to such lists and suggest essential reading.

What the teacher contributes

The teacher must bring a number of resources to the teaching of literature. Foremost of these is, of course, broad and deep reading, sound literary judgment, eclectic tastes, and an ability to recommend to students those works they are ready for and most likely to enjoy. The mature teacher has his private enthusiasms for Henry James, perhaps, or for Proust, Kafka, or Camus, but he does not force immature students to read these books. He has a broad enough reading background to remember that at thirteen or fourteen he may have thought Stevenson's *Treasure Island* or Pyle's *Men of Iron* exciting books; he may have become engrossed with a series of novels about Tom Swift before he was ready to tackle *Tom Jones*.

The teacher of literature needs three other important assets. If he is to handle modern novels which deal realistically with sex and social themes, he must be a mature person, at ease with language, and able to discuss such books without discomfort or embarrassment. He (or she) needs enough experience of life to be able to help young people understand such a book and gain a mature perspective of the slice of life it treats. Teachers who feel uncomfortable with such discussion usually prefer to work with less controversial books.

[13] See the listing of book lists at the end of Chap. 15.

Secondly, teachers who discuss with students books which treat the difficult topics of prejudice, intolerance, discrimination, and persecution must have skill and maturity if class discussions are to increase instead of lessen tolerance. They must be particularly skillful with language and must be able to understand how to help young people handle their encounters with words which lead to stereotyping and prejudice—such as the "loaded" terms for national, racial, and religious groups—and they must be able to show that some problems have no easy solution, but require understanding.

Instead of yielding to demands to ban such important works as *The Merchant of Venice* and *The Adventures of Huckleberry Finn*, teachers may help students to understand what they represent. Shakespeare reflects some sixteenth-century attitudes toward the Jew, but that does not prevent the play from being shown in Israel, and receiving great acclaim from Jewish audiences. Mark Twain, too, reflects attitudes toward the Negro characteristic of people in his own locale, but Huck's friendship for Jim speaks louder than his use of the offensive word "nigger."

The teacher of world literature or of books which present foreign countries or their peoples must know how to help students understand the wide cultural differences which such novels often represent. The reading of books alone will not in itself ensure increased understanding or insight. The teacher who deals with such books needs to understand the different ways men live and be aware of the anthropologist's view that no one way is inherently right or superior. He must recognize in himself the tendency to ethnocentric thinking, or the belief that his own way of life or the "American way of life" is the norm by which all cultures should be measured, and he must be able to help his students recognize the fallacies of this kind of thinking. He must help them to be free of the notion that their own race or nationality is superior and that all others are to be considered inferior. His students should understand the differences between race and nationality and the fallacy of using the term *race* loosely and inaccurately ("the dominant race," "the English race," "the Anglo-Saxon race," and others).

Finally, he must be able to help students free themselves from the tendency to think in stereotypes: the "typical" Frenchman, German, Chinese, or African. He (and they) must understand that while the novelist is often interested in types, one cannot accept any fictional portrait of a human being as a valid generalization of a national type. Mann's *Buddenbrooks* is a portrait of the bourgeois businessman in Germany, but his characters live as individuals; Pearl Buck's farmers in *The Good Earth* have the characteristics of many Chinese farmers, but they do not represent the Chinese people.

Evaluation

The most important test of the development of comprehension, critical judgment, and appreciation of literature is that of changes in students' reading tastes, their perceptiveness of talk about literature, and their ability to read more complex literary works with comprehension. Unfortunately, our usual tendency is to measure achievement by grades on quizzes and tests at the end of the study of a unit of literature, tests which are chiefly devoted to questions on plot, incident, and fact rather than on interpretation or critical comment.

Essay questions about literature are excellent preparation not only for college-bound students, but for all students who get too little practice in organizing an answer to a question which calls for facts and details. Students can be taught to handle such questions in ways that will improve their performance on tests and increase their expository skills as well.

The teacher will find a full range of sample questions on literature in the booklet prepared for teachers by the Commission on English of the CEEB. The essay questions and the sample answers rated by examiners from one to five, with the examiners' comments on the student's performance, illustrate what college-bound students may be expected to achieve in understanding of complex literary works—novels, plays, poems, and essays—as well as the command of language, sentence structure, organization, and logic demonstrated in the answers. Practice in writing answers to such questions should be a continuous part of work in the study of literature during the six secondary years, especially for college-bound youth. Individual chapters on the literary forms will show how these may be supplemented by short-answer quizzes, study questions, open-book questions, and the like. Chapter 16 adds suggestions about the uses of particular kinds of tests, and the adaptation of test questions to classes of different abilities.

The following example of a test question, a student answer which received a top rating, and the comments of the teacher-readers who framed the examination and read the answers, shows what good students may be able to achieve in ability to read and interpret a novel, and to discuss it in clear, logical prose. This is a sample question for eleventh graders from the *End-of-Year Examinations in English*. Although the work discussed is a novel, such a question serves equally well for any of the other forms of literature. Forty minutes is allotted to the question.[14] The student's answer earned a score of five on a rating scale of five (high) to one (low).

[Question:]
   A theme which writers have examined for centuries is the achievement of self-knowledge (a person's recognition of his own strengths and weaknesses, values and prejudices, aspirations, and fears). Inevitably this self-knowledge is achieved only after the person has undergone an ordeal which has forced him to reexamine his own values and those of the world about him.

---

[14] Question, answer, and teacher comments from *End-of-Year Examinations in English for College-bound Students, Grades 9–12*, College Entrance Examination Board, Princeton, N.J., 1963, p. 105.

[Directions:]

Write an essay in which you show how an author has dealt with this theme in a major work (novel, drama, long narrative poem, or biography). Identify the work and the character you are writing about and be *specific* and *thorough* in your examination of the way the writer has developed this theme. You may need to refer to the action and setting, or to symbolic elements of the work, but you should concentrate on the changes in attitude which the character undergoes. Show that you understand *the nature of his new self-knowledge*.

[Sample answer:]

Kurtz, in Joseph Conrad's *Heart of Darkness* is an example of a character who goes through a trying ordeal and gains a deeper knowledge of himself. The story itself is narrated by a seaman named Marlow, through whose eyes the reader sees Kurtz. Kurtz is introduced by hearsay as a universal genius. He is a bright young man sent into the heart of African darkness to gain experience in the trade of ivory and write a social report on native customs. His purpose is to gain self-education and self-knowledge.

The full irony of this situation is recognized when Marlow first meets Kurtz face to face. A row of dried heads on stakes around Kurtz's jungle hut testifies to the knowledge he has gained. Instead of leading the natives toward the civilization of the Europeans Kurtz has lost all trace of his old ways and become a king among the savages—a bloody tyrant of the darkness.

This condition does not seem to show any self-knowledge, and certainly while Kurtz is among the natives he does not worry about knowing himself. And yet when, as a dying man, he is enclosed in the cabin of a small river boat slowly winding its way back toward civilization, Mr. Kurtz is forced to consider. In the jungle he had considered only the values of his nearest neighbors. His own values and those of the world he left were allowed to slip away and become deformed. When his former way of life—the way of Europe— forces itself upon him he is forced to reexamine his actions and his double set of values. Conrad states that even the most civilized of men has a savage side of his personality he generally keeps subdued. Kurtz, on the other hand, has let his evil side dominate and has stepped one pace over the brink that separates civilized man from the animals. The trying experience of dying a slow death among his own people but as an outcast causes Kurtz to reexamine himself. He goes from a state of defending his own actions and demanding "only justice" for himself to a state of abject recognition. His final words are "The horror! The horror!" Kurtz truly gains self-knowledge by a trying experience and reexamination of his own values. But this is an ironic, tragic knowledge that comes for him much too late.

[Comment on sample 1:]

The strengths of this paper are its perceptive understanding of an exacting and appropriate work, its constant awareness of the demands of the question, and its intelligent use of relevant and illuminating details. The wording is exact without being pretentious; the sentence structure is firm; the style is disciplined. . . .

Maturely and perceptively the student works his way through the ironies and complexities of the book and of the character with complete accuracy and little simplification. He makes a valid and useful distinction between the kind of knowledge of himself, amounting to delusion, that Kurtz has persuaded himself of and the real self-knowledge that finds its anguished expression in "The horror!" He writes of the character with a detachment not devoid of sympathy of which only the rare student is capable. A less mature, less responsible reader might have indulged in moralistic comments on Kurtz's fall from grace. This student is too sophisticated to apply the "crime doesn't pay" tag to a subtle portrayal of human disintegration.

Of the standardized examinations in literature available, a great many test acquaintance with titles, authors, and mastery of facts about literature, rather than understanding of the work read. The following go beyond the recall of facts, and attempt to examine understanding of literature:

. . . *Cooperative Literary Comprehension and Appreciation Test,* grades 10–16, Cooperative Test Division, Educational Testing Service, Princeton, N.J., 1935–1951.

. . . *Interpretation of Literary Materials,* high school, college, grades 10–12, Cooperative Test Division (Subtest of Educational Tests of General Educational Development, United States Armed Forces Institute), Cooperative Test Division, Educational Testing Service, Princeton, N.J., 1944–1957.

The able teacher of literature may test himself as well as his students by the questions set in examinations such as these, and by the answers his students can give. Such mature understanding of a work of literature comes from classes in which there is ample reading and discussion of books to challenge the best minds in the class.

Above all, the teacher of literature must be one who loves books and can communicate his own enthusiasm about reading to his students without insisting that they enjoy the same books. He should be the kind of person described by a librarian, who says of her high school English teacher: "His enthusiasm for books, and his reading aloud, taught us to love books. He changed my life."

The teacher's role is of major importance in the success of any literature program. The books he selects to teach, the knowledge, wisdom, tolerance, and insight he brings to the teaching of these books and his patience and skill in guiding the reading and discussion of young people will determine primarily the kind of adult readers his English program will produce.

There is the world of the novel, and the world of the student. The teacher's job is to provide the bridge that links them. It is an old cliché of the profession that we need to "relate literature to life," but how this is done is not so easily said. The experiences of fiction are not always readily comparable with those in our own lives. Yet the reader who can see in the literary situation some analogy to his own struggles, problems, and strivings may find in the work of literature meaning that enlarges his own experience. He need not have had an encounter with a whale to see what it is to allow one maiming accident to darken his whole view of life; he need not have lived in pre-Civil War Missouri to know how it feels to want to be free of the "sivilizing" influences of adults and the restrictions of a narrow code of ethics.

If he is to become at home in so foreign a world as the China of *The Good Earth,* he must be able to share the universal human problem of a man wanting to build a life of his own, marry, and establish a family. If he is to read *Death of a Salesman* with understanding, he must be brought to feel that the problems of an aging salesman facing loss of a job, loss of the affection of his sons, and loss of his own self-respect are those which touch him, too.

The teacher who can bring literature to life for students has an unerring sense of the point at which the world of the student touches the world of the novel, play, short story, or poem. The chapters which follow explore some ways of accomplishing this important meeting of experience in the study of the chief literary types.

Selected bibliography

Dwight L. Burton, *Literature Study in the High School,* 2d ed., Holt, Rinehart and Winston, Inc., New York, 1964. Excellent suggestions for teaching literature to adolescents.

Northrop Frye, *Anatomy of Criticism: Four Essays,* Princeton University Press, Princeton, N.J., 1957.

Edward J. Gordon and Edward S. Noyes (eds.), *Essays on the Teaching of English,* Appleton-Century-Crofts, Inc., New York, 1960. Collection of essays delivered at the Yale Conference on the Teaching of English. Many on poetry, the drama, and the novel.

Hans P. Guth, *English Today and Tomorrow: A Guide for Teachers of English,* Prentice-Hall, Inc., Englewood Cliffs, N. J., 1964, chap. 5.

Charlton Laird, *The World through Literature,* Appleton-Century-Crofts, Inc., New York, 1957. A useful collection of essays on various national literatures.

Lewis Leary, *Contemporary Literary Scholarship,* Appleton-Century-Crofts, Inc., New York, 1958. A guide to the most useful books about the foremost literary genres.

Louise Rosenblatt, *Literature as Exploration,* Appleton-Century-Crofts, Inc., New York, 1938. Develops a theory of literature as experience and points out the necessity of interaction between reader and artist.

Edward Rosenheim, Jr., *What Happens in Literature: A Guide to Poetry, Drama, and Fiction,* The University of Chicago Press, Chicago, 1960. (Paper: Phoenix Books, 1961.)

Rene Wellek and Austin Warren, *Theory of Literature,* 3d ed., Harcourt, Brace & World, Inc., New York, 1964. An influential discussion of the New Criticism. (Paperback.)

CHAPTER *10*

The most influential books, and the truest in their influence, are works of fiction. They do not pin the reader to a dogma, which he must afterwards discover to be inexact; they do not teach him a lesson, which he must afterwards unlearn. They repeat, they rearrange, they clarify the lessons of life; they disengage us from ourselves, they constrain us to the acquaintance of others; and they show us the web of experience, not as we can see it for ourselves, but with a singular change—that monstrous, consuming ego of ours being, for the nonce, struck out.

ROBERT LOUIS STEVENSON [1]

The art of fiction

Fiction in the literature program

English teachers, trying to introduce their students to the great nineteenth-century novels beloved of earlier generations, are often disturbed at the seeming indifference of today's youth to the classics. There is considerable evidence to show that *Tess of the d'Urbervilles* and *Jane Eyre* can speak as eloquently to this generation as to the last. Unless young people become readers, however, social activities and the ever-present entertainment offered by television offer strong competition to the development of interest in reading.

One important reason for student indifference to great pieces of fiction is that the process of technical analysis or preoccupation with historical or biographical details has frequently become a substitute for experience with the work itself. Hamlin Garland's "Under the Lion's Paw," the story of a family's struggle for existence against the bitter experiences of drought, crop failures, and an unjust landowner, has been treated in the classroom merely as an example of "local color"; the poignant dilemma of the Jewish families in hiding in *The Diary of a Young Girl* has been presented as a lesson on fascism in Germany; stories whose characters elicit strong reactions are dissected for climax, the use of foreshadowing, or a chapter-by-chapter outline of plot.

[1] "Books Which Have Influenced Me," *Essays of Travel, and in the Art of Writing,* Charles Scribner's Sons, New York, 1923, pp. 317–318.

We can and should help students to gain insight into the writer's craft, but the secondary student is not yet ready to do graduate work; he must become a reader with ample experience of many books before he is ready for a course in the "New Criticism." In focusing primarily on close analysis of form, on history or biographical backgrounds, or on the analysis of symbolism, imagery, and structure, the teacher risks alienating the student from the human elements of fiction, and often leads him to believe that reading a book presents insuperable difficulties. Ninth graders have been sent symbol hunting in *Moby-Dick*, a novel with which many college students have considerable difficulty. Much reading of fiction in the classroom proceeds by circling the periphery of the work rather than by acknowledging that it involves people, experience, and life.

Program into practice

During each school year most teachers will include in the English program some works of fiction—both novels and short stories—which students will read closely and discuss together. This part of the literature program—often called intensive reading—requires that the teacher understand the capabilities of the class and consider what literary experiences students are ready for.

Selecting the novel

There are numerous problems in selecting a novel for class reading. Reading abilities may differ widely within one class. What appeals to girls (particularly at the junior high school level) seldom appeals to boys. Differences in ability and interest in a class can vary enormously. Teachers employ various stratagems in order to adapt selection to ability and interest and yet allow the profitable close examination and discussion of pieces read in common. The boys may read one novel and the girls another, learning much from each other's discussion. The class may be divided into three groups, with each group reading one novel, and all three novels concerning a common theme on which discussion centers. Often, reading centers around the unit theme, with all students reading certain selections in common.

The novel chosen should be a good one—one which deals with real concerns of maturing adolescents. The problems of Silas Marner, a voluntary outcast from society or those of Ivanhoe, a twelfth-century English knight, are remote from the compelling concerns of most young people. Those of Hester Prynne, of Maggie Tulliver in *The Mill on the Floss*, of Tess of the d'Urbervilles, and of Willa Cather's Antonia are, on the other hand, real, immediate, and meaningful. The books in which these characters appear deal in an artistic and adult way with the problems of relations between real men and women; moreover, they do not disregard love and passion—the subjects about which boys and girls at this age urgently seek information in cheap literature. These novels often show the young the difference between glamorized, lurid sex of the kind purveyed by some of the pulp magazines and books that deal honestly with the problems of real men and women.

When such novels as *A Tale of Two Cities, Ivanhoe, Silas Marner,* and other traditional choices are required by the course of study, the teacher needs to think through the same problems of introduction that he faces with any piece of literature: how can the student be made to feel that the life in the novel touches his own at important points and how can he be shown that his reading of the novel will contribute to his understanding of the world and people? If the teacher cannot help him answer these questions positively, it is probable that the syllabus should be changed. A good many "requirements" are still listed in courses of study not because of any real convictions of teachers that they are the best choice for the grade level, but simply because of inertia or delay in revising an outdated curriculum guide.

Handling reading.   The nature of the class, its previous experience with reading, the maturity with which it reads, the dependence or independence with which its members can work, all are matters which will govern the amount of time spent and the nature and depth of the reading they will be asked to do. Six weeks is usually far too long for concentrated study of a novel. Many teachers think that between five to ten days is ample time for discussion and reading. Some very complex novels may take three weeks. We can never teach all about any novel; some things have to be reserved for later reading and study of another piece of literature. If we do one novel in two weeks, we will have time to read three in the six weeks often allotted to such study.

In some classes, a major problem is to get students to read the novel assigned. Traditionally, coercive measures have been attempted. We have forced students to read by giving daily or weekly quizzes, we have cajoled and threatened, and still some students will not—or cannot—read. Often when such resistance is a problem, the assigned novel will be found far distant from the interests of today's boys and girls; often, too, it will be far beyond their reading comprehension. Some students can finish the book in three days; others will not have finished by the end of weeks of reading. In estimating the capabilities of the class, the teacher will have to decide how to handle reading time.

Some teachers assign the reading of a novel two weeks to one month in advance, advising students of the date the reading should be completed and planning with them how best to finish it. Fast readers may be told to put off the reading so that the book may be fresh in their minds. Slow readers will be advised to start at once. Questions to keep in mind while reading help focus the reader's mind on important points. The necessity of finishing the book on the date due is emphasized. Students cannot discuss what they have not read. Students may be encouraged to give a book one quick reading and then to review it slowly for more intensive study. Some teachers suggest a plan for having a student keep track of the chapter-by-chapter progress of reading of the members in the class.[2] The thing to be avoided is the snail's pace reading of a chapter a day or a minimal number of pages. Whatever will serve the reading of the book as a whole will necessarily avoid much of the elbow-jogging and nagging pressure to read chapters and pieces of the book, which often distorts the reader's view of the whole work.

Introducing the novel.   Getting the class ready to read the novel demands that the teacher engage the interest of the class in reading the work assigned and indicate how the reading may be profitable and meaningful for them. Too often the only introduction students get is having the books passed out and twenty-five pages assigned for Monday.

In many classes the teacher's best stratagem is to arouse curiosity about the book by reading the first few pages or chapters with the students. He may also allow them time to begin reading in class and, thereby, get them launched into the book.

Allowing the first few students who finish to talk with the teacher about the book often sets the pace for the rest of the class. Study guides with a few well-chosen questions for each chapter or for the whole book, may help readers to focus on important aspects of the novel.

Sample questions such as these may be used as a study guide for a novel such as Conrad's *Heart of Darkness:*

1. In his novel, *Heart of Darkness*, Conrad makes many references to the work's title. How many can you find and explain? In what contexts are they used, and to what do they refer?

2. Why does Conrad begin the novel on the Thames at sunset? How do you explain the references to the history of the Thames? To the Romans coming up the Thames as marauders? What are the parallels between Roman colonizers and the British in Africa?

3. What do you think Conrad refers to by the word "darkness"? What do you think he means by it?

For students who have difficulty with the novel, some sessions in which the teacher helps them to clarify important details may be helpful. The writing of brief paragraphs—not quizzes—may make clear whether they understand the setting, the major characters, and the developing conflict. They should be given an opportunity to raise questions in class about parts they do not understand. Slow readers may need help from the teacher in the form of reading aloud the opening descriptive scenes, talking over the first incidents in the book, and visualizing setting and characters.

Although some brief discussion about historical and social setting is needed if students are to understand *Ivanhoe, A Tale of Two Cities, Silas Marner,* or *Cry, the Beloved Country,* the leisurely stroll through the suburbs of Saint

[2] Walter Loban et al., *Teaching Language and Literature,* Harcourt, Brace & World, Inc., New York, 1961, p. 304.

Antoine, the heaths of Dorset, or nineteenth-century London is not for most secondary students. We need not feel guilty if we rush them over the heath to the spot where things begin to happen. The heath will stay there until we get back to it. The human dilemma in the novel is the first point of contact. Some kind of psychological bridge is needed between the experience of the student in the classroom and the experience of life in the novel he reads.

We may also ask young people to speculate about a central event in the story. One ninth-grade teacher of reluctant readers asked the class—largely boys—whether they thought it would be possible for an elderly man to go out alone in a boat on the ocean and bring back a large fish. They thought it was impossible and eagerly read Hemingway's *The Old Man and the Sea* to find out whether they were right. Older students may be asked whether a marriage such as that of Clym Yeobright and Eustacia Vye could work out (Hardy's *The Return of the Native*), whether a poor boy who inherited a sum of money might change (Dickens' *Great Expectations*), or what might happen to a poor family when the father finds a very valuable object (Steinbeck's *The Pearl*). The questions must obviously not detract from the suspense of the story, but they may be used to point up the conflict and start students wondering how the story works out.

Reading with comprehension

Young people need many experiences in discussing the various aspects of literature before they are ready to read a whole masterpiece with comprehension. For most of them, skill in reading fiction develops slowly, through a series of meetings with works of increasing difficulty. In a sense, good teaching of literature presents students with a "spiral curriculum" in literary comprehension. Each aspect of fiction may be discussed at varying levels of complexity as students look at short stories and novels in which these aspects are illustrated: setting, plot, characterization, point of view, symbolism, irony, style, and theme. As the student's ability to deal with abstract concepts grows, he will gain skill in reading with understanding.

Understanding clues to time and place. The young reader, longing for excitement and action in his reading, often skips or ignores descriptive writing which may set the tone or mood of the novel or short story. He must be helped to see the function of description in the novel and enabled to read quickly and perceptively the clues to time and place which will make the whole piece meaningful.

For the junior high school reader, it is fairly easy to perceive through the description of the Van Tassel farm, with its suggestions of ripeness, abundance, and prosperity, that it is a mouth-watering objective for the lanky Ichabod Crane as he woos the fair Katrina. Irving is a master of description. The sleepy village shown in the first few pages of "Rip Van Winkle" offers another illustration of setting which underscores the theme of the short story.

The teacher may help senior high school students understand setting in many ways. Sometimes he needs to read the first twenty-five pages or so of *The Return of the Native* with a bright class in order to help them see how intricately the heath is bound up with the motivation of the characters and with the events in the story. Few, except very good readers, can understand why Hardy takes so long to get at matters of interest, and many resent what they consider his dawdling over the story.

Some classes decide, although somewhat reluctantly at times, that the description of the heath is essential to the mood, atmosphere, and characterization in the novel, indeed, to everything that happens in it. They may be asked to list the incidents which are somehow related to life on the heath: the fire, Clym's furze cutting, Mrs. Yeobright's death, the reddleman's comings and goings. Skillful questioning by the teacher may elicit the information that not only is incident firmly tied to place, but the characters are what they are because of the heath: Eustacia, torn with desire to get away to the glamor of Budmouth; Clym, bound to it by ties of sympathy and concern for its people; Thomasin, who accepts it as her natural background.

Dickens' masterly use of fog in the opening chapters of *Bleak House* may provide for older readers insight into a physical setting and atmosphere which become symbolic of the people, events, moods, and attitudes in the novel. The paralyzing fog moves through London and Lincolnshire, enervating characters, preventing people from seeing themselves or others as they really are, keeping in its grip the dead hand of the law, the decadent aristocracy, and the impotent and unhappy few who cannot break away from its suffocating influence into redeeming action.

Practice in guessing clues to setting may be given by the teacher's reading of the introductory paragraphs of several short stories or novels, and asking students to guess (either in oral discussions or in writing) what the setting is. Benét's "By the Waters of Babylon," Clark's "The Portable Phonograph," Shirley Jackson's "The Lottery," and Poe's "The Fall of the House of Usher" serve as good choices for this kind of exercise. Older students may be asked to observe the mood of the story as they read "The Fall of the House of Usher," Willa Cather's "Paul's Case," or Forster's "The Machine Stops." Clues to time may be dealt with in similar ways. It seldom occurs to students that "The Portable Phonograph" or "The Machine Stops" must take place in some future time.

The "primitive level": understanding plot. In our zeal to develop critical readers of fiction, we often forget that the boys and girls in our classes are unsophisticated readers, with little experience before junior high school of reading a book for anything but its story. Although this is a valid reason for reading, they cannot remain at this point if they are to become critical and perceptive readers.

It is useful for students to see that this level of appreciation of fiction is but one of many and is a basic, even a primitive one. E. M. Forster reminds us that the story goes back to prehistoric times: "the primitive audience was an audience of shock-heads, gaping round the campfire, fatigued with contending against the mammoth . . . and only kept awake by suspense. . . .

We are all like Scheherazade's husband, in that we want to know what happens next." [3] The story as a series of events arranged in a time sequence is different, Forster holds, from the plot, which deals with events interpreted and with human motivation. " 'The king died and then the queen died' is a story. 'The king died and then the queen died of grief' is a plot." [4]

To stay at the level of plot is satisfying. Many readers never get beyond this kind of reading, and it serves an important purpose. Unless what happens is clear, the reader cannot go on to ask *why* these things happen, why they happen in this particular order, and what their significance is. In many great novels, the happenings are of central importance, and the power of the action is the major achievement of the writer. The whale hunt of *Moby-Dick*, the escape of Magwitch or the death of Miss Havisham in *Great Expectations*, Jean Valjean's rescue of Marius in *Les Misérables*—these things are the stuff of which novels were, and sometimes still are, made. Today's students, however, must, in general, become accustomed to novels in which literally nothing happens except in the minds of the characters; novels in which the daily concerns of living are the only events as in Joyce or Proust. Until we can appreciate such books as these, we are like Forster's shock-headed caveman gaping, "What next?" If we would appreciate the subtleties of character and situation, we must, as he says, come out of the cave and learn to read at many levels of understanding.

Early questioning about the novel or short story should establish whether the students have read enough to find out what happens, whether they really *know* what happens, and whether they understand the relationships between events. Thus, the first and elementary level of questioning is the factual level. Students have been known to be confused over what happens in *A Tale of Two Cities*. What does all the business about the mysterious traveling on the Dover Road mean? What does Tellson's bank have to do with the story? Who is Jerry Cruncher and what is his occupation: why does his "missis" keep flopping, and why does he resent it? In many classes discussion of the novel never rises above the level of "what happened?"

As soon as possible, students must be led beyond questions of "what" to questions of "why," involving character motivation. For young students embarking on a study of a complex art, the beginnings of discussion must be rooted in fact—partly because all interpretation rests on the accuracy with which the reader can understand what happened, and partly because students need a careful check to find out whether they understand the verbal symbols they have read. Many teachers are thrown off balance when, after carrying on a lecture on the symbolism in a great novel, they find that students do not have an elementary notion of the factual level of the book.

As the student begins to deal with more complex books, particularly those

---

[3] E. M. Forster, *Aspects of the Novel,* Harcourt, Brace & World, Inc., New York, 1927, pp. 46–47.
[4] *Ibid.,* p. 131.

in modern literature, he will find that events do not occur in an orderly time sequence. By the time he is a twelfth grader and from then on into adult life, if he is to read as mature readers do, he will deal with plots as difficult to follow as those of Conrad's *Lord Jim* or Faulkner's *Intruder in the Dust,* in which the novel shifts backward and forward in time. The development of a critical point of view about the perennial happy ending demanded by many high school students, and about the stereotyped plot, may be assisted by study of some of the plot summary exercises which teachers have used.[5]

Understanding point of view. The concept of the point of view from which a story is told is a significant part of understanding the writer's craft. Students recognize this artistic device but dimly, and it frequently confuses them. The literary critic who thought that too many martinis had been responsible for his confusion in reading Faulkner's *The Sound and the Fury* did not realize that the narrative is told by an idiot and the happenings are seen through the limited intelligence of the narrator.

In fiction it is difficult for immature readers to get accustomed to the various points of view a writer may assume in telling his story. Junior high school readers often object to the "I" who tells his own story, as in *Jane Eyre, David Copperfield,* and *Treasure Island*; they may prefer the less demanding approach of the omniscient author who tells us carefully *about* the characters, and often leads us to know what we are supposed to think about them. Immature readers tend to confuse the first person narrator with the author. It is difficult to get them to understand that Dickens did not necessarily himself undergo all that he recounts of David Copperfield's adventures, and that the madman who narrates "The Tell-tale Heart" is not Poe himself. (How many readers graduate from high school with the conviction that Poe was as mad as any of his characters?)

The simplest and most ancient point of view is that of the omniscient author—he who tells us about the characters and, in earlier fiction, comments on them, chides them, or tells us what to think of them. Thackeray pushes aside the acters on his stage to warn us that though Amelia Sedley is charming, she is a lightheaded sentimentalist, so infatuated with love for George Osborne that she cannot appreciate Dobbin's genuine affection. Similarly, Fielding interrupts the adventures of *Tom Jones* to comment—often hilariously—on manners and morals and to instruct the reader in what to think.

Even young students may speculate about the variations in point of view in the stories and novels they read. They may be asked to decide what a writer can tell if he chooses a narrator from among the characters. The first-person point of view, often disliked by immature readers, is easier for them to accept and to follow if they understand its important uses. A clear illustration is what

[5] See Dwight L. Burton, *Literature Study in the High Schools,* rev. ed., Holt, Rinehart and Winston, Inc., 1964, pp. 153–166. The publisher has given teachers permission to reproduce these exercises for class study.

it adds to the story of *The Adventures of Huckleberry Finn*. Most junior high school readers can see that what we know of Huck's education, attitudes, values, and character traits we learn because it is he who tells us the story; it is through his consciousness that we see the feud of the Grangerfords and the Shepherdsons and the shabby dealings of the King and the Duke.

Older students may observe how *Wuthering Heights* employs intricate devices in point of view. Mr. Lockwood tells the story, but information about what happened before his arrival at Wuthering Heights is filled in during his convenient illness by the Earnshaw nurse, Nelly Dean.

Studying characterization.   Readers can be led to see that character is revealed through action. Becky Sharp's immortal gesture of hurling the works of "the great lexicographer" out of the carriage as she leaves boarding school gives us in one flash a penetrating glimpse of her character; Mrs. Bennet's featherheaded reaction to Lydia's elopement in *Pride and Prejudice* and Jane Eyre's renunciation of Rochester show us what these people are.

Characters, like real people, also reveal themselves through what they say. When Huck Finn plays a practical joke on the faithful Jim, leading him to believe that his fear that Huck was drowned had its roots in nothing more than a dream, Jim's dignified rebuke to the boy who tried to "fool ole Jim wid a lie" shows us eloquently the affection and loyalty of the Negro for the white boy, as later, Huck's humbling himself to Jim in apology reveals Huck.

What characters say about other characters is a primary source of confusion for many literal-minded young readers. Thus even college freshmen are not on their guard when the barber in Lardner's "Haircut" describes the cruel practical joker, Jim, as "a card." Students often attempt to make the facts of the story fit that description, failing to realize that Lardner carefully builds a picture of Jim's actions that shows the sorrow his thoughtless clowning brings to others.

Sometimes characters are revealed as the omniscient author allows us to observe them through his eyes. As he comments, we learn what they are like.

Characters are also illuminated through the interior monologue (the thoughts that flow through their minds). We cannot read Joyce, Faulkner, or Virginia Woolf without understanding this stream-of-consciousness technique. As early as the seventh or eighth grade students may prepare for the encounter with modern fiction by reading Michael Fessier's "That's What Happened to Me" and understanding that the brave deeds and physical feats happen only in the boy's fantasy. Thurber's "The Secret Life of Walter Mitty" also provides such insights.

"What kind of person is this character?" "Why does he behave like this?" or "Why does he say this?" are all questions the mature reader must ask himself automatically about any work of fiction. Students can be taught to look behind surface actions or words to gain real insight into character. Even mature English teachers have been known to reject *The Catcher in the Rye*, with its powerful picture of adolescence, because they have misunderstood the main character. They denounce him for using "bad words," failing to see beneath his hostile behavior the troubled, sensitive adolescent, tender to all hurt things, who wants to be a "catcher in the rye"—a protector of innocent young children in danger from the evils of the world.

Many short stories provide good opportunities for youngsters to read for practice in interpreting character. Junior high school readers may read Marjorie Kinnan Rawlings' "A Mother in Mannville" to discuss why the orphan boy Jerry lies about having a mother; they may talk about the relationship of the two brothers in Irwin Shaw's "Strawberry Ice Cream Soda," and of father and son in Sarah Aldington's "Clodhopper." At the senior high school level, stories like Steinbeck's "The Leader of the People," Katherine Mansfield's "Miss Brill" and "The Doll's House," Lewis' "Young Man Axelbrod," and Willa Cather's "Paul's Case" provide good opportunities for discussion of character.

Interpreting figurative language and symbolism. Many students are accustomed to thinking that figurative language is something one learns in the study of poetry. Few can understand it well when it occurs in prose, and the tendency to read all prose literally is one of the chief limitations of poor readers.[6]

No reader can read effectively if all his interpretation is at the literal level. Great books are significant at various levels, and the good reader finds esthetic satisfaction and richness in his ability to comprehend literal, figurative, and symbolic meanings. The immature student is, of course, annoyed and baffled at being asked to read at different levels. Often this is the measure of his difference in ability from the gifted reader. Such students remind one of the plaintive remark of Jack Benny at finding himself drawn into a deep discussion of the symbolism in *The Old Man and the Sea*: "But I thought it was just a story about fishing."

Even young and immature readers can understand at a simple level that Jody's preoccupation with the fluttermill in the early pages of *The Yearling* and his indifference to it in the last chapter are symbolic of his growing up. They may see that various aspects of the setting of *Ethan Frome* symbolize the emotional condition of the characters: Ethan, who has been in Starkfield too many winters, is frozen in heart and tongue until the warmth of Mattie's love releases his natural emotions. His pitiful inarticulateness when he wants to talk to her about what he feels is related to the stark, bare, frozen landscape. The young can understand, with some help from the teacher, how feelings and speech, too, may be frozen in the human being.

More mature students may sense the impact of brilliant symbolic images: Per Hansa's dying with his back to the haystack and his face to the West in *Giants in the Earth*; the picture of the black plow, silhouetted against (and almost obscuring) the brilliant red sun in *My Antonia*, or, in the same work, the picture of the happy, maternal Antonia and her children bursting out of the fruit cellar to greet Jim Burden.

[6] See also the discussions of interpreting figurative language in Chaps. 3 and 11.

Teaching about style.   Style is another elusive quality of literature which it is difficult to teach the young to recognize. Adults, too, usually know whether or not they think a book well written, but they are seldom articulate about what makes it so.

Much oral reading by the teacher or listening to passages read on records can help the young ear become trained to recognize the subtle rhythms and cadences of prose. Some sessions of classroom discussion should be given over throughout the high school years to readings in which young people read out loud passages from books they have liked and think are particularly well written. During the junior high school years, little real analysis of style will take place, but the teacher will approach the subject of style inductively by asking students to observe certain details as they read, and to bring examples from their reading to the class. Some assignments such as those at the end of the chapter may help young people begin to develop the awareness of the writer's craft which leads to an appreciation of style.

Discussing theme in the novel.   We often tend to forget in our teaching how highly abstract is the theme of a great book. Even at the college level, trying to compress the main idea of a great novel or short story or play into a statement of theme is one of the most difficult things an English teacher teaches his students to do.

Is is fruitless for the teacher of English to expect students to express the theme of a complex book that taxes the judgment of competent critical minds. He must expect that during the high school years probably no student will be able to formulate a statement which coincides with that of a good critic. We would do well to remember that most adult readers do not consciously state the theme of every book, short story, or play they read. It is enough that high school students think seriously about the purpose of the novelist, and understand what he is trying to say. They should understand that what the artist says through the medium of language is a thing quite different from plot, from what happens to his characters, and from the ending of the book. During discussions, the skillful teacher will provide many experiences and activities which may prod students to search deeper into the author's purpose and urge them to try to state the theme of a book being read.

Students must come to understand that every serious writer of fiction has a personal view of life and of people, and that the writer selects setting, characters and incidents as a dramatic means of making a statement about the world in which we live. His work contains direct or implied statements of belief about human beings, society, or mankind. It is this central idea, this observation about life or about people, which is the theme of a work of art. Students may learn, too, that much popular fiction, written solely for purposes of entertainment, does not have such a controlling purpose or theme.

Practice in trying to state theme leads to increased awareness of its importance, and more perceptive attempts to put the generalization into words. Often the author himself states his theme, sometimes several times, either by commenting directly himself or else through the mouths of one of his characters. Hardy tells us frequently in *The Return of the Native* that the plight of man is a matter of indifference to the universe. Other novels of Hardy's state the same theme, and students may find it restated in many of his poems, among them, "Hap," "The Subalterns," and "The Convergence of the Twain." Wilder suggests that the theme of *The Bridge of San Luis Rey* is an answer to the question with which the book begins: "Either we live by accident and die by accident, or we live by plan and die by plan." His answer: "There is a land of the living and a land of the dead, and the bridge is love, the only survival, the only meaning. . . ." [7]

Students often think that a topical statement is a statement of theme. For them, the comment, "A picture of post-Civil War reconstruction in the South," states the theme of *Gone with the Wind*. This familiar pattern of the jacket blurb, or the advertising subtitle—the topical statement which indicates what the book is about—is quite a different thing from theme. Nor is a simple moral tag a theme, despite the fact that literature is still frequently taught with this concept. De Maupassant's "The Necklace" is *not* a story designed to teach us not to live beyond our means, although it is often presented that way to high school students. De Maupassant is saying, most critics think, that insignificant, trivial happenings can often give an ironic twist to the direction of a life. The theme of *The Scarlet Letter* is *not* that persons trapped in adultery will be punished, although that novel, too, is often taught from that moral point of view. Hawthorne's interest in the effects of sin and guilt on his characters is often obscured.

In *The Grapes of Wrath*, John Steinbeck is pointing out that human beings have a capacity to endure social injustice with courage and dignity. Hemingway writes of the courage with which men face death, and many young people can come close to stating the themes of his short stories and novels. They may see that the theme of *Silas Marner* is not that people should not value gold too much, but that a life in isolation is of little value to the possessor until made precious by human love.

The reader must begin to learn at an early age that it is possible, as well as satisfying, for him to understand what the author is trying to say in a significant work of fiction; however, until he has had more experience in reading he will not be able to state the theme of a complex work.

Evaluation

Some brief questions the teacher may ask to gain an idea of the student's grasp of plot or character are the following:

[7] Thornton Wilder, *The Bridge of San Luis Rey*, Grosset & Dunlap, Inc., New York, 1927, p. 235.

List the four or five most important happenings in the book (or short story) in the order of their occurrence.

List three adjectives which might describe the character of _____ in the story and explain each in one sentence.

Identify key characters in the novel or short story by indicating their importance to the story in a single sentence.

Explain in one or two sentences what key symbols in the novel stand for: Hester's scarlet letter, Queequeg's coffin, the spilled wine in *A Tale of Two Cities*, the "granite outcroppings" of *Ethan Frome*, Kino's pearl, in *The Pearl*.

Junior high school readers, or those who still read at a literal level, may be asked simpler questions about plot and character, multiple-choice or short-answer questions about events, the meanings of key words in the story, or the actions of the characters.

For readers of average ability and better, open-book questions may serve as good test questions after the study of a novel. They may be asked to trace through the book the development of a character, or the steps leading to an important climax or decision. The teacher may ask them to look back through the novel for instances of character change. They may, for example, chart the steps from Kino's finding the pearl to the ending of the book in which the baby dies and Kino throws the pearl into the sea; or they may chart the steps in the struggle of the old man to land the fish in *The Old Man and the Sea*.

Essay questions such as those suggested at the end of Chapters 9 and 15, and those suggested by the CEEB Commission on the English Curriculum for the *End-of-Year Examinations in English*, or for the Advanced Placement examinations, provide excellent samples of questions which may measure a student's breadth and depth of reading, his understanding of a complex novel, and of figurative and symbolic meanings. Edward Gordon has suggested five different levels of testing: (1) to remember a fact, (2) to prove a generalization someone else has made, (3) to make one's own generalization, (4) to generalize from the book to its application in life, and (5) to carry over the generalization into one's own behavior.[8] At least three levels are commonly used in essay testing. Students may be asked to remember facts from the books they have read: what difficulties did the characters encounter, what did they do about them, what did X do when . . . ; or to offer interpretations of behavior and character: why did Eustacia fail to answer the door when Mrs. Yeobright knocked? Why was Beret unable to adjust to her environment? What three ways of dealing with sin and guilt does Hawthorne show in *The Scarlet Letter*? They may be asked to select the incidents and details in *Silas Marner* which show Silas' isolation from his fellow men, to discuss its causes, or the ways in which he was brought back into communication with men. They may discuss Crane's view of courage in *The Red Badge of Courage* and show how he illustrates the various aspects of courage or the lack of it.

[8] Edward J. Gordon, "Levels of Teaching and Testing," *English Journal*, vol. 44, September, 1955, pp. 330–342.

The third level, the critical level, is one which some students are able to handle with intelligence. Here, the student may be asked to look at the book as a whole and to make some critical observations about it. (This level is comparable to Gordon's third and fourth levels.) They may be asked to explore several of the layers of meaning in Conrad's theme of darkness—the physical, the intellectual, the psychological, and the moral—to discuss what he says about human beings and society at each of these levels, and to discuss what he says about them in *Heart of Darkness* as a whole. A question of comparable difficulty may ask students to notice similarities in theme of several pieces of literature. The question may be put this way: the central character in each of several short stories we have read learns something about the adult world which disillusions him. What is his discovery, and what is the experience through which he learns it? (Faulkner's "Barn Burning," Hemingway's "My Old Man" and "The Killers," and Joyce's "Araby.")

Further examples of essay questions and testing techniques are provided in Chapters 9 and 16. Essay tests give students important opportunities to demonstrate their command of a subject, their reading comprehension, their observation of detail, and their ability to think critically and make sound judgments about the literature they read. Teachers will probably want to supplement the kinds of tests and questions suggested here with some of the standardized tests available in order to measure their students against those in other parts of the country through the use of standardized norms. Some of the best of these are suggested in Chapter 9, page 237.

The teacher of fiction introduces his students to the world of men and women, to their struggles and passions, decisions and indecisions, their strivings for love, fame, or happiness. As the student observes human beings and their interaction, their conflict with themselves, with each other, or with forces beyond their control, he learns much about himself, about life, and about his own values. The world of fiction can enlarge his concept of humanity, and of the dimensions possible to man's life. As he learns to look at the novel or the short story as a work of art, he becomes aware of the ways in which the artist has struggled to shape his view of the world and of human beings into significant form. But the central meaning of his experience with literature, the thing which will keep him reading, is finding kinship with men of all periods of time and of many different cultures, and his understanding of their search for answers to problems he recognizes as his own.

An approach to a novel: a student unit

The study unit which follows is a plan for teaching a novel to twelfth graders, developed by a student at the Harvard Graduate School of Education. The plan illustrates the student teacher's working out of the major matters for discussion in the novel, of largely inductive procedures, and of attention to meaning, style, and form. The plan has been condensed from its original form.

Cry, the Beloved Country: A Study Unit[9]

This paper is a plan for a unit of work centering on Alan Paton's Cry, the Beloved Country and bringing in relevant material from Africa. The work is planned for seniors in the college preparatory curriculum or for a very capable group of juniors. . . .

I think that the whole class would enjoy the story about the destruction of a way of life, concerning a Zulu minister who tries to save his sister and his son from the evils of modern city life, but who fails in both attempts. . . . In telling the story, Paton has drawn many effective contrasts: white against black, the rise of the modern city against the deterioration of the land, and the ruthlessness of commercialism against the close bonds of the tribe. There are many ideas for discussion here, for the situation in Africa has parallels all over the world. Paton also shows that wisdom can grow from sorrow and hope from destruction, for the minister returns to his home with an understanding of himself which he did not have before, and he has also formed a lasting friendship with the white man who lives near his village.

. . . The opening chapters set up the basic contrasts in the book, and also introduce the reader to the most important features of Paton's literary method. If the student reads these pages carefully and thinks about what is being done in them, he will be able to watch the ideas in them develop throughout the book and also gain a sense of Paton's organization.

Some of the questions which should be considered first are:

1. What is Paton trying to do in the first chapter? He describes the veld, certainly, but he does more than set the scene. Students should consider how much of an impact this description has for them. It would be a good idea to read this chapter aloud, substituting the impersonal "one" for Paton's "you" and omitting Paton's imperatives. For Paton gives a very personal picture of the land, and the reader is involved in this description to an extent that he does not at first realize.

2. The class should also consider why Paton writes of the land: "It is not kept, or guarded, or cared for, it no longer keeps men, guards men, cares for men . . . the men are away, the young men and the girls are away" (pp. 3–4). Students who have read the chapters as a unit will connect this statement with the conversation between Stephen Kumalo and his wife in the next chapter: ' "He is in Johannesburg," she said wearily. "When people go to Johannesburg, they do not come back" ' (p. 8). At this point the class might look at the way in which the city is treated throughout these chapters and see how the contrast between city and land is built up, as Kumalo leaves his home to go and find his sister and son.

3. This might lead into a discussion of Paton's method of characterization. What kind of a person is Stephen Kumalo? You learn about his gentleness through his conversations with his wife and with the small child who brings him the letter. You also learn a great deal about him by seeing him in contrast to Johannesburg. He is a simple, humble man who is overwhelmed by his new experience and easily duped by a member of his own race. (This point should be brought out, for it is an example of what the city can do to people's values; it is not just the white people who are cruel to the blacks.) It should also be noticed that Paton brings out a dualism in Kumalo's own character. Stephen is basically a humble man, but he cannot resist giving the other people on the train the impression that he is a man of the world, who makes frequent trips to Johannesburg. He

[9] By Barbara Zahner, reprinted from *The English Leaflet*, April, 1955, and Alan Paton, *Cry, the Beloved Country*, Charles Scribner's Sons, New York, 1948, and Jonathan Cape, Ltd., London, by permission.

will succumb to this kind of dishonesty throughout the book. This is one way in which Paton shows that Kumalo is a human being, not a cardboard character, and also shows that no issue in this book is clearly black or white, good or bad; all are complex.

4. Some discussion of Paton's language should also tie in here. When he uses native terms, what does he do besides give the reader a taste of the way a native talks? Are these terms integrated with the book? The class might look at the passage which describes Stephen's journey into the city.

5. Paton's prose style should also be considered. He has a varied style, for he suits his method to the scene which he is creating and to the idea which he wants to bring out in that scene. In many cases, his writing is very biblical. This is especially true of the first chapter, where he uses long sentences, made up of many short phrases, and containing many conjunctions. It would be a good idea to read the Twenty-third Psalm in connection with this chapter and see how similar the two pieces of writing are.

6. Paton also changes tenses in telling the story. Most of the narrative is in the past tense, but he is apt to switch to the present to create an instantaneous feeling for a scene, as in the description of Kumalo's arrival in Johannesburg.

. . . Class discussion should bring out such points as:

1. Stephen's search for Absalom. In how many different places did he have to inquire for him? With each new step in the search the suspense of the story is built up. Another contrast is brought in here, between Stephen and his brother John Kumalo, who has lost all sense of humanity since he came to the city and is exploiting the racial situation to gain power.

2. Stephen's temporary falling-out with Msimangu, the native priest who is helping him to find Absalom, should also be mentioned. . . . Paton gives a slight relief to the intensity of the search, showing at the same time how the search weighs on the nerves of these two men who are by nature so even-tempered. . . .

3. Students should also read aloud the section describing the living conditions for the natives in Johannesburg and the building of Shantytown. The paragraphs in this section would be excellent for choral reading, while the conversations could be taken by individual voices.

4. It would be interesting to see whether the class feels that there is any connection between the search for Absalom and the shooting of Arthur Jarvis, and whether they feel that the story is reaching a turning point. Paton gives no specific signs that the two events are connected, but the fact that the shooting follows so closely on the end of the day's search, and the newspaper account is described so fully, leads one to think that it is going to have major importance in the story.

5. These five chapters end on a note of despair, as Paton introduces his very lyrical paragraph "Cry, the beloved country, these things are not yet at an end. The sun pours down on the earth, on the lovely land that man cannot enjoy" (p. 72). Here one should recall the first chapter and see how much its meaning has increased. The class should also notice how it contrasts with the ending of the first assignment (first six chapters), when Stephen's hopes were so high. Here one begins to get a sense of the book's organization as a dream, in which success and failure follow each other throughout.

The basic themes of the book have now been established, and the class will also have explored the chief points in Paton's style and method of presentation. The following class discussions should center around these same areas. The class should watch the parallel development between Stephen's meeting and eventual reconciliation with Absalom, and James Jarvis' gradual acceptance of his son Arthur's support of the natives. James Jarvis' change in attitude is one of the most interesting parts of the book. Because he reads through his dead son's papers, he starts to look at the racial question in a new light. By the end of the book he has carried his son's philosophy into Ndotsheni, he has hired an agricultural expert to start building up the land, and he has given Stephen Kumalo the money for a new church. His new point of view and his friendship with Kumalo are the rewarding part of the book.

Class discussions should not only trace the development of this friendship, but should also notice that it is achieved only because Stephen Kumalo's son killed Jarvis'. There are many ways in which Paton illustrates the philosophy that hope comes through sorrow, but this is the chief one. The wisdom which both Kumalo and Jarvis have reached at the end of the book grows out of their suffering; it is their mutual suffering which unites them and which leads to hope for a better world. . . . Both Jarvis and Kumalo have a fuller understanding of the contrasts of which their worlds are composed, and can work to bridge the gap between the forces of destruction and creation. . . .

There is a great deal of material, in addition to the outside reading, which should be brought into the discussion of *Cry, the Beloved Country.* If the students live in or near a city which has good museums, they should take advantage of them. A trip to the African section of the Museum of Natural History in New York is better than any kind of writing for introducing one to the country and its people. The Museum bulletins, as well as magazines such as *Life* and *National Geographic,* have frequent articles on Africa, which should be brought into class if they are available. The same efforts should be taken to visit an art museum or find reproductions of African art. There are also good movies on this country.

I think that it is also important to bring in some discussion of contemporary life in America. Living conditions in many parts of this country are not very different from those in Johannesburg's Shantytown, and pictures might be brought in to illustrate this point. The American city has many of Johannesburg's evils. Juvenile delinquency grows in a big city under the same conditions of overcrowding and lack of equal opportunity for the minority groups. I think that analogies might be drawn here between the attitude towards minority groups in both countries; newspaper and magazine articles representing both the intolerant and unprejudiced points of view could be brought into class.

There are two other short pieces of writing which should be read in class, to bring variety into the discussion. One is the biblical story of Absalom. The other is a Public Affairs pamphlet written by Paton in 1951, on *South Africa Today.* This gives a brief, comprehensive treatment of all the problems in the novel and also contains illustrations. It is important to see how deeply a writer can be concerned with the problems of his world. Parallels could be drawn here to the Romantic poets' concern with the French Revolution, and particularly to Shelley's activities as a writer of pamphlets. It should be emphasized at the same time that the author's point of view will not have a lasting effect unless his writing is good.

When the class is discussing Paton's organization and style, parts of Maxwell Anderson's play, *Lost in the Stars,* which is based on the book, could also be brought in. The book's dramatic structure comes out very strongly when it is compared to *Lost in the Stars,* for Anderson has followed much the same pattern of organization. He has also kept many of the original scenes almost intact. The class might like to dramatize part of the book themselves or present scenes from the play in a school assembly. If they do not have a chance to stage the play, they might do a choral reading of two or three sections from the book. Students could listen to parts of the recording of *John Brown's Body*, if a phonograph is available, to see how effectively a choral reading with two or three solo parts can be handled. They should also have a chance to hear the music which Kurt Weill wrote for the play.

Student activities and assignments

The following sample assignments for the study of fiction may be supplemented by other excellent teaching exercises drawn from such resources as the articles on teaching literature in the *English Journal*, Margaret Ryan's *Teaching the Novel in Paperback* (see bibliography), and the chapters on teaching literature in the current methods textbooks suggested as resources in the bibliography of this chapter and of Chapter 17.

. . . Students may be asked to write a comparison of a book with the movie made from the book or with the televised version. What is retained? Left out? Changed? Why? How do you account for the changes? Did the original author have anything to do with the script?

. . . Students may discuss the inevitability of the endings in short stories or novels. Could Jody have kept the yearling, Flag? Could the men have escaped death in *The Bridges at Toko-ri?* Is it inevitable (according to Hemingway's design) that Catherine die in *A Farewell to Arms?*

. . . A few minutes of class time may be spent on asking students to recall the most vivid scenes they can remember from a book that has moved them. The teacher may contribute his own instances. Are the scenes sharp visual images or are they moving, dramatic, or exciting? Students may remember Hester on the scaffold at the beginning of *The Scarlet Letter* or in the woods with Dimmesdale; Tess sleeping on the altar at Stonehenge; Rawdon Crawley discovering Becky with Lord Steyne in *Vanity Fair*.

. . . Students may discuss their understanding of the endings of stories. At the end of "Barn Burning" we are not told what happens: there is a shot, and the boy walks off into the woods. Faulkner says "He did not look back." The teacher may help them see that Faulkner expects us to infer what has happened in the story from the fact that the boy has broken the code of "kin loyalty" to give warning that his father is about to burn a barn; he has allied himself with the forces of law and justice. His father is at least symbolically, if not in reality, dead to him. In "The Killers," students want to know, "Did Ole Andreson die?" They may discuss why Hemingway ends the story without telling us and be led to see that the author's main concern is not the fact of Andreson's death but the boy's awareness of evil and the attitudes of adults toward it.

. . . Students may be asked to draw a map of Egdon Heath or of Wuthering Heights, locating the houses and scenes involved. A few minutes in class spent on this activity provides the teacher with a good idea of his students' understanding of the setting and the relationships of characters in the novel.

. . . Another exercise through which students may grow in critical judgment is an assignment comparing abridged editions, editions of classics rewritten for lower grade levels, and comic-book versions with a real classic. The student's own criticisms of these significant differences between versions might be much more powerful antidotes to this kind of reading than any teacherish warnings against them. Immature students tend to equate books with movies: "I haven't read the book, but I've seen the movie." They consider any edition of a book—even the *Classics Illustrated*—equally as valuable as the original.

. . . A fruitful experience for more mature senior high school students may be a comparison of short stories in magazines with those in anthologies of short stories collected for their literary value. Many paperback editions of short stories and the collections prepared for high school students can be made to serve this purpose well, either with older students or with bright students who are good readers.[10] Major differences appear quickly in such a study. Attention can be drawn to differences in characterization (the emphasis on physical attractiveness and dress in most magazine short stories, contrasted with the more selective descriptions in most stories by master short-story writers); the significance of the theme of the story (is it merely boy meets girl, or will girl marry boss, or does it have to do with serious social, psychological, or moral problems?); the character of the ending: most students can readily see the differences between much popular magazine fiction, emphasizing happy endings, and the kinds of endings that many serious short stories have.

Analytical discussion of these differences demands insight; students are prone to generalize, or feel that they can easily tell a good short story from a mediocre one by one or two hallmarks. The exercise is valuable, however, in developing critical discrimination and could become more valuable if carried on from time to time with different materials: novels, plays, movies, poems.

. . . Ask students developing an awareness of style to recall a description of a person in a book they have read who seemed very real to them, a person they feel they could visualize vividly. Ask them to describe such a person for the class, or, if they can find the book, to bring it to class and read the passage. Students enjoy Irving's description of Ichabod Crane, Dickens' portraits of Uriah Heep, Betsy Trotwood, and Mr. Micawber, or Hardy's portrait of Eustacia Vye. The student's awareness of the writer's difficulty in creating a convincing portrait may be sharpened as they try themselves to write a description of a person.

. . . Other such sessions (and assignments) may focus on passages of description chosen for their beauty, their power, or their creation of atmosphere: the dance of the whooping cranes from *The Yearling*, the description of the Kentish marshes where Pip first meets Magwitch in *Great Expectations*, a storm at sea from Conrad, or the "trying out" of the whale oil from *Moby-Dick*.

---

[10] For instance, Frank G. Jennings and Charles J. Calitri, *Stories*, Harcourt, Brace & World, Inc., New York, 1957, for which the guide bound in the Teacher's Edition gives excellent teaching suggestions, and Edwin H. Sauer and Howard Mumford Jones, *Short Stories: An Anthology for Secondary Schools*, Holt, Rinehart and Winston, Inc., New York, 1963.

. . . The author's skill with dialogue may provide interesting discussion material for a class session if students are given time to think about the assignment and to bring samples to class. The writer's ear for the nuances and variety of human speech can be discussed as students compare bits of dialogue from Mark Twain, Dickens, Salinger, Hemingway, the Brontës, Steinbeck, Lewis, and other writers whose skill with dialogue is outstanding.

. . . Similar discussions may arise out of comparisons of passages selected for other qualities: exciting narrative, humor, moments of crisis and tragedy. Through these comparisons, young readers may become accustomed to noticing how an author selects and handles such incidents.

. . . Junior high school students may be given a list of sentences, chosen and duplicated by the teacher, which can be analyzed for style. They may be asked to see how the sentences would sound if they were rewritten in a different order and what difference the changes would make. Manipulating the sentences in different ways, changing order and sentence structure, and substituting different words with similar meanings will raise important questions of word choice and sentence and paragraph structure.[11]

. . . During the senior high school years, some time may be given to sentence analysis of such varied styles as those of Hemingway, Faulkner, Henry James, Wolfe, Conrad, and others. Discussions of how a writer gets effects—with the arrangement and suggestive value of words, the use of imagery, and the order, length, complexity, and rhythm of sentences—play a significant role in developing the student's sensitivity to the elusive quality called style.

. . . What authors have written about matters of style may be helpful for older students. Mark Twain's humorous "Fenimore Cooper's Literary Offenses" [12] and, for superior students interested in literature and in writing, the books or essays written on the author's craft by Henry James, Willa Cather, Joseph Conrad, and others may raise important points for discussion.

. . . Useful essays explaining the novelist's craft are included in Robert Scholes (ed.), *Approaches to the Novel*,[13] and William E. Buckler (ed.), *Novels in the Making*.[14] The teacher may read aloud illustrations from distinctive styles, or reproduce brief passages and ask students to guess their author, explaining the reasons for their choices. Sample passages from Hemingway, Faulkner, Wolfe, Twain, Poe, Hawthorne, and Dickens should be recognizable to good readers if the passages are well chosen.

. . . Students in all grades may be encouraged from time to time to try their hand at writing a passage of description, narrative, or dialogue. Virginia Woolf has commented that "the quickest way to understand the elements of what a novelist is doing is not to read, but to write; to make

---

[11] The suggestion on p. 161 that students try model writing to gain awareness of sentence structure and patterns is useful here.

[12] In E. B. White and Katharine S. White (eds.), *A Sub-Treasury of American Humor*, Coward-McCann, Inc., New York, 1941.

[13] Chandler Publishing Company, San Francisco, 1961.

[14] Houghton Mifflin Company, Boston, 1961.

your own experiment with the dangers and difficulties of words. Recall, then, some event that has left a distinct impression on you—how at the corner of the street, perhaps, you passed two people talking." [15] Reading sample passages (as suggested in these exercises) and then trying to write something like them may show the reader a good deal about the writer's craft.

Warnings against too much analysis should not be forgotten. The suggestions here are for exercises which may be used, with different materials, over the six years of high school. Each year, the teacher may give students a sampling of these exercises during the reading of short stories, plays, or novels, but they should always be a minor part of the work. If students could have such experience during each of their six years in high school, they could make steady progress with the critical skills which develop slowly. In these exercises, experience with literature comes first; then thoughtful scrutiny of examples drawn from reading, leading, finally, to the student's forming his own generalizations about style.

Selected bibliography

Elizabeth Drew, *The Novel: A Modern Guide to Fifteen English Master-pieces,* Dell Publishing Co., Inc., New York, 1963. Stimulating analyses of important books, many of them now being read in high schools.

E. M. Forster, *Aspects of the Novel,* Harcourt, Brace & World, Inc., New York, 1927. (Paper: Harvest Books.)

Edward J. Gordon and Edward S. Noyes (eds.), *Essays on the Teaching of English,* Appleton-Century-Crofts, Inc., New York, 1960.

Frederick Karl and Marvin Magalaner, *A Reader's Guide to Great Twentieth Century English Novels,* Noonday Press, Inc., New York, 1959. (Paper-back.)

Walter Loban et al., *Teaching Language and Literature,* Harcourt, Brace & World, Inc., New York, 1961, chap. 6.

Margaret Ryan, *Teaching the Novel in Paperback,* The Macmillan Company, New York, 1963. Invaluable guide to individualizing instruction in the literature program, and suggestions for reading the novel in depth.

James R. Squire, *The Responses of Adolescents While Reading Four Short Stories,* Research Report No. 2, NCTE, Champaign, Ill., 1964.

Jarvis A. Thurston, *A Checklist of Interpretation since 1925 of Stories and Novelettes,* Alan Swallow, Publisher, Denver, 1960. (Paperback.)

The teacher will want to consult one of the indexes to short stories in the library to locate the sources of short stories mentioned in this chapter.

---

[15] *The Second Common Reader,* Harvest Books, Harcourt, Brace & World, Inc., New York, 1960, p. 236.

CHAPTER *11*

What thou lovest well remains;

The rest is dross
What thou lovest well shall not be reft from thee

What thou lovest well is thy true heritage . . .

EZRA POUND [1]

Poetry

In the high school years, the primary aim of poetry reading should be pleasure: delight in sound, in rhythm and meter, in shared emotional experience, in the varied forms of verse. The student should encounter poems which present a rhythmic story to quicken his pulses, a lyric moment to touch his emotions, or a series of visual images sketched in graphic words. Stress on history, the biography of the poet, analysis of form and technique, complicated explication—all these often become a substitute in the English classroom for response to image and sound, and fail to produce the desire to hear the words again or to know them better.

Our chief allies in the cause of poetry as delight are the poets themselves. One distinguished poet, asked to explain Dylan Thomas to a teacher of poetry, gave sound advice: "Don't even try to understand him; just let him wash over you." Poets traditionally give such answers to those who would over-explain poetry, emphasize its cognitive meaning at the expense of its emotional one, or try to teach it overanalytically. MacLeish's stricture that poems "should not mean, but be" has become a canon for much twentieth-century poetry, and Frost's half-century battle with the "explainers" is well known.

---

[1] "Canto LXXXI," *Cantos of Ezra Pound*, New Directions, Norfolk, Conn., 1948, pp. 98–99.

Success in teaching poetry at the secondary level seems to lie primarily in two things. First, the teacher who would bring students and poetry together in pleasure must understand the students he teaches and be aware of their lives, thoughts, and emotions. His attention must be turned toward them constantly, rather than toward his own tastes, his own choices, and his own notions about what students should know. More than any other subject we teach, perhaps, the study and appreciation of poetry cannot be forced. The teacher must often be content with slow growth. The teacher who understands boys and girls well, who knows their inner thoughts and feelings, knows what delights them, moves them, worries them, or amuses them, has invaluable resources for selection of poetry which will have meaning for the young reader.

The second essential qualification for the teacher who would encourage a love of poetry in his students is an acquaintance with many poems. Only the teacher who has read poetry widely and with understanding, appreciation, and delight will know the right poem to introduce to the right child at the right time. The teacher whose mind is richly stored with lines of poetry and with the knowledge of poems of all kinds has the best chance of introducing a poem at the magical moment when it will linger in the memory.

We may look at a few such moments in the classroom. In an eighth-grade class, young people sit in a circle reading each other poems they have chosen. They talk informally about what the poems have meant to them and the reasons why they have particularly enjoyed one or another. A young dark-eyed boy glows as a classmate reads T. A. Daly's "Een Napoli." A newcomer to the United States, he has been until this time relatively silent and withdrawn in class. The poem moves him to speech, and with a rush of accented, somewhat broken English, he tries to tell the others about what he feels: "That's the way it is," he says. "That's the way it looks in Naples, and that's the way we feel about it now that we're here." Homesickness, pleasure, the need to share with someone the deep feelings that the poem awakens in him are all in his eager face. The poem has touched him deeply, and because he has told what it meant to him, the others see what poems can do to the individual.

In another classroom, a young student-teacher reads Alfred Noyes' "The Highwayman" to a group of ninth-grade girls. When he has finished, many of the girls are in tears. Wisely, he refrains from comment and, after letting the emotional impact be fully felt, talks with them informally about the dramatic situation in the poem. Later, recounting his experience to his methods class, he finds some of his fellow student-teachers horrified at what has happened. Several of the men declare they would have walked out of the class; some feel he should have chosen a less emotionally charged poem. The teacher explains that he thinks it is good for students to be moved to tears by a poem, and feels that the experience has prepared them to appreciate other, better poems. Class experiences like these help students feel the impact of poetry.

Poetry in the classroom

Although the young child responds to the sound and rhythm of poetry with obvious delight, the teen-ager, following peer-group custom, often groans when the subject is mentioned. Something has happened during the growing years to supplant spontaneous joy in the sound of language with a feeling of distaste for poetry. In a culture in which associations of effeminacy often cling to the poet, boys, needing to assert their masculinity, often reject poetry as unfashionable, sissy stuff. Girls, beginning to be aware of and to value masculine attitudes, frequently follow suit.

Another face of the problem is the difference between children's emotions, free, spontaneous, and uninhibited, and the new and complex emotions of the young adolescent, not yet understood or controlled. Poetry which touches these feelings deeply, as does much great love poetry, may strike a deep response in the adolescent, but he learns to conceal his feelings carefully lest he be laughed at by classmates.

Most of all, young people seem to dislike dissection of poetry. They complain about teachers who "pick the poem apart, line by line": on the other hand, they also complain that poetry is "hard to understand," and, at first, these two complaints may seem hard to reconcile. They can be understood, however, if the teacher realizes that although they often resent being asked to classify figures of speech, students often like to speculate about the meaning of a poem; they frequently enjoy letting their minds play with figurative language and talking about what it suggests to them. The teacher who wants to help the young enjoy poetry will handle the task of analysis with care, helping students find pleasure in the discovery of form, meaning, and sound, and seeing that they are always left with a pleasurable experience of the poem as a whole.

Most important, perhaps, is the teacher's realization that pleasure should precede analysis in the growth process. When young ears have been captured by the sound of poems they love, and when emotions have been touched, discussion of meaning may follow. The teacher can sense when students are ready for help with understanding. Good teachers learn to respect the silence which may follow the reading of a poem and which tells of the impact of the poet's words. They realize that such a moment is not the time to begin a lengthy explication.

The richness of modern poetry offers so much delight to young people who have learned something about reading it with understanding that there should be no reason for an exclusive diet of nineteenth-century didactic verse. Many high school students come away from their study of poetry knowing only Bryant, Longfellow, and Tennyson. Most encounter only a few poems of Frost, Robinson, and Emily Dickinson. Yeats, Eliot, Auden, and Hopkins are almost unknown. Teachers themselves are often unduly fearful of the reputed obscurity of modern verse and fail to realize how much truly great poetry there is which will excite modern youth. The teacher familiar with our literary heritage will want to present to students much of the best of Wordsworth,

Browning, Keats, Shelley, Shakespeare, Byron, Blake, and Donne. (The old favorites—Daly, Riley, Service, Field, and others—should not be overlooked. Often they form the first pleasurable introduction to poetry. The teacher whose tastes are more sophisticated should not scorn such beginnings.) Much has already been said about the great traditional poetry. The emphasis in this chapter is on modern poetry because it is less often taught in the classroom than poetry of an earlier age and because of its direct appeal to young people.

Why study poetry?

The practical young person in today's high schools wants to know why he is asked to study poetry. He wants to learn things which will help him toward his chosen goals: college, marriage, or a job. He has had, generally, little association with the relatively small minority of people who today read and enjoy poetry. He asks, as he must, if he would satisfy himself that the thing is worth learning, "What's in it for me?"

Many teachers feel that the best answer is contact with poetry itself. Its magic must be felt to be understood, and the best thing we can do is to make the English classroom a place where experience with poetry may work its own magic with young people.

One reason for studying poetry, however, students can understand relatively early. Browning's "Fra Lippo Lippi" states the aims of the poet: "For, don't you mark? we're made so that we love/ First when we see them painted, things we have passed/ Perhaps a hundred times, nor cared to see . . ."

Like the artist, but using words, the poet paints, and the images of the world we view through his eyes are things we have seen a thousand times but never noticed. The young reader can learn that, in John Holmes' phrase, the poet is one who sees the world "as if." The relations the poet sees, expressed in metaphor and simile, illuminate new perceptions of sight, sound, and touch. Through his words we see Humbert Wolfe's squirrel looking like a "small gray coffee pot," Cummings' spring world, "mud-luscious" and "puddle-wonderful," Yeats' old man, "a tattered coat upon a stick," or the plumet basilisk which Marianne Moore observes, feeling "like putty in the hand."

The student may reject the world of nature of the nineteenth-century Romantics, but he can understand why a modern poet describes an auto wreck, an express train, the wind sleeve at the airport, or the subway. The way the modern poet sees the things around him brings him close to today's youth. He makes poetry out of the world the student knows, the world of smoke and steel, of factory windows, of Buicks, bombs, and baseball. As Stephen Spender observes, ". . . the main task of the contemporary poet . . . is to transmute the anti-poetic material of modern life into transparent poetry." [2]

[2] Stephen Spender, *The Making of a Poem*, W. W. Norton & Company, Inc., New York, 1962, p. 43.

During adolescence many young people become aware for the first time that the poet probes the deepest human experiences— pain, grief, loneliness, despair, desolation. We want students to learn what John Ciardi has observed —that poetry adds to the "richness of man's awareness of what it is to be a human being on a tilted planet." What the poet observes about the physical world, his sense of wonder at sights and sounds, his perception of man's encounters with birth, death, love, and loneliness can show young people some of the pain and ecstasy of human life.

We teach poetry, too, because here, as in no other form of literature, the student encounters a new dimension of language. Appreciation of the poet's words can make him aware of the language he speaks as can no other school subject. "Poetry is language raised to the *nth* power," says a modern poet.

For many of our students, the contact with poetry will be deep and personal, something translated into experience, but not discussed in English class. The mathematical genius with a mediocre record in English confides to his girl that Emily Dickinson is "cool." A young mother, years after her first contact with Hopkins' tender "Spring and Fall: To a Young Child," uses his words to ask her newborn tearful infant, "Margaret, are you grieving?"

Some basic principles

Young people respond most readily to poems that deal with familiar experiences, poems they can understand. The reader first responds to the poem through the ear rather than through a study of prosody. Oral reading of poetry by the teacher and by students must provide the background for training in reading poetry silently. The silent re-creation of the sound of words in the mind's ear is a task of great complexity which students will master slowly. Experience with and response to poetry as sound and feeling provide the most meaningful beginnings to the young as they start their study of poetry; only if the experience is satisfying will the reader go on to study with pleasure and understanding the way in which the poet's struggle with form creates the work of art which becomes the poem.

Program into practice

Of basic importance to the program are the careful selection of poetry and the study of the poet's language and the sound of poetry. Activities such as choral speaking of poetry, memorizing poems, classroom discussion of poetry, and writing verse are also instrumental in developing appreciation and comprehension. Above all, the teacher's love for poetry and his sensitivity about the receptiveness of his students are key factors in developing the love of poetry in young readers.

Selecting poems

The selection of poems suited to the widely varying tastes of boys and girls during the junior high school years will have a great deal to do with whether students will enjoy reading poems. Junior high school girls often show a preference for sentimental, romantic, or imaginative poems, or those about people. Boys prefer sports and adventure, poems about the sea, or tales of heroic deeds. Both sexes enjoy storytelling poems, humorous poems, and poems about animals.[3] Many young readers respond to Elinor Wylie's "Velvet Shoes," particularly if the poem is read at the time when a recent heavy snowfall makes the sensory experience immediate and students can walk outdoors to see how it feels to be "shod in wool." The younger adolescent's interest in animals and pets brings response to such poems as Frost's "The Runaway," picturing a colt experiencing his first winter snow, to the proud spirit of Lindsay's "Broncho That Would Not Be Broken," and the plight of Lew Sarrett's motherless "Four Little Foxes."

Poems which say something about the world in which we live are also of interest to the young reader: Sandburg's "Clean Curtains," in which a mother struggles with city dirt; "Buttons," in which men are merely pins to be moved on a war map; or "Child of the Romans," in which the Italian railroad laborer looks through the train window at men and women eating steaks and strawberries; Lindsay's "Factory Windows," always being broken; Untermeyer's "Caliban in the Coal Mines," wishing for a handful of stars; or Langston Hughes' "Mother to Son."

Poetry which is very much of our time and place interests older youth: visions of the future like Benét's "Nightmare Number Three," and MacLeish's "Epistle to Be Left in the Earth," poems as modern as Shapiro's "Auto Wreck" and "Buick," or Fitzgerald's "Cobb Would Have Caught It," with its baseball refrain "Attyoldboy." Poems about war have a strong impact: Sassoon's "Does It Matter?" "Base Details," "Attack," or "Dreamers," Owen's "Anthem for Doomed Youth," "Arms and the Boy," or "*Dulce et Decorum Est,*" Graves' "It's a Queer Time," and Brooke's "The Soldier." More mature readers respond to Shapiro's "V-Letter," Jarrell's "Pilots, Man Your Planes" or "The Death of the Ball Turret Gunner," Viereck's "*Vale* from Carthage" or "Kilroy," and Peter Bowman's "Beach Red."

Other poems and subjects have strong appeal, too. Girls during the senior high school years respond to love poems, from the seventeenth-century writers to the moderns, and boys also secretly enjoy many of them. Marvell, Donne,

---

[3] See the discussion of children's interests in poetry in George W. Norvell, *The Reading Interests of Young People,* D. C. Heath and Company, Boston, 1950, pp. 97–98, and in his *What Boys and Girls Like to Read,* Silver Burdett Company, Morristown, N.J., 1958, chaps. 5–8 and 10–11. See also Elizabeth Rose, "Teaching Poetry in the Junior High School," *English Journal,* vol. 46, December, 1957, pp. 540–550, for further discussion of matters of motivation, selection, and teaching poems.

Drayton, Lovelace, and Suckling present attitudes toward love which may be contrasted with those of modern poets: Edna St. Vincent Millay's love sonnets, the love poems of Elinor Wylie, Cummings, Emily Dickinson, and Frost. The older adolescent, vitally interested in the subject of man's relation to woman, can find in poetry attitudes which range from cynicism and irony to adoration or tenderness.

Poems which explore the nature of man's relationship to God are important during these years: Thompson's "The Hound of Heaven," Pound's "Ballad of the Goodly Fere," Hopkins' "The Windhover" and "God's Grandeur," or Hardy's "The Oxen" find many willing readers. This age is interested, too, in exploring attitudes toward death. Therefore, such poems as Thomas' "Do Not Go Gentle into That Good Night" and "Death Shall Have No Dominion," Browning's "Prospice," or Whitman's "Come Lovely and Soothing Death," from "When Lilacs Last in the Dooryard Bloom'd," are usually well received.

In the senior high school years, good readers of poetry will find challenge in poems which repay rather close analysis and discussion for ideas. Some, expressing criticism of modern man, his values, his goals, and the society he lives in, may be studied in connection with novels and plays expressing similar themes. The ironic wit of Auden's "Unknown Citizen" or *"Mundus et Infans,"* Kenneth Fearing's "Portrait" and parts of Eliot's "The Waste Land," as well as his "The Love Song of J. Alfred Prufrock" and "The Hollow Men," are sometimes more frequently understood by modern youth than by their elders.

Developing understanding: the poet's language

Many young readers who can listen enthralled to the teacher's reading of a poem fail utterly when they confront the poem on the printed page. The ability to hear in the mind the voice of the poet or the musical quality of the poem requires something of the skill of the reader of music who can "hear" Beethoven's Fifth Symphony as he sits in the library reading the score. Like the musician, the reader of poetry must turn the black symbols on a page into sounds which can be heard vividly without the moving of a violin string or a muscle in the throat.

Although numerous problems confront the learner in his mastering the ability to read poetry meaningfully, experience in reading and discussing many poems can build such abilities gradually. With careful planning, the teacher can provide for help with the chief difficulties the language of poetry presents to the reader.

Figurative language.   One of the most important things students must learn about language in general and poetry in particular is the distinction between literal and figurative language. Struggling with nonliteral meanings is a primary problem of the young reader of poetry. It is because of his feeling of defeat in this struggle that he so often asks, "Why didn't he say what he meant?"

Immature and less able students must often be helped to understand the connection between the words of poetry and the words of everyday speech. One teacher showed his class this connection using homely slang comparisons, such as, "I feel like a worm," "She's a doll," or "We had a ball." He continued his illustrations by pointing out the difference between "I feel tired" and "I feel like a limp dishrag," and between "he ran fast" and "he ran like the wind." As students began to think of their own comparisons, they realized how rich everyday speech was in such vivid, picture-making phrases, and when they began to read the poem "The Highwayman," they were ready to notice the stable boy with hair "like mouldy hay," who listened, "dumb as a dog," to the soldiers, and the highwayman, riding "like a madman." Some of the better students noticed subtler metaphors in the "coat of claret velvet," and "the road was a gypsy's ribbon." Other teachers use the figurative language of the popular song for reference. One discusses with his class the impossibility of saying how it feels to be in love and plays a song from the musical *My Fair Lady* to show how language *can* communicate this kind of feeling: "I Could Have Danced All Night."

Imagery, metaphor, and symbol.   Only after students have learned to distinguish carefully between literal and figurative meanings in poetry and prose should they attempt the problem of distinguishing imagery, metaphor, simile, and symbol. The teacher finds such questions as these useful: What does this word make you think of? Why do you suppose the poet compares the squirrel to a coffee pot? Do you think it's a good comparison in this poem? What makes you think so? What do the names of the places "Nineveh," "Ophir," "Palestine" suggest to you in Masefield's "Cargoes"? What do the different cargoes suggest to you? Is there a difference between those in stanza one and two and those in the last? What is it? What about the sounds of the words "sandalwood, cedarwood, and sweet, white wine" as contrasted to "road-rail, pig-lead . . . and cheap tin trays"? Do you think Masefield indicates which cargoes he likes best? How? Does the poem suggest anything about time? How? Since the poem doesn't "say" as statement, good students may be pressed to sense the contrasts implied, by the sound and imagery in the poem, between a glamorous past and a practical, ugly present.

The student may be led to see that in many poems the aim of the poet is simply to present images: words which present a sharp, visual picture, a taste, a smell, or a touch: the ache of cold, the heat of the sun, the taste of plums or blueberries, the smell of wood smoke, the feel of silk or fur, the sound of a drum, of waves, of rain. Young people can thus learn that many poems use words which make the reader see things vividly, hear things clearly, smell things keenly, feel things sharply. When words are used in an attempt to evoke the memory of such sensory experiences, or to create them afresh, the device is called *imagery*. If they are asked to look back at the poems they have read, they can pick out examples of words or phrases which convey vivid images of sight, sound, or touch.

Students frequently fail to observe or understand metaphor outside the boundaries of poetry. The discussion of language in Chapter 3 may provide helpful illustrations for teachers to use in preparing their students for the study of poetry by calling their attention to the slang use of metaphor. Student speech is full of homely but pungent examples: "she's a doll," "the party was a blast," "he's a drip," "she's a brain."

The teacher should guide the students through poems with simple metaphors before complex ones are tackled. Sandburg's "Chicago" pictured as a "tall, bold slugger," a "hog butcher"; Elinor Wylie's image of snow ("veils of white lace"), the road in "The Highwayman" as a "ribbon of moonlight"; or Emily Dickinson's snake as "a whiplash, unbraiding in the sun," are all relatively easily grasped by most students, even in the junior high school years.

Older students may explore the rich implications of more complex metaphors in Hopkins' "The Windhover," Frost's "Desert Places," Jeffers' "Shine, Perishing Republic," Yeats' "Sailing to Byzantium," or Shelley's "Ode to the West Wind."

Symbolism is such an important device in literature, particularly in modern fiction, drama, and poetry, that young people should begin early to think of symbolization as an important function of language. Teachers may lead students to speak of the symbols they recognize in the world about them. The concept of the verbal symbol as a word which "stands for" an idea, a concept, a person, or an experience, may be grasped as students discuss common symbols in everyday life: the cross, standing for the Christian religion; the rose, symbolizing beauty, or the heart, standing for love. The teacher who starts a class thinking about this can soon cover the chalkboard with illustrations: advertising symbols, associated with firms or products; symbols for athletic teams, nations, occupations; status symbols.

Poems like Frost's "The Road Not Taken," "Fire and Ice," or "Nature's First Green is Gold" provide the teacher with useful illustrations of the poetic symbol at work. Students can usually grasp that because the road, in its function as a concrete object, is used to journey from one geographical place to another, it can take on the symbolic meaning of a road on which one journeys through life from youth to old age, success to failure. They also usually have little difficulty in understanding how fire and ice are related to passionate hatred and destruction.

Many poems of Frost's work in this way. A real object or event—a wall, a birch tree, a ladder against an apple tree, a glimpse of snow in a field— takes on added richness as its symbolic meanings unfold: it is the birch tree's setting the speaker firmly on the earth that we are to notice; the "Desert Places" are not only snow-swept wastes but the terrible interior loneliness of the human mind and heart.

Word order, syntax, and punctuation. Some readers never quite adjust to the fact that poets, in order to suggest meanings, take liberties with the conventional signs and signals of prose to fit the demands of form and idea.

Only in the last two centuries has it seemed important to poets to try to capture the order, rhythms, and idiom of everyday language and only in our century has this aim been achieved with masterly effect, as in the poetry of Robert Frost and William Butler Yeats.

There is evidence that the inversions of normal word order so common in poetry may present more serious obstacles to understanding than has been previously thought. One teacher's study presented a collection of poetic inversions to twelfth-year college preparatory students for interpretation. The responses to such a line as this from "The Ancient Mariner": "Ah wretch! said they, the bird to slay,/ That made the breeze to blow!" indicate something of the seriousness of the problem. Some of the questions and answers included the following:

Who is the wretch?
  The bird?
    They said, "Ah wretch!" to the bird they wanted to slay because he made the breezes blow.
    Ah, wretch that made the breeze blow, they said to the bird they were going to slay.
Why is he (she, it) a wretch?
  For making the breeze blow?
    Ah wicked one! they said, "the breeze has started blowing because you killed the poor bird."
  For wanting to slay the bird?
    They wanted to slay the bird who made the breeze blow.
  For slaying the bird?
    "You are a wretch," they said, "because you slayed the bird. Doing this made the breeze blow." [4]

In addition to learning to read sentences in inverted order, the student must also learn to pay attention to punctuation and often to syntax and ellipsis. Anyone who has heard the young student of poetry attempt to read it aloud notices how often he reads in a singsong voice, end-stopping lines, failing to note where a phrase carries over into the next line, stressing unstressed syllables, and committing other violations of form and sense. He must be taught to pay attention to the punctuation of poetry and to practice reading until phrases and word groups fall together naturally.

Developing appreciation: the poet's craft

Junior high school students usually spend time more profitably in becoming acquainted with many poems and experiencing pleasure in sound and rhythm than in studying prosody. When appreciation is assured, students are

[4] Bertram Mott, Jr., "Interpreting Poetic Inversions: An Experiment," *English Journal*, vol. 52, April, 1963, pp. 257–261.

ready to gain some knowledge of the means by which the poet gets his effects in the dimensions of sound and sense, of the details of the poet's craft. Much of this learning goes on indirectly through skillful inductive questioning as students read verse to sense rhythm, rhyme, and meter. Understanding increases enjoyment in poetry just as mastering the skill of swimming, tennis, or baseball increases pleasure in the doing of those activities.

Teachers who start students too early on the study of metrics risk deadening interest in poetry by focusing on matters which seem easy to teach: the memorizing of figures of speech, the number of feet in a line, or the identification of rhyme schemes. They are like James Thurber's Miss Groby,[5] who hunted for similes and metaphors as "little girls hunt for white violets in springtime." Those students who already know many poems and read with understanding can study metrics, and college-bound senior high school youth certainly should. The teacher's discretion will be the best guide with other students.

Rhyme.   Some poems rhyme, but not all of them do. The fact that not all poems rhyme is often a surprising revelation to junior high school boys and girls. Some students are so deaf to the sounds of rhymed words in poetry that when asked to supply the rhyming word that follows in verse with almost inevitable rhyme words (June-moon) they provide a word that jangles on the ear. They can be helped to notice this device in poems where the rhyming becomes a kind of game, as in the limerick, or in some of the patter songs from Gilbert and Sullivan, in which it is forced (*din-afore-Pinafore*). Some of the more whimsical poems of Robert Frost, such as "Departmental" in which the triple rhymes ripple delightfully (*ungentle-departmental, atwiddle-middle*) can also be used.

Older students may be helped to see that much of the best of modern poetry uses much subtler rhyming effects than the end-stopped forms of much children's verse. Slant rhyme (*study-lady*) or eye rhymes (*stone-gone*) are used with consummate skill in the poetry of Marianne Moore, W. H. Auden, Wallace Stevens, William Carlos Williams, and E. E. Cummings.

Meter and rhythm.   The student who has learned to hear and enjoy the music in verse—swinging, dancing, staccato, or stately rhythms—will probably be receptive to some study of how the poet achieves his effects. If he has observed that Lindsay's "The Potatoes' Dance" sets the feet to tapping, he may be asked to try to say how the poet makes us feel this. As he taps or moves in time to poems with strongly marked rhythmical patterns, he may notice that the beat is regular, so many beats to a line, as it is in music, in swimming, or in dancing. He probably knows the difference between rock 'n' roll and a waltz, between dancing to a "slow one" or to a twist tune, or he has noticed the way the conductor of the school chorus or band measures time

[5] In "Here Lies Miss Groby," *My World and Welcome to It,* Harcourt, Brace & World, Inc., New York, 1942.

with hand or baton. He can begin to learn that poetry, too, uses phrases or measures which create pleasing sound patterns. The teacher may have to help him discover the rhythms of everyday speech, pointing out how language works in stressed and unstressed syllables.

Counting the number of beats to the line and determining the number of accented or stressed and unaccented syllables are the keys to metrical analysis. Choral reading of strongly rhythmic poems with exaggerated stress (e.g., limericks, which go "da dée da, da dée da, da dée") will help. Long before the class is given the exercise of marking accented and unaccented syllables on the board should come the experiences of reading the poem together and learning to feel some bodily response to the beat of the verse. Exaggerating the stress on the accented syllables and lightening it on the unaccented can show students how several stanzas of a poem are usually sufficient to reveal the poem's dominant rhythmic pattern. A sharper ear will be needed to detect the devices many modern poets employ to give variation to regular patterns, which become monotonous if repeated too frequently.

The names of the principal meters are easily learned by students with vocabularies broad enough to recognize the prefixes of the terms: trimeter, tetrameter, pentameter, hexameter. The chief feet in English—iamb, dactyl, anapest, trochee—are probably best remembered by associating them with common names which exemplify them, iamb (Diane), dactyl (Frederick), anapest (Marguerite), trochee (David). Any good book on metrics will give the teacher or the student enough information to master the elementary facts of metrical analysis. From that point on, study should become increasingly more pleasurable as the trained ear listens, almost unconsciously, to the fascinating patterns the poet-craftsman employs to communicate sense through sound.

The teacher must always remember that the technicalities of scansion are of interest chiefly to those who already like poetry. They do not allow the student easy access to the poem. Those who have difficulty in developing a liking for poetry should not be forced to master the intricacies of technical analysis, nor should the teacher's effort to introduce poetry to the reluctant start with the study of metrics.

Sound and sense.   Students who have a feeling for poetry and who enjoy reading and hearing it will begin to notice how the poet uses sound to echo sense. Without necessarily being held responsible for the technical names, the reader may be led to notice the humming sounds that *m*'s and *n*'s in the language produce: "A drowsy numbness pains/ My sense, as though of hemlock I had drunk"; the sibilance of *s*'s in alliteration or consonance: "the silken, sad, uncertain rustling of each purple curtain"; the long *o* and *u* sounds which sound like the notes of a horn: "The golden gorge of dragons spouted forth/ A flood of fountain foam."

A simple poem for study is Sandburg's "Jazz Fantasia," in which the sounds echo those in the real world: the sound of the Mississippi steamboat,

272 Literature: appreciation, insights, and values

or the orchestra's horns. Students may also learn to recognize assonance (the repetition of interior vowel sounds as in "Upon the lonely, moated grange") and consonance, identical consonant sounds accompanying different vowel sounds (green, groan; lark, lurk). The effect of sharp plosive and dental sounds shocks the reader into attention to something unpleasant ("Dirty British steamer with a salt-caked smokestack . . ." or "to spit out all the butt-ends of my days and ways").

Young people can get much pleasure out of listening to poetry which emphasizes sound and even more out of reading it aloud, by themselves or chorally. Here the greatest enchantment lies for those of all ages. The power of sound is illustrated in the story Robert Graves tells of the effect that a reading given by Vachel Lindsay had not only on the Bloomsbury intellectuals, but on the grave, gowned dons of Oxford. Lindsay had them first listening, then intensely excited, and within forty minutes "roaring like a bonfire." [6] If a staid audience like this is capable of such response, teachers may well try for some of the excitement of poetic sound with today's teen-agers, who grow ecstatic over rock-and-roll stars.

Learning activities

Much class activity will probably center about listening to poetry read by the teacher or by actors or poets on recordings. When students have learned to enjoy poetry through hearing it, they may enrich their appreciation by learning to read it aloud well, by learning how to read independently for pleasure, and by participating in choral reading.

In addition to activities centered on hearing and reading poetry, students can profit from comparing and discussing poems. When they have gained experience in reading poetry with enough skill to understand and appreciate it, they can undertake memorizing and, perhaps, writing poems.

Listening to poetry: the sound of music. The young student can hardly know whether or not he likes poetry unless he hears a considerable amount of it read by a skillful and appreciative reader. This does not necessarily mean an intensely dramatic reader. Often a simple, perceptive reading of a poem is more effective than an overdramatic one. Although much poetry has been ruined by poor student reading, those who are willing to practice may learn much. One teacher of poetry maintains that "a poem in the mouth of the student is worth two read by the teacher."

The current wealth of recordings of poetry read by the poets themselves, e.g., Robert Frost, T. S. Eliot, Dylan Thomas, E. E. Cummings, and Marianne Moore, or by trained readers, are invaluable aids to the teacher of poetry.

---

[6] Retold by Archibald MacLeish in *Poetry and Experience,* Houghton Mifflin Company, Boston, 1961, pp. 44–46.

Both school and public libraries are acquiring ever-increasing collections of such recordings.[7]

Choral speaking. For some young people, group recitation of poetry is preferable to the solitary reading of a poem. There is comfort in the group and pleasure in the sound of words harmoniously spoken together. Choral speaking emphasizes the *sound* pattern of the poem, which is too often forgotten in classroom discussions of poetry read silently and discussed in intellectual terms. Many reluctant readers of poetry have become enchanted with the sound of poems said in unison, when attention is paid to the sound of the words, clear enunciation, the rhythm of the lines, and the mood that the poem often sets. There is evidence that if good poetry is chosen, this kind of group reading can be an experience of lasting meaning to the speakers. The sound of great verse, repeated over and over until it is part of the unconscious memory, is a delight for many people not otherwise distinguished by their love of literature or poetry.[8]

Discussing poems. Those classroom discussions of poetry which throw the burden of discovery on the boys and girls themselves lead to lively interest, closer analysis of meaning and imagery, and more understanding. Emphasis on enjoying, thinking about, discussing, and comparing interpretations of a poem will often lead to a much fuller appreciation of poetry. Even if the teacher does not agree with some of the interpretations given, he must encourage the student to trust his own judgment, to confront the poem with confidence that he can read it with pleasure and understanding. Unless he develops this confidence, he will not know what he thinks until he reads the critics or sees the poet's name.[9]

Writing poetry. To try to force poetry from young people is, many teachers feel, harmful and possibly damaging to a potential love of verse. Others believe, however, that writing poetry is pleasurable for young people and that it increases their feeling for poetry. One teacher encouraged his classes to write good poetry by creating an atmosphere in which the work of the writer might be kept personal and private (if the writer wished), by receiving every offering with respect and consideration, but reserving praise for

[7] A list of poetry recordings is given on pages 424–425.

[8] One student teacher pointed out parallels between choral speaking and the musical chorus: "It's fun to practice a popular number like 'Once in Love with Amy,' but after we've done it a few times, we're sick of it. With a Bach chorale, each rehearsal gets more exciting as the music means more to us. The more we practice, the more we appreciate its depth."
Suggestions for teaching choral speaking are given in Chap. 4, pp. 86–87.

[9] As I. A. Richards demonstrated in *Practical Criticism,* Harcourt, Brace & World, Inc., New York, 1929, even honors English majors at Cambridge University floundered in judgment when they faced poems they did not know. Not only did they fail to distinguish good poems from bad ones, but they could not read the plain sense of the poem, interpret figurative language, or keep from reading their own ideas (stock responses) into poems. Every teacher of poetry should know this book.

only the best, and by making sure that the best bits were heard and praised by the class.[10] The importance of honest comment about student verse is worth stressing. Young writers cannot stand harsh criticism, but much may be said to encourage the writer without giving unmerited praise. Some teachers wax enthusiastic about whatever is handed in; others, unable to distinguish true gold from dross, accord praise to much banal, sentimental writing. Most students are able to discern insincerity quickly and to recognize the mediocrity as well as the excellence of much student verse.

Verse writing is a helpful form of self-instruction in the craft of poetry. Some teachers suggest that students begin experimenting with the seemingly simple form of the Japanese *haiku*. The patterned arrangement of seventeen syllables in this slight form often intrigues students; its brevity keeps it from seeming formidable; yet many lovely images and ideas can be expressed within its limits. Another teacher asks her students to write an analysis of the process of composing the poem, giving reasons for choice of form, imagery, and idea. Such writing about the *process* of writing, when coupled with the student's struggle with form, helps most students achieve a much greater and more appreciative awareness of the poet's craft.

Memorizing poetry. The current reaction against requiring students to memorize poetry has its disadvantages. That forty students no longer learn by rote a poem without regard for its meaning is undoubtedly for the good. Much has been lost, however. As the sound of great music haunts memory's ear long after the sound waves are stilled, so the music of great poetry remains in the mind of readers who have loved it. Memorizing gives one a command of verse in a way that heightens appreciation and makes it possible to recall loved lines far from the book or the library.

The teacher can encourage memorizing in many ways. He may suggest that there is much poetry we like so well that we may want to keep some of it in our minds to remember at will. He may then set aside a certain day so that those who have memorized a poem may repeat informally what they have learned. He may say, "All of you who know a poem by heart may say it when we have our tape-recording session on Thursday." Since the desire to compete for the privilege of speaking into the recorder is often strong, younger boys and girls often respond to this approach.

Memory work can be easier and more satisfying for students if they learn techniques of memorizing. Some simple rules have been recommended by those who have studied this kind of learning. First, the learner is advised to read the passage to be memorized several times silently. Then he may say it in thought phrases, checking back to see whether he has missed a word or a line. Strict attention to meaning will help him immeasurably in remembering how the phrases go. Noticing meter and rhyme will also help. These latter clues (if they are present) will suggest what the rhyme word must be, or show that there

---

[10] Hughes Mearns, *Creative Youth*, Garden City Publishing Company, Inc., New York, 1926.

must be a different word to make the lines scan. Finally, he can recite the whole many times, polishing his phrasing and the tones in which he says lines or words, making sure that he is letter perfect and that his interpretation is faithful to the poet's intent in writing the poem.

Although students frequently resist memorizing verse, often the resistance is largely a pose. Generations of students have recognized the values that memorized verse has had for them, as great poems and passages from the Bible are treasured in the memory. Many students with high resistance to poetry may dislike memorizing verse, but many of these respond well to the group reading of poetry in choral speaking. Memory work should be encouraged but not forced; recommended, but not assigned except as an optional activity. The teacher who can encourage students to learn verse without demanding the rigorous recitations which used to produce fear will ensure that poems live in the memory of students.

Evaluation

Can an appreciation of poetry be evaluated? Many teachers think not. It is probable that we who teach poetry know little of what goes on in the minds and emotions of those to whom we teach it. So adroitly can adolescents mask their feelings from the teacher and from their classmates that real appreciation and understanding may frequently be carefully hidden.

Perhaps the only valid test of successful teaching is that which leads the young reader to continue reading poems after he is out of our classes. Those who go on to read, remember, and love poems they have talked about in class, those who continue to read other poems, widen their acquaintances with poetry, make poetry a part of their lives, are those who have passed the course with honors, whatever their grade.

We may learn much about how our students read poetry by asking them to write about a poem they have never read before. For younger students, this may be a relatively short and simple poem, demanding some small skill in interpreting figurative language, tone, and literal meaning. Brief lyrics with some complexity, like the simplest of Emily Dickinson or Robert Frost, may help the teacher to distinguish between those who can read figurative language with some skill and those who still read at the literal level.[11]

Imaginative teachers have invented other exercises which can be used to inform both teacher and student about the student's ability to understand poetry. One is the teacher-written parody or close parallel of a good poem. Students are given both versions on a sheet and asked to choose the version they like the best and explain why. A variation is the exercise which offers

[11] Examples of student analyses of poems in the CEEB *End-of-Year Examinations in English for College-bound Students, Grades 9–12,* illustrate the students' abilities in reading poetry.

several versions of the same poem or stanza. Analyzing why the poet made the changes he did is very informative.

One teacher gives a class a short poem in which blanks are substituted for key words, unusual adjectives, or verbs. Good discussions can ensue when students compare their choices of words with the original poem.

Even multiple-choice questions have been devised to confront the student with alternate readings of lines and interpretations of figurative language and meaning. Some of the test questions on standardized tests of appreciation are useful.[12]

The important thing about evaluation from the teacher's point of view is understanding the difficulties students have with reading. The kinds of test questions suggested here will turn up ample evidence about the difficulties young people have even in reading for the plain sense of poetry. Any real evaluation of understanding and appreciation in terms of a letter or a numerical grade has little validity. Most teachers prefer to avoid this kind of testing and grading and to assign grades to more objective and more measurable though perhaps less important matters than the appreciation of poetry.

The experience of delight in poetry is the right of young people in high school classrooms. The teacher who remembers that poetry is concerned with the deepest feelings and thoughts of men, and who knows and loves poetry, will have little trouble convincing adolescents of its meaning for them. The path to the poem through sound and feeling can provide the way for enjoyment of an ancient art, and appreciation of the rich heritage of verse in English. The teacher of English alone has the privilege of introducing youth to this heritage. It is a demanding, often difficult, but most rewarding experience.

An approach to a poem

Although much has been said in this chapter about the dangers of too much analysis of poetry, it is evident to most teachers that many students and often whole classes are curious about certain poems, and enjoy studying them carefully to see what they mean. The inductive approach to the poem does not burden the student with analytic lecture notes but helps him discover how the poem "means." The discussion of a poem which follows is not offered as a model for all class discussions of poetry, but as an example of a way of looking closely at a poem with a class when the time seems right to do so. The teacher will want to watch the section "Modern Poetry in the Classroom" in the *English Journal* for further illustrations of this kind of discussion of poetry.[13]

E. E. Cummings' little poem, "In Just-spring," looks strange on the

---

[12] For instance, *The Cooperative Literary Comprehension and Appreciation Test, Grades 10–16*, Cooperative Test Division, Educational Testing Service, Princeton, N.J., 1935–1951.
[13] See bibliography.

page to many a high school student. His first reaction (if he confronts it in print) may be to rebel against this strangeness with the kind of resistance which blocks understanding. Many teachers have found that even with junior high school students class discussion of this poem may help young readers feel that they can, by asking the right questions, learn to read much modern poetry of this kind by themselves. In planning a lesson of this kind, the teacher must think out a series of questions which can lead the student to discover how Cummings is working with language in the poem and how typography, punctuation, sound, inflection, and connotation all work together to evoke a memorably lyrical feeling of spring.

In Just-spring[14]

in Just-
spring   when the world is mud-
luscious the little
lame balloonman

whistles   far   and wee

and eddieandbill come
running from marbles and
piracies and it's
spring

when the world is puddle-wonderful

the queer
old balloonman whistles
far   and   wee
and bettyandisbel come dancing

from hop-scotch and jump-rope and

it's
spring
and
  the

    goat-footed

balloonMan   whistles
far
and
wee

This is a poem which could well be introduced to a class during the first days of spring when winter's snows or rains make the world *puddle-wonderful* so that young people will have seen on the way to school these puddles—

reflecting sky, perhaps?—and the children, newly liberated from winter-bound lives, come running with the boundless energy of children in the first spring weather, enjoying their marbles, their hop-scotch and jump-rope.

For younger students or for the more literal-minded classes—those who resist poetry or who tend to read so literally that something like this poem would seem formidable, the teacher may think it worthwhile to prepare the group for the poem by talking with the class about signs of early spring they have noticed, about the way they feel in spring (after a long, shut-in winter), and what things they remember with pleasure of their joy as children in the spring. (High school students like to think back to the time—years ago, of course—when they were children.) It is probable that from such discussion the teacher would get most—or at least several—of the things that Cummings uses in the poem. The feeling of release after winter is probably more characteristic of children in a climate with sharp seasonal changes; the balloonman will probably be recognized by city children rather than country children, but it will probably be the latter who respond most vigorously to the mud-between-the-toes image in *mud-luscious.*

Thinking aloud about such things (or writing them if this seems desirable) helps bring to consciousness experiences which may be drawn on in the discussion. The teacher who does not choose to give this much help to a class may let them start with the poem itself, providing a duplicated copy for each member of the class. Then he may begin by asking them if they notice anything interesting about the form of the poem on the page. They will probably notice the spacing—especially of *far   and   wee*—and the running together of *eddieandbill* and *bettyandisbel.* The teacher may leave these responses as questions to be returned to later. After the first speculation about the appearance of the poem, the teacher may read it aloud. Hearing the poem read should suggest some meanings to the class and clarify some things that might have puzzled them, such as the strange looking *bettyandisbel.*

The attention of the class may next be directed to questions about the time of year the poem talks about. They will easily see that it is spring, but they may be asked, Why "Just-spring"? Why the word "Just"? Why is it capitalized? If guesses are wild, or students are baffled, they may be reminded of some language analogies, for here Cummings uses what is ordinarily an adverb in quite a different way. Familiar contexts may help: *just a minute, spring is just around the corner, he's just leaving,* and other expressions which students recognize suggest *now,* the immediacy and intensity of the moment. They may be directed to the dictionary where they can distinguish between the adjectival senses of the word (which obviously do not fit the meaning here), and the adverbial senses, which do: *by a very little, precisely,* or *barely.* By trying these synonyms, they can see that it is the immediacy of spring which Cummings suggests; it is *barely* spring—that magical moment when winter changes —with a rush—into spring. As we read the poem, it is almost impossible to avoid letting the strong stress fall on *Just,* instead of on *spring. Just-spring* is a compound, then—a word invented by Cummings to suggest this particular time, and the capitalized *Just* makes us realize that this time of year is the real subject of the poem.

During discussion, young people often come to an agreement among themselves that the spacing of *far   and   wee* suggests the sound of the balloonman's whistle heard from a distance and coming nearer, and that the running together of *eddieandbill* and *bettyandisbel* suggests the breathless rush of children's speech. The slower students may take time to see that these queer-looking compounds are names, but the quick ones will help them.

The helpful teacher will let them play with associations to words suggesting sensory experience: *mud-luscious, puddle-wonderful*, even the motion suggested by the rhythm of the words *hop-scotch* and *jump-rope*. He may ask whether the balloonman is getting nearer or going farther off, and they may see that the spacing of "far and wee" decreases at each repetition, until the words are put in single lines in last position in the poem.

He will try to encourage discussion of the concrete images in the poem first and attempt to put off speculation about the balloonman until after other parts of the poem are clear. He is, of course, the central "fact" of the poem. Teachers may have to help immature students or those who have not read widely by supplying the most important clue to the poem, but older or more widely read children may be teased by the word "goat-footed." If the teacher asks them, "What does that word make you think of?" some student frequently remembers (dimly, perhaps) that someone—somewhere—in his reading was part man and part goat. Some may even remember Pan, and then associations may come tumbling: pipes of Pan, pipes of spring (the pipes being the balloonman's whistle).

Considerable help may then be needed if they are to put together the images of the poem into the meaningful order Cummings uses. First we meet the lame balloonman of the factual world with his familiar whistle, a common sign of spring, spelling enchantment and gaiety for the children; then the queer old balloonman (notice how each set of adjectives emphasizes oddity, unusualness, something unfamiliar); and finally, the word "goat-footed," which comes with a jarring impact. Obviously, we are no longer in the real world but are expected to take notice that something new is being said. When this adjective falls into place, the rest of the poem becomes clear; we see the connection between the balloonman and his whistle, first far off, then nearer, drawing the children from play to follow him and we remember Pan and his Pied Piper-like habit of enchanting youth with the music of his pipes.

The group may be encouraged to speculate on what the poet's purpose was. Is Cummings trying to describe the world in spring as it seems to a child? (They may see that the facts of the poem are those drawn from the child's view of the world.) Or does the poet want to suggest the fascination and enchantment of spring and its siren songs for youth? With most classes, arriving at this level of meaning will not be possible, though the bright may reach toward these speculations. The less bright or less mature may have gained much if they see the poem as a picture of the enchanted world of childhood awakening to the spring world and its delights. The young readers who can put these ideas about the poem together in class discussion will have learned much about the process of reading poetry for themselves with understanding and enjoyment. Certainly, the lesson should end with another reading, or perhaps two, of the poem by the teacher or perhaps by one of the students, to put the poem together again.

Student activities and assignments

Sample assignments in teaching poetry are suggested here. *The Explicator* and the *Exercise Exchange* offer excellent teaching suggestions and analyses. Such texts as those by Perrine, Brooks, and Ciardi (see bibliography) offer useful inductive exercises in helping students learn about metrics, figurative language, and theme in poetry. (The teacher will want to consult an index to poetry for sources of poems mentioned in this chapter.)

Stimulating independent reading

Let students browse in a classroom anthology for one of the following purposes and be prepared to report to the class or contribute to class discussion about what they find:

1. A collection of examples of effective imagery or striking metaphor.

2. Poems whose sound seems particularly effective.

3. A poem (or poems) which present ideas, sights, experiences, or situations they find interesting.

4. Poems which effectively communicate moods and feelings—sad, angry, loving, tender, happy.

5. Poems on a topic of interest for discussion (oral or written) with classmates. (Topics students have chosen include the following: war, death, love, social conditions, moods and feelings, animals, sports, the sea, people, the seasons, woods, humor, children, Lincoln, old people, mothers, fathers, etc.) Almost any of these topics would lend itself well to discussion in informal panel groups.

. . . Let students plan a report or a panel discussion in which they discuss a favorite poet, giving illustrations of his themes, and reading aloud some of the poems they like best.

. . . Ask students to begin to collect and make copies of poems they would like to keep in their own folders. They may individualize folders by designing attractive covers. Collections may be shared and added to, and poems may be commented on. A class project might be the editing of a collection of favorite poems of the class for an anthology to be kept in the classroom. Students may want to add brief editorial notes to some choices, explaining what the poem has meant to them.

Developing critical and esthetic appreciation

. . . Plan, with members of the class, panel discussions designed on one of the following patterns: discussion of poems on a topic or theme; discussion of a single poet; analysis of a poem for the class. Such poems as the following repay this kind of analysis and prove challenging for a group: Marianne Moore's "In Distrust of Merits," Auden's "The Unknown Citizen," Edna St. Vincent Millay's "Renascence," Benét's "Nightmare Number Three," Browning's "My Last Duchess" or "Fra Lippo Lippi," Yeats' "Sailing to Byzantium," Keats' "Ode on a Grecian Urn," Shelley's "Ode to the West Wind," Frost's "Directive," Eliot's "The Hollow Men."

. . . Encourage students to choose a poem to teach to the class. They should provide duplicated copies so that the class will be able to follow the discussion. Some comment on the metrical devices the poem uses, the effective images, literal and figurative meanings, and the theme of the poem provide good discussion topics.

. . . Let students prepare a reading of some of their favorite poems for a recording session with the class. Each student should have a copy of the poems he wishes to read and should have practiced his reading in advance. Selections of the best readings may be made so that recordings may be kept by the English Department for use in other classes.

Writing assignments

. . . Writing assignments may include an opportunity for free responses to poems: a comment on a poem which has particularly moved the reader (and why), some comparison of poems by different poets on the same topic or theme (love, the sea, moods and feelings, war). Some senior high school classes are capable of handling longer papers (making some use of biography or criticism) on poets: Frost, Emily Dickinson, Sandburg, Robinson, Browning, Wordsworth, Keats, and others are good examples. Such papers should minimize biography, except as relevant to the poetry, and focus on discussion of the poet's work, its central themes and significance.

. . . A different kind of assignment may be used to help clarify the links between the feelings, thoughts, and experiences of the reader and those expressed in some of the poems studied. The teacher may ask a class to write for a few minutes before the poems are read to the class. Such topics as these may help the student grasp the experience in the poem to be read:

> . . . If you could create a magic place where you could go when things get "tough," what would it be like? (Poems: Yeats: "Lake Isle of Innisfree," Coleridge: "Kubla Khan," Poe: "Eldorado," Tennyson: "The Lotus Eaters.")

> . . . Have you ever wanted to "get away from it all," to escape from the things that infuriate you about everyday life at home or in school? Some people do this in daydreams. Is there ever a disadvantage in doing this? (Poems: Elinor Wylie: "Sanctuary," Frost: "Birches.")

. . . Have you ever remembered a moment in which you were suddenly reminded of the fact that your parents loved you? What was the experience that made you realize this? (Poems: Edna St. Vincent Millay: "The Harp Weaver," Coffin: "The Secret Heart . . . ," Benét: "Nancy Hanks.")

. . . Have you ever had a thrilling experience you wish you could describe in words? A perfect downhill run in skiing, a perfect dive, an airplane ride, a horseback ride? (Poems: Benét: "The Horse Thief," McGee: "High Flight.")

. . . Have you ever seen a sight that was so beautiful that you wished you could describe it? (Frost: "Stopping by Woods on a Snowy Evening," Edna St. Vincent Millay: "God's World," Hopkins: "Pied Beauty" or "God's Grandeur.")

. . . Write a paragraph describing clearly how it feels to do one of these things you have experienced: walking in deep snow, flying in a plane, picking blueberries, feeling intensely cold, feeling very lonely, feeling very thirsty. Then read a poem in which a poet describes the same thing. (Poems: Elinor Wylie: "Velvet Shoes," McGee: "High Flight," Frost: "Blueberries," Shakespeare: "When Icicles Hang by the Wall," Frost: "I Have Been One Acquainted with the Night," Coleridge: "The Ancient Mariner.")

Selected bibliography

The teacher of poetry will want to consult the many articles on teaching poetry in the *English Journal* and the new department in that magazine sponsored by the NCTE Committee on the Reading and Study of Poetry in High School ("Modern Poetry in the Classroom").

George Warren Arms and Joseph M. Kuntz, *Poetry Explication: A Checklist of Interpretation since 1925 of British and American Poems, Past and Present,* rev. ed., Alan Swallow, Denver, 1961. An invaluable teaching resource for locating criticism and interpretation of specific poems. (Paperback.)

R. P. Blackmur, *Form and Value in Modern Poetry,* Doubleday & Company, Inc., Garden City, N.Y., 1946. (Paper: Anchor Books, 1957.) One of the standard books of the New Criticism.

Cleanth Brooks, *Modern Poetry and the Tradition,* The University of North Carolina Press, Chapel Hill, N.C., 1939.

———, *Understanding Poetry,* rev. ed., Harcourt, Brace & World, Inc., New York, 1950. One of the most helpful texts on interpretation of poetry.

John Ciardi, *How Does a Poem Mean?,* Houghton Mifflin Company, Boston, 1959. Excellent analysis of the creative process.

David Daiches, *Poetry and the Modern World,* The University of Chicago Press, Chicago, 1940.

Elizabeth Drew, *Poetry: A Modern Guide to Its Understanding and Enjoyment,* Dell Publishing Co., Inc., New York, 1959. A *must* for the teacher's library.

The Explicator, The University of South Carolina Press, Columbia, S.C. Contains analyses of poems.

Randall Jarrell, *Poetry and the Age,* Alfred A. Knopf, Inc., New York, 1953. (Paper: Vintage Books, 1955.)

Archibald MacLeish, *Poetry and Experience,* Houghton Mifflin Company, Boston, 1961.

Hughes Mearns, *Creative Power: The Education of Youth in the Creative Arts,* 2d rev. ed., Dover Publications, Inc., New York, 1959. Revised edition of a book first published in 1929. A discussion of the writing of poetry with a high school class.

Laurence Perrine, *Sound and Sense: An Introduction to Poetry,* Harcourt, Brace & World, Inc., New York, 1956. Excellent teaching exercises. (Paperback.)

I. A. Richards, *Practical Criticism,* Harcourt, Brace & World, New York, Inc., 1929. (Paper: Harvest Books, 1956.) An invaluable resource for teachers who would understand student reactions to poetry.

Morris Sweetkind, *Teaching Poetry in the High School,* The Macmillan Company, New York, 1964. (Paperback.)

CHAPTER *12*

It remains wonderful that mere puffs of wind should allow
men to discover what they think and feel, to share their
attitudes and plans, to anticipate the future and learn
from the past, and to create lasting works of art.

MAX BLACK [1]

Drama

Like poetry, drama is meant to be heard. Even more than poetry, perhaps,
drama requires of the reader the fullest coordination of the mind and senses.
For drama is meant to be seen, as well, and the reader must be actor, producer, stage designer, and even electrician, as he creates from the printed words
of the play the moving, speaking characters, the setting, and the actions the
printed symbols suggest. Reading a play, like reading poetry and fiction, is a
creative act, demanding the fullest imaginative cooperation between reader
and playwright.

Drama is available to our students in an unprecedented richness and
variety. Twenty-five years ago, most people in various parts of the country had
never seen a play performed. Today, community theater groups and road companies are common. Motion pictures, radio, and television have brought great
drama, ancient and modern, to the most isolated communities. Barrie's *Peter
Pan*, Shakespeare's *The Tempest, Macbeth, Hamlet, Romeo and Juliet,* and *A
Midsummer Night's Dream*, Ibsen's *A Doll's House*, Chekhov's *The Cherry
Orchard*, and Shaw's *Major Barbara* and *Don Juan in Hell* (from *Man and
Superman*) have been brought before television audiences.[2]

---

[1] Max Black (ed.), foreword to *The Importance of Language*, Prentice-Hall, Inc., Englewood Cliffs, N.J., 1962.
[2] See the discussion of the popular arts, Chap. 14, p. 337.

Reading the play in the classroom

The young reader meeting his first play finds that many of the devices which clarify meaning in the novel and the short story are missing. No author's description helps us visualize the scene and place of the drama that is about to unfold, except the usually brief stage setting given before the dialogue starts. Novelists may take many pages to create atmosphere and setting; most playwrights do it in a paragraph or two, and most of the detail is factual.

Anderson's *Winterset*, for instance, gives us in a few details a sketch of the river under the bridgehead, the gigantic span which seems to "lift over the heads of the audience," the rock barricade, the river bank, the shed for derelicts. We must infer the atmosphere of the play from the single street lamp, the glimmer of apartment-house lights, and the time: an early, dark December morning. The powerful visual effect of the stage setting, with its dark shadows, its thin lights, its looming bridge, gloomy shed, and apartment walls, must be created in our imagination.

Most young readers skip over setting as unimportant, finding it too detailed to follow and too factual to be interesting. Only when they learn almost automatically to fill in the visual details of light and setting for themselves will they read plays with full appreciation of their many dimensions. One way to help them create visual images of setting for themselves is for the teacher to draw in outline form on the chalkboard some of these details as the class reads the setting together. An artistic student may do the sketching at the direction of his classmates.

The reading of some settings of one-act plays may give students practice in learning to visualize setting and to anticipate the mood and tone of the play from a brief description. The settings of Susan Glaspell's *Trifles*, Synge's *Riders to the Sea*, Lady Gregory's *Spreading the News*, and O'Neill's *Where the Cross Is Made* are useful for this purpose. Students may discuss the details from settings of a number of plays to determine what kind of drama will follow. Will it be a tragedy or a comedy? How would the set make the audience feel? Depressed? Admiring? Sad? Happy? Awed?

Other settings may serve for discussion. That for O'Neill's *The Emperor Jones* tells us that the Emperor's throne is a "dazzling, eye-smiting scarlet," while orange cushions are placed on the seat and on the floor as footstools. In *The Glass Menagerie*, Williams tells us that the play, being a memory play, is dimly lighted. The dimly lighted interior suggests the world of fantasy and illusion in which Laura and her mother live, as the sharp and savage colors of the set of *The Emperor Jones* suggest something of the character of Jones himself.

The opening of the play

Students may begin to study how the dramatist uses exposition or dialogue at the beginning of the play to introduce the characters and bring us into the conflict. In *Macbeth*, a soldier reports the battle in which Macbeth has shown his bravery. The brawl in the streets at the opening of *Romeo and Juliet* tells us of the feud between the Montagues and Capulets. In *Hamlet*, we know of the ghost's troubled walking through the conversation of the guards as they walk on the battlements and from their report to Horatio who watches with them. In Wilder's *Our Town*, the Stage Manager tells us about the town and introduces the main characters to us, telling a little about each as they begin their accustomed actions of the day. The first few speeches, which introduce us quickly to the main characters and the central conflict of the play, require the dramatist's careful selection. He does not have the time to talk in leisurely terms about his characters as novelists do, or to describe settings and situations. He must select characters and details which will be most revealing, allow them to give us the facts which propel us into the center of the conflict, and get on with the play.

Studying character

Characters in drama reveal themselves for the most part in only one way in the printed play: through what they say. Through the author's stage directions we may get different ideas about them, their emotions, and their actions. The reader takes over the job of actor and director as he attempts to visualize how the character would move on the stage, look at someone, show nervousness, fear, or joy. In Besier's *The Barretts of Wimpole Street*, for instance, we have only their words to tell us of the emotions in Elizabeth and Henrietta during one scene in which they talk about defying their father. We are told that Henrietta speaks bitterly, stormily, defiantly, and earnestly during this time. We are told sometimes of the tones of voice the actors use when they fight, kneel, kiss, come in or go out, and so forth. But most of their tones, accents, pauses, actions, and movements we must fill in for ourselves.

Students may notice how a character's words reveal the kind of person he is. Amanda's fluttery prattle about her seventeen gentlemen callers in the first scene of *The Glass Menagerie* shows us her world of illusion and the nature of her plans for Laura as well as her inability to accept facts. In *A Doll's House*, Torvald's ponderous endearments to Nora tell us much about his condescension and his attitude of a father to a wayward child. Lady Macbeth's terrible "Unsex me now" speech reveals in a few words the coldness of her nature as Hamlet's soliloquy, "To be, or not to be," reveals his tortured mind.

What characters say about each other reveals much not only about other characters but about the speakers themselves. Lady Macbeth's "Yet I do fear thy nature; it is too full of the milk of human kindness to catch the nearest way," tells us not only about Macbeth but about her own willingness to "catch the nearest way" no matter what the cost. Mercutio's description of Romeo tells us about his infatuation with Rosalind and his tendency to fall in love easily, but it also reveals the speaker's wit and humor.

Actions provide another method by which the dramatist reveals character.

Even inexperienced readers may see that Nora's passion for macaroons presents her childlike nature. Laura's playing with the glass menagerie and turning on the phonograph to drown out the sound of quarreling between Amanda and Tom reveal her desire for escape into the world of fantasy. Eliza's hurling the slippers at Professor Higgins in Shaw's *Pygmalion* shows delightfully how the "squashed cabbage leaf" has turned into a woman with a mind of her own.

Clues to character are often subtle. Students need much experience in learning to watch for the word, phrase, tone, or gesture which indicates what characters are like and the sometimes small distinctions between them. Only when the play is read aloud by students who have practiced parts and studied carefully the characters whose role they are playing, do characters really come alive. Students may see a play raised to still another level of interpretation on the stage, or in recordings, as the skilled voices of great actors and actresses reveal new depths of character. When Judith Anderson plays Lady Macbeth, or when Laurence Olivier, Maurice Evans, or John Gielgud plays Hamlet, we realize anew the subtleties of Shakespeare's characterizations. As students begin to understand the revelation of character, they may gain valuable experiences in listening to recorded plays, especially those of Shakespeare, which have been done by different actors and companies. The differences in interpretation suggested by different readings of lines can provide a class with valuable ideas for discussion.

Studying action

There are more imaginative ways to study the plot and action of a play than the mechanical charting of rising action, climax, and falling action. It is said that Eugene O'Neill walked out of Professor Baker's class in playwriting at Harvard when a fellow student got up to put an outline of the plot of a play on the board. Students may discuss the first bit of evidence of conflict in a play (technically called the *inciting force*) as that which tells us something of what the action is to be about. In *The Barretts of Wimpole Street,* we see that the battle over drinking porter is one of the first evidences of conflict between Elizabeth and her father, one of the first scenes in which he imposes his will upon her. Trock's initial speech in *Winterset,* in which he flings defiance at the city and shows that he will buy his life at any expense, sets the mood and prepares us for the struggle. The witches' prophecy to Macbeth and Banquo, "All hail, Macbeth! that shalt be king hereafter," provides the initial incident which makes ambition begin to take shape in Macbeth's mind.

It is helpful to note with students the succeeding incidents which intensify the conflict and clarify the nature of the tensions between the opposing forces in the play. Only when students have seen what these forces are is the essence of the struggle clear. In *Macbeth,* it is personal ambition as opposed to moral law; in Bolt's *A Man for All Seasons* or Shaw's *Saint Joan* it is the struggle of opposing values. In *The Glass Menagerie,* Tom pits his realism against the world of illusion and false values his mother has built up.

The conflicting forces in modern drama are more often inward than outward. With the twentieth century, the drama in which conflict is chiefly psychological has become more important than that in which physical action or crises of situation are common: *The Glass Menagerie, The Barretts of Wimpole Street,* O'Neill's *Anna Christie,* and Miller's *Death of a Salesman* are such plays.

Students may spend a good deal of time reading plays and analyzing the nature of the conflicts they present, particularly as those conflicts become concerned with opposing sets of values and struggles for economic and social justice. In studying such conflicts, they may gain some of their most important insights into the nature of drama.

Studying atmosphere

The close reading of a play by senior high school students who have read many plays in junior high school will focus on some of the subtler aspects of drama, as well as the study of character and conflict. The teacher will direct their attention to atmosphere as it is used by some dramatists: the squalor and poverty of the environment of Rice's *Street Scene;* the fog and mist of the heath which darken the mood of *Macbeth,* and the chill vapors surrounding Elsinore where the ghost walks; the oppressive bright sunlight glaring on the scene of *The Emperor Jones;* the brooding, dark setting of *Winterset.* Some plays seem to depend little on atmosphere; in others, it is used powerfully to underscore theme and idea. The experience of students with the movies and televised plays may be used to illustrate the clichés of atmospheric devices which may be contrasted with the artistic ones of great playwrights. Murder is committed in storm and in rain in television mysteries as well as in *Macbeth;* the low keys of darkness, gloom, storm, rain, and fog are common devices whose effect on human emotions may be analyzed.

Studying form

Studying much of the technique of the dramatist need not be of first concern to the students or to the teacher. The study of the drama has too often taken the form of charting plots, making drawings of stage settings, and locating inciting forces, rising and falling action, climaxes, and catastrophes. There are some questions of form and structure, however, that the student will need to explore. He may be asked who in the play seems to represent the values the author stands for. They may then see the antagonist as the force or person who opposes that point of view. In *All My Sons,* Miller contrasts Chris' concern about the responsibility of man for other men with his father's anxiety about family security and position and the philosophy of business as usual.

With more sophisticated and widely read students, the structure and the tension of opposing forces in the play may be analyzed. Climax may be studied, even with younger students, in terms of the question, "At what point in the play are you fairly sure what the outcome will be?" They learn that the point of highest tension or conflict comes when things begin to turn in favor of or against the forces in conflict so that the outcome is predictable. In *The Barretts of Wimpole Street*, we know, when Elizabeth Barrett receives the letter from her father telling of his projected move away from London, that this will force her decision to marry Browning and ensure the defeat of her father. Macbeth, notified of the escape of Fleance, and breaking down in public in the banquet scene at the sight of Banquo's ghost, has started downward from the crest of his powers and fortunes.

Students should see that after the climax takes place some glimmers of hope or reversal may occur, as when Macbeth kills young Siward, but respite is only momentary and events rush to their inevitable conclusion. The rising and falling of tensions in the drama have their counterpart in our emotions and sympathies. Our own emotional responses may tell a clearer story about the play's climactic moment than our efforts at intellectual analysis.

The nature of tragedy

Students may be interested in learning about how concepts of tragedy have changed in our day. College-bound students may have studied the Aristotelian concept of tragedy as the fall of a man from high estate, the noble character destroyed by a tragic flaw: ambition, greed, impulse, or lust for power. From the time of the Greeks and Shakespeare, whose tragic hero was a king or a prince, a noble character, we have moved to the drama of the present and Arthur Miller's declaration that the common man, too, can be a tragic figure.[3] Students may be encouraged to discuss the modern conception of the tragedies which can happen to every man—the common man caught in the toils of an economic system, oppressive and unjust social forces, or persecution, or destroyed through weakness, delusion, or selfishness, as is Ibsen's Hedda Gabler, or Willy Loman.

Superior students may be able to discuss the Aristotelian concept of catharsis in tragedy: the purging of the emotions by pity and fear. After the teacher has raised the point for the class to consider, and asked the class how they feel at the end of a tragic play (such as *Hamlet, Macbeth,* or *Death of a Salesman*), he may get some verbal expression of that inexplicable feeling of satisfaction, of release of tension and spent emotion that the good reader experiences. When they have discussed how catharsis is possible, the teacher may read some of the passages from the *Poetics* in which Aristotle discusses why tragedy is greater than comedy. Further study may focus on the inevitability of the ending of tragedy. The very nature of tragedy is involved with the certainty of the ending. We are never in doubt as to what will happen. Anouilh

[3] Arthur Miller, "Tragedy and the Common Man," *Theater Arts,* vol. 35, March, 1951, pp. 49–91.

has expressed the essence of tragedy in the words of the Chorus of his *Antigone*:

> The spring is wound up tight. It will uncoil of itself. That is what is so convenient in tragedy. The least little turn of the wrist will do the job. Anything will set it going. . . .
>
> The rest is automatic. You don't need to lift a finger. The machine is in perfect order; it has been oiled ever since time began, and it runs without friction. Death, treason, and sorrow are on the march; and they move in the wake of storm, of tears, of stillness. Every kind of stillness. Tragedy is clean, it is firm, it is flawless. . . . Death, in a melodrama, is really horrible because it is never inevitable. . . .
>
> In a tragedy, nothing is in doubt and everyone's destiny is known. That makes for tranquility. . . .[4]

The dramatist's language

A study of the language of the playwright is an important part of the process of close analysis of a play. Students may notice as they read aloud that some characters talk in ordinary speech. They may observe ways in which language reveals character, and the power of rhythm and phrase to add a poetic quality to dialogue.

The rhythms of everyday speech are caught by Thornton Wilder in *Our Town*: the Stage Manager's "Now I'm going to tell you some things you know already. You know 'em as well as I do; but you don't take 'em out and look at 'em very often"; and by Miller in *Death of a Salesman*: "Figure it out. Work a lifetime to pay off a house. You finally own it, and there's nobody to live in it." But in both plays the characters are capable of poetic speech. There is Emily's poignant

> Good-by, good-by world. Good-by Grover's Corners . . . Mama and Papa. Good-by to clocks ticking . . . and Mama's sunflowers. And food and coffee. And new-ironed dresses and hot baths . . . and sleeping and waking up. Oh, earth, you're too wonderful for anybody to realize you. Do any human beings ever realize life while they live it?— every, every minute? [5]

And there is Linda's speech: "Willy Loman never made a lot of money. His name was never in the paper. He's not the finest character that ever lived. But he's a human being, and a terrible thing is happening to him. So attention must be paid." [6]

As we have seen, language, too, reveals the educational and social background of the characters as it does in *The Emperor Jones*, in *Street Scene*,

---

[4] Jean Anouilh, translated by Louis Galantiere, *Antigone*. Copyright 1946 by Random House, Inc. Reprinted by permission.

[5] Thornton Wilder, *Our Town*, Coward-McCann, Inc., New York, 1938, p. 124.

[6] Arthur Miller, *Death of a Salesman*, The Viking Press, Inc., New York, 1949, p. 56.

Kingsley's *Dead End,* Odets' *Golden Boy,* and many others. Students may learn about the Irish dramatist, John Millington Synge, listening with his ear to the wall in the huts of the peasants on the Aran Islands and capturing a poetic Irish speech in *Riders to the Sea* and *The Playboy of the Western World.* In *Riders to the Sea,* Maura, bereft of her sons and husband, makes a final speech that is poetic and eloquent: "Michael has a clean burial in the Far North, by the grace of the Almighty God. Bartley will have a fine coffin out of the white boards and a deep grave surely. What more can we want than that? No man at all can be living forever, and we must be satisfied." [7]

Classroom activities

The central classroom activity during the study of drama should be the reading of the play aloud. The teacher reads aloud often. When young readers are inept, when time is brief, or when illumination of character or lines is essential, the teacher's reading may clarify. The playing of recordings[8] which allow students to hear the reading of plays by good actors, dramatic companies, or the casts of movie productions is an important part of play study. When they have become familiar with the play and have been given time to practice, the students themselves may take parts and read. This oral reading of plays ought to be a central activity in the enjoyment of drama in the classroom.

Much of the poor reading of plays in class is a result of poor preparation and indifference on the part of students who do not know the play well enough to read it intelligibly. Some ways of encouraging good performance are the assignment of parts so that students can practice at home, the assignment of scenes to particular groups, and the appointment of a student director to coach the group. Allowing a group to work out its own production of a scene or a play to be recorded on tape for the class, or for playing before another English class in the school, encourages the creative class members. Where students can become involved in presenting a good production in competition with other groups or other classes, where they can become free and relaxed enough to enjoy the play through reading it aloud, appreciation of drama increases rapidly.

Junior high school students will need considerable help in learning to read the play. Class study of some simple one-act plays makes a good beginning for this kind of reading: students discuss how they learn what kind of persons the characters are and follow the action to the climax. During the first two years of junior high school, much of the reading of plays may be for enjoyment, with emphasis on the study of characterization and with questions designed to help students see what the conflict is about.

[7] *The Complete Works of John M. Synge,* p. 97. Reprinted by permission of Random House, Inc.
[8] See list on p. 424.

Ninth graders may, for instance, read Hart and Kaufman's *You Can't Take It with You*, and see the conflict between two philosophies of life. They may even be led to see that the play is not as important for characterization of an individual as of two different groups of people living for different goals. The play may be brought close to their experience through discussion of the problem of Alice in the play: should she renounce her happy-go-lucky family with its madcap ways in order to retain the love of wealthy Tony Kirby? (A bright class may see that a solution in which the Kirbys accept the way of life of the Sycamores is not at all a likely one.)

Older students may study character motivation and development, and the nature of the conflict: is it between man and man, man with himself, or man against outside forces? They may be asked to discuss whether the motivation is credible. They may analyze conflict by noticing in several plays what forces are pitted against each other. Do the characters bring their tragedies on themselves through something they have done? Through something they stand for or believe? Or is the tragedy inevitable because of social or economic forces beyond the control of the individual? What does the conflict involve: the struggle between love and lust for power (*Elizabeth the Queen*); the individual against tyranny (*Billy Budd*); the individual against society (*Inherit the Wind*); the individual with himself (*Hamlet; Othello*)?

Analyzing the ending of the play is important for students at all ages. Younger students may discuss the credibility of the happy ending (*You Can't Take It with You* or Van Druten's *I Remember Mama*). Students in senior high school may be asked whether it is credible that Nora would walk out on her family and husband in *A Doll's House*. They may be reminded of the early productions of this play in Germany in which Nora silently opened the door and reentered. They may discuss the irony of the ending of Heggen's *Mr. Roberts*, in which the man who wanted to see wartime action is killed drinking coffee in the officers' mess, or the fantastic symbolic ending of Giraudoux's *The Madwoman of Chaillot* when the Madwoman grandly sweeps all the materialists of Paris into the sewer. Are the suicides of Willy Loman (in *Death of a Salesman*) or of Hedda Gabler inevitable? The discussion of endings and the resolution of the conflict is of primary importance in determining the significance of the drama's total impact.

Other activities have been suggested as possible accompaniments to the study of drama. Many of these may be used as major activities to develop appreciation. As a brief introductory exercise or the culminating activity of a study of many plays, students may use the ideas and techniques they have studied in order to write a play of their own or to rewrite a short story or a scene from a novel into a play.

Junior high school students can often experience the feeling of dramatic conflict, the building of tension through incidents leading to a climax, and the resolution of struggle in drama through creative dramatics in which they write their own plays or adapt short stories for play presentation, or through role playing and sociodrama, in which they dramatize problems and conflicts of importance in their own lives.[9]

In order to help students become more critical and discriminating about plot and the significance of conflict, young people may be asked to record and analyze the plots of some of the favorite TV serials they watch. At any level in the secondary years, this can be illuminating. Even young students may see, through close analysis, the repetition of incident, the preponderance of violence, the stereotyping of character and situation, and the improbable resolution of conflicts.

Organizing the class for work

When the whole class reads a play together, as is frequently the case with a Shakespearean play or with other commonly taught plays such as *Our Town, Death of a Salesman,* or Anderson's *Elizabeth the Queen,* it may be encouraged to read the whole play quickly the first time to get the outlines of plot and action, and then to reread carefully to see how the playwright handles character, motivation, and action. Senior high school students may study the development of one important character: Lady Macbeth, Willy Loman, Emily (*Our Town*), or Queen Elizabeth (*Elizabeth the Queen*). They may be asked to take notes on their rereading, and study the play with study questions.[10]

Reading in groups

One of the most satisfying class experiences for students from the ninth grade on is the reading of several plays which illustrate one theme or which present a kind of problem. The teacher who is familiar with a wide variety of drama, particularly contemporary plays, may easily imagine a number of thematic groupings for this kind of discussion (see page 294). Several patterns of group organization may be worked out. The class may be divided into from three to five groups of five or six students, with each group choosing a theme and a list of plays illustrating that theme. Within the group, the plays may be assigned by choice, or the teacher may assign different plays to individuals in terms of their reading ability.

A variation of the pattern is for the class to be divided three or four ways, with each group reading a play: four levels of ability may be provided for in this way. The first pattern allows for more freedom of choice and provides for counseling so that students read within the limits of their understanding. Stu-

---

[9] See the list of "Guidance and Mental Health Plays" in the NCTE publication, *Guide to Play Selection,* 2d ed., Appleton-Century-Crofts, Inc., New York, 1958. Most of the plays mentioned in this chapter will be found in this source.
[10] See the sample questions at the end of the chapter.

dents may use the questions at the end of the chapter for individual reading and for group discussion and inform the group about the plays they have read through reports or a panel discussion at the end of their reading and discussion period.

A sample thematic play-reading unit

One of the most challenging themes for study for students from the ninth grade on is that of drama as a criticism of society. Some of our brightest students are deeply interested in questions of social issues and problems and the writings which discuss these issues. These questions concern less able readers and slow learners as well.

The plays of Eugene O'Neill, Clifford Odets, Arthur Miller, Maxwell Anderson, Robert Sherwood, Elmer Rice, John Galsworthy, Henrik Ibsen, and George Bernard Shaw are among those which have great impact on youth just beginning to experience the important social problems and issues explored by contemporary drama. The struggle against injustice, the effects of greed and materialism on the human spirit, the lonely battle of the individual who wishes to abide by moral rather than legal or social codes, the individual against tyrannical authority, the fight against poverty, unemployment, prejudice, discrimination, authority—all these appeal strongly to youth.

To young people the plight of Anouilh's *Antigone* is a moving one. Though the crime she dies for—the ritual burial of her brother—seems strange to young readers, the passion with which she declares herself against the practical Creon's setting of the state's welfare against (and over) the moral law is a moving and contemporary problem. Antigone, loving life and in love with Hemon, dies resisting tyranny. Her shouted "No" became a symbol of the French Resistance during the German occupation in 1944, as French audiences responded to Anouilh's words, "The whole sky has fallen on you and all you can do is to shout." [11]

Arthur Miller's *The Crucible* is moving in a similar way, as John Proctor tears up his confession of being in the devil's service in refusal to utter the lie that would save him from hanging.

Eliot's *Murder in the Cathedral*, Bolt's *A Man for All Seasons*, and Shaw's *Saint Joan* show men and women willing to die for their beliefs. Becket in *Murder in the Cathedral* chooses to give allegiance to God rather than to the King. Sir Thomas More of *A Man for All Seasons* goes to his death rather than acknowledge the legality of Henry VIII's divorce from Catherine of Aragon. Saint Joan rejects the intellectual arguments of her enemies. Lawrence and Lee's *Inherit the Wind* shows the individual standing against the community in his defense of scientific truth against prejudice; Rattigan's *The Winslow Boy*

---

[11] See E. Bradley Watson and Benfield Pressey (eds.), *Contemporary Drama: Eleven Plays*, Charles Scribner's Sons, New York, 1956, p. 113.

shows a family committed to a principle of justice even though the pursuit of the trial to clear their son's name sends them into bankruptcy and costs the daughter her lover. In Wouk's *The Caine Mutiny Court-Martial* and Levitt's *The Andersonville Trial*, the tyranny and brutality of distorted personalities given authority over men illustrates the rebellion of individual men against injustice. In a similar cause, Coxe and Chapman's Billy Budd strikes down the bullying Claggart, and Mio of *Winterset* dies in a defeating struggle against evil.

The problems of racial and economic injustice are presented in moving and meaningful terms in many contemporary plays. Lorraine Hansberry's *A Raisin in the Sun* portrays a Negro family striving for decent housing against the prejudices of the white community; Sidney Kingsley's *Dead End* shows what slum life can do to produce delinquency. The tragedy of Willy Loman in *Death of a Salesman* is that of the little man caught up in the pressures and values of a materialistic society. Rice's *The Adding Machine* has something of the same theme, portraying a life in which man is little more than a machine. Lillian Hellman's *The Little Foxes* and *Another Part of the Forest* are merciless pictures of the carpetbagger morality of a ruthless and greedy family who are willing to stop at nothing to get the money they want.

There is something in the drama of man standing alone as an individual against society for right, for justice, for social or economic equality, for truth, or for ideals that is stirring for modern youth. Some of the most powerful modern plays have used these themes, and they make a strong appeal at the time when idealism and the passion for justice and equality are at their height. Students who read and discuss these plays can gain insight into literature as a reflection of society.

Reading Shakespearean plays

The success that imaginative teachers have had in presenting Shakespeare to classes of all levels of ability indicates that the study of Shakespearean plays can be an enjoyable and stimulating activity for most students. Resistance to the study of Shakespeare is chiefly resistance to method: often the reading of a Shakespearean play becomes focused on memorizing the meaning of words no longer in the language. Too much time may be spent on the facts of the Shakespearean stage, the controversy over whether Shakespeare was Shakespeare, the dates and sequence of the plays, and the line-by-line analysis of meanings and figures of speech. Often students never come in touch with the real life of the play, or with the human dilemmas which make Shakespeare's world as contemporary as our own.

In both our world and the one he created, families are involved in a senseless feuding to prevent the marriages of young lovers, men are moved to brutal murders to gain power, and young men are appalled at corruption and licentiousness. As one teacher points out about teaching *Macbeth*: "Even with a reluctant group, it has been possible to awaken the desire to search out the themes, playing with 'done and undone,' with fatherhood and kingship, with good and evil, with the influence of the superstitions, or with Macbeth's sterility . . . where the disintegration of a human being is witnessed and understood. . . ." [12] The teacher who can show young people the universal themes, character traits and human dilemmas in Shakespeare and point out similar ones in the next street, the next block, or in the story in the daily newspaper will be able to interest students in the reading of Shakespeare.

Despite the conventional objections classes often raise about reading Shakespeare, classes of all levels of ability and interest have been led to the enjoyment of the plays by teachers who could bring them alive for youth. We have seen in our own time the tremendous popular response Shakespeare can command: the Shakespearean theaters in Stratford, Ontario, and Stratford, Connecticut, play to full houses. Joseph Papp's free productions of the plays in Central Park in New York City have met enthusiastic popular acclaim and have led to the showing of several plays in off-Broadway theaters during the winter season. Almost no Broadway season is without one Shakespearean play. The productions of *Macbeth, Romeo and Juliet, The Tempest,* and "The Age of Kings" series on television have commanded wide audiences. Movies have been made of *Hamlet, Romeo and Juliet, A Midsummer Night's Dream, Macbeth, Henry V,* and *Julius Caesar,* to name but a few. Broadway musicals have been adapted from *The Taming of the Shrew* (*Kiss Me, Kate*), *Romeo and Juliet* (*West Side Story*), and *The Comedy of Errors* (*The Boys from Syracuse*).

Shakespeare's language

The primary barrier between today's students and the enjoyment of Shakespearean plays is that of language. The blank verse of the plays is often read as prose by the immature reader; the differences between the language of the early seventeenth century and that of our own makes the reading of dialogue difficult for the nonverbal boy or girl. Teaching must assist young people to read Shakespearean language with understanding and pleasure.

Several kinds of assistance can be given students who find it difficult to read Shakespeare. The teacher may read aloud some of the first scenes of the play, asking questions, encouraging students to guess at meanings from contexts, talking a bit about the way language has changed since Shakespeare's time. One period might be fruitfully spent in such an exploration of the language of the play, with students attempting to locate lines they can understand with ease, lines which sound like contemporary speech, and those which can be understood in context except for one or two words. They may see that serious speeches in the play are most often in stately blank verse; humorous

---

[12] Charles Calitri, "Macbeth and the Reluctant Reader," *English Journal,* vol. 48, May, 1959, p. 259.

scenes are frequently in colloquial prose; other lines are astonishingly contemporary. Students frequently meet with astonishment and pleasure some well-known phrase which they greet with a gasp of recognition: "something is rotten in the state of Denmark," " 'tis caviar to the general," "out, out, damned spot," or "get thee to a nunnery."

The teacher might prepare a mimeographed sheet of fifteen or twenty quotations with a difficult or obsolete word underlined, asking students to guess at the meaning of the word from the context. Lines such as the following may be given to show students that they will need to practice guessing at meanings from context and that they may do so with a fair chance of being right: ". . . Tybalt would kill thee,/ But thou *slewest* Tybalt . . . ," or ". . . Else would a maiden blush *bepaint* my cheek. . . ."

Lines which might pass today for our own speech may be noticed, too:

O that I were a glove upon that hand,
That I might touch that cheek . . .

Give me my Romeo; and, when he shall die,
Take him and cut him out in little stars,
And he will make the face of heaven so fine
That all the world will be in love with night . . .

They will notice that modern girls do not talk that way, but the individual words are familiar ones.

Both good and poor students are likely to be baffled by the many mythological, historical, and biblical references in Shakespeare. Good students need to be challenged to check in a good dictionary on those essential to the meaning of a significant passage. It should go without saying that the teacher should have an easy command of these and be able to expand and interpret references, inspiring the readers to further exploration of these sources of allusions. It is significant for them to understand Hamlet's implied comparison of his father and Claudius with Hyperion (the Titan father of the sun god and the symbol of male beauty) and the satyr (the symbol of sensual ugliness) because it summarizes the feelings he has about the difference between the two men. It is not essential for them to know the story of Niobe to grasp the implication of Gertrude's following her husband's coffin, "Like Niobe, all tears," or to understand the reference to the players as "out-Heroding Herod."

Much Shakespearean study for young people is complicated by footnotes on all the literary and mythological allusions, which they are required to memorize. Such piecemeal memory work has little real relevance to an understanding of the play, and it obscures larger meanings. Here, certainly, the distinction between allusions which reveal character and casual references such as "foul as Vulcan's smithy," or "all Neptune's ocean will not wash clean these little hands . . ." should be made.

So, too, with the references to Elizabethan customs: e.g., falconry (*Romeo and Juliet*) or bear baiting (*Macbeth:* "They have tied me to the stake; I cannot fly, but bearlike I must fight the course . . .”). Good students who wish to pursue these references may do so; those who find the play hard going should be permitted to skim the references, concentrating on more important meanings. Slow students should have considerable help from the teacher.

Teachers may ask bright students to look for figurative language or the central metaphors of the plays studied in class. Caroline Spurgeon has pointed out how each of the plays contains dominant imagery: *Hamlet* is full of images of poison, corruption, and decay—of Denmark as an ulcer, or a tumor, which is infected. In *Macbeth,* the dominant image is that of the borrowed robes, the ill-fitting garments which “hang loose upon him like a giant's robe upon a dwarfish thief.” *Othello* abounds in images of toads, flies, goats, and monkeys—of references to lechery and animal breeding.[13] To see how Shakespeare has conveyed the essential atmosphere or theme of the play with such imagery is to enrich its meaning.

Much reading aloud of the play with the teacher's help in getting students over the hard places and frequent “translation” into idiomatic and colloquial English often makes the play memorable for students. Recordings help readers get the rhythms and sounds of the speeches by ear, the best way to learn them. One New York City teacher of a class of Puerto Rican girls of limited intelligence and very poor reading ability found that they responded with enthusiasm to *Romeo and Juliet* when it was read to them and later compared with the recording of Leonard Bernstein's *West Side Story.* The romance of the story captivated the girls; so did the rhythm of the language, read well by the teacher. We need not feel guilty if our students get their Shakespeare by ear: so did the groundlings; so, too, do present-day groundlings at amateur theater productions, the motion picture house, or before the television set.

If we can keep students reading carefully and wondering what revelations of character will come next; if we can lead them to understand the complexities of human nature that the plays reveal—the moral dilemmas of human beings who are like people we may know, facing problems we recognize, then the teaching of Shakespeare can be a means of fascinating discovery about people for today's high school students.

Evaluation

The problems of evaluating understanding of drama are not very different from those involved in testing student understanding of other types of literature. The suggestions for evaluation, study guide, and test questions given in Chapters 9, 10, and 16 will guide the teacher in constructing tests, and in using standardized forms of literary comprehension and evaluation. Students and teachers may evaluate the growth of the class in understanding and ap-

---

[13] Caroline Spurgeon, *Shakespeare's Imagery,* Cambridge University Press, London, 1935. (Paper: Beacon Press, Boston, 1958.)

preciating drama through observing whether students can turn to play reading with confidence and pleasure, finding in dramatic form the discussion of people, issues, and ideas they are exploring in fiction, biography, or nonfiction. Once the student has mastered the art of reading drama, he may turn to this form for reading for pleasure and intellectual stimulation as he does to fiction.

The dramatist takes the student into a swiftly paced world where he can live through the struggles and heartbreaks of men and women, their battles against fate, against each other, and against social forces which threaten them. In contemporary drama he can experience personal, psychological, social, and international problems, presented in human terms, and often he can precede or follow the reading of the printed play by seeing the movie or the televised performance. Drama as a medium for the discussion of ideas, and the human dilemmas of men of all times, should assume a position of central importance in the literature program.

Teaching the play *Death of a Salesman*

The following plan for teaching *Death of a Salesman* attempts to show how an important modern play may be taught at different levels to groups of differing abilities.

Defining purpose

Arthur Miller's richly symbolic *Death of a Salesman* seems ideally suited for adaptation to teaching at several levels. Its symbolism, probing of character, and searching examination of American values, and its subtlety in handling action, thought, and feeling, make it complex enough to be challenging to college-bound students. For terminal and slow students, it is suitable as a contemporary classic, one which has received critical praise as an outstanding drama of our time, yet simple enough in language to be readily comprehended at the literal level and challenging at its less complex symbolic levels. The language of the play is the idiom of everyday speech, yet the characters often rise to levels of eloquence, as in Linda's requiem speech and Charley's thematic statement of the salesman's character. For all students, it can be deeply moving emotionally. Willy's pathetic vacillation between love and hostility to those he loves, between hope and despair; Linda's constant appeal, "attention must be paid," her sympathy with Willy's anxiety about his job, and her efforts to sustain his dignity and pride are recognizable to students. Biff's struggle to find out who he is and to reach an understanding with his father is a familiar dilemma to many adolescents. Miller has drawn characters who are confused, fallible, but appealing human beings. We see their conflicting senseless dreams and poignant search for identity and security, for the good life, and enduring values. Like most of us, they are mixtures of love and hate, pride and humility, meanness and decency, selfishness and generosity. Because there is so much that we recognize of people we know in these characters, their plight is important. We care about what happens to them.[14] For many students the Lomans' problems will seem familiar; the longing for something better, the dreams of easy money, mixed with worry about whether the installment budget will stretch—these they have met in their own lives.

The play has value for today's students because it presents problems common to our society: the confused search for values in a materialistic world; the pressures of economic insecurity, impersonality, and anonymity in today's business world; the search for identity, and the attempt to maintain dignity in the lonely crowd. These are problems not only of the white-collar worker, but of the factory worker as well, not only of the well-to-do, but of the marginal worker fearful of being replaced in his job.

Through an objective look at the play's characters, students, under the direction of a skillful teacher, may learn to see themselves in new and important ways. For, like Willy Loman, many students believe that "the man who creates personal interest is the man who gets ahead"; they maintain that the important thing is to be "well-liked"; like Biff, they want to know who they are and to see themselves clearly. Lest they wake up like Willy in their mature years, deserving Biff's elegy ("He never knew who he was"), it is worthwhile for them to explore the attitudes and values in the play and through these to rethink their own. Late adolescence is the time for such search, when the maturing boy or girl organizes his own philosophy of life. This play can help him examine the values he chooses to live by. The play may profitably be taught in the eleventh or twelfth year.

Introducing the play

Teachers may prepare students to read the play by stimulating class discussion about the kinds of things parents want for their children, the things most people want out of life, or the goals they hold to be most important. After such discussion, students may be asked to read the play with the suggestion that it deals with some of the questions they have been discussing and that the characters in it choose what they want for themselves and their children. Students may be asked to read to see what choices the characters make and whether they agree with these choices. They may be urged to read the play quickly in order to find out answers to these questions. They may be warned, too, that they will find the play confusing as to time, for in some scenes past and present happenings are shown simultaneously. If the teacher prepares them for these shifts in time, illustrating how human beings often think

[14] One teacher of girls from wealthy families in a women's college reports that they tend to reject Willy and his family as improvident dreamers who ought to come to their senses. After expressing this point of view in their papers, the students listened to Arthur Miller's reading of the play on the recording. Several said they felt they had not understood the play and asked to be allowed to rewrite their papers.

of past and present happenings at the same time, they will not find the play confusing. Miller's explanation of the time sequence and the staging are illuminating.[15]

Discussing the play

After the first quick reading, students may be asked to take a few minutes of class time to write briefly their reactions to Willy, Linda, and Biff. Then they may discuss these questions: What kind of persons are these characters? How do they feel about each other? What does each want out of life? What is the central problem of the play? Who is the central character? Why? Is there ever a point at which we feel that things may go all right for the Lomans—Biff may get a job, Willy may be transferred to New York, Biff and Happy may start their sports store? At what point do things turn against Willy? How early do we know that he is really defeated? When do we get the first inkling of what he intends to do? (The teacher may select from these questions those which may most fruitfully be answered on paper before discussion starts and those which may be used in early discussion of the play. Probably the first four or five can be answered briefly by most students in all classes.)

Good students may be asked, in addition, to attempt to put into their own words what they think Miller is trying to show or say about people in the play. They may, in other words, try to state the theme. This is an excellent comprehension test. Many good readers can state the theme at the first quick reading.

When the teacher is satisfied that the whole class understands the main action, he may encourage the students to ask of the different characters, "What is he (she) like?" A discussion of the persons in the play will bring out most of the major points in the drama and students will go back to early happenings in the play to find instances which reveal character and action. Discussion of the characters, one by one, and their relationships to one another provides a valuable chance for talking about the play as a whole. With the poor readers, teachers will find that such discussion brings out innumerable errors of fact and interpretation in reading. Usually other members of the class can clarify a student's mistaken notion of what a character is like or what happens; there is always the text to return to if no agreement can be reached.

Teachers may ask the students to notice some of the devices Miller uses

---

[15] In the paperback edition (Bantam Books, Inc., New York, 1951) Miller has expanded his stage directions to make it easier for the reader to visualize the settings and transitions. He explains time in the play as a representation of the way human thoughts move from present to past almost in the same moment: "There are no 'flashbacks' here—we never go backward. It is simply that the past keeps flowing into the present, bringing its scenes and its characters with it—and sometimes we shall see both past and present simultaneously" (p. 4).

to unify the play, and his designing the structure of the play in two acts and a requiem. They may be asked where the first hint is that something will happen to Willy in the car. They should recall that the first speeches of Willy and Linda concern the possibility of an accident, that these speeches suggest Linda's apprehension and that there has been trouble before.[16] The first scene contains the seeds of the conclusion, when Willy rushes off stage and the car is heard roaring out of the garage. We are never allowed to forget the car, the possibility of accident, Willy's growing confusion, and the slow building of his determination to use that means of killing himself.

They may notice, too, that early in the first act, Willy talks about planting carrots in the back yard, and one of the last scenes shows him in the garden planting carrots by flashlight. The trip to Boston, which becomes a central force in the play, is suggested early when Willy talks about taking the boys to Boston with him, and by an early scene in which the Woman drifts into Willy's memory, thanking him for the silk stockings. We see Bernard as a boy, idolizing Biff, and being patronized by the Lomans, and we see him as a man, about to argue a case before the Supreme Court. There are many other instances that students may notice where there is a rounding out, a pulling together of themes, incidents, ideas, and character traits suggested early in the play.

Topics for discussion

With college-bound students who are good readers and who have had enough background in literature to be able to see in this play some relationships to other literary themes and ideas, a good deal of discussion can revolve around consideration of parallels. Some of the topics suggested in the introductory lesson may be explored more carefully: the nature of tragedy, the concept of the tragic hero, modern concepts of tragedy. Students may be referred to Miller's introduction to the play in *Theater Arts*, in which he explains his conception of Willy Loman.[17] Willy's plight may be contrasted with that of Hamlet, Macbeth, Othello, and Oedipus. Students should be encouraged to read many plays outside of class in order to bring in further contrasts from modern drama: O'Neill's *The Emperor Jones* and *Beyond the Horizon*; Miller's *The Crucible*, *All My Sons*, and *A View from the Bridge*; Ibsen's *The Master Builder* and *The Enemy of the People*.

Further discussion may revolve around the values illustrated in the play. Two universal themes are shown in the confusions of the characters in *Death of a Salesman*: the questions of what a man believes in and wants out of life and the Socratic admonition to "know thyself." Students may search out lines and incidents in which these two themes are exemplified: Willy's beliefs that "the man who creates personal interest is the man who gets ahead" and "a man

---

[16] Students may already be familiar with the literary device of foreshadowing.
[17] *Op. cit.*

can end with diamonds on the basis of being liked" are reiterated throughout the play; they have determined the way he lives his life and the way he has brought up his sons. He is a prime exponent of the false American dream:[18] his values are personality, charm, being "well-liked" and "known." His "I have friends" indicates he values friendship, but an analysis of his relationship with people indicates that he has no real friends. Through pride, he rejects Charley, the person who has offered him friendship and support, both economic and emotional. His adolescent dream of the "massive" funeral he will have turns into the reality of the empty cemetery in the requiem. Good students who have read Riesman's *The Lonely Crowd,* Whyte's *The Organization Man,* and Packard's *The Status Seekers* will see in these sociological analyses the characteristics of the false American dream Willy pursues, the dream which has proved empty for modern man. Ben is the symbolic exemplification of that romantic dream: "When I was seventeen I walked into the jungle and when I was twenty-one I walked out. And by God I was rich." Teachers may remind students of the source of this get-rich-quick American dream in its various American manifestations: the gold rushes in California and Alaska, boom-town life in America, real-estate booms in Florida, the stock market.

Other thematic ideas in the play may be explored by students whose wide reading allows comparison of this play with others they have read and whose ability to generalize and to see relationships makes such discussion meaningful. They may notice that the play's basic ironic contrast of dream versus reality has numerous aspects: (1) Sudden wealth (diamonds) versus the reality of a life in which each paycheck is stretched to cover the installment payments; where there is never quite enough money; where things wear out before they are paid for; where after twenty-five years of payments on the house they are "free and clear" only after Willy's death. (2) The promise of the past versus the stark and frightening reality of the present. The bright future envisioned for Biff and the dreams of success for the boys have turned into a bitter present in which one son is a drifter and the other a shallow philanderer. (3) Willy's dreams of popularity, success, and money, versus the reality of his friendlessness, loneliness, and ever-diminishing income.

Able readers may perceive the play's symbolism. They may explore the significance in the play of (1) Biff's tennis shoes (first marked with the University of Virginia, then, after the visit to Boston, burned). (2) The symbolism of the garden and Willy's preoccupation with seeds and planting: "Nothing's

---

[18] Teachers should contrast the dreams of the characters in this play with the statement by James Truslow Adams about the American dream in an epilogue to *The Epic of America:* ". . . the American dream, that dream of a land in which life should be better and richer and fuller for every man, with opportunity for each according to his ability or achievement. . . . It is not a dream of motor cars and high wages merely, but a dream of a social order in which each man and each woman shall be able to attain to the fullest stature of which they are innately capable, and be recognized by others for what they are, regardless of the fortuitous circumstances of birth or position." (Little, Brown and Company, Boston, 1931, p. 404.)

planted. I don't have a thing in the ground." (3) The symbolic import of Biff's compulsive stealing (getting something for nothing), which goes back to the theft of the football and is repeated in the stealing of the fountain pen when he applies for a job. (4) Linda's stockings, too, are symbolic. She mends them throughout the play, and the sight of them never fails to arouse in Willy feelings of remorse and guilt. They serve, too, to symbolize for Biff his father's infidelity to his mother.

The symbolism of the setting, of light, color, space, and sound is important, too. Most of this is suggested by Miller in his stage directions: The play opens to the sound of a flute "telling of grass and trees and the horizon." The set alternates between the memory scenes in which the leafy trees and open yard can be seen and the present with its "solid vault of apartment houses around the small, fragile-seeming home." (Students should be helped to see how the set underscores the theme: the promise of freedom and unlimited horizons of Biff's youth, the "vault" of the apartment houses suggests the imprisonment of the characters, their lack of "space," their economic and emotional confinement.) Youth (both Willy's and Biff's) gave a promise of freedom and space; maturity is hemmed in by confining reality.

Terminal and slow students may define some of the central conflicts in the play by listing some of the problems of each character. Many of these fall readily into the familiar categories of family, house, job, and future plans. They may compile some such list as this:

Willy: to make enough money to pay the bills; to see the fulfillment of his dreams for the boys; to work out his tangled relationship with Biff.

Linda: to encourage and support Willy; to see that the boys have some respect and feeling for their father; to keep Willy from committing suicide.

Biff: to find himself; to grow up; to try to sort out fact from the lies and dreams of fifteen years.

Happy: to get ahead in business; to keep his independence, his apartment, his car, his women.

A summarizing discussion of the play may ask students to state what they feel Miller is trying to say in the play. In the prefatory essay to the play in *Theater Arts,*[19] he has explained his purpose as that of raising the tragedy of the common man to the level of classic drama. His comments in the play about the empty dreams of getting ahead through competition, about rejecting the simple, free, and natural life where a man can be himself are clearly stated. The tragic flaw that destroys Willy, Biff, and probably Happy is the insistence on living in dreams rather than reality. Only Biff in the play fully realizes the falseness of this dream world, and we feel that it is too late for him to rebuild his life. The class may well conclude its discussion of the play by examining the values the play suggests chiefly by their absence in the characters: integrity, honesty, maturity, and loyalty.

[19] *Op. cit.,* p. 48.

Miller's play shows a large cross section of the modern metropolitan business world, where competition and the image of success are the basic facts of life, where a man's worth is measured by how much he makes a year, and how "well-liked" he is. Willy's sense of failure, not only for himself but for his boys, provides a poignant conclusion to the play when he kills himself to provide money for the rehabilitation of his wastrel son.

Student activities and assignments

These questions suggest the kinds of discussion about the plays that teachers can lead students to engage in. Through such teaching, the student discovers much about the meaning, the significance, and the literary form of the play. Listening to some of the many excellent recordings of plays,[20] both of contemporary works and of classics of the past, can lead students to a new awareness of dramatic form and structure, and the sound of the dramatist's language spoken by gifted actors can add a dimension to his study of drama.

. . . Follow the development of two (or three) of the main characters in the play. What kind of persons are they? What do they want in the play? How do we learn what they are like? (Make notes to show how we learn about them through what they say, what they do, what they think, or what other characters say about them.)

. . . As you read the play, make notes (referring to speeches and page numbers) of the dramatic actions which build to the highest point of tension in the play. Can you tell where you are first aware of what the real struggle is? Can you decide at which point in the play things begin to turn for or against the central character so that you are aware of how things will turn out for him? Does anything happen after this point to make you think things may not turn out this way? That he can escape his fate, get what he wants, or come out on top?

. . . What is the setting of the play? Is it important to the action? Is the playwright creating an atmosphere to influence the way you feel about the play, its characters, and its actors? What words would you use to describe the atmosphere—gloomy, depressing, gay and cheerful, starkly realistic?

. . . Can you locate any speeches or places in the play in which the author gives you clues as to what will happen later? Are there any hints of foreshadowing? (In *Death of a Salesman*, Linda's finding the rubber hose on the gas heater points to Willy's thoughts of suicide; in Lillian Hellman's *Another Part of the Forest* we are given hints about something in Marcus' dark past by the phrases, "the suspicion on your papa," and references to hot tar, clubs, and ropes.)

. . . Look for and mark speeches in the play in which you are given clues as to the author's theme. The theme of the play may be developed in a number of speeches or in one in which the author makes explicit his point

[20] Sources of information about recordings available are given on p. 424.

of view about life or the thing he is trying to say in the play. What speeches seem to indicate what this point of view or theme is? Does it seem to be a social message? A statement of belief in certain values? A point of view about life and the way it should be lived?

. . . Study the author's use of dialogue and language in the play. Is the language that of plain everyday speech or is it poetic? Does the way the characters talk indicate something about their education, their background, their social standing, their personalities or characters? If the author attempts dialect or regional speech, does this seem convincing or does it add too much to the difficulty of the play? (For example, *Pygmalion, The Emperor Jones, The Glass Menagerie, The Playboy of the Western World.*) In what plays is the speech poetic? (*Our Town, Winterset, Riders to the Sea.*) In what plays is the humor largely verbal, depending on wit, humor, irony, understatement? (*You Can't Take It with You, The Importance of Being Earnest, The School for Scandal.*)

. . . What is the nature of the conflict in the play you read? Do we see man struggling against the values of society, or of a group of people, or an individual? (In *Inherit the Wind,* Bertram Cates is in conflict with the views of a society which prefers to cling to outmoded beliefs rather than adjust to a painful new truth.)

Is the individual in conflict with himself, destroyed by something within him—perhaps the tragic flaw of the Greeks? Thus Willy Loman, Hedda Gabler, and the hero of Odets' *Golden Boy* are really self-destructive, defeated by some inner conflict that cannot be resolved. Does the conflict involve man against man? Antigone pits herself against Creon; Elizabeth Barrett fights her father's attempts to keep her dependent; Tom of *The Glass Menagerie* struggles with his demanding mother for his freedom; in *Winterset* Mio is pitted against Trock Estrella, the gangster, in the battle to clear his father's name.

. . . What is the nature of the values people fight for in the play? Money? Fame or success? Social ambition? Power? Personal honor or integrity? Love? The laws of God or the laws of man?

Selected bibliography

Eric Bentley, *In Search of Theater,* Vintage Books, Random House, Inc., New York, 1953. Stimulating criticism of the contemporary theater.

Cleanth Brooks and Robert B. Heilman, *Understanding Drama,* Holt, Rinehart and Winston, Inc., New York, 1948. "The Brooks-Heilman analyses are . . . unmatched" (Leary: *Contemporary Literary Scholarship*).

Committee on Playlist, *A Guide to Play Selection,* 2d ed., Appleton-Century-Crofts, Inc., New York, 1958. A useful source of information about plays and their sources for teachers. Contains an annotated bibliography of plays.

Edward J. Gordon and Edward S. Noyes (eds.), *Essays on the Teaching of English,* Appleton-Century-Crofts, Inc., New York, 1960. Contains some excellent comments on teaching drama, and on the close reading of plays.

Fred B. Millet, *Reading Drama,* Harper & Row, Publishers, Incorporated, New York, 1950.

Readings on Shakespeare

A. C. Bradley, *Shakespearean Tragedy,* Meridian Books, Inc., New York, 1955. A classic of Shakespearean criticism. (Paperback.)

Leonard F. Dean (ed.), *Shakespeare: Modern Essays in Criticism,* Oxford University Press, Fair Lawn, N.J., 1957. Contains essays cited by Harbage, Stoll, and Sewall. (Paperback.)

G. B. Harrison, *Introducing Shakespeare,* Penguin Books, Inc., Baltimore, 1947. Useful brief compendium of information for essential facts about Shakespeare.

Shakespeare in School and College, NCTE, Champaign, Ill., 1964. A collection of articles from the *English Journal* and *College English.*

Theodore Spencer, *Shakespeare and the Nature of Man,* The Macmillan Company, New York, 1949. (Paperback.)

D. A. Traversi, *An Approach to Shakespeare,* Anchor Books, Doubleday & Company, Inc., Garden City, N.Y., 1953.

Mark Van Doren, *Shakespeare,* Anchor Books, Doubleday & Company, Inc., Garden City, N.Y., 1953.

Margaret Webster, *Shakespeare without Tears,* The World Publishing Company, Cleveland, 1955.

CHAPTER 13

To read well, that is, to read true books in a true spirit, is a noble exercise, and one that will task the reader more than any exercise which the customs of the day esteem. . . . Books must be read as deliberately and reservedly as they were written.

HENRY DAVID THOREAU [1]

Nonfiction

The world of nonfiction, of the informative, argumentative or critical essay, the factual article, the biography of men and women, the fascinating book of true adventure—all these captivate many of our students more completely than the world of fiction, drama, and poetry. For many practical young people, products of a practical age, the challenge of ideas and the wealth of information presented by articles and essays, and the biographies of real men and women, will make up the larger part of their reading; only with reluctance will some of them enter the worlds of fiction or fantasy. The popularity of nonfiction today is a cultural trend observable in the increasing sales of nonfiction books—both hardcover and paperback—since World War II, with science, social science, and philosophy making dramatic sales gains. Television critics have observed that although television and the movies supply fantasy and fiction for today's audiences, they cannot compete in the field of nonfiction. Obviously, there are some programs which *do* compete with nonfiction books: the documentaries, the travel programs, and the biographical sketches of famous men and women.

An American Library Association report on the reading habits of the public at the end of 1962 showed that reading emphasis had shifted from westerns and light romance to art, travel, health, education, and domestic and

[1] *Walden and Other Writings,* Modern Library, Inc., New York, 1950, pp. 91–92.

international affairs. The public shows an increasingly greater interest in books on science, technology, and fiction dealing with politics and foreign relations.[2]

The essay

Most definitions of the essay agree on two characteristics: it is a reflection of the moods, thoughts, ideas, or opinions of an individual, and it reflects the personality of the writer through its style. In the essay more than any other literary form, in Buffon's much-quoted phrase, "Style is the man." In the essay we seem to meet the personality and mind of the author through language which is urbane and witty, reflective and serious, chatty, informative, incisive, or colloquial. In the best of essays, the writer is revealed as a human being: Lamb's personality has charmed generations of readers through the tenderness of "Dream Children" and the whimsicality of "A Dissertation on Roast Pig" or "The Superannuated Man"; the family adventures of James Thurber, E. B. White, Mary Ellen Chase, Shirley Jackson, and Clarence Day reflect, even if indirectly, the personalities and values of the writers. It is, of course, the meeting with a first-class mind which is most fascinating in the essay: we encounter the opinions—often idiosyncratic and individual, but always challenging—of people like Orwell, Aldous Huxley, Mencken, Chesterton, Belloc, Montaigne, or Addison.

It has been traditional in teaching to distinguish between formal and informal essays. The differences between the two are chiefly in subject, style, and structure. The formal essay treats a serious subject objectively, usually in a serious tone, and implies a distance between writer and reader. The style of the formal essay permits of no colloquialisms or contractions; its vocabulary is frequently erudite rather than popular, its sentences carefully balanced. The student is likely to meet the formal essay in "The Spectator Papers," or Lincoln's "Gettysburg Address," but few of the nineteenth-century formal essayists— Newman, Arnold, Huxley, or Ruskin—will be included in his reading unless he takes a college-preparatory course. Today's essays tend to be predominantly informal in style. Even when the modern essayist is very serious about an argument or an idea, he frequently takes a familiar, informal line with his audience and may employ colloquial speech.

Joseph Wood Krutch has observed that the personal or reflective essay today is a dwindling art form, not much in demand in the age of the informative article.[3] Publishers of magazines tend to reject essays and welcome, instead, the informative or argumentative article, more popular in national magazines with mass circulation. Despite the passing of the reflective essay

---

[2] Survey by American Library Association, reported in *Book Buyer's Guide*, vol. 66, February, 1963, p. 175.

[3] "No Essays, Please," in *The Saturday Review Reader*, Bantam Books, Inc., New York, 1951, pp. 147–154.

in the tradition of Addison and Steele, Hazlitt, Lamb, or Bacon, some of the best contemporary writing appears today in the form of thoughtful and critical essays by such writers as E. B. White, Joseph Wood Krutch, and Edmund Wilson.

While it is probably true that the leisurely, reflective essays many English teachers value—those of Lamb or Hazlitt, the embellished prose of Ruskin, the music of Pater—have less charm for today's younger generation than for an earlier age, the appeal of essays of all ages which explore problems of continuing concern to the young is strong to students who are just beginning to test their own powers of thinking and to clarify for themselves their opinions about such problems.

Biography and nonfiction

Biography and autobiography, the story of a life or lives, seem so close to fiction to young people that many of these books are commonly referred to as "stories." Certainly *The Diary of a Young Girl* reads like a novel, and the autobiographical sketches of Clarence Day, James Thurber, Kathryn Forbes, and others also read much like fiction. Maturer students prefer the serious treatment of the life of a famous historical personage, an artist, actor, or explorer. Some of the most popular nonfiction today includes the books of true adventure, exploration, danger, and courage, such as Heyerdahl's *Kon-Tiki,* Herzog's *Annapurna,* Tenzing's *Tiger of the Snows,* or Byrd's *Alone.* True accounts of personal experiences in wartime, travel, and daring or dramatic achievement provide the best of introductions to the world of nonfiction for the young reader.

Why teach nonfiction?

The study of essays in the high school years may provide the stimulation of new ideas, the enriching encounter with humor, the introduction to new worlds of thought in philosophy, ethical values, and social criticism. Because of its predominantly literal rather than symbolic content, many students find the essay a much easier form to read than the short story. As they put it, the authors of essays say what they mean, and he who can read may follow. This oversimplified approach to the reading of essays is refuted in classroom discussion, as students explore the figurative language in which many essayists express themselves and the deceptively simple phrasing of a complex idea which needs clarification. Even though students soon learn the error of their assumption that it is easy to read an essay, many find its wealth of ideas, reflections, opinions, and arguments a challenge to stretch the mind.

A chief reason for teaching the essay to all youth is that it is in this form that the reader encounters most of the information, opinion, and argument over issues and ideas about which he will have to clarify his own ideas and make up his mind during his adult years. Expository prose provides most of the material used in teaching reading for comprehension and much of that we use to teach the principles of writing, speaking, and listening. Colleges lay great stress on this form in freshman English. Recommendations to schools preparing students for college frequently emphasize the necessity for careful teaching of expository prose.[4]

Biography and autobiography are frequently taught as a means of extending the reading acquaintance of students with the wealth of books which provide glimpses of men and women in adult roles, their lives, their goals, their values, and their achievements. Biographies provide some of the best teaching about goals: in reading about those who have struggled against odds, the young person learns something about defining his own goals and working toward them. Through biography he "tries on," as it were, dozens of adult lives and roles he will never share, but which, nevertheless, enlarge his own world by showing him what it is like to be an artist, a scientist, an inventor, or a doctor. One of the tasks of the adolescent is finding heroes and models after whom to pattern his own life. Biography and autobiography serve this developmental need in important ways.

The search for values

The recent emphasis on teaching in the humanities may lead to the study of nonfiction as a means of examining philosophical and ethical values. Douglas Bush has called attention to the renewed importance of the search for humanistic values in a technological age:

> The "humanities" in the original meaning of this and kindred words, embraced chiefly history, philosophy, and literature. These were the studies worthy of a free man, that ministered to *homo sapiens,* man the intellectual and moral being, and not to *homo faber,* the professional and technical expert.
>
> The study of literature . . . has had to take over the responsibilities that used to be discharged by philosophy and divinity. . . . Most young people now get their only or their chief understanding of man's moral and religious quest through literature. . . . Most of the young people I see find in literature, literature of the remote past as well as of the present, what they cannot find in textbooks of psychology and sociology, the vision of human experience achieved by a great spirit and bodied forth by a great artist.[5]

The study of essays in the secondary school years may provide one of the chief sources of intellectual challenge for students as they explore a range of ideas and learn the excitement of mind meeting and arguing with mind. In the rich collections of essays available today, many of them in inexpensive

[4] See *High School–College Articulation of English,* NCTE, Champaign, Ill., 1961–1963, p. 4.
[5] Douglas Bush, "The Humanities," *The Educational Record,* vol. 36, January, 1955, pp. 64–69.

paperback editions, they may find master contemporary essayists arguing about numerous topics: living in an atomic age, the meaning of integrity, freedom of speech, literature and the art of writing, individual belief, science, education, mathematics, politics, and social injustice.

Program into practice

Studying the essay involves students in close, analytical reading. The personal, reflective, familiar, and literary essays require comprehension and an adequate vocabulary of the reader, but expository prose—the essay of argument and opinion—requires that the reader follow the reasoning of the author, that he recognize emotional appeals, and that he be able to make a logical analysis of reasoning. These are not simple skills. Yet, expository prose is the medium for most significant discussions of contemporary ideas, issues, and problems. The editorial, the scientific report, the argument, the analysis of a problem—all these require logical and critical thinking of the good reader.

The problems involved in teaching biography and other types of nonfiction are not so numerous. High school readers are not equipped, nor can they be easily taught, to make a critical analysis of a biography for accuracy of fact or the point of view of the author. They can make a beginning, however, by learning to check on the authority of the biographer and to look for possible bias or uncritical admiration. They can begin to apply some of the standards of style they have learned to the form and language of the biography. Most important, they can learn to be very clear as to the distinctions between biography and autobiography, and the reasons for which each is written.

Teaching the essay

The essay as a literary form need not receive much formal attention until the eleventh or twelfth year of high school. Before that time, the essay can be effectively included in thematic units where it extends the range of materials and points of view used to examine a theme. There are suggestions in this chapter for a number of thematic groupings into which essays would fit. Another possible kind of organization for the reading of the essay is for groups within the class to spend some time reading essays on a particular topic. The groups might be divided so that they may examine essays or nonfiction on numerous topics: science, the mass media, education, values, language, the arts. This kind of organization allows a group of students to compare the points of view of a number of people who have written on the same subject. Individual reports are possible, too, but less meaningful, probably, than the other possible ways of organizing reading. With capable college-bound students, some assignments for individual reading, and writing outlines, précis, or analyses of essays may be desirable in the later years of high school.

Although close reading of the essay and study of its style and structure should not receive much attention until the eleventh or twelfth year, there are many occasions during which a class, reading a piece of nonfiction together, may begin to develop some awareness of these elements. The study of paragraphs or brief essays for practice in reading comprehension, the use of models to teach various patterns of organization for writing, and the use of magazines and newspapers for the study of language all bring the essay into the classroom as an important part of language study during the six years of high school.

Today's collections of essays frequently include magazine articles, editorials, selections from autobiographies, pieces written by newspaper and magazine columnists, and criticism of books, movies, radio, television, and other mass media.

Students may investigate magazines and newspapers to collect and bring into class samples of writings in these forms. The teacher may have to gather other illustrations from sources he knows: the columns of James Reston, Walter Lippmann, Max Lerner, Harry Golden, Art Buchwald, and other syndicated columnists: the editorials in *The Saturday Review* and *Harper's*; the brief bits from "Talk of the Town" in *The New Yorker*; and some of the brief descriptive pieces in the editorial pages of the *New York Times* and the *New York Herald Tribune* are worth bringing to the attention of students.[6]

Teaching critical reading

Although the essay seems easy to read, many students who are not good readers seem to have difficulty understanding the plain prose sense of what they read. Even as college freshmen, they frequently fail to read an expository essay carefully enough to follow the logical development of its argument. Inadequate vocabularies often cause serious blocks to comprehension. The reader frequently cannot say what the central idea of the essay is, nor understand the relationship of illustrative detail to main thesis.

At some time during each year, it is probable that students will read together essays in one of the many good collections available at the high school level or in an anthology the class is using. This is an excellent point in the year's work to teach some of the basic skills of reading comprehension, to spend some time on vocabulary study, and to use some of the writing assignments during this period to help students practice some of the patterns of expository writing. Outlining, too, if not overdone, may be helpful in showing students the structure of a simple essay.

Some of the following points of emphasis in teaching the essay are helpful in assisting students to read with comprehension:

[6] Paperback collections of essays from *Harper's, The Atlantic,* and *The Saturday Review* appear frequently. For less able readers, *The Reader's Digest, Read,* and *Scholastic* magazines provide materials. (See bibliography of Chap. 5.)

1. Encourage students to state in their own words the central idea of the essay or the main point the author is making. College freshman composition texts frequently call this central idea the *thesis* of the essay. It is helpful to teach college-bound students this term and to encourage them to use it as they write their own expository papers. Frequently teachers can turn to other resources for practice in this kind of reading—to other essays in supplementary textbooks or in paperback collections, to the file of materials collected by the teacher, or to sample paragraphs duplicated so that each student may have a copy. Pages may also be projected by the opaque or overhead projector.

2. Using the same sources, the teacher can suggest that students study the essays or paragraphs to examine the nature of support for the main idea which the author offers. Are there examples? Details? Illustrations? Are there enough examples or illustrations to make clear the main idea or to give it adequate support?

3. Teacher and students may discuss the figurative language employed by the essayist. Winston Churchill's speech to the House of Commons after the evacuation of Dunkirk uses such figurative language: "The German *eruption swept* like a sharp *scythe* around the right"; "The whole *root* and *core* and *brain* of the British Army"; "hurled themselves in vain upon the ever-narrowing, ever-contracting *appendix* within which the British and French Armies fought." Such phrases as "hail of bombs" and "jaws of death and shame" provide other examples.[7]

One of the chief failings of college students in understanding expository prose is their inability to grasp a central metaphor when it exists. Such examples as Rachel Carson's chapter called "The Great Snowfall" in *The Sea around Us*, in which she pictures the continuous falling of sediments through the sea to the ocean floor as a continuous snowfall, illustrate the use of such a metaphor to clarify and make poetic a scientific concept. Students will encounter such examples in other essayists and nonfiction writers. The famous last passage in Thoreau's *Walden* suggests the theme of the book by the metaphor of the "strong and beautiful bug" which emerged from a kitchen table after sixty years:

> Who knows what beautiful and winged life, whose egg has been buried for ages under many concentric layers of woodenness in the dead dry life of society, deposited at first in the alburnum of the green and living tree, which has been gradually converted into the semblance of its well-seasoned tomb—heard perchance gnawing out now for years by the astonished family of man, as they sat round the festive board—may unexpectedly come forth from amidst society's most trivial and handselled furniture to enjoy its perfect summer life at last! [8]

[7] Winston Churchill, "The Miracle of Dunkirk," in Rewey Belle Inglis et al. (eds.), *Adventures in English Literature*, Mercury ed., Harcourt, Brace & World, Inc., New York, 1952, pp. 673–677.
[8] Thoreau, *op. cit.*, pp. 296–297.

Here Thoreau uses the figure of the "strong and beautiful bug" as a symbol of rebirth of the free, spiritual life of man emerging from the encumbrances of society into a true transcendental "perfect summer life at last."

Students may be reminded of the central metaphor of "The New Frontier" which the late President Kennedy used in his inaugural address, and they may be encouraged to notice others which are current in the daily newspaper or, perhaps, even in the everyday school life around them.

The essay provides suitable materials for the analysis of irony and satire, both difficult for immature readers to comprehend. The teacher may read aloud some good contemporary satire such as Orwell's *Animal Farm* or Thurber's *Fables for Our Time,* and ask students, as a test of comprehension, to state the central idea. For college-bound juniors or seniors, a good oral test is the reading of Swift's "A Modest Proposal," followed by the request that students write out their reaction to the author's argument. Ordinarily, teachers find that all but the best readers are horrified by the master satirist's proposal to sell children's skins for gloves, and many write angry diatribes against the immorality of his proposal. The essay is shocking enough to become a memorable illustration of the central characteristic of irony—the use of words which mean the opposite of what is said. Reading irony intelligently is a difficult skill for most students, and the essay provides challenging materials for the study of this verbal technique.

Many teachers have been successful in teaching students something about analysis of an argument through acquainting them with some of the central principles of logic. Students in the senior high school can learn to detect logical flaws such as begging the question, ignoring the question, the *argumentum ad hominem,* and others. Many of these fallacies can be observed in simple materials such as the advertising in newspapers, in magazines, and on television. Other tools for logical analysis come from the study of basic semantic principles—the "either-or" dilemma, slanting, loaded words, distinguishing fact from judgment and the like, discussed in Chapter 3.

Teaching about structure

Students from the ninth grade on and perhaps earlier can be taught a good deal about the structure of expository writing. The examination of an essay or a part of an essay which has one central idea and two or three supporting points provides a good illustration. Students can observe that the main idea sometimes comes first, sometimes as a summary sentence in the paragraph or essay, and sometimes is implied rather than stated. Most students do not need to learn the great variety of structural patterns for the paragraph commonly taught at the college level, but some of the simpler patterns should be familiar to them.

Readers in the junior high school may concentrate on observing how a writer develops an idea into a paragraph, how he directs the reader to follow his thoughts with transitional words, such as *then, next, first.* Senior high school students may examine more carefully a wider variety of patterns of development, with examples increasing in complexity from the tenth grade on.

The analysis of a paragraph is a convenient way to begin to teach something about the structure of the essay. As students examine a number of paragraphs—models chosen by the teacher for patterns of structure—they may see that sometimes the writer develops his ideas in chronological order, sometimes from general to specific examples, sometimes from cause to effect, and often, in familiar, informal, reflective essays, in a free association of ideas. For other patterns of structure, both in the paragraph and expository prose, the teacher may find examples and discussion in some of the many college texts designed for use in freshman English classes.

Often it is not until students begin to write expository essays of some complexity themselves that they can study profitably some of the subtler structures of the essay. During the eleventh and twelfth years, however, young people are capable of careful analysis of some great essays for both structure and style. They should have practice in outlining some essays in order to determine the main steps in the author's development of an idea. They can write précis or summaries in which they attempt to condense an essay from the original into a summary of one-third the length. Probably only the superior college groups need have much practice with the genuine précis, which requires that the writer retain the flavor of the original author's style. For all students, the exercise in compressing ideas without losing their essential meaning is excellent practice in both writing and reading.

Teaching about style

Some discussion about tone and diction is worthwhile for the class reading essays together. Such discussion is most helpful if there are numerous examples for comparison. If the teacher reads aloud a number of examples, poor readers will get a sense of the sound of the words and the beauty of the style. Most students can see the general differences between the conversational, informal contemporary style and the balanced sentences of Dr. Johnson or the rhythmic cadences of Stevenson's prose.

Beginning with the tenth grade, students should have some opportunity to make a close analysis of the styles of several writers. They may examine choices and connotations of words, the tone the writer uses, the use of detail, and the rhythms of the sentences.

Many close analyses of the one-paragraph Gettysburg Address have shown how Lincoln used a tightly constructed series of sentences to remind his audience of the past, of the present occasion and its purpose, and to inspire them with a sense of dedication for the future. Students may observe how his style varies from relatively simple sentences—"We are met on a great battlefield of that war"; "It is altogether fitting and proper that we should do this"—to

THROUGH HISTORY WITH J. WESLEY SMITH

"I think people will understand you better, Mr. President, if you just say 'eighty-seven years.' " Drawing by Burr Shafer; © 1958 *Saturday Review.*

those phrases in which he has inverted normal word order for emphasis—"little note nor long remember . . . ," "can long endure," "here gave their lives," "here dedicated." They may notice how he uses repetition for effect: "We cannot dedicate, we cannot consecrate, we cannot hallow . . ."; "of the people, by the people, and for the people. . . ."

They observe how he uses the latinate words "dedicate" and "consecrate" (with its religious connotations) thematically, repeating them several times. The prayerlike dedication occupies the final position in the brief essay and is stated in a long sentence—a series of four *that* clauses. Further, students may be asked to rewrite a few sentences of the address in their own words and to compare the two, noticing, for instance, the difference in effectiveness if one were to change "Fourscore and seven years" to "Eighty-seven years." [9]

---

[9] See the sample analyses of essays in Walter Blair and John Gerber, *Factual Prose: Better Reading I,* 4th ed., Scott, Foresman and Company, Chicago, 1959.

A comparison of a few paragraphs from Stevenson or Lamb, on the one hand, and White or Thurber on the other, will suggest some important differences between older writers and those of our time. The efforts of modern writers to capture the rhythms of speech and use colloquial diction rather than to strive for purely literary effects are noteworthy. In the eighteenth century, Johnson is said to have modeled his conversation on his writing, but in the nineteenth, Hazlitt complained of the Johnsonian style in terms a modern essayist might employ: "He uses none but 'tall opaque words' taken from the 'first row of the rubric': words with the greatest number of syllables, or Latin phrases, with merely English terminations. . . . How simple it is to be dignified without ease, to be pompous without meaning." [10] Rewriting proverbs or well-known passages from Shakespeare or the Bible[11] often shows more effectively than hours of discussion how important is the effect of certain arrangements of words. One book suggests rewriting "These are the times that try men's souls," into "Times like these try men's souls," "How trying it is to live in these times!" "These are trying times for men's souls," and finally "Soulwise these are trying times." [12]

Some exercises to develop an ear for style and sentence rhythm may be used with appropriate materials at different grade levels. Juniors and seniors may become aware of rhythm by hearing or reading aloud passages from some well-known examples: Churchill's Dunkirk speech,[13] passages from Shakespeare or the Bible, some anthologized selections from *The New Yorker*'s "Talk of the Town," some passages from *Time*. These may be contrasted with some of the most individual styles of the older writers: Thoreau's pungent comments in *Walden*, Johnson's "Letter to the Earl of Chesterfield," Stevenson's "Aes Triplex," or Ruskin's description of St. Mark's from *The Stones of Venice*.

Junior high school readers may be asked to observe as they read aloud from essays some passages in which the tone of the writer's voice is clear: serious, flippant, pompous, or ironic. They may notice, too, the writer's choice of words and the effect of connotative words, phrases, and of figurative language.

Although some attention may be given to this kind of close stylistic and structural analysis of the essay with good students, the main purpose of reading in this form should be to introduce the student to interesting minds and to the challenge of ideas. Teacher and students may search the anthologies for

---

[10] William Hazlitt, "On Familiar Style," in Wallace Douglas (ed.), *The Character of Prose*, Houghton Mifflin Company, Boston, 1959. (The article by Bonamy Dobrée, "The New Way of Writing," in the same text, is useful for high school students.)

[11] See the student paper on pp. 64–65.

[12] William Strunk, Jr. and E. B. White, *The Elements of Style*, The Macmillan Company, New York, 1959, p. 53.

[13] Such speeches are available in Edward R. Murrow's *Hear It Now*, and other recordings of famous speeches.

essays to be read and discussed in class, and group discussions of essays reflecting a range of opinions and ideas on art, education, contemporary culture, science, and politics may be arranged. The wealth of materials available today in essay collections makes it possible for students to read widely in this literary form, and to discover what men of all times have thought and said.

Unit: Teaching biography

During the junior high school years, most of the reading of biography and autobiography may be done as individual reading, sometimes in connection with thematic units and often as students report in groups or talk in panel discussion about the persons whose biographies they have read. Most students need little urging to explore this field. The individual book report, which often simply requires that the student read a "book of nonfiction," tends to be an occasion for tedious oral reports on the lives of Bing Crosby or Lou Gehrig. It is more conducive to thoughtful reading and reporting if the biographies that are used have something in common. Out of the rich selection of such writings, the teacher can easily present students with a number of books on a certain topic or theme, and students may choose in terms of interest to join the group working on a particular theme. Since the study of biography is easy to correlate with units on careers, a class might plan a series of panel discussions of the books they have read. Groupings such as the following may be suggested in terms of the interests and abilities of the class:

Great Americans

James H. Daugherty, *Daniel Boone,* The Viking Press, Inc., New York, 1939.

Helen Dore Doylston, *Clara Barton, Founder of the American Red Cross,* Random House, Inc., New York, 1955.

Esther Forbes, *America's Paul Revere,* Houghton Mifflin Company, Boston, 1946.

Douglas Freeman, *Lee of Virginia,* Charles Scribner's Sons, New York, 1958.

Shirley Graham, *There Once Was a Slave: The Heroic Story of Frederick Douglass,* Julian Messner, Publishers, Inc., New York, 1947.

Janet Elizabeth Gray, *Penn,* The Viking Press, Inc., New York, 1938.

Clara Ingram Judson, *Mr. Justice Holmes,* Follett Publishing Company, Chicago, 1956.

Ann Petry, *Harriet Tubman,* Thomas Y. Crowell Company, New York, 1955.

Vincent Sheean, *Thomas Jefferson: Father of Democracy,* Random House, Inc., New York, 1953.

Emma Gelders Sterne, *Mary McLeod Bethune,* Alfred A. Knopf, Inc., New York, 1957.

Henry Thomas, *Theodore Roosevelt,* G. P. Putnam's Sons, New York, 1959.

Scientists and inventors

Aylesa Forsee, *Louis Agassiz: Pied Piper of Science,* The Viking Press, Inc., New York, 1958.

Shirley Graham and George Lipscomb, *Dr. George Washington Carver, Scientist,* Julian Messner, Publishers, Inc., New York, 1944.

Joseph A. Kugelmass, *Louis Braille: Windows for the Blind,* Julian Messner, Publishers, Inc., New York, 1951.

Dean Lee Latham, *Young Man in a Hurry,* Harper & Row, Publishers, Incorporated, New York, 1958.

Sterling North, *Young Tom Edison,* Houghton Mifflin Company, Boston, 1958.

Constance Rourke, *Audubon,* Harcourt, Brace & World, Inc., New York, 1936.

Harry Sootin, *Michael Faraday,* Julian Messner, Publishers, Inc., New York, 1954.

Creative artists

May Lamberton Becker, *Presenting Miss Jane Austen,* Dodd, Mead & Company, Inc., New York, 1952.

Agnes de Mille, *Dance to the Piper,* Little, Brown and Company, Boston, 1952.

Jeannette Eaton, *America's Own Mark Twain,* William Morrow and Company, Inc., New York, 1958.

Moss Hart, *Act One,* Random House, Inc., New York, 1959.

Phyllis Jackson, *Victorian Cinderella,* Holiday House, Inc., New York, 1947.

Cornelia Meigs, *Invincible Louisa,* Little, Brown and Company, Boston, 1933.

Frances Winwar, *Elizabeth,* Harcourt, Brace & World, Inc., New York, 1957.

Teachers may plan to give assignments such as the following to eleventh or twelfth graders to encourage the reading of biography:

1. Read three biographies by different authors about a well-known figure and write a 300-word paper comparing them. Many fine biographies have been written about world-famous men and women: Jane Addams, Albert Schweitzer, Winston Churchill, Louisa May Alcott, Abraham Lincoln, Franklin Delano Roosevelt, Mahatma Gandhi, and others. Students may be asked to read these critically and compare the treatment of the life stories, interpretation of character, and author's attitudes toward the subject.

2. Autobiographies of Gandhi, Churchill, Schweitzer, Nehru, and others may be compared with the biographies. Books like the one Mrs. Eleanor Roosevelt wrote about her husband may also be included. Students should be urged to examine critically the attitudes of the writers toward their subject:

Is it one of hero-worship? Does the author show many sides of the subject's character or attempt to explain away criticism? Are there inconsistencies and contradictions between two lives of the same person? Where can these be checked to see what the facts are?

3. Ask students to read and report on a biography of a great American immigrant. The class may divide into panels according to their subjects: inventors (Pupin); philanthropists (Carnegie, Guggenheim); social reformers (Jacob Riis, Carl Schurz); scientists (John Muir, Steinmetz) artists (including musicians, architects, dancers, etc.); doctors; and others. Groups might examine the early experiences and education of the immigrant, his difficulties in adjusting to America, his encouraging experiences, and his attitudes toward his adopted country.

4. Suggest that foreign-born students choose a biography or book of nonfiction by an author who writes of the country of their ancestry. The book may be about a famous person of the country, about an American of the same descent, or a description of life in that country. In one class, two boys whose fathers came from Yugoslavia read Louis Adamic's books; a Chinese lad read Lin Yutang's *My Country and My People,* and a Chinese girl, Jade Snow Wong's *Fifth Chinese Daughter.*

5. Another group of panels or reports might be planned for students who have read a biography of someone who has achieved success in a career they would like to pursue. They may discuss the qualifications the person had, how he used his opportunities, his attitude toward education, and the personal qualities which brought success.

Critical evaluation of biographies.   From the ninth grade on, students may be encouraged to make critical examinations of the biographies or autobiographies they read in order to evaluate the book's worth. They may be asked to look for a list of the author's sources. The authority of the biographer may be checked in *Current Biography* or one of the other up-to-date references which gives biographical material about the writer. Often the book jacket or the introduction to the book will give some clue to the author's background, education, and experience. Douglas Freeman (author of *Lee of Virginia*) is a well-known historian; Esther Forbes (author of *Paul Revere*) a novelist well read in New England literature and history.

Students who begin to read biographies critically may be encouraged to answer several questions. Are the conversations and dialogues real (some biographers use quotations from the subject's letters in the dialogue), or has the writer invented them by imagining what might have been said? Does the author try to write the book as though it were a novel, or does he remind the reader that this is a factual treatment of a person's life? Does he deal with the entire life of the subject or with only a part of it? Can you tell, by comparing the biography with an encyclopedia treatment, whether the writer has over-emphasized some incidents? Distorted any historical facts? Tried to defend or explain his subject with undue partiality? What is the purpose of the biographer? Is it to explain, defend, reassess, whitewash, "debunk"—or can you determine another purpose? Does the author say what his purpose is?

In many such ways, the teacher may encourage students to read more critically in this important genre, and to develop the skills necessary to evaluate nonfiction.

Encouraging wide reading in nonfiction

The wide range of nonfiction includes rounding up criminals for the FBI, taking a submarine under the polar ice cap, conducting experiments during the International Geophysical Year, and photographing or capturing wild animals. It provides an ample field for reading through the high school years. Not only is nonfiction important because of its ability to widen horizons and extend reading interests, but it often is a means of encouraging students to read more demanding books than they are accustomed to tackling in fiction. From the eighth grade on, many students are reading books of adventure, humor, and family life which were written for the adult market. The popularity of such books as Heyerdahl's *Kon-Tiki* and *Aku-Aku*, Herzog's *Annapurna*, and others indicates that students can be led to enlarge vocabularies through adult reading. Some of the following topics will provide appropriate groupings for nonfiction for class discussion. The teacher will be able to add many other topics patterned after these.

Humor. One of the most neglected experiences in the literary background of young people in our schools is the wholesome enjoyment of humor. The times when a class may read aloud and enjoy a humorous piece of writing together are rare indeed. Students might proceed with more eagerness to serious study of the essay if some of their early experiences with the form in junior high school had given them the enjoyment provided by the oral reading of some of Stephen Leacock, Robert Benchley, James Thurber, or Cornelia Otis Skinner. A teacher's reading will bring out the absurdities of Thurber's "The Night the Bed Fell," "The Dog That Bit People," "The Night the Ghost Got In." "The Day the Dam Broke" provides a good starting point for discussion of mass behavior and mob psychology as Thurber describes the whole population of Columbus, Ohio, running east because of the false rumor set off by someone's misinterpretation of a word.

Students can read aloud themselves and enjoy some of the broader humor in Cornelia Otis Skinner's *Excuse It, Please* and *Our Hearts Were Young and Gay.* Her experiences in learning how to skate, ride a horse, and order a meal in a hotel room reveal the ability to laugh at one's own blunderings. This, too, is the charm of Leacock's timid adventure in opening a bank account or his "How We Celebrated Mother's Day."

The numerous books recounting family experiences are full of wholesome humor and lighten the frequent conflict the young are experiencing in their own relations with the family. Thousands of younger teen-agers have enjoyed books written primarily for adults: Jean Kerr's *Please Don't Eat the Daisies,* Shirley Jackson's *Life among the Savages* and *Raising Demons,* Day's *Life with Father* and *Life with Mother,* Gilbreth and Carey's *Cheaper by the Dozen* and *Belles on Their Toes,* and Kathryn Forbes' *Mama's Bank Account.* Many of these books are autobiographical; others are chiefly collections of sketches; most of them reveal warm, close family life despite the trials and frictions of family living. They provide an important kind of security and insight into the ways families get on together for readers of teen age.

The satire on modern psychology in Thurber's "Courtship through the Ages" can delight older students as can the descriptions of some aspects of college life in "University Days," in which the author describes his ineffectual attempts at focusing a microscope and relates a professor's assistance to a star athlete to enable him to stay in college. Senior high school students will enjoy the subtle humor in the essays of E. B. White, Betty McDonald's *The Egg and I* or *The Plague and I,* the Papashvilys' accounts of immigrant experiences in America, *Anything Can Happen,* and many of the subtler and defter satiric essays of James Thurber. A collection in the *Scholastic* units, *The Lighter Side,* will be enjoyed. Humor in recordings of verse, prose, and drama is also available.[14]

Regional life. Essay, biography, and narratives of personal experience provide valuable ways of acquainting youth with the flavor and quality of regional life in America and the customs and feeling of life on the prairie, in the mountains, the coastal towns and cities, and the great cities of America. Through such books we may experience the isolation of life in the Maine woods in Rich's *We Took to the Woods,* a Maine coast upbringing in Mary Ellen Chase's *A Goodly Heritage,* Southern life in Marjorie Kinnan Rawlings' *Cross Creek* and Frances Parkinson Keyes' *The River Road,* life in the Southwest in Carles' *Desert Country,* and Hilda Faunce's *Desert Wife.* Will James' *Lone Cowboy,* and *Roughing It* and *Life on the Mississippi,* accounts of the river life Mark Twain knew in his days as a steamboat pilot, are important pieces of Americana.

City life. Insight into city life in America can be gained, too, by reading the essays and biographies which reflect the feelings of those who have lived in America's cities, have either loved them, or felt cramped, hemmed in, or oppressed by them. E. B. White's *Here Is New York* and Kazin's *A Walker in the City* are among the best of these.

The world of nature. The reflective writers who delight in the world of nature have produced some of the most interesting books for the young reader, especially the junior high school student whose interest in animals and the natural world is keen. Rachel Carson's *The Sea around Us* has become a best seller, read with delight by young people as well as their elders for her memorably beautiful pictures of the beginnings of life in the sea and the

---

[14] See pp. 424–425.

gradual evolutionary process which produced land life. Her poetic prose in this book and in *The Edge of the Sea* invests natural science with beauty and wonder. Beebe's *Half Mile Down* and Cousteau's *The Silent World* are also fascinating for young readers intrigued by books about the underwater world. Essays on nature by Loren Eiseley, Donald Culross Peattie, John Burroughs, and John Muir will appeal to the student genuinely interested in nature. The engaging best sellers about the life of an otter—Maxwell's *Ring of Bright Water*—and about the lioness Elsa and her cubs in Joy Adamson's *Born Free* and *Living Free* have been popular with both children and adults.

Science. Young readers may be introduced to the world of science through the books on nature mentioned above. The dangerous separation between scientific and liberal education mentioned as a major conflict of our time by C. P. Snow in *The Two Cultures* suggests a need for wide reading about the world of physical science and invention for students of all grade levels. The biographies and autobiographies of men and women like Pupin, Steinmetz, Newton, Curie, Darwin, and others are significant for youth. The lives of humanitarian doctors and researchers: Marie Curie, Louis Pasteur, Dr. Walter Reed, the Mayo brothers, and Paul de Kruif's *Microbe Hunters* have provided important insights into the attitude of the dedicated scientist and researcher and the scientific tradition about international free exchange of knowledge about science.

More recently the biographies and essays of those men who worked on the atomic projects have become available, and some, like Norbert Wiener in "Moral Reflections of a Mathematician," have written of their spiritual conflicts while contemplating the future of a world influenced by their discoveries. The natural interest of many of our youth in science and the need for all youth to become more interested in scientific achievement and knowledge about science makes this area of reading interest a significant one for study in the classroom. Although not all students can be led to read many books entirely on science, the study of some of the important essays by scientists should be included. T. H. Huxley's classic "On a Piece of Chalk" and "The Scientific Method of Investigation" are important for twelfth graders to study.

Education. Some time in each high school year may well be devoted to a consideration by the class of the aims of education. A wide range of selections in essay and biography which raise these questions are readily available. Those which compare the kinds of education given children in different countries or in our own country in different times are usually exciting to younger readers. Mary Ellen Chase's picture of the Maine coast school she taught in is given in *A Goodly Fellowship*, Jesse Stuart's of the Kentucky hill schools in *The Thread That Runs So True*, Helen Keller's delight in learning words, Salom Rizk's experience in trying to learn English described in *Syrian Yankee* are all readable in the junior high school. Particularly interesting to children at this age are the reminiscences or autobiographical accounts of immigrants who have come to America in search of education.

Older students, college-bound, may well start thinking about their educational goals and exploring the many attitudes toward education men have taken since the days of the Greeks. The old question of vocational versus liberal education may be encountered beginning with Aristotle and Plato and continuing to the present in the writings of Jacques Barzun, Robert M. Hutchins, Mortimer Adler, John Dewey, and others. The great debates of the nineteenth century that took place in the essays of Newman, Arnold, Huxley, and others in the controversy over whether scientific education might be called liberal are worth reading for contrast. Many college-bound students will be interested in some of the sharp attacks on education in Barzun's *The House of Intellect* and *Teacher in America.*

Modern culture.   Bright students in the tenth grade, and good students in grades eleven and twelve may well study such important analyses of today's culture as Riesman's *The Lonely Crowd,* Whyte's *The Organization Man,* Margaret Mead's *And Keep Your Powder Dry,* Hortense Powdermaker's *Hollywood, The Dream Factory,* and essays by Lyman Bryson, Charles Siepman, Gilbert Seldes, and others. Readable studies of mass psychology by psychologists, sociologists, and anthropologists are available in paperbacks and are invaluable for the encouragement of critical thinking about the individual in a mass age. Books which analyze the influences working toward the subtle manipulation of public thought and taste such as Vance Packard's *The Hidden Persuaders* and *The Status Seekers* may also be important.

Exploring values.   A wide range of reading in nonfiction invites students to examine their lives, their beliefs, their ideas about society and about the good life—the great, universal ideas through which man has always searched for answers to the questions of the purpose and meaning of his life and the ways it should be lived. The imaginative teacher can think of dozens of thematic ideas around which the reading of students could be planned. For readers of all ages, the exploration of conceptions of personal honor, integrity, standards, and values are of great importance. Particularly moving for younger readers are books reflecting the courage, moral and spiritual, which sees individuals through personal tragedy or accident and the struggle for achievement despite handicap. Marie Killilea's *Karen,* Louise Baker's *Out on a Limb,* Ved Mehta's *Face to Face,* Hector Chevigny's *My Eyes Have a Cold Nose,* Katherine Butler Hathaway's *The Little Locksmith,* and John Gunther's *Death Be Not Proud* are all stories of those who have faced handicaps, physical or mental, with courage, endurance, and often humor.

Adolescence is the seed time for the development of a philosophy of living. We cannot and should not teach our students what values or beliefs to have, but we can introduce them to books which explore many ways of living and believing and encourage them to read about what others have thought important enough to live for and die for. These are the years when the search for personal faith is important. Many young people find answers as they explore the reflective essays and the life stories of those who have thought through these questions in books such as Lin Yutang's *The Importance of Living*, Catherine Marshall's biography of her husband, *A Man Called Peter*, Overstreet's *The Mature Mind*, Lippmann's *The Good Society*, the statements in *What I Believe* from E. M. Forster and David Lilienthal. Nehru's essays from prison, Gandhi's autobiography, Merton's *Seven Storey Mountain*, Aldous Huxley's *Ends and Means*, and Lippmann's *A Preface to Morals* all present various views of life and its goals. Superior readers among senior high school classes may read some of the discussions about the good life in Plato's dialogues.

Evaluation

Determining the student's growth in ability to read essays, biography, and other nonfiction intelligently and critically presents problems similar in kind to those discussed in chapters dealing with other types of literature. The kinds of tests suggested in Chapters 9 through 12 get at the same skills of comprehension and analysis which are developed through reading nonfiction.

The culmination of a six-year study of the essay and nonfiction in all its forms, from light humor to complex philosophical dissertations, can help the student become acquainted with men and ideas, and allow him to test his mind against the best minds of all times. As he searches for ideas and explores the various attitudes men have held toward life and the values for which they stand, he clarifies his own thinking and commitment to a considered philosophy of life. If it is true that the unexamined life is not worth living, then the adolescent will find that his examination of his own life and mind will help him take his place among men of reason.

World heroes and leaders: a unit of biography

From the tenth year on, a unit of study of biography dealing with some of the great heroes and leaders of the world may provide an important step in international understanding for students. Such a unit extends the horizons of the usual search for heroes from America to the world. American youth needs to know something of these men and women who have played a part in world history, contributed to its science or culture, or advanced the destiny of humanity in important ways. Students can easily be interested in such a topic if the teacher can lead them to the right resources. Today's literature is full of good examples.

In a thematic unit designed to emphasize literature for international understanding, a series of panel discussions on the lives of important world leaders might play a prominent part. Such panels might be introduced with a list of books, and an introductory statement patterned after those in the following groupings.

Doctors around the world

The work of great and dedicated doctors in many parts of the world has been one of the best means of furthering international understanding between peoples. You will find exciting and uplifting reading in these books which tell of their work. These are doctors whose work has furthered the well-being of people around the world.

> **Rachel Baker,** *First Woman Doctor: The Story of Elizabeth Blackwell,* Julian Messner, Publishers, Inc., New York, 1944.
>
> **Jacqueline Berrill,** *Albert Schweitzer,* Dodd, Mead & Company, Inc., New York, 1956.
>
> **Thomas Dooley,** *Deliver Us from Evil* (1956), *The Edge of Tomorrow* (1958), and *The Night They Burned the Mountain* (1960), Farrar, Straus & Giroux, New York.
>
> **Joseph Gollomb,** *Albert Schweitzer: Genius in the Jungle,* Vanguard Press, Inc., New York, 1949.
>
> **W. T. Grenfell,** *Adrift on an Ice Pan: A Labrador Doctor,* Houghton Mifflin Company, Boston, 1919.
>
> **Victor G. Heiser,** *An American Doctor's Odyssey,* W. W. Norton & Company, Inc., New York, 1936.
>
> **Albert Schweitzer,** *Out of My Life and Thought,* Holt, Rinehart and Winston, Inc., New York, 1949.
>
> **Gordon Seagrave,** *Burma Surgeon* (1943) and *Burma Surgeon Returns* (1946), W. W. Norton & Company, Inc., New York.
>
> **Henry Thomas,** *Sister Elizabeth Kenny,* G. P. Putnam's Sons, New York, 1958.
>
> **Alfreda Withington,** *Mine Eyes Have Seen,* E. P. Dutton & Co., Inc., New York, 1941.

Scientists around the world

Science is a truly international language. Some scientists have made discoveries which could have made them fortunes, but in the spirit of international science, they have offered their findings to the world. Others on this list have contributed in an important way to international knowledge.

> **Francis E. Benz,** *Pasteur: Knight of the Laboratory,* Dodd, Mead & Company, Inc., New York, 1938.
>
> **Eve Curie,** *Madame Curie,* Doubleday & Company, Inc., Garden City, N.Y., 1937.
>
> **Paul de Kruif,** *Microbe Hunters,* Harcourt, Brace & World, Inc., New York, 1926.
>
> **Elma Levinger,** *Galileo,* Julian Messner, Publishers, Inc., New York, 1952.
>
> **Fred Reinfeld,** *Young Charles Darwin,* Sterling Publishing Co., Inc., New York, 1956.

Alice Thorne, *The Story of Madame Curie,* Grosset & Dunlap, Inc., New York, 1959.

Antonina Vallentin, *The Drama of Albert Einstein,* Doubleday & Company, Inc., Garden City, N.Y., 1954.

René Vallery-Radot, *Life of Louis Pasteur,* Alfred A. Knopf, Inc., New York, 1958.

Political leaders who helped change the world

Some of these men led their own countrymen in a struggle for independence; others attempted to lead their countries toward democratic goals. All helped in some way to change the face of world politics and the shape of the future.

Nina Brown Baker, *He Wouldn't Be King,* Vanguard Press, Inc., New York, 1941.

————, *Juarez, Hero of Mexico,* Vanguard Press, Inc., New York, 1942.

Rachel Baker, *Chaim Weizmann,* Julian Messner, Publishers, Inc., New York, 1950.

Marcia Davenport, *Garibaldi,* Random House, Inc., New York, 1957.

Jeannette Eaton, *Gandhi: Fighter without a Sword,* William Morrow and Company, New York, 1950.

Louis Fischer, *Life of Mahatma Gandhi,* Harper & Row, Publishers, Incorporated, New York, 1950.

Shakuntala Masani, *Nehru's Story,* Oxford University Press, Fair Lawn, N.J., 1949.

Catherine Owens Peare, *Mahatma Gandhi,* Holt, Rinehart and Winston, Inc., New York, 1950.

Carlos Romulo and Marvin Gray, *The Magsaysay Story,* The John Day Company, Inc., New York, 1956.

Cornelia Spencer, *Nehru of India,* The John Day Company, Inc., New York, 1954.

Student activities and assignments

A number of topics for reading, panel discussions, and student activities have been suggested within the chapter. In addition, some of the following topics for discussion, reading, and writing in nonfiction are suggested here. The emphasis on topics exploring values is strong, as this is a major interest for students reading nonfiction (see page 325). Reading and writing are closely related in many assignments.

Examining values

Some papers during each year of high school may deal with the values students hold, their standards, beliefs, and ideals. Such units commonly come in the twelfth year, but this postponement ignores the fact that values are developing and changing during each year of adolescent growth. Discussion developing from the students' reading is an important factor in such change.

. . . The teacher who realizes the importance of pressing students to think through their own positions, as well as knowing those of others, may assign papers suggesting relationships between the ideas in the books they read and their own values. Thoreau's ideas on individualism and nonconformity, Emerson's on self-reliance, William James' on the "Moral Equivalent of War," James Truslow Adams' "The Mucker Pose," and others provide such stimulation.

. . . Junior high school students may read *The Ugly American* and *The Hidden Persuaders,* and older students may read and analyze *The Status Seekers, The Organization Man, The Lonely Crowd,* and *The Mature Mind.* They may hold panel discussions to argue the various criticisms of American values as reflected in these books.

. . . Young people enjoy arguing about what is really worthwhile in life; what one lives for (money? success? achievement? fame? position in society? contribution to society? security? personal comfort?). Themes on "What kind of life do I want for myself or my children?"; "How will my life be different from that of my parents?"; "I want my child to have a better life than mine"; "What I want out of my education"; and "What I want out of college" have led to reading in such collections of essays as those suggested below.

. . . Younger students will be concerned with problems of personal integrity, social values, and decisions about going along with the crowd or thinking for oneself. Older students will want to begin putting together a more organized philosophy of life, a pattern of values to live and act by, including those which affect his relationships with people in his society and the world in general. He may thus move from concern in the eighth grade with personal decisions about cheating to concern in the twelfth grade with international attitudes, world peace, and the morality of atomic testing. Reading, discussion, and writing on such topics can be continuous through the secondary years.

. . . One writing test used the theme topic "Three Days to See," and the National Council of Teachers of English Achievement Awards essay topic one year was "The Person Living or Dead I Would Most Like to Be." (The answers to this one ranged from Marian Anderson and Albert Schweitzer to Marilyn Monroe.) These topics seldom fail to elicit discussion of values, and frequently lead to the readings of biographies.

Stimulating critical thinking

. . . Students may read editorials and articles, or study the letter exchanges in local newspapers, *Time, The Saturday Review, Life, The Atlantic,* young people's magazines, or others. Let them locate the discussion of an issue which interests them and on which they are informed and write letters to the editor expressing an opinion. Such exchanges are often exciting, and students stand a good chance of having letters printed.

. . . Encourage students to read editorials or articles, and to write a paper of informed and considered opinion on a controversial topic appearing in the news: the court decision about whether parents of one religion should adopt a child of another religion, or color, or nationality; a political demonstration involving teen-agers; a decision to ban a book or a movie, or to raise the legal age for driving.

. . . Teachers may ask students to make a close analysis of some paragraphs, perhaps from the Declaration of Independence or the Gettysburg Address, to explore the meaning of words and ideas. Précis writing often helps good students to develop habits of analytical and critical reading.[15]

. . . Assign students an essay or article in which tone is distinctive and let them discuss how the writer gets his effect. Further close reading may show how sentences and paragraphs are related. Dr. Johnson's "Letter to the Earl of Chesterfield," available in a number of collections of essays, is a useful example for analysis.

. . . Provide students with study questions to discuss orally or in writing as they read biography and autobiography. What is the author's attitude toward his subject? Is it objective, one-sided, admiring, fawning, critical, derogatory? Does he seem to present only favorable facts, or does he mention unfavorable ones as well? Does he seem to invent dialogue and put words into the mouth of his subject?

. . . Ask students to compare a real and a fictionalized biography of the same person or a factual biography with an imaginative treatment. Dorothy Hewlett's biography of Elizabeth Browning (*Elizabeth Barrett Browning: A Life*) may be compared with Virginia Woolf's *Flush,* Rudolph Besier's *The Barretts of Wimpole Street,* or Frances Winwar's *Elizabeth.*

Among the sources of readings for the above assignments which may be useful to the teacher are the following:

> **Alice Baum** (ed.), *Nonfiction II,* The Macmillan Company, New York, Heritage paperback, 1961.
>
> **Jarvis E. Bush** (ed.), *Nonfiction I,* The Macmillan Company, New York, Heritage paperback, 1961.
>
> **Leon Edel et al.** (eds.), *Five World Biographies,* Harcourt, Brace & World, Inc., New York, 1961. (Caesar, Michelangelo, Napoleon, Madame Curie, Mahatma Gandhi.)
>
> **Jay E. Greene** (ed.), *Four Complete Biographies,* Globe Book Company, Inc., New York, 1962. (Winston Churchill, Helen Keller, Albert Schweitzer, P. T. Barnum.)
>
> ——— **and Murray Bromberg** (eds.), *Essays for Modern Youth,* Globe Book Company, Inc., New York, 1960.
>
> ———, *World Wide Essays,* Globe Book Company, Inc., New York, 1963.
>
> **Hans P. Guth** (ed.), *Essay,* Wadsworth Publishing Co., Inc., Belmont, Calif, 1962. (Paperback.)

---

[15] Richard D. Altick, *Preface to Critical Reading,* 4th ed., Holt, Rinehart and Winston, Inc., New York, 1960.

Louise Mountz, *Biographies for Junior High,* NCTE, Champaign, Ill., n.d.

New World Writing, Mentor Books, New American Library of World Literature, Inc., New York, 1952.

Russell Nye (ed.), *Modern Essays,* rev. ed., Scott, Foresman and Company, Chicago, 1957. (Paperback.)

J. B. Priestley and O. B. Davis (eds.), *Four English Biographies,* Harcourt, Brace & World, Inc., New York, 1961. (Shakespeare, Queen Victoria, Laurie Lee, Samuel Johnson.)

William M. Schutte and Erwin R. Steinberg (eds.), *Personal Integrity: Readings for the Composition Course,* W. W. Norton & Company, Inc., New York, 1961.

The various paperback editions of essay collections, especially those put out periodically containing selected essays from *The Saturday Review, The Atlantic,* and *Harper's* are especially useful.

The teacher will want to consult one of the indexes to essays and biography in the library for sources of titles mentioned in this chapter.

Selected bibliography

Richard D. Altick, *Preface to Critical Reading,* 4th ed., Holt, Rinehart and Winston, Inc., New York, 1960. Good exercises in close, critical reading.

Walter Blair and John Gerber, *Factual Prose: Better Reading I,* 4th ed., Scott, Foresman and Company, Chicago, 1959. Designed for college freshmen, the text contains exercises in close reading and sample analyses of essays.

Edgar Dale, *How to Read a Newspaper,* Scott, Foresman and Company, Chicago, 1941.

Wallace Douglas, *The Character of Prose,* Part IV of Gordon N. Ray et al. (eds.), *An Introduction to Literature,* Houghton Mifflin Company, Boston, 1959.

Herbert Read, *English Prose Style,* Beacon Press, Boston, 1952. (Paperback.)

R. W. Wells, "How to Read Your Newspaper," *American Mercury,* vol. 82, January, 1956, pp. 95–98.

CHAPTER *14*

The mass demand is not a proof of falling standards: it means that millions are being educated who would formerly have been left in the illiterate mass. . . . What we are seeing, is not a collapse of standards but a very rapid improvement. The crowds at the cinemas and the bus loads on the sightseeing tours are on the way up. They have already left the mass; they are individuals seeking ideas for themselves.

JOYCE CARY [1]

The mass media: print, sound, and picture

The mass media: a major cultural force

Comparatively few communities in the world today are out of range of the printed word, and still fewer are without the electronically reproduced spoken word. Radio has created a global community by bringing news to regions where no printed newspaper had been available until it was several days old. The Voice of America broadcasts have established communication channels between the free world and countries under rigid censorship. Television has become a world-wide force since Telstar made possible transmission of sound and picture to many different parts of the world.

The spoken word and the visual image on the motion-picture screen have effected significant changes in our ways of life and have become an even more powerful medium abroad for communicating images of American life to

[1] "The Mass Mind: Our Favorite Folly," Harper's, vol. 204, March, 1952, p. 27.

foreign people whose only concept of the United States is based on American films.

The revolution in the dissemination of the printed word is hardly less remarkable or influential. Newspapers and periodicals reach a large proportion of the reading public, although television has supplemented these as a medium both of information and entertainment. Inexpensive American magazines bring to a mass of readers short stories and articles ranging from the most stereotyped ephemera to fiction by America's finest writers and thought-provoking articles on science, psychology, philosophy, history, and religion.

Sharp criticism of the fare offered by television is continuous and healthy. The incidence of violence, murder, and mayhem has been a matter of concern since television became a major cultural force in American life. Conclusive evidence has not yet been presented about the effects that viewing such programs may have on children and adolescents. Although it has failed to prove that viewing is a cause of emotional disturbance or delinquency,[2] research indicates that it may "influence the way in which they find expression." [3]

Units on reading the newspaper intelligently are now standard in many English courses of study, but although television is said to engross one-sixth of a child's waking life from the early years to some time near the end of high school,[4] little attention is given in schools at present to improvement of young people's taste in television and the other media.

It seems clear that if schools are to produce citizens who are intelligent and critical listeners, readers, and viewers of the mass media, they must take some interest in recommending good entertainment, in developing standards of taste and appreciation, and in increasing the intelligent and critical use of the media.

The media in the English program

Whether we like it or not, newspapers, magazines, radio, television, and movies will be, for many students, the chief recreational fare of the adult years. If we do a good job of teaching students to grow into independent readers, we may do much to increase the reading of books and cut down the number of hours spent on these other activities, but the chances are that any dreams we have of returning to a book-dominated culture are illusory. Television and the movies constitute an important new language which our students will continue

[2] Teachers will want to be informed about this research. Frederick Wertham's *Seduction of the Innocent* (Holt, Rinehart and Winston, Inc., New York, 1954) is one of the best known attacks on television. Wilbur Schramm's *Television and Our Children* (Stanford University Press, Stanford, Calif., 1961) summarizes much of the research about the effect of television on children and adolescents.

[3] Leo Bogart, *The Age of Television,* Frederick Ungar Publishing Co., New York, 1956, p. 214.

[4] Wilbur Schramm (ed.), *The Impact of Educational Television,* The University of Illinois Press, Urbana, Ill., 1960, p. 216.

to use for significant parts of their education and recreation. We must hope to teach them to use it wisely.

Another imperative reason for including the mass media in the English program is that they will be for most of our citizens an important means of information, of news, and of extending their knowledge about what is going on in the world about them. This is a fact of modern culture that we cannot ignore. Unless we can give young people some direct training in using these sources intelligently and in improving habits of critical reading and viewing, we may have an illiterate and gullible public. Hopefully, our teaching of literature can produce students who are more widely read and better educated than those of other generations, but this alone will not help them use intelligently the new language of television, teach them to read thoughtfully and critically, or help them choose adult fare rather than violence and sensationalism in print or on film.

A last important reason for giving attention to these media in English classes rather than relegating such study exclusively to the departments of social science is that, wisely used, these media may directly reinforce the most important elements of the English program. These resources have been used by wise teachers to vitalize the teaching of speaking, reading, writing, and listening. They provide a textbook of constantly changing materials for the development of critical thinking and the study of language—the basic part of the English teacher's job.

For the large majority of our students, nonverbal, nonbookish, and practically oriented, the media serve as a force we can utilize to propel them in the directions in which we are trying to lead them—not very successfully, by all estimates—toward literacy and maturity. These resources represent the forces operating most strongly on our youth today; for the teacher they provide sources of information, entertainment, values, and intellectual challenge.

Goals for the program

A primary obligation of any study of the mass media is to train students to become more widely acquainted with the sources of information and more discriminating in their use. Surveys have shown that people get most of their information from the five- to fifteen-minute summaries of the news on radio and television. The adult who has not been introduced to other sources frequently clings for a lifetime to the tabloid newspaper, the picture magazine, and the brief news broadcast heard while the conversation at the family dinner table claims half his attention. To be literate, informed, and thoughtful about contemporary issues, tomorrow's adults must be able to know where to get information and how to interpret and judge it.

An important corollary to this goal is that students must learn how to evaluate the authority of sources of information and how to judge critically the quality and validity of the opinions expressed. Only carefully developed habits of critical thinking will serve to produce the kind of informed, thoughtful adults we wish our young people to become. There are abundant resources for developing these skills in the materials of the mass media.

A last and most important goal is that of utilizing the materials of the popular arts to improve skills and appreciation of language and literature. The mass media represent ways of using language and new forms of literature as well as old: not only the play, but dramatized novels, short stories, and biographies. Appreciation of these forms can be developed through practice in viewing and in reading the resources available in the popular media.

Program into practice

The amount and kind of attention devoted to study of the media should vary, obviously, with the age and ability level of the class, the nature of their viewing and reading habits, and the level of taste, appreciation, and critical skills they demonstrate. Some teachers like to incorporate study of these materials as units—to give a week or two, for instance, to the study of the newspaper, analysis of magazines, or the development of appreciation of television and the motion pictures. Others frequently use the media as a source of assignments and materials for study. Writing assignments, materials and topics for panel discussions, exercises in critical or appreciative listening, and viewing and criticizing programs presenting plays and dramatizations or readings of literature are an important part of the program in English.

A questionnaire at the beginning of the year can provide the teacher with valuable clues to student tastes and interests and an indication of reading and writing skills that need improvement.

Each of the media, too, demands some attention in its own right. The major emphasis during the school year should be on the kinds of activities listed above in which the materials of the media contribute to the development of the skills and appreciations we look for in every area of English, but each of the major media is, too, a language of a special kind, worthy of attention as an art form or an educational and informational medium. We need to appraise each for what it can contribute to the development of critical thinking and to cultural enrichment.

Teaching about television

The English classroom should be a source of information and preparation for selecting and viewing the best of television. Television committees are active in many classrooms, keeping students informed through bulletin-board announcements of forthcoming programs of special interest. The teacher of English should play an important role in recommending programs to students and in preparing a class for viewing what is to come or in following up in discussion a program that has proved somewhat confusing. Aware that a program on American cultural life or literature is to be presented the teacher may provide the students with a brief sketch of the artists and authors they may see on the program. Preparation for viewing Shakespearean plays, a novel to be dramatized, or some of the "Camera Three" programs available in many communities on video tape requires that the teacher provide students with background for viewing or information which will make the program understandable.[5] If discussion is to follow, the teacher will have to watch the program also. The lively talk that follows a performance which has excited students has often caught the teacher unprepared to deal helpfully with questions or to direct students in critical analysis of the content and technique of the program.

If enough advance notice of a program is available, as it often is in major productions, the teacher may assign the novel, play, or other work to be dramatized or read on a program and ask students to compare the televised version with the original. Class discussion about what parts of the novel or play may be kept, changed, or cut, will sometimes be profitable. Close analysis of a work of art may result from the discussion of form and structure, of dialogue and action. Students prepared in advance may use copies of the play to check scenes omitted and characterization or emphasis changed. Reading beforehand and checking afterward while the whole is fresh in the mind serves best. Some few excellent readers may be able to follow the play's text and watch the production at the same time. The teacher who alerts the class to forthcoming productions of Shakespearean or modern plays may plan such class discussions.

In addition to utilizing forthcoming programs for the study of literature, most teachers are aware of the powerful incentive to reading provided by television. The evening program which has held the interest of students can be used as a stimulus to further reading. The young viewers captivated by the dramatization of play, novel, or short story by a significant author may be sent to other works by that author. Some of the many documentaries or travel programs may provide the impetus to send viewers to books dealing with life in the countries presented: Africa, India, China, or Russia. The teacher who keeps informed about what is going to be presented will be able to follow up programs with reading recommendations. Really important books are worth a few minutes of mention during class time, even in the midst of another area of study.

Biography, essays, and nonfiction travel and adventure have their oral and visual counterparts in the offerings of television. Some interviews in the "Elder Statesman" series, which gave us Carl Sandburg, Robert Frost, Frank Lloyd Wright, Bertrand Russell, and Wanda Landowska, the "Wisdom" series, and "Small World," which did the same with other men and women in the arts, politics, and diplomatic life, are available to schools.[6]

---

[5] Sources of information are the advance information bulletins of the Columbia Broadcasting System, the National Broadcasting Company, and local or regional educational networks.
[6] See bibliography for resources of these materials.

The English teacher, fully aware of the poverty of television's "wastelands," may yet applaud the literature that television has made available for the first time to thousands of viewers and use in his courses what it offers each year of the finest of motion pictures of the past, dramatizations of novels of Hemingway, Wilder, Faulkner, Fitzgerald, Melville, or plays by Shaw, Ibsen, Giraudoux, Sophocles, O'Neill, Shakespeare, Chekhov, and Ben Jonson. His students may hear live poets, writers, or actors reading from the works of great writers from all centuries. The televised three-hour film version of Sir Laurence Olivier's *Richard III* in 1956 drew an estimated daytime audience of twenty-five million viewers, more than the "probable combined total of audiences for stage productions of all Shakespeare's plays since he wrote them." [7]

Using television drama as a springboard for the study of the play, teachers have assigned and discussed the viewing of such television classics as Paddy Chayefsky's *Marty*, Gore Vidal's *Visit to a Small Planet* (television's most literate satire, according to Postman), Reginald Rose's dramas of social criticism, *Twelve Angry Men* and *Tragedy in a Temporary Town*, James Costigan's *Little Moon of Alban*, and many of the plays available on such programs as "Hallmark Hall of Fame," "Camera Three," and others. Community educational television makes available some of the best drama filmed by the British Broadcasting System, and national networks have collaborated with the Lincoln Center for the Performing Arts, the New York City Center, and the Metropolitan Opera Company to bring opera, light and serious, and musical comedy to the television screen: *Oklahoma!*, *The King and I*, the light operas of Gilbert and Sullivan, *South Pacific*, *My Fair Lady*, and others.

Radio, having staged a comeback in the era of FM broadcasting and transistor sets, commands a large audience of young people, not only for popular music and jazz, but also for opera, symphonic and chamber music, discussions of civic and international problems, forums, drama, poetry readings, and book discussions. New directions in radio programming make possible a wider range of cultural and educational resources for today's youth.

Perceptive critics of the new media—Marshall McLuhan, Patrick Hazard, and Gilbert Seldes among others—have urged that schools and colleges give serious attention to these "newer languages" (in McLuhan's phrase) of the popular arts, which provide an important bridge to the study of classic and contemporary drama for the English curriculum. [8]

Developing critical appreciation. Television affords the teacher an ideal medium, high in interest, for helping students develop standards of critical judgment applying to the written word as well as the video screen. Junior high school students may be encouraged to watch a serial program for some weeks, analyzing its value as to plot, character development, stereotyping, motivation,

[7] Neil Postman et al., *Television and the Teaching of English*, Appleton-Century-Crofts, Inc., New York, 1961, p. 37.
[8] The books by Postman, McLuhan, and Boutwell in the bibliography provide useful exercises for teachers and illustrate ways of using the mass media to develop critical appreciation of literary forms.

"All the kids in Advanced English—*that's* who call it a Boob Tube!" Drawing by P. Barlow; © 1962 The New Yorker Magazine, Inc.

realism, the kinds of problems treated, the credibility of incidents, and the resolutions of the problem. Students entering their teens grow increasingly critical and discriminating about the programs they watch. When the plots or situations of some of the programs are subjected to objective scrutiny, stereotyping and formula plots often become obvious.

In the junior high school, students may be divided into groups according to choice to study certain programs: westerns, family comedies, mysteries, science fiction, crime or detective stories. One group may take such comedies as "The Munsters," "My Favorite Martian," or "Lucy"; another, "The Fugitive" or "The Man from U.N.C.L.E."; another, "Bonanza" or "Gunsmoke."

They may be asked to observe the kinds of problems the programs present and the way they are solved. Each group may look also at characterization: what is the hero like; the villain; what kind of fathers and mothers do the family comedies present? What about little brothers and sisters? What kinds of adolescents are presented? Bright students may look more critically at some stylistic aspects of the program such as dialogue, some of the subtler stereotypes, and the formula plot which fits into the pattern of the fifty-two-minute hour, or the twenty-seven-minute half hour. Students may look, too, for some of the devices television uses to suggest character quickly. Numerous critics have called attention to those used in the westerns: the heroes wear white hats and are clean shaven; the villains are unshaven and wear dark clothes. (Someone has pointed out that the "good guys" also eat apples.[9])

Students at the senior high school level may attempt to look for formula plots in "Perry Mason," "The Defenders," "Ben Casey," "Mr. Novak," or the current TV favorite. Analysis of comedy styles of television comedians, comparisons of the various news programs, of news announcers or of the hosts of various shows may be illuminating, too. Committees may be appointed to listen for several weeks to sample the programs of three or four TV news analysts, rating them on objectivity and fair coverage.

A little noted aspect of television watching among young adolescents is the conflict between the increasing demands of school work and their habits of spending much of their leisure time watching television. Surveys show that the hours of watching decrease as youngsters enter the teens, but many young people, beginning to be aware of new responsibilities and a sense of purpose in their lives, are troubled by the amount of time they waste on television. Some are highly critical of the way they waste time, recognizing that they really care little about seeing the program shown, but that they have not developed the self-discipline to change viewing habits. Some discussion of this problem in class, coupled with suggested solutions, would be helpful to youth. Suggested supports to good intentions may be a schedule for homework, a rationing of time so that they see only selected programs each week, and class evaluation of the programs they do see. If even a few students in a class are discriminating in their choices and critical of mediocre fare, they can be influential in changing group tastes for the better.

Developing appreciation of motion pictures

Although the world of the movies impinges less strongly on the English classroom than that of television, it too offers a visual "literature" which has been acclaimed as a new art form. At their best, movies can, like television, supplement and reinforce the development of critical judgment and appreciation. The obvious point at which the motion picture meets the classroom world is in the adaptation of novels and plays to the screen. Many of the novels and plays students commonly study in school have been filmed: *Great Expectations, David Copperfield, Jane Eyre, Wuthering Heights, Pride and Prejudice, The Good Earth, Macbeth,* and *Julius Caesar*—all these and many others are now available to our students. Some of the finest American and foreign movies are available for watching on television also, although many of them are presented so late in the evening that they are of little use to our students.

---

[9] Teachers should be familiar with Gilbert Seldes' analysis of the western as a kind of Everyman morality play in *The Public Arts,* Simon and Schuster, Inc., New York, 1956, p. 25.

Resources for study.   There are many resources to help the teacher of English develop appreciation for the art, both visual and literary, of the good movie. Films designed to teach certain aspects of the art of the film—direction, photography, characterization, and theme—are available for classroom use.[10] Various handbooks are helpful in teaching students something about screenplay appreciation.[11] Often films used in classes are shown chiefly to illustrate the book about to be studied, and little attention is given the film as an art form. Here is a chance for valuable comparisons between what the novel and the film can do; the student should learn the limitations and resources of each and the important differences between them as art forms. These distinctions are important to students who tend to equate reading the book with seeing the movie.

Some of the writing and discussion about the movies may well center on the differences between Hollywood's "spectaculars," with lavish sets, highly paid actors, and huge mob scenes, and inexpensively made films with non-professional actors which have been artistically satisfying, such as *The Quiet One,* De Sica's *The Bicycle Thief* (considered one of the best movies ever made), and others.

In the senior high school some study of the documentary as a film and television form is important. Students may begin with the familiar "Twentieth Century," discussing what problems in selection would arise in trying to compress the significant points of a decade like the 1920s or an era of historic significance such as "The Rise of Hitler," "The Crisis at Munich," or "The Battle of the Bulge" into a twenty-seven-minute broadcast. Other television documentary programs such as "CBS Reports," NBC's "White Papers," and special programs on problems like water conservation and the population explosion may provide a background for the study of some of the great motion-picture documentaries available for showing in schools or occasionally rerun on television: Pare Lorenz's *The River,* with its poetic script and musical score by Virgil Thomson, his *The Plow That Broke the Plains,* and the outstanding films by one of the greatest of the documentary artists, Robert Flaherty: *Louisiana Story, Nanook of the North,* and *Man of Aran.* The late Edward R. Murrow's "See It Now" programs, no longer presented but available on video tape, are some of the best of these, according to Gilbert Seldes, who calls attention to the brilliant technique which created virtually a new art form.[12]

More and more of the fine films no longer available in commercial houses are being shown on television or are available through state-university film libraries, public libraries, or at inexpensive rentals through the numerous centers distributing films for educational purposes. Industry makes a wide variety of films available to schools, many of which are shown to classes with little

---

[10] Teaching Film Custodians, 25 West 43d Street, New York 36, N.Y.
[11] William Lewin and Alexander Frazier, *Standards of Photoplay Appreciation* (see bibliography), is a standard guide.
[12] Seldes, *op. cit.,* p. 206.

benefit except to the advertiser. A few, such as a history of the oil industry, have won praise for artistry. Many educational films produced for public health and welfare organizations and some commercial films are often worth studying. *The Quiet One* is available in some communities through mental-health organizations. *The Brotherhood of Man* provides a fine introduction to some units on intercultural understanding; many short films, such as the classic *The Red Balloon, Moonbirds,* and the Mr. Magoo series, are available through public libraries.

Questions students may discuss about the translation of a novel to the motion-picture or television screen may center on characterization: Have the characters been brought to life as the author created them, or have they been changed in the screen characterization? Have any characters been left out or added? What effect do these changes have on the presentation of the story? What accounts for the changes?

Changes in plot and action: Are there any important incidents in the book which are omitted in the film version? Have any been added? Is the ending the same, or has it been changed? If changed, what accounts for the change, and what is its effect on the theme of the novel?

Photography: What is the effect of the addition of the visual image (often in color) to your own images of character and scene in the book? Which do you prefer? Does the scene on the wharf, in grayed blues, at the beginning of *Moby-Dick* add to your appreciation of the novel? The shots of the moors in *Wuthering Heights*? The lyrical shots of the Italian countryside in the *Romeo and Juliet* filmed in Italy?

Studying about the newspaper

Teaching how to read the newspaper efficiently and critically and using newspaper resources for many of the subjects for the study of language have been discussed elsewhere in this book.[13] Study of the newspaper as a vital part of American life and an important means of information about national and world affairs is included somewhere in most English curricula. Thoughtful and critical reading of the newspapers, an essential qualification for a citizen in a democracy, is not taught through one unit of study in the junior and senior years but through training in the development of good reading habits during the six years of high school. The newspaper provides many resources for the study of language.

A sequential program in reading the newspaper

More thoughtful and critical readers of the newspapers can be trained during the six years of high school through the use of materials appropriate to the

---

[13] See Chaps. 3 and 5.

interests and abilities of each age group. Some suggestions for such a program follow.

Seventh and eighth grades:

1. The use of advertising, sports, features, and news stories to study connotative, denotative, and figurative language, varieties of usage, and the difference between reports and judgments. Older students, from grade nine on, may study more subtle uses of these kinds of language in news of greater complexity—controversial issues of national and international importance—in editorials and columns.

2. A study of the difference between a news article on a relatively uncontroversial issue (the death of a famous personage; an accident) and an editorial on the same subject.

3. Making a study of the newspaper to develop locational skills: using the index, finding news items quickly, gaining familiarity with the parts of the paper regularly devoted to certain features.

4. Making a comparison of the coverage of a disaster—a fire, a flood, or a hurricane—to see what proportion of news is devoted to factual reporting, human-interest stories, or pictures.

Ninth and tenth grades:

1. Comparing the extent and accuracy of coverage of local, national, and regional news in two or three newspapers and one or two of the news weeklies; observing facts omitted or added, differences in interpretation, analysis of pictures and headlines to study emotional appeals, and attitudes toward the news on the part of the publication.

2. Developing familiarity with the technical aspects of the newspaper, the principal sources of news, and the ways in which news is gathered and edited. Ninth and tenth graders of average and above-average ability should be familiar enough with a variety of newspapers to answer the following questions:

> . . . What are the chief sources of news represented in your own local newspaper: Associated Press, United Press International, coverage by local reporters? How do syndicates like the Associated Press gather and disseminate news? How is news gathered from the cities and towns in your area? What sources are used for foreign news? Washington news?
>
> . . . What is the balance of local or regional news, national news, and international news in your local paper? How much space is given to international news? Where does it appear? Students should have a chance to compare this coverage of space allotment to different kinds of news in local papers, large-city dailies, and papers of national importance such as The *New York Times*, the *New York Herald Tribune*,

the *Christian Science Monitor,* and others. These three are the most readily available in large metropolitan areas and in libraries.

. . . What are the differences in the treatment of news on any one day in a tabloid, a small-town paper, a large-city paper in the state, and a newspaper of national importance? What accounts for the differences?

. . . How many syndicated columns appear in your newspaper? What is their source? What topics do they discuss?

. . . Who owns the newspapers in your community? What are the political affiliations of the newspapers? Are these observable in the selection, editing, and reporting of news? In the editorials and cartoons? Can you detect efforts to sway your opinion, to influence your feeling about a political candidate or a controversial issue? How?

Eleventh and twelfth grades:

Although the teacher should attempt to find out how much study of the newspaper students have had before entering these grades and attempt to evaluate their proficiency in the skills of reading and interpreting the news, some critical attention to newspaper study should take place in these years. It is at this time that students are most capable of profiting by intensive study of the newspaper as an opinion-molding force in a democracy. They can compare the papers they know with great national and international papers and become capable of critically reading and evaluating the presentation of news. These years mark the last chance that schools will have to train the majority of youth in the reading habits they will use as voters and as citizens to form their opinions on important issues.

It is during these years, too, that students must learn to compare and judge the treatment of news on controversial social or political issues in several papers. It is during these years that the student should form the habit of reading a good newspaper which gives objective treatment of the news, rather than limiting himself to the narrow scope of a largely pictorial tabloid or to the brief reports given by radio or television. Where local newspapers are inadequate, the teacher may direct students to a good national paper such as the *New York Times* or the *Christian Science Monitor.*

The ideal reader-citizen is aware of the traditions, guarantees, responsibilities, and history of a free press, is well aware of the pressures which operate on it, and of the threats of censorship from various pressure groups and agencies. He knows who owns the newspapers in his area, and how that ownership is reflected in the selecting and editing of news. He knows which papers represent major political parties, groups, or financial interests. Readers of this kind can exert a formidable influence on the shape of the world to come because they cannot be manipulated by a press reflecting the voice of pressure groups, the violent tirades of dictators, or the propaganda devices of unscrupulous politicians or financiers.

Eleventh-grade students studying American literature and American history need to be fully informed about the constitutional guarantees of the freedom of the press established in the Bill of Rights.[14] They should know something of the history of these freedoms and of the struggle to preserve them and know what limitations have been put on these freedoms from time to time. During the study of American literature, they will read about the era of the muckrakers and their role in American social history and become acquainted with some of the great reporters of that era. Through reading Lincoln Steffens, Upton Sinclair, and others, they will learn what the era of yellow journalism was like and will be ready to study the steps which led to reforms in newspaper codes. In the eleventh or twelfth year they should be introduced to some of the biographies of American and international news reporters and the kind of excitement and dedication of the lives of many of these men: William Shirer, Eric Sevareid, Walter Duranty, Ernie Pyle, and others.

Twelfth-grade students should become acquainted with some of the great international papers: the *Manchester Guardian* (highly respected by newsmen for generations), the *Times* of London, *Le Monde* (of Paris), and others. A study of foreign-language papers for format, pictures, headlines, and style is instructive, too.

A unit taught in the twelfth grade may serve as a culmination for the preceding years, filling in gaps and clarifying information studied earlier. Where the English syllabus provides for a sequence of instruction in critical reading of the newspaper ("democracy's textbook"), students can develop the skills needed for effective participation in democratic life. Such instruction is essential for American adults.

A unit on the study of the newspaper, wherever it is included in the course of study, should cover such topics as these:

1. A careful study of the space allocated to major news stories in different papers for one day or one week. The class should have available a sampling of papers to examine. If enough papers are available, the class may be divided into groups for study, with each group including a local daily, a large-city newspaper from another city in the state, the *New York Times*, the *New York Daily News* or another tabloid, and the *Christian Science Monitor*. Each group may take one area of the news: international news, state political news, local news, national news, sensational news—disasters, riots, robberies, murders. The study may include the column space allocated to each story, the size of the headline, the placing of the news—front page or small column on the last page.

2. Each group may make a careful study of the language used in the news it has evaluated for space. Evidences of editorializing and distortion may be collected for a report by the group to the class. They may observe that editorial-

---

[14] The teen-agers questioned in the Purdue opinion poll did not know, apparently, that a free press is guaranteed by the Bill of Rights. (See H. H. Remmers and D. H. Radler, *The American Teen-ager*, The Bobbs-Merrill Company, Inc., Indianapolis, 1957, p. 52.)

izing may be done in subtle ways, such as the choice of a word for a headline or the publication of a picture placing someone in an unfavorable light.

3. The group may compare the treatment of news studied in the daily papers with the same topic in several news weeklies (*Time, Newsweek*) and journals of opinion (*The New Republic, The Nation, The Reporter, The National Observer, The Commonweal,* and others). What differences are there in coverage? In emphasis? In objectivity? In kinds of opinion expressed?

4. Each member of the class may take one well-known reporter, columnist, or reviewer for intensive study: book reviewers, television and drama critics, science and education editors for the *New York Times* and other large papers, authors of syndicated columns. A close analysis of each writer should reveal something of his style of writing, his objectivity, and his background and knowledge of the field.

5. A careful study of levels or varieties of usage and style may be made in such a unit. Are prominent personages called by their first names? By their nicknames? Is there much slang or colloquial language used in the news reports? In editorials? Is there a difference in the level of usage between the tabloid and the paper of international repute? What accounts for it?

With such topics for discussion, a class may become familiar with some important critical criteria for judging a newspaper. Most students realize for the first time in such study the limitations of the small local daily which may have been their main news source until the unit began. They will come to know several papers more thoroughly and have some basis for judging a paper.

Studying periodicals

Teen-agers entering high school are beginning to become regular consumers of many of the magazines which offer, in cheap form, fantasy, escape fiction, purportedly "true" romances, detective stories, crime stories, and others. Adults have deplored for years the amount of violence, sex, horror, and sadism purveyed in many of the pulp magazines, but little assistance has been given to young people in teaching them to evaluate such magazines and to detect formula plots and efforts to manipulate the emotions of the readers. Some attention to the vast flood of periodical literature available to children for twenty-five cents or less is warranted in an area where newsstands are filled with sensational literature.

Most students fail to know, too, some of the most valuable magazines in our culture today, those which take the most independent stands in presenting opinion well supported by facts; those which make available some of the best writing of fiction writers, and articles by leaders in the field of public opinion, cultural affairs, politics, and major educational and social problems. Some of the writing found in our periodicals is shoddy and sensational, but much of it is very good. Stories by Hemingway, Faulkner, Marjorie Kinnan Rawlings, Stephen Vincent Benét, and others have first appeared in *The Saturday Evening*

Post; Hemingway's *The Old Man and the Sea* was first published in *Life,* and some of our finest novelists, poets, and short-story writers have appeared first in the pages of *The New Yorker, Harper's, The Atlantic,* and others.

Some teachers have been successful in getting junior high school readers to look critically at the content of the "pulps" by having them analyze the appeals of the advertising. In fact a number of magazines, from *True Romances* to *The New Yorker,* may profitably be analyzed from this point of view since it is obvious, even to the very young, that advertisers write for the kind of audience they know will be drawn to the magazine. Even the uncritical reader is often shocked by the advertiser's assumptions about public credulity. Young people grow critical and sophisticated about advertising appeals long before they can transfer such critical attitudes to other materials.

An examination of magazine fiction can provide training in the appreciation of fiction. Even young and uncritical readers can detect the differences between plots and endings in stories in the true-romance and love-story magazines, and those in the "slicks" like *Mademoiselle, Good Housekeeping, The Ladies' Home Journal,* and *The Saturday Evening Post.*

Wise teachers can use information about magazine tastes to recommend books which treat the same kinds of subjects in a maturer and more artistic way. Teen-age stories by Mary Stolz and Betty Cavanna are often appealing substitutes for some of the pulp fiction; books by reputable writers of science fiction can replace stories the pulps offer, and there are better mysteries, westerns, crime and sports stories. Many teachers find it preferable to introduce young people to books which treat relations between men and women honestly than to leave them to a diet of the frankly sensational fiction which purports to inform them about adult life and offers them cheap fantasy instead.[15]

Students need to be informed, too, about the many magazines which play an important role in examining more fully than other media the social, cultural, and political issues of the day. It is important for students to see that some of the independent journals may voice unpopular opinions that newspapers, under pressures from advertisers and groups of various kinds, cannot afford to express. One exercise that may lead to such a discovery is the study of an important problem as treated in an assortment of periodicals: *Time, Life, Newsweek, The Atlantic, Harper's, The New Republic, The Nation, The Commonweal, The New Yorker, The Reporter, U.S. News and World Report, Current History, Business Week, Fortune.* Students may examine current issues, usually available in libraries, or choose a topic treated in back issues. They will need to use their library skills with reference materials such as *The Readers' Guide to Periodical Literature, The Education Index, The Public Affairs Information Service,* and others. It is best if they can begin such an assignment with a topic which is controversial but not too heavily loaded emotionally, such as that of medical care for the aged, fluoridation, the use of insecticides, or the Peace Corps.

---

[15] See Chap. 15 for treatment of this topic, with suggestions for readings.

Junior high school students may study the treatment of the President's family, the physical fitness campaign, or juvenile delinquency.

Studying all the media

At least some of the activities during the school year may be designed to help students compare the treatment of one issue or subject in all the media. An examination of humor may include study of film and television comedians, those who are heard on radio and those humorists who write for newspapers or magazines or draw cartoon or comic strips: Charles Addams, George Price, Jules Pfeiffer, Peter Arno, Al Capp, Walt Kelly, or Charles Schulz—all these are worth study.

Comparison of the range and quality of news coverage on radio and television, in newspapers and news weeklies is a topic of importance for students at all grade levels. Careful comparisons will reveal that many of the radio news broadcasts use the news highlights from the morning newspaper, but that the total article contains relevant facts which the brief minute or two of radio time cannot cover. Television provides the visual record of historical events or disasters. Most valuable to uncritical readers is this close analysis of the differences in scope and depth of coverage in the news which will emerge as a pattern if the class is assigned the task of comparing various types of papers and radio and television coverage.

Students may be asked to read the chapter called "What We Read, See, and Hear" in *The Mature Mind* and examine the treatment of news for a few days in the light of Overstreet's comment that newspapers have a vested interest in catastrophe and emphasize life in its violent and hostile aspects more often than in its cooperative, friendly, or constructive ones.[16] More mature students may analyze the appeals of advertising and entertainment in films and television: do these media offer fantasy, daydreams, and escapism, or do they offer a meaningful interpretation of life?

One teacher opened a semester's work with a one-week unit on comic books and found in the class addicts who were uncritical devourers of the genre. The class focused on such questions as: Why do we read them? Why do adults read them? Why do parents object? What kinds of comics are there? Who reads which type? What are typical comic-book heroes like? What do they have in common? What values do they support? To what extent, if at all, are our own standards shaped by their conduct? This teacher believes that increased awareness of esthetic form in the media leads to deeper appreciations of traditional literary forms—fiction, poetry, and drama.[17]

Another teacher describes an elective course in the mass media designed to develop critical thinking and focused on exploration and discussion of such

[16] H. A. Overstreet, *The Mature Mind*, W. W. Norton & Company, Inc., New York, 1949.
[17] Patrick D. Hazard, "Behind the Tinsel Curtain," *English Journal*, vol. 45, March, 1956, pp. 134–144.

questions as "Can or should the number of hours allotted to westerns and easterns (big-city crime) be curtailed?" The class learned about the shortcomings of chain ownership of newspapers, the difficulties of independent ownership of papers, the role of the advertiser, and the significance and responsibility of a free press.[18] Still another teacher encouraged her class to participate in panel discussions reviewing the reading of the class in magazines, comic books, and their watching of television and movies. The boys in this tenth-grade class were extremely critical of the "trash" they claimed the girls were reading, and pointed out to the attentive girls that such reading would give them "crazy ideas." Such opinions carried weight with the audience, and led the feminine contingent, at least, to a closer scrutiny of its reading and viewing habits.

As illustrated in the chapters on the teaching of language and literature in this book, the materials of the mass media can support and enrich the teaching of English and assist in producing better informed, more discriminating adult citizens. Whether we like it or not, the popular arts are among the most potent forces now shaping the intellectual and cultural tastes of our students. We ignore them at our peril. If we fail to recognize this important part of twentieth-century life, we stand little chance of sending mature and literate students into an automated world of increased leisure. If we help them acquire the new literacy in print, sound, and picture, they will leave the classroom as the kind of people visualized by Joyce Cary as having left the mass and become "individuals seeking ideas for themselves." [19]

Student activities and assignments

Teachers will find it helpful to look over the teaching areas in English to see where media materials may be utilized in developing the language skills. The suggested activities marked with one asterisk are suitable primarily for use in the junior high school; those marked with two in the senior high school; those unmarked may be used at either level, making adjustments for materials of greater or lesser complexity and maturity.

Speaking:

. . . Participating in panel discussions of problems raised in newspapers, periodicals, TV, or movies—problems relevant to teen-age privileges and restrictions, teen-agers in the news, social problems: the legal drinking age, driving privileges, drag racing.

. . . Developing skills in speaking through mock forums, panels, debates, quiz programs: "Face the Nation"; "Meet the Press"; or "CBS Reports."

. . . Planning interviews and news reports and commentaries modeled after radio and TV talks.

[18] Lieber Anker, "English V: Rocket to Critical Thinking," *English Journal*, vol. 50, January, 1961, pp. 34–43.
[19] *Loc. cit.*

. . . **Presenting interviews and dialogues or conversations modeled after "Youth Forum" or "Open End."

. . . Choosing several magazine short stories, and giving the class a brief synopsis of the plot. The narrator should stop at a point near the conclusion and let the class guess how the story's conflict is resolved. The ease with which many of them can guess the endings of such stories without reading them speaks eloquently about the stereotypes employed in much light magazine fiction.

Listening:

. . . *Listening to news or public speeches and training oneself to remember and report accurately on what was heard.

. . . *Listening critically to analyze bias, distortion, or slanting in public informational and political speeches and news commentaries.

. . . Listening to recordings of actors reading poems, short stories, plays.

. . . Developing awareness of language usage, vocabulary, dialectal differences, pronunciations, regional accents, and differences among varieties of usage.

. . . Listening regularly to one analyst or commentator to detect bias, opinion, political affiliation, or prejudice on an issue of importance.

. . . *Listening to news commentators handling a complex and controversial issue for degree of subjectivity or objectivity.

. . . *Listening critically to the dialogue on different types of programs: westerns, detective stories, "doctor" and "lawyer" programs for clichés, usage, or dialect.

Reading:

. . . Reading books recommended by the teacher for those whose TV tastes lie in the following areas:

Westerns: Schaeffer's *Shane,* Clark's *The Ox-Bow Incident,* Wister's *The Virginian.*

Crime and detection: Chesterton's Father Brown stories; Doyle's *Sherlock Holmes,* Whitehead's *The F.B.I. Story.*

Westerns featuring Indian characters: Richter's *Light in the Forest,* LaFarge's *Laughing Boy,* Clark's *Little Navajo Bluebird.*

Animal stories: Enid Bagnold's *National Velvet,* Street's *Goodbye, My Lady,* Gipson's *Old Yeller,* Marjorie Kinnan Rawlings' *The Yearling,* Clark's *Track of the Cat,* Knight's *Lassie Come Home.*

Family situation comedies: Gilbreth and Carey's *Cheaper by the Dozen,* Day's *Life with Father,* Anna Parrott Rose's *Room for One More,* Ruth McKenney's *My Sister Eileen.*

Documentaries on life and conditions abroad: novels with settings in foreign countries (see Chapter 15); biographies of foreign political leaders; nonfiction travel and adventure books (see Chapter 13).

Social-issue programs: novels, biographies, and nonfiction dealing with these problems or with the lives of those who have had a role in solving them (see Chapter 15).

Drama, poetry, novels, short stories, humor, biography, and essays: reading the originals or other works by the same authors.

. . . Reading magazines and newspapers and viewing movies and television may be used to develop some of the following reading skills:

Comprehension: reading cartoons, interpreting figurative language,
skimming newspaper and magazine articles for facts, developing locational skills by searching for materials, understanding wit, allusion,
irony, satire, humor; understanding symbolism.

Critical reading: (1) evaluating fairness and comprehensive coverage
of an issue; (2) looking for writer's intention: reading between the
lines, detecting prejudice and distortion; (3) comparing validity of
arguments in controversy; evaluating different points of view; drawing
inferences; (4) evaluating authority of writer; checking on sources of
information and accuracy of presentation.

Writing:

. . . Outlining speeches given on radio or television.

. . . Writing a critical analysis of a family, teen-age, animal story, western,
science fiction, domestic situation, or doctor or lawyer program. (See the
student paper on pages 351–352.)

. . . Writing a TV or movie script based on a short story, novel, or play, or
scenes therefrom.

. . . Writing a critical comparison of the TV or movie version of a play,
novel, series of sketches, or biography of a famous person.

. . . Writing assignments suggested by topics of news on TV: some aspect
of integration, housing, juvenile delinquency, political life, or other issue of
public interest treated on TV.

. . . **Writing a critical analysis of television, newspaper, or magazine
(and perhaps movie) coverage of an important political or social issue: the
launching of a new space vehicle, the President's message to Congress; an
international crisis.

. . . ** Comparing the coverage of an issue in American media with that in
the comparable media of one country or several countries abroad.

. . . Writing a critique of a popular TV figure or a movie actor, producer,
or director.

. . . Writing endings for some of the plot-summary exercises suggested in
Literature Study in the High School[20] or for some which the teacher makes
up. Discussion of the endings will provide material for comment on attitudes and values as well as serve to develop literary discrimination.

. . . Viewing programs directed at smaller children for their possible
effects, and writing a review and recommendations for children, for their
parents, for adults, or for teen-agers. Students may compare their judgments with the recommendations in such magazines as *The National
Parent-Teacher, The Catholic Transcript,* or *Scholastic* magazine.

. . . Writing letters to television executives about programs especially liked
or disliked. A barrage of letters has been known to keep a fine program on

[20] Dwight Burton, *Literature Study in the High School,* rev. ed., Holt, Rinehart and Winston, Inc., New York, 1964, pp. 153–166.

the air despite limited public reception, or to recall one which has been withdrawn. Letters may be sent to the account executive of the sponsoring company, or more effectively, to the president and vice-president in charge of programs at the major broadcasting companies: the American Broadcasting Company, 7 West 66th Street, New York, N.Y.; the Columbia Broadcasting System, 485 Madison Avenue, New York 22, N.Y.; and the National Broadcasting Company, 30 Rockefeller Plaza, New York 20, N.Y.

. . . *Writing an evaluation of magazines published for a special audience or covering a special field: sports, outdoor life, science, teen-age life, movies, news, fashions, social issues.

. . . **Writing a criticism of the presentation of a social issue, a current event, or a documentary purporting to give facts—either a cross-media approach or criticism of one program.

. . . **Writing a critical analysis of advertising for magazines, newspapers, or television which uses one of the following appeals: fear, desire for status or for popularity, appeals to the "masculine" man or the "feminine" woman; desire for success; anxieties about self (bad breath, BO); desire for sex appeal, for wealth, or power. What values or penalties are implied in such advertising?

. . . **Writing a paper about the characterization of the members of an ethnic group in popular fiction, television, and/or the movies. Do such characters have major or minor roles? Are they heroes, villains, servants, unskilled workers? Students should indicate clues to ethnic background: names, occupation, character traits, appearance, membership in organizations, etc. They should note the degree of approval, sympathy, or lack of sympathy in the treatment by the author. Is the character presented as a worthy person, or an object of condescension or ridicule? [21]

. . . Writing about the characterization of one kind of person in modern magazine fiction: the college professor, the secretary, the career girl, the young businessman, the teen-ager, the small brother or sister, the young mother.

The following paper is an example of student response to the kind of assignment suggested on page 350: an analysis of westerns.

Same Time, Same Station[22]

"Howdy, Mister Dillon. . . . They Went That-a-Way. . . . Them's Shootin' Words, Padnoh!" These are common excerpts from a major form of entertainment in our country today, the Western. Millions of people, be they office workers, professional men, or just

[21] Assignment adapted from a study of stereotypes in magazine fiction by Bernard Berelson and Patricia J. Salter, "Majority and Minority Americans: An Analysis of Magazine Fiction," *Public Opinion Quarterly,* vol. 10, 1946, pp. 168–197, reprinted in Bernard Rosenberg and David Manning White (eds.), *Mass Culture: The Popular Arts in America,* The Free Press of Glencoe, New York, 1957. This book contains valuable analyses of the popular media, including comics, mystery stories, and advertising.

[22] Paper by ninth-grade student, reprinted from *Pegasus,* vol. 1, June, 1963, King Philip Junior High School, West Hartford, Conn.

ordinary John Q. Americans, stare attentively at their television sets for hours at a stretch, watching Westerns. They watch the inevitably white-hatted "good guys" (though now with the more educated, adult-appealing cowboy such as Paladin, this normal color pattern may differ somewhat) meet up with the inevitably black-hatted "bad guys."

Our hero is direly tested. He is insulted, betrayed, ambushed, roughed-up and has a rather unpleasant go of it for the first half-hour of the program (now that they are first-rate entertainment, many of our Westerns have progressed from the half-hour to the more sophisticated hour variety). By the start of the second half of the show, though, you can always expect our hero to be showing his true colors. By the time the show has progressed fifty minutes, our hero has the band of desperadoes in jail and has thoroughly regained face. After going to the saloon for his hearty milk on the rocks, he manages to leave a shiny silver bullet, or his card for the townspeople to remember him by, and then rides off into the sun, madly kicking his pure white steed and shouting "Hi Ho Silver" at the top of his lungs.

The word *cowboy* is automatically associated with our country just as bagpipes automatically bring Scotland to mind. Just about everyone enjoys a good Western with all of its commonplaces: the saloon, old Doc somebody, the livery stable, the barroom brawl, and the inevitable showdown on Main Street at high noon.

Are they realistic? Of course not. I doubt if there ever was a cowboy who could quote Shakespeare as accurately or as eloquently as does Paladin each Saturday night at nine-thirty. But the Western does serve its purpose. It provides an escape from today's modern, complicated world to an exciting, romantic one. For one hour (between the commercials) you ride your easy chair through the dusty prairies. That glass of Coke in your hand becomes a shot of whiskey, and your belt becomes a holster.

Finally, when your one-hour romp through the "badlands" is over, you leave your trance. But don't despair! Next week, same time, same station, you'll ride the wide-open range again. You'll dodge bullets, drink whiskey, and doff your ten-gallon white (of course!) hat when Miss Kitty passes.

Selected bibliography[23]

Leo Bogart, *The Age of Television,* Frederick Ungar Publishing Co., New York, 1956.

William D. Boutwell (ed.), *Using Mass Media in the Schools,* Appleton-Century-Crofts, Inc., New York, 1962.

Ernest Callenbach, *Our Modern Art, the Movies,* Center for the Study of Liberal Education for Adults, Chicago, 1955.

The Educational Media Index, vol. 5, *The English Language,* McGraw-Hill Book Company, New York, 1964.

Films for Classroom Use, Handbook of Information on Films for Education, Teaching Film Custodians, Inc., 25 West 43d Street, New York 36, N.Y. Published each month.

Patrick D. Hazard, "The Public Arts and the Private Sensibility," in Lewis Leary (ed.), *Contemporary Literary Scholarship,* Appleton-Century-

---

[23] See also the list of suggested films and recordings on pp. 423–425.

Crofts, Inc., New York, 1958. A thoughtful evaluation of the relationships between the public arts and the humanities.

Arno Jewett (ed.), *Recordings for Teaching Literature and Language in the High School,* Federal Security Agency, Office of Education, Bulletin no. 19, Government Printing Office, Washington, D.C., 1952.

William Lewin and Alexander Frazier, *Standards of Photoplay Appreciation,* Educational and Recreational Guides, Summit, N.J., 1957. Textbook for junior and senior high schools designed to raise standards of taste and appreciation of movies.

The Motion Picture and the Teaching of English, NCTE, Champaign, Ill., 1965.

Neil Postman et al., *Television and the Teaching of English,* Appleton-Century-Crofts, Inc., New York, 1961.

Bernard Rosenberg and David Manning White (eds.), *Mass Culture: The Popular Arts in America,* The Free Press of Glencoe, New York, 1957. Contains valuable analyses of the popular media, including comics, mystery stories, and advertising.

Gilbert Seldes, *The Public Arts,* Simon and Schuster, Inc., New York, 1956.

Francis Shoemaker (ed.), *Communication and the Communication Arts,* rev. ed., Bureau of Publications, Teachers College, Columbia University, New York, 1957. Articles discussing communication in a number of disciplines.

Wilbur Schramm, *Television and Our Children,* Stanford University Press, Stanford, Calif., 1951. Summarizes much of the research about the effect of television on children and adolescents. A useful study for the teacher of English.

Harold Spears, *High School Journalism,* rev. ed., The Macmillan Company, New York, 1964.

Studies in the Mass Media, NCTE, Champaign, Ill. Although this is no longer published, past issues contain valuable study guides to televised or screen plays made from books and plays.

CHAPTER *15*

I read Shakespeare, Thackeray, Eliot, Dickens and the Brontes, Hawthorne, Cooper, and Robert Louis Stevenson. I do not remember that I was conscious of any difference in treatment between *Bleak House* and *Little Women*, between George Eliot and Sophie May, that I regarded one as duller than the other, more difficult to get into. They were all stories. If they took me into a different world and kind from the one I knew, I gloried in the swift and certain transference.

MARY ELLEN CHASE [1]

The individual reading program

The omnivorous reader described to us by Mary Ellen Chase is common among high school students, and often he is unknown to his teachers, who may know little or nothing of what he is reading. Such readers read insatiably, and often without discrimination at first. As their experience with books widens, they grow increasingly critical, choosing more carefully, rejecting inferior works, and building discriminating tastes. Such students will be lifelong readers, turning to books in the adult years for wisdom and delight. The creation of such readers is the aim of the individual reading program.

In earlier chapters we have seen how reading skills may be developed through a good developmental program and we have observed the ways students learn to read with comprehension and appreciation in the different types of literature. The three important strands of the reading program have been described in Chapter 5: (1) teaching the skills of reading for speed and comprehension, (2) intensively studying literature for appreciation, and (3) getting individual students to read so that they develop lifetime reading habits.

[1] *A Goodly Heritage*, Henry Holt and Company, Inc., New York, 1932, pp. 46–47.

All three strands of the program overlap at many points, and all three play an important role in producing the kind of reader we imagine as our ideal—he who reads skillfully, clearly comprehending what he reads; who understands, appreciates and finds satisfaction in literature as an artistic creation; and who is a mature, self-directed reader, making reading a continuing leisure activity and turning to books for understanding of himself and the society in which he lives.

This third strand—getting students to do extensive individual reading—is that phase of the program most often neglected or omitted in the average secondary school program. The close reading of selected classics is, in most schools, the foundation of work in literature. Recent emphasis on the importance of developmental reading has led many teachers to assume responsibility for helping all students gain practice in the skills of speed and comprehension. Important as both these aspects of reading are, however, we recognize today that young people also need the opportunity to range freely among books, to follow individual tastes and interests, and to learn to select their own reading wisely. As they talk about books with their friends, they discover the satisfactions of becoming independent readers who find reading an important part of their lives.

The reading skills program is discussed in Chapter 5 of this book. Part 2, dealing with the types of literature, is devoted to discussion of close reading, and intensive study of each of the various types. Chapter 14 has suggested ways in which the popular arts of picture, sound, and print can provide new perspectives for the study of literature and stimulate interest in reading. The present chapter will focus on the third strand of the reading program, discussing ways in which a strong program of individual reading can become a significant part of the course in English, serving to enrich and broaden literary experience, and to produce mature readers for whom reading and books will serve an important humanizing function.

The need for an individual reading program

Traditional courses in literature, requiring that all students read the same novels and allotting five or six weeks to a detailed analysis of a book, have been notoriously unsuccessful in producing students who leave high school with a taste for reading and a habit of regularly reading good books as part of their leisure recreation. Polls have indicated that only one-quarter to one-third of American adults read as much as a book a month.[2]

Although America ranks high among the countries of the world for the amount spent on books, per-capita reading figures place us fifth as a book-

[2] Bernard Berelson, "Who Reads What Books and Why," *Saturday Review*, vol. 34, May 12, 1951, p. 8; and John Timmerman, "Do Illiterate A.B.'s Disgrace Us All?" *College Composition and Communication*, vol. 8, February, 1957, pp. 50–56.

reading nation. More than a quarter of our college graduates have not read a single book in the last year.[3] Even among our educated citizens, the independent reading of worthwhile and challenging books has never been a distinctive part of our contemporary culture.

The demand by colleges for students who have read widely, intelligently, and with comprehension, and the decreasing reliance of college-entrance examinations on single classics has made possible great variety in the choice of books for student reading. Increasingly, such examinations have demanded breadth of reading and less detailed analysis of any one book. The increasing availability of good contemporary books in paperback editions and inexpensive hardcovers makes it possible for young people to explore their interests and plan their own programs of reading. Studying literature in thematically organized sequences or units is becoming an increasingly common pattern for high school courses of study.[4] New emphasis on independent study programs in high schools makes such a plan for reading both possible and desirable.

There are a number of reasons why our existing reading programs do not produce enough adult readers who value good reading as a recreation. Foremost among these are the wide differences among students in reading tastes and interests, making it unlikely that the choice of any one novel will interest a whole class. Other disparities are common: there are wide differences in reading interests between boys and girls, especially during the junior high school years. Secondly, not all students are ready for the same book at the same time. The book chosen for the class of thirty or forty will prove too difficult for the poor readers and too easy or simple in plot for the top students. Then, too, many readers who are not interested in the book the teacher selects will read avidly if allowed to choose their own books. All of these reasons indicate that at least some part of the year's work should be devoted to a program which allows some freedom to read according to interest and to discuss books with classmates.

There is considerable evidence to show that such programs do increase student reading—sometimes with dramatic results. Many teachers have learned that when students are permitted to range among books at their level and are allowed time to read in class, they will read with enthusiasm. One teacher conducted an experiment with 115 eleventh-grade students who had ten copies each of twelve different books in their classroom. The students were told that they could read for as long as they remained interested in the books and that their marks would not be changed by anything they did during the period. They read 424 books in thirteen days, an average of almost four books to a student.[5]

[3] Jacob M. Price (ed.), *Reading for Life: Developing the College Student's Lifetime Reading Interest*, The University of Michigan Press, Ann Arbor, Mich., 1960, p. 4.
[4] See Chap. 1, p. 11.
[5] G. Robert Carlsen, "Literature and Emotional Maturity," *English Journal*, vol. 38, March, 1949, pp. 130–138.

In another experimental program, designed to provide enriched cultural experiences for college-bound students whose background in English was less than adequate, a group of forty-four students read a total of 700 books in eight weeks. During the intensive reading course, students wrote, read, and talked about books from eight in the morning until midafternoon. Discussions of books carried on through the dinner hour, often until ten in the evening, and on several occasions until one or two in the morning, with the teachers often called back by the students to take part in the discussion.[6]

In a junior high school in New York City, the books taken from the library during the first week of the new free-reading program rose from 40 to 1,000. During the first year, the minimum number of books read by any one child was eight and the maximum number, forty-two.[7]

Book reports and reading

The traditional provision for wide reading in most English classrooms is the book report. Students are required to read a book every month or so and to make reports, oral or written, which serve as a check on their reading of the book. Often the teacher provides a complex and detailed outline in which the student is asked to discuss theme, style, author's purpose, principal characters and setting, and review the plot. Oral book reports, intended to interest students in the books others are reading, are frequently a trial for both student and teacher, as a succession of nervous and awkward adolescents stumble painfully through a retelling of the plot of the book, stopping short of the climax to say, "If you want to know what happens, read the book."

Many teachers feel that the book report does not serve the purposes for which it is designed. As a check on whether the student has read the book and a device to promote further reading, it has obvious limitations. Most teachers are familiar with the various subterfuges which are substituted for reading: students tend to select the shortest and easiest books; synopses of plots are available in libraries, or are passed from student to student; parents can often be persuaded to read the book and describe it; book jackets yield comments which can be worked into the written report. These and other ruses become a substitute for reading, which frequently turns the book report into a game of matching wits with the teacher. The traditional written or oral book report frequently penalizes the student for reading: most adults would probably read less if they were required to write a report of 300 words about each book or to stand, face an indifferent class, and give a talk. A committee discussing life-

---

[6] (Program at Dillard University, New Orleans, during summer of 1959.) Frank Jennings, "How Free Can a Guided Reading Program Be?" in a speech before the New England Association of Teachers of English, December 5, 1959.

[7] Many of the suggestions in this chapter were made by Mrs. Doris Coburn, director of the program at P.S. 65, New York City. See Elizabeth Rose, "Literature in the Junior High School," *English Journal*, vol. 44, March, 1955, p. 145.

time reading habits called such reports "one of the most effective devices to condition young people against books." [8]

There is strong evidence that such practice limits the reading even of good students rather than extends it. One twelve-year-old put away her copy of *David Copperfield* to finish during the summer because the assignment for her monthly book report was the reading of a mystery story; a group of ninth-grade girls discussing books about romance commented, "We don't read teen-age romances much any more. The books we like are those which adults read —*Gone with the Wind* or *A Lantern in Her Hand*—but they're too long, and you have to stop and think. So we may go back to the Betty Cavanna and Mary Stolz books for a book report or something like that." Still, even within the traditional pattern of the monthly oral or written book report, ingenious teachers have often found ways of adding variety and informality to the requirement and providing for the kind of sharing of books which encourages reading. Numerous articles list ways to add interest and variety to book reporting. [9]

Principles for the program

Teachers in many schools have found it possible to increase student reading significantly by putting into operation a few important principles of an individual reading program. Among them are these:

Freedom of choice.   Students are allowed the greatest possible freedom of choice in choosing the books they will read.

Time to talk.   Students are encouraged to talk with each other about the books they have read. The exchange of opinions, reactions, and ideas about reading provides the primary motivation for further reading. The powerful influence of group opinion and pressures to do as the group is doing provide invaluable motivation for more and better reading, and taste improves as students freely and honestly exchange their reactions to what they have read.

Time to read.   Time is provided for reading in class. In many homes today, large families, crowded living conditions, the rival activities of occupants, and the ubiquitous noise of radio and television make reading almost impossible for many of our youth. Finding time to read is most difficult precisely for those young people who have the most trouble with reading in

---

[8] Jean D. Grambs (ed.), *The Development of Lifetime Reading Habits,* a report of a conference published for the National Book Committee by R. R. Bowker Company, New York, 1954, p. 6.

[9] See Jerome Carlin, "Your Next Book Report," *English Journal,* vol. 50, January, 1961, pp. 16–22; and Howard S. Rowland, "Alternatives for the Book Report," *English Journal,* vol. 51, February, 1962, pp. 106–113.

school. Class time in which to browse through several books and to select one and start it may provide the needed impetus toward getting into a book that one can finish independently.

Reading guidance. The guidance of a teacher who has read widely in books for adolescents and knows their reading tastes, the books that are available to them, and the right book to recommend to the right child at the right time is the key to a successful individual reading program. Few English teachers have read widely enough to be able to offer the highly individual guidance needed to challenge the interests and tastes of a group of adolescent boys and girls. Teachers who assume the role of guiding reading find it necessary to know what books students are reading, to read many, skim others, and become familiar with still others through reading reviews and the descriptions in reading lists. Few kinds of preparation are so demanding for the English teacher, yet few are more rewarding when a reluctant reader samples and finishes a book.

Aims of the program

The chief aim of the program is to produce readers, students who will find lifelong pleasure in reading for ideas, for information, and for the insights which may produce more humane, civilized human beings. Young people learn that books can help them find answers to personal problems and perplexities, illuminate otherwise inaccessible areas of human experience, and help them develop a set of values by which to live. Habits of continued good reading usually produce readers who can discriminate between poor and mediocre literature and that of lasting value and quality. They recognize the means the artist uses to make form and style serve idea and imagination. Such readers grow into adults who find reading a humanizing and civilizing leisure-time pursuit.

Program into practice

A program designed to encourage reading and provide for growth includes a series of activities for the student, and well-defined responsibilities for the teacher. The student needs to set goals, to browse and choose books to read, to begin and continue to read, to participate in discussions with other students about books, and to keep such records as will help measure growth in reading. The teacher's responsibility is to act as a resource person with a wide knowledge of books adolescents like, to stimulate interest in reading by introducing books to students, and through selection and discussion of literature to help students reach for more challenging books.

The student's responsibility

Setting goals. No student can become an intelligent, self-directing reader without defining for himself what his goals are in reading. For many poor or indifferent readers in our classes, the initial aim may be simply to find some books which can be read with interest and pleasure. Better readers often indicate the desire to begin reading adult books, to explore books of a different type, or to become acquainted with a new author. Good readers are often interested in planning for themselves a reading program which will acquaint them with the books commonly found on college lists or the books which will help familiarize them with their literary heritage or with the writers and ideas that are current in contemporary literature.

When students are given a chance to voice their ideas, many will show that they have already well-defined interests that they are eager to explore. Some want to read to find answers to problems—social, religious, or personal. Others, on the brink of maturity, want to find out through the vicarious experience offered by literature the demands adult life will make of them as husbands and wives or parents, soldiers, or citizens. Some have strong intellectual interests in science, history, philosophy, or sociology. Whatever these interests, even though they are as basic as finding a book that can be read through to the end, a successful program encourages students to clarify their goals in reading and to change them as they grow in maturity.

Browsing and choosing. A second significant step in the development of independent readers is the opportunity to browse among books which have been introduced by a teacher or a librarian, made available in the library, or selected by the student himself on a trial basis. Students need the chance to select and discard, to attempt, reject, and choose again. In the traditional literature program, the student is given one book, chosen by the teacher, which he must read, study carefully, and pass tests on. In individual reading, there is freedom to choose, sample, and select according to interest.

The ungifted in English may have potential ability but lack the zeal that makes the avid reader. Teachers who have been gratified by the results of a program of individual reading have observed that when the pressure is off, students often read eagerly. "They discover that by seeking they can ultimately find a book that has impact for them. They slowly move toward more variety in their reading and more subtle presentations. At least half ultimately try books that are too difficult for them, or that they do not initially like but think they ought to read." [10]

Students need the experience of looking through many books, sampling parts of the book, learning to read reviews, exchanging reactions to books with other students, and finding, through these and other means, the books which are most important for them. More mature readers can gain experience in using book lists and reading the reviews in newspapers and magazines. Many

[10] Robert Carlsen, "English for the Ungifted," *English Journal*, vol. 50, May, 1961, p. 329.

will turn to an adult whose taste they can trust for recommendations. The English teacher should be such an adult, ready to guide and suggest, rather than to make unrealistic demands that all students read and enjoy a narrowly restricted list of classics.

Reading and more reading. Reading increases when young people have a time and a place to read. Teachers who allow a weekly or biweekly period for reading in class find that many students are drawn into books they might not choose to attempt at home. The competing interests of family, school, and social life make it imperative that some time in school be allotted to individual reading. Such time in the English program provides the teacher with important opportunities for guidance, talking with students individually or in small groups, checking reading records, or putting books into the hands of boys and girls. As students develop more interest in reading and increased ability to read independently, less class time may be given to reading and more to discussion of books.

Discussing books. If the contagious enthusiasm about reading is to exert its influence to the full, young people must have the opportunity of talking freely about the books they have read and enjoyed. Since group opinion is of prime importance, such word-of-mouth recommendation is one of the most powerful persuaders for increased reading among teen-agers. The impulse to share with friends the excited reaction to a book is as natural to boys and girls as it is to adults. The individual reading program, then, must provide time and opportunity for talking about books in informal situations, frequently in small group meetings of the class, in which five or six young people reading the same book or the same type of book may talk together. Boys and girls to whom the oral book report is a monthly nightmare can talk informally together with enjoyment about books and present panel discussions before the class.

Many classrooms offer the maximum disadvantages for such discussion: too many students, immobile desks, young people without much self-discipline or self-control. Yet even in overcrowded schools, boys and girls can be seen talking together with enjoyment about books, stimulating each other to further reading and growing in their ability to evaluate the merits and disadvantages of the books they have read. Even at the junior high school level, four or five discussion groups in classes as large as thirty or forty have been managed. Since this kind of talk is a privilege for most of them, they are willing to pay for it with lowered voices and the maximum control of confusion and noise.[11]

Keeping reading records. An important substitute for formal book reporting is the keeping of such reading records as will help students plan, record, and evaluate their own reading. Such a record is valuable to both student and teacher. To the student it indicates achievement in books finished and steps taken toward more varied and more mature reading. To the teacher it shows which books were attempted and put aside and those which were

---

[11] Chap. 4, pp. 80–81, offers more detailed suggestions for carrying out group procedures.

finished with satisfaction. Some check of the student's understanding of the central facts about the book may be given on the record: the date of the setting, the nationality of the author, the type of book (adventure, science fiction, animal story), the name of the author, the title, and the date of publication. Cumulative reading records[12] are kept by the guidance department or the English teacher; more informal records may be kept on a mimeographed form in the student's theme folder. Reporting provides an important means of self-evaluation for the student. As he becomes increasingly responsible for his own growth, and proceeds to more demanding books on the reading ladder, he will become an increasingly self-directing reader.

The teacher's responsibility

The teacher who puts into operation a successful program of individual reading has two important qualifications: the first is his love of books, enthusiasm for reading, and a wide reading background in literature of all kinds and of all times; the second is his understanding of adolescents, their interests, needs, and problems, and the ability to communicate excitement about books and ideas to them. Books must be recommended to young people not because the teacher likes them, not because students "ought" to read them, but because they serve an immediate need in the lives of youth. Nor does this mean servile pandering to interest alone. This task of keeping alive the electric communication between students and books is one of the most important functions of the teacher of English.

Yet many teachers feel inadequately prepared to assume such a role in the classroom. No teacher ever feels that he knows enough books. A planned program of reading is an essential part of professional growth, but the beginning teacher may not have read widely enough outside of his required program to introduce a variety of books to youth. It has been said that the teacher of English needs to know at least two hundred books high school students like in order to make valid recommendations to young people. The inexperienced teacher needs to tap a variety of resources in order to give the boys and girls in the English classroom the kind of guidance they need. Book lists provide invaluable help, but the teacher must also have read many of these books.

One way in which teachers rapidly increase their knowledge about the books students like is to allow boys and girls to talk freely about them. By talking with students, reading book reviews, and studying and comparing book lists, teachers may gain a general knowledge of books boys and girls like and choose those he needs to know. By making it a point to skim regularly a number of books in each of the categories which commonly interest boys and girls, by visiting book stores and libraries with good collections, and by preparing book talks periodically for English classes, the teacher rapidly widens his acquaintance with books. Often a teacher may win acceptance of increased

---

[12] Available from the NCTE, Champaign, Ill.

reading among students by saying frankly to a class, "I don't know enough about the books you like. Tell me some of your favorites. If you recommend some books, I will read them so that we can talk about them." The idea that students can make a teacher read a book provides a delightful reversal of roles for young people. Any teacher who is willing to listen to student recommendations and take them seriously will have taken an important step toward getting reluctant students to read.

Making books available.   A teacher's primary step is that of bringing students and books together. The chief obstacle to increased reading in most schools is the lack of enough books to provide for a wide range of individual tastes. Teachers who wish to start an individual reading program must learn what resources are available and work to bring books within the reach of boys and girls. Ingenious teachers have done this in many ways. Some have charged out twenty or thirty books on their own library cards as a loan collection for a class for a month or so. Most libraries are willing to make such arrangements, and teachers have reported getting books returned in good condition. The various paperback book clubs represent another valuable resource. In some schools students have contributed a certain amount each year or month to buy paperback books for a classroom collection; some buy from the book-club list and contribute the books to the classroom library when they have finished, inscribing their names on the flyleaves as the donors. Discarded books are brought in from home libraries; book drives yield contributions which can be added; classes raise money to buy books through cake sales or paper drives.

Efforts to collect books for schools in culturally deprived communities have brought results when members of the community were asked to donate books; PTA groups have made sums available each year to the English teachers in some schools for classroom library purchases, and other civic organizations have donated books or money; the Junior Chamber of Commerce has organized a project called "Operation Bookshelf" to provide books for school and classroom libraries.

The continuing problems of nonexistent or underequipped school libraries and the lack of classroom libraries for the teacher of English are diminishing in many schools as teachers demand such resources for their classroom. Often books are lacking because English teachers have never asked for them or because they have given priority to expensive sets of anthologies, grammar textbooks, or reading machines. Such purchases are often based on the assumption that every child must be reading the same book at the same time. Fortunately, publishers are currently making available inexpensive editions of short stories, essays, plays, poetry, and novels, or collections of plays or novels. As administrative support for libraries increases, flexibility is increasingly possible in the choice of reading for students.

Finally, teachers can play an important role in encouraging students to buy books and to build up their own libraries. The rise of membership in paperback book clubs is encouraging evidence that students will buy and keep the books they like. More and more schools are making paperback books available for purchase within the school, sometimes in the library, frequently at the cafeteria candy counter. One report suggests that schools take just as much interest in encouraging students to buy books as in encouraging them to buy candy.[13] In one school, profits from the student-run bookstore enabled the school to offer a $500 scholarship to a worthy senior; during the second year, two scholarships were offered.[14] Where administrators have not seen the advisability of encouraging book buying in the school, English teachers have worked with local drugstores to see that books recommended in school are available for purchase. English teachers who are themselves buyers and readers of books can find ways of bringing books and students together.

Introducing books to readers. A book in the hands of a boy or girl is worth two on the shelves of the town or school library. The teacher who can recommend a book, read bits of it, and put it immediately into the outstretched hands of an eager reader has increased the chances that the book will be finished. For many years teachers have tried to develop readers by offering mimeographed lists of required classics which must be obtained at the town library. Enthusiastic readers follow up such recommendations, but many bright students and almost all reluctant readers find in such an approach no challenge to read. Imaginative teachers can think of dozens of ways of introducing students to books. Here are some that have worked:

1. Instead of ordering a copy of a novel for every student in the class, order five copies of six or seven titles and let students exchange books.

2. Establish a classroom library by some of the means just suggested and allow class time for browsing, selecting a book, and starting to read.

3. Plan book talks in which brief and interesting introductions to ten different books are provided during a class period. Read tantalizing bits from some of the books.[15] Allow the students who are interested to borrow the books to read outside of class.

4. Arrange with the school librarian to allow you to select a sampling of books that might suit your students and bring them to your room to allow students to sample and choose.

5. Arrange with the school librarian for a period at least once a month during which your English class may visit the library, exploring and sampling books or reading (*The Literature Sampler*, Secondary Edition, grades 7 through 9, Encyclopaedia Britannica Press, 1962, offers a planned program for such sampling).

[13] Grambs, *op. cit.*, p. 19.
[14] (Herkimer Central School, Herkimer, N.Y.) See Norman R. Lee, *Paperbacks for High School: A Guide for School Bookstores and Classroom Libraries,* Syracuse University Press, Syracuse, N.Y., 1962, p. 29.
[15] A sample of such a book talk is included in the pamphlet, *Richer by Asia,* prepared by a Committee of the Young Adult Services Division of the American Library Association, American Library Association, Chicago, 1959.

6. Invite the librarian into your classroom to give a book talk and to recommend books to your students.

7. Plan with the high school librarian to involve a class in reading widely to decide which books should be bought with money allotted for recreational reading.

8. Provide a "Reading Aloud" bookshelf in your classroom with books of humor, adventure, or other kinds suggested by students for class sharing.

9. Stock a leisure-reading shelf in the classroom with attractive books and encourage students to bring the books they are reading with bookmarks showing where they are. Students who finish their work early may browse on the shelf or pick up the book they are reading and start where they left it last time.

10. Encourage the school to hold a book fair or to install a folding bookstore for the sale of books within the school. Book fairs which can be set up in the school for a day or so provide an important stimulus to reading and book buying. Local jobbers, paperback publishers, or wholesalers will usually arrange such fairs, delivering and collecting the books, and handling business details. Several companies now offer folding bookstores which can be set up in cafeterias or school libraries. Schools sell books, send the companies a percentage of the total, return unsold books for credit, and reorder when necessary.[16]

Stimulating interest.   The teacher who keeps students reading is one who not only knows which books to introduce to the young, but what these books offer that relates directly to the consuming interests of adolescents. The teacher who knows what these are can ask the right questions and guide discussion of books in ways that keep students pursuing their interests with deeper and better books.

Exploration of student interests is a first step for the teacher in helping students find books they will like. Many teachers develop interest inventories to gather such information. Teachers may discover something about reading interests through discussing the choices of girls and of boys for their three favorite books, book characters, kinds of books, magazines, television programs, or movies.[17]

Some teachers prefer informal methods—observing the things boys and girls talk about spontaneously in the classroom, the hobbies, interests, or problems they mention in their themes or in class discussion.

Other means may be used to spark interest in reading books and articles which are available to students. News items about an American family who adopted a Korean war orphan may lead to the reading of Helen Doss' *The*

---

[16] See "Paperbacks Guide," *Studies in the Mass Media,* vol. 4, December, 1963, for suggestions about book fairs. A model design for a folding bookstore may be found in Lee, *op. cit.,* pp. 13–14. See also Alexander Butman (ed.), *Paperbacks in the Schools,* Bantam Books, Inc., New York, 1963.

[17] See Lou La Brant et al. *Your Language, Book 1,* McGraw-Hill Book Company, New York, 1956, p. 87.

Family Nobody Wanted; items about unusual pets can lead to the reading of books about animals. Feature stories about hairbreadth escapes, daring rescues, disaster relief, or the most recent war news, class discussions about social problems, about prejudice, injustice, education, vocational goals or values can lead to the reading of important books if the teacher makes the right suggestions. His job is to seize the moment of interest, recommend reading in which the student can follow those interests, and suggest where copies of the book can be found. Such clues to further reading may lead farther than we think, and the student who is an avid reader may pick up even indirect suggestions. One college student reported that she first read Sigrid Undset because of a sentence she corrected in a grammar exercise which asked, "Have you never read *Kristin Lavransdatter?*"

For teachers who want to create interest in reading, particularly among reluctant readers, some of the following ideas will work. Many of them may be put into operation by students working individually or in committees to prepare files of materials, exhibits, or bulletin boards:

1. With the aid of students, collect back issues of used magazines which can be brought into the schoolroom, used for leisure-time reading, or added to the files for future reference. Copies of *The Atlantic, The Saturday Review, The New Yorker,* or *Harper's* are useful for college-bound classes of older students. For younger students or slow readers, such magazines as *The Reader's Digest, The Saturday Evening Post, Popular Mechanics, Outdoor Life, Field and Stream, Seventeen,* and others are popular. As the magazines become used, the best articles may be clipped and filed in file-sized cartons for other readers.[18] Such articles may lead to the reading of books on the same subject.

2. Make bulletin-board committees responsible for preparing displays to create reading interest. The school or town librarians sometimes contribute discarded book jackets, and magazines may provide illustrations suitable for many types of books—sports, sea or animal stories, romances.

3. Have good readers prepare selected readings from favorite books to record on tape for playing to classes.[19]

4. Work out a class project in which students make out 3 x 5 cards about books they have liked, giving essential information and a personal reaction to the book. A class file built up through student recommendations is an invaluable resource in stimulating reading interest.

5. Divide students into reading-interest groups to prepare a book list of recommended books in various areas: science fiction, sea stories, animal stories, family stories, or adventure. A list may be compiled of titles and annotations signed by the young reviewers and the lists included in a manila or heavy paper folder decorated with an appropriate picture and interest-arousing title.

---

[18] Olive S. Niles and Margaret J. Early, "Adjusting to Individual Differences in English," *Journal of Education,* vol. 138, December, 1955, p. 19.

[19] Oral readings and sociodrama, too, may be used. See Chap. 4, pp. 87–90, for suggestions.

6. Invite to the English classroom or to the school assembly speakers who can interest students in an area they can follow up through reading. Exchange students and teachers from foreign countries can arouse interest about life in the country from which they come. A hall or library exhibit about books dealing with these countries arouses interest in these books. Speakers on travel, on scientific matters, on the humanities, or on social problems can stimulate reading if books are suggested and made available.

7. Follow up television offerings with recommended reading. Travel and adventure programs will stimulate interest in books of this kind; popular current programs such as the shows dealing with doctors, nurses, medicine, lawyers, and scientists can all be used to stimulate interest in biographies or fiction which deal with similar topics. The student who is a fan of Ben Casey or Dr. Kildare may be invited to compare the incidents in these programs with those in the biographies of Albert Schweitzer, Victor Heiser in *American Doctor's Odyssey,* Tom Dooley, or the Mayo Brothers, or in such novels as Lewis' *Arrowsmith* or Cronin's *The Citadel.* Bulletin boards or library exhibits may feature books which tie in with such programs.

8. Keep students informed of plays, novels, short stories, and biographies scheduled for television treatment and encourage the reading of the book before viewing the show. Through such timely suggestions, students have been led to read such plays as Patrick's *Teahouse of the August Moon,* Rostand's *Cyrano de Bergerac,* and Ibsen's *A Doll's House,* and such novels as James' *The Turn of the Screw,* Hemingway's *For Whom the Bell Tolls,* Wilder's *The Bridge of San Luis Rey,* and many Shakespearean plays.[20]

9. Observe the choices students make in ordering from one of the student book clubs or the high interest they show in a book of good current fiction. When five or six students have read the same book, suggest that they present a brief panel discussion on the book for the class, or talk about it with the teacher.

10. In some classes of reluctant readers, few students will own library cards or be familiar with the local library. Many will not know what the inside of a bookstore is like. Teachers often arrange to take such classes to the library for an introductory visit, making it possible for them to explore the resources of the library, take out cards, and become acquainted with the librarians. The library then ceases to be the formidable place it often is for some children.

11. Suggest reading as a follow-up of current movie offerings. *El Cid, Ben Hur, Ivanhoe, Moby Dick, The Old Man and the Sea,* and others have been followed by heavy demands for the books. The World Heritage Film and Book Program offers such a tieup between the film and the book.[21] *A Tale of*

---

[20] See p. 351 for sources of information on programs.
[21] Sponsored by Metro-Goldwyn-Mayer and Scholastic Book Services, 904 Sylvan Avenue, Englewood Cliffs, N.J.

Two Cities, Kim, Captains Courageous, The Good Earth, Julius Caesar, Pride and Prejudice, and others have been among the offerings. Paperback copies of the book are offered through the book clubs at the time the films are shown, and study guides are available for the teachers.

12. "Plant" ideas for writing or discussion which may lead to further reading. Pen-pal or World Tape[22] correspondence may lead through discussion to interest in reading books that describe life in different regions of the country, or in different countries of the world. Some teachers have asked students to write a description of a book they would like to read if someone were to write one to order for them and have recommended books which fit the descriptions. Questions raised in discussions about literature studied in common may lead to suggestions for individual reading. "Did pioneering really involve such hardships as those described in *Giants in the Earth?*" may lead to the reading of Aldrich's *A Lantern in Her Hand,* Lane's *Let the Hurricane Roar,* Richter's *Sea of Grass.* Questions about how it feels to experience prejudice, discrimination, physical handicap, love, adventure, danger, and war lead to books on these topics. Ingenious teachers can add dozens of ways to keep alive the interest in books and to help young people encourage each other to read further.

Guiding growth. The ability of the teacher to offer encouragement and to exert a steady pressure on students to read better and better books is a key factor in the successful direction of individual reading. Without the help and encouragement of someone who can provide information about more challenging books, young readers may continue reading at the same level indefinitely: the same authors, the same types of books, with mediocre books read out of inertia or ignorance. They seek the comfort of the familiar or have difficulty finding other books equally satisfying. Most young people want and need direction and accept it eagerly from an informed teacher who treats their reading interests with respect and who suggests rather than requires certain choices.

Continual individual guidance of this kind is essential. The teacher must be ready to suggest that the boy who can read only Zane Grey westerns may find pleasure in comparing these with some true stories of western ranch life: Moody's *Little Britches,* or Will James' autobiography, *All in the Day's Riding.* Such readers may move on to a biography of Cochise or Wyatt Earp, Schaeffer's *Shane,* or even Clark's *The Ox-Bow Incident.*

The eighth- or ninth-grade girl who is still fascinated by the teen-age dilemmas portrayed by Betty Cavanna or Anne Emery may be urged to move on to adult fiction. Biographies and nonfiction have proved favorites at this age: the Freedmans' *Mrs. Mike,* Louise Dickinson Rich's *We Took to the Woods,* Katherine Pinkerton's *Wilderness Wife,* Anna Perrott Rose's *Room for One More,* or Jade Snow Wong's *Fifth Chinese Daughter.* Adult novels such

[22] See pp. 95 and 155 for details.

as Lewis' *Arrowsmith*, Rose Wilder Lane's *Let the Hurricane Roar*, Dorothy Canfield Fisher's *The Deepening Stream*, Tarkington's *Alice Adams*, and Edna Ferber's *So Big* often provide the kinds of satisfactions the young girl searches for in teen-age fiction.

When students realize that they may read books in the area of a particular interest on different levels of difficulty, they are usually responsive to the suggestion that they move from easier books in one category to those which are more advanced. Usually the teacher's comment "I think you are ready for a more grown-up book; why not try————?" is sufficient challenge. Sometimes the teacher may say, "This book is rather difficult, but I think you might like to try it." Libraries sometimes use the title "Books That Stretch the Mind" for a display of such books.

Most young people enjoy feeling that they can read some of the books adults like. Fortunately some of these are written so that even young readers can understand them. Hersey's *A Bell for Adano*, Michener's *The Bridges of Toko-ri*, Hilton's *Goodbye, Mr. Chips*, Helen Doss' *The Family Nobody Wanted*, Hemingway's *The Old Man and the Sea* and Stuart's *The Thread That Runs So True* can be read by students of seventh-grade level of reading ability.[23] Teachers may also successfully use the lure of competition: students will often struggle to read books too difficult for them if other students they admire are reading them. Finally, boys and girls will attempt books of increasingly greater difficulty if they are engrossed in a subject or a topic. The seven-year-old, eager to use his new microscope, struggles to read an article on chemistry in an adult encyclopedia. The twelve-year-old fascinated by history begs his teacher for "a list of books about the American Revolution," and the boy who wants to be a doctor reads every biography he can find about doctors in action. Girls develop similar intense interests in books about the ballet, about family life, about nursing, about horses, actresses, or famous women; boys about hot rods, hunting, westerns, undersea adventure, and science fiction.

Many teachers use the concept of the "reading ladder" to show students that they may find books on a subject or theme that interests them at three or four different levels of difficulty. The book list, *Reading Ladders for Human Relations*, provides such lists for books on several themes,[24] and the teacher may make up others by using lists which give the recommended grade place-

---

[23] The American Library Association publishes periodically a list of "Easy Adult Books for Slow High School Readers." Suggestions for slow readers are also given in Ruth Strang et al., *Gateways to Readable Books: An Annotated Graded List of Books in Many Fields for Adolescents Who Find Reading Difficult*, The H. W. Wilson Company, New York, 1958. See other references in Chap. 5, p. 121.

[24] See Muriel Crosby (ed.), 4th ed., American Council on Education, Washington, D.C., 1963. The introductory chapters suggesting ways of using books and short stories and questions for discussion are particularly helpful for teachers. The pamphlet, "Literature for Human Understanding," by Hilda Taba et al. illustrates class discussions which can be used with such books. (American Council on Education, Washington, D.C., 1948.)

ment of books. Students wanting to read books about family life may be provided with such a ladder as the following:

Easy Reading.[25] Eleanor Estes: *The Moffats*; Laura Ingalls Wilder: *Little House in the Big Woods*; *On the Banks of Plum Creek*; Louisa May Alcott: *Little Women.*

Intermediate Reading. Helen Doss: *The Family Nobody Wanted*; Gilbreth and Carey: *Cheaper by the Dozen*; Day: *Life with Father*; Ruth McKenney: *My Sister Eileen*; Sally Benson: *Junior Miss*; Marjorie Kinnan Rawlings: *The Yearling.*

Senior Reading. Harper Lee: *To Kill a Mockingbird*; Betty Smith: *A Tree Grows in Brooklyn*; Llewellyn: *How Green Was My Valley*; Jessamyn West: *The Friendly Persuasion*; Pearl Buck: *The Good Earth*; Gladys Hasty Carroll: *As the Earth Turns.*

Mature Reading. Galsworthy: *The Forsyte Saga*; Sigrid Undset: *Kristin Lavransdatter*; Mann: *Buddenbrooks*; Asch: *East River.*

In some classes, students make their own ladders of books on topics that interest them; in others, teacher guidance is frequently directed to helping students move one step up the ladder.

During the class hours set aside for individual reading, the teacher may offer tactful guidance by noting the absorption or indifference with which various young people approach their books, stopping to encourage the reluctant reader by showing interest in his choice, or recommending one or two books as next choices for the student who is reading eagerly. The interest of the teacher in what young people are reading and on-the-spot recommendations are invaluable aids to further reading.

Using reading lists. Reading lists are generally more helpful to the teacher than to the student. Young people need practice in learning how to use published lists. If they check ten or twelve titles they might like to read and find none available in the local libraries, they may become quickly frustrated. Teachers often prefer to make their own lists in order to select books for a particular class and to indicate those which may be found in the school or town library or those available in paperback.

Teachers need to understand and teach students about how lists are compiled and what they are useful for. Frequently the lists are intended to suggest books to be ordered for school or classroom libraries. Sometimes the categories and choices are suggested by the curriculum rather than because they represent the real reading interests of young people. *Quo Vadis* or *Ben*

---

[25] Many kinds of titles of these groupings are possible. Most teachers working with adolescents find it best to use a title which indicates something of reading difficulty without labeling the book "primary reading" or "junior reading." Older students who read below grade level are sensitive about such categories. Most lists should carry some indication of books which should be recommended only to mature readers. The student's emotional and chronological maturity and his previous reading experience will guide the teacher in making recommendations.

Hur may be kept on a list because of the demands of the Latin or the history teacher. Many students prefer to use book lists which represent choices made by adolescents themselves.[26] Class sessions in which students examine and evaluate various lists to determine their purposes, usefulness, and limitations give important help to junior and senior high school students learning to become self-directing readers.[27]

Guiding discussion. Discussion about books must have some structure or it will become random and profitless. Guiding talk about books demands the teacher's greatest skill. In the beginning, students will focus chiefly on plot, as they do in oral book reports. Through skillful questioning, the teacher can lead them to consider the motivation of characters, the problems characters have and the ways they attempt to solve them, or the complications of personality and behavior which lead to conflict.

At the junior high school level, when reading interests are usually widely varied, discussions may lead to an examination of recurring plot patterns in the books about sports, science fiction, or "teen-age romances." Good readers often lead the less observant to notice weaknesses of form, style, or stereotypes of plot and character and to demand more challenging reading.

Such growth is shown in a panel discussion on science fiction by a group of ninth-grade boys. Their questions dealt with comparisons of fiction and fact. They had checked with their science teachers to determine whether some of the incidents described could actually happen and found that some could be verified and others could not. Some, having read as many as forty-five books, had become critical enough to discuss some plot and character stereotypes: "the main character is usually between seventeen and twenty-three and gets by on his brains and courage"; "he is always getting into tight jams he gets out of."

They were aware of similarity in the materials of science fiction: typical situations were space travel, lost kingdoms under the sea, going backward or forward in time, colonizing another planet, or interplanetary visitations. They discussed with interest whether scientists were represented as heroes or villains. Asked by the teacher whether the reading of science fiction had been worthwhile to them, they saw it as valuable in stimulating their interest in checking the differences between scientific fact and fiction and leading them to want to read more nonfiction books of scientific interest. Many felt that these books had interested them in reading more about the possibilities of space travel, of life on other planets, and of scientific invention. Their discussion revealed their growth in literary discrimination between fantasy and realistic fiction, and between characters who were credible and those who were types. They had moved beyond the stage of obsession with fantasy to a critical demand for more intellectually challenging reading.

[26] For instance, *Books We Like,* published by the Illinois English Association, available through the NCTE, and the lists published by the Boys Clubs of America.
[27] See the list of book lists at the end of this chapter.

372 Literature: appreciation, insights, and values

Students gain insight into literature as they learn to look in many types of novels for the conflict of the story, for the way it is resolved, and learn to judge whether the resolution is consistent with the development of character throughout the book. Through applying standards of literary judgment to many novels read by different members of the class, individual readers collect a wide variety of illustrations and grow used to asking these critical questions of themselves as they read. At each grade level, questions for discussion must be phrased in such terms that students can deal with them, but central questions of form and content in the novel can be asked of any books they are reading.

Instead of talking about "style," "climax," "conflict," or "theme," junior high school students look at the novels they read to see whether the way characters talk or behave seems real or resembles the way people they know talk and act. They may discuss at what point of the book things seem to be most tense or exciting, state the central problem in the story, and discuss the way in which it may or may not be solved. For senior high school students, talk about the books they are reading individually can deal with many of the problems of comprehension, form, and appreciation discussed in the intensive reading of a single novel.[28]

Evaluating the individual reading program

Traditionally, tests on literature the class reads together and grades on oral and written book reports have provided the chief instruments of evaluation of response to literature in English programs. Important as they may be in their ways, these forms of measurement tell us little about the student's reading. They do not indicate whether he reads voluntarily, reads much or little, whether he is growing in his ability to read more difficult books, or staying at the same level for months or even years. Neither do they indicate much about whether students are growing in taste, appreciation, and comprehension or whether they are becoming more independent in choosing and judging books.

The questions we really want answered in evaluation of reading are these: Is the student reading more or less than usual? Has he progressed up the reading ladder from easy books to more difficult ones? Has he shown ability to read complex books with more understanding? Has he shown growth in independent choosing of his reading or in planning ahead for what he will read next? Has he developed well-defined reading tastes and interests? We may observe many of these things through listening to him in discussion and through observing his choices, his comments about books, oral or written, and his ability to handle books with unfamiliar settings, characters, or situations. His growing competence with differing types and his understanding of character and of the significance of idea or incident provides additional evidence of growth and maturity in reading.

[28] Such questions are suggested in Chap. 9.

The teacher may glean valuable information about what the student gains from his reading by asking him to write briefly and informally on topics such as the following: "The Best Book I Ever Read," "A Book That Changed My Thinking," "The Best Children's Book I Ever Read," "The Person in Literature I'd Like to Be Like," "A Book That Shocked Me," "A Book Which Helped Me Grow Up," "The First Adult Book I Ever Read," "A Book That Influenced Me." Comments by students on such topics often indicate the role a book plays in changing reading habits, overcoming the antipathy to a long book, or starting a reading interest to be explored later.

One group of high school seniors made these comments: "*Andersonville* has gotten me very interested in books of the Civil War era, and I intend to read as many books about the Civil War as I can." "I liked *A Farewell to Arms* because, for the most part, it takes place in Italy. I am of Italian descent and have heard of many of the places and customs in Italy." "Through reading *The Red Badge of Courage* I think I matured along with Henry as only then did I fully realize how such a thing as war could change a person." "In the reading of *Exodus*, I conquered a fear of long, pagey books and learned of a people and era I had known nothing about." "*Exodus* will influence me never to be prejudiced against anyone regardless of religion, race, color, or creed." "During my junior high school years, I never read a book unless it was assigned. Not so with *Battle Cry*. In the first sitting I read over a hundred pages, which is very unusual. Every spare minute would find my nose in *Battle Cry*, and I read five hundred pages in a week. I enjoyed the book so much that I am going to read *Exodus*."

Some teachers have gained important insights into what books have meant to their students by encouraging them to write their reactions to the book, their honest responses to people and situations. Students freed to write of what the book means to them (avoiding the clichés about style and theme) reveal much of importance about their reading. These papers are invaluable for showing the teacher the growth in basic reading skills and for demonstrating the results of the program to administrators. Checks on growth in comprehension, vocabulary, and reading skills can be made through such instruments as the standardized tests described in Chapter 5.

Self-evaluation

The student's own evaluation of his progress is often more effective and more important to his growth in reading than his scores on standardized or teacher constructed tests. Periodic evaluation, informally written or discussed in conference with the teacher, forces the student to look at his own growth, to take responsibility for improvement. Students may be asked to write evaluations of their own reading at intervals, answering such questions as these: Are you satisfied with your reading during this term? How many books have you read? Are you reaching toward more difficult books? Have you read anything by an author who is new to you? A new type of book? Any books on the

"For Mature Readers" list? Which types of books do you read too much of? Which have you avoided? Are you having difficulty finding books you especially like? What can you do to improve your reading? Which books do you plan to read next? What kind of reading do you feel you need help with? Do you want any recommendations for books to try next?

Such questions may provide suggestions for the student's evaluation. He should not be forced to answer all, but he may attempt to answer most of these for himself and many for the teacher with the understanding that they will be used to help him in planning for his own future reading. It is probable that few youngsters in school ever take an over-all look at their own reading or realize that there are criteria for evaluating it. Where reading can serve to enhance self-respect and contribute to individual development in such a way that the student himself can see his growth, it is likely to be more satisfying and to grow increasingly mature.

Group evaluation

In addition to the individual's study of his reading, most classes will profit from a group evaluation. Booklets, charts, maps giving locations of novels read, and time charts indicating books read representing different periods of history often point up both growth and the limitations of the reading done by the class. Records showing types of books read, authors who are most popular, places read about, books set in different regions or countries, and the number of books the class has read on a list of 100 books recommended as good reading often indicate to the whole group the breadth or provinciality of its reading. Older students and college-bound classes should measure reading critically against college reading lists.

A method both of evaluation and of stimulating further reading is a class card file in which students reading a book make out a card with a brief comment about it. As three or four cards accumulate on a particular book, students will like to compare reactions and perhaps plan a panel discussion on a book which provokes contradictory responses.

The changing tastes of the class during the period of a semester or a year often serves as a good yardstick for the progress of the class in maturity in reading. The real evaluation of growth in a program of this kind may not be made for many years. The test of an individual reading program is whether it produces readers who continue to read long after the school years are over and who remain thoughtful, lifelong readers. One follow-up study of an outstanding program showed that it produced readers who read well above the national average for adults.[29] The most important contribution such a program

---

[29] Evidence of the superior results of an individual reading program in producing mature adult readers is given in the follow-up study of a three-year experiment at Ohio State University High School in Margaret Willis' *The Guinea Pigs after Twenty Years,* Ohio State University Press, Columbus, Ohio, 1962.

can make is to the individual emotional and intellectual development of young people. The assistance it can give in helping them make with assurance and self-confidence the transition from adolescence into maturity will help ensure the development of lifetime reading habits.

A program of thematic units for individual reading: grades 7 to 12 *

Grade 7.   **A Time for Growing**

The family of man

Gilbreth, Frank, and Carey, E. G.:
   Cheaper by the Dozen
Benson, Sally: *Junior Miss*
Day, Clarence: *Life with Father*
Rose, Anna P.: *Room for One More*

Doss, Helen: *The Family Nobody Wanted*
McKenney, Ruth: *My Sister Eileen*
Saroyan, William: *The Human Comedy*
Buck, Pearl: *The Good Earth*
Steinbeck, John: *The Pearl*

Animal lore

Knight, Eric: *Lassie, Come Home*
Salten, Felix: *Bambi*
Henry, Marguerite: *Misty of Chincoteague*
Kjelgaard, Jim: *Big Red*
Gipson, Fred: *Old Yeller*
North, Sterling: *Rascal*

Bagnold, Enid: *National Velvet*
Rawlings, Marjorie Kinnan: *The Yearling*
London, Jack: *The Call of the Wild*
O'Hara, Mary: *My Friend Flicka*
Street, James: *Goodbye, My Lady*
Steinbeck, John: *The Red Pony*

Exploring space

Clarke, Arthur: *Islands in the Sky*
Bradbury, Ray: *The Martian Chronicles*
Heinlein, Robert: *Farmer in the Sky*

L'Engle, Madeleine: *A Wrinkle in Time*
Verne, Jules: *20,000 Leagues under the Sea*
Wells, H. G.: *The War of the Worlds*

Facing handicaps

Baker, Louise: *Out on a Limb*
Killilea, Marie: *Karen*
Keller, Helen: *The Story of My Life*
Putnam, Peter: *"Keep Your Head Up,
   Mr. Putnam"*
Chevigny, Hector: *My Eyes Have a Cold Nose*

Marshall, Alan: *I Can Jump Puddles*
Gunther, John: *Death Be Not Proud*
Mehta, Ved: *Face to Face*
Hathaway, Katherine Butler: *The Little
   Locksmith*

Grade 8.   **Accent on Youth**

Teenagers around the world

Daly, Maureen: *Seventeenth Summer*
Stolz, Mary: *The Seagulls Woke Me*
Gray, E. J.: *Sandy*
Summers, James: *Tougher Than You Think*
Krumgold, Joseph: *. . . And Now Miguel*
Larsson, Gösta: *The Wonderful Boat*

O'Dell, Scott: *Island of the Blue Dolphins*
Pak, Chong-Yong: *Korean Boy*
Ullman, James Ramsey: *Banner in the Sky*
Frank, Anne: *The Diary of a Young Girl*
Af Gejerstam, Gösta: *Northern Summer*
Godden, Rumer: *The River*

* The arrangement is in the approximate order of difficulty.

A program of thematic units for individual reading: grades 7 to 12 (continued)

Enduring hardships

Sperry, Armstrong: *Call It Courage*
Frank, Anne: *The Diary of a Young Girl*
Malvern, Gladys: *Jonica's Island*
Kipling, Rudyard: *Captains Courageous*

Benary-Isbert, Margot: *The Ark*
Williams, Eric: *The Wooden Horse*
Moody, Ralph: *Man of the Family*
Del Castillo, Michel: *Child of Our Time*

American youth

Wouk, Herman: *City Boy*
Steffens, Lincoln: *Boy on Horseback*
McCullers, Carson: *The Member of the Wedding*

Coffin, Robert T.: *Red Sky in the Morning*
North, Sterling: *So Dear to My Heart*
West, Jessamyn: *Cress Delahanty*
Sandburg, Carl: *Always the Young Strangers*

Adjusting to change

Shotwell, Louisa: *Roosevelt Grady*
Wong, Jade Snow: *Fifth Chinese Daughter*
Means, Florence: *Shuttered Windows*
Sone, Monica: *Nisei Daughter*

Richter, Conrad: *Light in the Forest*
Lewiton, Mina: *The Divided Heart*
Moody, Ralph: *Little Britches*
Cronin, A. J.: *The Green Years*

Danger and mystery

Chesterton, G. K.: *The Amazing Adventures of Father Brown*
Scoggin, Margaret: *The Lure of Danger*
Pease, Howard: *The Dark Adventure*

Doyle, Sir Arthur Conan: *The Complete Sherlock Holmes*
Floherty, John: *Men without Fear*

Grade 9. The Many Faces of Courage

The soldier

Tregaskis, Richard: *Guadalcanal Diary*
White, W. L.: *They Were Expendable*
Howarth, David: *We Die Alone*
Trumbull, Robert: *The Raft*

Considine, John, and Lawson, Ted: *Thirty Seconds over Tokyo*
Pyle, Ernie: *Brave Men*
Hersey, John: *Into the Valley*

The civilian in wartime

Hersey, John: *A Bell for Adano*
Frank, Anne: *The Diary of a Young Girl*
Keith, Agnes Newton: *Three Came Home*

DeJong, Dola: *And the Field Is the World*
Klein, Gerda: *All but My Life*

The pioneer

Lane, Rose Wilder: *Let the Hurricane Roar*
Rolvaag, Ole: *Giants in the Earth*

Richter, Conrad: *Sea of Grass*
Aldrich, Bess Streeter: *A Lantern in Her Hand*

A program of thematic units for individual reading: grades 7 to 12 (continued)

The explorer

Balchen, Bernt: *Come North with Me*
Dansing, Alfred: *Endurance*
Dufek, G. J.: *Operation Deepfreeze*
Repplier, Agnes: *Père Marquette*
Kugelmass, J. A.: *Roald Amundsen*

Benét, Laura: *Stanley, Invincible Explorer*
Herzog, Maurice: *Annapurna*
Heyerdahl, Thor: *Kon-Tiki*
Byrd, Richard: *Alone*

The doctor

Dooley, Tom: *The Night They Burned the Mountain; Deliver Us from Evil*
Lewis, Sinclair: *Arrowsmith*
Hilton, James: *The Story of Dr. Wassell*
Baker, Rachel: *The First Woman Doctor*

Grenfell, Wilfred T.: *Forty Years for Labrador*
Heiser, Victor: *An American Doctor's Odyssey*
Seagrave, Gordon: *Burma Surgeon*
Gollomb, Joseph: *Genius of the Jungle*

Those who achieved

Saint-Exupéry, Antoine de: *Night Flight; Wind, Sand, and Stars*
Curie, Eve: *Madame Curie*
Eaton, Jeannette: *Gandhi: Fighter without a Sword*

Oursler, Fulton: *Father Flanigan of Boys' Town*
Roos, Anne: *Man of Molokai*
Kennedy, John: *Profiles in Courage*

Grade 10. A World I Never Made

The search for identity

Conrad, Joseph: *The Secret Sharer; Lord Jim*
McCullers, Carson: *The Heart Is a Lonely Hunter*
Wolfe, Thomas: *Look Homeward, Angel*

Salinger, J. D.: *The Catcher in the Rye*
Joyce, James: *A Portrait of the Artist as a Young Man*

The fall from innocence

Golding, William: *Lord of the Flies*
Knowles, John: *A Separate Peace*
Steinbeck, John: *The Pearl*

Lee, Harper: *To Kill a Mockingbird*
Salinger, J. D.: *The Catcher in the Rye*
Conrad, Joseph: *Heart of Darkness*

The fight against prejudice

Tunis, John: *A City for Lincoln*
Jackson, Jesse: *Call Me Charley*
Thompson, Era Bell: *American Daughter*
Kugelmass, J. A.: *Ralph Bunche: Fighter for Peace*

Anderson, Marian: *My Lord What a Morning*
Embree, Edwin: *Thirteen against the Odds*
White, Walter: *A Man Called White*
Uris, Leon: *Exodus*
King, Martin Luther: *Stride toward Freedom*

A program of thematic units for individual reading: grades 7 to 12 (continued)

The search for a life of significance

Landon, Margaret: *Anna and the King of Siam*
Stuart, Jesse: *The Thread That Runs So True*
Lewis, Sinclair: *Arrowsmith*

Bartholomew, Carol: *My Heart Has Seventeen Rooms*
Gibson, William: *The Miracle Worker*
Najafi, Najmeh: *Reveille in a Persian Village*

The face of war

Maclean, Alistair: *Guns of Navarone*
Michener, James: *The Bridges at Toko-ri, The Bridge at Andau*
Hersey, John: *Hiroshima*
Remarque, Erich: *All Quiet on the Western Front*
Crane, Stephen: *The Red Badge of Courage*
Uris, Leon: *Battle Cry*

Hemingway, Ernest: *A Farewell to Arms; For Whom the Bell Tolls*
Shaw, Irwin: *The Young Lions*
Wouk, Herman: *The Caine Mutiny*
Boulle, Pierre: *The Bridge on the River Kwai*
Lord, Walter: *Day of Infamy*
Cozzens, James Gould: *Guard of Honor*

Grade 11. America Is Promises

America contains many diverse groups

Edell, Celeste: *A Present for Rosita*
Sterling, Dorothy: *Mary Jane*
Saroyan, William: *My Name Is Aram*
Housepian, Marjorie: *A Houseful of Love*
Forbes, Kathryn: *Mama's Bank Account*
Papashvily, George and Helen: *Anything Can Happen*
Cather, Willa: *My Antonia; O Pioneers*
Wong, Jade Snow: *Fifth Chinese Daughter*

Asch, Sholem: *East River*
Farrell, James: *No Star Is Lost*
Sinclair, Jo: *Wasteland*
Kazin, Alfred: *A Walker in the City*
Heyward, DuBose: *Porgy*
LaFarge, Oliver: *Laughing Boy; The Enemy Gods*
Rizk, Salom: *Syrian Yankee*
West, Jessamyn: *The Friendly Persuasion*

Americans live in diverse regions

Stuart, Jesse: *Hie to the Hunters*
Annixter, Paul: *Swiftwater*
Steinbeck, John: *Of Mice and Men*
Lewis, Sinclair: *Main Street*
Fisher, Dorothy Canfield: *Hillsboro People*
Guthrie, A. G.: *The Big Sky*
Chase, Mary Ellen: *Silas Crockett*
Jewett, Sarah Orne: *The Country of the Pointed Firs*

Sandburg, Carl: *Always the Young Strangers*
Marquand, John: *The Late George Apley*
Walker, Mildred: *Winter Wheat*
Erdman, Grace Loula: *The Edge of Time*
Suckow, Ruth: *The Folks*
Smith, Betty: *A Tree Grows in Brooklyn*

A program of thematic units for individual reading: grades 7 to 12 (continued)

America deals with social problems

Steinbeck, John: *The Grapes of Wrath*
Petry, Ann: *The Street*
Baldwin, James: *Notes of a Native Son; The Fire Next Time*
Farrell, James: *Studs Lonigan*

Sinclair, Upton: *The Jungle*
Dreiser, Theodore: *An American Tragedy*
Faulkner, William: *Intruder in the Dust*
Wright, Richard: *Black Boy*

America deals with racial and religious tensions

Lee, Harper: *To Kill a Mockingbird*
Hobson, Laura: *Gentlemen's Agreement*
Graham, Gwethalyn: *Earth and High Heaven*

Sinclair, Jo: *Wasteland*
Hansberry, Lorraine: *A Raisin in the Sun*
Hughes, Langston: *Not without Laughter*

The not-so-ugly Americans

Lederer, W. J., and Burdick, Eugene: *The Ugly American*
Cole, Samuel: *Preacher with a Plow*
Dooley, Tom: *The Night They Burned the Mountain*

Vining, E. G.: *Windows for the Crown Prince*
Buck, Pearl: *Fighting Angel*
Bowles, Cynthia: *At Home in India*
Seagrave, Gordon: *Burma Surgeon*

Grade 12. The World Is Wide

The shadow of the future

Wells, H. G.: *The War of the Worlds*
Huxley, Aldous: *Brave New World*
Shute, Nevil: *On the Beach*

Frank, Pat: *Alas, Babylon*
Golding, William: *Lord of the Flies*
Orwell, George: *1984*

Men, women, and marriage

Wharton, Edith: *Ethan Frome*
Maugham, Somerset: *Of Human Bondage*
Ibsen, Henrik: *A Doll's House*
Hardy, Thomas: *The Return of the Native; Tess of the d'Urbervilles*
Galsworthy, John: *The Forsyte Saga*

James, Henry: *The Portrait of a Lady*
Austen, Jane: *Pride and Prejudice*
Marquand, John: *H. M. Pulham, Esquire*
Flaubert, Gustave: *Madame Bovary*
Undset, Sigrid: *Kristin Lavransdatter*
Bennett, Arnold: *The Old Wives' Tale*

Parents and children

Marquand, John: *B. F.'s Daughter*
Miller, Arthur: *Death of a Salesman*
Farrell, James: *Father and Son*
Lawrence, D. H.: *Sons and Lovers*
Balzac, Honoré de: *Père Goriot*

Butler, Samuel: *The Way of All Flesh*
Meredith, George: *The Ordeal of Richard Feverel*
Turgenev, Ivan: *Fathers and Sons*
Mann, Thomas: *Buddenbrooks*

A program of thematic units for individual reading: grades 7 to 12 (continued)

Political and social change

Dinesen, Isak: *Out of Africa*

Orwell, George: *Animal Farm*

Saghal, Nayantara: *Prison and Chocolate Cake*

Chang, Eileen: *The Rice Sprout Song*

Paton, Alan: *Cry, the Beloved Country*

Sholokhov, Mikhail: *The Quiet Don*

Silone, Ignazio: *Bread and Wine*

Malraux, André: *Man's Fate*

Tolstoi, Leo: *War and Peace*

Suyin, Han: *Destination Chungking*

Koestler, Arthur: *Darkness at Noon*

Pasternak, Boris: *Dr. Zhivago*

Forster, E. M.: *A Passage to India*

Social and economic injustice

Dickens, Charles: *Oliver Twist; Bleak House*

Steinbeck, John: *The Grapes of Wrath*

Zola, Emile: *Germinal*

Hugo, Victor: *Les Misérables*

Sinclair, Upton: *The Jungle*

Solzhenitsyn, Alexander: *One Day in the Life of Ivan Denisovich*

Koestler, Arthur: *Darkness at Noon*

Shaw, Les: *Rickshaw Boy*

Markandaya, Kamala: *Nectar in a Sieve*

Man's search for faith

Marshall, Catherine: *A Man Called Peter*

Greene, Graham: *The Heart of the Matter; The Power and the Glory*

Maugham, Somerset: *The Razor's Edge*

Merton, Thomas: *The Seven Storey Mountain*

Lagervist, Pär: *Barrabas*

Lewis, C. S.: *The Screwtape Letters*

Liebman, Joshua: *Peace of Mind*

Yutang, Lin: *The Wisdom of China and India*

Schweitzer, Albert: *Out of My Life and Thought*

MacLeish, Archibald: *J. B.*

Shaw, G. B.: *Saint Joan*

Bolt, Robert: *A Man for All Seasons*

Eliot, T. S.: *Murder in the Cathedral*

Selected bibliography

Dwight L. Burton, *Literature Study in the High School,* rev. ed., Holt, Rinehart and Winston, Inc., New York, 1964.

Jean D. Grambs (ed.), "The Development of Lifetime Reading Habits," R. R. Bowker Company, New York, 1954. A report of a conference published for the National Book Committee.

Lou La Brant, *We Teach English,* Harcourt, Brace & World, Inc., New York, 1951.

Walter Loban et al., *Teaching Language and Literature: Grades 7–12,* Harcourt, Brace & World, Inc., New York, 1961, chaps. 6 and 7.

George Norvell, *The Reading Interests of Young People,* D. C. Heath and Company, Boston, 1950. A useful study to direct selection of books for young people.

Jacob M. Price (ed.), *Reading for Life: Developing the College Student's Lifetime Reading Interest,* The University of Michigan Press, Ann Arbor, Mich., 1960.

Esther Rauschenbush, *Literature for Individual Education,* Columbia University Press, New York, 1942.

Aids for selecting books for adolescents

A Basic Book Collection for High Schools, regularly revised. American Library Association, Chicago.

A Basic Book Collection for Junior High Schools, regularly revised. American Library Association, Chicago.

The Booklist and Subscription Books Bulletin, American Library Association, Chicago.

Books for the Teen Age, issued annually. New York Public Library, New York.

Books for You, an annotated book list for the senior high school, periodically revised, NCTE, Champaign, Ill. 1964 edition published by Washington Square Press, Pocket Books, Inc., New York.

Books We Like, Illinois English Bulletin, vol. 42, February, 1955, Urbana, Illinois. A reading list of books endorsed and annotated by high school students.

Otis W. Coan and Richard G. Lillard, *America in Fiction: An Annotated List of Novels That Interpret Aspects of Life in the United States,* 4th ed., Stanford University Press, Stanford, Calif., 1957.

College and Adult Reading List of Books in Literature and the Fine Arts, Washington Square Press, Pocket Books, Inc., New York, 1962.

Committee of the Young Adult Services Division, American Library Association, *African Encounter: A Selected Bibliography of Books, Films, and Other Materials for Promoting an Understanding of Africa among Young Adults,* American Library Association, Chicago, 1963.

Muriel Crosby (ed.), *Reading Ladders for Human Relations,* 4th ed., American Council on Education, Washington, D.C., 1963.

Good Books: Recommended Cadet Reading, Department of English, United States Air Force Academy, Colorado Springs, Colorado, 1960.

Jean Carolyn Roos, *Patterns for Reading: An Annotated Book List for Young Adults,* American Library Association, Chicago, 1961.

Eleanor Walker (ed.), *Book Bait: Detailed Notes on Adult Books Popular with Young People,* American Library Association, Chicago, 1957. Book list compiled for Association of Young People's Librarians.

J. Sherwood Weber (ed.), *Good Reading,* Mentor Books, New American Library of World Literature, Inc., New York, 1964.

Your Reading, an annotated book list for the junior high school, periodically revised. NCTE, Champaign, Ill.

CHAPTER 16

Wondrous the English language, language of live men,

Language of ensemble, powerful language of resistance,

Language of a proud and melancholy stock, and of all who
aspire,

Language of growth, faith, self-esteem, rudeness, justice,
friendliness, prudence, decision, exactitude, courage.

WALT WHITMAN [1]

Planning the year's work

The need for a sequential program

For the English teacher, intelligent planning proceeds from a clear concept of the goals of the English program and an understanding of the adolescents in the classes for which he will plan learning activities. Often, the course of study is determined by the choice of novels and plays that has been made beforehand, but even within the narrow restrictions of such a course of study there is always room for and need for planning.

The teacher must determine the order and method of teaching and adapt materials to particular classes. Through such planning, he gains the confidence that the teacher who is only a step ahead of his class cannot enjoy. Well-organized materials, clearly defined goals, and an ordered sequence of activities provides security for both students and instructor. The teacher whose work is properly organized gains control of his classes and is able to communicate to students his command of his subject.[2] Plans do not force the teacher into rigid patterns of instruction or deprive him of freedom and spontaneity; they

---

[1] "As I Sat Alone" (1856).

[2] Teachers who must take a position at short notice will gain security from a short-term plan—even for a week—while they prepare for the rest of the semester or the year.

rather increase his flexibility by providing a point of return from digressions.

Studies of the learning process tell us that students learn best and retain most when they can fit their newly acquired learnings into an ordered structure of experience. The best planning provides sequential and interrelated learning experiences which allow students to see where they are going and to understand what they have accomplished as the term progresses. Such an organization makes learning meaningful and memorable.

The examination of the learning process in Chapter 2 and its implications for adolescents (page 36) points out some basic concepts for planning curricula and units.

Clarifying objectives

Intelligent program planning in English requires a clear idea of teaching objectives as they are conceived of in modern educational theory. The new emphasis on programmed instruction, demanding a knowledge of the sequential steps of learning and of the ends toward which teaching and testing are directed, has forced educators to formulate a clear definition of the objectives of teaching. One of the most significant statements comes from the Committee of College and University Examiners who were charged with the responsibility of formulating a theoretical framework to clarify the relations between testing and education. The committee listed these objectives as significant: the acquisition of knowledge; the development of intellectual abilities and skills (problem solving, critical thinking, etc.); the cultivation of the ability to abstract, analyze, synthesize, and evaluate.[3] These skills and abilities are a subject of study among teachers and groups engaged in curriculum planning.

The units, lessons, curriculum designs, and tests suggested in this chapter emphasize the kinds of processes in learning which leaders in the profession feel should become an integral part of the curriculum: knowledge of the structure of a subject, critical thinking and problem solving, the development of basic concepts about a subject through inductive procedures, the observation of relationships between subjects and recurrent themes in literature and the arts.[4] The teacher who is aware of these objectives has a clearer idea of the way to structure classwork in order to achieve these ends. The curriculum-study centers of Project English and the summer institutes and in-service workshops for teachers sponsored by NCTE and the CEEB have provided direction for individuals and groups charged with the responsibility of planning new curricula. At these study centers, college and high school teachers of

---

[3] See Benjamin S. Bloom (ed.), *Taxonomy of Educational Objectives*, Longmans, Green & Co., Inc., New York, 1954.

[4] See Northrop Frye (ed.), *Design for Learning*, University of Toronto Press, Toronto, Canada, 1962; Jerome S. Bruner (ed.), *The Process of Education*, Harvard University Press, Cambridge, Mass., 1960; and the series of volumes published by the Commission on the Curriculum of the NCTE. See Chap. 1, p. 7.

384 Literature: appreciation, insights, and values

English cooperate in sharing ideas about the aims, purposes, content, and methods of the English program.[5]

What planning involves

At whatever point the teacher starts planning, he must keep in mind that the year's work for his class represents part of a larger design—a three-year junior or senior high school sequence or, as is becoming more common, an uninterrupted six-year course. He must also have a thorough acquaintance with the state course of study in English, as well as that prescribed for his town, school, and grade level. This is essential information for the teacher in order to avoid needless duplication and waste of time in teaching units of study or pieces of literature allocated elsewhere in the curriculum. For the beginning teacher, planning will probably mean outlining a flexible general framework with some fixed units, activities, and tests, and filling in details when he knows the classes he will have.

Planning is a matter of timing and classroom management. Without a feasible timetable, the teacher will find the term ended before he has finished the work outlined in the course of study. He may find grading sheets or report cards due before sufficient evidence for grades has been accumulated. Many a teacher has discovered at the end of the first semester that students have not had much work in spelling, vocabulary work, or writing, and that nearly half a year has been spent on the colonial period in American literature.

Planning before the year begins

An important part of the teacher's planning takes place before he outlines specific lessons or units, and often before he knows what classes he will have. A study of materials, resources, and course outlines will provide the limits within which he must work during the year. Such planning includes the following:

Examining the syllabus. A careful examination of the course of study, if there is one, should reveal what work in literature, language, and composition is to be covered in each class. A study of the six-year syllabus, if one exists, can tell the teacher something about what work his students will have had, and what they will take up in the following year. He should learn, too, how rigidly he must adhere to the course of study, and where he will be permitted to choose his own materials.

Exploring resources. The teacher will want to know as much as he can about the availability of books in the school and town library, what the book-

---

[5] See the discussion of such resources for the teacher outlined in Chap. 1, pp. 19–20.

room contains, whether reference materials, films, projectors, and other equipment are available in the school or in the town, and how he may make arrangements for their use. He should learn something about the community and its students, the kinds of guidance and social services provided by school or town, and the consultant services available in state or regional centers.

Planning before meeting the class.   Planning before meeting the class involves the teacher in selecting a range of literary materials which might interest groups such as those assigned to him. He may include in his plan a sequence of lessons in writing and the study of language and decide what kinds of speaking activities the class will carry on: panel discussions, committee projects, and individual reports. Refinements, changes, additions, and deletions from these general plans may be made following the first meetings with the class and acquaintance with the students in these groups.

In most schools there will be a schedule for major pieces of literature required by the course of study. If the teacher knows that his class will use the copies of *Hamlet* during the first half of the third marking period, he can arrange to plan reading and writing assignments accordingly. He will probably want to sketch in the preliminary plan the number of themes he will require during the year, class time to be allotted for reading and discussion of books, or a unit for which he has prepared materials.

Setting long-range goals.   Even without knowing the individuals in the particular groups of students he will meet in September, the teacher may begin to determine, long before that time, some of the major materials and activities he will want to use during the year. He may find it useful to draw up a time chart, blocked out into marking periods, on which he fills in what he will want to do in each of his classes during the major time divisions of the year.

During the early days of the term he can find out much about his students through informal speaking and writing activities and discussions of reading tastes, vocational goals, and leisure-time activities. Some teachers draw up charts containing the names of all the students and the kinds of usage problems or difficulties with mechanics and sentence structure which are most frequent with them. Often the student may keep such records himself on a page in his notebook.[6] From such diagnostic procedures the teacher can find out the students' major difficulties and begin to plan work which will help with the most serious problems.

The broad outlines for any course will cover work in composition; the reading of literature, both group and individual; the study of language, including vocabulary work and the conventions of punctuation, spelling, grammar, and usage; speaking activities; and practice in listening. Topics to be considered in planning are the best means of developing taste and appreciation in literature, ways of increasing power and command over language, the kinds

[6] See Fig. 16-1.

Figure 16-1 A sample "error grid" for student themes. The numbers refer to types of errors, and the student keeps a record of frequency of his errors as they occur: run-on sentences, fragments, comma errors, and other mistakes in grammar, spelling, paragraphing, or punctuation. From Eric W. Johnson, "Stimulating and Improving Writing in the Junior High School," *English Journal*, vol. 47, February, 1958, pp. 68–77.

1	2	3	4	5	6	7	8	9	10	11	12	13	14	15	16	17	18	19	20	21	22	23	24	25	26	27	28	29	30	31	32	33	34
		MARKS				SPELLING														COMMAS													
DATE	SUBJECT	CONTENT	SPELLING	GRAMMAR	OTHER	coming	tries	ie‑ei	stopped	undone	OTHER	¶	cap.‑l.c.	K	ref.	rep.	r.‑o	frag.	w. o.	1. yes,	2.,Jim,	3. May 1,	4. introd.	5. appos.	6. said,	7. series	OTHER	•	can't	John's	∧		
10/7	Tying a shoe	III	III	II		⫽		/	⫽		⫽⫽	/	⫽		/	⫽ /	⫽	/	/	⫽			/		/	///	⫽	/	/	///	⫽		
10/12	Monkey at zoo	II	III	IV		⫽ /	/	///			/// ⫽		⫽			/// /	/// /	⫽		///		/	/			/// /	/// ///	⫽ /	/				
10/17	Never again	II	III	IV		///		///	/		/// ///		///		/	⫽ /	/// ⫽	/		/// /		/	/	⫽		⫽	/	/	⫽	⫽ /	⫽		

of materials which will challenge students to develop writing skills. The teacher will want to plan the reading activities to allow for teaching basic skills, class reading for appreciation, and individual reading.

Some kinds of reading should come early in the year—probably short stories—paving the way for the more complex forms of the novel, the play, and the poem. Working always from the simple to the complex, the teacher plans in these ways the major outlines of the year's work.

Involving students in the planning.   Students are seldom consulted about their own needs and goals, yet most have well-defined and very sound ideas about what these are. Those who have a chance to share in the planning usually become much more deeply involved in their work and assume more responsibility for their own learning than those who follow a plan made for them. Although the teacher must assume final responsibility for over-all planning, the students, within limits, can offer valuable suggestions as to their needs for work in reading, writing, and speaking.[7]

Getting students to think through their goals, to have even a small voice in determining what they shall learn, and to identify the work they need inevitably has a salutary effect on student attitude. Adolescents are realists. They neither need nor want to plan their own programs, but they do appreciate being given even a small element of choice in what they will study.

Teachers may learn much if students are given a chance to express honestly their evaluation of activities which have most and least value for them. One study of students' opinions about English showed that non-college-preparatory students prefer many of the English activities which offer variety and freedom from the textbook. Both boys and girls rated as most useful such activities as taking part in introductions and conversations, conquering fear of giving talks before the class, and increasing vocabulary.[8]

Students may be asked at the beginning of the year to suggest ideas for projects and units they would like to study and to outline the kinds of work they need. Those which seem of value to both students and teacher may be considered for classwork. If there are several proposals for topics of nearly equal value, students may be allowed to make the final choice. Chapters 4 and 6 suggest numerous other ways in which students can assume responsibility for classroom routines of checking assignments, papers, and books and managing bulletin boards.

Planning instructional units

When the teacher has blocked out the plan in rough form for the year's work, he is ready to start planning instructional units in some detail. The new

[7] See also Chap. 4, pp. 79–81.
[8] "Opportunities for Enterprise in the Teaching of English," in Olive S. Niles and Margaret J. Early, "Adjusting to Individual Differences in English," *Journal of Education,* vol. 138, December, 1955, p. 64.

teacher may want to plan only one unit for the first year of teaching. He may work that one out carefully, developing plans, exploring resources, reading widely to collect materials which will be useful to his students. As the years go by, he will want to add new units each year until he has many resources and unit plans ready for adaptation to individual classes.

Designing a thematic unit around an idea expressed in several novels, plays, short stories, or poems clarifies for students the various ways man has expressed his most important ideas and shows the existence of universal themes in literature that transcend time and form.[9] The numerous suggestions for reading units given in the previous chapter may suggest to the new teacher a topic for reading which will allow students to choose books according to their interests and to discuss these choices. From time to time they will write papers about their reactions to the reading.

The term *unit*, used with many meanings in the teaching profession, refers to a unified series of lessons planned around a topic, theme, a type of literature, or the development of a skill. Some teachers speak of a unit on language or composition, meaning a period of four to six weeks spent on a series of related lessons devoted to a single language skill: writing, speaking, or reading. Others develop units centered on the study of the newspaper or the development of taste in television and the movies, the study of a single literary type—poetry or short stories, or a single work of literature—a Shakespearean play or a novel.

Today many teaching units are centered around the study of a topic ("Growing Up," "Family Life around the World," or "Famous Americans") or the reading interests of young people (animal stories, humor, adventure). The thematic unit, in which students explore a literary theme or idea expressed in many literary forms, has become increasingly popular, especially with Advanced Placement and honors classes. Such units include topics like "The Search for Identity," "The Consequences of Evil," or "The Individual and Society." One such course, an eleventh-year curriculum planned in thematic units, centers around four major themes for the year, and includes books read in common and materials from which students may select readings (Table 16-1). Other such thematic units are suggested in Chapters 12, 13, and 15.

A good unit plan gives the superior student freedom to move ahead, working at his own pace on challenging topics, while the less able student works to the limit of his capacity, contributing what he has learned from the reading of less difficult materials.

Many student-teachers are required to write unit plans for their courses in methods of teaching English or their student teaching. Such a plan usually includes the following features: a preface indicating the grade level and range of abilities of the class for which it is designed; the time to be allotted to the study; a clear descriptive statement of the scope, purposes and content of the

[9] See discussion of unit teaching in Chap. 1, p. 11, and the thematic units suggested in Chap. 15, p. 356.

unit; a list of clearly defined objectives, including the topics the unit will cover and the skills it will develop; a list of the materials and resources to be used; a description of the way the unit will be introduced to the class; a list of the activities, group and individual, through which the objectives will be reached are also included; and, finally, the kinds of evaluation which will be made.

The same unit may be taught at differing levels of ability by adapting the reading materials and topics for discussion to the students in the class. Thus, a unit on "Family Life," commonly taught at the seventh- or eighth-grade level, and using such books as *Cheaper by the Dozen, Life with Father, As the Earth Turns*, or *Mama's Bank Account*, might well be adapted for much older students by using books as Lawrence's *Sons and Lovers*, Galsworthy's *The Forsyte Saga*, Mann's *Buddenbrooks*, and Asch's *East River*.

Choosing the unit topic places important responsibilities on the teacher. Unless the topic or theme chosen is suitable for the ability of the students, it may not lead to broadened interests, wider reading, and growth in language skills. Some units are too easy to challenge a class to read and think. An over-emphasis on topics of teen-age interest can keep students reading books they should have outgrown and result in discussion of matters of minor importance.

Whereas some such "teen-age" units may be valuable at the seventh- or eighth-grade levels, they should be replaced by problems of greater significance by the time students are in senior high school.

A unit, however interesting, is of little value unless it contributes solidly to the intellectual development of the students engaged in its work. Deciding on a theme which can lead to maximum growth in all areas of the language arts is of major importance in successful unit teaching.

Defining the scope of the unit.   Constructing units calls for careful planning of the objectives, information, and skills to be taught. In a twelfth-grade unit on "The Individual's Search for Values" students may (1) explore a range of values by which men have lived in the past; (2) read in contemporary literature and philosophy to define the chief values men seem to live by in the twentieth century; (3) evaluate the values discovered through reading to determine which seem most permanent and worthwhile; (4) clarify their own values or philosophy by which to live.

The teacher also defines specifically the topics and skills which the unit aims to cover and develop. An eighth-grade unit on "Who Are Americans?" may suggest the following: understanding the kind of life from which the families settling America have come, the kinds of adjustments immigrants must make, and the experiences of discrimination they encounter. Such a unit may work on several of the basic reading skills: learning to skim rapidly for essential facts, to increase vocabularies, and to read regional dialect with comprehension.

Introducing the unit.   The unit plan describes the way in which the teacher introduces the unit to the class. Sometimes an interesting bulletin-

Table 16-1. Outline of Eleventh-year English Curriculum

Theme	Key books	Additional honor-class books	Large-group lectures	Partial list of additional materials
Is there a pattern?	Our Town Moby Dick The Bridge of San Luis Rey and two outside book reports	The Flies No Exit Caligula Mourning Becomes Electra Hedda Gabler	Sources of T. Wilder What is man? Symbolism Classicism: Literature Art Music Greek mind and Greek thought Determinism: in historical theory, in scientific theory TV Humanities Films	To Wilder, "Thoughts on Playwriting" Interview of T. Wilder by R. Goldstone Sartre, "Existentialism" W. James, "The Will to Believe" Excerpts from Camus, "The Myth of Sisyphus" D. Thomas, "And Death Shall Have No Dominion" Velasquez and Titian paintings I Pagliacci by Leoncavallo Excerpts from Aristotle, Poetics and Ethics; readings on Greek background, example: Edith Hamilton, The Greek Way "Abstraction in Art" Tenets of Classicism

Topic	Readings
Interpersonal communication problems in man's modern society	Anderson, *Winesburg, Ohio* Miller, *Death of a Salesman* Lewis, *Babbitt* Carson McCullers, *The Heart Is a Lonely Hunter* (read out of class) One additional book report
Three types of man as defined by Riesman in *The Lonely Crowd*	T. S. Eliot, "The Hollow Men" Excerpts from Masters, *Spoon River Anthology* Excerpts from Hawthorne, "Ethan Brand," and Whitman, "I Hear America Singing" Fearing, "American Rhapsody" Excerpts from Kazin, *On Native Grounds* Excerpts from I. Howe, *Sherwood Anderson* Excerpts from Schevill, *Sherwood Anderson* Excerpts from *Huckleberry Finn* Rodin, *The Thinker* Story of David in the Bible Wagner, *Parsifal*, story and music Van Gogh paintings Excerpts from Thoreau, *Walden* Excerpts from Riesman, *The Lonely Crowd* Chapter 18, Ayn Rand, *The Fountainhead* Thoreau, "Plea for John Brown"
Psychologists on the problem of communication	

Table 16-1. Outline of Eleventh-year English Curriculum (Continued)

Theme	Key books	Additional honor-class books	Large-group lectures	Partial list of additional material
Men in Conflict	Thoreau, "Civil Disobedience" Thoreau, Walden Ibsen, Enemy of the People and two outside book reports	Camus, The Plague	Transcendentalism Pragmatism "The Great Chain of Being" in Shakespeare, More, Burke, etc.	Excerpts from Emerson, "Self-Reliance" Excerpts from Brooks, The Flowering of New England Excerpts from Spiller, Cycle of American Literature, Parrington, Main Currents in American Thought, Matthiessen, The American Renaissance, and Literature and the American Tradition Eliot, "The Love Song of J. Alfred Prufrock" Emerson, "The Transcendentalist" S. Paul, "Resolution at Walden" Milton, "On His Blindness" Paintings and artistic position of Whistler, Rouault, and the Futurists Excerpts, Fischer, Gandhi Excerpts, Tolstoi's letters to Gandhi Excerpts, More, Utopia Excerpts, Burke, The Real Social Contract Excerpts, Shakespeare, Troilus and Cressida and Richard II Excerpts, Kant, "The Metaphysics of Morals" Excerpts, Milton, "Aereopagitica" Arguments for censorship of the press (Every student reads and does some critical research on Hamlet)

Individual in Search of His Identity	(read outside of class)		Excerpts from critical material on *Hamlet*
Hamlet	O'Neill, *The Great God Brown*	Huckleberry Finn—two lectures	Brownfield, "Comfort Is a Thing Called Friends"
Huckleberry Finn	Salinger, "For Esme—with Love and Squalor"	*Hamlet*—critical theories and debates	Suspended explanation of J. D. Salinger
The Catcher in the Rye and one additional book report			"Love Calls Us to the Things of This World"
Also—Salinger, "A Perfect Day for Banana Fish"		Catcher—taught in large groups by the senior teacher	Chapter from Hesse, *Siddhartha*, "The Awakening"
			Excerpts from Saint-Exupéry, *The Little Prince*
			Cummings, "Pity This Busy Monster Manunkind"
			Excerpts from Ferlinghetti, *A Coney Island of the Mind*
			Donne, "No Man Is an Island"
			Carson McCullers, "A Tree, A Rock, A Cloud"
			The Sermon on the Mount
			Pound, "Ballad of the Goodly Fere"
			Excerpts from O'Neill, *The Great God Brown*
			Frost, "The Road Not Taken"

SOURCE: Peggy R. Meisel, "An English Curriculum for the Eleventh Grade," *English Journal*, vol. 52, March, 1963, pp. 186–195. (Details of the plan are explained in the article.)

board display or attractive reading materials on the reading table may arouse students' curiosity about the reading to be done. At times the teacher's reading of a brief selection to the class stimulates interest in reading about certain problems.

Teachers have used some of the following kinds of introductions to units:

. . . Bulletin boards featuring clippings, book jackets, pictures, and articles designed to arouse interest in the topic to be studied.

. . . The reading of a short story, poem, or challenging article to arouse interest in the subject of the unit. One teacher led a class into a unit on the topic "Immigrants into Americans" through reading Robert Lawson's *They Were Strong and Good* (The Viking Press, Inc., New York, 1940). Discussion of the book led to curiosity about the countries from which the students' parents had come and the experiences of new immigrants to America.

. . . An exploration of student tastes in television has led into a unit on understanding and appreciating good dramatic offerings on television.

Creative teachers watch for class interest in significant topics and capitalize on situations which suggest the need for further work in an important area.

Among the materials recently developed for teachers planning thematic units are the following:

Bantam Learning Units, Bantam Books, Learning Units Division, New York. These include *How to Read a Play: Introduction to Drama, The Art of Drama; How to Read, Study, and Enjoy the Short Story: An Introduction; The Art of the Short Story; The American Novel: Melville, Dreiser, and McCullers; Introduction to Russian Literature; Youth and Society;* and *The Individual and Society.*

Scholastic Literature Units, Scholastic Book Services, New York. Among these are units on *The Family, Animals, Moments of Decision, Frontiers, Mirrors, Survival,* and *The Lighter Side.* Both *Scholastic* and *Bantam Units* include a bookshelf of paperback books for the class.

Other useful resources are the paperback Literary Heritage series of the Macmillan Company that is organized around both periods of literature and types—short stories, drama, nonfiction, and poetry. The units in *Understanding the Novel: A Seminar Approach,* of Doubleday and Company, offer another type of reading unit, based on comprehensive and close reading of the novel.

Unit activities. The work of the unit usually involves the student in most of the language activities in the English program. Among the most important of these are reading (both selections read by the class as a whole and books, articles, and other pieces read by individuals and chosen because of interest) and writing (brief reports on outside reading or compositions in which the student analyzes his reaction to a piece of literature he has read).

Listening activities usually include listening to recordings of works of literature or to records or tapes of materials related to the topic of the unit. There should be ample opportunity for students to speak as they carry on the work of the unit: panel discussions on literary topics, individual reports on reading, oral reading of scenes from a play or a novel, tape recording of student discussions, role playing and dramatization of scenes from books, or choral speaking. Language study, too, is usually closely related to the work of the unit, as students listen critically to speeches to improve usage and examine their papers for form, content, mechanics, and expression.

Culminating activities. Many plans attempt to synthesize and summarize the work of the unit in an activity which provides a goal toward which students may work and serves as a focal point for the contributions of individuals and groups. This activity may be the production of an assembly program or a dramatization for another class, talks to be given before a wider audience than the class, the production of a class newspaper or pamphlet including the best of the papers and reports written for the unit, the preparation of a bulletin board or exhibit for the classroom or the school hall, or the collection of materials in a notebook or folder for each individual student.

The worth of a project of this kind is in the part it can play in synthesizing and making memorable the work of the unit. To be valuable, the project should demand a maximum effort from students. Activities should be language-centered. Students can learn much while they are planning together to produce a play, a class magazine or newspaper, or a series of panel discussions. Too often, however, the amount of reading and writing students do is sharply limited because too much time is spent on elaborate projects involving much cutting and pasting of pictures, making papier-mâché models, sand tables, posters, murals, and exhibits involving a large amount of time with little resulting growth in the basic language skills. The teacher must decide whether the unit project will be worth the time and effort expended on it, and whether it will demand the greatest intellectual growth of the student.

Organizing the class for work.   The work of the unit may be carried on in several ways: some activities will involve the whole class meeting together for discussion of common readings, for writing, testing, or other work in which the class is involved as a group. Some reading and writing activities will be carried out in small groups and committees assigned to particular projects or organized to discuss selected readings or a topic or idea. Some of the work of the unit will be carried out in individual assignments, as students read, write papers, give reports, or carry on a project requiring independent work. Ideally, the good unit provides for work both in small and large groups and for independent study. A wise handling of these various kinds of activities allows the teacher to meet students either in individual conferences or for help in small groups, where more individualized instruction is possible.

Planning the single lesson

For the beginning teacher, the requirement of the daily lesson plan adds one more task to the formidable array of those he is already trying to accomplish. He observes skilled veteran teachers who appear to have little need for a detailed written outline of the lessons they teach. Yet even such teachers frequently use notes and questions to guide their discussion of a piece of literature or to chart their progress in teaching a lesson on language or composition. Teachers who do not appear to use written plans usually have clear mental outlines of their teaching procedures. Just as the skilled writer frequently works without an outline except that in his mind, so do such teachers work to achieve well-organized lessons.

Planning is a necessity for the beginning teacher, who must keep many things in mind at once. He is engaged in remembering the names of the boys and girls before him and in trying to recognize them as individuals. He must consider how his lesson is going, be sure enough of his questions to handle student answers intelligently, and feel competent to stimulate discussion without knowing just what answers will be forthcoming. He needs at the same time to be aware of student reactions, to observe students who are inattentive, talkative, or indifferent, and to judge how students are responding to his teaching. The young teacher who uses a well-organized, though brief, outline of his plan brings with him the self-confidence born of good preparation and leaves an important part of his mind free for matters which come up in his dealing with the class. As the preliminary sketch is to the artist, the blueprint to the architect or the carpenter, and the outline to the writer, so is the lesson plan to the creative teacher. Occasionally a good lesson comes from spur-of-the-moment inspiration; however, most well-organized, effective teaching comes from careful, thoughtful, creative planning of procedures, activities, and questions.

Introducing the lesson. The skillful teacher makes certain that the class understands the central aim of the lesson and sees the relationship between what students are to study and what has gone before. The teacher may bridge the gap between the previous lesson and the present one by a brief introductory comment. As he teaches *Great Expectations,* for instance, the teacher may say, "Yesterday, we talked about Pip, Estella, and Miss Havisham, and the things each one wanted out of life. Today we will take a look at some of the other characters who influenced Pip's life." He may prepare students to think about the next day's discussion by giving students an idea of the topic, and directing students on how to study: "As you prepare for class discussion tomorrow, go back over the book to watch how Pip's values change through his experiences with Magwitch, his stay in London, and his relations with Joe, Miss Havisham, Magwitch, and Estella." In such ways the teacher helps students understand the planned continuity of discussion of a novel and ensures the orderly progression of the plan of discussion.

Teachers often lead students into the day's work by a challenging question which focuses attention on the subject for discussion and engages interest in learning. The introduction to a lesson in which the teacher plans to discuss students' compositions may begin by pointing out the gains students have made in the present assignment over the previous ones and then suggesting two topics for improvement—those which are to be the subject of the day's work.

The art of questioning. The heart of the daily lesson, or indeed, of all teaching, is the teacher's ability to ask the kind of questions which lead students to think rather than to recite memorized facts. Even today it is possible to find schoolrooms in which most of the teaching of English is centered on the recall of facts, rather than on the discussion of ideas. This process has been called Gradgrindism, after the character in Dickens' *Hard Times*. Readers of that book will remember how Mr. Gradgrind's questioning of the unfortunate Sissy Jupe led him to the despairing conclusion that "Girl number twenty" was unable to define a horse and caused him to turn to a more satisfactory student:

> "Bitzer," said Thomas Gradgrind. "Your definition of a horse."
>
> "Quadruped. Graminivorous. Forty teeth, namely twenty-four grinders, four eye-teeth, and twelve incisive. Sheds coat in the spring; in marshy countries, sheds hoofs, too. Hoofs hard, but requiring to be shod with iron. Age known by marks in mouth." Thus (and much more) Bitzer.
>
> "Now girl number twenty," said Mr. Gradgrind. "You know what a horse is."

Mr. Gradgrind's assumption that the ability to master facts leads to knowledge is no longer valid. Good teaching encourages good thinking, and the teacher's aim is to use each lesson to stimulate students to think.

Student-teachers and those who are just beginning their teaching often cling to the security of a detailed list of twenty-five or more factual questions, often those which can be answered by a simple *yes, no,* or one or two words. Such questions as "What was the color of Johnny Tremaine's hair?" "Where did Jody find the fawn?" "What happened after . . . ," and "What did (character's name) find when he . . ." all too frequently are found on such lesson plans.

The teacher can suggest by the language of his question whether he is interested in hearing what a student thinks or merely asking the student to recite an answer which repeats the teacher's ideas. The characteristic form of many questions is, "Now give me the definition of a noun," "Give me three characteristics of Romantic literature," or "Tell me the names of the principal characters in *Silas Marner*." These questions imply that the purpose of the student's response is to give the teacher what the latter wants to hear, rather than to provide a contribution to the thinking of the class.

Some questioning about fact is, of course, necessary in teaching literature, particularly with less able students. Students must understand what happens in a novel, a play, or a short story before they can interpret why it happens or what the characters' are like. Frequently, however, students can learn to look back over the novel they have read and select details which can help to interpret the motivation of a character or throw light on the author's development of suspense in the plot. Although emphasis on fact is usually thought of as a check on assigned reading, thought questions demanding a meaningful and intelligent organization of factual detail serve as an even better test of reading and comprehension. Such questions as "How does Shakespeare show us the gradual development of Macbeth's ambition?" require the student to synthesize details by pointing to lines, speeches, and incidents through which Shakespeare shows us this trait. Other examples: the student may be asked to list the major incidents which contribute to Jody's growing up in *The Yearling*, to show the main incidents leading to Silas Marner's isolation and those which help him return to human fellowship, or to contrast Eustacia's values with Clym's in *The Return of the Native*.

Getting students to ask questions is a mark of superior teaching. Teachers who encourage students to question the decisions, actions, and motivations of characters are directing the thinking process.

The teacher who demands thinking rather than reciting builds his lessons around five or six thought-provoking discussion questions. He uses factual questions as checks on comprehension or interpretation when students seem to be misinterpreting important points, moving too far from the text, or giving other evidence of sketchy or careless reading or thinking. Unwittingly, the teacher may determine the answer he will get by the wording of his questions. The "loaded" question colors the attitude of the student before he answers. If the teacher asks "Why is Ma Baxter such an unpleasant (or hard or cold) woman?" the words he has chosen have a strong emotional "charge" that will influence the attitude and response of the student toward the character. As teachers, we are less interested in determining how students *should* respond to literature than in how they actually *do* respond, and it is only by skillful, nonloaded questions that we can find out.

The slanted question may also stop thinking rather than encourage it. Such questions as "Why do you think Sidney Carton was a good man?" "Why do you think X's decision was the right one?" or "Why do you disapprove of X's actions?" determine what the student's response will be. They usually arise from the teacher's determination to get a particular kind of response to the piece of literature from the students and the emphasis in such questioning is on forcing the students to give the expected answers. Such teaching prevents real thinking and honest response to literature. It encourages students to make judgments rather than to try to understand character. Such questioning often turns into what Madison Avenue calls the "hard sell," in which the teacher attempts to force his own interpretation of a piece of literature on the students, and then requires that they reproduce it for him on a test.

What psychologists call the open-ended question provides one of the most useful tools for the teacher. These are carefully phrased to avoid slanting thinking and to elicit the student's real thoughts and feelings about what he has read. "What did you think of (name of character)?" "Why do you think he acted as he did?" "What did you think of his decision?" and the like are questions which allow the student to respond without having been forewarned as to what he is expected to think or what the teacher thinks.

In judging questions the teacher needs to ask himself their potential value for stimulating thought and discussion in the class. He will see that some questions lead to a very limited response ("What happened to Mrs. Yeobright on the heath?"), whereas others direct students to look for complex character motivation ("Why does Eustacia encourage Wildeve's attentions?").

One of the difficulties of the beginning teacher, and of many experienced ones, is in recognizing when student discussion is pertinent, fruitful, and productive of thinking. The teacher often feels an uncritical glow of satisfaction when an otherwise apathetic class becomes involved in interested talk. The beginner often says, "Well, at least I got them talking." A moment's thought suggests that there is something more involved, something that should be ever present in the mind of the teacher who is trying to encourage students to talk freely in discussion. Both students and teacher should want and need discussion that says something and leads somewhere. Talk can be merely a discharge of energy, sound and fury signifying nothing, or it can be a means to help students develop profounder insights into literature or to analyze critically their own ideas and responses. The teacher's role is all important. He must guide the class, turn back those who would digress, stimulate students to probe deeper rather than to accept facile generalizations and easy answers. If discussion does not produce critical thinking, it is of little value.

Summaries and assignments.   Most good teachers like to conclude a lesson by indicating to students what the major points of the discussion have been and showing them how these points relate to what has gone before and what will come afterwards. Each step in the discussion of a play or a novel should provide this kind of relationship so that students may discern pattern and order in their learning. Although talking over a short story or a poem may take but a single class period, students need to be aware how the piece being studied fits into a larger design for learning and to realize what they have gained from the lesson.

Students need to be made aware of progress in learning. Too often lessons follow one another without apparent meaning or reason; assignments are given without any explanation of why the work to be done is important, and the student is expected to carry out instructions without knowing what he is learning or why and how it may be valuable to him. When students understand the reason for their lessons and recognize the direction and plan of the work to be done, their learning becomes more significant.

Evaluating growth in the unit

Formal and informal measures of achievement may be used to evaluate student growth during the time spent on a unit of study. The degree of improvement of skills in reading and writing may be estimated by teacher-constructed tests and quizzes on the readings studied during the unit. The papers

Drawing by Ed Fisher; © 1958 *Saturday Review*.

the student has written may be preserved in the students' folders, where they serve as measures of progress both in mechanical skills and form, and organization of content and ideas. Spelling and vocabulary tests given at the end of the unit of study may provide further useful measures of growth. An estimation of progress in the ability to speak easily before a group, to organize and present an oral report clearly, to participate intelligently in a panel discussion, and to work effectively with others in group and committee work in carrying out assignments for the unit are other effective checks on growth in oral language skills. The sections on evaluation at the end of the chapters devoted to reading, listening, writing, speaking, and literature suggest further examples of types of testing techniques.

Teaching units planned to develop language skills, problem solving, and critical thinking about language and literature should become important parts of the curriculum in English at each grade level. As the beginning teacher gains the confidence born of practice, he will want to look beyond the individual lesson or unit plan to block out a year's work in a sequence of units and activities. Such courses of study for a year's work become part of the larger pattern of the six-year, or the kindergarten-through-twelfth-grade English program. New programs being designed to emphasize developmental and sequential learning and the mastery of a progression of concepts hold the promise of training youth in the language arts and skills necessary to effective personal, social, and intellectual life in the modern world.

Planning the sequential curriculum

Curriculum revision is underway in most schools, at the local, state, regional, and national levels. Teachers from every level are participating in this kind of planning. The quality of such curriculum guides and the plans envisioned for the six years of secondary school vary widely. In some communities pressure of competition with other communities, or the desire to revise a guide quickly —perhaps because of an impending evaluation—leads to hastily contrived and ill-considered plans. Often a single teacher is assigned to rewrite the curriculum guide or the course syllabus for a year's work; often the teacher does this revision in addition to a full schedule of classwork. Often, too, revision consists merely of adding new texts to the course outline or substituting some required classics for others.

Seldom is curriculum revision accepted both by administrators and teachers as a project worthy of time and effort on the part of teachers and consultants who can talk, plan, and exchange ideas about a desirable program. Such a task today should be more than the patching of an outdated course of study, or the work of a single individual whose judgments will affect the teaching of a number of teachers and the learning of hundreds of students. Good revision takes time, effort, study, research, and the combined efforts of the best minds willing to engage in the project. Harold Martin, speaking to college teachers for the Commission on English of the College Entrance Examination Board, charged them with the responsibility of sharing in the important work of the secondary schools' curriculum revision, and reminded them of "an obligation to the guild, to the profession, an obligation to help all those who teach English to teach it soundly and imaginatively. . . ." [10]

Some outstanding curriculum guides have resulted from the careful planning and combined thinking of teachers from every level. In some states groups from state departments of education, from college and university faculties, and from the classrooms of secondary and elementary schools meet together to plan sequential curriculums from grades kindergarten through 12. Where leaders

[10] Harold C. Martin, "The Status of the Profession," *College English*, vol. 50, April, 1961, p. 455.

in the profession have taken an active role in such planning, or where groups of teachers at all levels have been granted time and money to free them for the job, some superior plans have resulted.[11] The pages which follow illustrate some of the plans resulting from such collaboration.

Some of the new plans focus on the development of concepts rather than on a body of information to be mastered. Learning activities are directed toward helping the student grasp key concepts in language, composition, and literature through illustrative learning experiences. The development of such concepts through a sequential curriculum is a primary aim in the Georgia plan (Table 16-2). A subdivision of Concept 1 ("Each language has its own peculiar structure") lists the ideas to be developed sequentially throughout the grades: e.g., "The structure of English is revealed through the sentence," "Sentences are generated regularly from basic patterns," etc. After defining the basic concepts, the guide goes on to list a series of twenty-three learnings to be developed through work in the grades for the development of Concept 1.[12] Such a curriculum is both "spiral" and sequential.

The list of concepts about language as worked out by one teacher, and the papers based on these concepts written by eleventh-year students, appear in Chapter 3, pages 63–65. Nonsense words, poetry illustrating the use of figurative language, and an exercise in style consisting of the rewriting of a passage from the Bible are some typical assignments.

The composition sequence outlined in the Portland, Oregon, plan illustrates another type of planning in developmental and sequential patterns (Table 16-3). Of the sequence illustrated here, the *Guide* observes that the study of composition ideally will be related to what the students study in language, and that literature will be used as subject matter for writing and for models of student work. Problems of usage will be discussed as they occur in student writing.[13]

Still another sequential program in writing developed for grades 7 through 12 contains the following features: beginning study of formal paragraph in the seventh grade, moving in later grades to different patterns of development; mastery of the form of business and personal letters by end of the eighth grade; study of transitions and topic sentences in the ninth grade; two-paragraph themes in the ninth grade to five-paragraph themes in the tenth grade; and essays of 500 to 800 words in the eleventh grade. In the twelfth grade, students would move on to analysis, critical writing, reference papers, and argument.[14] Sequential programs in language, composition, and literature are included in Chapters 3, 6, 13, and 15.

[11] For example, the group which worked out the Portland, Ore., *Course of Study* discussed in the following pages.

[12] *English Language Arts Curriculum Guide,* Georgia Department of Education, Atlanta, 1962, p. 8.

[13] *Guide for High School English: Grades 9–12,* Portland Public Schools, Portland, Ore., 1962, p. 11.

[14] Clarence W. Hach, "Needed: A Sequential Program in Composition," *English Journal,* vol. 49, November, 1960, pp. 536–547.

Table 16-2. **Concepts Chart**

A. Language	B. Literature	C. Composition
Language, oral and written, is the medium of communication. Each language has a history and a recognizable structure. It functions variously as it is directed toward the accomplishment of different purposes.	Literature reflects human experience—the life of a people. It reflects certain constant human concerns. It deals with value judgments. It selects from human experience and orders that experience.	Composing in speech and in writing is a purposeful ordering of experience, to clarify thought, to communicate thought and feeling, to express oneself. The composer's experience and his reactions to it provide the basis for composing.
1. Each language has its own peculiar structure.	1. Literature reflects universal elements in human experience.	1. Composing requires something to say.
2. Each language has dialects.	2. Literature reflects the culture.	2. Composing involves purpose.
3. Modern languages are the result of historical development.	3. Literary works may be classified by type-form.	3. Composing involves arranging selected material into a recognizable order.
4. Speech is primary. Writing symbolizes speech/thought.	4. A literary work has structure.	4. Composing is usually done within recognizable patterns (types).
5. Language changes.	5. Literature affects the culture.	5. Composing involves the development of an individual style.
6. Language has differing social functions.	6. The relationship of the reader to the literary work is individual and personal.	
7. Words convey meaning at various levels of literalness and abstraction.		

SOURCE: *English Language Arts Curriculum Guide*, Georgia Department of Education, Atlanta, 1962, p. 8.

The Portland language guide plans a sequence of study during the four years to focus on the following areas:

Ninth grade: syntax; the nature and development of language.

Tenth grade: lexicography and meaning.

Eleventh grade: linguistic geography and dialect.

Twelfth grade: history of the English language; the nature of correctness in language.[15]

The ninth year thus attempts to provide a basic understanding of English sentence structure and an analytical and descriptive study of language. The

---

[15] *Guide for High School English, op. cit.*, p. 1. "Language Studies for English Classes."

Table 16-3. Summary of Composition Sequence

	Basic sentence / Technical skills	Sentence structure / Basic paragraph	The longer composition / Organization	The longer expository paper
Focus	Basic sentence / Technical skills	Sentence structure / Basic paragraph	The longer composition / Organization	The longer expository paper
Assignments	Frequent paragraphs, with emphasis on sentence patterns	Frequent paragraphs with emphasis on sentence and paragraph structure	Frequent paragraphs and short themes Longer papers (300–600 words), at least four per year One reference paper (750–1,000 words) Papers related to study of literature	Frequent paragraphs and short themes Longer themes (500–750 words) related to study of literature, at least four per year

Rhetoric	Sentence
	  Completeness
	  Sentence revision
	Other applications of grammar study, e.g., use of sentence patterns, including passive and expletive patterns
	Coordination, subordination, modification
		Paragraphs
		  Generalizations and support
		  Main idea and unity—topic statement
		  Development and substantiation of a topic idea
		  Coherence—links and transitions
		Sentence
		  Coordination, balance, and parallelism
		  Subordination and modification
		  Diction—applications of language study, lexicography
			Theme
			  Organization—compare with paragraph organization
			  Selecting and limiting topic
			  The main idea
			  Planning and the outline
			  Developing an idea
			  Transitions, introductions, conclusions
			Sentence
			  Predication
			  Choice of appropriate patterns
			  Evidence—fact and opinion in compositions
				Point of view
				Tone
				Style
				Devices for unity in longer paper
				Validity of evidence
				Diction—application of language study, nature of correctness
				Clichés, triteness
				Figurative language
				Economy

Usage and mechanics			
Proofreading	Verbs	Adjective-adverb distinction: form	Review and treatment of individual problems
Spelling, including plurals, compounds, possessives	Principal parts, e.g., lie, lay	Function words	
Manuscript mechanics—capitals, word division, abbreviations, numbers, italics	Tense, consistency	Completeness in comparisons and other constructions	
Punctuation	Subject-verb agreement	Punctuation	
Between main clauses	Pronouns	Brackets, parentheses, colon, dash	
After introductory elements	Case	Semicolon with groups containing commas	
Dates, addresses	Agreement, consistency	Review and treatment of individual problems	
Comma in series	Punctuation		
	All interrupters		
	Quotations		
	Review and treatment of individual problems		

SOURCE: *Guide for High School English, Grades 9–12,* Portland Public Schools, Portland, Ore., 1962, p. 11. The Summary of Composition Sequence outline indicates the general progress of the four years. It is a kind of table of contents for more detailed suggestions in the sections of the *Guide* for each year (p. 14).

study of the nature and development of language includes such topics as non-linguistic and linguistic systems of language or communication, understanding the ways in which we use language, and the study of growth and change in the language.

The tenth year concentrates on dictionary study, the nature and processes of lexicography, the history of linguistic change as reflected in the dictionary, and the study of usage. In grade eleven, traditionally given to the study of American literature, the guide focuses on linguistic geography and dialect. Literary selections illustrating American regional dialects provide an important part of the reading.

During the study of English literature in the twelfth year, language study is centered on the history of the English language, a unit of two weeks for the backgrounds of Middle English before the study of Chaucer, two days a week during the study of Chaucer, and two days a week during the study of a novel, *Hamlet,* or *Oedipus* (total time: eight weeks). Detailed suggestions for teachers, recordings, bibliography, and topics for discussion are provided in *Language Studies for English Classes,* a compilation of excerpts from the *Guide for High School English.* Materials for the explication of literature and detailed materials for language study are included.[16]

Testing and evaluation

The problems of testing in the different areas of English have been dealt with in individual chapters. Something remains to be said about the role of testing in English, its functions and purposes in the program. Testing in most programs is probably chiefly designed for purposes of grading. Because of administrative and parental pressures for adequate support of the grades given students, frequent testing takes place, and marks at the secondary level are usually given in percentages. The question, "What does a grade in English mean?" has been raised frequently in the profession.

One critic of marking systems points to seven ways in which teachers may inadvertently grade dishonestly: (1) by abdication (putting together crude and inadequate tests at the last minute, and tailoring the course to ready-made tests; (2) by using the "carrots and clubs" system (grading on extraneous factors—deportment, penmanship, covers for reports, extra credit for reading; (3) by default (maintaining that tests are meaningless, and giving so few that students' grades depend on an overly small sample of their performances);

---

[16] The *Guide* materials were developed by a Curriculum Planning Committee with professional advice and assistance from Prof. W. Nelson Francis, Brown University, Prof. Robert Gorrell, University of Nevada, Prof. Carroll E. Reed, University of Washington, and Prof. Paul Roberts, Director of the Linguistics Program, Consiglo per gli Studi Americani, Rome, Italy. Curriculum consultants were Marian Zollinger, Supervisor of Language Arts, and Elsie May Cimino, Assistant Supervisor of Language Arts, Portland, Ore., Public Schools.

(4) by becoming testing zealots (grading everything except classroom posture); (5) by changing the rules in mid-game (shifting grading standards up or down to threaten or encourage students); (6) by being a psychic grader (considering that tests are superfluous and inferior to intuition); and (7) by anchoring the grading system "in the rainbow of an impossible perfection" (no one gets an A; few, B's, and many fail). Such abdication of responsibility by teachers, the author maintains, results in grades becoming more important than learning, and distorts the real aims of education.[17]

The sample tests available such as the CEEB *End-of-Year Examinations in English,* illustrated in Chapters 8 (page 207) and 9 (pages 235–236), the Advanced Placement examinations in English, the practice tests used for the College Entrance Examination Scholastic Aptitude and Achievement tests are useful for the teacher of good students, and many questions are adaptable for use with less able students.

The teacher will want to select carefully from the many good standardized tests available. The evaluations of such tests by professional consultants are available in the *Mental Measurements Yearbook.*[18] They provide a useful indication of the strengths and weaknesses of the test, and a judgment as to whether it measures significant material. Examinations planned for use in schoolwide testing in English should be checked in such a source.

An essential part of any planned program for a year will include careful preparation and consideration of the tests to be used. If planning is haphazard or nonexistent, testing may be equally random. Too much time may be spent on tests that do not teach, or which do not yield any relevant information about pupil performance except the ability to remember facts, to repeat generalizations the teacher has made, or to guess the kinds of questions the teacher is likely to ask. The teacher needs to distinguish between the kinds of questions which test recall of fact, those which sample unimportant or irrelevant bits of information, and those which call for verbal reasoning, interpretation of meanings, and the observations of similarities and differences—generally considered one of the highest intellectual functions. Good essay tests demand of the student (1) the ability to abstract information from reading, and to discriminate between important and unimportant details; (2) the ability to organize knowledge into a clearly developed answer; (3) the ability to make valid generalizations and to support them with concrete details or relevant evidence; (4) the ability to stick to the point and to deal logically with the question; (5) the ability to remember facts and relate them to relevant generalizations. Essay testing is commonly encountered throughout the student's college career. All college-bound students should encounter this type of testing in high school,

[17] Summarized from Orville Palmer, "Seven Classic Ways of Grading Dishonestly," *English Journal,* vol. 51, October, 1962, pp. 464–467. Mr. Palmer is editor for College Board programs of the Educational Testing Service, Princeton, N.J.
[18] See Oscar K. Buros (ed.), *Fifth Mental Measurements Yearbook,* Gryphon Press, Highland Park, N.J., 1959. See also third and fourth yearbooks.

and non-college-bound students will profit greatly from writing and discussing such essays.

One expert in testing believes that the best tests consist of writing problems set by asking the student to read passages and answer relevant questions about them: the meaning of words in context, the interpretation of words or phrases, the analysis of ideas, attitudes, assumptions, and the comparison of likenesses and differences. Such a test, he believes, examines both reading comprehension and writing ability, and provides lively teaching materials of high interest to students. Suggestions for constructing such questions are given in his article.[19] Suggestions for making tests—especially objective tests—are provided in a pamphlet published by the National Council of Teachers of English.[20] Teachers would do well to review these aids before planning the testing program for the year. Good tests perform a genuine teaching function that no mass-produced short-answer tests on literature, grammar, or usage can serve.

Selected bibliography

Abraham Bernstein, *Teaching English in High School*, Random House, Inc., New York, 1961. An informally written approach to teaching English with illustrations of practices in large city schools.

Dwight L. Burton and John S. Simmons (eds.), *Teaching English in Today's High Schools: Selected Readings*, Holt, Rinehart and Winston, Inc., New York, 1965.

Commission on the English Curriculum, *The English Language Arts in the Secondary Schools*, Appleton-Century-Crofts, Inc., New York, 1956.

Northrop Frye (ed.), *Design for Learning*, University of Toronto Press, Toronto, Canada, 1962. "Among the more important of recent analyses of curriculum."

Edward J. Gordon (ed.), *Writing and Literature in the Secondary School*, Holt, Rinehart and Winston, Inc., 1965. A collection of talks given at the Yale Conferences on the Teaching of English.

Hans P. Guth, *English Today and Tomorrow: A Guide for Teachers of English*, Prentice-Hall, Inc., Englewood Cliffs, N.J., 1964. A thoughtful discussion of content, method, and objectives.

David Holbrook, *English for Maturity*, Cambridge University Press, Cambridge, England, 1961.

J. N. Hook, *The Teaching of High School English*, 2d ed., The Ronald Press Company, New York, 1959. A practical, down-to-earth approach to teaching English.

[19] Paul B. Diederich, "Making and Using Tests," *English Journal*, vol. 44, March, 1955, pp. 135–151.

[20] Robert B. Carruthers, *"Building Better English Tests: A Guide for Teachers of English in the Secondary Schools*, NCTE, Champaign, Ill., 1963. See also Edward J. Gordon, "Levels of Teaching and Testing," *English Journal*, vol. 44, September, 1955, pp. 330–342, discussed in Chap. 9, pp. 251–252.

Albert R. Kitzhaber et al., *Education for College: Improving the High School Curriculum,* The Ronald Press Company, New York, 1961.

Lou La Brant, *We Teach English,* Harcourt, Brace & World, Inc., New York, 1951. A stimulating book pointing out the responsibilities of the teacher of language.

John S. Lewis and Jean C. Sisk, *Teaching English 7–12,* American Book Company, New York, 1963.

Walter Loban et al., *Teaching Language and Literature: Grades 7–12,* Harcourt, Brace & World, Inc., New York, 1961. A comprehensive book with excellent suggestions about teaching, and numerous student assignments.

Patterns and Models for Teaching English—1964: A Report of the NCTE Committee to Report Promising Practices in the Teaching of English, NCTE, Champaign, Ill., 1964.

Promising Practices in the Teaching of English: A Report on Selected New Developments in the Teaching of English, NCTE, Champaign, Ill., 1963.

M. Jerry Weiss (ed.), *An English Teacher's Reader,* The Odyssey Press, Inc., New York, 1962.

CHAPTER *17*

As kingfishers catch fire, dragonflies draw flame;
As tumbled over rim in roundy wells
Stones ring; like each tucked string tells, each hung bell's
Bow swung finds tongue to fling out broad its name;
Each mortal thing does one thing and the same:
Deals out that being indoors each one dwells;
Selves—goes itself; *myself* it speaks and spells,
Crying *What I do is me: for that I came.*

GERARD MANLEY HOPKINS [1]

The teacher and the task

What does it mean to be a teacher of English today?

Teachers of English today embark on a career of great responsibility and importance. Those who will leave their imprint on today's youth are dedicated, serious human beings with great competence in their fields, a sensitive understanding of youth and its problems, a creative approach to teaching, and a conviction that the subject they teach is "the central humanistic study" in the curriculum.[2]

The creative English teacher today finds himself in an exciting environment. As we have seen in Chapter 1, more widespread experimentation is going on currently than we have seen since the progressive education movement of the thirties. Change is in the air, and the concern for improved methods and materials of instruction and for higher standards in the teaching of English is general.

[1] From *Poems of Gerard Manley Hopkins,* Third Edition, edited by W. H. Gardner, Copyright 1948 by Oxford University Press, Inc. Reprinted by permission.
[2] The Harvard Committee on General Education, *General Education in a Free Society,* Harvard University Press, Cambridge, Mass., 1945, p. 107.

National recognition of the growing significance of English as a subject of importance for all American youth has focused attention on the need for fully qualified teachers of English and generally higher standards of preparation for teaching the subject.

Although today there are many more full-time English teachers than ever before, it is still all too common that English classes are assigned to teachers of other subjects. Teachers of Latin and French, history, mathematics, or science may take a class in English, and even the football coaches may do so. In many schools, English classes are still taught by teachers on temporary certification in English or those who have the very slender minimal requirements which are still demanded in some states. The discouraging administrative attitude that anyone who can speak English can teach it is slowly becoming a thing of the past. The public is demanding better teachers for its children and has shown increasing concern about the quality of English teaching in the schools and the qualifications and preparation of those who teach the subject.

The making of a teacher of English

For the first time, an attempt has been made by the Committee on National Interest of the NCTE to suggest a national standard of preparation for teachers of English. Those preparing to teach and those whose college preparation for teaching is well behind them may do well to check their own training against the "Standard of Preparation to Teach English" which the Committee has formulated. Of the teacher of English, they say:

> Much of the basic knowledge of English as his native language—which he understands, reads, speaks, and writes—he should have by the time he enters college. Likewise, by that time he should have read a number of major works that belong to English and American literature and some foreign pieces in the original language or English translation. He should consequently have developed a fair ability to judge and a taste to choose among literary works. During his four or five years of collegiate study, he should extend and sharpen his fundamental knowledge of the English language and literature and should acquire the special knowledge of English, together with the science and art of teaching it, which he will need for his work in the elementary or secondary school.[3]

The training the English teacher needs is summarized in a careful survey of the requirements of the job by the consultants in a recent study, who urge "the equal importance of work in language, rhetorical theory, and advanced expository writing." [4]

Those making recommendations today for improved preparation for tomorrow's teachers of English emphasize the importance of broad backgrounds

---

[3] *The National Interest and the Teaching of English*, NCTE, Champaign, Ill., 1961, p. 40.
[4] Albert R. Kitzhaber et al., *Education for College: Improving the High School Curriculum*, The Ronald Press Company, New York, 1961, pp. 90–91.

of study in language, literature, and composition. Twenty-nine colleges associated with Harvard University in its Master-of-Arts in Teaching Program recommend that the teacher of high school English should have a year's work in each of the following: prose fiction, intensive reading of poetry, advanced composition, structure and history of the language, Shakespeare, major figures of American literature, and sufficient knowledge of a foreign language to provide good judgment in reading and evaluating translations.[5] The teacher of English should have the following qualifications, according to the NCTE Commission on the Curriculum in a study of *The Education of Teachers of English:*[6] extensive training in his teaching major: in the English language, in composition, in literature, in speech, in dramatics, and in journalism. He should have at least the following: freshman composition (one year); the English language (three courses); expository writing (in addition to freshman courses); other advanced writing (two or more courses); journalistic writing (one course); rhetorical theory and practice (one course); logic (one course); semantics (one course); evaluation and improvement of student writing (one course). The program in literature should include courses in English and American literature, world literature, Shakespeare, genre and major writers courses, period courses, literary criticism, and literature for adolescents.

The teacher of English: professional

The present or future teacher of English measuring his qualifications against these suggested requirements for his profession should begin to fill in the gaps in his background and training. If we were to think about the kind of person we would have teaching English to American youth, we might construct an idealized portrait of the teacher of English. No single individual could incorporate in his character, personality, and experience all of the qualities, abilities, and knowledge suggested here, but the sketch will serve to suggest to beginning teachers the concept that preparation for teaching English is a life-time job.

The teacher learns as he grows. Many of our finest teachers have chosen their profession for just this reason: it provides them with the opportunity to read, study, and live a life rich in the satisfactions of reading and writing. It should be comforting to the beginning teacher to know that at no period of his life does the teacher of English feel really adequately prepared for his task. The English language and its literature is a subject almost without boundaries, rich, complex, ever varying, and fascinating.

Ideally, the preparation of the teacher of English for his job begins in childhood, as he learns his language from those who use standard English

---

[5] From recommendations published in a new report on the academic preparation of teachers, reported in *Council-Grams*, NCTE, Champaign, Ill., March, 1963, p. 14.
[6] Alfred H. Grommon (ed.), Appleton-Century-Crofts, Inc., New York, 1963, chap. 5.

with ease and grace and as he grows up sharing a delight in reading with those who love books. Nor is college graduation the end of his preparation, but a beginning of a life spent enriching his knowledge of language and literature. The English major preparing to teach should plan to improve in the areas in which he is weak. He needs the following proficiencies in spoken and written English, in reading competence, in listening, and in knowledge about his language.

Spoken English

The successful teacher of today's youth should, first of all, be one to whom young people may talk comfortably, to whom the avenues of oral communication are easily open. Realizing the intimate nature of the spoken words, this teacher knows that oral communication is usually his first access to what goes on in the hearts and minds of the young, to what might be revealed or concealed behind the spoken symbols. He knows how language starts in the infant and develops with the child; he knows the closeness of the mother's tongue to that of the young person and of the sensitive nature of this tie.

Oral language, together with gesture and facial expression, is the immediate medium through which the teacher will establish (or will fail to establish) rapport with a class group or with an individual student. The teacher's words, if they are harsh and strident, can close quickly all doors to further learning. His words, if they are pleasant and agreeable, may invite students to the wonders of language. Not only the words he chooses, but also the tone of voice in which these words are spoken, are very important in setting classroom atmosphere. The tone in which words are spoken is indeed sometimes stronger than the words themselves.

The teacher's greatest classroom asset is the ability to read aloud well, to be able to enchant students with the power of the sound of language in poetry and prose. The teacher who has a fine voice will be able to quell the noisiest class, to wield his magic with the dullest and most indifferent students. Some few lucky teachers are born with this talent, some achieve it through patient practice, and many have the necessity for learning it thrust upon them by the often-expressed desire of the classes they teach: "Read it to us, please." Thomas Wolfe has described such a teacher in *Look Homeward, Angel*—one whose reading "passed through their barred and bolted boy-life" and "opened their hearts as if they were lockets." [7]

The teacher of English will be better prepared for his task if he is a good conversationalist, a skillful leader of discussion, a competent parliamentarian, an able director of choral speaking, sociodramas, or plays. Some of these skills are those he brings to his job; others he acquires through practicing them with the young people he teaches.

---

[7] Thomas Wolfe, *Look Homeward, Angel,* Charles Scribner's Sons, New York, 1929, p. 314.

Written English

A teacher of the language arts should be able to write legibly and correctly, to have at his command the rules of good usage, grammar, punctuation, capitalization—all the technicalities and mechanics of writing. If his command is not automatic, he will find that his hasty writing on the chalkboard or on student papers will contain misspelled words and errors in punctuation or sentence structure, all readily recognizable by his bright students, who may not hesitate to correct him. Even the teacher in a hurry should have such automatic command of basic conventions that he does not make mistakes.

Correctness in writing is a requisite of the teacher of English, but he cannot be content with correctness alone. If he is to teach writing effectively, he should himself be able to handle words easily on paper. This does not mean that he must be able to write novels and poetry. It does mean that he should be an interesting writer of letters and informal essays, and that he should be able to write clear expository prose.

The teacher of writing should himself be consciously aware of the pains and struggles connected with writing. This awareness comes especially if the teacher himself has published something and knows the many distractions one can find to delay the serious business of putting pen to paper or fingers to keyboard. Through the remembrance of his own difficulties he can sympathize with and encourage the young person who says, "But I have nothing to write about" or "How can I begin?" The teacher should not only feel the pangs of writing but he should also know the satisfaction one has when the writing progresses and the paper becomes a finished article or chapter or report. If he will write with and for his students from time to time, he will find that his efforts are rewarded by increased interest and increased willingness on the part of his students to undertake the tasks of writing.

Competence in reading

Beside these competences in and attitudes toward speaking and writing, the teacher of English must have developed the habit of reading deeply and widely and must know the techniques of rapid and efficient reading. Since the teacher of today's youth is living at a time when there appear each year more than ten thousand book titles that cost less than a dollar, he must learn to select and read with discrimination and to skim much that he need not read carefully. He must be sensitive to the power and pitfalls of the written word; he should have a working knowledge of semantic concepts and a high degree of skill in critical reading.

The teacher of English should have a sound knowledge of literary history, surely more than the piecemeal information he might get from a college survey course. His preparation should include a rich background in English and American literature, some knowledge of European literature—French, Italian, Russian, German, Scandinavian—and some of the great writings of the

Orient, such as the *Bhagavad Gita,* the *Ramayana,* or the *Analects* of Confucius. His reading interests should include modern literature as well as older classics; he should know both current writers and the great thinkers of the past.

Wide reading in literary criticism should have prepared him to read great literature with understanding and appreciation of both content and form. He should have enough skill and perception about what makes a literary work of art to be able to help his good students read literature with close attention to matters of form and to understand the difficult abstractions of tone, style, symbol, and structure.

Competence in listening

In this listening-looking world of today, an English teacher is not sufficiently prepared for his task through reading alone. In addition to knowing and caring about books, the teacher of the present-day adolescent must be well acquainted with all of the audiovisual forms of communication: the motion picture, the radio, the stage play, television. He must know something of the movie stars young people admire and the kinds of pictures in which their favorites appear as well as something of popular radio and television programs. Only with this knowledge can he hope to begin at youthful levels of enjoyment and raise these interests to more mature levels. The teacher of English today knows how to judge each of the newer forms of communication and how to relate them to his teaching of the young, who have grown up with these media and are unaware of their tremendous force.

Knowledge about language

The teacher of English today can no longer confine his knowledge of so powerful an instrument as the English language to a few rules of grammar, usage, and the mechanics of punctuation. He must know much more about language growth and structure than he tries to teach youth. The teacher of English must know something about the development of the English language and the structure of the English sentence. He should understand the importance of language in national and international affairs, the place of the English language in the world scene, and be informed about the findings of modern linguistics. A knowledge of the intricate nature of language and of the importance of words in ordering and disordering our lives is necessary for today's teacher of the language arts.

Teacher of English: the whole person

Ideally, the teacher of adolescents is a person who is able to move rather easily between two worlds, the world of the thinker and the world of the doer. He is one who is secure, self-sufficient, with enough inner resources to enjoy long periods spent alone correcting papers, reading for pleasure or professional growth, and writing. He is, also, when occasion or his social or professional needs demand it, able to enjoy the stimulation of good company, pleasurable association with young people, or friends both inside and outside the profession, as well as satisfying participation in community affairs and professional organizations.

Much harm has been done to the public image of the teacher of English by those who, unable to live in the world, have used the teaching of English as a retreat from reality into the world of books or those who have become pedantic scholars. Equally harmful to the dignity of the profession is the teacher who never grows up, either as teacher or as person, who remains an intellectual dilettante, teaching the books he read in college, remaining unaware of recent developments in his field, or who prefers a hectic social life to growth as a mature, well-read person. Incomplete, too, both as teacher and as person, is one who lives too much of his life in the classroom, whose only emotional life is that lived vicariously through his students, whose only interests are in professional matters and in the students he teaches.

Overinvolvement in the profession is a danger. The English teacher does not have time to be an organization man, spending his life at committee meetings and conferences. He needs, as did Thoreau, a broad margin to his life. The teacher who is not affiliated with a group of English teachers, however, misses important sources of stimulation and ideas about teaching and fails to contribute to efforts for higher professional standards.

There is danger that those of us who teach English may live too much in a verbal world, losing contact with the world of things, of nature, and of touching and seeing. The teacher who can turn from correcting papers and reading books to planting tulips or tomatoes or building a stone wall will feel himself firmly rooted in the real world. He will be prepared to talk with children whose lives are similarly rooted in tangible reality. As one teacher of literature said, "How can an English teacher introduce students to the *Odyssey,* to that wonderful world of physical action, unless he has himself felt a blow on the jaw while boxing or the ache of muscles from long swimming?"

Experiences which may enrich the background and life of the teacher of English come from many directions. The young person who comes to the profession with a wide background of work, of travel, or of army life has something to give his students that many lack. Some of our most successful teachers are young men who have had the kind of experiences which have given them insight into the lives, the values, and the problems of the large section of our population who live by factory or manual labor.

The teacher who knows what it is like to work on an assembly line in a factory, as a camp counselor, a playground director, a nurse's aid, a librarian has an understanding of the world of work into which many of his students will go that the teacher with an academic background alone can never have. One young teacher, unusually sensitive to the problems of the near-delinquent children in her junior high school classroom, says that these "latchkey" children became different persons to her after a summer as playground director, during which she saw them locked out of houses while their parents worked, forced to find food for themselves, and made responsible for younger brothers and sisters similarly neglected.

All this means that the teacher who has had varied experience in working with his hands and working with a variety of jobs may have a better chance to find ways of relating books and language to the life experiences of many children in our schools than he who comes to teaching with book learning alone.

This detailed picture of the kind of teacher of English needed today is a formidable one. No one individual can possess all of these qualities, nor is it necessary that he should. For the teacher of English should be, above all, an individual, a person unique and interesting. The young person, measuring himself against this ideal and finding that he meets most of its standards, may well approach his vocation with pride. Those who fall short of the standard will be many, perhaps most of those preparing to teach, or now teaching in English classrooms. Those who are discouraged at their failure to measure up may feel reassured by recalling that no teacher of English was ever made in four or five years of college. The teacher, like the doctor, the minister, and the lawyer, grows through experience, through continued reading in his chosen profession, through maturing as an individual with broad interests and achievements. As with other professions, the materials of the English teacher's craft are continually changing, and the need to keep up with professional advances is imperative. He who spends a lifetime of instructing youth teaching the same books, whose lesson plans endure with scarcely a modification from year to year, whose ideas about his profession never grow or change, will probably find his teaching routine, dull, and largely unrewarding. Many such teachers have learned to hate their craft and even to feel strong antipathy to and impatience with the youngsters whom they teach.

Above all, the teacher must love the subject he teaches. Delight in literature alone is not enough. The teacher is one who can communicate this delight to youth through finding the literature suitable to their stages of growth. He must love the language he teaches, its written and spoken forms, its structure and history. Of the love for language, good writing, and good literature that the English teacher needs, J. B. Priestley says: "To any English teacher who, deep in his or her heart, does not share that love, I would say: 'for your students' sake, your own sake, and indeed for God's sake—change your subject!' " [8]

Planning for professional growth

The kind of teacher who grows with his profession will be he who sets clearly outlined goals. He must have a clear image of the teacher-person he

[8] J. B. Priestley, "Life, Literature, and the Classroom," *Harbrace Teacher's Notebook in English,* unpaged reprint, Harcourt, Brace & World, Inc., New York, Winter, 1960.

hopes to become, lest the many demands on his time and energy pull him in too many different directions until he attempts everything and achieves little. He will be asked to judge contests, to revise curricula, to join the salary committee, to collect for the Cancer Drive, to gather properties for the town's little-theater production, to teach Sunday School, to sponsor a Brownie troop. The experienced teacher who wants to continue to grow must take stock from time to time and evaluate his development as a teacher. The most successful teachers are always searching, seldom satisfied with their work. They plan for growth through reading and studying, through interest in the profession, and through experience.

In addition to personal growth in breadth of interest and experience, most teachers who are serious about their jobs carefully plan a program of reading and study which will supplement the beginnings they made in various subjects in college. If they are wise, they will have left college with the nucleus of a good professional library—the books they acquired through reading in various courses and those they added to their libraries to read for pleasure. They will have made a conscientious effort to buy books which might be useful in their teaching libraries. The availability today of paperback editions not only of fiction, general nonfiction, poetry, and drama, but also of scholarly texts of literary criticism and studies in language makes it possible for a teacher to own a library several times the size of one he might have had fifteen years ago.

For many teachers, the end of college provides a sense of freedom and anticipation that the time has now come to read the books he has been forced to put aside in order to finish required reading. Without planning, this sense of freedom often proves illusory, and the impulse to read is often dissipated by random sampling of ephemeral best sellers. The teacher with a purpose takes stock of his past reading, looks honestly at the important gaps left in his undergraduate work, and plans his reading to continue his education and improve his preparation for teaching. The kinds of reading he must do for professional competence are widely varied, as a look at the following areas suggests.

The good teacher of literature is one whose reading includes *Alice in Wonderland* as well as *War and Peace, The Wind in the Willows* as well as Shakespeare's plays. Since parents seldom read aloud to children these days, and since reading as a family pastime is almost a thing of the past, a teacher who enjoys the classics of childhood and can introduce them to youth may provide the only chance for young people to know and love these books.

It has been suggested in Chapter 15 that extensive acquaintance with the books adolescents are reading is a primary resource of the teacher who provides the needed guidance for the individual reading of his students. The suggestions in that chapter indicate how he may extend his acquaintance with such books without taking too much time from the other tasks he faces.

But the teacher cannot limit his reading to the books that his students should know. He must also find time for wide and deep reading on his own level. He may take stock of what he has already read, using a list like the paperback *Good Reading*[9] or a list of the great books of the world to see the extent of his reading in the literature of the various periods, genres, and nations. A planned program of reading, estimating a fair number of books to be read in a summer or in a year, will provide a goal to work toward.

In addition to the literary classics, the teacher must read for his profession, too. Just as the mediocre or inferior teacher is often content to rest on the scattered knowledge he has accumulated during his college days, so many teachers often teach for a lifetime on what they learned in one course of methods during their undergraduate years. Recent studies of English teaching, for example, have indicated that many school curricula in English are set up without any recognition of recent research in grammar, usage, linguistics, reading methods, or semantics.[10]

Professional reading is essential for the teacher who wants to keep informed about new developments in the teaching of his subject. Journals in English, as well as in education, psychology, sociology, or curriculum and methods, contain fruitful ideas for the teacher searching for methods of enriching his teaching. New textbooks provide helpful teaching suggestions and new bibliographies. A library of such resources should be as much a part of the English teacher's equipment as the new piano in the music department or the laboratory equipment for the science teacher. In many schools, such books are purchased for the library; in others, they are provided for an English Department library, and in still others where such resources are scarce, teachers cooperate to share the expenses of subscriptions to magazines and the purchase of books.[11]

How does the English teacher find time for the reading he wants to do and must do? Precious time may be gained by planning work ahead so that not all papers or time-consuming assignments fall due at the same time. It is gained by working out timesaving devices for correcting student writing;[12] by finding an isolated spot at school or at home for reading student papers protected from the interruptions of overly social students or colleagues; by foregoing the relaxing but vapid television program in favor of a stimulating book. Most of all, it is gained by giving reading the primary place among the daily tasks which need to be done and by refusing to put it off for the magical moment of "free time" which may never come. Such time for reading can be found. Many of our busiest and most competent teachers *do* find the time, and some of those who are most active in teaching, committee and organization

---

[9] See *Good Reading*, book list prepared by the Committee on College Reading, New American Library of World Literature, Inc., New York, 1960, or *The College and Adult Reading List*, Washington Square Press, Pocket Books, Inc., New York, 1962.

[10] Suggestions for professional reading in the areas of English are given at the end of each chapter.

[11] The need for such resources is indicated by the observations of several members of the Executive Committee of the NCTE that in some schools English teachers are unaware of their national organization and its publications.

[12] See Chap. 6, pp. 147–148, for some suggested techniques for saving time.

work, and in speaking and writing for publication are also those whose breadth of reading is most remarkable.

Membership in the profession

Although some of our greatest and most beloved teachers have been persons well adapted to the contemplative and often lonely life of the reader, scholar, or writer, some of the most valuable members of the profession have been those who share their thoughts and experiences through participation in organizations designed to stimulate teachers to exchange ideas about good teaching and to learn about new developments in the field. Many teachers look upon the conferences, meetings, and workshops sponsored by such groups as important sources of stimulation and a means of sharing ideas and problems.

The person dedicated to his task is eager to make his contribution to the profession through working for better teaching conditions, better standards of preparation and performance, and improved methods and materials for teaching. It is the strong, vocal, influential city, state, regional, and national English organizations which have been chiefly responsible for the strides we are making today in improving the status of the profession. Pressure for smaller classes, better standards of preparation for those in the profession, and foundation support for experimental projects in English have come largely from the work of individuals and groups in these organizations. Although the teacher of English may not like to think of himself as a joiner and though there is a grave danger in overinvolvement in organizational work, the dedicated teacher is usually one who makes a contribution to these efforts to improve the status of the profession. He can be more helpful still if he will write for professional journals, volunteer for committee work, or share in some of the projects sponsored by his English organizations.

"This I believe . . ."

This chapter has tried to suggest the qualities we may wish for in the persons who teach English to America's youth and some of the ways in which they can develop these qualities, competences, and skills. Teachers of English find themselves in a world in which many conflicting voices proclaim this or that magical answer to the oldest problems of the teacher. There are those who believe in a panacea for all the difficulties with the language our young people have: it may be linguistics, psychological counseling, semantics, teaching machines, guidance, phonics, reading accelerators, more writing, less writing, special grouping, classes for the gifted, classes for the retarded, teaching by television, or something else. Overwhelmed by the seemingly insoluble problems of the first years of teaching, the young teacher may grasp at any straw and accede to any innovation to help him find a way out of his dilemmas.

Not unless he has himself developed a clearly thought out philosophy of teaching English, based on what he knows of adolescent growth, development, and of the ways in which students learn, is he likely to choose and act wisely. Only then can he make sound choices among the many methods, techniques, and materials he will be asked to use, or support his choices with valid reasons.

Furthermore, his philosophy needs to be one fitted to the system of education in which he teaches—not a system suitable only for an intellectual, social, or economic elite, but one providing opportunity for all who would gain by it. The way to excellence need not be emulation of the British or the Russians; it needs to be sought within the framework of the democratic system of education that is inherent in America. The teacher does not gain status because he teaches Milton's "Samson Agonistes" or Spenser's *Faerie Queene* in the ninth grade, but because he can seek and encourage excellence in the most unpromising students.

Those who work with young teachers like to remind them that the job they prepare for is a responsibility and a privilege rather than a right. He who is unwilling to face the implications of his job and to embark on his profession with a sense of dedication should turn to one in which the minds and hearts of our youth are not so deeply involved.

We can look ahead to important and far-reaching changes in the teaching of English. Larger classes and changing school populations will pose new problems in many schools, but new resources and new tools will make easier many parts of the teacher's work. The English teacher, better prepared than ever before in the subject he teaches, stands in the center of the curriculum. It is he who will free the youth's tongue to speak, help him shape thoughts into written words, and open his eyes and his mind to the power of language and the world of books. If he does his job well, he provides the challenge which can help turn the indifferent student into the educated man, and introduce the bright students to new worlds.

It is within his power to determine whether young people will leave his classroom hating English as a narrow and dull subject, composed of drill in grammar, spelling, and punctuation, and plentiful red-penciled corrections on every paper, or whether they will leave with a love of reading, respect for and appreciation of the written and spoken word, and a feeling that their lives have been enriched by experiences in English.

Because he deals with the thoughts and feelings of his students, and of the writers of all ages, the English teacher has, more than most teachers, the power to change lives for the better. The teacher of high school English stands in a special relation to his students during their growing years as they turn to adults outside the family for guidance and inspiration.

In an automated world, where more and more of the world's work is done by pushing buttons or operating machines, the teacher of English deals as an individual with individual human beings. Behind the closed classroom door or even in front of a television camera, he is still a craftsman and an artist. His responsibility is a great one; his need for dedication is a certainty. The teachers of English who live in the memories of their students may say with Hopkins: "What I do is me; for that I came."

Selected bibliography

Jacques Barzun, *House of Intellect,* Harper & Row, Publishers, Incorporated, New York, 1959.

————, *Teacher in America,* Doubleday & Company, Inc., Garden City, N.Y., 1955.

Mary Ellen Chase, *A Goodly Company,* The Macmillan Company, New York, 1960. (Paperback.)

Alfred H. Grommon (ed.), *The Education of Teachers of English for American Schools and Colleges,* prepared by the Commission on the English Curriculum, NCTE, Appleton-Century-Crofts, Inc., New York, 1963. Volume V of the Commission series deals with important questions of the preparation and continuing education of teachers of English.

G. B. Harrison, *The Profession of English,* Harcourt, Brace & World, Inc., New York, 1962.

Gilbert Highet, *The Art of Teaching,* Alfred A. Knopf, Inc., New York, 1950. (Paperback.)

Irving C. Poley, *Speaking of Teaching,* Germantown Friends School, Philadelphia, 1957.

Robert C. Pooley (ed.), *Perspectives on English,* Appleton-Century-Crofts, Inc., 1960. A group of essays by distinguished teachers of English.

"Preparing the Beginning English Teacher," *Illinois English Bulletin,* vol. 51, November, 1963, pp. 3–50.

Appendix

Suggested films and recordings

The English teacher will want to consult other sources for further suggestions. The Schwann Long Playing Record Catalog (131 Clarendon Street, Boston) contains complete listings of recordings. Many of these resources may be ordered through NCTE. (See also the Chapter 14 bibliography.) Some of the most useful are:

Annotated List of Recordings in Language Arts, compiled and edited by NCTE Committee on Recordings, Champaign, Ill.

The Educational Media Index, vol. 5, "The English Language," McGraw-Hill Book Company, New York, 1964.

Films for Classroom Use: Handbook of Information on Films for Education, Teaching Film Custodians, Inc., New York.

The Motion Picture and the Teaching of English, NCTE, Champaign, Ill., 1965.

Recordings for Teaching Literature and Language in the High School (Arno Jewett, ed.), U.S. Office of Education, Government Printing Office, Washington, D.C., 1952.

Resources for the Teaching of English, NCTE, Champaign, Ill. Published annually, listing records, filmstrips, and other materials available through NCTE.

Language

Films

Language in Action Series (Dr. S. I. Hayakawa), 13 half-hour films, Indiana Audio Visual Center, Bloomington, Ind.

Language and Linguistics (Dr. Henry Lee Smith), 13 half-hour films, Indiana Audio Visual Center, Bloomington, Ind.

Talking Sense (Dr. Irving J. Lee), 6 half-hour films, Indiana Audio Visual Center, Bloomington, Ind.

Recordings

Spoken English, album to accompany the *Guide to Modern English* program, 2 records, Scott, Foresman and Company, Chicago.

A Thousand Years of English Pronunciation (Dr. Helge Kokeritz; Lexington 7650-55), 2 records, Education Audio Visual.

A Word in Your Ear: A Study in Language from *The Ways of Mankind* album, National Association of Educational Broadcasters, Urbana, Ill.

Literature

Films

The Humanities Program Series, Encyclopaedia Britannica Films, Wilmette, Ill. (Series 1: The Theatre, twelve 30-min films, including *Our Town, Hamlet,* and *Oedipus Rex*; Series 2: The Novel, Art, Architecture, and Poetry, eleven 30-min films.)

Of Poets and Poetry, eight 16-mm kinescopes, 29 min, NET Film Service, Indiana University, Bloomington, Ind.

Portraits in Print, ten 16-mm kinescopes, 29 min (Milton, Defoe, Goldsmith, Coleridge, Irving, Byron, Hawthorne, Thackeray, Hugo, Dickens), NET Film Service, Indiana University, Bloomington, Ind.

Shakespeare's London and *Shakespeare's Theatre,* 2 tape, filmstrip sets, Educational Audio Visual, Inc., Pleasantville, N.Y.

Recordings: General

Cambridge Treasury of English Prose, vol. 1: Malory to Donne (TC 1054); vol. 2: Burton to Johnson (TC 1055): vol. 3: Defoe to Burke (TC 1056); vol. 4: Austen to Brontë (TC 1057); vol. 5: Dickens to Butler (TC 1058), Caedmon.

The Enjoyment of Poetry and *An Introduction to Poetry,* to accompany the *Literary Heritage Series,* The Macmillan Company, New York, 1964.

Many Voices, albums (8 records) to accompany Laureate Edition of *Adventures in Literature,* grades 7–12, Harcourt, Brace & World, Inc., New York.

Many Voices, albums 1–6 to accompany Olympic Edition of *Adventures in Literature,* grades 7–12, Harcourt, Brace & World, Inc., New York.

Prose and Poetry Enrichment Records Series, 6 albums to accompany the *Prose and Poetry Series,* The L. W. Singer Company, Inc., Syracuse, N.Y.

Recordings: Drama

Ages of Man (OL 5390) and *One Man in His Time* (OL 5550), selections from Shakespeare read by Sir John Gielgud, Columbia.

Death of a Salesman and *The Crucible* (SA 704), read by Arthur Miller.

Don Juan in Hell (OSL 166), 2 records, Charles Boyer and others, Columbia.

Othello (SL 153), Paul Robeson, Uta Hagen, José Ferrer, Columbia.

Shakespearean plays recorded by The Shakespeare Recording Society.

Recordings: Fiction

Dickens' Duets (SA 736), scenes from Dickens' novels read by Frank Pettingell, Spoken Arts.

Emlyn Williams Presents Charles Dickens (SA 762), Spoken Arts.

Mark Twain Tonight! (OL 5440), read by Hal Holbrook, Columbia.

Recordings: Poetry

Dylan Thomas Reading His Complete Recorded Poetry (TC 2014), 2 records, Caedmon.

Great American Poetry (TC 2009), two 12-in. records, Caedmon.

Great Poems of the English Language, 3 vols., Poetry, 475 Fifth Avenue, N.Y.

Negro Poetry for Young People (FC 114), Folkways.

Poems of T. S. Eliot (SA 734), read by Robert Speaight, Spoken Arts.

The Poetry of William Butler Yeats, read by Cyril Cusack, Caedmon.

Robert Frost Reads His Poetry (TC 1060), Caedmon.

Treasury of Modern Poets (TC 2006), two 12-in. records, Caedmon.

Index